W9-BCW-293

DISCARDED
JENKS LRC
GORDON COLLEGE

A TALE OF TWO CONTINENTS

A TALE OF TWO CONTINENTS

A Physicist's Life in a Turbulent World

Abraham Pais

PRINCETON UNIVERSITY PRESS

PRINCETON, NEW JERSEY

JENKS L.R.C.
GORDON COLLEGE
255 GRAPEVINE RD.
WENHAM. MA 01984-1895

Copyright © 1997 by Princeton University Press
Published by Princeton University Press, 41 William Street, Princeton, New Jersey 08540
In the United Kingdom: Princeton University Press, Chichester, West Sussex

All Rights Reserved

Library of Congress Cataloging-in-Publication Data

Pais, Abraham, 1918–

A tale of two continents : the life of a physicist in a turbulent world / Abraham Pais.

p.   cm.

Includes index.

ISBN 0-691-01243-1 (alk. paper)

1. Pais, Abraham, 1918–   .   2. Physics—History.   3. Physicists—
United States—Biography.   I. Title.

QC16.P24A3   1997

530′.092—dc21

[B]   96-39313

QC
16
.P24
A3
1997

This book has been composed in Berkeley Medium

Princeton University Press books are printed on acid-free paper and meet the guidelines for
permanence and durability of the Committee on Production Guidelines for Book Longevity
of the Council on Library Resources

Printed in the United States of America by Princeton Academic Press

2   3   4   5   6   7   8   9   10

To IDA, JOSHUA, LISA, AND ZANE,

And in memory of all on our side who fell

in the Second World War

Contents

Acknowledgments

MY DEEP gratitude goes to those whose generosity, wisdom, knowledge, and criticism have helped me in preparing this book.

Conversations with my friend Tineke Strobos, who saved my life, have refreshed my memory about events in Holland during the Second World War. Jaap Polak, survivor of Bergen-Belsen, has generously put at my disposal his excellent library of books on the fate of the Jews in that war. Rigsantikvar Olaf Olsen has answered many questions about Denmark's history.

Special thanks to Paula and Fred Morgan, editors of *The Hudson Review,* who excerpted and published in their literary magazine fragments of this book (Spring 1993 issue). Its reception has been a great encouragement to me.

I am greatly beholden to the Alfred P. Sloan Foundation for a grant that has aided me in many phases of preparation. I thank Jan Maier for her excellent help in the preparation of the book's manuscript. It was a pleasure to have the thoughtful editorial help of Alice Calaprice.

My dear wife Ida's wise critique of the manuscript and her gentle care have sustained me throughout my labors.

The stupendous arrogance of such a record!
What should it contain, then? A pedestrian
reckoning by the sun, or aphoristic flights, or a
momentous study of my excretions covering
years? A digest of all three perhaps. One can
hardly tell. No matter.

—Lawrence Durrell, *The Black Book*

What gives a man worth is that he incorporates
everything he has experienced. This includes the
countries where he has lived, the people whose
voices he has heard. It also takes in his origins,
if he can find out something about them. By this
is meant not only one's private experience but
everything concerning the time and place of
one's beginnings.

—Elias Canetti, *The Play of the Eyes*

Prologue

Rabbi Zusia said: "When I appear before the
Almighty, I am not afraid to be asked: 'Reb
Zusia, why have you not been like Abraham,
the patriarch, or like Moses, our great teacher?'
The question I truly fear is: 'Reb Zusia, have
you truly been Reb Zusia?'"

—OLD CHASSIDIC TALE

FAMILY and friends have often urged me to write the story of my life, saying that this would be an unusual tale. "Yes, that is perhaps so; I'll think about your suggestion," I would reply, but I would not follow up. I did not like the idea of an "I, I, I" book, putting myself center stage.

There came a time, it was 1990, when I had finished writing my biography of Niels Bohr and was thinking about what to do next when Ida, my wife, asked if this was not the right time to start my autobiography. I said to her that I would take a month to consider her suggestion with care, after which I would make a decision.

During those days of reflection I made a discovery, perhaps known to others but new to me: I need not put myself center stage but can rather place myself at the side, like a Greek chorus. As the curtain rises, I can walk to the center and speak as follows: I wish to tell you of happenings in the twentieth century, as I witnessed them and reflected upon them. You will see me return to center stage, but only occasionally. Once that imagery had gotten hold of me, I went back to Ida and said yes, I shall try.

What, in my lifetime, has happened in the world? Over 80 international conflicts, including 2 world wars, more than 120 new nations formed, 1

Great Depression, 1 U.S. president assassinated, 1 resigned, 1 black woman elected U.S. senator, 2 women appointed to the U.S. Supreme Court, 1 polio and 1 AIDS epidemic, 1 royal abdication, 7 men (or were there 8?) who married Elizabeth Taylor, over 300,000 new words added to the *Oxford English Dictionary* (including two created by me), a civil rights movement, a women's movement, billions of hamburgers sold at McDonald's, the beginning of space exploration, the invention of the microchip, the discoveries of DNA and of quantum mechanics—to give but a pretty random sample.

The curtain is still down as I walk to the center of the proscenium and say this. For most of my life I have been a professional theoretical physicist and have actively participated in revolutionary developments in this field, notably discoveries of new, unforeseen forms of matter. It is inevitable that I shall have to speak of those events, and I shall do so. I am aware, however, that what scientists do is a mystery to many of those I hope to reach with this book. Fear not, kind reader, I shall not scare you off with steganography. Moreover, in the text I have marked with an asterisk all sections that deal with specific scientific subjects in layman's terms. If these are still too hard to swallow, just skip them and read on. (It would please me, however, if you would be willing to give these starred entries a try.) I will also try to bring science to life for you in other ways than telling of its contents, to wit, by recalling some of its most prominent practitioners I have had the good fortune to have known, men like Albert Einstein, Niels Bohr, Robert Oppenheimer, Andrei Sakharov.

A word about the title of this book. "Two continents," as I use it, has multiple meanings. First, I am at home and have homes both in Europe, where I was born and raised, and in America, where I made my career. But I have also lived most of my life within the continent of science which, alas, is at some remove from the continent of daily life. You may well have read biographies of scientists who found their destinies revealed to them as young children. I am not one of those. My own revelation came only after some time of university studies, when I attended a lecture in which I first heard how the results of certain experiments could be coded in terms of a curve, and how then a certain theory produced the same curve. Right then and there, this confluence between the continent of the outside world and the continent of the mind made me decide that this was to be my career. Only in my late twenties did I first encounter the great men I mentioned above. Only in my early thirties did I find my own niche—as a pioneer in

the branch of physics dealing with newly observed submicroscopic particles. These facets of my development are woven into the story that follows.

In thought I have started this story many times—lying awake at night, or
on walks in the woods. Twice I even began to write something down. The
first time was on June 22, 1958, the day after my son, Joshua, was born in
Princeton, the first American-born in the line. He and his mother, Lila, were
still in the hospital. The house on 94 Battle Road was silent as I sat on the
porch, contemplating the life that had just begun. It was then that the urge
came, overwhelmingly, to "talk" to Josh about those strange events of my
past, to make him the partner of a heritage. And yes, I did write some pages
but I don't know what happened to them.

Then Joshua came home and there was so much to be done, and all was
new, and why bother with the old and the dead, when new life came
streaming into our home—why bother.

In the late 1960s I tried again—I am not sure why. Was I depressed
because I was nearing fifty, and did I feel that it was a way to reconcile
myself with my natural decline? I don't quite know but do recall an event
that was perhaps decisive.

Shortly before, I had told some of my earlier experiences to a dear friend.
She listened quietly, and I felt she had understood something. The next
evening she took me to a poetry reading by Anne Sexton. As we sat down,
she turned to me and said: "I think you ought to write of what you have
seen." That quiet statement in a festive atmosphere stirred me. Shortly afterward, I sat down and wrote a few pages—also lost.

Another thirty years have gone by. It is now or never.

Autobiographical elements are present in books I have written before, in my
Einstein[1] as well as in my Bohr biography,[2] and also in *Inward Bound*, a
history of the structure of matter and the nature of physical forces as these
developed in the twentieth century.[3] I believe that it makes for better and
more lively reading if authors purposely inject themselves into books of
that kind, as long as they remain out of the spotlight. (Deliberately or not,
every author is of course present in every book he or she writes—even in a
scientific text.) These personal details were only very fragmentary, however. There was no natural reason for including many other events from my
past, some pleasant, some (to put it mildly) unpleasant. These happenings
are recounted in this book, written not because this author thinks he is all

that important but rather because they may yet serve as another small contribution toward illuminating our turbulent century.

As I am about to begin, a maxim of La Rochefoucauld comes to my mind: Old people like to give good counsel because they are no longer capable of setting a bad example.

Now the curtain rises.

BOOK THE FIRST: EUROPE

1

Descent

I, ABRAHAM (friends call me Bram), am the son of Jesaja,[1] son of Abraham, who was a diamond cutter, son of Jesayas, also a diamond cutter, son of Benjamin Pays—who was married twice and had eleven children from his first and seven from his second marriage—son of Nathan Pais, son of Benjamin Paes, son of Nathan Paes.[2] All of these ancestors, as well as I myself, were born in Amsterdam.

The reason I can trace my paternal ancestry that far back is that all of these Paises belonged to the Portuguese-Israelitic, also called the Sephardic, congregation Talmud Torah of Amsterdam and were registered in its record books, which have been preserved.

I have not been able to follow my lineage to still earlier times. It is certain, however, that my ancestors came to Amsterdam from the Iberian peninsula at some time after the 1590s, when the first Sephardic Jews reached the Low Lands (now the Netherlands and Belgium) via the Friesian town of Emden, most probably from Portugal. (The early spelling "Paes" perhaps indicates earlier Spanish origins.) Many Sephardim fled from Spain to Portugal after the Inquisition began. To this day the telephone book of Lisbon shows a long list of Paises, a name which in Portugal dates back to medieval times. In 1160, a Gualdim Pais established the Templar Order of Christ near where, in 1345, the town of Tomar was founded—by a Dom Pais, according to an inscription on his statue in the town's main square. I do not think that these gentlemen are ancestors of mine, however.

The arrival of Sephardim in the northern Netherlands marked the founding of the oldest emancipated post-Renaissance Jewish community in the Western world. Later it would sometimes be called the Jerusalem of the North.

In 1519, the humanist and scholar Erasmus of Rotterdam wrote in a letter: "If it is Christian to hate the Jews, then we are all of us outstanding Christians."[3] Nothing unusual about that. There were only a few Jews to hate in his environs, however. Before 1500, one finds only scarce and scattered references to the presence (and persecution) of Jews in the area now known as the Netherlands. Of the few Jews who lived there, most disappeared after 1544, when Emperor Charles V, king of Spain, who also ruled over the Netherlands, issued a decree ordering their expulsion from the region. By that time they had already suffered a similar fate in Spain.

The Spanish Inquisition, initiated in 1478, "had been originally devised for Jews and Moors, whom the Christianity of the time did not regard as human beings."[4] It brought to an irrevocable end the golden age—the thirteenth and fourteenth centuries—for Jews and Arabs living in Spain; many Spanish Jews converted to Catholicism in order to escape horrible brutality. These neo-Christians were known as Marranos, which is Spanish for swine. Most remained secretly faithful to Judaism, however; thousands were caught and lost their lives at the stake. Those who continued openly to profess Judaism were expelled from Spain by the royal edict of March 31, 1492, four months before Columbus set sail on his first voyage of discovery of the New World. Many fled to Portugal where, shortly afterward, they were again forced to renounce their faith. In 1536, the rule of Inquisition was also introduced in Portugal, causing some to flee, others once again to become Marranos.

Meanwhile, the Inquisition had extended its activities to the persecution of Christian heretics. Recall that the sixteenth century was the age of the great religious and political revolution known as the Reformation, spearheaded by men such as Martin Luther and Johannes Calvin. The new Protestantism found a large following in the Netherlands; the Inquisition reacted there accordingly, ably sustained by Philip II, son and heir of Charles V, with its customary cruel tortures and executions.[5] These events caused the peoples of the Low Lands to rise up in arms, led by William (the "Silent"), count of Nassau, prince of Orange. In 1568, the eighty-year war with Spain began. Up till then the Low Lands had been an agglomerate of regions ruled by counts, barons, and other nobles. Now it became one nation, "the Netherlands," which initially comprised both Holland and Belgium. William, known to the Dutch as "the Father of the Fatherland," wrote that he was prepared to stake "his person and all that is in his power to commence and maintain the liberty of religion and of the fatherland."[6]

In this favorable climate the first Sephardim settled in Amsterdam, from where the Spaniards had meanwhile been expelled. By 1612 about 500 were already living there.[7] In 1618 they inaugurated their enlarged synagogue on the Houtgracht.[8] It was there that in 1642 Rabbi Manasseh ben Israel welcomed William's son, Prince Frederick Henry, who was accompanied by the queen of England;[9] also here, on July 27, 1656, the infamous ban on the Sephardi Baruch Spinoza was pronounced. Rabbi ben Israel played an active role in the readmission of Jews to England—from where they had been expelled since 1290—when in 1655 he visited London at Cromwell's invitation.[10] Sephardim were also the first Jewish settlers in New York (in 1654).

The Portuguese synagogue of Amsterdam, inaugurated in 1675, unharmed by war and occupation, stands today as one of the world's most renowned synagogue buildings. Its services are still held in a Hebrew that, apart from small variants, is identical to the Iwrith now spoken in Israel. As I remember from my youth, however, announcements to the congregation were made in Portuguese; for example, "Mincha a una hora e mea" (the afternoon prayers will start at one thirty). I also remember the melody and text of the Sabbath prayer for the House of Orange, also in Portuguese: "A Sua Majestade, a Rainha dos Paizes-Baixos, e Seu Real Consorte," etc. (To her majesty the Queen of the Netherlands and her royal consort). On high holidays, the Sephardim would greet each other not with a hearty "Gut Jomtov" but rather with a formal "Boas Festas." When in 1887 the male synagogue choir was formed, it was given a Portuguese name: Santo Serviço. A photograph[11] shows my father as second conductor; later he became first conductor.

In the Holland of my youth, half the Dutch Jewish males were engaged in petty trades. Sixty percent of those employed in the diamond industry, and twenty percent of all art and antique dealers, were Jews.[12] Jews belonged in modest numbers to the middle class (from which I hail) but mostly to a large proletariat, all of them led by a handful of well-to-do men.

As to our language at home, my parents, grandparents, and their friends spoke only Dutch, never Yiddish or Ladino, its Sephardic equivalent. (Until about the middle of the nineteenth century, Portuguese had been the Amsterdam Sephardim's everyday language.) I grew up in a religious but strongly assimilated milieu.

My mother was Ashkenazi. Her maiden name was Kaatje van Kleeff. She was called Cato, more often just To. All I know of her ancestry is that her father, Levi, was a diamond cutter. She met Isaiah, my father, when both were studying to become elementary-school teachers. I have never heard anyone call him Isaiah, however; he was always Jacques, and so he signed his letters. Mother taught school until she married my father, on December 2, 1916.

My father was also an elementary schoolmaster, and later headmaster. In addition, he was headmaster of the Sephardic Hebrew school—all this until the Second World War. After the war he became the secretary of the Sephardic congregation of Amsterdam, the executive officer in all secular matters. He was a much respected and greatly beloved man in that community, always ready to listen to and counsel people who would flock to him with their worldly problems. He was formally named a rabbi posthumously. At his funeral we carried his coffin to the Portuguese synagogue and set it down in front of its main doors. (No dead body is ever allowed inside an orthodox synagogue.) Then the doors were opened. Candles had been lit inside. Next, the chief rabbi proclaimed my father a rabbi. Thereafter we brought his body to the serenely beautiful Sephardic cemetery, founded in 1614, in Ouderkerk aan den Amstel, a village just outside Amsterdam. There both he and my mother now rest in peace.

2

Early Years

I WAS BORN in my parental home in Amsterdam, Pretoriusstraat 24, then a pleasant tree-lined, cobblestoned street. That was on May 19, 1918, in the closing months of World War I, during which Holland had managed to remain neutral.

According to my mother, the first comment she heard about me came from Dr. Trompetter, just after he had delivered me: "Look at those big eyes!" The earliest photograph of me that I own shows me lying on a scale, staring at the world with intense curiosity, one of the few commendable qualities I never lost. My mother has told me that I was "clean" (no more diapers) within six months, a source of pride to her. Like so many Dutch women, she had a compulsion for cleanliness.

On November 1, 1920, Annie, my sister and only sibling, was born. Much later my mother spoke to me about that event. She and my father were still in bed that morning when she told him to get up and fetch the doctor: her time had come. My little bed stood in my parents' bedroom. Soon after my father had left the room in haste, my mother's water broke. I stood up in bed and watched in amazement, yelling at her: "You pig!" I myself have no recollection whatever of that day's events. This is perhaps curious, since I do remember what happened right thereafter.

I had been brought to my mother's parents' home to stay for the next few days. One evening, my grandmother put a plate of food in front of me, but I refused to eat. When in her grandmotherly fashion she urged me to take the food, I became enraged and threw the full plate onto the floor. I can still see the mess of broken shards and scattered food. As a young child I would occasionally throw such tantrums, as the time I threw a wooden ball from a bowling set at a boy with whom I was playing. Fortunately he ducked; unfortunately the ball went through a big window. I would get quite pale during such outbursts—they came to an end when I was about seven—and had to sit down afterward to rest. It strikes me that these earliest memories are rather angry ones.

At age four I started kindergarten or, as Amsterdam schoolboys called it, *kakschooltje* (little shit school). The only memorable event of those two pleasant years was that I made my first lifelong friendship, with Max Dresden, born on the same street as I, and only one month older. We became inseparable, going later to the same elementary school and high school. At about age nine we moved to another apartment, on the Linnaeusparkweg, also in Amsterdam. At about the same time, Max and his family moved to that street as well. One early recollection: like all the boys around me, I had an intense interest in dirty language. One day Max triumphantly marched up to me and declared: "I know what fucking means." It took some time to get this important information out of him.

Max and I also started our university studies together, in physics, in Amsterdam. In those years we became part of the first generation of hitch-hikers, traveling through Belgium, France, and Switzerland, often sleeping in haystacks on farms—which is comfortable but do not ask how we smelled. Such trips helped solidify our high school knowledge of foreign languages. When you drive with a trucker through France you speak French or else. When you are picked up by an Englishman in a classy automobile—as happened to us in the Rhône Valley in Switzerland—you speak English. One summer day we were near the Vosges in northeastern France, sitting at a roadside, having our gourmet lunch of bread and cheese when suddenly, out of nowhere it seemed, a French soldier stood before us and asked what we were doing there. Our reply appeared to be acceptable to him. He walked off and suddenly vanished again. Only later did we understand that we were having lunch in the middle of the Maginot Line, built before the war to protect the eastern border of France.

After a few years at the university, Max and I parted our ways when, mainly because of the threat of a European war, he left for America. In later years we have seen each other off and on, to our pleasure—most recently as emeritus professors.

Back to the earlier years. At age six I entered elementary school. I had not learned to read earlier but quickly picked it up. Within a few months I was reading books. According to my mother, after having finished my first book I said to her: "I never knew that reading was so wonderful." Soon I had to be rationed to one book per day. When I was smaller, I had played with my few toys, blocks, a Meccano set. But now I just read. First, the traditional Dutch children's books, which include neither *Hans Brinker and the Silver Skates* nor the story of the boy with his finger in the dike—these tales are unknown in Holland. Then I took interest in books about American Indians written by the German author Karl May—who had never set foot in America—and the great characters such as Winnetou, chief of the Apaches, Old Firehand, and Old Shatterhand. I read everything by Jules Verne and by Paul d'Ivoi, and then I discovered detective stories, including those by the Dutchman Ivans and by Edgar Wallace (the latter in translation, of course). On occasion I would pick up adult novels being read by my parents, with particular interest in the erotic passages. My mother once found me absorbed in one such book and took me aside, explaining that what was written there was not what went on in the real world. I reassured her with barely hidden smugness that, yes, I understood that. Once I got hold of a copy in Dutch of Krafft-Ebing's *Psychopathia Sexualis,* and became furious when I saw that all the juicy parts were in Latin.

At school I became a smart, rather arrogant kid, always learning fast, especially arithmetic. I was always number one in my class, through high school, doing poorly only in physical education.

In my young days Holland was a stable, bourgeois, and very rich country with little upward mobility. It was then the world's third largest colonial empire, still possessing the Netherlands East Indies (now Indonesia) and the West Indies, Suriname, and Curaçao. My parents could always make ends meet, but well-to-do they were not. We lived in a modest-sized apartment heated with coal stoves. As was quite common, we had no hot water, nor did we have a telephone.

In those years we always had a live-in maid. Most often these young women were German, eager to escape from the economic ruin in their homeland following the First World War, working in Holland at modest salary but with plentiful good food. The maid and my mother kept busy all day long. Every day the bed linens were hung out of a back window. Every day the apartment was dusted and cleaned. Silverware was polished. There was constant washing of clothes and dishes. Once a week the street in front of the house was scrubbed. My mother did the cooking herself.

My parents never owned a car; in my young days that was a prerogative of the rich only. A radio came later. I remember being invited to the home of friends—I must have been less than ten years old—and hearing my first broadcast crackling from a crystal set. Like most middle class homes, ours had no bath. My mother bathed us children in a zinc tub in the kitchen, while she and my father went to a nearby "bath house," a tidy place that provided shower rooms. Only after the Second World War did my parents have a shower in the home; also a telephone. They were past forty when they went abroad for the first time, to Paris. (Note that the distance from Amsterdam to the Dutch border is about the same as from New York to Philadelphia.) It was a big to-do; aunts and uncles, Annie and I came to the railway station to wish them *bon voyage*.

The years of my youth were harmonious and without a care. Home life was tightly knit. My father was a truly religious Jew. My mother later told me that she did not share those sentiments, but that nevertheless she always participated. The rules of eating kosher were strictly observed, which meant that we had four sets of dishes, plates, and cups: two for the regular year, one for meals with meat, one for dairy foods, and another two just for the week of Passover, when the regular plates were stored in the attic and the special ones, never touched by anything that contained yeast, were brought down. Friday evenings were special—finer foods, and the table set with the best linens.

Once a year, during Christmas vacation, my parents took Annie and me to the movies, a tremendous treat for us. We saw Charlie Chaplin, or Laurel and Hardy, or Pat and Patachon, the Danish comedians. Saturdays, my father's one day off, activities were limited by religious constraints. Sundays, while Father taught Hebrew school—he was a hard-working man—Mother took us for a walk, sometimes to Artis, the Amsterdam zoo. My main recollection about weekends is that they were endless and that nothing happened. My parents never took us to any of Amsterdam's renowned museums, or to a theater or concert. In the summer they rented for four weeks a house in one of Holland's beach resorts. To defray expenses we always had one or two paying guests along, boys or girls from better-to-do families.

I was a pudgy little boy, most often the shortest one in my class. The pudginess began to change when at about age ten I started to swim (though I always remained a shorty). That became my favorite sport. Some years later I joined Het Y, a prestigious Amsterdam swimming club. It was at a time when Holland produced the best women swimmers—world record holders such as Iet van Feggelen and Willy den Oude, both of whom I got to know personally. Every afternoon after school I swam for two hours. I became a decent water polo player. The proudest time of my young life was a match of Y II, when I played center forward and scored two goals against HPC (the Hague Polo Club) in a play-off game for the championship second division of Holland. In 1946, while I was in Copenhagen, I received a call from the trainer of the Dutch national team which was about to play Denmark. One of the players had become sick on the plane, I was told, and I was asked to stand by as reserve. Regretfully, that player recovered in time.

Now about my relatives. My father had two sisters and three brothers, and my mother two sisters and one brother, most of them married with children. Relations were comfortable all around, but there was none of that running in and out sometimes found in families. Ours was a quiet home. The only standard visits were those of my grandparents on the Sabbath afternoon. Saturday evening was bridge night, rotating between my parents' and other couples' homes. My father played very well.

The ties to my sister were a fairly common blend of sibling rivalry and great fondness. We did not have much in common. While I spent most of my out-of-school hours with my nose in a book, and with swimming, she, a pretty girl, would charm others. She did all right in school, but tended to be lazy. I was my parents' pride, the smart kid on the block. They doted all too much on me.

My mother was the stronger and more disciplining of the two. My father worshipped her, and she was devoted to him. I remember that my father was really furious with her only once—when she bobbed her beautiful long dark hair which had been held up in a bun. When my father came home and saw what she had done, he did not speak to her for several days.

My mother tended toward emotional restraint. Once I came home and told her that my friend so-and-so had done this, my friend had said that. She told me not to call him friend but comrade since I did know him that well—advice of questionable value. I also remonstrated strenuously against her attempts to teach me French.

My early relations with my father were much colored by his religiosity. From age four on he took me along to the synagogue every Saturday morning. I did not know any Hebrew yet and found the whole thing confusing and unpleasant. Because I went to a public elementary school which was open Saturday mornings, I had to miss those hours, which angered me. As my father and I walked to the synagogue, my classmates passed on their bikes, which I was forbidden to ride on the Sabbath. I hated to be different. My father taught me Hebrew (he had written a Hebrew school primer), and I learned to read it, but with little understanding of meaning. Nevertheless I became religious for about a year (I was about eight or nine), saying prayers at home every morning. Then I abruptly lost all religion.

I remember how that came about. It was on a Saturday afternoon. My parents were in the living room; the maid had the day off. Suddenly the thought came: What would happen if I lit a match—strictly forbidden on the Sabbath? I went to the kitchen, struck a match, blew out the tiny flame, and ran like hell. No ghastly repercussions. That was the end of that. I still feel it was a privilege to have gone through my liberation as a personal act.

When, many years later, I told this story to my late friend, the physicist Isidor Rabi, he told me of his similar experience. As a boy he too had regularly gone to the synagogue. On the Sabbath morning there comes a moment during the service when the Kohanim (the priests, all those named Cohen or Kohn) congregate in one area, cover their heads and faces with the prayer shawl, and then recite a benediction. The purpose of the covering is that during these moments they should be protected from the strength of God's light shining on them. In turn, the members of the congregation look downward so as to be protected from the strength of God's light transmitted by the Kohanim. One Saturday morning Rabi asked himself: What would happen if I look at the Kohanim but only with one eye? He did. Nothing happened. That, for him, was the end of that.

In spite of having abandoned—for good—religion, I continued to go to the synagogue with my father until well into my high school years. In the home I abided by the rules of orthodoxy. At age thirteen I went through the rituals of the *bar mitsvah,* the formal initiation to manhood, which included the recitation on a Sabbath morning of the weekly *haftarah* (which means "finish" and is taken from the Prophets) before the assembled congregation. In later years I had nothing more to do with Jewish orthodoxy. In fact, whenever I see it practiced I have only one reaction: I find it stifling. Just look at what its inflexibility is doing to Israel these days. Yet wherever I am, be it in Holland, or the United States, or Denmark—my three main centers of residence—I always feel first and foremost a Jew. It is a tribal feeling that mostly lies quietly right below the surface, but it has never restricted my choice of relationships or environment.

I was about ten years old when I experienced a crucial revelation: that my parents are good people, but that they cannot help me find my own way in life. I was on my own now and must seek for myself who I should be and what I should do. And this I did.

At age twelve I finished elementary school, passed the examination for admission to high school, and entered an HBS, a higher burgher school (how Dutch an appellation; such a school is now called Atheneum), on the Mauritskade in Amsterdam. That school—one of several types of high school—had a five-year curriculum with an emphasis on basic subjects.

I think back to those high school years with immense gratitude. This is what I was exposed to: algebra, including trigonometry, geometry, plane and solid, biology, Dutch, French, German, history, and geography, five years each. Four years of English. Physics and chemistry, three years each. Two years of mechanics, including one year of calculus. No electives—you were just told what to do.

My classmates and I worked hard, but there remained time for play. I swam every weekday. I also gave tutoring lessons to younger children, thereby earning much-needed pocket money; part of it was set aside for summer travel, the rest went for the usual diversions. I also had girlfriends in those years, but that was oh so innocent. . . .

When at age seventeen I passed the final examinations (as number one in my class—it might perhaps have been better for my soul if I had not always been number one, but what can you do), I could express myself, reasonably though not fluently, in three foreign languages: English, French, and German.

A main event of that period was my first exposure to good music at age fifteen, when we still had no radio in the home. Until then my only acquaintance with music had come from some years of violin lessons. Neither my abilities, nor my teacher, nor my instrument was of the best quality, and after many arguments with my parents I gave it up. My greatest regret about my childhood is that I never learned to play any instrument passably.

Then came the "youth concerts," a few concerts a year offered to all high school students in advanced grades in Amsterdam. One evening I entered for the first time the Concertgebouw, Amsterdam's famous concert hall, filled with youngsters on that occasion. The orchestra was tuning up. Then Willem Mengelberg, the conductor, entered. The first number on the program was the overture to "Oberon" by Carl Maria von Weber.

They began to play.

I began to cry.

I had never heard anything so beautiful. A new world of experience had opened for me.

To conclude the recollections of my early youth, I want to say a word about the Dutch language. On visits to Holland, which have become less frequent as time has gone by, I feel very deeply that Dutch is the language closest to my heart, even though by now I am much more comfortable expressing myself, verbally and in writing, in English. What then causes these feelings about Dutch? I think it is because I can understand so well and still participate in Dutch small-talk. It is so cozy, so full of redundancy, a type of talking that does not excel at succinctness but gives a particular color to communication. When I discussed this point once with the eminent American author Garrison Keillor, he remarked that the only place in the world where he could always join in the small-talk was in his native Minnesota, and that, for that reason, Minnesota would forever be his home. That is just how I feel about Holland. People like myself, who truly feel at home in several countries, are not strictly at home anywhere. Yet the native country remains special.

3

Bachelor's Degrees in Amsterdam

ANYONE who had successfully passed the final examinations at a high school of the kind I attended was automatically entitled to enter the Dutch university of his or her choice. One neither applied for admission nor went for interviews, as in the United States. All I had to do, and did, was go to the municipal comptroller's office of the city of Amsterdam, armed with my high school diploma, three passport pictures, and four hundred guilders (the fee for one year's admission), present all that to a man behind a little window, and presto, I was a registered student at the University of Amsterdam. Founded in 1877, it was then still a municipal institution, but became part of the national university system in 1971. The price of admission was quite a sum for my parents. I continued to live in the family home, so there were no additional expenses for bed and board.

When in the fall of 1935 I started my university studies, I was not very clear about my professional goals. In my boyhood years I had read a two-volume, richly illustrated book on the Netherlands Indies (now Indonesia) written by Hendrik Colÿn, a member of the "Antirevolutionaries," one of the quaint small Calvinist political parties of the time, who later became prime minister. That book's vivid descriptions made such an impression on me that for years I entertained the hazy idea of becoming an explorer. (I can still recite the names of Java's volcanoes hammered in at high school: Salak, Gedeh, Tangkoeban Prahoe, Papandajan, Merapi. . . .) I had also played with a simple boys' chemistry set, and, while in high school, Max Dresden and I had tried to read an elementary Dutch book on relativity theory. We got stuck, however, on the meaning of symbols such as g_{11} and g_{12}. These, we thought, were misprints. Should powers of g not be written as superscripts, g^{11}, g^{12}? Ah, those years of innocence, when tensors were still in our future. . . .

In high school I had a very good chemistry teacher. It was from him that I received my first primitive introduction to atoms and molecules and simple instances of their intercombinations. We also performed elementary experiments. All of it was a lot of fun. Physics, on the other hand, was pretty dull, it seemed to me then. You learned of heat and electricity and optics and all that, but our teacher treated them as one separate subject after another, without even giving hints of the underlying principles that made those various topics into a coherent whole. But I did grow fond of mathematics.

All in all, I knew I wanted to become a student of the exact sciences, though I did not yet have a precise plan of action. Accordingly, I began by taking chemistry and physics as major subjects (knowledge of physics was important for chemistry, that much I knew), mathematics and astronomy as minors. In addition I began to follow on a voluntary basis a course on the fundamentals of philosophy for first-year students. That experience marked the beginning of my lasting distaste for philosophy; I dropped out after a few lectures.

A sizable part of the chemistry curriculum consisted of laboratory exercises, which I handled tolerably well, though not expertly. The first-year lab course was in inorganic chemistry, the second in organic chemistry. My contact with the organic part cured me once and for all of any desire to become a chemist. (I recall that this conviction arose in me in the course of having to synthesize allyl alcohol.) I found organic chemistry—as it was taught to me then—inordinately boring. You had to cram fact after fact into your head with little indication of the whys and wherefores. Early in my second year I made up my mind: chemistry was not for me. And I now began to concentrate on mathematics and physics.

In my second year I also began attending graduate courses. One of these was given by Roland Weitzenböck, a Prussian-born German army officer in the First World War and a rather curious duck. His lectures consisted of a recitation of pages from his textbook on the theory of invariants.[1] The most fascinating part of his book is the preface. Write in sequence the first letters of its first twenty-one sentences and you read: *Nieder mit den Franzosen*— down with the French. If you find this hard to believe, get a copy of the book from some good library and see for yourself.

My undergraduate physics education, solid as could be expected in Holland, included an obligatory laboratory course. My first exercise was to determine how much heat it takes to melt a given amount of ice. I knew the right answers from the books, but with the best will in the world I couldn't get closer than about 75 percent of the right value. With fear in my heart I handed in my lab report with that result. My lab instructor later told me that my answer was quite satisfactory. It is not all that easy, he assured me, to come close to the correct value for such an elementary experiment with the rather primitive tools put at my disposal. He also said that for those who reported the correct value, he wrote a note behind their names: Watch out, this one has finagled the answer.

At this point I will briefly digress to reminisce about the Dutch chess craze of 1935–37.

In 1935, Max Euwe, an Amsterdamer with a Ph.D. in mathematics from the University of Amsterdam and a recognized chess master, challenged Alexander Alekhine, the reigning world chess champion. It became a gruelingly long battle lasting thirty games. The interest in Holland in this event was enormous, leading many people to take up chess for the first time. In one of the university's physics laboratories, students would sit in front of chessboards analyzing the moves of which they were informed by telephone. This went on until the professor forbade the presence of chessboards in the workplace. So the students bought thin portable boards that could be folded and put in one's pocket—and the games went on.

Euwe won nine games, lost eight, and drew thirteen. He was the champion. Great joy in the nation. In 1937 a rematch, requested by Alekhine, was played. This time Euwe lost.

I watched all this with interest but, unlike my friends, never sat down in front of a chessboard, for the following reason. Earlier, when I was about twelve years old, my friend Dresden and I had begun to play chess together. For some time we were about evenly matched, until something odd began to happen. Dresden started winning practically all our matches. This puzzled me, and after a while I asked him what he was doing to win all the time? He grinned and at first wouldn't say but then told me the secret. He had gotten hold of a book on chess openings and in that way knew how to obtain decisive advantages against ignorant me. I asked if I could borrow the book; he let me have it. I sat down all alone in front of a chessboard and went through many openings. I can still recall some of their exotic names, such as Nimzo-Indian, Tarrasch, Sicilian, Caro-Kann. Those hours of study impressed me greatly and led me to make up my mind: no more chess for me. I had begun to understand the nobility of the game and its demands on study and concentration. This was no kid stuff, it was a profession. Since I felt I could not give chess the devotion it deserved, I rather gave it up altogether, and have never again played it. It has gone likewise for me with checkers and with bridge. The only game I have continued to enjoy is an infrequent hand of poker.

Returning now to my activities as a student. In the winter months of 1936–37 an event occurred that brought my study plans into focus. Some time during that period George Uhlenbeck came to Amsterdam to give two guest lectures. Since the spring of 1936 he had been the professor of theoretical physics in Utrecht. His talks dealt with beta-radioactivity, the spontaneous emission of an electron plus a neutrino by certain specific kinds of atomic nuclei. In 1934, Enrico Fermi had incorporated the neutrino, a massless particle, into a systematic theory of beta-radioactivity. Uhlenbeck was among the first to work out consequences of Fermi's quite recent theory. In his first talk he discussed the pertinent experimental facts. In the second, he reported his own analysis of those data. These two lectures were my first exposure to science as it is in progress at the frontier of knowledge.

In later years I came to know other physicists who were at least as distinguished as Uhlenbeck. I have never, however, met anyone who could lecture better on science than he. His calmness, his style—systematic without a trace of pedantry—compelled me not to miss a word he said. That was a fairly rare experience, since I have a propensity for following my own line of thought during lectures, at the cost of missing what I have come to hear. Not only the style but also the contents of those two talks captivated me entirely. I am sure I understood only a fraction of what I was exposed to (I do not remember whether I had even heard of a neutrino at that time) but, curiously, that did not seem to matter to me. As I sat there in the auditorium of Clay's laboratory, I had the intense experience that here and now it was revealed to me what I wanted to do, had to do. From that time on I have never wavered in that conviction.

On February 16, 1938, I obtained two bachelor's degrees, with majors in physics and mathematics, minors in chemistry and astronomy. In that academic year I continued to take graduate courses in Amsterdam, including those in physics given by Johannes Diderik van der Waals, Jr., the one and only professor of theoretical physics, the son of the great van der Waals who in 1910 had received a Nobel Prize for his equation describing the thermodynamic properties of gases and liquids. I found the lectures by his son dull and uninspiring. As I learned later, he was averse to the more modern aspects of physics such as the quantum theory. It soon became obvious to me that he was not the right man to guide me in further studies of theoretical physics. So I went to see some graduate students to ask for guidance as to how to proceed next. They advised me to try and become a graduate student with Uhlenbeck in Utrecht. Accordingly I wrote to him, asking for an interview.

I shall come back in a later chapter to what happened as a result of that letter, but first I will turn to describing some of my extracurricular activities.

4

Of Music, Films, and
Other Diversions

STUDENTS from Amsterdam University could buy concert tickets at a very considerable discount. I liberally availed myself of this opportunity, inspired by my first exposure to good music gained from the high school youth concerts. Many were the evenings on which I would take my bicycle and ride to the Concertgebouw in the van Baerlestraat, chain it to a lamp post, and enter. Biking was the main mode of transportation for the middle- and lower-class Dutch. It was joked in those days that at birth a Dutch baby would come out riding on a bike.

Never in later life have I been as frequent a concert goer as in the years 1935–40. I should like to relate some of my principal musical experiences of that time.

One day a friend asked me if I would like to have his ticket to a Segovia concert, as he himself could not go. "Who is Segovia?" I asked. "A classical guitarist," he told me. I had never even heard of the existence of classical guitar music. Well, why not, I thought, and accepted his friendly offer.

So, once again, I wended my way to the Concertgebouw, which houses a large hall for main concerts and a small hall for more intimate recitals. I went to the small hall, expecting Segovia to play there, but it was closed. On to the large hall. As I entered I was astonished to see that it was packed. Most of the podium, normally reserved for the orchestra, was now filled with chairs, leaving open only a fairly small square area in which stood one chair. Before long, Segovia came down a set of steps, a handsome dark-haired man, wearing a flambard, holding his guitar. He sat down on that single chair, and almost at once began to play. His first number was a Busoni transcription of a Bach chaconne. As had happened to me once before, I started to cry. How could a single man make such heavenly music which to me sounded as if it was created by a small ensemble? Even after Segovia's favorite final encore, the Dance no. 6 in E Minor by Granados, people seemed reluctant to leave the hall.

The very next day I went to a music store and bought myself an inexpensive guitar. For some time thereafter I took lessons but did not get very far. Yet my love for the guitar never waned. In later years I have bought better guitars, but they did not improve my playing by much. I did get familiar with a sufficient number of basic chords, however, and learned to accompany myself singing folk songs of many nations. It was not great music but nevertheless gave me pleasant hours.

Only one more time was I moved to tears because of music. That happened when for the first time I attended a recital by Pablo Casals and heard him play the third Bach suite for unaccompanied cello. When, much later, I spent an afternoon with him, I used that occasion to express my immense gratitude for that experience.

Other strong memories. The Amsterdam debut of a young violinist named Yehudi Menuhin playing duets with his sister Hepzibah at the piano. Sergei Rachmaninoff appearing with the Concertgebouw orchestra, a tall, slender, austere-looking man with salt-and-pepper hair cropped short, wearing a white tie and tails and a red sash to which a decoration was attached, probably czarist. I can still hear the soft "Aahh . . ." that went through the audience as he began his encore with his well-known prelude.

Year after year I attended recurrent performances of great choral works, Bach's *Passion According to St. Matthew* in the Concertgebouw, his *Passion According to St. John* in another hall, the *Vrÿe Gemeente* (both sung in German, of course). Around Eastertime it became the standard custom among my friends and me to address each other melodiously in *recitativo* à la Bach rather than in regular speech.

Also from that time stems my first acquaintance with another wonderful kind of music, American jazz, which I have loved ever since. That came mainly via radio, but I also recall having heard the saxophonist Coleman Hawkins play in a small Amsterdam dive.

In those years I also became a movie buff as well. It was a very rich period in the development of this young art form.

The United States brought us various new categories of light comedy: Chaplin with *City Lights* and *Modern Times*; the Marx Brothers introduced new heights of zaniness in *A Night at the Opera* and *A Day at the Races*. Of British contributions I remember Leslie Howard in *The Scarlet Pimpernel* and *Pygmalion,* Alfred Hitchcock's *The Thirty-Nine Steps* and *The Lady Van-*

ishes. In the beginning 1930s Germany had produced some outstanding movies as well, such as Fritz Lang's *M* with Peter Lorre as the psychopathic child killer, and *Der blaue Engel* with Marlene Dietrich and Emil Jannings. The greatest contribution of that period, if not ever, made by German film was in my opinion *Dreigroschenoper* (Threepenny Opera), a nonpropagandistic, cynical view of capitalist society's power play, and of love, set among thieves, and starring Lotte Lenya, who sang the pirates' song, and Ernst Busch rendering the ballad of Mackey Messer. This film carries the magic of high art.

To my taste, by far the finest movies of the period were French, superbly acted and directed. Among those masterpieces I remember Jean Renoir's *La Grande illusion,* with Eric von Stroheim and Jean Gabin; Harry Baur in *Crime et châtiment;* and the work of Marcel Pagnol, notably *La Femme du boulanger,* with Raimu, whom Orson Welles has called the greatest actor who ever lived.

It was an ongoing feast to see all those movies—many still steadily played in revival houses—as they first appeared.

For the first time during my Amsterdam student years I also began to visit museums, the Rÿksmuseum (National Gallery) which houses the most complete collection of Dutch painters from the fifteenth to nineteenth centuries, and the Stedelÿk (municipal) museum, where modern art was and still is on display. (Amsterdam's fine van Gogh museum dates from the postwar years.) Ever since that time I have been an avid contemplator of the visual arts, the world over. Only after having visited major museums abroad did I become aware of the important Dutch pioneering role in how to hang paintings so that they are provided with proper space and lighting.

Of my extracurricular reading in those years, the most important to me was my first exposure to the writings of Sigmund Freud, who was then still alive. I began with his introductory lectures on psychoanalysis, a fortunate start. I always read him in German, and have become convinced that it is sufficient ground for learning that language to read the man in the original; I greatly admire his literary style. As to contents, it was as if a new world opened for me. At the same time, I had the distinct sensation that I somehow already knew what he was conveying—except for the fact that I had never consciously phrased it.

It was not long after I had begun these readings that, one day, a young man came into the room in which I was sitting, deeply absorbed in Freud. He had been visiting the family of my girlfriend and came to say good-bye. I did not care much for him but nevertheless intended to say something friendly. Instead I found myself saying, "I am glad you are leaving." He could not have been more stunned than I was. In a flash it came to me: this is precisely one of those slips I had just been reading about. It was as if I confirmed experimentally what I had been confronted with.

Then I turned to Carl Jung who, in little time, began to enrage me. Whereas Freud wrote in scientific style, clearly stating his assumptions and his verifications thereof (never mind that not all of these have held up), Jung introduced mystical, unverifiable elements. What was all that non-sense about the collective unconscious? How do you *know?* From then on, I have continued to look upon Jung as a sort of charlatan.

5

First Contacts with Zionism

WHEN in 1935, at age seventeen, I entered the university, Hitler had been head of the German state for two-and-a-half years. Right after he had come to power, the Reichstag building in Berlin had burned down. Holland took special notice of that event since the fire was supposed to have been set by a Dutch communist. All political parties except that of the national socialists had been dissolved. The destruction of German cultural life, until then among the best of its kind, was in progress. The *Beamtengesetz* (civil service law) of April 1933 permitted university authorities to fire staff on grounds of politics and/or race. Another law enacted that same month restricted membership in student organizations to "Aryans" only. The next May the infamous book burning took place. Life for Jews in Germany had become extremely difficult if not impossible. Mass emigration, both legal and illegal, of German Jews had begun.

I followed reports of these events in Dutch newspapers but, like most Dutch people, felt that they took place far away, even though Amsterdam lies only one hundred miles west of the German border as the crow flies. I was of course concerned about the fate of the German Jews—without, however, sensing in any way that they were "some of us." There was rather a contrary response among many Dutch Jews to the influx from the east, to wit, that these "aliens" might arouse anti-Semitic reactions among the Dutch, which might backfire on the Jews in Holland. In 1938 the Dutch government actually closed its borders to this kind of immigration, for reasons that were not just economic. In 1939 it founded a central refugee camp, residing under the Department of Justice, for Jews who had fled from Germany. The camp's name (taken from a small nearby town in the northeastern Netherlands) came to be hated and feared during the next five years: Westerbork.

I may note that anti-Semitism did exist in Holland, but only in a mild

form. The Dutch did have their own national socialist party, the NSB, founded on May 14, 1931, by a man named Mussert. It was never more than a
small lunatic fringe affair laughed at and/or hated by nearly all the Dutch.
During World War II some of its members volunteered for service in the
German army. In any event, Dutch anti-Semitism, whatever its extent,
never caused me any personal difficulties.

That was the situation in Holland regarding Jewish problematics when,
as a first-year student, I came in contact with Zionism for the first time.

The Zionist world organization was born in 1897, at the first Zionist
congress, held in Basel.[1] Two years later a Netherlands branch was founded, the NZB. The call for this action sets a significant tone: "Zionism as an
indication for a new fatherland has no purpose for Dutch Jews. They are
free people and belong to *their* country. We hope, however, that they will
strongly support this effort which is undertaken in the interest of their
unfree religious brethren."[2] In the 1930s the NZB had between three thousand and four thousand members—less than 3 percent of Dutch Jewry.
There was considerable anti-Zionist sentiment among Jews with strong as-
similationist and/or socialist convictions.

The NZB comprised an agglomerate of factions such as the Mizrachi,[3]
which maintained the traditional religious values, and the socialist-Zionist
oriented Po'ale Zion (workers of Zion). My father was a dues-paying member of the Mizrachi but did not actively participate in any Zionist-oriented
work. Like quite a number of NZB members, he expressed solidarity by
membership only, and that was that. I have no recollection of discussions
on Zionism in my parents' home.

In addition to the NZB there existed a Zionist student organization (NZSO)
and the Jewish Youth Federation (JJF), which embodied Zionist youth clubs
from various parts of Holland.

It was through the NZSO that I came in personal contact with the Zionist
movement for the first time. In the fall of 1935 I was approached by one of
its members who inquired if someone might come and talk to me. I said he
was welcome to do so. Shortly afterward I had a visit from Jaap van Amerongen, a senior NZSO member. My friend Dresden, who had also been
approached, joined us at my home. Jaap began by asking us if we had any
interest in Zionism. I replied that I neither cared nor knew in any detail
what the movement was really about. (Neither did Dresden.) Whereupon
Jaap said that this was not uncommon, that he had not come to propose
that we join the NZSO, but rather to invite us for a series of instructional
discussions that would take place a few evenings a month throughout our

first year as students. After that time it was left to us to decide whether or not we wished to join. It all sounded very reasonable and potentially interesting, and we accepted.

Those discussion evenings marked the beginnings of a lasting change in my perceptions of Jewry. Up till that time my only contact with Judaism had been the stultifying exposure to orthodoxy. Now it began to dawn on me that to be a Jew, to experience Jewishness, did not necessarily mean to be religious. To be sure, religion had been the main force that had caused the Jewish identity to be maintained throughout the diaspora. Had the Jews not carried their constitution, the Torah, on their backs through centuries of wanderings and persecutions? That constitution, however, was the law of a tribe, and one could be—feel to be—a member of that tribe even if those ancient laws had faded, if not vanished, as a determinant of one's personal conduct.

These changes in attitude and sentiment, beginning roughly in the early nineteenth century, the age of enlightenment and emancipation, had a variety of consequences. There were those who opted for assimilation to their host country, sometimes combined with continued adherence to one or another liberalized modification of Jewish religious custom. I have always felt averse to the assorted versions of reform Judaism which, so the joke goes, replace the Ten Commandments with ten suggestions. As said before, strict religious positions are not mine, yet I have an abiding respect for the tough old Jewish religious stance.

Quite a different consequence of the change in attitude to what it means to be a Jew was the rise, late in the nineteenth century, of the Zionist movement. As is well known, the root idea of Zionism was, from the outset the establishment of a Jewish homeland in Palestine. It was conceived as a secular, politically oriented national movement, in contrast to earlier migrations by Jews who came to Palestine either to live according to religious precepts and to die there, nearest the place of the Last Judgment; or who went, often driven out by pogroms, to cultivate the land according to the agrarian traditions of the biblical Jews. Zionism introduced an entirely new ideal, that of a sovereign Jewish nation-state. The motivation was obvious. The wandering Jew could only become a settled Jew, no longer constantly threatened by persecution and expulsion, if he had a corner of the world to call his own. The Zionist idea never was to establish a grand refugee camp, but rather to find a place on earth where the Jew could finally unpack his belongings, including perhaps his Torah, and live not only in peace but also with dignity.

The father of political Zionism was Theodor Herzl, who concisely formulated the question of the Jew. At about the same time, Ahad Ha'am,[4] a rabbinical scholar turned agnostic, began to raise a distinct issue, the question of Judaism or, as it is sometimes called, spiritual or humanistic Zionism. "He no longer believed . . . that God had created the Jews and set them apart; on the contrary, the Jewish people, in his view, had given authority to their unique moral values by inventing the God who commanded them."[5] Ahad Ha'am has written: "Judaism was born in a corner and has always lived in a corner. . . . History has not yet satisfactorily explained how it came about that a tiny nation . . . produced a unique religious and ethical outlook . . . which has remained so foreign to the rest of the world, and which to this day has been unable to master it or to be mastered by it."[6]

Ahad Ha'am believed in the Palestine solution, but not as a homeland for all Jews. For this there was simply no space, he said. He was also among the very first to raise the issue of the local Arabs, warning against the ill-perceived slogan that Palestine was a land without people waiting for a people without a land. In his view, only a select elite should move to Palestine to establish a spiritual center influenced by both Jewish and European culture. "In the modern era of disbelief, he said, religion was no longer preserving the Jewish people. Jews needed to find some other source of communal energy. . . . Judaism [should] aspire to make the Jewish people to a spiritual elite on the way to perfecting all of mankind. . . . He defined for [the Jews] the fundamental human questions: the source of community, the meaning of faith in a disbelieving world, and the relationship of morality to power."[7]

Ahad Ha'am, a self-taught polyglot, published only in Hebrew. "In his hands, the language of Hebrew finally and irrevocably left the Middle Ages."[8] He was a driving force in making the revival of the Hebrew language a central aim—attained since—of Zionism. His impact on Israel's culture has been profound. Yet he remains virtually unknown in the West.

There clearly exists a range of options between the extremes of purely political populist and purely spiritual elitist Zionism, a subject of much debate when I first became exposed to these issues. In the NZSO discussion evenings, I learned of Herzl's and Ahad Ha'am's views and of points in between. I became aware of a major issue that had hardly been discussed in Holland before the 1930s but that now, in view of the political developments in Europe, became topical: Can one reconcile being a Zionist with loyal Dutch citizenship? I attended a few NZB meetings which made clear to me a divergence between the generations: the older Zionists had not yet moved away substantially from the position, quoted before, that their movement was essentially in support "of their unfree religious brethren."

The position of the NZSO and the JJF had turned more radical, however. They never denied the obligation of loyalty to Holland but stressed that their traditions, culture, and future were not the same as those of the other Dutch. As one of them wrote: "We can appreciate the national holidays of the others but they are not ours." Such opinions were not appreciated by the NZB. In 1939 they would call a young Zionist on the mat for having written that the flags of the *galuth* (diaspora) are not our flags.[9]

I also became aware for the first time of the *chalutz* (pioneer) movement, which aimed at preparing Jews for settling in Palestine by means of *hachsharah,* or schooling in the Jewish background, including the study of Hebrew, as well as menial labor. In Holland this organization had begun in the 1920s, mainly in support of the young *Ostjuden,* Jews from the East, who had fled pogroms. In the thirties, increasing numbers of Dutch Jews joined, often working for some years on Dutch farms in order to acquaint themselves with agricultural methods. By 1936 about 1,200 Jews from Holland (roughly one percent) had emigrated to Palestine.[10]

I attended a few meetings of Zionist youth clubs in Amsterdam, encountering there for the first time young Jews who had been directly exposed to the Nazis; for some reason, the 1930s were the JJF's most flourishing time.

The result of all these experiences in my first student year was the realization that my earlier contacts with Judaism, those realized by going to the synagogue with my father, had little to do with the life of the modern Jew. I liked the new exposure—to Sephardim, Ashkenazim, to Dutch Jews and Ostjuden alike. They taught me ideas and songs, and conveyed a lively spirit. So after my trial year, I joined the NZSO.

By then I had already begun to acquire a circle of Zionist student friends. On evenings we would meet frequently in the basement of the spacious house where Jaap van Amerongen lived (his father was a wealthy diamond trader), a place which we called "The Catacombs." There I met for the first time Lion Nordheim. A deep friendship with him developed, which later would cause the most tragic moments of my life, as I shall relate further on.

Lion was born in 1910, in Arnhem, the son of a well-to-do antique dealer. In his high school years he joined the local Zionist youth club. When he moved to Utrecht to study law he joined the NZSO. A bright, eloquent, and learned man who read widely, especially on Zionism and philosophy, he became president of the JJF in 1934.

After leaving the catacombs, Lion and I would often walk home together,

I accompanying him to his apartment, he then following me to mine, often several times back and forth. I learned much from our discussions and could well appreciate why Lion was widely respected as the leading ideologue of the more radical type of Zionism.

A small circle of catacomb members would meet regularly in the home of Síeg Gitter for joint reading and discussions. We took on Spinoza's *Ethics*. Those were wonderful get-togethers, though I do not remember a word of what Spinoza wrote. I also took Hebrew lessons again, with Leah Neubauer, Síeg's fiancée and later his wife. I did get a bit further than I had been under my father's earlier tutelage, but regrettably never came to master the language. Síeg and Leah have remained good friends of mine throughout the years. They now live in Ramat Gan, Israel. Síeg is professor of medicine at Tel Aviv University. In the spring of 1990 Ida, my wife, and I had the pleasure of taking them out to dinner in a little restaurant right below Suleiman the Magnificent's wall surrounding the Old City of Jerusalem.

In those prewar years I became active in the youth movement. For some years I was a member of the board of the JJF, which involved visiting youth clubs in various parts of the country and giving speeches. I have two special memories of that time.

One was a visit from Zalman Rubashov, a *shaliach,* or emissary, sent from Palestine. His purpose was to mediate the tensions between the JJF and the NZB regarding radical Zionism. Much later he became the third president of Israel (1963–1973). By then he had changed his surname to Shazar. He was the first of five presidents of Israel I have met in my lifetime.

The other was a visit from Menachem Ussischkin, a venerated leader of the Zionist organization who had emigrated to Palestine already in the 1880s. He was the senior fund-raiser of the world organization. In 1921 he had accompanied Chaim Weizmann and Albert Einstein on their joint trip to the United States, aimed at soliciting financial support for the movement as well as for the Hebrew University. The JJF board had organized a luncheon with Ussischkin, during which our president gave a feisty speech in which he said we must raise funds for this, we must raise funds for that. After he sat down, Ussischkin turned to him and said only this: "Sie wollen *mich* überzeugen?" (You want to convince *me?*)

At one point, *Hanoar Ha'owed* (The Workers' Youth), the youth branch of the socialist Zionists in Amsterdam, was in need of a new chairman. I was asked to take on that task. Like so many youths of that era, I had socialist leanings but had never been then, nor was I later, a devoted Marxist. I had tried to read *Das Kapital* but soon had given up—it was simply too dull for

me. In any event, I felt I had to and did take on the chairman's job. This
meant that, for a few years, I had to chair a meeting every Saturday night
from September to June, arrange for a speaker, lead in singing the wonderful
songs of the movement (I even remember a Yemenite song), join in dancing
the *horrah,* and so on. It was time-consuming but on the whole a fine experience. Among my bitter memories of the war is the fact that most of those
kids, my kids, were later taken to German "labor camps," never to return.

It was also through my Zionist connections that I met Tineke Buchter.

She is non-Jewish and was a girlfriend of Jaap van Amerongen's youngest
sister, still at the end of her high school years when we first met, a beautiful
young woman with great style. Already then she had strong emotional involvements with Jewish issues. I still remember an occasion on which she
recited a medieval Dutch poem: "*'t en zÿn de Joden niet, Heer Jesu, die U
kruisten . . . ik ben't*" (It was not the Jews, Lord Jesus, who crucified you . . .
it is I). I fell in love with her and courted her. It was my first serious
involvement with the opposite sex. It took time, but eventually we became
attached, unofficially engaged one might say. After finishing high school
she became a medical student. Already then her main interest was psychia-
try; today she is a distinguished analyst. It was Tineke who introduced me
to the writings of Freud. Once she took me to the university's anatomical
laboratory to show me the cadaver which she was assigned to dissect. I had
never seen anything like it. Thoughts of illness and death had always made
me acutely uncomfortable but, surprising to me, I found the experience
utterly fascinating.

When I told my parents about Tineke, my father became furious. He did
not wish to see his son attached to a *shiksa* (a non-Jewish female) and
absolutely refused to receive her in our home.

During the summer of 1940 Tineke and I were together in a Dutch beach
resort. On a walk along the beach I saw my parents sitting on the sand. I
turned to Tineke and told her I would now introduce her. So I did. My
parents reacted politely; the ice was broken. Soon she was able to visit me at
home. In the course of time no one came to adore Tineke more than my
father. More about her later.

My Zionist experiences naturally raised the question for me: Should I consider moving to Palestine? I decided: no, principally because of my growing
involvement with science. Let me now return to where I left off on that
subject, the time when I had obtained my bachelor's degrees.

6

Utrecht: M.Sc. and Ph.D.

AS ALREADY mentioned at the end of chapter 3, I had written to Professor Uhlenbeck in Utrecht, asking if I could come for a visit to discuss my study plans. After some weeks of impatient waiting I received a letter inviting me to come over on a specific day. When the time had come, I took a train to Utrecht and walked from the station to Bÿlhouwerstraat, where the physics laboratory was then situated (it has since moved to other quarters). Uhlenbeck shared one room there with his assistant. I knocked at the door of room 220, went in, stumbled over the threshold (I must have been nervous), and, Charlie Chaplin–fashion, fell right down in the presence of the professor: a glorious beginning. I quickly composed myself, was invited to sit down, then told Uhlenbeck of my hopes to become a graduate student in theoretical physics under his guidance.

Uhlenbeck's response was unexpected. "If you like physics," he asked, "why don't you consider becoming an experimentalist? Or if you like the mathematical aspects of theoretical physics, why not become a mathematician?" In explanation he noted that the practical future for a theoretical physicist in the Netherlands was extremely limited. At that time there were only five professorates in the subject in the whole country. Accordingly, chances for a continued career were quite slim. Experimental physics as well as mathematics opened many more possibilities, for example in industry. Furthermore, he added, theoretical physics is very difficult, it would be a life of toil with many frustrations and disappointments.

I was quite taken aback and mumbled, "But I like theoretical physics so much." Uhlenbeck's reaction was again unexpected. "If that is really true," he said, "then by all means become a theorist; it is the most wonderful subject you can imagine." As he later told me, his preliminary attempts at dissuasion were exactly like those he himself had been exposed to when he wanted to start his own graduate studies, adding that he used the same routine whenever anyone applied to study with him.

Having gone through these preliminaries, Uhlenbeck said next that he wanted to tell me about his current research. The subject was cosmic rays, radiations of photons and various other species of particles that come from outer space and are detectable on earth. In particular he was interested in a recent paper by the Russian physicists Landau and Rumer on so-called showers, processes in which radiations entering the upper atmosphere generate many additional particles when colliding with air molecules farther down. Uhlenbeck outlined the theoretical treatment on the blackboard, while I sat and listened, occasionally asking for more explanations or information which he patiently provided. Some mathematical tools (integro-differential equations—never mind if you don't know what these are) were new to me, so I had to keep my wits together, following not only the physical reasoning but also the mathematical analysis. I did not do all that badly, but after an hour became tired of the intense discussion. Uhlenbeck imperturbably went on, however. After another hour I was dazed but told myself to hang in there, boy, this is trial by fire. This went on still a bit longer, then the professor stopped, gave me the reference to the paper we had been discussing,[1] told me to study it and come back in two weeks. I sort of staggered out of the room, unable to concentrate on anything but getting back to the train station.

Years later I told Uhlenbeck how that first afternoon with him had affected me. He told me with a smile that he had gone through the very same treatment, had the very same reactions, when he had visited his revered teacher, Paul Ehrenfest, for the first time. Ehrenfest in turn had received the same treatment from the great Ludwig Boltzmann in Vienna. This tradition is part of teaching in the grand old style, concentrating on but very few students. In my time I was the only student Uhlenbeck had taken on. Because of that privilege I may count myself as a spiritual great-grandson of Boltzmann. Meanwhile the old style has gone forever, I think, because of the large number of students now clamoring for higher education.

All through the spring term of 1938 I paid regular visits to Uhlenbeck; I had dropped out of taking graduate courses in Amsterdam. After further discussions on cosmic rays, Uhlenbeck said he would soon put me on a problem in that field. But first I had to study the textbook on quantum mechanics by Hendrik Antony Kramers, a professor in Leiden and Holland's most prominent theoretician of the period. I did all right. During one of my visits to Uhlenbeck, the door to his office suddenly opened, no knocking first, and a man stormed in without saying hello, planting himself squarely in front of the blackboard. After a few moments' study of what was written there, he turned to Uhlenbeck and finally spoke: "You need a *schlei-fenintegral,*" a technical mathematical term. It was Kramers. I would meet him later many times, as we shall see.

It was springtime when Uhlenbeck told me that the following fall term he was taking a leave of absence to become a visiting professor at Columbia University in New York. That was of course a disappointment for me. He gave me a list of things to study and work on. That fall I enrolled in the University of Utrecht but continued to commute from Amsterdam. I was permitted to use Uhlenbeck's office, which I had all to myself (Boris Kahn, his assistant, was in Bristol for postdoctoral work).

During Uhlenbeck's absence, Hendrik Casimir, then reader at the University of Leiden, came to Utrecht twice a week to give a course on quantum physics. From him I got my first instruction in atomic structure and atomic spectra. These were lucid lectures from which I benefited much, as also from private discussions afterward. It was from Casimir that I for the first time heard stories by someone who had been in personal contact with Niels Bohr.[2] In addition I took courses in mathematics, which was to be my secondary subject for the master's degree.

I was also obliged to do one year's experimental work in the Utrecht laboratory. This brought me in contact with Leonard Salomon Ornstein, the professor of experimental physics, a scientist of distinction who had started his career as a theorist. He took to me and would almost daily visit me in Uhlenbeck's office for a chat. He was also prominent in the Zionist organization, so we had a lot to talk about.

My experimental work ended abruptly and prematurely when I caused a catastrophe. I was assigned as "slave" to a senior graduate student who was performing a series of experiments in beta-radioactivity for his doctoral thesis. He was supposed to educate me in the workings of his apparatus; I was to obey orders to assist in all kinds of ancillary matters. One of these was to keep a careful eye on a huge bank of batteries, several yards long, which were coupled in series so as to provide a very steady DC voltage. When my boss was absent I was to keep check on this affair. Since this only involved reading off some meters once in a while, I installed myself with a theoretical physics monograph to read in the meantime. I remember being deeply absorbed in *Leçons sur la théorie des spineurs* by Élie Cartan when suddenly a flame shot through the battery bank from one end to the other. My inattention had killed every battery in the setup. With fear in my heart I immediately went to a higher-up to report what had happened. In no time Ornstein, a man known for his ferocious temper, appeared in my work space. He examined the damage, then furiously turned to me and said: "Out you go, and don't come back to do any more experiments." That was the end of my brief career as an experimental physicist. I had not completed my year, but fortunately that was not held against me for my master's requirements.

Nevertheless, my contacts with the experimental physicists remained good. The Utrecht laboratory was especially renowned for precision measurements of intensities of spectral lines. In Uhlenbeck's absence, people would come to me with questions about spectra. This forced me to study the subject further, and for some time I was the resident expert on the theory of spectra.

Another event brought me in close contact with experiment—though I was obliged to keep my hands off the apparatus. In February 1939 I read a now famous article in the journal *Nature* which explained the principles behind nuclear fission. I became quite excited and ran into the laboratory to tell my friends, suggesting that we should have a look at this phenomenon ourselves. We had all the necessary tools available for a primitive test: some uranium, a source of neutrons, and an oscilloscope. Willem Maas, a fellow graduate student, aimed the neutrons at our uranium and detected what happened on the screen of the oscilloscope. There we saw them: huge spikes on the screen that we had never seen before. We could of course not prove in this way that these spikes appeared because in fission uranium nuclei split into two nearly equal halves (plus some debris), yet it was obvious that what we saw could not be understood in terms of nuclear reactions we had known until then. It was that simple.

Shortly thereafter, Uhlenbeck returned from America, where he had learned about fission. We had long discussions on this brand-new branch of nuclear physics. He told me of a meeting in Washington, D.C., he had attended, where Bohr and Fermi had for the first time made public the news about fission, and how American newspapers had immediately picked this up as a piece of sensational news.[3] He also told me of sharing an office at Columbia University's Pupin Laboratory with Fermi, who had just escaped from Italy with his family. (The reason for his flight was that Mussolini's government had recently enacted anti-Semitic laws—and Fermi's wife was of Jewish extraction.) One day, he said, Fermi and Uhlenbeck had been discussing fission. Fermi got up, walked to the window, looked out, and said something like: "Do you realize, George, that fission may make possible the construction of bombs so powerful that just a few of them can destroy this whole big city?" Which goes to show that there was nothing secret about atomic weapons: the issue was obvious to the physicists, and even I, a youngster, at once understood the import.

Shortly afterward I met the nuclear physicist Frédéric Joliot, son-in-law of the late Marie Curie. He had come to visit Uhlenbeck who afterward told me of their discussions. It turned out that facilities on a military airfield had been made available to Joliot for doing undisturbed fission research under military protection. Joliot, a confirmed communist, had been given a fine car for personal use. When Uhlenbeck asked him if that would not change if the communists came to power, he replied, "Oh no, they will realize that I deserve a car because of my importance."

Back to Uhlenbeck's return from America. He also brought another piece of news that was most unwelcome to me: while in the States he had accepted an offer to return to the University of Michigan in Ann Arbor, where he had been employed before, from 1927 to 1935. He was to leave Utrecht in the summer of 1939. Until then, he promised me, we would do a lot of physics together.

The first thing I was told to do was make some calculations concerning fission. I had to compute a certain curve that displays the force between two fission fragments. The curve was expected to exhibit one minimum. Enthusiastically I started to work. Lo and behold, my curve showed two minima! Excitedly I went to tell Uhlenbeck, who snapped: "Impossible. You've made a mistake." Back I went to check. The two minima remained. Again I went to see Uhlenbeck, more timidly this time. Together we went through the calculations, then saw what had happened. I had used a book containing Kobayashi's mathematical tables of Bessel functions. My fake second minimum was due to an error in one of the printed tables, which I could have spotted myself—but what young kid doubts the printed word? It was a lesson for me always to use horse sense to anticipate roughly the answer to a calculation before one starts to sweat it out.

During that spring of 1939 Uhlenbeck gave a course called *Capita Selecta,* selected topics. He had chosen to lecture on the still quite young theory of the electron and the positron (a particle just like the electron except that it has an electric charge of opposite sign) developed by Paul Dirac. One of my life's strongest emotional experiences related to science occurred when for the first time I understood Dirac's equation for those particles.

Uhlenbeck had been one of the discoverers of a property of the electron called spin. Roughly speaking, it says that an electron spins around an axis while moving in some orbit or other, in some ways similar to the earth's rotation around an axis while moving around the sun. Uhlenbeck's discovery in 1925 had been the result of an analysis of certain spectroscopic phenomena which showed that an electron *had* to spin—but not *why* it did so. Then, in 1928, Dirac came forth with an equation that explained why. Finding this very tiny, compact equation was one of the most important discoveries in twentieth-century theoretical physics, made by a twenty-six-year-old man whom I would get to know very well later on. I was deeply moved when I first grasped how that equation works. It is such a simple equation, yet so rich in implications—it is beautiful and elegant.

What does a scientist mean when he or she says that a mathematical equation is simple, or beautiful, or elegant? Can such an inherently nonscientific appreciation be shared with the nonscientist? In explanation I should like you to imagine that you have a friend who has devoted himself to the study of the Chinese language. One day the friend comes to you and says, "Look at this Chinese poem here. It is so simple, so elegant, so beautiful." You will tell him, "I must take your word for it but cannot share your appreciation because I do not know Chinese." You will appreciate what your friend has in mind even though you cannot follow why he has those emotional responses. It is likewise with the language of mathematics. You will have to study for years in order to reach the possibility—not even the certainty—of developing the rewarding capacity for appreciating simplicity, elegance, beauty in a language that, so regrettably, has scared off so many.

Among my assignments for obtaining the master's degree was giving a few theoretical seminars. My first one was on fission. I was well prepared, I thought, and began my talk, writing formulas on the blackboard as I went along. Uhlenbeck interrupted almost at once: "First tell us what the problem is," he said, "then state your conclusions at once. Only thereafter should you go into details of the derivations." I followed instructions, but still the professor interrupted me several times with comments like: "You must explain in simple language, not show how smart you are." It was a most instructive and illuminating experience, and I have taken it to heart ever since. Uhlenbeck also taught blackboard techniques which, he later told me, he had learned from Ehrenfest, one of the best physics teachers in the early part of the twentieth century: "Start on the top left corner, prepare your written comments so that by the end of your talk you are at the right bottom corner. Never, never erase anything while making your presentation." Such advice may seem simple, almost trivial, but it is crucial for keeping your audience's attention, for not distracting them, as many otherwise good physicists do by holding a piece of chalk in one hand and an eraser in the other while they lecture. Among the debts of gratitude I owe to this great teacher is this style of presentation. I still get agitated when I listen to young physicists in action who are out to show how clever they are, how much they know, without apparent regard for the limited capacity of almost every person in the audience to absorb what they are saying.

I was also obliged to give a general colloquium in front of all local physicists, not just theorists, plus, possibly, outsiders. As a topic I had chosen the theory of a particle called the meson, another quite novel subject in the 1930s. My only recollection of that event is meeting Ornstein afterward; he asked me—he was known for rough language—if I really believed in all that shit.

Among my other tasks was assisting Uhlenbeck with certain calculations on the behavior of cosmic rays as they pass through a sequence of absorption layers made of different materials. That work was published later.[4]

Then the time came for Uhlenbeck's departure. I vividly remember our last encounter on Dutch soil. I thanked him for all I had learned from him. His final words to me were: "We shall meet again." That remark has given me added courage during the subsequent dark years. He left by boat in August 1939, only weeks before the outbreak of the Second World War. The next time we were to meet was in September 1946—in New York City.

In the preceding period I had learned more of the mathematical techniques of theoretical physics from Uhlenbeck than I would ever after from anyone else. I would have benefited much more in this respect had he not departed. In later years I have always felt that I did not master mathematics well enough for physics purposes. I have come to the conviction that a theorist can never know enough mathematics, yet, paradoxically, he can easily know too much of it. Mathematics should always be treated by physicists as a tool, not as a purpose. As Kramers once said to me, mathematics should forever be an unrequited love to the physicist, like a woman worshipped from afar.

From the experiences of the past year, I came to understand that theoretical physics was to be my life's way, wherever it might lead me. I could not reconcile this choice with a life in Palestine. Earlier I had given serious thought to emigrating, but now I decided that I could not possibly do so and also pursue science with the passion I had begun to lavish on it. I have never regretted that choice.

Before his departure, Uhlenbeck had arranged my first academic appointment, a quite modest one, of course. His earlier assistant Kahn had left to
become *lector* (associate professor) in Groningen. He had been succeeded
by Kees van Lier, a student with whom Uhlenbeck had published a nice
nuclear physics paper.[5] During academic year 1939–40, van Lier was on a
leave of absence, and Uhlenbeck saw to it that I became his temporary
replacement. As a result, I now received my first salary, small but nevertheless most gratifying. And so it may be said that at age twenty-one, still only
a graduate student, I began my academic career. In September 1939 I
moved to a rented room in Jutphaas, a suburb of Utrecht.

I devoted the fall of 1939 to preparations for my master's degree in
Utrecht. I now had regular discussions with Ornstein to give me some guidance in my independent physics studies. However, before leaving, Uhlenbeck had spoken about me to Kramers in Leiden who had said he would be
willing to receive me now and then for discussions. So a few days a month I
journeyed to Leiden, also attending on occasion the famous so-called
Ehrenfest colloquium. My talks with Kramers showed him to be a man of
quite unusual depth in his thinking, not only on physics but also in regard
to numerous other aspects of human culture. He was very musical and, as I
was soon to hear for myself, played the cello very well. I remember a story
he once told me about music. One evening he was attending a concert of
music he was particularly fond of. Suddenly, in the middle of it all, he got
up and left, because, he told me, he had found himself sitting there calculating in his head the energy levels of an oxygen atom, unable to concentrate
on the music at the same time. That was too much for him. He never went
to a concert again but continued to make his own music because that he
could do with undivided attention.

My acquaintance with Kramers grew into a friendship that would last
until his death in 1952.

Meanwhile, steps were being taken to find a successor to Uhlenbeck. As a
result, Léon Rosenfeld, professor of physics in Liège, Belgium, was invited
to spend a few days in Utrecht and give a colloquium.

In this colloquium, which I of course attended, Rosenfeld reported on
very recent work which he and Christian Møller were still doing, dealing
with the meson theory of nuclear forces.[6] We had several detailed technical
discussions during his stay. One of the topics was the quadrupole moment[7]
of the deuteron, the nucleus of heavy hydrogen, the simplest of all composite atomic nuclei, consisting of one proton and one neutron. I found those
talks stimulating but quickly realized that Rosenfeld belonged to a different

breed of physicist than Uhlenbeck. He was more the *savant,* the learned scholar, than the enterprising explorer. He was more philosophically inclined and also a rather outspoken Marxist. Wolfgang Pauli once described him as the square root of Niels Bohr and Léon Trotski.[8]

On April 22, 1940, I successfully passed the examination for the master's degree. It consisted of several written tests in mathematical subjects and lengthy oral probes conducted by Ornstein.

On May 7, 1940, the minister of education sent a letter to Rosenfeld that was signed by Queen Wilhelmina. It begins with the usual salutation: "*Wÿ Wilhelmina, by de gratie Gods Koningin der Nederlanden, prinses van Oranje Nassau, enz., enz., enz., hebben goedgevonden en verstaan . . .*" (We Wilhelmina, by the grace of God, Queen of the Netherlands, princess of Orange Nassau, etc., etc., etc., have approved and understood . . .). It was the official document approving his appointment to professor in Utrecht.[9]

On May 9, 1940, I sent a letter of congratulations to Rosenfeld in Liège. The day before I had also written to him, asking if I might be permitted to continue my studies under his direction if and when his appointment were to come through.[10]

On May 10, 1940, German armed forces invaded the Netherlands, Belgium and Luxembourg. After brave resistance, the Dutch army capitulated on May 15.

Mail delivery between Holland and Belgium was now interrupted for several months. When in August 1940 I was able to write to Rosenfeld again, I had to report a tragedy: "The capitulation of Holland has caused a great psychic shock to some people. . . . This shock has been too severe for some. In this connection it is my sad duty to report to you the death of van Lier."[11] He had committed suicide.

"I have been appointed his successor and I hope that you would be willing to accept me in that position."[12] Rosenfeld did so. He arrived in Utrecht in September.

I now began work on my doctoral dissertation. The problem Rosenfeld had proposed to me was an outgrowth of his program with Møller. The latter had made an attempt[13] to formulate their version of the meson theory in terms of a specific five-dimensional description, the so-called de Sitter space, in which the universe is supposed to possess a fifth dimension confined to a very small extension.[14] It is qualitatively analogous to replacing an infinitely thin spherical surface, analog of the usual universe, by a spherical shell of finite thickness, analog of de Sitter space. Superstring theories, the recent vogue, are in a sense further extensions of this type of theory to spaces with even more than five dimensions.

What Rosenfeld wanted me to do was to formulate this meson theory in terms of another version of five-dimensional theory known as projective relativity theory. When that was done, I had to tackle another, distinct, problem: using this theory, to calculate the probability for the disintegration of deuterons when irradiated by energetic photons.

I now had to learn a lot, to begin with, projective relativity, a seductively elegant generalization (as is also the de Sitter version) of Einstein's theory of general relativity, of which I already knew a fair amount from self-study, but not enough. These five-dimensional theories[15] had been invented as kinds of unified field theories which aim at unifying gravitational with electromagnetic phenomena—Einstein's dream, not successfully realized to this day. I delved into this subject, helped in particular by very clear papers written by Wolfgang Pauli,[16] little suspecting that, some forty years later, these studies would help me greatly in preparing a difficult chapter of my Einstein biography.[17]

Next, I had to learn meson theories, about which I already knew a bit but not enough. It is a subject that belongs to the broader category of so-called quantum field theories, a topic on which Rosenfeld was an expert. That part of physics was to become the center of my later research interests. Finally, I had to learn how to handle the deuteron, which led me to studies in nuclear physics. All in all, it was a fruitful area of problems for a beginning theorist.

Van Lier's suicide was only the beginning of my brushes with death. There would be so much more of that in the following five years—and much closer to home still. Later in 1940 another event occurred which directly affected my life and career.

The first months of German occupation of Holland passed without major difficulties for Dutch Jews. But then, in November 1940, the Germans issued a decree banning Jews from all civil service positions, including all academic posts (see the next chapter). That meant the end of my assistantship at the University of Utrecht, to which someone else was appointed in my place (to my regret I cannot remember his name). At the suggestion of Rosenfeld, an understanding *sub rosa* was reached whereby this person was to share with me his assistant's salary—to which he graciously consented.

The decree also meant that Ornstein was fired from his professorship and his directorship of the laboratory. He was not even allowed to enter his own place of work any longer. He became a broken man. He died on May 20, 1941, only sixty years old.

I had grown to like Ornstein very much, and his death shook me up. My work had to go on, however. Neither van Lier's suicide, nor my own dismissal, nor the death of Ornstein held me back from my researches. My preparations for the doctorate were soon affected, however, by yet another development.

According to a further German decree, July 14, 1941, was to be the final date on which Jews would be permitted advancement to the doctor's degree. Along with the burdens of a substantial research program there now arose the external pressure of a deadline—not, one might say, an ideal atmosphere for doing research. I doggedly went on, however, deciding to beat the Germans at their own game.

As I now look back, half a century later, to those days as a youngster, it strikes me that my situation then, though far from ideal, offered one tremendous advantage. Hell-bent as I was about getting the work done, I had little emotional energy to waste on the constraints of everyday life, nor on fearful anticipation of what might happen next. Indeed, my strong attachments to science provided me throughout the war years with a sort of protective emotional shield from the events around me.

My further account of the war days and the German occupation can be found in the next chapters.

Throughout my career I have worked hard, but never more so than in early 1941, particularly because of the deadline I had to face. Toward the closing stages, when I had to do the actual writing, I worked for weeks on end until two in the morning, until I literally could not move my hand any more to write the next word; then I went to bed and got up again at five to continue.

I spent some time during that period in a house in the country, near Amsterdam, that belonged to Tineke's family. One day, it was the 22nd of June, I was sitting at a table outside, hard at work, when someone rushed in, excitedly. Had we heard? German armies had invaded Russia. I did not look up, and said: "Then they will lose the war," and kept writing.

I made the deadline.

On July 9, 1941, at 3 P.M., I began the defense of my doctor's thesis in the Aula of Utrecht University on Domplein. It was a public affair. Among the substantial audience were my parents, my sister Annie, Tineke, more family, friends from Amsterdam and Utrecht, and fellow students. For the first time in my life I had to be in white tie and tails for the occasion. (The next time would not be until forty years later, at a Nobel ceremony in Stockholm.) I rented that outfit. Lion Nordheim and Sieg Gitter acted as my paranymphs, men who had to assist and support the promovendus. They, too, were in white tie and tails. At three the doors of the Aula were opened and the university beadle entered, carrying a staff which he banged three times on the floor. Whereupon the *rector magnificus* of the university came in, followed by about a dozen professors, Rosenfeld of course among them, all in black togas. After some preliminaries, a few professors began questioning me, addressing me as *hooggeachte promovendus,* highly esteemed promovendus. I replied, beginning with *hooggeleerde* (highly learned) opponent. The last examiner was Rosenfeld, who queried me on technical issues. This went on for about an hour, whereupon the beadle entered again, once more banged his staff three times on the floor, and proclaimed: *Hora est,* the hour has come. The professors withdrew for some ten minutes, during which I stood chatting with family and friends. Then they returned, and Rosenfeld pronounced that my defense had satisfied the faculty, that I now was entitled to call myself Doctor of Philosophy. (Two weeks later I received my Doctor's Bull written in Latin. It still hangs in my study at home.) A reception in another part of the building followed.

Then a number of us took taxis to the railway station and went to Amsterdam, where Tineke and Marie, her mother, had made arrangements for a festive dinner in their home, attended by them, my family, and some close friends. I remember it as a happy evening. But more clearly than anything else I recall one thing: I was exhausted. Tineke and I took a short vacation together afterward.

As to my actual doctoral thesis, it had been available as a printed monograph at my thesis defense.[18] (The last part of my labors had been the misery of reading proof.) It is dedicated to my parents and to Tineke. It contains three chapters, written in English. At Rosenfeld's request I had written for openers a short autobiographical sketch in Dutch instead of the customary preface. The concluding summary of the thesis is of a nature that must be extremely rare: it is written in Latin. Not only was this Rosenfeld's idea, but he actually wrote it. He did so because I never studied Latin (nor Greek), being an alumnus of a type of high school which, as the Dutch say, breeds barbarians.

In my opening sketch I had thanked Rosenfeld: "His support, his encouragement, and especially the interest which he always showed in my person have helped me through many a difficult moment. It is of particular value to me that I found in him someone who not only taught me much about physics, but with whom I at the same time have been able to have contact in other domains. The cordiality which he and his wife always have shown me has been a great support to me in difficult times." I concluded my sketch with these words: "I regret that, because of circumstances, the problems treated in this dissertation have not been dealt with in the way I intended to. I hope, however, to return later to these questions." There is no doubt in my mind that the thesis could have benefited from more time than circumstances of war allowed me to spend on it.

In the years 1941–43 I actually published four papers based on my thesis work, including corrections to some errors I had made earlier. The first paper[19] deals with an improved general formulation of projective relativity theory, the second and third[20] with the application of the theory to meson fields, the last with the theory of the photodisintegration of the deuteron.[21]

7

War

*I can also bring to mind some pleasant goods
and some inevitable evils, which, when I turn
my thoughts backward, strike terror in me and
astonishment that I should have reached this
age . . . wherein . . . I am still travelling
prosperously forward.*

—BENVENUTO CELLINI IN HIS AUTOBIOGRAPHY,
TRANS. BY J. A. SYMONDS

7.1 OMINOUS RUMBLINGS

NOT SINCE October 1830, when the fall of Antwerp sealed the independence of Belgium from Holland, had Dutch armies faced action in the field. Holland had remained neutral during the First World War. Peace had reigned for more than a century when it came to an end at about four o'clock on the morning of Friday, May 10, 1940.

On April 28, 1939, Hitler delivered the last great peacetime speech of his life before the *Reichstag* (parliament) in Berlin. An American reporter then stationed there has called it "probably the most brilliant oration he ever gave. . . . For sheer eloquence, craftiness, irony, sarcasm, and hypocrisy it reached a new level he was never to approach again. . . . It was broadcast not only on all German radio stations but on hundreds of others throughout the world; in the United States it was carried by the major networks. Never before or afterward was there such a world-wide audience as he had that day."[1]

I, too, was among the listeners to this long speech, which lasted over two hours. Having heard several of Hitler's earlier addresses, I also believe that this one was his most remarkable. I of course was never happy with what he said but even so could not avoid being spellbound by his delivery.

This address contained for the first time publicly expressed threats against Poland, specifically German demands on Danzig (now Gdansk), which had been detached from Germany by the Treaty of Versailles to become a *Freistadt* (free city) under the supervision of the League of Nations. The treaty had, moreover, created the "Polish Corridor," separating Danzig from Germany by a strip of land that gave Poland access to the Baltic Sea. Not only did Hitler want Danzig to revert to Germany, but he also had in mind to build a super motor highway and a double-track railroad through the corridor, thus linking Danzig and East Prussia once again with the Fatherland.

Already in November 1938 Hitler had issued a top secret directive to his armed forces ordering surprise attacks on Danzig, followed in early April 1939 by another such directive to prepare for the destruction of all Polish armed forces.[2] As was his custom, he continued for almost a year to talk with the Poles about some negotiated agreement, however.

On August 23, 1939, Joachim von Ribbentrop, the German minister of foreign affairs, arrived in Moscow at noontime for discussions with Stalin on a German-Russian nonaggression pact. This move had been prepared by a variety of earlier diplomatic exchanges. Late that night the pact was signed, as was a secret additional protocol defining the respective spheres of influence. (This last document remained unknown until after the war.) That done, Stalin proposed a toast to the health of the Führer; Ribbentrop in turn proposed a toast to Stalin.

In 1941 Stalin said that the pact had served to prepare his forces for defense if fascist Germany risked attacking.[3]

After the war, Ribbentrop was arrested in a Hamburg boarding house on June 14, 1945. He was sentenced to death by an international military tribunal. At 1:11 A.M. on October 16, 1946, he ascended the gallows to be hanged.[4]

I heard the news of the pact as I came back to Amsterdam from a day in the country with Tineke, and then said to her: "This is it. War will break out in a matter of days."

September 1: Germany invaded Poland.

September 3: Britain and France declared war on Germany.

World War II was upon us.

Since I always read the newspapers, I was aware of all the events recapitulated above. I knew that the world was in turmoil, but I lived under the delusion that this was *the* world, not *my* world. In that regard I was not all that different from the rest of the Dutch. We lived in a little country that was intellectually alert, yet asleep, by and large, regarding the possible impact on us of international events. We lived complacently in a country with a very high standard of living, bourgeois and self-satisfied in outlook.

How shortsighted we were.

7.2 DAYS OF WAR IN THE NETHERLANDS

We all know, and can probably answer, questions like: Where were you when you first heard of the assassination of JFK? I know where I was on that occasion—but I also remember vividly where I was when I first heard that World War II had broken out.

It was on an Amsterdam street called Het Rokin. I was walking along, minding my own business, when suddenly I saw people rushing toward a poster that was being put up—I still remember precisely where. It was a newspaper bulletin that brought those of us present the first news of war. I also clearly recall my first reaction. It was one of thrill, intense excitement, rather than fear or gloom.

For many years it had been Dutch foreign policy, successfully implemented during World War I, to maintain strict neutrality. The reasons were, in the first instance, economic. Holland needed Germany for its important transit trade, and it needed Britain for maintaining the security of the Dutch East Indies, now Indonesia. Recall that at that time little Holland was the world's third largest colonial empire. Nevertheless, on August 28, 1939, a few days before the outbreak of hostilities, the Dutch government had ordered the mobilization of the armed forces—but purely as a preparatory defensive measure.

On November 5, 1939, a German anti-Nazi colonel warned the Dutch and Belgian military attachés in Berlin to expect an attack on November 12. This, however, did not come off.[5]

By January 1940, intelligence sources reported that the Germans were concentrating some fifty divisions on the Dutch/Belgian frontiers.

On April 9, German forces invaded Denmark and Norway. After two hours of combat, Denmark capitulated. "In those few hours of fighting the Danish army put up just enough resistance to escape complete dishonor."[6] The Norwegians fought back until well into June, whereafter the king and his government officials fled to London.

Also in April, the Dutch government declared a state of siege in order to deal with German espionage. Twenty-one prominent Dutch Nazis were arrested.

On May 3, the German colonel warned again: the attack would begin on May 10. On May 9, the Dutch military attaché in Berlin called his Ministry of Defense: "Tomorrow at dawn. Hold tight."[7] At that stage the total strength of the Dutch armed forces was 300,000 men.

This time the information turned out to be accurate.

Neither I nor any other Dutch citizen, for that matter, was aware of that warning. May 9 was in fact a happy day for me. That morning my friend Lion Nordheim had received his long-wished-for "Certificate," a document issued by a British governmental office stating that he was permitted to emigrate to Palestine. I believe that it was also on that very day that he became engaged to Jaap van Amerongen's older sister, with whom he had been in love for years, as all his close friends well knew.

That evening they and a number of their friends converged on the terrace of the Lido, a restaurant near the Leidsche Plein, to celebrate the happy events with a drink. Tineke and I were there, also Sieg and Leah and others. Then and there we pledged: whatever happens—ten years from now we shall meet in Palestine. In May 1950 I did indeed ring the doorbell of the Gitters' Tel Aviv apartment—but some of those present that May 9, 1940, would be killed a few years later.

Afterward we went out for dinner and stayed together until late. Then I went home and to bed right away.

It was two in the morning of May 10.

Between three and four, German planes began dropping three hundred bombs on Schiphol, Amsterdam's airport,[8] completely destroying all its facilities. I heard nothing, since I was a deep sleeper.

I remember a story that circulated in Holland during the war days. I cannot vouch for its veracity but here it is.

In the early dawn of that same May 10, a policeman was patrolling along the banks of the river Maas, near Rotterdam, when he saw a small rubber boat on the river coming toward the grass embankment. A few men got out and clambered upward on the grass. As every Dutchman knew, wherever there was public grass you inevitably would find a small marker which said: "Forbidden to walk on the grass, Article 364 of the penal code." So the police officer addressed the men somewhat like this: "Hey, you, what do you think you are doing?" Whereupon one of the men drew a pistol and shot and killed the policeman. The men were German soldiers who belonged (and this is fact)[9] to a company that had landed on the river in antiquated seaplanes. True or not, the story illustrates correctly how unexpected the invasion was for the good citizens of Holland.

It must have been about 5 o'clock when my father came into my bedroom and said (verbatim): "Bram, get up. There is war." I responded with a grunt, then, seconds later, I sat up and said: "*What* are you saying?"

All of us got dressed and had breakfast, after which my father and I took our bicycles and made our way toward the Dam, Amsterdam's main square, where the Royal Palace (not the residence, which is in The Hague) is situated. Many people did what we did, driven, as it were, to the center. The mood was quiet and solemn. Many policemen lined the streets, all wearing helmets instead of their usual caps, something I had never seen before. We came to the Dam, got off our bikes, and strolled around a bit, exchanging a few words here and there with equally subdued fellow citizens. Then we rode back home. It remained ominously quiet in Amsterdam during all the war days. All schools were closed. Occasional air alerts would break the silence, with sirens wailing up-down-up-down, but in fact in all those days not one bomb fell on our city.

On that tenth day of May I was just nine days shy of my twenty-second birthday. At age eighteen I had passed obligatory medical tests to determine if I was fit for military service. I was, but received deferment as a university student, to be called up only after I had obtained my master's degree which I had already received the preceding April. When war broke out I had not yet been notified where to report for duty, and for the five years following the capitulation there was no Dutch army. So, through a confluence of events, I never became a soldier. Nor in fact have I ever fired a shot with a pistol or rifle: hunting was something that never interested me in the least. As Einstein told me on a later occasion, Walther Rathenau, at one time Germany's foreign minister and a Jew, had once told him that when a Jew says he likes to hunt he is a confessed liar.

Nevertheless, I felt I ought to make myself somehow useful during the war. Upon contacting fellow students I learned that a request had gone out for volunteers to help prepare protective measures for university buildings. I went to the Oudemanhuispoort, where Amsterdam University's central building was located, and offered my services. I was asked to help hoist sandbags to the building's roof as protection against possible fire that might result from bombing. I did so and—perhaps it seems odd—had an absolutely wonderful time doing those menial chores: first of all, I had never done anything like it, and second (which dawned on me only later), it was a fine way to deflect thinking about all kinds of grim things related to the situation.

While this was going on, we were invited to attend a briefing on civilian preparedness in one of the lecture rooms. The speaker impressed on us the need to be alert for fifth columnists (a term dating from the Spanish Civil War) who were expected to be present in many places. He further stressed not to take any personal action but rather to warn a policeman or a soldier. I remember one bizarre incident he recounted. Somebody walking under a railway overpass had heard footsteps on the train tracks and duly alerted an armed soldier, who also heard the noise and took up position. At one point the soldier could see movement on the tracks and fired, wounding another soldier on a roof who had been assigned to guard the overpass. The noise on the track turned out to have been made by a stray goat.

I next outline briefly the military developments.[10]

"The conquest of the Netherlands was accomplished in five days largely by parachutists and by troops landed by air transports behind the great flooded water lines . . . To the bewildered Dutch was reserved the experience of being subjected to the first large-scale airborne attack in the history of warfare."[11] A whole army corps consisting of two divisions had landed behind the lines. The Dutch fought courageously. In a directive issued on May 14, Hitler stated: "The power of resistance of the Dutch army has proved to be stronger than was anticipated."[12]

Back to May 10. A few hours after the invasion had begun, the German ambassador in The Hague delivered a statement that German troops had entered to protect Dutch neutrality against an Allied invasion aimed at the Ruhr Valley. The Dutch government indignantly rejected these inane allegations but now, after the event, requested urgent help from British and French forces. They never came.

On that first day, the German air force destroyed most of the Dutch military planes. German parachutists who had landed near The Hague with orders to capture the queen and the government were shot. Other parachutists landed and captured the Moerdÿk Bridge over the Maas, the crucial link between the northern and southern parts of the country. These tactics ruined Dutch plans for a concerted defense of "Fortress Holland," the country's central section, protected by inundations and fortified defense positions.

On May 12, Crown Princess Juliana and her family were transported to England by British destroyer. Bernhard, her husband, immediately returned to join Dutch troops fighting in Zeeland, the southwestern province.

On May 13, the queen and the cabinet ministers likewise left for England. Staying behind were the secretaries general and the permanent undersecretaries, the highest remaining Dutch authorities in the country. Proclamations of the queen and the commander in chief announcing these departures were made public on May 14.

On the morning of May 14, I, following the example of many other Dutch, went to a savings bank to pick up the small amount of money I had on deposit there. As I took my place in the queue I saw ominously thick black smoke rising from the north. This caused great excitement among all those waiting in line. Several said they had heard that this was the result of heavy fighting between German and British troops, which had landed in the meantime. The source in fact turned out to be the British military, but not combat troops. Early that morning one of their demolition squads had arrived with orders to destroy immediately all Dutch petroleum supplies.

This first confrontation with false rumors would be followed by many, many more in those war years. Few if any had evil intent. It is most striking how desire can overwhelm reality in people.

On May 14 it became evident that the military situation was hopeless. All Dutch naval ships were ordered to leave for England, where they arrived safely. At 1:30 P.M. on that day, the bombardment of Rotterdam began; it ended up destroying one-eighth of the city, causing one thousand deaths, and making eighty thousand people homeless. Along with the bombardments of Warsaw and Coventry this event became a symbol of German ruthlessness.

At 10:15 P.M. the commander in chief of the Dutch armed forces addressed the nation on the radio. "We have had to lay down our arms because it could not be otherwise."[13]

On the morning of May 15 the Dutch commander and some of his staff met with a German general and his advisers in a school building in Rÿsoord near Rotterdam. The two sides were seated at separate tables, facing each

other. The German general declared, "Ihre Truppen haben tapfer gef-
ochten" (Your troops have fought bravely). The Dutch commander replied:
"Ich danke" (I thank you).[14] Otherwise the entire proceedings were devoted to the formulation of the instrument of surrender of all troops except
those fighting in Zeeland, which capitulated three days later. All Dutch
troops were declared prisoners of war. A few weeks later they were released,
however, but of course their weapons were confiscated. As to the German
forces, they had lost five hundred planes and sixteen hundred prisoners of
war to the Dutch.

That night many Dutch people destroyed anti-Nazi books and
newspapers.

The number of suicides among Jews in Holland during May 1940 has
been estimated to be about two hundred.[15] The only one of these I knew
personally was my friend Kees van Lier (see chapter 6).

Tineke has recently reminded me that on the day of the capitulation, she
and I went to the Dam square, like many other Amsterdamers, and there
remembered what the poet Heinrich Heine had said: "When the world
comes to an end I shall go to Holland. Everything there happens eighty
years later."

It must have been very shortly after the capitulation when, as I walked on
an Amsterdam street, I saw a huge German tank rumbling by, a helmeted,
grim-faced soldier looking out of the turret. I can still remember the exact
spot where I was at the time. I have never forgotten my unanticipated reaction to that sight. I said to myself: "I am a Dutchman," whereupon my
thoughts continued along lines something like this: "You silly little fellow,
of course you are a Dutchman. So what else is new? Why didn't you ever
have that thought before? Why now?"

I found the answers during the next five bitter years: that part of your
being which gets challenged the most becomes most prominent in your
feelings.

8

Occupation of Holland

I MUST NOW write—in this and the next chapters—of years of heroism and treachery, of noble sacrifice and the crassest egotism, of oppression, hunger, and starvation, of life on the brink of death, and of murder at rates never seen before.

So it was in all countries of occupied Europe. Worst off in the West was Holland. There are two principal reasons for this.

First, by a decree of May 18, 1940, Hitler appointed Dr. Arthur Seyss-Inquart, Austrian minister of the interior and a confessed Nazi, as *Reichskommissar* of the Netherlands. He became the chief of the German civil authorities, the highest German position in the land. That kind of regime was much worse than the military administration that ruled Belgium and France. The military had one overriding aim: to keep things quiet so that troop movements will not be hampered. The institution of civil leadership in Holland, on the other hand, was but a first step toward the Nazi aim of incorporating the country into a greater German *Reich*. As an early step, these civilians—if you pardon the expression—laid down the rules for paying the financial costs of occupation, which, for the duration of the war, would amount to about two-thirds of Holland's national income.[1]

Second, Holland's geography was the worst possible under the circumstances: no hills or forests to hide in, bounded to the east by Germany, to the north and west by the sea, to the south by two other occupied countries. Escape was not impossible but extremely difficult. Few dared, even fewer succeeded.

All over occupied Europe, the Jews' fate was particularly awful, nowhere worse than in Poland. Worst off in the West were again the Jews of Holland.[2] Their story will be the subject of the next chapter. Here I will make only a few preliminary remarks on the subject.

Why did the Dutch Jews fare so singularly badly? The reasons are complex. Holland's German civil administration and its geographical features were no doubt contributing factors, but that is only part of the answer. When the question was put to some of the Dutch Jews who managed to survive the extermination camps, one answered: "The Dutch suffered more than all the rest. They thought too much of their wives and children, and that was the reason why they perished." Another called them "a soft bunch, unused to cutting hay and felling trees or to the stark terror of nazi brutality. . . . They [quickly] gave up or grew weak and sick or made fatal mistakes through carelessness or indifference."[3] A doctor found the answer in the sudden change of diet—from the fatty meals of former days to the almost total lack of fat in the camp food. "It was said that Poles and Russians, coming as they did from countries with a harsh climate and a lower standard of living, were better able to endure hardships, more capable of taking care of themselves, of escaping notice and of fending for themselves. Not much less adaptable were the Greeks, followed by the Slovaks, the Germans, the Czechs—in that order—with the Dutch at the very bottom of the list." Another survivor remarked that the Dutch Jews "lacked the animal cunning, the stubborn urge to survive at any price, if necessary at the expense of others."[4] Let it be stressed that such comments referred to a majority but not by any means to all of the Dutch Jews.

In order to express some views of my own I interject an occasional fictitious dialogue between a questioner (Q) followed by my reply (P).

Q. Do you agree with these observations?

P. I note them respectfully, am inclined to believe that they contain more than germs of truth, but am unable to say that I accept them categorically. Remember, I myself have been spared the camps.

Q. Does the last comment on survival at the expense of others not raise profound questions about moral behavior?

P. They certainly do. I have witnessed enough to have an opinion on this point. We are dealing here with places and times in which the normal rules of social intercourse have broken down completely, as the result of actions not by but against the Jews—and others. I am sure that most Jews would not pride themselves for the ways they behaved in those extreme circumstances. I would urge you, however, not to condemn them but try—you won't be able to but try anyway—to imagine what it is like when it is your life or your neighbor's, when you are going mad with hunger. I will quote to you a line from the beggar's ballad in the *Dreigroschenoper*: "Erst kommt das Fressen und dann kommt die Moral" (first stuff your belly, and only then talk of morality). Note that the verb *fressen* is the German word most commonly used to refer to the way an animal eats. Try to imagine that you and those around you have in fact become animals, driven only by their survival instincts.

I now leave the Jewish predicament for later except for an occasional mention of events that affected the life and behavior of both the Jews and their non-Jewish surroundings.

After the capitulation of the Dutch, it took German forces less than six weeks to achieve all the objectives of the military campaign that had begun on May 10. Belgium capitulated on May 28, Paris fell on June 14, an armistice with France was signed on June 21. Meanwhile, the "miracle of Dunkirk," the successful evacuation, between May 26 and June 3, of British forces on the continent, had taken place.

I spent the day after the fall of Paris with Kramers, in the study of his home on the Poelgeesterweg in Oegstgeest, a suburb of Leiden. The plan had been to discuss some physics issues, but neither of us felt like doing that. The loss of Paris had hit us, as it did so many other Dutchmen, very hard. I do not think that any one of us had really believed that our country could successfully withstand the German onslaught. But Paris stood as the symbol of Western culture. I think that none of us had reckoned with Paris falling into German hands—and so quickly, at that. So my visit to Kramers turned into hours of gloomy reminiscences about the City of Light. I do not mean to exaggerate when I note that the fate of Paris hit us harder than even the fall of Holland.

The only inspiriting events in those months were the first war speeches delivered by Churchill, the prime minister of Britain since May 10, given when Britain stood alone. These have become classics of oratory. On June 4, in the House of Commons: "We shall fight on the beaches, we shall fight on the landing grounds, we shall fight in the fields and in the streets, we shall fight in the hills; we shall never surrender." On June 18, at the same place: "Hitler knows that he will have to break us in this island or lose the war. . . . Let us therefore brace ourselves to our duties, and so bear ourselves that, if the British Empire and its Commonwealth last for a thousand years, men will say: 'This was their finest hour.' "

Those speeches, still widely remembered, the texts of which were broadcast in full on the BBC, gave me strength, as they did to untold many others. Here, in days when spirits were so very low, came a voice of firm resolve that spoke without bombast and without at all gilding the lily. Life was going to be tough. Survival of the self, as of civilization, crucially depended on the ability to face the realities of the situation. That was the spirit of Churchill's addresses. I shall never forget them.

All through the war the BBC Home Service programs were the best and most realistic sources of information. I listened to them as much as I could, clandestinely of course. There were voices I became familiar with, such as Joseph McLeod (I hope I am spelling his name correctly), a regular newscaster, and Raymond Gram Swing, an American war correspondent who frequently spoke on the radio. From him I heard for the first time English spoken with the distinct American accent that I have grown to know and love in later years.

From June 1940 on, the Dutch government in London sponsored a daily fifteen-minute radio program, called Radio Oranje, to which I listened but only infrequently. I did not care for their attempts at bringing optimism, even cheer, to our occupied country. I did like the broadcasts in French (also over the BBC), not so much for their content as for their talent in saying nothing in the most elegant way. How well do I remember the way they concluded their broadcasts, which went like this: "Ceci termine notre cinquième bulletin d'information en langue française. Bonjour mesdames, bonjour mesdemoiselles, bonjour messieurs."

On July 19, in the last of his great *Reichstag* speeches, Hitler made his final peace offer to Britain. It was rejected. Then came the battle of Britain.

I shall of course not need to describe here step by step the progress of the war, and so return once again to the events in Holland. I cannot resist, however, to add one joke about the *Blitzkrieg* which I heard told those days over the BBC.

A man is sitting in a barber chair, getting shaved, when somebody runs in and yells: "Mr. Brown, Mr. Brown, your house is on fire!" The man jumps up from the chair, his face still half-lathered, a towel still around his neck; he dashes out of the shop, and starts running. After half a mile he suddenly stops and says to himself: "Why should I run? My name isn't Brown."

During the summer of 1940 there was calm, by and large, in Holland. There was one kind of nuisance though: rationing had begun, of tea, coffee, and bread in June, of rice in July, of meat in September, of cheese in October.[5] These restrictions were not—not yet—severe, but they were irritants to the Dutch, heavy eaters as they are.

I spent part of that summer in Zandvoort, the beach resort nearest to Amsterdam. Of those days I remember in particular the occasion when I saw a detachment of the SS *Totenkopf* (death head) *Husaren* march along the boulevard bordering on the North Sea. They were singing the *Engeland Lied,* the defiant song in which the Germans announced their intent soon to invade England—which never happened. I can still sing that song in its entirety, including the boom-boom pauses. Its refrain ends like this:

> Reich mir deine Hand
> Deine weisse Hand
> Leb' wohl mein Schatz—boom—boom
> Leb' wohl mein Schatz leb' wohl
> Lebe wohl
> Denn wir fahren
> Denn wir fahren
> Denn wir fahren gegen Engeland, Engeland.

(Give me your hand, your white hand, good-bye my darling, for we are sailing against England.) One thing you had to concede to the German troops: they could sing, so very well. I remember so many of their songs: the Horst-Wessel song, "Die Fahnen hoch, die Reihen fest geschlossen" (The banners high, the ranks firmly closed); "Today we own Germany, tomorrow the whole world"; "Es war ein Edelweiss"; many others.

The first major Dutch protests against German rule were the result of the decree of November 1940 banning Jews from all civil service positions. I have already mentioned in chapter 6 how this affected my own assistant appointment at the University of Utrecht. The news reached the Dutch universities on the 22nd of that month.[6] On the 25th, the students of the Institute of Technology in Delft went on strike, but the faculty did not yet respond. In Leiden, Rudolph Pabus Cleveringa, dean of the Faculty of Law, was asked by his faculty to take over the classes of his famous Jewish colleague Eduard Maurits Meyers. He did so, and on the 26th he conducted the first and, as it turned out, the last of these classes, with words honoring Meyers: "The German actions are beneath contempt . . . this noble son of our people, this man, this father to his students, this scholar, whom foreign usurpers have suspended from his duties . . . a man who, as all of us know, belongs here and God willing, shall return to us."[7] After which the audience rose and spontaneously burst out in the *Wilhelmus,* the national anthem. Within days, thousands of Dutchmen had read duplicated copies of this speech. Other universities reacted less strongly. In Amsterdam the rector declared an early vacation.

As a result of these actions, Delft and Leiden were closed, and Cleveringa was sent to prison for eight months. Delft was reopened later. In the autumn of 1941, a secretary general announced his intention to replace some Leiden professors by NSBers; a mass resignation of faculty followed, eighty percent by May 1942. Leiden therefore remained closed for the duration.

Among the notable Jews who lost their positions as a result of the November decree was Lodewijk Ernst Visser, president of the Dutch Supreme Court, a man of impeccable integrity who had set his heart on militant opposition.

On October 22, 1941, the Germans decreed that Jews were to be debarred from participation in nonprofit organizations, which included the Royal Dutch Academy of Sciences. As a result, five non-Jewish Academy members resigned, among them my friend Hans Kramers.[8]

Meanwhile, the next major protest had taken place, the 1941 strike in Amsterdam, in which Jews and Gentiles acted in concert. In January of that year harassment of Jews by NSB thugs had turned violent. The Jews refused to knuckle under, however. "Determined to defend their hearths and homes—however poor—they formed the first resistance groups in the country."[9]

Amsterdam's Gentiles, too, became enraged. One of them expressed his feelings by chalking on a wall: *Blijf met je moffenpoten van onze rotjoden af* (Keep your Hun's paws off our rotten Jews).[10]

> Q: "Rotten Jews," doesn't that sound anti-Semitic?
>
> P: Let me remind you once again that I am describing a society to which the normal rules of human conduct do not apply. In normal times "rotten" might arouse the righteous indignation of the Antidefamation League, that rather silly organization. You should further know that *rotjoden* is a century's old appellation of Jews in Holland, a gentle expression of disgust that was common in Western Europe, even in Holland, which can justly pride itself on a history of tolerance. Note also that the writer mentioned *our* Jews, a term that connotes an element of solidarity, if not of some affection. Such apparent contradictions were not that rare. Another example: a Gentile who actively helped Jews once said, "They're a lousy lot, but of course we must help them."[11] People like that actually belonged to a minority of Gentiles whose

moral values were stronger than their dislikes. Believe me, the Jews would have fared much better had this attitude been more widespread.

In 1941, Gentile reactions went well beyond the verbal. Some joined the Jews in street battles against NSBers, in particular Amsterdam's dock-workers, a vigorous and tough breed. On February 11 they descended on the Waterlooplein, the main square in the Jewish quarter, armed with cud-gels, chair legs, or whatever else came to hand (but no firearms). In pitched battle, one NSBer was severely wounded and died soon afterward. He was buried on February 17.

It is known that the Germans were quite taken aback. Never before, ei-ther in their own or in occupied countries, had they met with physical counteraction by Gentiles in support of Jews.

On February 19, a German patrol entered a Jewish-run ice cream parlor in south Amsterdam which earlier had been badgered by NSBers. The owners had installed an ammonia flask as a defense measure, which was set off when the Germans came in, spraying them with the irritant fluid. As a result, one of the owners was arrested and, on March 3, executed. He was the first Jew from Holland to come to this end.

On February 22 and 23, the Germans hit back with the first *razziahs* against the Dutch Jews. They picked up 425 young males who ended up in the concentration camp Mauthausen, near Linz in Austria. Only one of them survived.

The response to these actions was the great February strike of the 25th and 26th, mainly in Amsterdam. The Germans, once again taken by sur-prise, declared a state of emergency. Machine guns were set up in various spots as a threat; no shooting followed. Strikers were arrested all over town and brought to the Lloyd Hotel, which had been converted into a prison. By the end of the second day, the strike was broken by intimidation. Those arrested were held until mid-March, then sent home.[12]

I spent those days in Tineke's home in central Amsterdam. At one time, looking out of the window, I saw trucks racing toward the small square in front of the house, then stopping. German *Grüne Polizei* (Green Police) jumped out, started to cudgel passing Dutchmen, and dragged them into trucks. It was the first time I saw such physical violence with my own eyes. I remember how I trembled with rage.

On the 25th of February of every year since 1946, thousands upon thou-sands of Amsterdamers gather on the Jonas Daniel Meyerplein, the square where the four hundred young Jews had been collected before being carted off. On December 19, 1952, Queen Juliana unveiled a memorial statue on the square. It depicts a defiant dockworker, sleeves rolled up, arms half-spread. When you walk by there, pause a moment to remember those brave and selfless Gentiles who had stood by their Jewish brothers and sisters.

The other major strike in Holland, this one nationwide, began on April 29, 1943, and lasted for about a week. It was the largest strike against the occupiers, not just in Holland but in all of Western Europe. This time the Dutch did not react against the NSB but against the Germans.

By that time the tides of war had turned against Germany. On the night of May 30, 1942, the British had carried out their first one-thousand-plane night-bombing raid (on Cologne). A good number of those planes flew over Holland. By then few if any took the trouble to get out of bed and into an air-raid shelter. I would listen to the planes' droning, feel less isolated, and contentedly turn over.

In November 1942, the African campaign of the Germans collapsed when they withdrew from El Alamein. On February 2, 1943, the last German troops in Stalingrad surrendered. That dated the beginning of German despair, as could be gleaned from the slogan, heard on the radio and seen on posters: "Victory at any price." Speaking of morality in wartime, such a sentiment was not exactly moral either.

In Holland, the German military setbacks had begun to radicalize the resistance movement. Rationing had become increasingly strict. In July 1942 the systematic deportation of Jews had begun (to which I shall come back later).

The April-May strike was the Dutch response to the German decree ordering the reinternment of all who had served in the Dutch forces. The unstated motivation behind this move was to supplement the labor force in Germany. The ensuing strike involved hundreds of thousands of workers. The Germans declared a state of police siege. Many Dutchmen were arrested, eighty were executed, sixty were killed in random shootings.[13] The strike was quelled. But the bitter anger against the Germans had now risen to new heights.

I lived in hiding at the time of the strike (my experiences during the hiding period are discussed in chapter 10) and recall that the resentment about what was going on in our country was tempered by good news from the fronts. On May 13 all German forces in Africa capitulated, in the night of July 9–10 the Allies landed in Sicily, two weeks later Mussolini was forced to resign, then he was arrested. His fall caused great joy in the Netherlands and led practically all of us to assume, prematurely, that the war was almost over.

The news of Mussolini's overthrow led my host to break open and share with me one of his last bottles of whisky. That evening I got very, very drunk, a rare occurrence for me. One of us would raise his filled glass, then pronounce "Benito, finito," and gulp down his drink. Whereupon the other would make the same toast. Many Benito, finitos were thus exchanged, and it all ended by both of us staggering to our beds in a happy stupor.

There are so many other topics bearing on the years of occupation that deserve telling about in detail. If I do not do so it is, first, because they involve events that I was not directly involved in and, second, because I can refer the reader to an excellent account in English.[14] I cannot pass over these subjects in complete silence, however, and have therefore adopted the compromise of detailing them in telegram style.

The role of the churches: they were the source of the most pervasive and influential opposition to Nazi ideology. The resistance: as a movement it never grew into an effectively organized, unified organization, though there were numerous acts of sabotage and other bravery by single resistance fighters or small groups. Executions involving both them and innocent hostages. According to official Dutch estimates, two to three thousand Dutchmen were executed in Holland, six hundred died in concentration camps, about twenty thousand were imprisoned in Holland or Germany.[15] Practically all of these were non-Jews. Revelations of sensitive information under torture. Betrayals, not by NSBers only. A marked increase in juvenile delinquency and black market dealings by teenagers.

A flourishing underground press. The day after the capitulation, the first clandestine handbills appeared. By the end of 1940, some sixty underground periodicals were being published; total circulation: 450,000 copies, each one read by several families. Resistance groups occasionally seized the presses of some regular newspaper, forcing the personnel to print underground copy. Not to be outdone, the Germans published fake issues of such papers in order to confound the readers.

Several newspapers of those illegal times continued to become important dailies after the war, such as *Het Parool, Trouw, De Waarheid*. The first two are still published, the last one folded in 1990. Also, the student paper *De Vrÿe Katheder* continued after the war (I wrote for it in 1945 and 1946).

Pamphlets and books were produced illegally, too. In this category falls the one and only poem I have ever written that was actually published. It bears the English title, "We Lose It Not as Long as We Can Smile," a line from Shakespeare's *Merchant of Venice*. It was signed with my underground name, Adje (diminutive for Arthur) Pot. I have been told that this screed was republished after the war in a volume of resistance poetry which, however, I have never seen.

To conclude this chapter, I turn to the final and by far the grimmest times of the occupation. This period began on September 5, 1944, the day remembered in the annals of the Netherlands during the war as *Dolle Dinsdag* (Crazy Tuesday), and ended with the capitulation of the Germans eight months later.

At noon on June 6, 1944, Churchill rose in the House of Commons "to announce that during the night and early hours of this morning the first of the series of landings in force upon the European continent has taken place. . . . The whole process of opening this great new front will be pursued with the utmost resolution."[16] D-Day was in full swing. I need not recount here the often and well-told story of the next few months' successful campaign. A few main dates will suffice.

June 13. The first V1's are dropped on London. These bombs were so named by Hitler, because, in his flush of ruination, he hoped they would be only the first in a series of terror weapons that would drive Britain out of the war. Londoners called them "doodle bugs" or "buzz bombs." They were pilotless jet-propelled aircraft. About 2,400 of them got through. "This new form of attack imposed on the people of London a burden perhaps even heavier than the air-raids of 1940 and 1941."[17] With the help of radar and proximity fuses, the defense mastered these bombs by late August.

Another German aerial attack weapon, the V2, began hitting London on September 8, others were aimed at reconquered Antwerp. These were twelve-ton steerable rockets with a one-ton warhead, moving with a maximum speed of about 4,000 miles per hour. About five hundred of them per month got through on all targets combined. Launching sites included positions in Holland. They posed a high nuisance value; defense was difficult.

August 25. Allied troops enter Paris, finding the city largely under control of the French resistance.

September 4. Antwerp falls. Thus the Allies are now quite close to the Dutch border. On that same day Radio London reports that the southern

Dutch city of Breda has been freed. This erroneous report was the cause of *Dolle Dinsdag,* September 5.

In the preceding I have already taken note of astounding unfounded war rumors. These were nothing compared to what was happening now. Never, to this day, have I heard or come under the spell of rumors like those that spread all over Holland on that crazy Tuesday, nor can I imagine to behold the likes of them again. How well I remember that day![18]

In Rotterdam it was said that the Allies had taken the nearby Moerdÿk Bridge. In Amsterdam it was alleged that The Hague and Rotterdam had been liberated. I was told that Allied troops had passed Utrecht, twenty-five miles south of our city. Near the main bridge on the Amsterdam-Utrecht road, people were actually waiting that day, flower bouquets in hand, to welcome the victors. Dutch national flags appeared, including the *oranje, blanje, bleu* (orange, white, blue), the royal colors. Even the enemy reacted to the magic power of the rumor mills. German troops began hasty withdrawals from coastal regions, trains packed with NSBers were leaving for Germany.

Another phenomenon worth recalling was the appearance of those who later were called "September artists," people who all of a sudden became active patriots and tried to enlist in resistance groups. Most of them were well meaning, but traitors too tried to join the fray, to save their hides.

We lived in a dream that day. All of these stories were fabrications. This is what did happen.

On September 12 American troops crossed the Dutch border in the south of the province of Limburg. On the 14th, Maastricht, the first major Dutch city, was freed. On the 17th, Americans were parachuted near Nÿmegen. British and Polish troops came down near Arnhem, where they managed to hold on to the northern end of a crucial bridge over the Rhine but were unable to dislodge the Germans from the city itself. The battle for Arnhem, one of the most dramatic of the whole war, lasted until the 25th, when the gallant troops were ordered to withdraw. When the dust settled, the southern part of the Netherlands, the region below the arms of the Rhine had been liberated; the northern part remained in German hands. Further frontal advances came to a complete halt.

The northern part became known as the *Festung* (fortress) Holland. It included Amsterdam as well as Rotterdam and The Hague.

The Germans returned. Sabotage by the resistance increased markedly. Levels of cruelty and killings rose sharply. Just one example: In the little town of Heusden, situated near the Rhine front, citizens would spend the night in the town hall to shelter themselves from bombardments. On the night of November 4–5, the Germans blew up the hall's tower so that the Allies wouldn't be able to use it as a lookout post. The 134 Heusden citizens gathered in the hall were killed.

And so we, in the *Festung,* moved into the winter of 1944–45, times of cold and famine, when approximately fifteen thousand people in northwest Holland alone died of hunger.[19]

We had nothing.

There was no more electricity and gas, no more coal or other standard heating fuels. If you had some candles or a petroleum lamp you were lucky and used them sparingly. Night fell at four o'clock in the afternoon.

People tried to cook and keep warm by burning wood, often acquired by plunder and pillage. Park benches vanished, sawed to pieces. Wood was stolen from houses that stood empty, including support beams and stairs. As a result, houses collapsed, often killing people foraging there for wood. That is why especially in the Jewish quarter, where inhabitants had been deported, all that remained of quite a number of houses were piles of rub-ble. In those days one could see signs on some house doors warning: This house is inhabited.

There was no wood for coffins to bury the dead. "There only was the granite floor of Amsterdam's Zuiderkerk [church] where bodies were de-posited, sometimes 60 or 70 of them together . . . where they would some-times lie for weeks [while] rats would trip around between the cadavers."[20] There were many clandestine burials, enabling next of kin to retain the deceased's ration coupons.

Cooking was most often done on small (maybe eight inches high) cylin-drical stoves that had to be continuously fed with splintered wood. Soap or other cleaning substances were no longer available.

Food supplies were below subsistence levels. In the first quarter of 1945 all you could get officially—that is, with ration coupons—was 969 grams of bread and 1,000 grams of potatoes per person, per week.[21] Which would not at all guarantee that you would be able to find even that small allotment in stores, where even food substitutes could no longer be had. Dogs and cats were eaten. "In The Hague a horse was killed in a street, by a falling bomb. Even before the smoke had risen the animal was carved up by passers-by who departed triumphantly with a bloody horse's leg tied to their bicycles"[22]—which of course no longer had any tires. Have you ever tried horse steak? Tastes fine.

Black markets flourished. A loaf of bread went for the equivalent of thirty dollars; a pack of lousy cigarettes for forty to fifty; a box of matches, three dollars.

Then came the big hunger marches, the searches for food. Thousands, tens of thousands of city dwellers went to the countryside, in long, gray processions of ill-fed, poorly dressed people, on foot or on bikes. If you had a pushcart, you were like royalty. Automobiles or trains? No more for ordinary citizens, whether poor or rich.

Such trips could take days. People would fall by the wayside and die. You bartered with the farmers, offering your silverware, jewels, whatever was of some value. I could not go—being in hiding—but contributed my tuxedo, for which I got a bag of potatoes, a fine deal I thought. There were good farmers and bad farmers—those who were greedy—as there were gentle and overly aggressive trekkers. You slept in barns on the way, tying your bounty to your body with rope to avoid being robbed, which could happen anyway. In February and March 1945 the number of food hunters dropped sharply when snowy and icy roads made the trips well-nigh impossible.

There were only two kinds of staple foods left to us. One of them was sugar beets, normally used for cattle feed. They were cooked on the little wood stoves, producing a thick, brownish, sweet syrup that would be poured off in a pan. That w   the good part. You also ate the residual mush—not so good. The ot .er staple was flower bulbs. Have you ever eaten cooked tulip bulbs? They have a sickeningly sweet, mealy taste. I hated them—but ate them.

Those who suffered most in those months of what truly was horror were the poor and, across the population, babies and the very old. There were numerous cases of edema. Hans Kramers suffered from it. As to yours truly, I would wake up in the morning with only one thought: food. Nor was I able to think of anything else during the long, endless, slow-moving day. When I lay down at night, I had only one thought: food. It was then that I made up my mind: If I pull through this I shall have no special demands for fine foods. But I shall never, never be as hungry again as I am now.

In those bitter days you could experience instances of true generosity. Also of explosions of anger and irritation. Yet all such emotional ups and downs were embedded in a deep sense of solidarity. I was reminded of this when sometime after the war I read these words by Jean Paul Sartre (presumably in his *Chemins de la liberté* but I am not sure): the French were never as free as under German occupation. Meaning that there was one bond overriding all other sentiments that tied all the French together: hatred of a common enemy, resolve to dislodge him. So it was with us in the hunger winter.

On April 10, 1945, Churchill sat down to write a letter that began as follows.

> *Prime Minister to President Roosevelt.*
>
> The plight of the civil population in Occupied Holland is desperate. Between two and three million people are facing starvation. We believe that large numbers are dying daily, and the situation must deteriorate rapidly now that communications between Germany and Holland are virtually cut. I fear we may soon be in the presence of a tragedy.[23]

Thus Churchill's last letter ever to Roosevelt dealt with the plight of my little country. Two days after those lines were written, the president suddenly died.

On April 17, Churchill spoke in the House of Commons about the world's loss. His long eulogy ended as follows: "In Franklin Roosevelt there died the greatest American friend we have ever known, and the greatest champion of freedom who has ever brought us help and comfort from the New World to the Old."[24]

Of the war's end I shall at this point only recall that Arnhem finally fell on April 14, that negotiations with the German authorities in Holland began in that same month, and that on May 4, 1945, all German troops in northwestern Europe surrendered, taking effect in Holland on May 5.

In the next chapter I shall have more to say about these last months, after having explained my own situation in those days. You see, I had spent those days in a Gestapo prison.

9
Sho'ah

Sho'ah (Hebr.): destruction, ruin; catastrophe,
cataclysm, disaster; darkness; pit, abyss.

—R. ALCALAY, *The Complete*
Hebrew-English Dictionary

9.1 "THE IMPOSSIBLE REAL"

THE YEAR is 1991. It is a cool December day here in Copenhagen, weather I like best. A gentle mist hangs over the city. My wife Ida and I have had breakfast together. Two lit candles stand on our table, a common Danish custom. I have been out with Sidse, our dog, for my customary morning walk in the park surrounding Frederiksberg Castle. Sidse is a dachshund, a pedigreed hunting dog, so she always gets quite excited at the same place, where she can smell that foxes have crossed. Returning home, I have my morning coffee. Now I sit at my desk in our home, feeling at peace with myself and the world, turbulent though it is today. Ida is busy nearby in her own study.

My room is tranquil and beautiful. Walls are painted a deep red. On the floor of unfinished wood lies an antique red Afghan rug. Sidse lies next to me in her basket, snoozing away. On the walls are pictures of family and friends, an old Turkish Kaiseri rug which I picked up years ago in Geneva, a small piece of wooden sculpture by Louise Nevelson given to me on receiving the American Book Award in 1983, and a copy of a cartoon of me by David Levine, which had appeared in the February 26, 1987, issue of the *New York Review of Books*. On my desk stands a picture of my wife and son, taken on a boat while we were cruising Roskilde fjord.

There are several bookcases, an easy chair, and a couch. On my shelves stands one of the two copies of my cherished encyclopedia, the thirteenth edition of the *Britannica* of 1925 (superior in my opinion to the much-touted eleventh of 1911, because the former is a reprint of the latter plus an additional two volumes covering events between 1911 and 1925). My other copy is in our Manhattan apartment. Looking out of the windows, I see fir trees. French doors open to a balcony overlooking our garden.

Life has not always been easy, but on the whole it has been good to me these postwar years. I now have a family which I love dearly. My work as a physicist has been successful, all in all. Since 1978 I have devoted most of my efforts to writing books on subjects bearing on the history of science. A biography of Niels Bohr came out a few years ago and has received good reviews.

Now I sit at my desk, smoking one of my favorite Caminante cigars, planning to map out the contents of the present chapter. This chapter and the next one will be the grimmest part of this book and the hardest to write. It will deal with the fate of the European Jews during the Second World War, discussing in more detail what happened to the Jews of Holland. The next chapter is devoted more specifically to what befell my family and me.

I cannot think of a greater contrast than that between my present life, so full of happiness and contentment, and those years of the past, so full of suffering and sorrow.

Why, at this point, should I thinly sketch my present frame of mind (about which more later on)? Because "witnesses . . . are concerned less with the past than with a sense of that past in the present."[1] It seems proper to me, therefore, to preface my testimony with an outline of how that present looks and feels to me. Note also that this particular part of my past has receded behind half a century of largely positive experiences, so that recollections have necessarily dimmed.

If I am to succeed in conveying next what happened then, it is important—as always—to have the facts straight, but even more essential to bring back to life the emotional states of earlier times. I doubt very much that I can do so in ways that are satisfactory to me—but shall endeavor to come as close as I am capable of doing now.

It is not an easy task. I have often heard it said that witnesses to those past disasters believe it is impossible to really make clear to interested outsiders what he or she has experienced. I am no exception. When I hear myself talk to others about those earlier experiences of mine, I invariably have a peculiar sensation. I hear my own words, know that I speak the truth as honestly as I can, yet cannot believe what I hear myself saying. In other words, the me of those days has become totally estranged from the me of today. Schizoid reactions like these are fairly common among survivors, as recorded case histories have shown me. For example, a woman who had gone through it all once said to her interviewer: "I'm gonna tell you something now. If somebody would tell me this story, I would say 'She's lying, or he's lying.' Because this can't be true."[2] This same interviewer has written: "It is not surprising to hear witnesses in oral testimonies confess that sometimes they do not believe their own stories."[3] Another author has coined an elegant expression for this sort of experience—"The impossible real."[4] That same sense of unreality was experienced by those who have suffered similarly at other times and in other places. Take, for example, the case of Terry Anderson, the American who was taken hostage in Lebanon and held captive for nearly seven years. On March 15, 1992, only three months after his release, he wrote in the *New York Times:* "The pain, frustration, rage, and loneliness of those years seem as though they happened in some other world, not my real one."

Many of those who have had to face the hard task of how to survive survival have developed curious warps in their personalities. I, for example, do not find it easy, as said, to communicate my experiences—yet when I do, I feel no pain. It does not hurt me to write these lines. Not that I talk that often about the war, but when I do I observe myself mentioning quite casually facts and figures about those genuinely dear to me who were murdered.

I have noted several times earlier that the normal values of human conduct do not apply to the times of stress in war. I will now add that—as my own behavior illustrates—the same appears to be true of some aspects of the behavior of survivors, as I will make evident with an extreme example.

Recently I read an interview with a Jew who, as a boy, had been deported from a Polish ghetto to a death camp together with his family. There it came to pass that he had to say farewell to them even as they walked to the gas chambers. "Then, in a matter of minutes, my mother, my father, my brother, died. And I didn't even think one second about them. Nothing. It must be nature's way. If I started to think, maybe I couldn't begin to handle it." When asked if he felt guilty about not having deep sorrow over the loss of his family, he replied, "I feel very guilty that when I said good-by to my mother, the words I said were stupid. . . . Other than that, no guilt. Why? Should there be? I couldn't help anything." When asked what were those last words, he paused for a long while, then replied, "I hate to repeat them to you."[5] Though I have never been witness to a scene that gruesome, I can nevertheless feel how that boy felt, though words to describe that feeling fail me.

Only twice in all those later years was I able to reach the enormously strong pains and hurts that lie hidden within me at all other times.

The first occasion this happened was on one of my several stays in Jerusalem, when I visited for the first time the memorial Yad Vashem. The name means "a monument and a name," a superbly chosen quotation from Isaiah 56:5: "I will give in my house a monument and a name better than sons and daughters. I will give them an everlasting name that shall not be cut off." The memorial is built on a hilltop near Mount Herzl in Jerusalem. A seventy-foot-high pillar dominates the site. The plan for this memorial was adopted by the first postwar Zionist congress, held in London in August 1945. On August 15, 1953, in an atmosphere of solemnity, the Knesset unanimously passed the Yad Vashem Law 5713-1953, which outlined the objectives and the organizational framework. Article 4 of the law states one of the purposes: "To confer upon the members of the Jewish people who perished in the days of the Holocaust and the resistance the commemorative citizenship of the State of Israel as a token of their having been gathered to their people." The center includes a Hall of Names, where more than two million pages of testimony bearing the names of Jews who died or who fell in the resistance are filed. A research center deals with ongoing investigations of Nazi crimes. Its library contains about 50,000 volumes. Nearby is a forest where one tree has been planted, marked with a name plate, to honor each of the over three thousand "Righteous Gentiles" of record, brave non-Jews who at great personal risk had hidden Jews from the Nazis or had helped them in other important ways.

The most impressive and moving part of Yad Vashem is its Memorial Hall (Ohel Yizkor). Its interior, the dome and floor both made of granite, gives on purpose a sinister impression, meant to convey aspects of concentration camps. It is sparsely lit, to bring into focus the eternal flame burning in the center of the floor, in front of which ashes of murdered Jews are interred.

After entering the Memorial Hall, I was given a *keppel*, a head covering for male Jews; Gentiles are also obliged to wear one when entering a Jewish place of worship or sanctuary. I walked up to a balustrade, behind which lies the message of the memorial, chiseled in the floor's granite. It is stark and extraordinarily powerful—only the names of twenty-two camps: Auschwitz, Belzec, Bergen-Belsen, Buchenwald, Chelmno, Dachau, Drancy,

Flossenburg, Kaiserwald, Majdanek, Mauthausen, Natzweiler, Neu-
engamme, Ravensbrück, Sachsenhausen, Sobibor, Stutthof, Szebnie, Theresienstadt, Treblinka, Westerbork, Zemun.

When I stood there, reading those names, something completely unexpected happened to me that has never occurred before or since. I started
yelling loudly. No tears. These were the wounded cries of an animal. Even
as I was doing so, I could understand what was happening to me. After
many years I had finally come in touch with pains, deep inside, which
cannot be expressed in ordinary words and in daily settings.

Reflecting on this inadequacy of language, I am reminded of several interviews with prominent artists which I have seen and listened to on television
in the course of time. They were people quite capable of expressing themselves in speech, but when it came to answering questions about what they
tried to express on their canvases, they were at a loss for words. It struck me
then that artistic expression may not always be amenable to transliteration
—another category of instances where words fail.

I have visited Yad Vashem twice thereafter. On the second visit I only
wept quietly. On the third I did not even do that, just stood there in a
solemn, somber mood. Which only corroborates the well-known fact that
repeated exposure to events or their images diminishes their impact. That
was also evident to me as I walked through Yad Vashem's exhibit of photographs (I believe they are mostly from Bergen-Belsen), showing emaciated
human beings, barely alive, and piles of corpses. While these pictures never
fail to make an impression, they affected me much less strongly than the
starkness of the Memorial Hall. I had seen the pictures too often, there and
elsewhere.

It seems to me that the total absence of any such death camp photographs
only serves to enhance the Frenchman Claude Lanzmann's *Sho'ah*, his monumental documentary film about the extermination of the European Jews,
to my taste the most powerful and moving account of those events. Seeing
the film on television in 1991 provided the second occasion for reaching my
old pains.

The film consists of a series of interviews both with survivors from and
with people who lived near the camps, interspersed with pictures of those
camps, not as they were then but as they look now, and with shots of trains
moving toward one campsite or another. For hours I sat transfixed, watching the stories unfold. Two of them hit me most particularly.

One was an interview with a middle-aged Jew who, as a young boy, had
been adopted, so to say, by German camp personnel because he could sing

their songs so well. As a kid he had been ordered time and again to sing for them. Lanzmann had brought him to one of the places where he had done so, and there asked him to repeat a song. There the Jew stood, pathetic, singing "Wenn die Soldaten durch die Stadt marchieren" (When the soldiers march through town), etc., a song I too remember so well from those days. That memory made me burst out in tears. It was as if I saw myself standing there, singing. Odd, isn't it, this response not to a song I particularly cared for, but to a song of *theirs*.

The other interview that affected me was with a man who had been a barber before being deported and who in camp had been assigned to cutting off the hair of women, for reasons of "hygiene." Actually, the women were about to be gassed; their hair was subsequently sent on for industrial purposes. The Jew's barber shop was situated right next to the gas chambers. He and his fellow workers were strictly forbidden to talk to the women, all of whom were naked by then, on pains of being gassed themselves. At one point our man sees the wife and sister of his best friend enter, both of whom he knows quite well. He cannot say a word to them. Then he sees them march off to their doom.

Up to that moment the barber had spoken casually, almost businesslike, about his experiences, as he had also done in earlier parts of the documentary. When, however, he came to the point of describing how he saw those two women walk to the gas chambers, he fell apart completely, overwhelmed by the pain of memories. The very same happened to me as I sat there by myself in my beautiful room, watching him. For a long time I sobbed uncontrollably. It was not because of the scene he was describing— to repeat, I never was in a camp myself—but because of the sequence: his first talking casually, then breaking down, resonated with my own hurts, likewise hidden most of the time.

Are there lessons to be drawn from this past, which—in the words of one survivor—"already seems so thoroughly unreal, as if it no longer belongs to the experience of our generations but to mythology"?[6] I certainly have learned from it. Yet I have my doubts that I have been of much use to others in that respect. Again I associate myself with yet another survivor, "Can anybody understand [that]? I don't know. And that's probably the biggest tragedy I face, because I cannot relate or convey my experience to another person and make him, you know, better."[7]

I feel that common language is inadequate for a description of that period, which is simply too singular to be described in terms such as horror, tragedy, disaster. Those words sound too worn to me to serve their well-meant purpose. For the same reason I refuse to use the H-word, in writing as well as in speech. I have a visceral dislike of people like Eli Wiesel, professional *shiva*[8] sitter, who make a living from H-word tales.

It has been said that people should know of these facts to help prevent them from recurring. I doubt that this is an efficient means for counteracting historic forces. Amidst all these tragedies one is confronted with instances of true courage, sacrifice, even heroism. It has been said that these demonstrate the invincibility of the human spirit. I don't quite know what this exalted expression is supposed to mean.

If I am not clear as to whether this past contains lessons, and if I am not sure that my language has been adequate, then why did I write of these memories at all? It is, I think, an attempt at showing how a life beginning with a carefree youth, followed by catastrophe, can reshape itself into a fascinating career, ultimately leading to the scenes of happiness and fulfillment with which I started this part of my story.

9.2 THE FATE OF EUROPE'S JEWS

Casualty figures of World War II are usually quoted in round numbers: 17 million military casualties, 30 million civilians killed, among the latter 6 million Jews.

During the opening days (November 1945) of the Nuremburg trials of Nazi war crimes, the prosecution stated that "of the 9,600,000 Jews who lived in the parts of Europe under Nazi domination, it is conservatively estimated that 5,700,000 have disappeared . . . [of whom] 4,500,000 cannot be accounted for by the normal death-rate nor by immigration; nor are they included among the displaced persons. . . . Most of them have deliberately been put to death by the nazi conspirators."[9]

This declaration clearly shows that it is not well known how many Jews lost their life due to the Nazi death machines. Several uncontrollable factors have contributed to this imprecision. Prewar estimates of Jewish populations in Eastern Europe differ widely. Nor is it known how many were murdered during round-ups in ghettos or by firing squads, nor how many died from disease, hunger, and neglect. Whatever the size of these uncertainties, it was the fate of the Jews to suffer the most systematic and largest-scale extermination of a race and the eradication of its culture in human history.

Nor should either Jew or Gentile ever forget that "in addition to the six million Jewish men, women, and children who were murdered at least an equal number of non-Jews was also killed, not in the heat of battle, not by military siege, aerial bombardment or the harsh conditions of modern war, but by deliberate, planned murder." These were civilians belonging to specific European nations, from West to East. An exception were the Gypsies, who "like the Jews were marked for destruction by the Nazis. . . . Like the Jews, the Gypsies had to face a combination of artificially intensified 'race' hatred, meticulous planning, continual deception, and overwhelming military power. . . . By 1945 more than 220,000 of Europe's 700,000 Gypsies had been murdered by the Nazis."[10]

These large numbers, whether precise or not, are numbing. All the same they are to be remembered for a measure of the size of the calamity, even though they do not in the least suffice to convey fully what went on in those days. Fear, pain, sorrow cannot be expressed in terms of statistics. I shall nevertheless add just a few more cold data, concerning events in particular countries.

Nowhere was the slaughter more complete than in Poland, where the Jewish population had been estimated at 3,350,000 in 1939, of which 50,000, less than two percent, were still alive in 1945, compared with an almost ninety percent survival rate in Bulgaria and Russia—which were never fully occupied—and fifty percent in Hungary, but only fifteen percent in Yugoslavia and ten percent in Austria. In Western Europe, Holland was worst off: fifteen percent survived, compared with Belgium (forty-five percent) and France (seventy-five percent).[11]

The Jews of Germany itself (reckoned with the borders of 1938) fared in some ways the best. A census taken in 1933 showed 500,000 "pure" Jews living there. By the outbreak of war, emigration had already reduced this number to a bit over 200,000—the German Jews had had the "advantage" of earliest exposure to the Nazis. In 1945 there were 80,000 Jews in Germany, but note that this included 60,000 displaced persons.[12]

I continue this sparse review of wartime Europe as a whole with a brief chronology.

November 1939. The wearing of the yellow star by Jews becomes compulsory in Poland, followed by the same measure in the greater Reich (September 1941), France, and Holland (June 1942). This event is reflected in a peak in the suicide rate in Berlin.[13]

April 1940. The first enclosed and guarded ghetto is established, in Lodz (Poland). The Warsaw Ghetto is sealed off the following November.

July 31, 1941. By order from Hitler, Goering sends a directive to Heydrich, chief of the *Sicherheitsdienst,* better known as the Gestapo, commissioning him to take charge of "the execution of the intended Final Solution of the Jewish question." This document appears to be the first in which the term "final solution" is used.[14]

September 1941. Experimental gassing of Jews starts at the camp in Auschwitz.

January 20, 1942. Heydrich convenes a meeting of fifteen representatives of various ministries, the SS (the Nazi elite corps), and the Gestapo at the offices of the Internationalen Kriminalpolizeilichen Kommission, Am grossen Wannsee 56-58, in a pleasant suburb on the southwestern fringe of Berlin. This gathering had originally been planned for the previous December 9 but had to be postponed because of the Japanese attack on Pearl Harbor on December 7 and the German declaration of war on the United States on the 11th.[15]

Heydrich opened the meeting with a long talk in which he outlined the strategy for the Final Solution. First, transport the Jews of conquered Europe to the East, there work them to death, and exterminate those who survive. Long before these plans could be implemented, however, it was decided to dispatch Jews by quicker means: through mass slaughter by flying squads of special *Einsatzgruppen* (task forces); and by poisoned gas, in gas chambers to be constructed for that express purpose. Heydrich put in direct overall charge of these operations his underling SS *Obersturmbannführer* (lieutenant colonel) Karl Adolf Eichmann, an Austrian Nazi, a native of Hitler's hometown of Linz and by then head of section B4 of Bureau IV of the *Reichssicherheitshauptamt* (Gestapo headquarters), the section dealing with Jewish affairs. It was Eichmann who wrote the fifteen-page protocol of the Wannsee meetings, which still exists.

July 1942. Deportation to the East of Jews from Holland and France begins, followed in August by those in Belgium and in November by those in Norway.

I shall come back in the next chapter to what happened in the camps.

July 24, 1944. Soviet troops are the first to liberate survivors from a camp, the one at Majdanek.

January 26, 1945. Russian troops liberate the camp at Auschwitz.

April 15, 1945. British forces liberate Camp Bergen-Belsen.

To conclude these general cursory remarks on the fate of Europe's Jews, I turn to these questions: How much did the Allies know of the Final Solution? When did they know it? What did they do about it?

In June 1942, the Polish authorities in London received a report from occupied Poland which confirmed that Germans were murdering Jews throughout that country. On June 29, the World Jewish Congress held a press conference in London on the Polish situation; one speaker mentioned gassings in Chelmno and a total number of estimated deaths of over one million. On June 30, the London *Times* carried a headline: "Massacre of Jews/Over 1,000,000 dead since the war began." The *New York Times* of that day placed the news on the bottom of page 7. That "newspaper of record" was anxious not to appear too Jewish. In general, the American press treated news of Nazi murders in a far more muted way than did the British.[16]

On August 1, 1942, the chief of the Geneva office of the World Jewish Congress received word "that a plan had been discussed in Hitler's headquarters for the extermination of all Jews in Nazi-occupied lands." The message was forwarded to Rabbi Stephen Wise, American Jewry's most prominent leader, who in turn transmitted it to Undersecretary of State Sumner Welles.

In November 1942 the American legation at Berne, Switzerland, transmitted to Washington four affidavits confirming the original report.[17]

On December 13, 1942, Edward R. Murrow said on a CBS broadcast, "Millions of Jews are being gathered with ruthless efficiency and murdered. . . . The phrase 'concentration camps' is obsolete. . . . It is now possible to speak only of death camps."[18]

On December 18, 1942, British Foreign Secretary Anthony Eden made a declaration (simultaneously released in Washington and Moscow) to the House of Commons in which he proclaimed that the Allies had received numerous reports of Nazi atrocities against the Jews. Eden mentioned the wholesale deportations from all occupied countries to Eastern Europe "in conditions of appalling horror and brutality." In Poland, "which has been made the principal Nazi slaughter-house, the ghettos established by the German invaders are being systematically emptied of all Jews except a few highly skilled workers required for war industries." The declaration spoke of many hundreds of thousands of victims. When Eden was done, the House of Commons stood in silence.

On January 21, 1943, Undersecretary Welles received another cable from Berne: Jews were being killed in Poland at the rate of six thousand a day.[19]

On April 19–29, 1943, the Anglo-American conference on refugees took place in Bermuda. Jewish representatives were excluded from the meeting. The delegates would not discuss a Swedish offer to accept forthwith twenty thousand Jewish children from occupied Europe. A big point was made of shipping difficulties which precluded immediate rescue. The most important objective was stated to be to return the Jews in large numbers to their own countries after the war. Afterward, the meeting was heavily criticized for lack of meaningful proposals of rescue and for its apparent purpose of saving itself from public censure rather than the Jews from immediate death. One American reporter angrily wrote that at the conference it had been considered "almost improper to mention the word Jew."[20]

On November 1, 1943, the Declaration on Atrocities was issued after the interallied conference on war crimes, held in Moscow, failed to indict the Nazis for the murder of Jews.[21]

On March 30, 1944, Eden made another declaration to the House of Commons. At about the same time, the Russian Politburo explained the extermination of the Jews as a phase in the historical struggle between fascism and progress; in other words, Jews were not being massacred because they were Jews but simply as anti-Fascists.[22]

On July 11, 1944, Churchill wrote in a memorandum to Eden: "There is no doubt that this is probably the greatest and most horrible crime ever committed in the whole history of the world, and it has been done by scientific machinery by nominally civilized men in the name of a great state."[23]

Late in 1944, a Hungarian Jew came to Cairo, where he called on Lord Moyne, resident British Minister, with a proposal that came straight from Eichmann: exchange one million Jews for ten thousand trucks that would be used only at the Eastern front. The good lord's only response was: "What shall I do with those million Jews? Where shall I put them?" (*Note:* Moyne was assassinated by the Irgun shortly afterward.)[24]

And so, while Jews were dying like flies, the West and the East did absolutely nothing. They could have bombed railway functions along the routes over which Jews were carried to their death, but did not. They could have bombed the gas chambers, but they did not.

Why not? The reasons appear to be complex. There certainly was anti-Semitism in high circles. There was the overriding, principal aim of the war: to defeat Germany, which provided a reason (excuse?) for not diverting any war effort for other purposes. There was the admittedly stupendous problem of how to handle a million or so displaced people. There was a tendency to decry reports of atrocities as propaganda, especially in the American press (see, e.g., a *New York Times* report of Babi Yar!).[25] Toward the very end of the war it became publicly known that the U.S. Office of War Information had suggested to the press to contain and even suppress references to the murder of Jews, the argument being that such stories would be "confused and misleading if it appears to be simply affecting the Jewish people."[26]

And isn't it extremely saddening (to put it mildly) that Churchill, in his monumental six-volume history of the Second World War, mentioned the plight of the Jews only once, in the memo quoted above—and this in volumes published after ample opportunity for further reflection? And also that his victory speech of May 15, 1945, contains no reference at all to the tragedy of the Jews?[27]

When the time came for all to see what had happened, it caused profound shock.

I conclude this section with the response of an American major on entering a camp in April 1945: "I couldn't believe it even when I saw it. . . . I couldn't believe that I was there looking at such things."[28]

I can well believe him.

9.3 THE FATE OF HOLLAND'S JEWS, MAY 1940–JULY 1942

In my experience, the surviving Jews from Holland (and quite probably those from elsewhere as well) can be divided into three categories.

First, those who remained in Holland afterward. Of these, many adjusted rapidly (which does not mean fast) to a life that had to go on. Those who had lost children found outlets for their need to love by adopting de facto (not before the law) surviving children from others who had not returned from the camp. My own parents participated in creating such a contracted family, not by taking in a child but by regular visits with children. They became adoptive grandparents.

Next, those who lived through it all in Holland but left the country soon afterward had much more difficulty adjusting. I am one of those.

Finally, there were the Dutch Jews who had been abroad while the catastrophe occurred but lost some or all of their families. They had more serious problems than all the others in coming to terms with the past events. The reasons are, I am convinced, that they had to submit to the esemplastic power of the imagination, a process which causes great psychological strains that can only partly be alleviated by talking to others, or by reading. Perhaps more importantly, they experience, even more than those who were there and made it, the guilt of being a survivor. What have I done to deserve to live while those dear to me were killed? They often experience quite unreasonable feelings of deep shame when asked, "And what happened to you?"

What, in fact, did happen? When I write that more than four out of five Dutch Jews did not survive, I speak the truth but not the whole truth. When I add facts and dates that are part of recorded history—as shortly I shall—I will augment the truth, but still it is not all of it. The whole truth, a chronicle of the sufferings of 100,000 victims up to their last moments, cannot be given. Yet it is empathy with individual feelings that brings one closest to the reality of past times. That is why the diary of Anne Frank, the young Jewish girl from Amsterdam (born in Germany, from where she and her family had fled in 1933) who recorded her feelings while in hiding, has touched more people more deeply than any impersonal historical account ever can.[29] It seems to me that the greatest value of her moving account lies in making it clear that even those days were not all pure anguish. Happier experiences of the kinds common to all of us are woven into a background of great tragedy.

In the next chapter I shall turn to my own personal experiences. But now—some facts.[30]

Already during the war days fear, if not panic, was rampant among Dutch Jews. Many flocked to North Sea ports, hoping to escape to England. Few made it; most had to return home dejectedly. Calm and balance returned fairly quickly, however, because of the unforeseen circumstance that nothing at all happened to them—at first. There were no pogroms, there was no persecution. Not until two months after the Dutch capitulation was a decree made public that affected the life of some, not many: the prohibition of ritual slaughter. Another three months went by until, on October 22, 1940, the first really major anti-Semitic action was taken: all businesses owned by Jews, or having at least one Jewish partner or director, or having predominantly Jewish capital or Jewish shareholders, all as of the preceding May 9, must be so registered. It was the prelude to the systematic plunder of Jewish property that was to follow.

This proclamation was the first in which Jews were openly named.[31] In fact, one article of the decree spelled out who, according to the Germans, was a Jew: those having three or more full Jewish grandparents, or, if only two of them were, if they belonged to a Jewish congregation or were married to a Jew. Later on, one instead of three Jewish grandparents would do. Did the Jews comply? Yes sir, they did, dutifully filling out forms in quintuplicate.

In November, the dismissal of Jews from all civil service posts was ordered, as already discussed in chapter 8. That, more or less, sums up what happened in 1940. As the year drew to an end, many Jews still hoped that the Germans had now done their worst—as they would, time and again, after each next phase in their destruction.

Then came 1941. The year began with one of those measures that would have caused a major outcry in ordinary times but that, under the circumstances, caused only a small ripple: as of January 5, Jews were forbidden to go to the movies. All cinemas were forced to put up signs saying "Für Juden verboten," banned to Jews. It is a trivial thing that I would remember the name of the last movie I saw before the ban went into effect: *Dorothea Goes Wild*, an English or American film.

This decree was like nothing compared to the next one. Effective January 24, all Jews, full, half, or quarter, must register themselves in writing, on forms available at assigned offices. Did we register? Yes sir; with few exceptions, we did, about 140,000 of us, my family and I included. As a reward for our efforts, we received an identity card, like all Dutch people, but ours bore a distinguishing mark: a large J stamped in black. As I do my best to remember the responses to those ID cards, I cannot remember any Jew who realized at that time that this measure would set a mortally dangerous trap.

As mentioned in chapter 8, harassment of Jews had led, on February 11, to pitched battles in which Gentile joined Jew. The next day the German authorities called in some leading figures in the Jewish community to demand the immediate formation of a Joodse Raad (JR, Jewish Council) to act as responsible representatives of Amsterdam Jewry, charged with preserving order in their community. SS *Hauptsturmführer* (Captain) Ferdinand Aus der Fünten was assigned to be in charge of dealings with the JR. Councils of this kind were no novelty; they had been instituted earlier in other occupied regions.

The JR was organized soon afterward. It consisted of some twenty members and had two co-equal presidents: Abraham Asscher, a leading figure in the diamond world and in public life; and David Cohen, a professor of history at the University of Amsterdam until he was sacked by the civil servants decree. At first glance this Council, which soon became responsible for Jews in all of Holland, may seem to be an example of what sometimes has been called "reasonable collaboration," meant to act in the interest of the general population or of special groups. In the event, it turned out to be nothing of the kind.

One by one they came, the anti-Jewish measures, as 1941 wore on. *April:* Jews are no longer allowed to change domicile from Amsterdam to other parts of the country. They have to surrender their radio sets. *May:* They are no longer admitted to public parks, baths, and swimming pools. *Autumn:* Their children must leave public schools. Special schools for them are organized. *Finally, on December 5:* the first measure bearing on deportation—all non-Dutch-born Jews in Holland must report for "volunteer emigration."

And yet, most Jews in Holland still kept looking for a brighter side. "They pinned their hopes on the likelihood of Germany eventually losing the war, and consoled themselves with the knowledge that, however bad the situation, it could have been much worse."[32]

Then 1942. That was the year in which the Germans finally unveiled in full their evil designs. Remember that in the beginning of 1942 the Wannsee Conference had taken place—of which we, of course, knew nothing.

On January 5, the JR was ordered to supply fourteen hundred unemployed Dutch Jews for transport to labor camps in the Dutch province of Drente. The JR first tried to oppose this project, then tried delaying tactics; finally, it gave in on the grounds that refusal might endanger many more people. Eventually they sent a warning letter to those called up which said in part, "If you refuse, we shall no longer be able to do anything for you, and you yourself must bear full responsibility for the consequences."[33]

During the following months, thousands more were called up. Everyone's fitness for work had to be checked by a medical board. Smarter ones of course tried tricks to be exempted. In those days the following joke was told. A doctor asks one man if he suffers from headaches. "No." "Trouble walking?" "No." "Heart trouble?" "No." "Then I have to reject you because you must be crazy."

The noose tightened further early in 1942. Jews scattered all over Holland had to move to Amsterdam, this creating a virtual ghetto. A ban on mixed marriages came into force. In April, Aus der Fünten informed the JR presidents that Jews will have to wear stars. The order, published on May 9, stated that all Jews must wear a star when appearing in public. It shall be a black, six-pointed star on yellow cloth, the size of a palm, and bearing the black inscription Jood (Jew), to be affixed to the outer clothing of the left breast. Vigorous protests by the JR led nowhere, of course. The order that the Council shall distribute the stars could in fact not be refused, as the presidents explained to their staff, "since otherwise many Jews would have been unable to obtain their stars and would have been thrown into gaol."[34]

Leaving aside any judgment on the JR position, not wearing a star did turn out to be mortally dangerous.

So, like all of us, I wore my star; I still have several of them. My initial reaction of discomfort vanished rapidly. A spectrum of responses came forth from the non-Jewish Dutch. Quite a few showed their solidarity. Men would lift their hats when passing Jews. Others would come up to shake the hands of Jews. The most touching story I know is of a young Gentile boy who came up to a Jewish lady to tell her that his school class had decided to keep Jews company so they wouldn't feel lonely. Reactions among the Jews themselves also varied widely. Inevitably new jokes emerged. The star was called Ordre pour le Sémite, a pun on the German Ordre pour le Mérite. The Waterlooplein, the main square in the Jewish quarter, came to be known as Place de l'Étoile.

In June, a series of orders went into effect that aimed at further isolating the Jews: curfew for Jews from 8 P.M. to 6 A.M.; bicycles to be handed in; shopping in non-Jewish businesses prohibited, as was use of trains and all other public transport and of public telephones; private phones are disconnected.

The next month the wholesale deportation of Holland's Jews began.

9.4 Deportations, July 1942–September 1943

On June 26, Aus der Fünten summoned representatives of the JR to his office, to tell them what was about to happen next. "Police controlled labor contingents" of men and women of ages sixteen to forty would be sent to Germany. This, he said, was no more than labor service. He wanted to know how many people per day the JR could "handle."[35]

The usual song and dance followed. The JR protested, the Gestapo rejected, the JR came up with a proposal: 350 persons per day. Aus der Fünten wanted 4,000, to be deported starting July 15. The JR sent out forms, provided by the German authorities, to 4,000 people. The text began as follows: "Summons. You are called up for forced labor in Germany [first lie] under police supervision [second lie]." Once again, the Germans camouflaged their aims. The forms went on to state, "You must present yourself for personal and medical inspection at Camp Westerbork" (see chapter 10); the Germans had taken over the camp that July 1942. The call-up form ended like this: "The home must be left in good order, closed, and the keys must be taken with you." Those keys had to be handed over in the camp, so that the Germans could leisurely rob the Jews of their belongings.

On July 14 the Germans raided the Jewish quarter and took 700 hostages, threatening to send them to a concentration camp if the 4,000 did not turn up.

Reactions were fear, panic, and, ultimately, resignation. "If they need us for work, it is in their own interests to treat us well." False rumors flew: the British will bomb Amsterdam's central railway station, point of departure; the railway workers will strike; the invasion will begin just in time. The JR begged the Jews to think of the 700 hostages.

And so they departed. The first train with 1,000 Jews left the night of July 14–15. On the 15th the hostages were released.

That was just the beginning. Call-ups by the thousands followed. Some responded, others did not. The result was that in the summer of 1942 the Germans instituted raids, dragging men and women of all ages, children and grandchildren included, out of their homes. They were first gathered in the Hollandse Schouwburg (Dutch Theater), and from there shipped to Westerbork. By the end of August, over 10,000 Jews had already been deported farther eastward.[36]

Meanwhile, others continued to respond to call-ups. They, too, had to report to the Schouwburg first. Among my indelible memories is seeing a man, his wife, and two little children walking on the Plantage Middelaan, burdened with hand luggage, on their way to the theater. Even now I can see the expression of sorrow on their faces as they walked to a doom worse, so much worse, than what they had been told to expect.

Then came the stamp episode.

On September 8, 1942, Asscher and Cohen called on Aus der Fünten to protest the raids and to suggest call-ups only. The only concessions they obtained were that those working for the JR, or for the Jewish community (rabbis, teachers, etc.), as well as baptized Jews, those in mixed marriages with children, and those doing work relevant to the German war effort— notably in the diamond, old metal, textile, and rags industries—would get a special stamp on their ID card stating "Inhaber dieses Ausweises ist bis auf weiteres vom Arbeitseinsatz freigestellt" (Holder of this ID card is until further notice exempt from mobilization for labor).

The JR asked for 35,000 exemptions, which excluded three-quarters of the Jewish population. The Germans allowed them half that number. These were given their stamps beginning in September.

It was a German move in which cleverness matched cruelty. It was clever because it deflected most Jews' anxieties of facing deportation to a scramble for exemption. "When the first stamps were issued, the scenes at the Jewish Council were quite indescribable. Doors were broken, the staff of the Council was attacked, and the police had often to be called in. . . . The stamps quickly became an obsession with every Jew."[37] This made it easier for the Germans to pick up those who missed out. It was cruel because a stamp only meant that execution was deferred. A year later or less, practically all protection by stamps would cease to exist. In the following chapter I will tell what the stamps did for my family and me, but for now I turn to the odd stories of the foreign Jews.

These people, small in number, were the first to be exempted. When this category was announced, "Jews tried desperately to become citizens of Bolivia, Paraguay, and Haiti—though they could not always spell these names correctly. Passports were smuggled to them from abroad or forged in Holland; forgery [also of false ID and ration cards] had in fact become a large-scale industry."[38] The Germans were actually aware of these chicaneries but closed an eye, hoping to exchange German internees for these pseudo-nationals. The trick did save lives.

The most bizarre of the efforts to "become" a foreigner was the claim by a group of Portuguese Jews, natives of Holland, who asserted not to be Jews at all, racially that is, but of Moorish descent! They enlisted Dutch anthropologists and so managed to obtain a report stating that "so-called Portuguese Jews cannot by any stretch of the imagination be classified as Jews and they show strong affinities with Western Mediterranean races."[39] They were also able to obtain support from the Portuguese government. Four hundred of them (ten percent of all the Sephardic Jews in Holland) managed to satisfy the criteria, which included marriage to a "Portuguese" and seven Portuguese grandparents. So they did obtain their foreigner exemptions. But what good did it do? They were the last to be gassed at Auschwitz.

The raids to erase the Jews from the map of Holland went on, with relentless brutality. The biggest raid, on October 2–3, 1942, netted 13,000 people, according to an official German report. The cynicism of the phrase "mobilization for labor" was never better demonstrated than in March–April 1943, when Jews in hospitals all over Holland were taken away. In May the JR was directed to name 7,000 of its staff for deportation. It did, and they went. So it went on until September, when the last big raids took place, and 3,000–5,000 were picked up. In that month the JR was dissolved and its presidents were deported: Asscher to Bergen-Belsen, Cohen to

Theresienstadt. Both survived. A few Jews were still left, however, notably the "Portuguese" and the diamond workers. But in 1944 their turn would come too.

Where did they end up?

Sixty trains carrying over 60,000 Jews went to Auschwitz. Nineteen trains with over 34,000 went to Sobibor. Almost 4,000 ended up in Bergen-Belsen, nearly 5,000 in Theresienstadt. And so this city, Amsterdam, my city, to which its ten percent Jewish citizenry had lent a special vibrancy, was now practically empty of Jews. D-Day came in their absence.

Except for those in hiding.

We called them *onderduikers,* divers. Their actual number is uncertain; the figures most often quoted are around 25,000. The number caught is even more uncertain, ranging from 10,000 to over 15,000.

Every diver who survived has his or her distinct story to tell. Of being ever mindful of the constant dangers of discovery. Of loneliness and adjustment to a radical change in lifestyle, for diver as well as host. Of living in sometimes very cramped spaces. Of tensions with hosts, or among themselves if there were more than one, itself not a good idea. Of those who became ill or went mad, or even some who died. Of betrayals.

There were also problems common to all divers. How to find a place to hide? Note the article in the underground newspaper *Het Parool* of July 14, 1942, which told that it was most often the people in the poorest homes who threw them open to the hunted. It used to be said in those times that the poor offer you shelter, the rich someone else's address. Bless the poor.

Hiding cost money. There were many hosts who were quite generous in that respect, but also those who fleeced the diver. Then there was the problem of how to obtain ration cards and false papers. That too involved money.

There were a few who could have found and would have been able to afford a hiding place but chose of their own free will not to do so, an example being my late friend Boris Kahn, erstwhile assistant of Uhlenbeck (chapter 6). In discussing the hiding option with me, he said to me that he would not follow that path because he would go stir crazy hiding in a small space for a long time. When I said he had enough to divert himself by doing some physics, he told me, "No, that won't do." He would rather work outdoors at forced labor. And so he went, never to return.

It will be obvious that impecunious Jews had the hardest time financially, if they could manage at all. Also, these were the people who had the fewest contacts with potential hosts and with the resistance. As was the case with obtaining exemption stamps, the large Jewish proletariat was, once again, by far the worst off.

This concludes my account of the darkest hours in the history of the Jews in Holland. I have not gone into great detail but believe that the preceding information gives the overall picture. Before I turn to my family's and my own experience, I first want to add a few comments on the reaction of the Dutch community at large to the persecutions, and on what we in Holland knew about what was happening in the camps.

Deeply felt Dutch hostility toward the Germans and the beginnings of large-scale resistance were strongly influenced by their treatment of the Jews. I do not believe the Germans ever understood the intensity of those feelings, though they translated themselves into active assistance in only a small fraction of the population. One cannot emphasize enough the gratitude and respect for that help, given at grave risk and often at personal sacrifice. Yet it should neither be forgotten that there is much to criticize as well. Some police officers acted heroically, but others slavishly assisted the Germans in rounding up Jews, some doing so with glee and cruelty. Train personnel could have sabotaged the departures to and from Westerbork—but the trains kept running on time. The Dutch Red Cross behaved miserably. "An unbiased non-Dutch observer has expressed the view that when it came to receiving parcels [in camps] the Dutch either got nothing or least of all,"[40] the latter in comparison with other nationalities. Another witness said about a postwar transit camp, "The French and Belgian Red Cross were there, but the Dutch Red Cross was, as ever, conspicuous by its absence."[41]

The Dutch cabinet-in-exile in London was not much better. In February 1943 this august body rejected a proposal for exchange of Dutch Jews with Germans in Surinam (then still a Dutch colony). Although the Jews were probably worse off than the rest of the population, "it is questionable whether this entitles them to privileged treatment."[42]

What did we in Holland know about the killings in the East, and when did we know it? On July 24, 1942, Radio Oranje asked, "Just how does it help the German war effort to herd together thousands of defenseless Jewish Poles and do away with them in gas chambers? How does it help the war effort when thousands of Jewish Dutchmen are dragged out of their country?" Important. Note that gassing is only mentioned insofar as it concerns Polish Jews. The Dutch were only told what they already knew. Did the government-in-exile not know that all Jews were exposed to gassing? Could they not guess? Or were they worried that the Dutch Jews might get privileged treatment after all?

On October 9, 1942, Anne Frank noted in her diary, "Whatever will it be like in the distant and barbarous regions they are sent to? We assume that most of them are murdered. The English radio speaks of their being gassed."[43] So there was some information but, believe it or not, people simply could not believe it. After the war the Dutch wartime prime minister said that he could remember reading a pertinent document dated October 5, 1943, and finding himself, even at that late stage, "utterly unable to believe in the mass extermination of West European Jewry."[44]

Jaap Polak, a Dutch-born Jew, now a New Yorker and a friend of mine, has told me of a discussion he had some time after the war with another Dutch Jew who had spent the war in London, where he worked and broadcast for Radio Oranje. Jaap asked him why that radio service had never told straight out what was happening to Holland's Jews in the camps. That very intelligent man (I know him) was silent for a long while, then said: "I could not and would not believe it but, even if I had believed it, the Dutch government would have forbidden me to tell it." Here we meet once again with the all-pervasive theme, the difficulty if not complete inability of survivors, whether Jewish or Gentile, to believe even in the face of incontrovertible evidence. As to the Dutch government-in-exile, well, frankly, to hell with them.

I call the last witness in the matter of what we knew. In a long postwar memoir on events in Holland, a well-known Jewish lawyer from Amsterdam who was deported to Bergen-Belsen has written: "Murder on the scale that took place was unimaginable, even when in September 1943 . . . the BBC gave precise information. My own diary, kept in Bergen-Belsen, shows that there we heard for the first time on November 8, 1944, of the gassings in Auschwitz."[45] He knew it in 1943 but only began to believe it in 1944.

This is the main message I have been trying to convey repeatedly: the real is impossible to those who have seen it definitively documented and even to those who, like me, have witnessed part of it. Yet it is real.

I conclude with a word on the Jewish Council, the JR.[46] The reader may have noticed some irritation on my part when writing about the activities of this body, which was so representative of bourgeois Holland's respect for any kind of legality. I want to stress that neither then nor later did I ever believe that the members of the JR should stand accused of crimes. Recall that the Germans forced the formation of the JR in 1941, at the time of their earliest anti-Jewish measures in Holland. That was a time when some degree of collaboration still seemed reasonable. Note also that the JR was the only intermediary through which any Jew could appeal to the Germans. No one, *but no one*, foresaw what the next two years would bring. The JR's actions were always intended to prevent worse. Who could know that the worst would happen? I shall not argue against the view that the JR's position became ever more shortsighted as time went by. But evil it never was.

10

Wartime Experiences of My Family and Me

10.1 UNTIL MARCH 1943

THIS PART of my story starts in the autumn of 1941, since I have nothing to add to what I wrote earlier (chapter 6) regarding my war experiences up until the time I received my Ph.D. My first topic is one which, as such, has nothing to do with war: sex.

It was in the autumn of 1941 that I lost my virginity. I had by then reached the ripe age of twenty-three, not an unusual age for sexual initiation for people of my generation. I believe it is necessary to touch on this subject—and the role sex played in my later life as well—even though to me it is not a favorite topic of writing or conversation. I never talk about sex, not even to close friends. Yet in an honest story of my life, its mention cannot be avoided.

My very first time was like what, in the American vernacular, is called the original amateur hour. I count myself most fortunate that the lady in question took this in good grace and continued to receive me. Thereafter there were no problems. I shall forever be grateful to her.

At that time Tineke and I had already begun to drift apart somewhat. That nothing ever came of our relationship was entirely due to my considerable immaturity at the time. Yet we remained close, and her most important role in my life was yet to come, as will soon become evident. We remained close until I left Holland at the beginning of 1946, to return only for short visits. Today Tineke is an esteemed psychiatrist, also a grandmother, living near New York City. We continue to see each other occasionally, have tea or dinner together, and, of course, talk of old times. Our bonds remain strong. She was and still is one of the most important persons in my life.

But to return to the subject, my sex initiation occurred not long before I went into hiding, so you can imagine that hiding did not make life too easy for an aroused young man approaching his mid-twenties who had had a taste of sex.

After the war I had some catching up to do. I have no idea how many relationships I have had since, except that there were many, never simultaneously but one after the other, almost never one-night stands. But there were also periods, some of them lengthy, during which I was all alone. Throughout my life I have been too shy to ever "pick up" a woman to whom I had not been properly introduced. I am, in fact, convinced that shyness, which was particularly pronounced in my younger years, held me back at an earlier stage—not from girls but from sexual encounters.

Until well into my middle years, I have quite often experienced my strong physical urges as painful, as a burden, wishing so much for calmer, more serene spirits.

Most of my relationships came to an end mostly because of my inability to commit myself fully. When my partner became too amorous, I felt the need to run. I believe I may say, though, that I treated my women friends decently for as long as it lasted. At any rate, the result has been that I spent the greater part of my life as a bachelor.

Behind all this lay my overriding absorption in physics, which held me back from investing in human relations of all kinds. I was in fact thirty years old when for the first time I experienced very intensely what it really meant to fall in love. The result was total helplessness on my part in this new situation; and it came to nothing. But it was an important late lesson.

The combination of my devotion to science and my earthy desires often led to the following sequence of events. When I had no partner, I would soon become restless and could not concentrate well on my work. Then I would meet someone; we had—nearly always—very pleasant times. As a result I threw myself with renewed vigor into my work, tending to neglect the woman as a result. Naturally this was not to her liking and she would leave me, almost always without bitterness or harsh words. Then the cycle would start all over again.

That is essentially all I shall have to say, here and later, about my relations with the opposite sex, with the exceptions of my marriages, about which I shall write in due course.

As I reread these last few handwritten pages, I am not impressed. I find them lacking in expressions of passion, of painful moments, and especially of tenderness and love. In a way I am not there. I have found it too personal and too difficult to re-create all those feelings on paper. It has to suffice to say that I am capable of those emotions and have experienced them, at times intensely.

So there I was, in the autumn of 1941, with my Ph.D. in my pocket but without a job, having at my disposal only the modest amount of half my earlier assistant's salary (chapter 6). I had, however, ideas on how to continue the lines of physics research begun in preparation for my doctorate and went to work on those. Sometime between then and June 1942 (I don't remember precisely when), when Jews were forbidden to use trains, I moved back from my room near Utrecht to my parents' home in Amsterdam. In the intervening period before June, I would regularly travel to Utrecht to discuss my research with Professor Rosenfeld, my promoter. He and his wife were gracious in offering me a place to sleep in their home so that I could spend an extra day or two talking about my work. Both are gone now. My memories of them are affectionate and respectful.

As mentioned before, in the autumn of 1941 Jewish children were barred from public schools; the Jewish community now provided schooling for them. Teachers for these schools were in demand. I felt I should participate; I could also use the few extra guilders. I still have a yellowed letter dated May 3, 1942, confirming that I was teaching mathematics in the youth center at Plantage Franschelaan 13, as well as at a center for adult education at Nicolaas Witsenkade 14. I also have an identity card dated October 13, 1942, issued by the JR and signed by Presidents Asscher and Cohen, which states, in Dutch and German, that I am an *Oberlehrer* (secondary teacher) who is *unentbehrlich* (indispensable) for the education of Jewish pupils.

Almost from the start I had to walk to get to my place of work. In June, use of all public transportation became forbidden to us. In addition, I had to turn in my bike at that time (see the preceding chapter). I still have the receipt for delivery of my beloved old bicycle.

The really bad times had meanwhile started. Since May I had worn a star. In July deportations were initiated. In September the stamp drama began. The first in my family to get a stamp was my father. Between June and September he had received four different bilingual legitimation cards: two issued by the Office of Social Affairs of the city of Amsterdam, and two by the JR, stating that he was *Religionshauptlehrer* (headmaster for religious education). Then, on September 30, he received the stamp in his ID card stating that he was exempt, until further notice, from mobilization for labor. The stamp was numbered 82.226. It was one of the so-called 80.000

series, issued to those connected with the JR. If my father counted among these, it was not because of any involvement with deportation measures but simply because he taught at a Jewish school.

For that same reason an 80.000 stamp, no. 85.303, was issued to me as well, on October 6. On February 11, 1943, mine, however, was upgraded to a 40.000 stamp, no. 40.874, one of the 640 stamps[1] in that most coveted category of all: Jews enjoying various forms of German protection.

The institution of that classification had been the result of initiatives by the (Dutch) Secretaries General of the Interior, and especially of Education, Science, and Cultural Affairs. These men had been able to convince the Germans that there was a small group of Jews who had contributed so much to advancing Holland's cultural life that they deserved preferential treatment. What had brought little me into such company? Recall that I had been a university assistant, an appointment which in its time had gone to the Minister of Education in The Hague for approval, so that I was registered as a Jew who had lost a nationally recognized position. My assistantship in physics may actually have added very little to the culture of the Netherlands, yet this official registration sufficed to make me a candidate for a 40.000 exemption.

I now leave my own story for a while to tell what happened to Annie, my sister, who was nearly twenty when the war came to Holland. Already earlier, in October 1939, she had become engaged to Herman de Leeuw, a young Jewish businessman. I believe that he too had managed to obtain an 80.000 stamp. People used to pull strings in those days. In any event, on a day in May 1942, they married. I recall how my family, Tineke included, first went to Amsterdam's city hall for the civil wedding, then to the Sephardic synagogue for the religious ceremony. There she sat, my pretty little sister, under the *chuppah*,[2] wearing a lovely white dress—with a star attached. Afterward we had a fine dinner. I do not remember where that took place, but can recall the main course: sweetbreads, hard to get in those days, with peas-in-the-pod.

Annie's marriage abruptly transformed her personality. From a rather indolent girl she turned into a young woman who took charge. How well I recall looking at her with new respect and increased affection! Because of her marriage she shared the protection of her young husband's stamp.

One late evening around the end of 1942, I was in my upstairs room in my parents' home when suddenly I heard yelling and shrieking in the room next to mine, in the house next door. It was the bedroom of an old man in his eighties, a Jew. I knew at once what was happening: Germans had come in to take him away. There I stood, one ear glued to the wall, listening to those terrible and frightening noises that went on for some twenty minutes. Then all became silent. The next morning I learned that I had guessed correctly. My old neighbor, in his nightclothes, had been clinging to his bed, refusing to move and yelling for mercy. He was gone. The Germans had struck only meters away from me.

My father had three brothers and three sisters, all married. My mother had one brother and one sister, both unmarried, and another sister who was a widow. My mother's father, well into his seventies, was my only grandparent then still alive. I had five cousins in all. Of these, only one sister of my father and her two children survived (she had been married to a non-Jew), as well as one cousin from my mother's side who went into hiding. The other seventeen family members were deported and never returned. How could these gentle people possibly have harmed Germany? It is the kind of question every survivor keeps forever mulling over when thinking of close ones lost.

Soon after I started courting Tineke Buchter, it became my custom to go to her home at Nieuwe Zyds Voorburgwal 282 on Saturday afternoons and stay over until Sunday. Tineke, a non-Jew strongly involved with Jewish issues, lived there with her mother, Marie (who was divorced), of whom I also became very fond. Marie's mother would often also be there, a spry, corpulent, determined little lady whom I also liked greatly. All of this began before the war. After the summer of 1940, when my parents had accepted her, Tineke would come to our home on Friday nights for the weekly festive Sabbath dinner and would stay over.

   Tineke and Marie's home became a haven for hunted people practically from the day of the capitulation. In these first days of occupation, those who sought refuge were not so much Jews as those who feared incarceration because of their political convictions. As the situation grew more and more threatening for Jews, they were hospitably taken in, not so much for prolonged stays as in transit to hiding places. Especially Tineke, but also Marie, became increasingly active in helping to find suitable premises.

   When deportations started in the summer of 1942, I began to think seriously of going into hiding myself. I had sworn to myself that I would never respond to any order to move to a place where Germans would have direct control over my movements. My exemption stamps gave me some respite, but I never for a moment believed that their guarantee would last indefinitely. I first discussed my hiding plans with Tineke, who fully agreed with them and pledged her help. Some time thereafter I talked it over with my parents, urging them to make similar plans. I vividly recall their response. My father said he felt he had to go to a labor camp when called up because of his intense feelings of solidarity with his fellow Jews. Whereupon my mother said, "Go if you want to—but I won't." In the event, she prevailed. I did not have such discussions with my sister because after her marriage she and her husband had moved into an apartment of their own.

In the fall of 1942, I was unofficially informed that I was under consideration for a high class 40.000 stamp. That would give me extra respite, but my mind was nevertheless made up. At an appropriate moment I would go into hiding. Tineke had meanwhile arranged for a place for me. I began to make preparations. Little by little I would bring clothes of mine to Tineke's home for temporary storage. Next came my better books—with my name on the flyleaf cut out. I left behind books of my youth, the adventures of Pietje Bel, of Dik Trom, of Prikkebeen, as well as my study books from student years. All those are lost now. In later years I have wished off and on to hold them in my hands again. This is one of the ways—not the worst— in which I feel cut off from my childhood.

Then I began to take some lessons in indoor physical exercises from a Jewish acquaintance, since I wished to be prepared for keeping physically fit during a period of confinement that might well be prolonged. A student friend of mine gave me a pair of lightweight dumbbells for exercise purposes; these too were duly stored with Tineke.

At that juncture an unforeseen alternative came my way. My close friends Sieg and Leah Gitter (see chapter 5), now married, had begun planning their escape from Holland via Belgium and France to Spain. They came to ask me whether I would like to join them—at their own rather substantial expense. I asked for one day's time to think this over.

I decided to decline their truly generous offer. At that time I was deeply immersed in theoretical physics research. I could neither imagine abandoning that work nor see how I could concentrate on it while being "on the road." That, much more than the obvious risks of the enterprise, held me back. So there came a day when I embraced each of them and from the bottom of my heart wished them bon voyage. They did make it to Spain, and from there to Argentina.

In 1943 I made my own move—inside Holland.

On January 13, the Secretary General of Education, Science, and Cultural

Affairs signed a letter addressed to me, written in German. At the heading
was written: *Betrifft Arbeitseinsatz* (concerns mobilization of labor). The text
read: "Hereby I inform you that I have drawn the attention of the [German]
general commissioner for special affairs to your situation. He has agreed to
give the matter special consideration." It was the formal announcement that I
would get a 40.000 stamp which, as mentioned, I indeed received in February. While I was of course pleased, I did not change my plans.

On March 12, I received a form letter signed by the Secretary General of
the Interior, this one in Dutch. It said: "I have the honor to inform you that
you will neither be transported to Amsterdam nor put to work in a work
camp abroad." The mention of transport did not apply to me but to Jews
living outside the capital. The reference to no deportation had to do with
the decision made meanwhile to move all holders of 40.000 stamps to De
Schaffelaar, a small chateau in Barneveld, a little town in the province of
Gelderland, this to prevent their accidental capture in *razziahs* (round-
ups). Some had moved there the previous December; the rest had to move
in March. That, I decided, was the ideal moment for me to go to the hiding
place Tineke had arranged for me. If people wondered where I was, my
parents could simply say that I had gone to Barneveld. On March 19, I
arrived at my hide-out.

Before going on, a few words about the fate of the Barnevelders, as those
who went there came to be called.[3]

They lived in an island of tranquility, cut off from the rest of the world.
Life was not unpleasant. Schooling for children and evening lectures for
adults were organized by the participants themselves. Food was tolerable.

So it remained until September 29, 1943, the day on which the JR in
Amsterdam was dissolved. On that same day, Germans arrived in Barneveld
and gave the inmates thirty minutes to pack for transport to Westerbork. In
September 1944 they were transported from there to Theresienstadt, the
better-class concentration camp. From there, some were brought to Switzerland in the spring of 1945; the others were liberated by Soviet armed
forces and returned safely to Holland.

Had I gone to Barneveld, I would also most probably have survived.

10.2 I GO INTO HIDING. MY SISTER IS DEPORTED

My new home was a patrician house on one of Amsterdam's famous old
canals, Keizersgracht 499, not far from Anne Frank's place of hiding. My

host, Mr. Koehorst—I called him Pa—was a gentleman tailor who had his atelier downstairs. The family consisted of his wife, Ma, two sons—Lou, a few years younger than I, and Rob, his younger brother—and one daughter, Alwien, about my age, a very pretty young woman. The family quarters were in the building's top two floors. I had a pleasant room on the top floor to myself. It was on the whole a cheery family, though I could feel some tension between the parents (who divorced after the war). We took our meals together, otherwise I spent my time in my own room.

I had a false identity card, under the name Arthur Meerwaldt, M.D., with of course my own picture inserted. The card, provided by Tineke, was most probably a real card voluntarily "lost" by its owner, who could apply for a new one. From now on I was called Ad or Adje. On arrival I still had my own valid ration card. Later I would get one that had been stolen from a card distribution office. A financial arrangement with my hosts had been agreed upon, whereby I paid them a reasonable monthly sum in payment for boarding expenses. The money came from the sale of my father's stamp collection. He had been a collector since he was a young man, though he had spent only modest sums of money on his hobby. Still, he had a very presentable assortment, neatly gathered in a set of albums. For example, he had a complete set of Dutch stamps from the first issue on (dating, as I recall, from the 1850s). In those war days there was great demand among the well-to-do for diamonds and for stamps, since both these items take up very little space and so could be stored in tiny containers that were fire- and bombproof—and they could easily be hidden. At that time the value of my father's collection must have risen to many thousands of dollars, which provided for the material security for our family.

And so I settled into a life that may be called carefree considering the circumstances. I developed regular routines. Every day, all through my years in hiding, I did forty-five minutes of physical exercise before breakfast, in front of an open window with curtains closed, and another forty-five minutes in the late afternoon before dinner. I devoted hours of each day to research, helped by the few books I had with me. These included one I had specially bought recently, in preparation for my isolation: volume 24, part 1, of the *Handbuch der Physik,* an 800-page tome that contained the best summaries of what was known about quantum physics to date. It is by far the most expensive book I have ever bought; it still graces my shelves in my present university office. If I had need for books not in my possession— that happened only infrequently—Tineke would fetch them for me in the "U.B.," the university library. I would interrupt my studies once in a while for a chat with Lou, who worked at home as a tailor in his father's business. I would also spend long hours reading belles-lettres.

Especially in the beginning, I keenly felt the restrictions imposed on my movements: I was never on the streets and could not enjoy casual encounters with friends and acquaintances. This lack of stimulus caused me to do something I had never done before: I kept a diary, in which I wrote regularly during the remaining war years, noting events, unbosoming feelings, recording reflections. Shortly after the war, in a fit of melancholy, I burned those diaries. It was an irrational and in fact futile attempt to rid myself of very painful memories. Now I find the act both understandable and quite regrettable. Had I not done so, I would now have documents about the daily life of one who lived practically next door to Anne Frank—but who survived. Those lost diaries would certainly have been a valuable help in the present undertaking.

On May 19, exactly two months after I vanished from the surface of the earth, I reached my twenty-fifth birthday. My hosts made it a pleasant day for me, but of course no family and friends dropped in, nor did letters arrive in the mail. Not one person of my past life knew where I was, except for Tineke. That was one of the crucial precautionary rules of the times. The less you knew, the better, in case you got caught. Not even torture can make one confess what one doesn't know.

Dear Tineke saw to it, however, that I would get an occasional letter that she would pick up for me. I still have one of those, birthday greetings from my sister, Annie, written the week after May 19. She began by sending greetings for "two birthdays"—Tineke, two years younger, and I were born on the same day. She further wrote that the following week she would be celebrating her first wedding anniversary with family and friends, and that she would miss me greatly that day. Her letter went on to describe a visit to our father at his school for Jewish children. Just after she had arrived, the air-raid alarm had sounded. A war plane went right over the school; some machine-gun bullets hit the playground. Many children became hysterical; one fainted. The letter continues: "Jews who had been baptized Christian must leave next Friday. They received a call-up at their home address, just like we did." It ends: "Perhaps we shall soon be together again." This letter is the last memento I have of my dear sister.

Two weeks after she had written it, she was dead.

Killed.

The German letter of call-up to Annie and Herman is lost, but I still have an accompanying printed notice in Dutch, dated May 23, signed by the two

JR presidents. It says: "On the strength of the accompanying call-up, the German authorities order you to appear on Tuesday, May 25, between 8 and 18 hours, at the constabulary barracks, Polderweg, to be put to work in Germany. . . . You should note that the sharpest possible measures will be taken against you if you do not appear."

As soon as I learned of Annie's call-up, I made plans to meet with her. I do not recall the specific arrangements. In any event, one day very soon afterward I went to my parents' home, on a borrowed bike and without a star. There I found Annie waiting for me. I took her to my old room upstairs, where we sat down and talked. The gist of what I said was to urge her most strongly not to go to the camps but rather to go into hiding with her husband. I was in a position to suggest this because Tineke and I had discussed their hiding option some time earlier, whereupon she had come up with a concrete proposal for a hiding place.

Annie said no, she could not do that, because Herman had refused to entertain the idea on grounds I had heard earlier from others: being cooped up would drive him crazy. What could I say?

Even though information on gas chambers awaiting Dutch Jews had not yet reached us, all my instincts had told me: Don't go. But what arguments could I marshall against a young woman's desire to stick it out with her husband? I simply did not know what more to say to her. So we sat and talked some more about this and that. Then I took her in my arms and hugged her. For the last time. Then I said good-bye to my parents and left forever the home of my teenage years and returned to my hiding place.

A few days later, Alwien came into my room to tell me that Annie and Herman had departed. My reaction was what I believe amounted to hysterics. For minutes on end I cried but also laughed and felt completely irrational. Then, exhausted, I calmed down.

A few days later, my parents received a postcard from barracks 64, Westerbork, written by Herman. It lies here in front of me, and says: "Dear parents, just back from a soccer match which we lost, 4–3, at the last moment. It was a great match. Annie looks well and is a wonderful and dear woman. . . . We laugh a lot. . . . Westerbork agrees much better with us than we anticipated. . . . Food is good. Do not worry about us. Now I say farewell and hope to see you soon. Annie is very well [last two words underlined]. Kisses." It was the last sign of life we ever had from them. When the war was over, I did everything possible to find out what happened to them, but nowhere could I obtain any information. Fifty years later, in the fall of 1991, I found out.

10.3 SOBIBOR

With typical thoroughness, the Germans had introduced a classification of *Lager,* camps where Jews and others were confined, into a variety of categories, from *Aufenthaltslager* (places to stay), to concentration camps, to *Vernichtungslager* (extermination camps), the principal settings for the "Endlösung der Judenfrage," the Final Solution. There were six of the latter camps. The oldest, Chelmno, 60 miles west of Warsaw, began to operate in late 1941. The other five were as follows (distances always calculated from Warsaw): Auschwitz-Birkenau (Oświecim-Brzezinka), 120 miles to the southwest, also in part concentration camp, "the largest death center the world had ever seen";[4] Treblinka, 30 miles to the northeast; Sobibor, 80 miles to the southeast, 5 miles from the town of Wlodawa; Majdanek, near Lublin, 60 miles to the southeast; and Belźec, near Lemberg (Lwow), 125 miles to the southeast.[5]

When on January 26, 1945, Russian forces first entered Auschwitz, they found only 2,800 invalid survivors. In 1946, *Obersturmbannführer* (Lieutenant-Colonel) Rudolf Hoess, the camp commander, earlier a convicted murderer, would boast at the Nuremberg trials to have superintended at Auschwitz the extermination of two and a half million persons, not counting one-half million who had been allowed to succumb to starvation.[6] Present estimates, varying to within twenty percent, put the number of people killed in Auschwitz at about one million.[7]

The capacity for death at Auschwitz far exceeded those of the other killing centers. The method used was to drop crystallized prussic acid, known as Zyklon B, through an opening in the death chambers. "When the Soviets moved in, twenty-nine of the thirty-five store rooms had been burned down. In the six remaining ones the liberators found part of the camp's legacy: 368,820 men's suits, 836,255 women's coats and dresses, large quantities of children's clothes."[8]

The first camp to be liberated by the Western Allies was Bergen-Belsen at Celle, near Hannover, in western Germany. When on April 15, 1945, British troops entered the German camp, administration had already broken down completely. Food supplies had been shut off, the starving inmates were left to their own devices, spotted typhus and diarrhea raged unchecked, tens of thousands of corpses rotted in barracks, and, on dung heaps, rats attacked living inmates (dead ones were eaten by starving prisoners). The British troops found 2,800 women, 12,000 men, and 13,000 unburied corpses. Another 13,000 died within a few days of liberation. After the camp was freed, every rag and stick had to be destroyed by fire.[9]

Holland had to make its contribution: 3,722 Jews were transported from there to Belsen. Of these, 2,184 survived, the highest percentage of Jews from Holland as compared with those sent to any of the other camps. Of the 62,000 Dutch Jews sent to Auschwitz, only 1,000 survived.[10]

Of the camps mentioned, Auschwitz has become the lasting symbol of the Final Solution. It was there that the Russians found survivors who could testify to what had happened. It was also there that they found the killing machinery largely intact, as well as materials that give silent testimony to the plunder of the dead.[11] It was about Auschwitz that Hoess, its commander, testified about freely in Nuremberg. Moreover, the ex-Auschwitzers have established a number of national committees that, every year on January 26, organize memorial meetings, events that are fittingly mentioned in the press.

By comparison, the other killing centers have garnered much less public attention. Perhaps the least known of all is Camp Sobibor on the river Bug, even though several hundred thousand Jews were killed there too. One can understand why not much has been heard of Sobibor. First of all, when the Russians reached it, they found no signs of survivors, nor, in fact, of a camp. Already in the fall of 1943, orders had come from above to destroy the camp without leaving a trace. The same happened in Treblinka and Bełżec.[12] This was done because by that time the German armies were already retreating from Russia. On the preceding July 15, Soviet forces had launched their first summer offensive and had since retaken Smolensk and Charkov. The areas of the three death camps in eastern Poland were therefore increasingly exposed to recapture, and the German authorities were determined to keep their annihilation operations a deep secret.

After *Vernichtungslager* Sobibor had been razed, the entire terrain was planted over with saplings by thirty Jewish forced laborers, all of whom were shot in November 1943. It was as if the Final Solution had never taken place there. "Sobibor was Himmler's best kept secret."[13]

On the camp site now one can only find a commemorative plaque which reads: "Sobibor. In this place stood a Nazi death camp from May 1942 to October 1943. In it, they killed 250,000 Russian POWs, Jews, Poles, and Gypsies."[14] This is a lie, since no Poles or Russians were exterminated there. Poland, a notoriously anti-Semitic nation, would not even see fit to record who were the only sufferers.

A second reason for history's comparative silence about Sobibor is that

among the millions of pages of German documents captured by the Allies in
1945, only three short documents refer to it.[15] Finally, there were very few
who, after the war, could tell what happened. The best count of Sobibor
survivors is forty-six.[16] As a result of all these circumstances, only a small
fraction of the voluminous literature on camps is devoted to Sobibor.[17]
From these books and articles I was able to compose the following picture.

The building of the camp began in March 1942. *Obersturmbannführer*
(Lieutenant Colonel) Christian Wirth was in charge of this construction
project as well as those in Belżec and Treblinka. The camp covered an area
of some 170 acres and was surrounded by three seven-foot-high electrified
fences. Between the middle and the outer fences lay a path that was constantly patrolled.

Extermination started in May 1942 and lasted until October 1943. The
Croat-born *Obergruppenführer* (Lieutenant General) Odilo Globocnik directed all *Einsatz* (action) Reinhardt massacres and thus oversaw the killings in Sobibor. The camp had its own commander, first *Hauptsturmführer*
(Captain) Franz Stangle, then *Hauptsturmführer* Frank Reichleitner. The
camp staff consisted of thirty SS men and about one hundred Ukrainians.
Many tasks were performed by a number of Jewish inmates, who never
numbered more than one thousand; two hundred of them worked near the
gas chambers, on the disposal of corpses and on the sorting of clothes. An
unknown number of Gypsies and of people declared insane or incurable
(such as sufferers from tuberculosis) were also killed in Sobibor.

In these and related activities, German officialdom systematically aimed
at leaving as few traces as possible. In their documents, there is never any
mention of *Endlösung* but rather of *Sonderbehandlung* (special treatment).
Incurables were sent to "clinics." Transports to camps were labeled *Arbeitseinsatz*. Such camouflage reached its extremes in the camps, where they
had a further purpose: to keep the Jews calm and as long as possible unaware of what was in store for them. This way they could not warn the next
arrivals of what had just happened to their predecessors, and revolts could
be avoided. For example, the arrival platform—transports came by train,
most often in cattle cars—at Treblinka was disguised as a normal railway
station with signs like "To Warsaw" and "To Bialystok."[18]

These precautions were especially elaborate in Sobibor.[19] The arrival
platform was situated in the *Vorlager* (front camp), the only section visible
upon detraining. The rest of the camp was hidden by wooden fences. The
various buildings in the *Vorlager* bore such signs as *Die Heimat Gottes*
(God's Fatherland), *Das Schwalbennest* (The Swallow's Nest), *Zum lustigen*

Floh (The Merry Flea). Various crossings were marked with wooden signposts reading: to the baths, to the casino, to the bowling alley. "The newly arrived would be addressed via loudspeaker by an official who told them that they would be transferred to work camps in nearby Wlodawa. Families would be kept together. Those who worked hard would be awarded certificates of good conduct. Meanwhile, they had all come a long way and would no doubt welcome a good wash in the bath house."[20]

From the *Vorlager* the victims walked along the Himmelfahrtallee (Ascension Boulevard), passed Lager 1, where the sorters and other Jews working as shoemakers, dressmakers, electricians, bakers, etc., were housed, to come to Lager 2, where inmate *Kommandos* deposited the luggage which the newcomers had brought with them and sorted their contents. Here also room was provided for tables and benches to write letters—never sent off.

For almost all comers, their day of arrival in Sobibor was also their day of death. The assembly-line procedure went like this. Lager 2 contained barracks in which one had to strip. From there one walked to the strictly isolated Lager 3, which bore the sign *Lazarett* (infirmary) over the entrance gate. Women's hair was now cut. Then everyone entered the *Badehaus* (bathhouse), a single building, surrounded by flowerbeds, that contained the six gas chambers, each one—camouflaged to the end—equipped with dummy shower fittings, each one with a capacity for exterminating five hundred to six hundred people at a time. Jews were driven into the chambers by Ukrainians wielding truncheons and whips and holding dogs. Those who had been unable to walk—the sick, the old, the little children—were shot separately behind the gas chambers.

After the chambers had been loaded, doors were shut and gassing began. Carbon monoxide from engine fumes was fed into the chambers, causing death in fifteen to thirty minutes, unless an engine broke down. An SS man would look through a spy hole in the roof to make sure that everyone had suffocated. That done, doors were opened and Jewish special *Kommandos* entered, wearing gas masks and gumboots and carrying hoses to remove blood and defecation. "The twenty or so Jews who were made to clear the gas chambers were shot every few weeks and made up again by a selection from among the sorters."[21] Some *Kommando* members were ordered to check teeth for gold fillings and crowns; these teeth were ripped out with pliers. The corpses were transported to open pits, where they were cremated. "Those selected for these tasks knew they had just another 4 to 6 weeks of life left to them. Quite a number, it would seem, lost their minds or committed suicide."[22]

These gassings, this hell on earth, came to an end when on October 14, 1943, several hundred Jews staged a revolt, described in the following "Report of the Security Police in the Lublin district—October 15, 1943 (City of Lublin)":

> On October 14, 1943, at about 5 P.M., a revolt of Jews in the SS camp Sobibor, twenty-five miles north of Chelm. They overpowered the guards, seized the armory, and after an exchange of shots with the camp garrisons, fled in unknown directions. Nine SS men murdered, one SS man missing, two foreign guards shot to death.
>
> Approximately 300 Jews escaped. The remainder were shot to death or are now in camp.[23]

Many of the three hundred escapees were subsequently murdered or betrayed by Polish and Ukrainian anti-Semites. Only forty-six survived.[24]

Between March 2 and July 20, 1943, nineteen trains, carrying 34,294 Jews, left Westerbork for a voyage lasting three days and three nights, making the 1,100-mile trek eastward to Sobibor. According to a man who was in Westerbork through this March–July period: "Not only after the war was the name Sobibor virtually unknown; the same was true in Westerbork during the war. The name was never mentioned in relation to the nineteen trains to Sobibor. There was reference to Auschwitz, even occasionally to Riga, but never to Sobibor. I can state this so firmly since I had transport duty in Westerbork on departure of all these nineteen deportation trains."[25] As far as I have been able to ascertain, the only Jews from Western Europe to end their trip and their lives in Sobibor were those on the nineteen trains from Westerbork.

A Polish-born survivor who saw the Jews from Holland arrive in Sobibor has said: "The Dutch bounced off the trains in furs and silk dresses or woollen suits, carrying their valuables. Unlike the Polish Jews, they were, for the most part, well educated, not Orthodox, and totally western. . . . They had not been prepared for Sobibor by ghettos, typhus, starvation, fear and hatred, slow death, bullets, whips."[26] Of the more than 30,000 Jews from Holland, only two survived, both women: Ursula Stern, German-born, and Saartje Wÿnberg.[27] They had been in the group of three hundred escapees.

Already before V-E Day, the Dutch government-in-exile had discussed the need for setting up an institution that would gather and analyze information on war events in Holland. As a result, the Rÿksinstituut voor Oorlogsdocumentatie (Netherlands State Institute for War Documentation) was officially founded on May 8, 1945, within a week following the end of the war in Europe. It has since obtained and catalogued documents that can fill a mile and a half of stacking space. The Institute is now housed in Herengracht 474, Amsterdam.[28]

I remained in Holland for most of the eight months following the end of the war. As mentioned earlier, during that time I had tried without success to find out about the fate of Annie and her husband after their departure from Westerbork. I do not remember whether or not I contacted the Rÿksinstituut at that time. In any event, it was a new venture then, not yet well organized. In later years I heard the Institute mentioned several times. As I started preparations for writing this chapter, it struck me that I ought to make a last try at finding out about my sister. Accordingly I wrote to Amsterdam, asking whether they had the information I so much wanted. On September 25 I received an answer. The relevant phrase: "Your sister Anna de Leeuw-Pais and her husband Herman de Leeuw were deported from Westerbork to Sobibor, where they died on June 4, 1943."

How could this date be fixed with such precision? Because it must have been known at Westerbork that they were among the 3,006 Jews who left Westerbork on June 1, and because Jews were gassed on the very day of arrival at Sobibor.[29] I had heard of Sobibor by the time I received the letter but did not know much more about it than its name. Since then, I have read all I could lay my hands on about that camp, so that I now have an inkling of the environment in which Annie and Herman spent their final hours.

I could no longer weep by the time I received that letter. I have in fact often wondered through the years why, after the day the news of Annie's departure had caused me to respond hysterically, I have never again felt the acute pain of her loss. It was as if her earlier existence had become a sealed-off part of my soul. Subsequent reading about the reactions of other survivors has made clear to me that my own was not rare. By the time the information about Annie's death reached me, she would have been seventy-one years old had she still been alive—and my last memory of her is as a young woman of twenty-three. I was therefore not surprised at my own calm when the news reached me in 1991. After having read the letter, a copy of which I immediately sent to Tineke, I became silent and withdrawn for days on end, recalling especially my last talk with Annie. Once again I asked myself, as I had done so often during the past half-century: Should I have insisted more emphatically that she should go into hiding?

Since the receipt of that letter, I have tried numerous times to imagine what it must have been like for the young couple. In thought I have tried to walk with them to those gas chambers in Lager 3, holding Annie by the hand and talking softly to her. My powers of imagination fail me, however. For me, a survivor, that reality is too impossible.

10.4 MY PARENTS GO INTO HIDING

I return now to my war experiences in Holland and how my parents managed to survive the war.

I have before me two documents addressed to my father. The first, dated July 4, 1943, was signed by the secretary of the Portuguese-Israelitic parish in Amsterdam. It states that both my parents appear on a list, presented to the Portuguese government, of persons being considered for possible emigration to Portugal. It is a bit of a puzzle to me how my mother, who was Ashkenazi, made her appearance on that list.

The second document, dated July 10, 1943, and signed by an official of the JR, states: "It is with pleasure that we can inform you that the department of education of the municipality of Amsterdam has informed us that you will receive an *Ausnahmebescheinigung* (certificate of exemption)." I do not remember what that exemption meant. Recall, however (see sec. 9.4 of chapter 9), that by September 1943 the deportation of Dutch Jews was virtually complete and that already in July the situation had become extremely critical. I had continued to urge my parents by letter to go into hiding as well, informing them that Tineke had a place waiting for them. My sister's departure in late May had finally convinced them. In the summer of 1943 they went.

Their home was on a farm near the village of Hillegom, near Haarlem. They now assumed new identities; I still have their false IDs. My father became Fredericus Leonardus Groenewege, born in The Hague, *Stucadoor,* whitewasher, by profession. My mother was now Elisabeth Elerie, born in Usquert, in the province of Groningen. I also still have her *Stamkaart* in my possession, a document needed for obtaining new ration cards when the old ones expired. By the strict rules of the game, I of course did not know where they were, except that it was somewhere outside the city. Knowledge of hiders' whereabouts could in fact be exceedingly dangerous. If someone did know, and that person was caught by the Germans, then the person hiding had at once to move elsewhere, since no one, however trustworthy, should be expected to remain silent under torture.

The following true story will illustrate that in those days knowledge could have mortal consequences. One day, *lange Jan* (tall John), as he was known, was walking along on a street in Amsterdam. I had met him earlier and knew that he was an important figure in the resistance movement in our city. At one point on his walk he noticed that he was being followed by two Gestapo men, and began to run. Then they started to run. Lange Jan ran into a house, up the stairs. The Gestapo men followed him inside. Jan climbed all the way to the roof, the other two still on his heels. Since he could not risk being captured, as he knew a lot, he took his own life by jumping off the roof. The ending of the story is even more bitter. Sometime later it became known that the Gestapo had not been after him, they in fact did not know who he was, but had started pursuit after they saw him trying to elude them.

All through the rest of the war, my mother walked freely outside, as her appearance was not markedly Jewish. Since the farmer's family was Catholic, so was my mother, who passed for a cousin of the farmer's wife. She was supposed to be an evacuee from a region the Germans had requisitioned for military purposes. My father, on the other hand, had to stay hidden indoors during the day, but could also come out during dark evenings, when he could walk around on the farmer's land. My mother could therefore do her share of the shopping. She would also regularly visit a village store where she could borrow books at a modest cost. This led to one of her more hilarious war experiences. One day she asked the store owner if he knew anything about a certain book she had chosen. "I do," the man said, "but I must warn you that this one is on the Catholic Index of forbidden books." "In that case," my mother replied, "I shall of course not take it along."

Reading became my parents' main diversion. In addition, I had undertaken to teach my father English. He and I each had a copy of the same textbook, which contained many exercises. My father would study a chapter and write out the assignments. These reached me by courier. I would check them and on the next occasion return them with corrections.

My father, an inveterate smoker, also developed the hobby of planting tobacco, which he would tend himself during the evening hours. When the leaves were mature, they were brought inside and hung on the attic to dry. When that was done, my father had something for his pipe. I too got a share, finely cut, to roll into cigarettes. These tasted awful, but it was the only tobacco available to me.

Their life at the farm continued in peace and quiet until the spring of 1944, when German Army personnel came into their area to begin construction of launching sites for V2 rockets, which (see chapter 8) in September of that year, began to hit London. It now became far too dangerous for people in hiding to stay close to that area, since residences could be expected to be thoroughly searched for hidden weapons and unauthorized persons. Once again, Tineke went into action, finding them this time a flat in the town of Heemstede. There they stayed safely until the end of the war. It was there that I saw them again for the first time after the war, having come on a borrowed bicycle.

The rest of this chapter is about my own wartime experiences.

10.5 THE TALE OF THE FIVE HIDING PLACES

By the time I went into hiding, it was already clear that Germany would lose the war, though nobody could foresee how long our misery would last. By then the Germans had been driven out of Africa and out of Stalingrad, and Mussolini had fallen.

Soon after I had arrived on the Keizersgracht, a special place had been constructed where I could hide in case of a German raid on the house. In an attic next to my room, a wooden wall panel had been cut loose, behind which there was a tiny space in which I could crawl if necessary. A lock had been attached to the inside of the panel so that I myself could close off the wall once I was installed. I regularly trained myself to go rapidly through the necessary motions.

Life during the next months was a period of calm and routine. I had one wonderful diversion throughout that period. I have said that only Tineke knew where I was. That was not quite the whole story. One other person knew: Hans Kramers, the physics professor with whom I had become on increasingly good terms ever since my first visits to him in Leiden in the autumn of 1939 (chapter 6). Ever since his university had been closed down by the occupying powers (chapter 8), he had been forced to seek income elsewhere. As a result he became a consultant for the Bataafsche Petroleum Maatschappij, one of Holland's major corporations, bringing him once a week to that company's offices in Amsterdam. By contacting Tineke he had learned of my whereabouts. After consultation with my hosts, it was arranged that he would come and visit me once a week, on Mondays, after having finished his consultant's duties. He and the Koehorst family took to each other, and Hans—as I now called Kramers—was invited to stay for dinner on the days he visited me.

Kramers and I would of course talk physics. In particular we had intense debates on questions having to do with the theory of the electron.[30] Other subjects came up as well. Naturally we argued about the war situation. One day the discussion turned to music. Kramers said that my hiding period would be a good time for me to learn to play an instrument, and he offered to give me instruction on the cello, his personal favorite. I said that sounded great, except that I had no cello. That was not a problem, he replied, he knew a music store in Amsterdam where one could be rented. Shortly thereafter Rob, the younger Koehorst son, was delegated to visit that store and rent an instrument. Now I had a wonderful new pastime. The noises I produced caused no problems. My hosts told neighbors in passing that Rob had taken up the study of the cello. And so my life went on, by no means unpleasantly, until one Monday in November 1943, when disaster struck.

It was about six o'clock in the evening. We were at dinner, Kramers included, when the bell rang. Whenever that happened, at an unusual hour like this, one of the Koehorst children would go down to open the door in person. There was a special button near the front door which, on being pressed, sounded an alarm upstairs. When it rang, I ran from the table (someone at once took my plate away) to my hiding place. On my way upstairs I heard German spoken below, so I knew that it was the Gestapo. I opened the panel in the attic wall and crept inside behind it. Then, dammit, I was so nervous that I could not work the inside lock. I therefore held the panel in position by hand. That way it did not fit perfectly; a narrow open crack remained.

The Gestapo people came upstairs and went into the attic. One man carried a strong torchlight which he at one point shone straight at my panel. I could see the light through the crack—I can still see that light even as I write these lines. He played the light around for a while. Then they left. For the moment at least, I had escaped the most dangerous situation in my entire life.

I kept sitting in the tiny space, practically bent over double, holding onto the panel, when I heard the door to my room, which lay at the other side of my hiding spot, open softly. Someone entered, I did not at first know who. Then that person sat down on a small bench that stood right at the wall behind which I was folded up. The person began to read, not loud but quite softly. It was Kramers. Earlier he had lent me a volume of Bradley's *Lectures on Shakespeare*. What this good man was doing now was reading to me from that book, in order to calm my nerves.

Sometime between ten and eleven one of the sons came to the attic to tell me that the coast was clear and I could come out. I vividly remember that I believed to have been cooped up for some fifteen minutes. In actual fact it was four hours.

It was obvious that I had to leave the Koehorst home, but I could not depart at once. It was late at night now, and a person on the virtually deserted streets could attract too much attention. So I rested, remaining fully dressed, until the next morning. Tineke and Marie had been alerted meanwhile. Shortly after 8 A.M. I went by bike to their home.

Either that previous night or the next day (my memory is understandably hazy), the Gestapo ripped off the floor of Pa Koehorst's atelier downstairs. There they found hidden a quantity of ladies' fine fur coats and other valuables that well-to-do Jewish clients of Mr. K. had asked him to hide for them. As a result of that discovery, Pa was sent to prison, where he was kept for about a year.

After only a very brief stay in Tineke's home, I went to my next hiding place, an apartment on Admiraal de Ruÿterweg. I deeply regret having forgotten the names of my hosts. I now lived with a couple and their two daughters. The husband had an office job. The younger girl was about fourteen, the older about seventeen. It was a quite modest-sized flat in which, however, I had a small room to myself, all I needed.

It was a friendly family with whom I had very pleasant relations. A shadow hung over their life because the older daughter was epileptic. Her attacks were fairly frequent, at times several per week. Occasionally I would be all alone with her in the home when one of these episodes occurred. I had seen what one should do: pillow under the head; place something between her teeth to prevent her from biting her tongue; hold on firmly to both arms, sitting on the lower legs if necessary—all this to prevent the poor girl from hurting herself. When it was over, see to it that she rested quietly on top of her bed. I had a curious feeling of inadequacy, being unable to do more for her while she was in her epileptic state.

During my stay in my second hiding place, I continued my regimen of physical exercises. I also listened to the BBC—including Churchill's occasional addresses—lying on my hosts' bed, a blanket covering me and the small radio set. What I remember most particularly about that period is an enormous amount of reading. Tineke knew a man who lived nearby who had a quite decent private library, and who had been kind enough to make a list of his books, at Tineke's request. That list was for me; I would select books, Tineke would fetch them for me. My recollection of what books I read those days is poor. All I remember are wonderful hours with Tolstoi's

War and Peace and with many of the writings of Dostoyevsky. The library also contained a four-volume German edition of the complete plays of Ibsen. In one week I read all of those. In spite of all these ways of keeping my mind occupied, I could not quite escape feelings of monotony. By way of mild diversion I decided to grow a mustache, just to look different. I nurtured this growth for a month or so, then shaved it off.

From that period dates one of the most important discoveries I ever made, and which forever changed my life. It concerned new insight into the process called thinking. Since my earlier years, at the university and especially in preparing my doctoral thesis, thinking had taken on ever-increasing importance in my way of life. In those years, I had to tell myself: Now sit down, young man, forget everything else and concentrate on your thoughts. Diversions could not only easily deflect me but would also cost time and effort afterward to return to the thinking mode.

Now, in hiding, it all worked differently. I would get up, exercise, have breakfast, then sit down at my little worktable and, presto, thoughts emerged totally unforced, by themselves, you might say. It was as if it was not I who did the thinking but as if thinking took place independently of my willingness to think. It was, in other words, as if the self became the passive receptacle of thoughts that came independently of any effort by me. That was the most important positive experience of my years in hiding.

The influence of isolation on the creative thought process has been experienced frequently. Isolation is intimately related to the emergence of religious visions. It has been written that Moses wrote the words of the Covenant, the Ten Commandments, during his solitary stay of forty days and forty nights on Mount Sinai, in the presence of only the Lord (Exodus 34:28). And that Jesus stayed in the wilderness for forty days (Mark 1:13). According to orthodox Buddhist belief, the Buddha Gotama remained in deep meditation under the Bo tree for seven times seven days and nights.

The most famous example of the positive influence of isolation on progress in science may well be the case of Isaac Newton, who in the 1660s was forced to live in seclusion on his mother's estate at Woolsthorpe for the greater part of two years, after the great plague closed Cambridge University. "That a youth should immediately after graduation retire to a lonely village and there, unaided, make three capital discoveries[31] in science, is nothing short of miraculous."[32]

One also finds the isolated state of the individual described in stories and novels. In several books by Charles Morgan one finds a poignant term for the resulting state of grace: singleness of mind, in particular in his *The*

Fountain. Here the author describes the experiences of a British officer who, during World War I, spends a number of years interned in a small chateau in Holland. That novel, which I read for the first time in the 1950s and have reread several times since, has made a deep and lasting impression on me. I find it puzzling that Morgan's novels are so little known. Those days of untrammeled thinking have taught me to appreciate quiet evenings spent by myself at home.

My absorption in my own thinking once led to an embarrassment. Normally I had the freedom of walking around the whole apartment. I was confined to my own room when my hosts had guests, however, having to take off my shoes to minimize noise. That was the situation when, one day, deep in thought and oblivious to my surroundings, I stepped out of my own room and, in stockinged feet, entered the living room where my hosts were having tea with a couple of visitors. All in the room, including myself, were quite startled. My hosts simply had to explain the situation. Fortunately, their guests, very decent people, understood at once. Nor did my stupidity have any further consequences. Afterwards, I offered my apologies and pledged that never again would I cause similar embarrassment.

The 6th of June 1944 came, D-Day. On the BBC a name was mentioned that I had never heard before: Eisenhower. I still have an old notebook filled with calculations and a notation in the margin of one page: D-Day. All over Holland, rules of curfew were tightened. That meant nothing to me, of course. In fact, my focus on work, thinking, and reading was not interrupted in the least.

On July 20, a German attempt was made to assassinate Hitler while he was in his headquarters at the *Wolfsschanze* (Wolves' Entrenchment) in East Prussia. In the course of the day, the BBC broadcast the news which, however, was still quite vague. We kept the German radio going all day. Just after midnight, Hitler himself came on the air. In a curiously hoarse voice he told the world that a bomb had exploded two meters away from him, that he was unhurt, and that the criminal elements responsible would be destroyed without mercy. It was the last time I would hear that hated voice.

That event did not interrupt my concentration either.

Then came *Dolle Dinsdag* (Crazy Tuesday), September 5, 1944. Gone was my focus and singleness of mind, never to return for the remainder of the war. In chapter 8 I already recounted the story of that crazy day. Like practically all Dutchmen, I was in a state of turmoil. At that time there was no doubt that Germany was well on its way to defeat. On that day it seemed as if we would be free within hours. Imagine my feelings. After having been cooped up for a year and a half, I would freely be walking the streets again! All of a sudden every additional minute of waiting for that glorious moment became agony.

Years later I was reminded of those explosive feelings when I read the account of slavery in the United States by Alexis de Tocqueville in his book *Democracy in America.* De Tocqueville pointed out that people can endure a state of enslavement for an unlimited time. When, however, they become aware of the possibility that this state may not endure, their lives suddenly become unbearable. That was exactly my experience on that Tuesday in September. But I had yet another very hard eight months to live through before it was all over.

Later that September I received an unexpected piece of news. My mother was coming to Amsterdam for a brief visit and hoped to see me. A meeting was arranged through the kindness of the Schönitzer family, friends of Tineke and Marie, who lived on the same street where I was hiding. My mother was to arrive there at an appointed hour, and I was to join her there shortly afterward. (It was of course out of the question that she would come to the place where I was staying.) It was impressed on me that I walk leisurely to that house, so as to avoid attracting attention.

And so, for the first time in I no longer remember how many months, I walked on a street. On arrival I thanked the hosts—whom I also knew— and embraced my mother, who looked well. We sat and talked for about an hour. Then she left. I was to wait a while longer before returning home myself.

Then the doorbell rang. The wife peeked out of the window, then, looking scared, turned to me and said, "Quick, to the basement. There are two men at the door whom I've never seen before." It was the Gestapo. I ran into the basement, unprepared for the situation, looked around, and saw a large vertical box of the kind used for storing clothes. I opened its lid, wormed myself inside, pulled some women's dresses over me, and waited.

Minutes later the cellar door opened and the men came in.

What I experienced next is unique in my life. I had the intense sensation of leaving my body and becoming a spectator of what was happening to me. The men puttered around in the cellar, never opening the box in which I was hiding, then left. I do not recall how long I stayed in the box, but after a while someone came down, called me, then told me I could come out. The coast was clear.

I went upstairs and had to sit down. My strange mental state had disappeared meanwhile, to be replaced by limpness and exhaustion. I was given a shot of brandy, waited a while longer, then returned to my own residence.

No one ever found out what brought the Gestapo there at that time—minutes after my mother had left. She too returned safely to her home.

Not long after, for reasons I cannot recall, I left the home on the de Ruÿterweg, where I had spent nearly a year of my life in the company of good and kind people. I stayed next in the home of a psychiatrist and his family in the Lairessestraat. After a brief sojourn I moved again, this time to a house on the Herengracht.

That was an altogether different type of hiding place. The house was in the hands of the resistance movement. It was situated opposite Amsterdam's central telephone offices and was intended to serve as a base when orders came to occupy that vital communications center. The basement of the house was a storage place for weapons to be used on that occasion. The inhabitants included a number of people in hiding like myself.

It was there that the hunger winter of 1944–45 (chapter 8) hit all of us hard. It was cold; we often spent the daytime hours huddled in blankets. It was also dark—gas and electricity services had been suspended. Fortunately, the resistance people had provided us with a lot of candles, which enabled us to light one room. I have memories of those evenings spent together, cheery in spite of everything. It was the time during which I, like nearly all the Dutch, could think of only one thing: food. There was not much energy left for my beloved physics or for reading.

From that period dates a special kind of Dutch gallows humor. A sample: if you had three more days to live, what would you do, and with whom? Another: after the war is over the Dutch government sends a questionnaire to all citizens. It starts out as follows: name? date of birth? domicile? have you been in prison? if not, why not?

Early in 1945 I changed hiding places again—for the last time. Once again, the style was different. Together with three friends from the Catacomb days (chapter 5), I rented an apartment on the Hobbemakade in Amsterdam. The three were Lion Nordheim, my admired friend from prewar days, the leader of the young radical Zionists (chapter 5), whom we last met on May 9, 1940, on the evening before the German invasion of Holland (chapter 7), when we celebrated his engagement to Jeanne van Amerongen, whom he had married later that year; Jeanne herself; and her youngest sister, Truusje. We had the apartment all to ourselves. Jeanne and Truusje went out freely on the streets. They had of course false identity documents and, blonde-haired and blue-eyed as they were, could easily pass for Gentiles. Lion, who had a very pronounced Jewish physiognomy, and I stayed indoors.

I need to explain the layout of our domicile. First of all, the place was a trap; there was no possibility of hiding anywhere in case of unwelcome visits. We had a living room, kitchen, bath, and three bedrooms, one for Jeanne and Lion, one for Truusje, and one for me. It should be noted for what follows that there were no intimate relations between Truusje and myself.

The lifestyle differed from that in my earlier sanctuaries in that we had occasional friendly visitors. One of these was Bert Broer, a Gentile friend of mine from my undergraduate years in Amsterdam. He would turn up once in a while to discuss physics problems. Another was a young Jewish woman whom I shall call Miriam. She had been engaged to a Gentile who was active in the resistance. Both were caught; her fiancé was executed. She had been in prison until a German official proposed that she become an informer, to be installed in an Amsterdam apartment. She accepted and escaped soon afterward. Now she was at risk, but nonetheless went freely outside. (I seem to remember that she had dyed her hair blonde.) She too would visit us occasionally.

Life was on the whole uneventful. I spent much of the daytime in my room with my physics calculations, which I copied in notebooks, and with my diverse reading. So it went on until one day in March, I believe it was the fifteenth.

That morning we had a visit from Miriam, who stayed for a while and then left. A bit later Johan van de Kieft came to see Lion and me. He was an important figure in the resistance movement, in contact with London. (Right after the war he became chairman of the socialist faction of the upper house of the Dutch parliament, and from 1952 to 1956 was minister of finance in the so-called third cabinet Drees.) The purpose of his visit was to discuss a draft bill, under consideration by the Dutch government-in-exile, which dealt with the fate of Jewish children who had been hidden during the war but whose parents had been deported and would probably not return. The issue was: Who should be responsible for them after the war, the natural parents if they returned, the foster parents if they so desired, or the Jewish community at large? This complex and delicate problem had been discussed among resistance leaders since early 1944. On February 14, 1945, they had sent a proposal to London providing for the establishment of the *Voogdÿraad OPK* (Guardian Commission for Wartime Foster Children).[33] Van de Kieft wished to discuss the issue with us because we had been assigned (I do not remember by whom) to represent the Zionist youth movement with the resistance.

That was my closest involvement with that movement. I never participated in sabotage or use of arms. There were Jews who did so, however. One of them, Philip de Leeuw, was a friend of mine also from the prewar period. I was at his religious marriage in an Amsterdam synagogue early in the war, where he appeared in the uniform of a reserve first lieutenant. He was a brave man. In November 1944 he participated in an attack on a Dutch railway line, was caught, and was executed that same month.[34]

After van de Kieft had left, Lion and I talked things over and decided that a memorandum should be prepared for use by the resistance. Lion said he would write it and started at once, while I repaired to my own room. Shortly afterward lunch was ready. As we sat down to our frugal meal, Lion put his unfinished writing in his jacket pocket—instead of storing it in the cache we had prepared for sensitive material.

10.6 WEEKS IN PRISON. WAR'S END

After lunch Bert Broer came to see me. That day we discussed a paper recently published by the great German physicist Werner Heisenberg and a coworker, H. Koppe, on the theory of superconductivity.

When the bell rang, I did not pay attention. Only the ladies were permitted to open the door. Moments later the room to my door opened. There stood a tall man in SS uniform, the skull and bones symbol on his cap, a drawn revolver in his hand.

My first reaction was a quick look at the window. Could I jump out? Impossible.

Not saying a word, the SS man moved his revolver to indicate that Bert and I should go into the hallway. The women and Lion were herded in there as well, rounded up by another German.

My strongest recollection of the next moments is the total collapse of Lion. I was of course frightened out of my wits, but that was as nothing compared to his behavior. He was visibly in total panic, had lost all semblance of composure, and moved erratically, causing one of the Germans to hit him in the face, sending his glasses flying. I heard Jeanne pleading with one of the men, offering diamonds to let us go, an offer that enraged them.

Next we were led down the stairs. Two cars were waiting. We three men were shoved in one, the women in the other. As we drove off, I experienced fears more intense than I have ever felt in my life. It was a degree of fear that caused physical pain. My body ached all over.

As I heard later, the women were driven to the women's prison. I did not see them again until May, when it was all over. We were taken to Gestapo headquarters (I believe it was on the Apollolaan), where the three of us were shoved into separate rooms.

As I was waiting for what was to happen next, I remembered some advice given me by resistance members on how to behave in such situations. First, and most important, try not to show fear. Behave politely. Ask for an interpreter who could translate spoken German into Dutch, the purpose being to gain time for replies. I actually never asked for that favor.

A man in mufti came in. I jumped to attention. As he paced slowly back and forth in the room, he began to interrogate me, speaking in conversational tones, never raising his voice. He first asked me if I was a Jew. I said no, I was not. Whereupon he ordered me to let down my pants. In Holland in those days circumcision was a procedure applied to Jews only. So I said, "All right, I am a Jew. But I am also a physicist, and all I did in that apartment was to pursue my research, as you can verify from the papers and books in my room." The questioning went on, the man keeping up his slow pacing. At one point, when he came quite close to where I was standing, he slapped me hard in the face, then continued his movements as if nothing had happened.

It was a shattering moment. The pain was only minor. Rather, it was the shock effect of experiencing an abrupt and unexpected interruption of a basically conventional situation, two men talking, by an act of very brief but violent aggression. Its purpose was obvious: not so much to cause physical pain as to make me lose my mental equilibrium. Even though the man had succeeded in doing so, it did not interrupt the continuing interrogation, with the questions now turning to my possible dealings with the resistance. I denied any such involvement.

The man left. I waited again. After a while I was ordered out of the room, whereupon I met Bert and Lion again, the latter looking ashen. Once again we were shoved into a car which brought us to the Weteringsschans, where we entered a building that before the war used to be the city's House of Detentions but had meanwhile become a Gestapo prison. We three were pushed into a cell and the door was banged shut and locked. I had arrived at my next war residence, cell IB4.

It was no longer possible to have me transported from there to one of the camps in the East. On March 9, tanks of the U.S. Ninth Armored Division had crossed the Rhine over the still intact Ludendorff Bridge at Remagen, southeast of Bonn, near the Dutch border. On March 24, General Patton and his troops had occupied another bridgehead, at Oppenheim, and his tanks were already moving to Frankfurt. The night before, General Montgomery's armies had crossed the lower Rhine and were headed into the north German plain. *Festung* Holland was cut off.

When we arrived in our cell, another man was already there. He at once began to tell us of his capture earlier that day. Having finished, he started the same story all over again. This went on for a while. It was not, one might say, an ideal ambiance for us who had just gone through the most wrenching experience of our lives. After a time, we simply told the chap to shut up, which, to our relief, he did.

We got nothing to eat that night; the first food we received came twenty-four hours later. When it came I was surprised to note that, in spite of a normally strong appetite, I had not even noticed earlier the absence of anything to eat.

The small cell contained four cots, a portable latrine, and a washbasin. I fell into an exhausted sleep that night, to be awakened by banging on the cell door, which then was opened. Like the others, I continued to lie on my cot, awaiting developments. Moments later a prison guard came in and started yelling at us. Didn't we know that we had to get up on the double when the cell was opened, quickly get dressed, place the latrine outside the door, then stand at attention to await cell inspection? No, we didn't know, but of course we learned quickly.

It had weighed heavily on my conscience that I had dragged Bert Broer into this predicament. It came as a relief when, two days later, a guard came in and told him that he was to be released forthwith. Bert was good enough to visit Tineke to tell her where and how we were.

The days then took on a regular routine. Meals were miserably small. In the late mornings we were let out of our cell for airing and walked around for a short while with other prisoners in a small yard surrounded by high walls. It was beautiful spring weather. We could see a triangular piece of pure blue sky through our small barred window. As I looked out one day, I saw a gull flying in my field of vision. I stood hypnotized, watching the gull glide effortlessly back and forth. What harmony, what freedom that single gull represented in my little patch of sky. Never have I seen a more beautiful view of nature than that solitary bird.

Days in prison were mostly quiet, but nights were bad. We would hear heavy metal doors clanging, shouts, shrieks. We knew that some poor bastard was being taken away, but had only grim forebodings as to where. The monotony of the days was broken by periodic interrogations that took place inside the prison building. Sometimes Lion, sometimes I, was taken out of our cell. I was brought to a small room and remember one setting in particular.

As I came in I saw a man sitting behind a desk, leaning back, relaxed, with hands clasped behind his neck. The room was otherwise bare, as was the desktop, except for a revolver lying in the middle. I stood in front of his desk, at attention as always. The man began to speak. "You will now tell me all you know about the resistance," he said calmly, "and you will speak the truth. If you do, it will help your situation considerably; if you don't, I shall shoot you right here in this room." My instincts told me: this is intimidation, stay calm, look the man in the eyes, firmly but not aggressively. I remember how the thought came to me: he is the animal in this circus, you are the tamer, look at him like the animal trainer stares steadily at his beast. I replied to his question as I had done before: "I had nothing to do with the resistance. It is true that I am a Jew. But I am just a young scientist absorbed in my work, as can be seen from the papers found in my room. I am just a *weltfremd,* unworldly, young man." That worked.

Another day it was Lion's turn. When he came back that time, he did not walk but rather stumbled into our cell, quite pale and deeply shaken. "What happened?" I asked. His reply: "I've been condemned to death."

My immediate very brief reaction was and still is astounding to me. It was as if, inside my head, a blinding light shone and a voice spoke: I SHALL LIVE. I had not been condemned.

Lion had fallen on his cot. I picked him up and cradled him in my arms, as one does a young child. I spoke calming words to him; I do not recall what I said. He quieted down somewhat but remained deeply withdrawn and hard to reach those next few days, staring out of our little window, unseeing.

A few days later the cell door opened at an unusual hour. We jumped to attention. There stood the guard and next to him a man in SS uniform who, I later found out, was the prison commander. The SS man looked us over, head to toe, one after the other. Then, silently, he pointed to me, indicating that I was to step out. Oh my God, I thought, now it is my turn.

Never saying a word, the commander indicated that I was to follow him. We walked through a corridor, cells on both sides, until we came to a metal door. He opened it, I stepped through, he locked it behind me. Next a second door, same procedure. Then we came to an ordinary wooden door.

He opened it, shoved me through, then said only: "*Fahrräder reparieren,*" repair bicycles, and walked away.

I looked around me in amazement. I was in a good-sized hall; bicycles were standing along the wall. In the center about half a dozen men were at work on some of them. They were obviously prisoners since, like myself, they looked dishevelled and were unshaven. Two *Grüne Polizei* (Green Police) were sitting at ease, a rifle on their shoulders, smoking cigarettes.

I went up to one of the prisoners and asked what I should do. Pointing to a tall, thin man who also was busy, he said, "Talk to Jan. He's in charge." I walked up to Jan and said, "I'm supposed to work here but don't know from shit about bicycle repairs." Jan turned out to be an amiable fellow from the Jordaan (derived from the French *jardin,* garden), a workers' quarter in Amsterdam renowned for its special kind of slang and for the tough customers living there. Jan gave me some pointers and soon I was busy. I felt happy to have something to do and to have so much company. Some hours later I was brought back to my cell.

About happiness while in prison. From that period I have learned that even in times of misery there are good days and there are bad days.

The next morning I was returned to the bike hall. It was then that I learned of Jan's brilliant idea of how to smuggle messages out. He had been put in charge because in real life he had his own bike shop. Every once in a while he would walk up to the guards and inform them that such and such a bike needed work that demanded special tools that weren't available here. But if someone would ride the bike to his shop and would tell the repairman there that Jan had said to fix the bike free of charge, then the job would be taken care of. Meanwhile, prisoners wrote messages on scraps of paper with a pencil stub someone had swiped. These were inserted between the inner and outer tubes and sent to the outside world.

Some days later—we were now well into April—I found upon returning to the cell that Lion was gone. "Where is he?" I asked the man who had been with us from the beginning. He told me that two guards had come in and had ordered Lion to take his things along and come with them. He did not know anything more. I sat down on my cot, in despair. What else could I expect but the worst?

A day or so later the bike repair adventure came to an end when an SS officer marched in, walked up to Jan, smacked him over the head, and told him that our courier service had been uncovered. Everyone was ordered back to his cell, and that was the end of that.

Another diversion came along shortly afterward. One day my cellmate and I were ordered out of our cell and together with more prisoners were marched to the exit door. Outside stood a horse-drawn truck. All of us were put in, a tarpaulin was thrown over us, and off we went, to be brought to a house somewhere in Amsterdam South. We got out, were ushered inside, then given instructions: there were cellars full of potatoes that had started to sprout; they were to be put in bags, carried up some stairs, then emptied into a courtyard. There we had to remove the runners, rebag the potatoes, and return the bags to the cellars.

I remember sitting outside, a pleasure in itself. It was a balmy spring evening. The fellow sitting next to me turned out to be Hermann Schey, a Jew and well-known basso, whom I had heard sing a number of times in the Concertgebouw. We were talking of music when suddenly another prisoner moved over and whispered that he had just heard bad news—President Roosevelt had died. It must have been about April 13 when we heard.

By now it was late April, and one last time I was taken out for a chore. A number of us were marched through Amsterdam to the port area, under guard by the *Grüne Polizei*. I engaged in an amiable chat with one who was walking alongside me. Our job was to unload freight from a small German ship. In the course of the day the captain gave each of us a big slice of brown bread, saying, "*Wer arbeitet soll auch essen*," he who labors should also eat.

In order to explain what happened to me next, I must relate what Tineke had been up to during this time.

On May 13, 1988, friends and colleagues of mine had organized a one-day symposium in honor of my seventieth birthday. (Later I shall tell more about that meeting.) In the evening a festive dinner was arranged for well over one hundred guests. In the course of that event, a number of people spoke. None touched me more than Tineke. When she had finished, several guests were crying. My heart was full and my voice quavered as I spoke to thank her. From the text of her speech, combined with conversations we had in later years, the following picture emerges about her wartime endeavors.

First, she had an amusing anecdote about me. One morning, while she was still in bed, the doorbell rang. "Who is there?" "Open up. Police," a man said in Dutch. Tineke and Marie, her mother, were fearful that this had to do with hiding Jews. The man came in and said he was from the vice squad. Complaints had been received that Tineke was visible, in the nude, as she was making her morning toilet. She solemnly promised never to expose herself like that again. I was in the house at the time and, curious as always, stood near a door to listen. The door had an opaque glass panel through which my silhouette was clearly visible. I sprang away when the man came by but was properly read the riot act by Tineke afterward not to be so stupid again.

After the war Tineke and Marie drew up a list of people who at one time or another had been hidden in their home. Their count ran up to about one hundred names. I never knew more than maybe half a dozen of these people, since, quite properly, the others' identities were not revealed to me. One I knew, Hans de Jong, a wealthy industrialist, had been betrayed by his bookkeeper, leading to a house search by the Gestapo during which Tineke was thrown against a wall, headfirst. Marie was hiding elsewhere at that time. Tineke asked and was permitted to call her grandmother's house to tell her that she could not come for dinner that evening. The person answering said, with great presence of mind, "But you were not supposed to come for dinner. Do you have visitors? Shall I call your mother?" "Yes," Tineke said. At that point the Gestapo man broke off the conversation, and left. A week later Tineke and Marie were ordered to appear at their headquarters in The Hague for a long interrogation concerning Hans and to be instructed on how to recognize Jews and report them. They were shown photographs of eye shapes as true criteria of Jewish physiognomy. Then they were let go. Apparently the Gestapo had swallowed whatever Tineke had told them earlier.

In all, Tineke's home was raided eight times by the Gestapo. That they never caught anyone was due to telephone calls she and Marie would receive, always from the same Dutch person beforehand, who would say, "You are going to have visitors," then hang up. Now, fifty years later, Tineke still does not know who that man was or where he spoke from.

Right after my three friends and I had been captured, Tineke had gone to the house on the Hobbemakade where we had been living. As she rang the bell the door was opened by a Gestapo agent. She was arrested on the spot, then interrogated at length. They had found men's socks and women's underwear in the same room of the house, concluding that Lion had been sleeping with Jeanne, whose story that she was Aryan had meanwhile been believed by the Gestapo. So the tragic situation developed that the Germans considered Lion, properly married to a Jewish woman, to be guilty of *Rassenschande,* racial disgrace. (That is why earlier I made a point of noting that Truusje and I were not intimate.)

That, I am sure, is why the Germans had it in for Lion rather than for me.

There may well have been the following additional reasons. It was Lion rather than I who had in his pocket the draft reply to the resistance about the Jewish war orphans. It was Lion who fell apart in the presence of the Gestapo who, animals as they were, could smell fear. Finally, it was he who looked so very Jewish.

After hours of interrogation, Tineke was let go with the warning that she would be watched, that she was probably Jewish herself, or hid Jews, or had a Jewish husband.

At this point I want to note that Kramers, advised by Tineke of my capture, had meanwhile written (in German) to Heisenberg, probably stressing that I was a talented apolitical young physicist, or words to that effect. Kramers had sent a copy of the letter to Tineke. As he later told me, he did receive a reply. Heisenberg understood, he wrote, was very sorry, but could not do anything.

It was Tineke who got me out. She had gotten hold of the name and address of a high Nazi official in Amsterdam and decided to call on him. She was indeed received in his office. On his desk stood a photo of Goering, with the dedication "*Für meinen Freund*" (to my friend). Tineke was afraid that the man would ask for sexual favors, yet she was prepared to grant them if necessary. (What a woman.) Fortunately, he did not. She showed him her copy of Kramers's letter to Heisenberg and asked for his help. After reading the letter the man did not say a word to Tineke, but picked up the phone to call the Weteringsschans. "*Hast du einen Jude Pais dort?*" ("Do you have a Jew, Pais, there?") Yes, they did. "*Lass ihn gehen*" ("Let him go").

So it came about that I gained my freedom because of physics, and because of the devotion of Kramers and, above all else, of Tineke.

On one of the last days in April I was taken out of my cell, IB4, and brought to the office of the prison commandant. He told me I was free but would at once be picked up and shot if I committed any act against Germany. I stepped out of his office and was brought to a small window near the exit, behind which sat a scribe who I knew must be a prisoner. He had to register my departure. I whispered to him, "Where is Lion?" He replied, also in a whisper, "He was shot several days ago." Then the small outer gate was opened. I stepped out on the street.

For me the war was over.

For maybe ten minutes I stood motionless in front of the prison on that sunny spring day. I felt no joy, I did not feel sad. I felt nothing.

It is a state, called anhedonia by William James, in which one is incapable of experiencing emotions of whatever kind. In my case that was due to exhaustion, hunger (I never was thinner than at that time), feelings held back for too long to be readily reachable, and to the shock I had just had hearing the news of Lion's death.

Then I started walking—to Tineke's home, where else? No longer wearing a star, I went through the Leidsestraat, crossed the Koningsplein. When I rang the bell, there was pandemonium, laughing, crying. I was embraced by Tineke and by Marie and hugged them both.

In the living room, there was a familiar sight: a wood-burning furnace, on top of which rested a tiny wood-burning stove with a big simmering pan of diced sugar beets. I was given a cup of the brownish, intensely sweet beet liquid and drank it. It tasted like ambrosia. I washed myself (with cold water, of course), then sat down. The first thing I had to tell them was about Lion. They already knew: when Tineke had gone to the German official to plead my case, she had also tried to help Lion and was told of his execution.

Across the street from the house, there was a newspaper office which I knew to house a barbershop on the ground floor. I said I was going there to be shaved. I went into the shop, told the barber that I had just come out of prison, and asked if I could have a shave. The man's response can only be called loving. He led me to the barber chair, made me sit down, and said he still had one bar of shaving soap, which he only used on special occasions. Feeling ever so much more cheerful now that my dirty beard was gone, I got up and asked how much I owed him. "This one is on the house," was the barber's reply. We warmly shook hands and I left.

I spent the next few weeks in Tineke's and Marie's house. We no longer feared raids. I could come and go freely. First I had to catch up on the news; I was told that Allied troops had already penetrated *Festung* Holland. No Allied forces had yet reached Amsterdam.

Negotiations between the opposing powers had begun. As a result the Germans gave permission for Allied planes to fly over Holland in order to drop crates of food by parachute. This relief came none too early. By late April the food average available per capita in the cities of western Holland was 225 calories per day, which means a loaf of bread a week and two potatoes per day.[35] Only later did we learn that on April 28 the last kilograms of potatoes were distributed. By May 5, the final slender reserve would have been gone.[36]

Sunday, April 29, 1945, is an unforgettable day for all who were then living in Amsterdam. Everybody was on rooftops, waiting for the planes to come. There they were, large, low-flying bombers. Everybody wept. By early May, 1,400 Flying Fortresses and 180 British Lancasters had dropped 1,200 tons of food in western Holland.[37]

On the afternoon of April 30, Hitler had taken his own life.

On May 7, a German general and an admiral arrived in a little school-house in Reims, France, where they signed the document of unconditional surrender of all German forces.

On that same day Tineke and I left the house, intending to walk to the quite nearby central square, the Dam, which is flanked along one side by the Royal Palace, and which is the traditional gathering place for momentous events. We never got there. We had barely started on our way when shots rang out. Marie had opened a window and was yelling to us, "Come back, come back!" As we were running back, a man we knew fell, shot to death. What had happened was that drunken German marines, barricaded on and near the Dam, had opened fire with hidden machine guns.[38] Cross-fire began as armed members of the underground shot back. We later heard that several people were killed on the Dam. So it came to pass that I saw for the first time war dead after the war was over.

On May 8, V-E Day, Canadian tanks of the *Régiment de la Chaudière* entered Amsterdam. That midnight the guns of Europe fell silent. After twelve years, four months, and eight days, the Third Reich had ceased to exist.

10.7 THE FATE OF THE GERMANS

Here I record the fate of some of the Germans, most of them mentioned in this chapter, who played a role in the persecution of the Jews and/or were in authority in wartime Holland.

Ferdinand Aus der Fünten, in charge of the Gestapo in Amsterdam. Condemned to death in Holland. Sentence commuted to life after reported intervention by *Reichskanzler* Konrad Adenauer. Released from a Dutch prison in Breda on January 27, 1989. Expelled to Germany that same day as undesirable alien. Died April 1989.

Friedrich Christiansen, air force general, commander of the Wehrmacht in Holland. Tried in Holland. Sentenced to twelve years in prison, July 1948.

Adolf Eichmann, in charge of the Final Solution. Seized in Argentina in May 1960 by Israeli agents. Put on trial in Israel and condemned to death. Conviction affirmed in 1962 by Israel's Supreme Court. Hanged in Jerusalem that year.

Odilo Globocnik, organizer of *Aktion* Reinhardt. Contradictory accounts: either killed by Italian partisans in May 1944; or took poison in June 1945 to avoid arrest by a British patrol.

Rudolf Hoess, commander of Auschwitz. Condemned to death in Poland. Executed 1947.

Anton Mussert, Dutchman, head of the NSB, the Dutch national socialist movement. Condemned to death by a Dutch high court. Executed by bullet, May 1946.

Hans Albin Rauter, SS and police leader for Holland. Condemned to death by a Dutch high court, April 1948. Executed the following November.

Franz Reichleitner, at one time commander of Sobibor. Died after the war without having stood trial.

Arthur Seyss-Inquart, Reichskommissar for occupied Holland. Sentenced to death by the international military tribunal at Nuremberg. Hanged October 1946.

Franz Stangl, at one time commander of Sobibor. In 1970 sentenced to life in prison by a Düsseldorf court. Appealed the verdict. Died in Düsseldorf prison in 1971 of natural causes.

Christian Wirth, in overall charge of Belżec, Sobibor, and Treblinka. Killed in 1944 during a battle with Italian partisans.

10.8 THE FATE OF OTHERS

Upon their return from camps, Abraham Asscher and David Cohen, erstwhile presidents of the Jewish Council, were requested to appear before a Jewish Honor Council specially constituted for that occasion. This body strongly criticized their actions, but did not condemn them. They were, however, forbidden to serve on Jewish community boards for five years.

The Dutch government arrested the two men, but released them soon afterward without having instituted legal action.

On December 10, 1990, I sent a letter to the Netherlands State Institute for War Documentation, asking for information about how, in March 1945, it had come about that Lion, Jeanne, Truusje, and I had been arrested and about the details of Lion's execution.

I received a reply, dated January 14, 1991, part of which follows:

We have not found any data in our collections concerning the arrest of you and the other three hiders.

On orders of the Sicherheitspolizei, 25 so-called *Todeskandidaten* [death candidates] were taken away on April 15, 1945, from the House of Detention at the Weteringsschans in Amsterdam. Seven persons of this group, among them your cellmate Lion Nordheim, were brought to Wormerveer, where immediately upon arrival they were executed by bullet. The other 18 persons were likewise executed in St. Pancras. Both executions were meant as reprisals for attacks on railroads.

Todeskandidaten is the designation for prisoners who would be executed in any case.

After the war, the Dutch government commissioned a monument at the site in Wormerveer where the seven were mowed down by bullets. Every year a brief ceremony takes place there on April 15, the day of execution, during which the flag is raised.

Lion's remains rest in the Jewish cemetery in Muiderberg.

On September 12, 1988, I sent off a letter to the Director, Department of the Righteous, Yad Vashem. Part of the letter follows:

The purpose of this letter is to propose a person as most worthy to be recognized by the Designation of the Righteous and to suggest that a tree be planted in her name at Yad Vashem. She is Tina Buchter Strobos, M.D. . . . I owe her my life. We have ties that will never break. . . . It would be silly to make comparisons with other rescuers, of whom I have known several. But I have never known anyone with Tineke's moral nobility.

I have a copy of the letter, dated January 22, 1990, sent by the director to Tineke. Part of it reads:

I have the pleasure to inform you that the Special Commission for the Designation of the Righteous, at its session of November 28, 1989, decided to confer upon you and your mother Marie [posthumously] its highest expression of gratitude: the title of Righteous among the nations. . . . Your name [will be] inserted in the Garden of the Righteous, Yad Vashem, Jerusalem.

11

War's Aftermath:

A Last Lesson in Dutch History

U PON FREEING *Festung* Holland, the Allied troops, mainly Canadians, encountered a starving population beset by weakness and sickness and having neither heat nor light. Yet most of us still had the energy to cheer our liberators and express our gratitude. An American journalist wrote from Utrecht: "It is not possible to give the emphasis with which time and again we heard the same words—'We waited so long for your coming.'"[1] Otherwise all of us were deeply weary.

The region held captive for so long was not all that large (Holland's total area is 125,000 square miles) but it housed over four million people. The population density of the Netherlands at that time was seven hundred persons per square mile, the highest in the world; within the *Festung,* the density was twice as high, with half of the population living there. Thus it was no small undertaking to restore normalcy to my country.

My country. Funny expression. It has now been almost forty years since I swore allegiance to the Constitution of the United States, for reasons of attachment and conviction and not just for convenience. Yet I feel no contradiction in still writing or speaking of Holland as "my country." I should enlarge on that and will, later on.

Already before war's end, reports of the severe famine had reached the Allied forces. I have already mentioned the food drops by American and British planes during the last days of the occupation. Furthermore, "in anticipation of the relief of the occupation, the Supreme Headquarters of the Allied Expeditionary Force [SHAEF] collected a team of expert nutritionists, food supplies, and transport facilities. The experts prepared to carry out, immediately upon liberation, a survey to determine the extent and the effects of the famine, and the best means of providing relief."[2]

The team of experts reported as follows:

> Fall of bodyweight was progressive and rapid. All the characteristic signs of calorie-deficiency appeared: undue fatigue on moderate exercise, feeling cold, mental listlessness, apathy, obsession with thoughts of food, etc. In the beginning men especially were affected.
>
> It is easy to write now that each person got 400 calories a day. In practice it was quite another thing. Each Thursday there was published the list of the coupon-numbers that were valid for the next week's food. One planned to divide that food over the week. The ordinary person, however, often consumed in two or three days all that was given for the whole week. Consequently there was an enforced fast for 4 days until the next rations were available. This seriously aggravated the situation. People sought food everywhere in the streets and the surrounding countryside. Anything edible was picked up in this way and they were lucky who found a potato or two or a handful of greens.
>
> In January 1945 the first cases of hunger oedema appeared and were admitted to the hospitals. Soon the numbers multiplied. Little relief could be offered these patients. Even in the hospitals there was little food. The nurses and physicians worked day and night without supplementary rations. Their menu for example was: one slice of bread and one cup of tea substitute for breakfast; two potatoes, a little bit of vegetables and some watery sauce for lunch; one or two slices of bread with a cup of coffee substitute and a plate of soup for dinner. This soup was frequently made with sugarbeets by the Communal Kitchen. For hospital patients, however, there was a little more food available, so something could be done for them. . . . Weight loss averaged about 15–20% of total body weight. Hunger oedema appeared in January 1945 and by May 1945 had affected an estimated 10% of the city population. Menstrual irregularities, retarded menarche, or amenorrhea were reported in 50% of all women examined. . . . During the famine, the groups with increased risk of dying were males, those at either extreme of age, and the less prosperous classes.[3]

As an example of one not belonging to the latter, my friend Hans Kramers was suffering severely from edema toward the very end of the war.

The influence of famine in Holland on fertility and fecundity was the subject of detailed studies:

Fertility varied closely with food rations at the time of conception through most of the years 1944–46. In the famine area, nine months after the onset of acute starvation, a distinct fall in the number of births began. . . . At the height of the famine, births in the affected Dutch cities were reduced to about one-third of the expected number. . . . In May, with relief of the famine midway through the month, the number of births conceived at that time rose at once, and by June the number was at pre-famine level.[4]

Note, however, that "above a minimal threshold level nutrition is not a critical factor in fertility. Indeed, the postwar rise in fertility occurred throughout the Western world, including the United States, where there had been no war-time nutritional deprivation."[5] The general conclusions were these:

Infertility and infecundity caused by starvation is rapidly reversible. A steep rise in conceptions immediately after the liberation marked the restoration of susceptibility to fertilization. The main contribution to the rise in conceptions was made by couples both of whom were resident in Holland throughout the famine period. The rise preceded in time a more gradual rise that followed the return home of soldiers, prisoners, deportees, and refugees. The immediate recovery of fertility indicates that there was also immediate physiological recovery of sexual activity, normal ovulation, and fecundity in general.[6]

In April 1992 I was in Holland to give a lecture on "American Science and World War II," and to receive the annual prize of the Physica Foundation of the Netherlands. I used the occasion to visit the archives of Amsterdam's university library in order to browse through Dutch newspapers of 1945 for the purpose of refreshing my memory about events following shortly after the liberation. Here are some, printed in *Het Parool*; all dates are from 1945.

May 7. The first newspapers reappear, some for the first time legally. They consisted of one sheet printed on both sides. I remember being astonished to see a good-sized photograph of Queen Wilhelmina in the first postwar issue of *De Waarheid* (The Truth), the communist newspaper. The prewar communist press had been strongly anti-royalist. That picture was perhaps the best symbol of the unifying force of war events, which drew all Dutchmen together in a national cause. Note that, after the 1941 invasion of Russia by Germany, Dutch communists were among those most active and brave in the resistance.

May 9. Distribution of imported foods begins. These were basic items— K-rations, canned beans, powdered milk, and the like.

May 15. Movie houses will reopen in a few days, thanks to generators made available by the Canadians. I recall the thrill of seeing movies again after nearly five years. My first visit was to Cineac, a cinema showing mainly newsreels, where I saw the liberation of Paris in black and white. My first real movie, seen with Tineke, was *I Married a Witch,* with Alan Ladd and Veronica Lake.

May 18. Announcement that on May 21 the first coal for heating will be distributed.

June 2. The first train arrives at Amsterdam's Central Station, carrying repatriates.

June 14. The first coffee will be available between June 17 and 23, all still on ration coupons.

June 15. The first freighter enters the port of Amsterdam.

June 18. For the first time since October 1944 trams (on electric power) run again in Amsterdam.

July 15. Electricity and a few hours of gas are restored to Amsterdam's citizens. How happy I was to have my first real light to write by!

September 8. A survey of the food situation. The lowest week ever was May 6–12: 230 calories/day. By late June we had 2,500 calories/day each. The famine was over. The very good harvest of that year was a further great help.

September 13. Announcement that as of September 20 all old paper money will lose its value. We had to continue to use the miserable coins made of zinc minted in wartime.

September 15. The universities of Leiden, Amsterdam, Delft, and Nijmegen will be reopened. On *September 18* the queen is present at the opening ceremonies in Leiden. I go to the opening ceremonies in Utrecht, in the Domkerk, the city's principal church.

September 21. The first forty "real" cigarettes (Craven A, Gold Flake, Players) are available on the tobacco ration coupon.

December 8. As of December 1 it is possible to request a coupon for buying a bicycle with rubber tires. Not only had the Germans requisitioned bikes in large numbers, but the Dutch who were fortunate enough to keep theirs had no tires for them.

11.2 HOLLAND'S MATERIAL WAR DAMAGES

According to a *New York Times* report of June 25, 1945, these were estimated at 15 billion guilders (a bit over 8 billion dollars), at 1938 levels—

half of the 1938 national property of the country excluding colonial investments.

This figure does not include what the Germans took in factories, ships, railways, and from individuals. Four thousand factories were plundered bare, including the installations of the large steel works as well as their large stocks of iron and steel. Four thousand church bells were carried off. Maritime losses: 90 sea vessels, 200 coastal vessels, 17 seaworthy tugboats, 2 large dry docks, several hundred fishing boats. Precious libraries and art collections were stolen, as were of course all goods belonging to deported Jews. Citizens were robbed of 50,000 bicycles and hundreds of thousands of radios.[7]

Other once-occupied countries registered large material losses as well. At an international conference on restitutions by Germany, held in Paris in November 1945, Holland put in a claim for 26 billion guilders; other countries came with still higher claims. Also discussed at the conference was the search in Germany for stolen valuables. Holland was more successful than other countries in retrieving these, including libraries and artworks.

Actual subsequent restitution amounted to only four percent of the Dutch claim.[8] In later years the Federal Republic of Germany paid out 700 million guilders to the Dutch government, of which twenty percent was earmarked for distribution among Jewish survivors.

11.3 THE RESTORATION OF GOVERNMENT

On May 14, 1945, the prime minister of the war cabinet tendered his and his colleagues' resignation to Queen Wilhelmina. The first postwar cabinet began its functions on June 23. On June 27, the new prime minister addressed the nation, expressing as his first concern the reestablishment of law and order: "We know that at several places there are restless groups of the population, prepared to take justice into their own hands."[9] This unrest was so prevalent that it was clear that the country could not be governed in normal ways. During the first months after the liberation, the principal instrument for sanitizing the situation was the so-called *Militair Gezag* (Military Authority), answerable to the Cabinet and remaining operative until March 1946. Its tasks included the arrest of those who during the war years had done "wrong"; the cleansing of all internal governing bodies, town councils, mayors, the police, and so forth of undesirables; and the assistance with food distribution to the starving. Most important, the *Gezag* was the liaison with SHAEF, the central organization that assisted in the restoration of economic normalcy in the once-occupied Western European countries.

Sometime later, Holland became one of the beneficiary nations of the Marshall Plan, as proposed by Secretary of State George Marshall in his Harvard address in June 1947. Within the framework of that plan, Holland received nearly one billion dollars, eighty-four percent as a gift, the rest as a loan—a wonderful, much-needed small injection.

Only after Holland was somewhat back on its feet was it possible to hold general elections. The difficulties of organizing them had been monumental, since many voter registration lists had been destroyed to prevent the Germans from organizing forced labor corps. Thus the first postwar elections were not held until May 1946.

11.4 The Return of the Jews

Of the about 110,000 Jews deported to the camps from the Netherlands, 2,361 men and 3,089 women returned, including the 918 still present in Westerbork at the time of liberation. Almost none of them were over age fifty or under sixteen. (Another 30,000 never went to camps, having died, fled the country, or gone into hiding.) The Portuguese-Jewish community, in particular, was sadly diminished. It is not known, however, if all those who returned from the camps registered their names as Jewish survivors.[10] "There were many cases of people who had somehow managed to keep up their spirits in the camps themselves, only to break down utterly after the liberation, often because of unbearable loneliness and terrible fear of strangers. . . . No wonder so many committed suicide."[11]

Those who kept going often showed symptoms that would have appeared odd if one were unaware of how much they had been through. A Dutch doctor has written:

> Possibly there is someone in your vicinity who has been to a concentration camp or who was locked up in a little attic for years. Perhaps he is difficult and a little strange in his manner, has a number of symptoms characteristic of the concentration-camp syndrome: he flares up, he becomes melancholic and cannot carry on a normal conversation without suddenly losing the thread, he likes to be alone at one moment and at others cannot bear to be left. Confining spaces, for instance telephone booths, oppress and frighten him; he may

even refuse to enter a cinema. One drink, if only a glass of beer, and he is tipsy. Perhaps he cannot stand coffee; that, too, is not uncommon. He is always tired and will sometimes burst into tears for no reason at all; he may start sweating, without any physical exertion. And this list is far from complete.[12]

Not only emotional but also material problems awaited the returnees. "For many Jews, and especially for the well-to-do among them, it was a strange experience to re-enter society without even the bare necessities, with not much more than the clothes—and what clothes!—on their backs."[13] Complex legal questions were often raised when reclaiming property, as for example when it was necessary to prove the death of a parent or spouse, often an impossible task. Relief came when on June 2, 1949, a law was passed to the effect that missing persons in certain categories could be assumed dead.

Next I need to discuss a subject that still makes me sad and angry: the unexpected and striking anti-Semitic reactions during the summer of 1945 among many of the Dutch toward the returning Jews. This attitude was already evident during the war, as shown by the March 15, 1943, diary entry of an honest official: "We must restrict the influence of Dutch Jews, so that they do not have too big a say in politics and in the social and economic field (a bit tricky, this)."[14]

Many instances are on record of neo-anti-Semitism immediately after the war. For example: in the formerly illegal student paper *De Vrÿe Katheder,* now a legal monthly, of July 1945, it was reported that a Jewish woman was told in a shop that "'it is a pity that so many of you have returned alive.' . . . Nobody from the public present found it necessary to protest." The Dutch-Jewish historian Presser recorded a number of similar pronouncements told him by witnesses: "All the good Jews are dead. It is the bad ones who have come back . . . There are still too many Jews in the Netherlands . . . Jews should always remember how thankful they need to be—they could very soon exhaust others' sympathy . . . Jews ought not to be in such a hurry [to claim their possessions back] . . . What happened during the occupation was repugnant, but all the same we're better off without them."[15]

Another author mentioned the case of a woman returnee who sat on a bench waiting for a bus. A non-Jewish lady told her to stand, that "others are entitled to this seat." The Jewish lady explained that she is very weak, having just been released from the hospital after treatment for exhaustion.

She is told: "They should have kept you in a concentration camp; we have enough of your kind here."[16]

Stateless Jews, legal prewar residents, had particularly unpleasant experiences.[17]

A number of ugly incidents also occurred when Jews tried to retrieve possessions left with non-Jewish acquaintances. Just one example. A young woman visited a neighbor with whom clothes, jewelry, and furniture had been stored. She was cordially received and shown that all had been kept in good order. A week later the woman came back with a truck and driver to collect her belongings. The neighbor told her: "We have nothing from you, out with you." The police were unable to help since no formal proof of ownership existed.[18]

Also from 1945 dates a "well-meaning" newspaper article in which Jews were advised "to give as little cause for friction as possible. . . . They should try to acquire some of our greater sense of modesty."[19]

Government agencies did nothing to ameliorate relations, continuing the policy (adopted during the war; see chapter 9, sec. 9.4) not to treat the Jewish part of the Dutch population in any special way. That may be good and well, but couldn't the authorities have expressed publicly, just once, a few kind words of welcome back and have called on all Dutch citizens to do likewise? I have not seen any statistics of the frequency with which these deplorable incidents occurred. However, I would be gravely remiss if I did not also mention that there were numerous instances in which returning Jews were cordially received.

Nor should it be forgotten that these events are insignificant when compared to what happened farther east. "Even after the liberation, Jews were still being murdered in Poland, where a daylight pogrom was organized, not by professional criminals, but by young mothers, by students of Polish literature, by devout Catholics who prayed to God before the massacre. And not only did they murder the Jews, but they also indulged in an orgy of torture, in a veritable witches' sabbath—in July 1946, barely a year after the end of the war."[20]

Disquieted and angered by these happenings, a group of intellectuals from Amsterdam—non-Jews, with a few exceptions—organized a group in 1945 to discuss the question, "Antisemitic attitudes in the Netherlands?" Their findings and those of others strongly indicate that at play were psychological phenomena of considerable complexity.[21] I will mention some frequently cited factors. The Nazis introduced, so to say, the Jews to Holland, in the sense that Jews were not that widely recognized as a minority group before 1940. Regarding what befell them during the war, one should remember the old saying that it is in the human spirit to hate those whom it has wronged, if only by not sufficiently lending a helping hand. The isolation of the Jew during the war led to a decrease of fear or hatred of Jews to be replaced by feelings of superiority relative to the Jew, since pity breeds contempt rather than respect. The war caused a marked rise of Dutch nationalism, into which the Jew fit less readily. For the Jew, persecution dominated all other aspects of the occupation; for the others, it was but one aspect among many.

Note finally that right after the war it was not yet widely and fully known how gruesomely the Jews had been treated—and that the victims themselves were not yet ready to talk much about those experiences. As one Jewish woman put it: "After the war we remained silent. We did not tell our children. We could not talk about it. You felt that after the war you could not come out with stories about the camps. Nobody would believe it."[22] Once again it was the impossible real (chapter 9, sec. 9.1).

Postwar anti-Semitism was widespread if not written in the banners of political movements as it had been in the 1930s. Neo-fascist organizations did crop up, however, including in Holland.[23] In 1953 two Dutchmen sent out a call for the reestablishment of the NSB. It reads in part:

> The undersigned act in the conviction that, in spite of enormous errors made in the recent past by people and parties, the national socialist as well as the fascist ideas continue to be driving forces for millions of Europeans. These two world views appear—notwithstanding the tragic errors which have led to such a great catastrophe—to be capable not only of restoration but also of inner renewal. . . . Democracy leads in the long run to chaos and decline, as we have been able to note increasingly in Western Europe in recent years. Communism with its colorless masses is in certain respects the extreme consequence of democracy. As a reaction against these trends, there arose in the '20s and '30s fascist and national socialist movements. By means of the idea of leadership one wished to restore man's personality and give him once again a sense of responsibility. It lies in the line of history that these systems had to arise, and it is equally clear that they will replace the stagnant democracies.[24]

Some months later these two men were brought to court and condemned to two months in prison. Their movement was forbidden. The Dutch minister of justice declared that fascist-tainted organizations must be considered "an intolerable challenge."[25]

Will there ever be an end to anti-Semitism? A silly question. During the

week before Christmas 1991, a soccer match took place in Amsterdam between Ajax (Amsterdam) and Feÿenoord (Rotterdam). The Feÿenoord sup-
porters, about twenty thousand of them, bellowed "Jewish dogs" every time
an Ajax player had the ball. When the Ajax player happened to be black, he
was a "Jewish nigger." This in nice, tolerant Holland. Now, in the 1990s, we
live in blessed times when racial protests and violence directed against ethnic minorities have become disturbingly widespread.

In the 1980s important changes toward Jewish survivors began to take
place, however.[26] They are now no longer exclusively seen as victims or
patients with various traumas, but have rather suddenly become venerated
witnesses, invited by newspapers and television stations to speak of their
experiences. Oral history projects have been organized in the United States,
England, France, Holland, and Israel whose goal it is to interview survivors.
Almost no one refuses to be questioned. They now want to talk about their
past, because they have become aware of the interest in their stories. No
doubt these changed attitudes have emerged because many of the survivors
are now very old. They have finally broken their silence, in the interest of
their children and grandchildren, and, more generally, in the interest of
future generations.

12

My Final Months in Holland

12.1 SOME PERSONAL EXPERIENCES, MAY–SEPTEMBER 1945

I MENTIONED earlier that during the war I began to keep a diary, which to my regret I later burned (chapter 10, sec. 10.2). Right after the liberation I began another one. This one I have kept; it is before me now. The first entry begins as follows:

> *May 27, 1945.* In view of (provisional) loneliness I begin a second diary. The past weeks were characterized by a hangover mood. Discrepancies between liberation and views of liberation during the occupation. The prison adventure has made me looser with regard to many problems of life: I now live much more day by day. Tonight I am going to do physics again. [I also note right away an entry on *June 10*]: There is a lot of *risjes* [yiddish for anti-Semitism], as I heard yesterday, very strongly in the NBS [Dutch forces of the interior, the collective name for organized resistance groups]. Have noticed little of that myself. But then I close myself off again with theoretical physics.

I have kept the diary going through later years. In the course of time it has turned more and more into a log book, written quite irregularly, full of gaps that neglect events I can still recall and find interesting. It has always been more important to me to live through events than to record them.

The first order of business for both my parents and me was to find a place to live. The apartment they had left in the summer of 1943 had meanwhile been occupied by others. A legitimate claim to that space could no longer be made.

It was typical of my parents' personalities that my mother would be the one to take on the task of finding a new residence. After the war they stayed for a while longer where they had been hiding, in Heemstede. As soon as it became feasible, my mother began to take day trips by train to Amsterdam, walking through the city, ringing doorbells to ask if the person who came to the door knew of any vacant apartments. Demand for these was high. There were no advertisements of any kind, let alone for much sought-after living quarters, in the newspapers yet. I do not recall how long she kept this up, but in the end she did find a place. It was a very nice apartment at Weesperzÿde 139, overlooking the Amstel River. It consisted of two large rooms, a small room, a kitchen, and a toilet, in which they installed a shower. That was the first time in their lives—they were now in their early fifties—that they had a bathing facility in their own home. Another novelty: their first telephone was installed.

I have already mentioned (chapter 1) that right after the war my father found a new position, as secretary of the Portuguese-Israelitic community. It was ideally suited to his temperament and interests.

Fortunate circumstances made it much easier for me than for my parents to find a place to live. I was quite friendly with Bram van Santen, a wealthy Jewish businessman who had survived the war by hiding. After the liberation he reestablished his business in the same building he had used before. He offered me the top floor rent free, a generous proposal which I accepted happily and with gratitude. So my first postwar address became Herengracht 555, centrally located around the corner from Thorbeckeplein, an old square. Next I rented a pushcart, which I took to the front of Tineke's house, where I loaded it with my possessions, mainly clothes and books. This done, I merrily pushed it through Amsterdam's streets until I reached my abode on one of the old canals. Several trips up the stairs, and I had a home, installed with my modest amount of personal belongings.

The strongest of my memories of these earliest postwar days is that I would meet people on the streets, classmates from high school, fellow students, neighbors from previous addresses, recognize them, place them in proper context—but I had forgotten their names, every single one of them. Apparently my years in hiding and months in prison had completely erased that kind of memory. I had to relearn my environment, familiar though it was on the whole. On July 22 I noted in my diary: "At present I have the sensation of being a stranger in Amsterdam. I see a certain street and suddenly feel that I look at it with the eyes of a stranger who sees a cityscape well known yet at the same time unknown to him. I am thoroughly alone. A stranger." A few days later I copied out a sonnet by Baudelaire which begins with these lines.

Que diras tu ce soir, pauvre âme solitaire,
Que diras tu, mon coeur, coeur autrement flétri?

(What will you say tonight, poor solitary soul,/What will you say, my heart, heart previously faded?)

I also find a note to the effect that several young women of my acquaintance spoke of wanting to die. One word keeps recurring for several months in what I then wrote: loneliness. Revived sexual activity did cause relief, but not enough.

Yet my life was not all that sad or dull. A lot was going on in Amsterdam. On May 19 (my twenty-seventh birthday), the papers announced that Amsterdam would become a leave center for Allied soldiers.[1] These men brought a lot of action to our city, including a flourishing black-market trade. It is no exaggeration to say that women went wild over them. I have never seen the likes of it. Not just the more, shall we say, accessible ladies who could be had for a pack of cigarettes or for that great novelty, nylon stockings; no, young women of my acquaintance were easily seducible and seduced as well. The reasons were obvious. After months if not years of battle, the soldiers were hungry for women. They were on the whole a vigorous breed, illuminated by the glow of victory. They naturally appealed much more to Dutch women than we Dutchmen, worn down by hunger and fatigue. I noted in my diary the substance of a talk I had with a member of the Jewish Brigade. He told me that the women of Holland were more readily available than those he had met in any other European country.

On June 30 I had an experience that taught me that some of our liberators were tough customers. I had gone for an evening walk and was crossing the Thorbeckeplein when I was approached by two Canadian soldiers. Did I have any liquor to sell? "No," I replied, "I don't, but have a bottle of whisky in my apartment and would be glad to invite you up for a drink." They accepted and up we went. We sat down in my darkening room (I had no electricity yet), and I poured drinks for them and myself. At one point I turned around. Whereupon I received a blow on the head with a heavy object. I passed out. When I came to I was lying on the floor, blood streaming from my head. The Canadians were gone. So was my bottle of whisky. I managed to reach a doctor who cleaned and bandaged the cut on my skull. The moral I derived from this adventure was to treat our esteemed foreign guests with a more generous amount of circumspection.

The next evening I attended the first postwar concert in the Concertgebouw, with Yehudi Menuhin as soloist and Tineke as my guest. I made my appearance wearing a rather formidable bandage and recall—so does Tineke—how upset and frightened she was when she saw me in my picturesque headdress. I had to assure her that I would survive.

A final note concerning the military presence. On September 4, Field Marshall Sir Bernard Law Montgomery visited Amsterdam accompanied by Prince Bernhard, the first visit to our city of any Allied army chief since war's end. "Huge, wildly cheering crowds lined the streets,"[2] I among them. In early October, Dwight David Eisenhower visited Amsterdam and The Hague, and I had my one and only look at the Supreme Commander of the Western Front.

I wrote earlier how right after the war I had tried unsuccessfully to get news about the fate of my sister Annie and her husband. I visited offices where lists of names were available of survivors and of those known to have perished. None of these gave the information I was after. This search was one of the reasons why I reported for volunteer duty at Amsterdam's Central Station, where, beginning in early June, trains with camp survivors began to arrive. Those were strong and moving experiences, especially when I could welcome someone I knew. I remember in particular meeting one person, still clad in the pajama type of clothes so familiar from camp pictures. I kissed him on both cheeks and hugged him. He told me that he had spent some weeks in a transit camp, which explained why he no longer had that haggard camp look. I asked him and others, whether I knew them or not, if they had ever met Annie and Herman de Leeuw while in camp. No one had.

I do not recall whether or not my parents also went on a search. They probably did. It is most remarkable—though, as I found out much later, not uncommon—that they would never, absolutely never, mention their daughter, at least not when talking to me. It was only many years later, after my father's death, that I asked my mother about this. She told me that they never talked about her between themselves either but that, every night before going to bed, my father would take off his glasses and carefully place them underneath a picture of Annie that was standing in their bedroom—a small act presumably of great symbolic significance.

In later years I often asked myself whether I should not have broached the subject to them. I still don't know how to answer that question.

Sometime in July I decided that the walls and ceilings of my apartment needed a fresher look. So I bought cans of whitewash, borrowed a ladder and brushes, and set to work. I had been at it for some time when I found myself lying on the floor, whitewash spattered over me. I had fallen off the ladder and fainted. Not being the fainting type, then or later, I decided I had better consult a doctor. He examined me, reassured me that there was nothing seriously wrong, but that I simply had not yet sufficiently recovered from the famine to partake in the activities that had caused my minor accident. He urged me to take some time off for recuperation. This I did, finding hospitality on the farm that had been my parents' first hiding place. There I slept a lot and was fed very well, getting milk, butter, and cheese aplenty, and I took leisurely walks around the area. On one of these strolls, I encountered and got in conversation with members of the Jewish Brigade who were stationed nearby. These were Jews from various European countries and from South Africa who had volunteered for service in the Allied forces. Most of them were committed Zionists who had enlisted in the hope that their action would promote chances for establishing a Jewish state. They invited me for lunch several times, then invited me to lecture about the history of the Jews in Holland during the war years, which I did. I had of course much to tell and was gratified by their obvious interest and their many questions afterward. In my diary I find several of their names: "Noach Ukrainitzer, with that wonderful uncomplicated self-assurance . . . Lawi, who wanted to teach me Hebrew . . . Schelasmitzki, who wanted to empty out all of Palestine to help the Jews here . . . the ambitious captain, Tycho—the South African Major Liebman."

I stayed on the farm for a week, then returned to Amsterdam, much refreshed.

*12.2 First Publications: Planning for the Future

Early in June I went to see Rosenfeld, my adviser, who asked me to return at once to my assistant position (chapter 6). I accepted with pleasure. Then we turned to a discussion of future postdoctoral research opportunities.

All through the war I had had the firm conviction that I would survive, though I was not fool enough to think this was certain. Yet I had (and still have) strong survivor instincts and a will to live. While in hiding I had already promised myself to get out when the war was over. A discussion about where to go next was therefore a most welcome undertaking.

Rosenfeld made two suggestions: go either to Niels Bohr in Copenhagen, or to Wolfgang Pauli, who was then at the Institute for Advanced Study in Princeton. Since it was not clear what the possibilities would be, he proposed that I send letters of application to both places, and that he would independently write a letter of recommendation. I thanked him warmly for his suggestions, both of which sounded fine to me.

A week after this discussion, Rosenfeld met with the Dutch-born American astronomer Kuiper (a professor in Chicago), who was on a scientific fact-finding mission in Europe. As a result, Kuiper promised to talk about me to Samuel Goudsmit, head of Alsos, whose mission it was to find out what progress, if any, German scientists had made in making atomic weapons. He was an American scientist but a native Dutchman stationed in Paris at that time.

Meanwhile, I wrote letters to Copenhagen and Princeton, and also to the Institute for International Education in New York, under whose auspices I would study if I were accepted by an American institution. On July 8 I wrote in my diary: "I am now sitting with papers to fill out, from the Institute for International Education. Fifteen scholarships for U.S.A. available for the Netherlands, for all universities and all disciplines. Damned little chance. I hope of course to be among the elect."

At that time I had already begun to prepare for publication the work I had been engaged in during the previous few years. The prospect of going abroad spurred me on to get these papers out of the way.

(*Note to the reader:* From here on I will occasionally refer to scientific issues, which I will do in the simplest possible general terms, adding technical footnotes that may be of possible interest to cognoscenti.)

The first paper I sent off dealt with the theory of the scattering of protons by neutrons. Early in June it went by Red Cross mail to England—postal connections with foreign countries still demanded improvisation. The envelope, addressed to Dirac, one of my early heroes (see chapter 6) in Cambridge, contained a covering letter from Rosenfeld, who in July received a reply: Dirac had submitted my article for publication in the *Proceedings of the Cambridge Philosophical Society*.[3]

In July I gave my first two public lectures on physics. First I spoke in Leiden, invited by Kramers, whom I was very happy to see again. (At that time I did not yet know about his intervention with Heisenberg on my behalf.) I noted that he was quite tired and did not look well. Later I spoke at a meeting of the Dutch Physical Society in Amsterdam. On both occasions my topic was the nuclear physics part of my doctoral thesis.

In August my friend and former cellmate Bert Broer and I turned in a short paper to van der Waals, the professor of theoretical physics in Amsterdam, who had consented to present it to the Royal Dutch Academy of Sciences. It deals with some delicate problems stemming from the fact that light quanta, or photons, have zero mass.[4] How can a particle like the photon have zero mass? To answer this question, one needs the theory of relativity.

Also in August I finally finished a set of three papers that contained the results of my main research while I was in hiding, which deals with issues in what is known as quantum field theory. The best-known example of such a theory is quantum electrodynamics, a theory based on the set of equations one obtains after applying the rules of quantum theory to electromagnetic phenomena. At that time, theories of that kind had already booked many successes but had also led to vexing difficulties, notably that the masses of basic particles like the electron or proton are predicted to be infinitely large. It was a problem that Kramers and I had discussed heatedly during his visits to me in my hiding place.[5] My three papers dealt with the beginnings of a method I had worked out for remedying that difficulty.

The question was: Where should this bulky material be published? Eventually it appeared in 1946, as a ninety-page monograph in the *Transactions of the Dutch Academy of Sciences*.[6] I also sent a short note with the main results to the *Physical Review,* America's leading physics journal.[7] Later it was determined that my method was not the right way. Progress has since been made regarding the difficulties of infinite masses but as a matter of principle they remain unsolved to this day. While my method was not the answer, my logic and calculations had been in good order. That can and does happen fairly often in physics. In any event, I still feel quite good about those early attempts of mine.

Two more papers complete the list of the work I did in Holland. One dealt with the instability of a species of particles known as neutral vector mesons, and appeared in *Nature* in December.[8] The other, a sequel to my work in quantum field theory, appeared in June 1946 in the Dutch journal *Physica.*[9] The purpose of mentioning all these publications is less to advertise them as important than to show that I had not sat still during the war years. In fact, my years in hiding turned out to be quite profitable for my further career.

On June 16, 1945, I noted in my diary: "The *Physical Review* issues of 1944 and first half of 1945 have arrived. Little news, we will catch up quickly." There was in fact just one paper that caused much excitement.[10] It was written by Lars Onsager, a Norwegian-born theorist from Yale, and reported the first exact calculation of a nontrivial phase transition. (The most familiar—and still not calculable!—phase transition occurs when a liquid is heated to the boiling point, where it starts the transition to another phase, a gas.)

I had been particularly eager for further news about nuclear fission, the great discovery of 1939, and the subject of my earliest theoretical calculations (chapter 6), and was astonished to find that not a single *Physical Review* publication dealt with the subject. It was entirely inconceivable that fission had not been researched further in the years 1941–45. What was going on? Were the Americans pursuing the subject secretly? Were they making the bombs that physicists had already speculated about in 1939? I was not the only one to be puzzled by this silence. As I found out only in 1990, a Russian nuclear physicist had made the same observation and the same guess already in 1942—which he at once reported to Stalin.[11]

I forgot about the whole business until I opened the Dutch daily *Het Parool* of August 7, 1945, and saw the headline, "The First Atomic Bomb on Japan," followed by the report that on August 6, at 8:15 in the morning local time, Hiroshima had been destroyed by what we later heard was a uranium-235 bomb. On August 9, I wrote in my diary: "Dammit, I was right. . . . Oppenheimer is in charge of the American project. . . . Testing stations in New Mexico . . . a second bomb [this one made of plutonium] has hit Nagasaki." On August 26, I recorded a conversation with Kramers on the construction of atomic weapons and added: "I will find my place anywhere. Nuclear physics, the science of the future. Lucky kid."

The news of the atomic bomb was of course of high interest to the public at large, in Holland as everywhere else. So it happened shortly after the first newspaper reports that I was approached by acquaintances on the editorial board of the monthly *De Vrÿe Katheder*, with the request to write an article for their paper on the new weapon. I accepted, and thus got my first taste of a task which, from the start and for the rest of my life, I have found important and difficult: to instruct the general public on scientific issues. In my first effort (which appeared on August 31),[12] I began by giving people a feeling for numbers: 100,000 atomic nuclei laid side by side cover the diameter of an atom; 100 million atomic diameters together span one centimeter. I knew enough of the physics to give a crude picture of how a bomb works. I ended by stating: "If one could master the difficult task of using fission for peaceful purposes, then man will be more powerful than ever before. Numbers speak better than words. A one-liter can filled with uranium oxide powder contains enough power to keep a thousand 50-watt lightbulbs burning for a full year, or to bring to a boil two million two-liter pots filled with ice water. . . . One awaits with intense interest what will be the Allies' uranium policies." Rereading the piece after all these years, I find it not too bad for my first try at a new kind of communicating.

During that summer of 1945 I became the resident Dutch expert of my generation on nuclear matters. In October I wrote again.[13] The English title "Share the Atom," a quote from a speech (August 21) by Vernon Bartlett in the House of Commons, indicates the theme: international relations. I ended as follows: "The nuclear physics discoveries could lead to international and economic cooperation. It can also happen, however, that one or more of the great powers will try to sabotage such urgently necessary solidarity. If that happens one will be able to say of modern physics that in much wisdom lies much sorrow" (a quotation from Ecclesiastes).

In November, a third piece of mine came out,[14] this one the result of having read the official U.S. government report *Atomic Energy for Military Purposes: The Official Development of the Atomic Bomb under the Auspices of the United States Government, 1940–1945.*[15] It was written by Henry De Wolf Smyth, with whom I would be friends before long. Only a few copies of this very important document were available this early in Europe. It was a small book eagerly devoured by physicists. Kramers had lent me his copy. Rosenfeld, just back from a brief trip to Copenhagen to celebrate Niels Bohr's sixtieth birthday, told me that in Bohr's institute the report was literally chained to a wall in order to give everybody a chance to see it. Remember that at that time there were no copying machines yet.

This time I ended my article like this. "Let us hope for grand gestures by the major powers which would render science again as free as is ardently hoped by all who love her."

12.3 A Trip to France and England

After the authorities had approved the resumption of my assistantship in Utrecht, I made arrangements to take up my function there. I was given Uhlenbeck's old room (he was in the United States now) as my office. I also found a room in town, rented from a Mr. Keizer, who had a well-known butcher shop on the ground floor. It was a nice, light, top-floor room at Vischmarkt 9, on one of the few old canals that give some atmosphere to Utrecht, which I otherwise found a monumentally uninteresting city.

My encounters with members of the Jewish Brigade had stimulated me to write to several Dutch friends who had moved to Palestine, asking for information about the Hebrew University in Jerusalem. If memory serves me, I do not believe, however, that I was all that serious about emigration. My ties with Zionism had loosened both because of the catastrophes of years past—"my" Zionist youth organization, Hanoar Haowed, had been dissolved since most of the kids had perished—and because of my ever-growing involvement with science. Nevertheless, late in 1945, events brought me for one last time in close contact with Zionist organizations.

In October I received an invitation to represent Holland at international conferences of Zionist student organizations to discuss postwar issues. The meetings were to be held first in Paris, then in Manchester. I thought this sounded interesting and accepted.

Travel in those days was complicated. First I needed a document stating that I was politically reliable. This brought me to the headquarters of the Netherlands Security Service in Scheveningen, near The Hague, where I obtained a paper stating (in English): "This is to certify that nothing is known against . . ." With that in hand, I could obtain a passport (I still have it) with an exit visa: "For departure and reentry in the territory of the Netherlands Kingdom in Europe, which is in a special state of martial law." All that red tape was of course intended to prevent people who had done "wrong" during the war from sneaking out of the country.

Finally I obtained visas from the British Embassy in The Hague and the French Consulate in Amsterdam. One thing helped: I never had to wait in line to obtain all these documents and stamps. Foreign travel was still a rarity. Only after all these formalities was I ready to take off.

On December 13, I left for Paris by Pullman, changing trains in Brussels. Three hundred miles and seventeen hours later, after having passed two lengthy border inspections, I arrived at the Gare du Nord. Rosenfeld had written to several distinguished scientists on my behalf. So it could come about that on my first day in Paris I was received by Paul Langevin at his home on Rue Vauquelin. He was a friendly old man, one of France's finest scientists of the century. It was a great privilege to meet him almost at the end of his life. That evening I settled into a modest hotel room, where during the night I was entertained by the voice of an American soldier who was spending time with a lady in the room next to mine: "There's nothing to be afraid of. . . . You are a lady and I shall treat you like a lady." The next day I was cordially received by some of my hosts and spent long hours in the Louvre.

The conference began the day thereafter. I do not remember much of what went on except that we worked hard and that a press conference was held. So it went on for a few days. Only in 1992 did I find out that a young woman I had met at those meetings later married the violinist Isaac Stern.

On December 20 I took the boat train to London. Of that journey I remember only one thing: being sick as a dog during the Channel crossing. From London I went right on to Manchester, where I met Blackett. Once again I have no recollection of the details of our hard work. Thereafter, a two-day visit to Cambridge, where I spent one afternoon with Dirac, a hero of mine since my graduate school days (chapter 6), and I also paid a long visit to the famous Cavendish Laboratory.

The most intense experience of that trip abroad resulted from my visit to the Picasso exhibit at the Victoria and Albert Museum in London. The intensity of his paintings affected me profoundly. I knew at once that I had encountered the work of genius—whatever that word may mean—and I have since then been a great admirer of his. Those sentiments did not change at all after Françoise Gilot, one of his ex-wives, told me, much later, what a son-of-a-bitch he was in personal life. His oeuvre has retained a great influence on my perceptions of twentieth-century art.

Which reminds me of a news item I saw a day or so later in a London paper. It was a picture of a boy of maybe six standing in front of a Picasso canvas in the museum. The caption read: "Johnny, son of air commander so-and-so says 'I don't understand it.'" I hope for you, Johnny, that later in life you will have learned to appreciate that, when seeing (or hearing) a work of art, you should let your feelings reign freely, leaving the mind altogether out of it. Trying to understand while experiencing takes away from your feelings, which should be important to you. We physicists say: feeling and understanding are complementary, both are important but—at a given moment—one excludes the other.

Before setting out on my trip, I had been in touch with one of my acquaintances from the Jewish Brigade who regularly flew an air courier service between Amsterdam and London. He had offered to fly me back. I met him at Croydon Airport and walked with him to his plane, a quite small, lightweight affair. He and I were the only people on board. No seats, no seat belts, just a bench. We took off for what was the first airplane trip of my life. We were barely in the air when I became very sick. No air-sickness bag. I made a mess. My friend just sat at the controls, grinning. After we had come down at Schiphol Airport, he told me, "Now you know the two stages of air sickness." "And what are they?" I asked. He replied, "In the first stage you are afraid of dying; in the second you are afraid you will not die." I apologized for my poor show, thanked him warmly, and got myself back to my room on the Herengracht.

12.4 DEPARTURE

Already in early September I had received a letter from The Hague informing me that the minister of education had recommended me for support from the Institute for International Education. Two weeks later I received a cordial letter from Niels Bohr, inviting me to spend two years at his Copenhagen institute. He had secured a grant for me from the Rask Ørsted Foundation (named after renowned early nineteenth century Danish scholars, a linguist and a physicist). In October I had a letter from Uhlenbeck inviting me to Ann Arbor. Thus things were looking good. Nevertheless, I could not make plans yet, since I had had no reply to my Princeton application. I was much encouraged by a letter received in November from Pauli, telling me that he was personally in favor of my coming to Princeton.[16] About my long papers on quantum electrodynamics, which I had sent to him at Rosenfeld's suggestion, he wrote: "Your work seems to be very carefully done."

When I came home from London in late December, there was a letter from Princeton in my mailbox, written by Frank Aydelotte, director of the Institute for Advanced Study from 1939 to 1947. I had been accepted for a one-year stay on a stipend of $1,800. In addition, the support from the Institute for International Education, which was contingent on my acceptance by a U.S. academic institution, had come through. So there I was, a potentially rich young man with two offers for a research position, one in America and one from Denmark. I immediately consulted Rosenfeld on what to do. His advice was: accept both. I should immediately go to Denmark, explain the situation to Bohr, and ask if I could stay there for one year, then go to Princeton, then return to Copenhagen for the second year. That sounded like good advice to me.

The next few weeks were truly hectic. Letters of acceptance had to be written. A formal request for leave of absence from my assistant's position in Utrecht had to be made. I had to make arrangements for my living quarters in Amsterdam and Utrecht. Tickets had to be bought. Good-byes had to be said to family and friends.

I went to see Rosenfeld once more to express my gratitude for his great help. He had prepared a letter which I was to take along and personally give

to Bohr. In 1992 I obtained a copy of it, now in the Niels Bohr Archive. It is
a splendid handwritten document, written in eighteenth-century Danish. It
reads in part as follows, in translation:

> Your magnificence, the Director, and honored and highly learned pro-
> fessors at Copenhagen's Institute for theoretical physics . . . My servant
> named Abraham Pais, who brings you this document, wishes and desires
> nothing but to drink from the cup of science, which, with great zeal and
> profundity, you keep filled with the purest and noblest nectar; I believe he is
> capable of doing so . . . Utrecht, dated January 26, in the year of our Lord
> 1946.

On January 25, 1946, I left Holland. I could not know then that I had just
completed spending the last full month of my life in my native country. I
have been back there many times since, but only for, at most, a few weeks at
a time.

13

Getting to Know
Niels Bohr

13.1 MY FIRST DAYS IN DENMARK

ON JANUARY 24, 1946, I flew from Amsterdam to Copenhagen. I had
been afraid that the misery of my first air trip to London would repeat itself,
but this time all went fine. My first view of Copenhagen from the air consisted of three high smokestacks from the H. C. Ørsted power plant—an
example of how vividly one can remember trivial details. We landed in
Kastrup, where, only ten days later, the first commercial flight from New
York to Denmark would arrive; flying time: 17 hours, 30 minutes.[1]

I took a bus from the airport to the terminal in town, and from there a
taxi to the Institut for Teoretisk Fysik, as Niels Bohr's institute was then
called. (In 1965, when Bohr would have been eighty, it was renamed Niels
Bohr Institutet.) I presented myself to Fru (Mrs.) Betty Schultz, a kind and
formidable lady who was Bohr's secretary from 1919 until his death in
1962. She welcomed me cordially and told me that I was the first of the
post-World War II generation to come to the Institute from abroad for
postdoctoral study. Next she informed me that a room was being held for
me in the *pension* of Frøken (Miss) Margrethe Have on Fridtjof Nan-
sensplads Nr. 5. I proceeded there, settled down, then, together with my
fellow boarders, had my first Danish dinner.

That evening Frøken Have invited me to her room for private tea and
kager, the justly renowned Danish pastries. Her English was quite decent.
She turned out to be a real character, with very outspoken opinions, particularly about renowned physicists who had boarded with her in the course
of the years. About Werner Heisenberg she said: "Too much Nazi. [Violent
motion with a poker.] I don't want to have any Germans here any more."

She told me that many Germans had fled to Denmark after the Russian invasion of their country, and that some two hundred thousand—five percent of Denmark's population—were still there. British and American authorities told the Danes that they were not allowed to send these Germans back, costing the Danes a lot of money and causing them some grief. I asked whether British and American soldiers were liked here. (Copenhagen, like Amsterdam, had become a rest-and-recreation center.) "Very popular. My maids go out with them every night. I should be glad if the soldiers went home."

Early the next morning I went back to Fru Schultz's office and asked if I might call on Professor Bohr. She told me to wait in the journal room adjoining the library, and she would call me as soon as Professor Bohr was free to see me. I sat there and read for a while, then someone knocked at the door. I said come in. The door opened. It was Bohr. My first thought was: what a gloomy face.

Then he began to speak.

Later I have often been puzzled about this first impression, which vanished forever the very moment Bohr started to talk to me that morning. True, one might correctly describe Bohr's physiognomy as unusually coarse or rugged. Yet his face is remembered by all who knew him for its intense animation and its warm and sunny smile.

On that first day at the institute I met Niels's brother Harald, a renowned mathematician whose looks (unlike Niels's) reflected the brothers' Jewish ancestry from their mother's side. I also had discussions with Christian Møller, whose papers on the quantum theory of scattering were familiar to me. We talked about the work I had done during the war and also about his current interest in so-called S-matrix theory, a wartime contribution by Heisenberg. I recall finding the discussion interesting but had no great expectations of Heisenberg's new ideas, a judgment that has turned out to be not far off the mark.

I spent the next day, a Saturday, taking long walks through Copenhagen, which at once I found to be a pleasant city. I still do. The first thing I did that morning was to go into a bookstore and buy a Danish-English pocket dictionary, which I began to use immediately to decipher signs in shop windows. So it happened that the first Danish sentence I learned was: *Sig det med blomster,* say it with flowers.

That evening I went to the Cinema Triangel (long since gone) to see *Maanen er skjult* (The Moon Is Down), an American movie adapted from a Steinbeck story. I discovered that reading Danish subtitles to the English-spoken words provided another entry into the language. So did my attempts at reading Danish newspapers, which I did not find that difficult, since the language has massive amounts of English, German, and, remarkably, especially Dutch cognates. *Speaking* Danish was quite another matter, however. It is well known that Danes swallow parts of the written word when talking, which makes it much more difficult to understand the spoken language than the written one.

Yet I gained the unwarranted reputation of being the Institute's visitor who learned Danish faster than any of my foreign predecessors, probably as the result of the following. It was a rule of Frøken Have that she be notified in advance if one could not come for dinner. One day soon after my arrival I was invited to dinner that evening by a Danish colleague, and I accepted. Since I was at the Institute at that moment, I had to telephone the Have home. I went to Fru Schultz and asked to use her office phone, for which she gave permission. In those days the Copenhagen phone system was only semi-automatic. You lifted the receiver and dialed two letters that indicated a section of Copenhagen. I dialed Øb for Østerbro. An operator came on the line and said Øbro. I then gave her the number, which I had learned to say in Danish for precisely such occasions as the present one. So I said: *tre og tredive to og halvtreds* (3352), and was connected. When I hung up I saw Fru Schultz looking at me with unconcealed admiration: "You speak Danish!" That was nearly all I could say at that time—but that is why I became known as the fastest learner of the language.

Another useful expression I learned to use early was *Tak for sidst* (thank you for last time), which is what you say on the first occasion you meet someone who had earlier invited you to his or her home. It is a good example of the Danish custom of pushing courtesy to extremes.

13.2 How Denmark Survived the War

Not long after my arrival in Denmark, I caught my first glimpse of what it had experienced during the war—much different from what happened in the Netherlands. In the course of time I pieced together how Denmark had fared in those years. A thumbnail sketch follows.

On September 1, 1939, the Second World War broke out. The period between late September, when Germany had completed the conquest of Poland, and April 1940, when hardly any military activity occurred in Western Europe, became known as the "phony war." Meanwhile, however,

Germany had started planning to strike northward, the major military target being not so much Denmark as the Norwegian Atlantic coast. During that period, on February 2, 1940, Churchill met with Scandinavian journalists and said in part: "I could not reproach Denmark if she surrendered to Nazi attack. . . . Denmark is so terribly near Germany that it would be impossible to bring help. Personally I would in any case not undertake to guarantee Denmark. . . . The question for Denmark is to find a balance. . . . We get some bacon and butter and the Germans get some. . . . That is perhaps the best way. Denmark has a pact with Germany but I do not doubt that Germany will overrun Denmark on the day that it will suit them."[2]

That is exactly what happened. On April 9, 1940, at 4:15 A.M., German forces began the occupation of Denmark. During a few hours of scant resistance, Danish casualties amounted to sixteen killed, twenty-three wounded. "In those few hours of fighting the Danish army put up just enough resistance to escape complete dishonor."[3] At 6:20 the Danish capitulation was broadcast to all military units. The Germans pledged respect for Danish neutrality (!), noninterference in internal Danish affairs, and maintenance of the Danish army and navy on active-duty status. The positions of parliament and king were to remain unaltered. Life in Denmark did not at once change drastically after the occupation. There was not even a ban on listening to the BBC.

The Danes became restive as Germany began to experience major military setbacks. Anti-German demonstrations and strikes increased in number, as did acts of sabotage. In August 1943 the German authorities demanded that the Danish government declare a state of emergency and impose capital punishment for acts of sabotage. The government rejected this ultimatum, then resigned. On August 29 at 4 A.M., the Germans declared martial law.

The position of the Jews in Denmark now became perilous.[4] By August 1943 there were 8,000 of them, 6,500 native born, of which 1,500 were half Jewish, and 1,500 were refugees (all in round numbers). Their problems up till that time had been no more severe than those of other Danes. Their civil rights had remained protected under Danish law, they had retained their jobs and had continued to conduct religious services. This situation, idyllic compared to what was happening elsewhere, came to an end on September 28, when a direct order from Hitler for the deportation of all Danish Jews reached Copenhagen. On that very day Georg Ferdinand Duckwitz, a high German official, informed two Danish political leaders that the rounding up of Jews was to begin at nine o'clock on the evening of October 1. For this act his name will live in the history of the Danes and of the Jews. (He also helped prevent catastrophic action by the Germans during the last days of the war.)[5]

On the evening of September 29, two German freighters docked in the port of Copenhagen for the purpose of transporting the Jews to Germany. On that same day Niels Bohr fled Denmark.

Next followed the greatest mass rescue operation of the war: the transportation of nearly all Jews to Sweden, where 7,220 of them arrived safely. It is a tale of improvisation and great courage from the side of the resistance movement, only slightly marred by the occasional greed of some fisherman who asked for too much money.

At 8:35 on the evening of May 4, 1945, the BBC broadcast to Denmark the news that the German High Command had surrendered all German forces in Denmark to Field Marshal Montgomery. The next day the first British troops arrived at Copenhagen Airport.

When, nine months after its liberation, I came to Denmark, I found it to be a land of milk and honey. I am not sure, however, that many Danes would have shared that judgment, since their standards of comparison had to be so very different from mine. I have already described the material impact of the war on the Dutch. Let me outline next what befell the Danes in that respect.

During its hours of war, Denmark suffered nothing like Rotterdam's terrible bombardment. In fact, all during 1940–45, the damage caused by German bombings was minor. With respect to food, some rationing had been introduced as early as 1939. Until about 1960 Denmark was predominantly an agricultural society, self-supporting for all basic foods. As a result, between 1939 and 1944 the average caloric intake per person dropped by only about ten percent and was essentially unchanged in the countryside![6] Rationing was still enforced when I arrived in Denmark. I received the necessary coupons, which I handed to Frøken Have. At that time weekly allowances included a half pound of butter and a half pound of coffee.

From the very beginning I was greatly impressed by the quality of the Danish food, an enormous improvement not only over the hunger winter of 1944–45 but also over the still austere conditions in Holland in the half year after the end of the war. Above all, I loved the *frokost* (lunch), consisting of *smørrebrød*, literally buttered bread, the famous Danish open sandwiches. To this day I know of no better lunch anywhere in the world.

In those days I ate like a wolf but was surprised to notice that nevertheless I kept losing weight. A medical doctor gave me the explanation. In the year before coming to Copenhagen, I had lived nearly exclusively on carbohydrates, and lousy ones at that—sugar beets, flower bulbs. My weight loss was the result of the transition to a high-protein diet.

I had gone to see the doctor for a different reason: I had noted that my heartbeat was at times irregular. He reassured me that I had no organic problems. It was a matter of nerves, presumably an aftereffect of the war. He prescribed phenyl ethyl barbiturate tablets. Before long all was well.

13.3 VARIA FROM MY DANISH SOJOURN

Right after my first encounter with Bohr, he went to Norway for a brief trip. After his return he was very busy with plans for the extension of his Institute, so for the first month or so I did not see much of him. Bohr's preoccupation with the Institute's extension gave me my first insights into one trait of his personality: his fondness for taking part in deliberations on construction. Much later his wife recalled: "The Institute was always building. As soon as they finished one thing they were starting another. Oh, I hoped I should never see an architect again. . . . But he liked it; he liked architects, and he liked handwork to occupy himself with, and he liked to see it. He certainly took part in every little detail; it amused him. . . . It must have taken a good part of his time, some of his time. But it was a relaxation for him."[7]

I shall return below to my most important experiences in Denmark: my contacts with Bohr. But first a few personal impressions of Denmark.

13.3.1 On the Landscape

Helped by newly acquired Danish friends, I began to explore Copenhagen's environs. One of the most pleasing features of the city is that the outdoors are so near at hand and so easy to reach by public transportation. Just to the north one can go for walks along the Øresund, the sea arm that separates Denmark from Sweden, which you can easily see just a few miles across the water. Visits to Dyrhaven, the deer park, only a bit farther up the road, became another of my favorite promenades. In its middle stands the Eremitage, a pretty, eighteenth-century royal hunting lodge, from which you have a great view of surrounding forests and the Øresund.

I have often been asked how Denmark and Holland compare. Both countries are small, flat, and beautiful in what I would call an undramatic way. Both are monarchies (Denmark is Europe's oldest), with the ruler's rights and privileges strictly circumscribed constitutionally. The respective climates are on the whole alike: moderate, lots of rain. There the similarities end. In Denmark, unlike in Holland, you are never far from water: the North Sea west of Jutland (and stretching down to Holland), sea arms, fjords, lakes. Woods and forests are common in Denmark, rare in Holland. Holland's population density is high, Denmark's is low. Light plays a special, though distinct, role in both countries' environments. The Dutch light, soft yet strikingly clear, has been immortalized by the seventeenth-century Dutch landscape painters. Denmark is equally famous for its *lyse natter*, light nights, of midsummer, when the sun sets after 10 P.M. and it never gets fully dark. By contrast, in winter all daylight is gone by 4 P.M., which explains, I guess, the Danish fondness for candlelight in the home.

13.3.2 New Friendships

After several brief and pleasant encounters with members of the opposite sex, I met Inger, who was to be my girlfriend for the duration of my stay in Denmark. She was the daughter of a judge and herself an air stewardess on DDL, Det Danske Luftfartselskab, or Danish Airways, a company that in August of that same year was absorbed by SAS, the Scandinavian Airlines System. She was bright, cheerful, and pretty, and would spoil me by bringing home fruits and other delicacies from her flights to France or Italy. She was also an expert kayak rower, able to paddle standing up, with one foot in each of two kayaks. I was impressed enough to try it too, but after not more than five paddle strokes I could see that I was unable to prevent the two light boats from moving away from each other. I plunged into the water, to my humiliation and Inger's great delight.

Those were happy days. We kept writing to each other after my departure from Denmark. She married not long after. She died young. Her memory remains precious to me.

I became good friends—and still am—with Niels Bohr's son Aage, who was then a physics graduate student. We would talk shop; I would also query him about Denmark and its traditions. He was to become a fine physicist, receiving a share of the Nobel Prize for 1975.

Meanwhile, new people from abroad had begun to arrive at the Institute.

One of them Res Jost, from Switzerland, Ph.D. from Zurich, became the most important friend of my life; our friendship grew and lasted until his untimely death; I miss him much. I also became friends with Lamek Hulthén, a Swede from Lund who was ten years older than I.

I have a few memories of parties given by friends. On one occasion we went to our places at the dinner table, where a beer and a small glass with akvavit stood waiting for each person. One guest, a Swedish physicist whom I knew to be quite composed if not stiff, asked the hostess for two more akvavits, which he placed neatly next to the first. When the time came for the hostess's *skaal* (toast) of welcome, he picked up his first glass and emptied it bottoms up, then did the same with the second and third. He remained his quiet self for a few moments, then burst out in loud song, and for the rest of the evening was the life of the party. When I asked the woman seated next to me to explain this uncommon behavior, she replied that there was nothing unusual about that. Give a Swede a few strong drinks, she said, and only then does he come to life. I have not been able to gather enough statistics to verify this, but my wife assures me that this is correct.

At another party, a guest inadvertently toppled his wine glass, leaving a large stain on the well-set table. Without a moment's hesitation, the hostess threw the contents of her glass on the table as well. I was greatly impressed by that gesture, clearly designed to put an embarrassed guest at ease.

On yet another occasion I arrived late at a gathering where a Norwegian, who clearly already had a few drinks under his belt, was among the guests. I introduced myself as a Dutchman. He then said to me, loudly, for all to hear: "The Norwegians are great drinkers, aren't they?" I said yes, they were. "The Dutch are great drinkers too, aren't they?" I said yes, they were. "We must show them, won't we?" I said yes, we must. Then, to my horror, he proceeded to fill two beer glasses with akvavit, handed one to me and said: "We shall drink bottoms up, won't we?" What the hell was I to do? I was young, I was challenged, I had no choice. So both of us did as announced; the rest of the crowd looked on expectantly, then applauded. For a minute or so I felt nothing unusual, but then became so drunk that I lost control over my limbs. Trying to go through one open door I found myself going through another. After some time, some guests took pity on me, bundled me into a taxi, accompanied me home, saw me safely up the stairs, and dumped me on my bed, fully dressed. I fell into a stuporous sleep from which I awoke the next morning, feeling quite all right. I did not even have a hangover. I swore to myself, however, that never, ever, would I be that drunk again. And so it has been.

13.3.3 Physics. First Encounter with Pauli

With all this gallivanting, did I find time to do any physics? You bet I did; in fact, I worked hard during the Copenhagen period.

My first project was a collaboration with Hulthén. It was a lengthy computational affair dealing with neutron-proton scattering, a problem that had interested me earlier (chapter 12, sec. 12.2) and on which I had published one of my first articles.[8] Both of us felt extremely bold in pushing our calculations all the way up to proton energies of 25 million electron volts—at that time experiments could not yet reach beyond energies of almost 10 million volts. Nowadays we can accelerate protons to energies one billion times higher.

At that time, we did not have the benefit of electronic computers. All we had was a Marchant machine, a piece of equipment the size of a large typewriter. It worked slowly but was the fastest computer available at the time. It operated on electric current and literally hammered out numbers accompanied by machine-gun-like noises. For scientists there were no good old days . . .

Hulthén and I proceeded by taking turns, one dictating the input numbers, the other banging on the Marchant; I insisted that dictation should be in Danish. At one point Hulthén did the dictating, calling out digits that I would code. One of them I understood to be eight, so I pressed the 8-key. When after a few hours we made some spot checks, we found curious irregularities. It did not take us long to find out what had happened: the Danish word for the digit one is *et,* which is pronounced like the English "eight." I should have pressed the 1-key instead of the 8-key! Having learned that lesson, I apologized to my collaborator, begging him to continue nevertheless in Danish, which he graciously consented to do.

Our results were published in a paper that appeared in the *Proceedings* of the first international postwar physics conference, held in Cambridge, England, in July 1946.[9]

Meanwhile I had also begun to work together with Møller. I noted earlier that he and I had independently worked on different versions of five-dimensional relativity theory,[10] and that this had been one of the topics of my Ph.D. thesis (chapter 6). Our joint effort dealt with an interesting consequence of Møller's version: the electron appears there not as an object all by itself, but as the lowest mass particle of a particle family. In physical terms, the electron is the lowest state of a mass spectrum. Similarly, the proton-neutron, collectively called nucleon, and the meson should be respective ground states of other particle families. We obtained a formula which gives the mass values for members of all those family members.

At that time there was completely confused information about possible "new" particles seen in cosmic radiation. Our analysis of these particles and their decay modes could therefore simply not survive. (This work was done before the π-meson and μ-meson had been properly identified.) Nevertheless our paper, also published in the Cambridge conference *Proceedings*, contains a contribution that will last forever.[11] We felt it necessary to introduce a collective name for all "light" particles, those in the electron-neutrino family. After consultation with a learned acquaintance, we settled on the name lepton (from the Greek λεπτός = small). As a result, our paper contains one footnote: "For the 'light' particles we propose the name 'leptons.'" That word has meanwhile found its way into the *Oxford English Dictionary*. Some years thereafter, mass spectra would play an important role in my further work.

One evening in early 1946 I met Pauli for the first time, at a dinner party in Bohr's home. At that time he had already long been recognized as one of the major figures in twentieth-century physics, not only because of his own contributions, but also because of his critical judgments—which could be quite sharp, but nearly always to the point—of others' work. He was known as the conscience of twentieth-century physics. He had shown genuine interest in my work (see chapter 12, sec. 12.4) and was clearly pleased to meet me. He was kind enough to invite me for dinner the next evening at Krog's fish restaurant, one of Denmark's finest eateries. In the course of that meal I witnessed for the first time his chassidic mode, a gentle rhythmic rocking to and fro of the upper torso. Something was on his mind. He began to talk of his difficulties in finding a physics problem to work on next, adding "Perhaps that is because I know too much." Silence; more rocking. Then: "Do you know much?" I laughed and said, "No, I don't know much." Another silence, while Pauli seriously considered my reply, then: "No, perhaps you don't know much, perhaps you don't know much." A moment later: "*Ich weiss mehr*" (I know more). That was said in the Pauli style, without aggression, merely an expression of a statement of fact. I would see much of him in later years.

While I think back with pleasure on the two collaborations just mentioned, and to that first encounter with Pauli, these events cannot be compared in significance with the main experience of that Copenhagen period: less than a year after I had been held in a Gestapo prison I became, for a number of months, the closest collaborator of one of the greatest figures in twentieth-century science. Let me now introduce him.

13.4 What I Knew about Niels Bohr and When I Knew It

When I first arrived in Copenhagen, my knowledge of Bohr's achievements was quite fragmentary. I knew that in the 1920s and 1930s he had made his Institute (officially opened in 1921) into the Mecca of theoretical physics, especially quantum physics—but not that Heisenberg's seminal paper on uncertainty relations (1927) and Dirac's fundamental first paper on quantum electrodynamics (also in 1927) had both been written in Copenhagen. I knew of course—as does every theoretical physicist—that Bohr had been the first to apply the quantum theory to the structure of the atom, introducing some of the most audacious new postulates ever to enter physics: that electrons orbiting around the nucleus of an atom can only do so in a discrete set of orbits, in contravention to the then generally accepted tenets of a kind of physics—which we now call classical—that allows for a continuum of orbits; and that electrons in a higher orbit will jump into a lower one under the emission of a light-quantum, a photon (the existence of which had been postulated by Einstein in 1905). I knew that Bohr's ideas had been amazingly successful in explaining the properties of hydrogen, the simplest of atoms, but not that he had gone on to lay the foundations of the theory of the periodic table of elements, the main subject of his lecture given on accepting the Nobel Prize (1922). (Bohr was the first Nobel laureate I came to know personally. By last count I have met ninety-four more.)

These contributions by Bohr had made him famous in the world of science, even though this work, like that of his illustrious predecessors Max Planck and Albert Einstein, suffered from serious inconsistencies. Bohr, more aware of these paradoxes than anyone else, had spent enormous efforts at finding their resolution. It was not he but Heisenberg and Erwin Schrödinger who in 1925–26 discovered the new physical laws, called quantum mechanics, needed to end this veritable crisis. A close coworker of Bohr described Bohr's reactions: "He was very tired that time, and I believe that the new quantum mechanics caused him both much pleasure and very great tension. He had probably not expected that all this would come so suddenly but rather that he himself perhaps might have contributed more at that time. At the same time he praised Heisenberg almost like a kind of

Messiah and I think that Heisenberg himself understood that that was a bit exaggerated."[12]

Bohr was, then as always, full of praise for others' good work. He wrote to Einstein that Heisenberg's contribution "represents a most significant . . . exceptionally brilliant . . . contribution to the general problems of quantum theory."[13] In a letter to another colleague, Max Born, about Dirac: "Apart from his outstanding talents . . . he is a very likeable man . . . just now he is writing a beautiful paper on radiation and collisions [i.e. on quantum electrodynamics]."[14]

As often happens in moments of great scientific upheaval, discovery does not necessarily mean understanding what has been discovered. After 1926 the understanding and interpretation of quantum mechanics became Bohr's most important task. He threw himself onto the problem of the logical-philosophical basis of the new theory, which he achieved by introducing a new concept: complementarity. I shall explain a while later what this notion consists of.

When in my graduate student years I was taught quantum mechanics by Uhlenbeck, I had heard nothing about complementarity and doubt if he ever even used the word in his course. Nothing unusual about that. Complementarity, which Bohr himself considered his main contribution, is in fact not mentioned in some of the finest physics textbooks. The superb *Lectures in Physics* by Richard Feynman serve as but one example.[15]

Why this silence? The reason is that complementarity will not help you in your quantum mechanics calculations nor in setting up your experiments. Physics is more than just assimilating and developing facts, however. One should also once in a while reflect on the meaning of what one is doing. In that respect, Bohr's considerations are extremely significant. But at the time I came to Denmark I was—as is typical for most youngsters— more interested in finding answers than in pondering about fundamentals. In a word, complementarity arguments were too "philosophical" for my taste.

Nevertheless, already in 1946 I knew more about complementarity than most of my generation, because my teacher Rosenfeld had often talked to me about that subtle subject. Starting in 1931, Rosenfeld had been Bohr's closest collaborator all through the thirties (see chapter 6), visiting Copenhagen for periods lasting from a few days to half a year. (During that period, Liège in Belgium was his main base of operations.) In the course of time, Rosenfeld had become the self-anointed defender of the complementarity faith, *plus royaliste que le roi,* managing at the same time to hold strong views on dialectical materialism. As already mentioned, Pauli once called him "the square root of Bohr times Trotsky."[16] I must confess that in my Utrecht years complementarity interested me as much as communism—very little.

Because of my interest in nuclear physics, I was aware of Bohr's important contributions (dating from the mid-1930s) to the theory of nuclear reactions, processes initiated by making atomic nuclei collide with one another. Because of my interests in nuclear weapons (chapter 12, sec. 12.2), I knew that in 1939 Bohr had been the first to understand the crucial role for that process—and for making atomic bombs—of the rare isotope uranium-235.[17] As it has turned out, that was the last major discovery in his life.

Clearly, then, I did not come to Copenhagen quite unprepared. Yet there were so many facts about Bohr I was quite unaware of at that time: that Copenhagen had no physics institute or laboratory at all until Bohr took the initiative for founding one; that he administered the Institute himself and was its fund-raiser; that after the Nazis had come to power he was quite active in support of refugee scientists; that in the 1930s he had been instrumental in arranging for a team to work on biophysical topics at his Institute; that there the isotope tracer methods had been pioneered, now so vital to science and medicine. I knew only vaguely of Bohr's involvement with atomic weapons. Perhaps most important, I had no idea of Bohr's humane qualities.

I knew considerably more by 1986, when I sat down to begin work on my Bohr biography.[18] (I remember the day I started—it was the first of June.) But it was only four years later, when the end of that labor was in sight, that one day I said out loud to myself: Now I know who Bohr was.

The basis for my insights into Bohr's personality and oeuvre was laid during those months I worked closely with him—which I am now about to describe.

13.5 WORKING WITH BOHR

13.5.1 Bohr's Later Years

Bohr was sixty years old when I first met him, but he was still in full vigor, still running up steps two at a time. From that year on I was to see him off and on, mainly in Denmark and in the United States, until his death in

1962. He will therefore reappear in later chapters, but here I will give a sketch of him as a public figure during those later years of his life, beginning with his experiences during World War II.

Bohr spent the early war years in Copenhagen, managing somehow to keep his Institute going. Among the memorable events of that period was a letter from a colleague in England which Bohr received via underground channels. It contained an invitation to come to England and "to assure you that if you decide to come you will have a very warm welcome and an opportunity of service in the common cause."[19] Bohr decided to decline the offer because he felt it was best for Denmark that he stay. In his reply he further stated—in veiled language—his belief that it would not be possible to make atomic weapons: "I have to the best of my judgment convinced myself that in spite of all future prospects any immediate use of the latest marvelous discoveries of atomic physics is impracticable."[20]

Nevertheless, Bohr left Denmark half a year later. He had to. In September 1943, the time of the planned deportation of Danish Jews, he was informed that, being half Jewish, he ran grave risks of imprisonment by the Germans. He and his family fled to Sweden, from where he was flown to London.

Right after his arrival in England, Bohr was informed that a joint Anglo-American project for producing atomic bombs was underway with no definite results yet, however. This news astonished him greatly since, as noted, he had been quite dubious about practical applications of the fission process. He was asked to join the project as consultant and accepted. From then until August 1945 he made numerous trips back and forth between London and his U.S. headquarters in Washington, D.C., and between Washington and Los Alamos, always accompanied by his son, Aage.

Bohr played only a minor role in the actual weapons program. From 1943 onward his major concern was less with the war effort than with the radical changes in the postwar political climate that could be anticipated because of new weapons. These, he became convinced, might actually hold out a promise for improved international relations precisely because of their unmanageable threats to the security of nations. He further believed it necessary for the Western leaders to consult the Russians at once on this issue, because, he reasoned, if one deferred such contact until after the war, serious distrust would disrupt relations between wartime Allies, with potentially grave consequences.

Being a man of action, Bohr started attempts at bringing his ideas personally to the attention of Winston Churchill and Franklin Roosevelt. These efforts date back to a time when the first atomic device had not even been tested. In 1944 he had personal meetings with the two war leaders. For complex reasons,[21] his attempts to convince these great statesmen of his ideas failed completely. Times were simply not yet ripe for such wisdom. In later chapters I shall have more to say about Bohr's continuing efforts at promoting "glasnost."

In June 1945 Bohr was back in London. In August, Hiroshima and Nagasaki were atom-bombed. Later that month Bohr returned to Denmark.

By 1946 Bohr was already a public figure of the first rank, with he and Margrethe, his wife, often being called Denmark's second royal family. High dignitaries visited his home. From Denmark, the king and queen, cabinet ministers, and ambassadors came for dinner. On his seventieth birthday in 1955, the king and queen came to congratulate him, and the prime minister addressed the Danish people by radio to honor him.[22] Foreign notables visited Carlsberg, among them Queen Elizabeth II and Prince Philip of England, the queen of Siam, the crown prince (now the emperor) of Japan, Jawaharlal Nehru, prime minister of India, David Ben Gurion, prime minister of Israel, and Adlai Stevenson.

For years the academic world had already recognized Bohr with honorary degrees and election to learned societies abroad. Special honors of a different kind also came. In 1947 the king of Denmark conferred on him the nation's highest distinction, the Order of the Elephant, which obliged Bohr to adopt a coat of arms. In 1957 he received the first Atoms for Peace award, in Washington, in the presence of President Eisenhower, who, in addressing him, called him "a great man whose mind has explored the mysteries of the inner structure of atoms, and whose spirit has reached into the very heart of man."[23]

After Bohr's death, President John F. Kennedy wrote to Mrs. Bohr: "I am deeply saddened by Professor Bohr's death. American scientists, indeed all American citizens who knew Doctor Bohr's name and his great contributions, have respected and venerated him for more than two generations. . . . We are forever indebted to him for the scientific inspiration he brought along on his many visits to the United States, and especially for his great contribution to the atomic center at Los Alamos. Please accept my condolences and deep sympathy."[24] Other messages included those from the prime minister of Israel, the king of Sweden, and the chancellor of West Germany.[25]

I now return to earlier times and the national scene on which Bohr had become a hero. In 1959, when the newspaper *Politiken* celebrated its seventy-fifth anniversary, its readers were asked to vote on which men and women had made the greatest impact on developments in Denmark during that era. Among the thousands of answers, Bohr topped the list with a sizable majority. This national adulation had already begun in the 1920s. From that period dates the "story that a young man arrived in Copenhagen and took a taxi to Bohr's institute; and the taxi man wouldn't take any money because it was to Bohr's that he had driven—and the veriest business man knows all about him."[26]

Along with all these consuming events, the Bohrs still found time and took pleasure in receiving physicists, junior and senior, in their home.

Which brings me back to my own experiences in 1946.

13.5.2 Our Collaboration

As already mentioned (sec. 13.3), I saw little of Bohr in my first month at his Institute. My real contact with him began on February 24, when I was invited for Sunday dinner at the Bohr home, Gammel Carlsberg, a rather palatial house known as the Aeresbolig, the Residence of Honor. It is situated on the grounds of Denmark's largest brewery. Jacob Christian Jacobsen, its founder, had left his huge fortune to the benefit of Danish science. He had established the Carlsberg Foundation, administered by a board of directors chosen from among the membership of the Danish Academy of Sciences, which in the course of time has dispensed I do not know how many millions of Kroner in support of science. According to the foundation's Annual Report for 1991, about $10 million was disbursed in grants in that year alone.

Jacobsen also gave liberally for maintenance of Danish cultural monuments. Best known are his contributions to the rebuilding of Fredensborg, one of Denmark's most beautiful castles, which had burned down in 1859, and to the founding therein, at his initiative, of Denmark's museum of national history, now the home of national relics from the introduction of Christianity to the present. He was the greatest Maecenas in Danish history. In 1991 the foundation paid $3 million to maintain Fredensborg. Jacobsen had declared in his will that after his and his next of kin's death, his home, Gammel Carlsberg, should be offered free for life to the Danish man or woman most prominent for his or her activities on behalf of science, literature, or the arts, that person to be proposed by the Academy's membership for approval by the Carlsberg Foundation's board. In 1931 Bohr had been chosen. He would live in Gammel Carlsberg until his death.

That Sunday evening I had my first opportunity to talk physics with Bohr in his study. I told him of my work on quantum electrodynamics carried out during my years in hiding in Amsterdam. While I was telling him about what I had done, he smoked his pipe; he looked mainly to the floor and would only rarely look up at the blackboard on which I was enthusiastically writing down various formulas. After I finished, Bohr did not say much, and I felt a bit disheartened with the impression that he could not care less about the whole subject. I did not know him well enough at the time to realize that this was not entirely true. At a later stage I would have known right away that his curiosity was aroused, as he had neither remarked that this was very interesting nor said that we agreed much more than I thought—his favorite ways of expressing that he did not believe what he was told.

After this discussion we went back to the living room to rejoin the company. Then, as on later occasions, I felt fortunate to be, for a while, in the invigorating atmosphere of warmth and harmony that Mrs. Bohr and her husband created wherever they were, but above all in their Copenhagen home. The conversation now turned to more general topics, and that evening I caught a first glimpse of Bohr's intense preoccupation with the problems on the international political scene, which looked so profoundly different from the way it does today. The Nuremberg trials of German war criminals were still in the headlines. The United Nations counted only fifty-four member states. These aspects of the world situation of course also interested Bohr, yet his thoughts were focused on one central idea: the unique opportunities for an open and peaceful world due to the advent of atomic weapons. He had failed to convince Churchill and Roosevelt of these far-seeing visions—but he had by no means given them up. For now I shall only record the deep impression which Bohr's sense of urgency on this issue made on a young man who had just emerged from life in occupied Europe. "The release (by the U.S.) of atomic data for purely scientific purposes is but a side issue. The essential point is the political issue. The current political problems of Poland, Iran, etc., however important, are but side issues." Such remarks may now seem obvious. They were not at all so widely accepted then. On such topics, as in matters scientific, Bohr's strength lay in the single-minded pursuit of one given theme. At the time he was still optimistic that in not more than a year or two such views as he then expressed would find acceptance by the governments most vitally concerned.

It would be wrong to suppose, however, that evenings at the Bohrs were entirely filled with discussions of such weighty matters. Sooner or later, for the purpose of illustrating some point, or just for the pleasure of it, Bohr would tell one or more stories. I believe that at any given time he had about half a dozen favorite jokes. He would tell them; we would get to know them. Yet he would never cease to hold his audience. For me, to hear again the beginning of such a familiar tale would lead me to anticipate not so much the dénouement as Bohr's own happy laughter upon the conclusion of the story.

Shortly thereafter, on the second of March, the twenty-fifth anniversary of the Institute was celebrated. True to Bohr's style it was an intimate occasion, the high point of which came as Bohr reminisced about the people and the events of that heroic period. There was no pomp, only a few brief speeches. It was my pleasant task to express the gratitude of the first install-ment of postwar visitors from abroad. That evening Parentesen, the stu-dents' club, held a festive meeting. It began with a lecture by yours truly on "It Happened in Holland," held in the Institute's Auditorium A, renowned for the international gatherings held there since 1929, in which the cream of the world's theorists participated. Afterward we went upstairs to the *fro-koststue* (lunch room) for a feast. It was then that I learned to sing "Vid-enskabens Fædre" (the Fathers of Science), of which the last verse is ren-dered while the participants stand on their chairs, beer in hand: "*Nobelmanden Niels Bohr ved veg blandt alle vildspor . . .*" (. . . knows the way amidst all false tracks). It gave us all a sense of pride to have Bohr in our midst at that moment, also standing on his chair.

During the following weeks it became clear that Bohr had become quite interested in the problems of quantum electrodynamics I had mentioned to him. Every now and then he would call me into his office to have me ex-plain one or another aspect of them. He was particularly intrigued by the arguments which showed that many elementary particle problems are fun-damentally quantum problems that cannot be dealt with by the methods of classical physics. This view was not as widely accepted at that time as it would be two years later, when the modern version of the theory known as the renormalization program started to develop.

Then, one day in May, Bohr asked me whether I would be interested in working with him on a daily basis during the coming months. I was thrilled and accepted. The next morning I went to Carlsberg. The first thing he said to me was that it would only be profitable to work with him if I understood that he was a dilettante. The only way I could react to this unexpected statement

was with a polite smile of disbelief. But evidently Bohr was serious. He
explained how he had to approach every new question from a starting point
of total ignorance. It is perhaps better to say that Bohr's strength lay in his
formidable intuition and insight rather than in erudition. I thought of his
remarks of that morning some years later, when I sat at his side during a
colloquium in Princeton. The subject was nuclear isomers. As the speaker
went on, Bohr got more and more restless and kept whispering to me that it
was all wrong. Finally, he could contain himself no longer and wanted to
raise an objection. But after having half-raised himself, he sat down again,
looked at me with unhappy bewilderment, and asked, "What is an isomer?"

Before turning to the substance of our collaboration, I should like to note
that every once in a while Bohr would interrupt our discussions on scientific issues with digressions to political questions that were important to
him. I recorded in my diary some things he said:

> My position is complicated. I am the only one outside England and America
> who is familiar with the atomic bomb projects. My public statements are
> therefore carefully scrutinized. . . . America has offered their atomic secrets
> to the U.N. provided there will be international control. We should act on
> this, and quickly. It is a unique opportunity for organizing global peace. We
> should urge that these matters will be settled before other countries have the
> bomb,[27] because otherwise the situation will become dangerous, and will
> turn into a poker game of gamble and bluff. It should be important to all
> parties that the American proposal be accepted. I have serious doubts about
> Baruch,[28] who once said to me that he preferred an honorable war over a
> dishonorable peace.
>
> . . .
>
> I have talked with Roosevelt about these matters. His death [in 1945] is one
> of our great losses. Truman is an unimportant figure, chosen as vice-
> presidential candidate because stronger men would have disturbed the bal-
> ance between Republicans and Democrats.
>
> . . .
>
> I am in contact with various statesmen regarding the atomic issue. I am
> optimistic over the future course of events. In half a year from now nobody
> will talk about anything else but the atomic bomb. I hope that all will be
> settled in one or two years. If not, then there will be unimaginable suffering. A
> new war will last just one day. America is afraid to be at a disadvantage
> because of its concentrated industrial areas.
>
> . . .

Aage and I traveled like postal packages. When we came to New York we got a body guard who brought us to Chicago. There we were delivered to Secret Service men who brought us to the mountains [Los Alamos]. We went back and forth perhaps ten times between Los Alamos and Washington.

Now to science. The first order of business was to assist Bohr in the preparation of the opening address to the international conference in Cambridge, mentioned earlier. Bohr planned to make a number of comments on the problems of the quantum theory. I must admit that in the early stages of the collaboration I did not follow Bohr's line of thinking a good deal of the time and was in fact often quite bewildered. I failed to see the relevance of remarks such as, for example, that Erwin Schrödinger was completely shocked in 1926 when he was told of the probability interpretation of quantum mechanics, or references to some objection by Einstein in 1927 which apparently had no bearing whatever on the subject at hand. It did not take very long before the fog started to lift, however. I began to grasp not only the thread of Bohr's arguments but also their purpose. Just as in many sports the players go through warm-up exercises before entering the arena, so Bohr would relive the struggles which took place before the content of quantum mechanics was understood and accepted. I can say that in Bohr's mind this struggle started afresh every single day. This, I am convinced, was Bohr's inexhaustible source of identity. Einstein appeared forever as his leading spiritual sparring partner; even after Einstein's death he would argue with him as if he were still alive.

I can now explain the principal and lasting inspiration that I derived from the discussions with Bohr. In Holland I had received solid training as a physicist. It is historically inevitable that men of my generation received quantum mechanics served up ready-made. While I may say that I had a decent working knowledge of the theory, I did not fathom—nor could I have—how very profoundly the change from the classical to the quantum mechanical way of thinking affected both the architects and the close witnesses of the revolution in physics which took place in 1925–27. Through steady exposure to Bohr's "daily struggle" and his ever repeated emphasis on "the epistemological lesson which quantum mechanics has taught us," to use a favorite phrase of his, my understanding not only of the history of physics but of physics itself deepened. In fact, the many hours that Bohr spent talking to me about complementarity have had a liberating effect on every aspect of my thinking.

Of course, the purpose of the foregoing remarks is hardly to edify the reader with what goes on in my own mind. Rather, they are meant to exemplify the way in which the direct close contact with Bohr affected physicists of the post-quantum mechanical era. To earlier generations he had been a leader in battle at the frontiers of knowledge. This was no longer so in the times I am referring to and thereafter; such is destiny. To those of us who knew him then, Bohr had become the principal consolidator of one of the greatest developments in the history of science. It is true that, to the end, he was one of the most open-minded physicists I have known, forever eager to learn of new developments from younger people and remaining faithful to his own admonition always to be prepared for a surprise. (In these respects he was entirely different from Einstein.) But inevitably his role in these new developments shifted from actor to spectator. Bohr created atomic quantum physics and put his stamp on nuclear physics. With particle physics, the next chapter, the post-Bohr era, begins. The Cambridge paper of 1946 actually represents Bohr's furthest penetration into the more modern problems.

13.6 A PHILOSOPHICAL DIGRESSION

Young as I was, I taught Bohr more techniques of theoretical physics than he taught me. Yet I learned immensely from discussions with him. It was he who urged on me the need to think a theoretical problem through to the end before sitting down to make calculations. Several times he showed me how to do so. He was better at making qualitative estimates of what the answers should be like than anyone else I have ever known.

Even more important were the many hours during which Bohr explained to me his philosophical ideas that go by the word "complementarity." Before explaining what these are about, I wish to note that much of what has been written about this topic for general audiences is of very poor quality. I think in particular of erroneous attempts to link Bohr's philosophy to Oriental mysticism.

Bohr's complementarity provides the basis for understanding the curious behavior of matter, electrons for example, to appear under certain circumstances as particles, under others as waves. From the point of view of classical physics, this presents a grave paradox. Particles are not waves, waves are not particles. The new quantum mechanics provided the mathematical tools for coming to grips with this situation. When Bohr entered the arena, one knew how to calculate this particle/wave behavior without yet understanding the deeper meaning of this duality.

That comprehension was Bohr's contribution, first enumerated in 1927.[29] From that time on and for the rest of his life, Bohr focused on the language of science, the way in which we communicate. Right away, in 1927, he had stated his main theme: "Our interpretation of the experimental material rests essentially upon the classical concepts."[30] Even though it sounds simple enough, it is also most profound. Let me enlarge. In the classical era one verified the validity of theories by comparing them with experimental observations made with balances, thermometers, volt meters, and so forth. The theories have been modified in the quantum era, but—and that was Bohr's point—their validity continues to be verified by the same readings of a balance's equilibrium position, a thermometer's mercury column, a volt meter's needle, and so on. The phenomena may be novel, their modes of detection may have been modernized, but detectors should be treated as classical objects; their readings continue to be described in classical terms.

"The situation thus created is of a peculiar nature," Bohr remarked. Consider, for example, the question: Can I not ask for the quantum mechanical properties of a detector, say a volt meter? The answer is yes, I can. Next question: But should I then not abandon the limited description of the volt meter as a classical object, and rather treat it quantum mechanically? The answer is yes, I must. But in order to register the volt meter's quantum properties, I need another piece of apparatus with which I again make classical readings.

On another issue of language, Bohr said (I paraphrase): The question, Is an electron a particle or is it a wave?, is a sensible question in the classical context where the relation between object of study and detector either needs no specification or else is a controllable relation. In quantum mechanics that question is meaningless, however. There one should rather ask: Does the electron (or any other object) *behave* like a particle or like a wave? That question is answerable, but only if one specifies the experimental arrangement by means of which "one looks" at the electron.

To summarize, Bohr stressed that only by insisting on the description of observations in classical terms can one avoid the logical paradoxes apparently posed by the duality of particles and waves, two terms themselves defined classically. Wave and particle behavior mutually exclude each other. The classical physicist would say: If two descriptions are mutually exclusive, then at least one of them must be wrong. The quantum physicist will say: Whether an object behaves as a particle or as a wave depends on your choice of experimental arrangement for looking at it. He will not deny that particle and wave behavior are mutually exclusive but will assert that both are necessary for the full understanding of the object's properties. Bohr coined the term "complementarity" for describing this new situation: "The very nature of the quantum theory forces us to regard particle behavior and wave behavior, the union of which characterized the classical theories, as complementary but exclusive features of the description. Complementary pictures of the phenomena only together offer a natural generalization of the classical mode of description."[31]

In the course of time, Bohr improved and refined the language of observation, culminating in 1948 in his precise definition of the concept "phenomenon":

> Phrases often found in the physical literature, as "disturbance of phenomena by observation" or "creation of physical attributes of objects by measurements" represent a use of words like "phenomena" and "observation" as well as "attribute" and "measurement" which is hardly compatible with common usage and practical definition and, therefore, is apt to cause confusion. As a more appropriate way of expression, one may strongly advocate limitation of the use of the word phenomenon to refer exclusively to observations obtained under specified circumstances, including an account of the whole experiment.[32]

Bohr's usage of "phenomenon" is the one now subscribed to by nearly all physicists.

These considerations by Bohr mark him as not only a major figure in physics but also as one of the most important twentieth-century philosophers. As such he must be considered the successor to Kant, who had considered causality as a "synthetic judgement a priori," not derivable from experience. Causality is, in Kant's own words, "a rule according to which phenomena are sequentially determined. Only by assuming this rule is it possible to speak of experience as something that happens." This view must now be considered passé. Since Bohr, the very definition of what constitutes a phenomenon has wrought changes that, unfortunately, have not yet sunk in sufficiently among professional philosophers.

Again according to Kant, constructive concepts are intrinsic attributes of the "*Ding an sich*" (thing in itself), a viewpoint abandoned by quantum physicists. In Bohr's words: "Our task is not to penetrate in the essence of things, the meaning of which we don't know anyway, but rather to develop concepts which allow us to talk in a productive way about phenomena in nature." After Bohr's death, Heisenberg wrote that Bohr was "primarily a philosopher, not a physicist," a judgment that is arguable yet particularly significant if one recalls how greatly Heisenberg admired Bohr's physics.

Do we now possess the last word on quantum mechanics? I have seen too much to believe that anyone has the last word on any scientific issue, but I do think that Bohr's exegesis of the quantum theory is the best one we have to date. His writings on the subject are dense. I, however, have had the great privilege of Bohr's patient and repeated verbal explanation of these fundamental ideas.

13.7 WORKING WITH BOHR, CONTINUED

After we worked together for a month or so, Bohr suggested that we "lay aside titles," as the Danes say, which means that one addresses the other person in the familiar "thou" form. I recall how in the beginning I twisted sentences around in the most awkward ways, to avoid the formal form of address; but I got used to it in the end. (Today the familiar form has come in almost universal use, somewhat to my regret.) Sometime thereafter, Mrs. Bohr, a kind, gracious, and formidable lady, likewise suggested I use the "thou" form. I tried my best to do so, but simply couldn't and soon gave up the attempt.

In June the Bohr family moved to their summer house, situated on a property (still owned by the family) in Tisvilde in Sjælland, forty miles northwest of Copenhagen, close to the seashore. In 1924, when Bohr acquired the house and the land, it had been an old gamekeeper's home, a thatched one-story house called Lynghuset, the heather house. It stood in a forest grove of scattered high pines on heather-covered hilly grounds. It was an untouched landscape then (no more so, alas) that attracted artists, many of whom became good friends of the Bohr family.

Close to but separate from the Bohr house stood a small one-room cottage, Pavillonen, the pavilion, ideal for undisturbed work. "In this beautiful area that he loved so much [Bohr] found rest and recreation. . . . [Here he found time] for a bicycle ride in the woods, bathing from the beach, and ball games at which he was skilled up to late in life."[33]

In the course of the years, many young physicists had come out to Tisvilde to discuss scientific matters. That June, Bohr invited me to come and stay in the country with the family, so that our work could continue. I was of course happy to accept. During the following month or so my relations with Bohr deepened, and friendships developed with Margrethe, his wife, and with Aage, who was there during that entire period. Also the other sons, Hans, Erik, and Ernest, would turn up for longer or shorter visits. During that period I was witness to the strong and happy ties between parents and children. I myself was taken in as part of the family. That Tisvilde episode was altogether a wonderful experience. My memories of those weeks belong to the best of my life.

A good deal of the day was spent working in the pavilion; Aage would often join in as well. One morning we were interrupted by a maid who came to ask if the professor would kindly open a can of sardines for lunch. With his customary total concentration Bohr set himself to that task while I looked on. When I saw that he was making a mess of it, I said, "Here, let me do it." (Formality was never called for in my relations with Bohr.) I easily managed to do the job. Bohr looked at me in awe, then said: "Now come with me." Up to the house we marched, Bohr carrying the sardines on a plate, the maid and I following him. When we came to the kitchen where Margrethe was preparing lunch, he exclaimed: "*Margrethe, Margrethe, nu skal du se hvad Pais har gjort!*" (Have a look at what Pais has done!) It was one of those charming little events that made Bohr so dear to all who knew him personally.

Afternoons we would go for a swim and often we would work more at night. In fact, after Aage and I had retired to our bunks in the bedroom we shared, Bohr would still come in sometimes, in a shoe and a sock, to impart to us just one further thought that had occurred to him that very minute, and then would keep talking for an hour or so.

Evenings were spent in the family circle, chatting about issues large or small. Teasing belongs to the style of the Bohrs. When Niels was the target, he would say: "You never can make me a bigger fool than I am in my own eyes." When differences of opinion arose, he would often quote a dictum he was fond of: "It is not enough to be wrong. One must also be polite."

Sometimes Bohr would tell anecdotes about Einstein, or Dirac, or others. One I remember is about David Hilbert, the renowned mathematician from Goettingen, being asked his opinion about the question: Do animals have ethics? "*Aber nein,*" replied Hilbert. "Surely morals as an aggressive weapon is an invention of man."

A recurrent theme during those evening discourses was what one might politely call Bohr's lack of faith in professional philosophers, best illustrated by one of his favorite definitions. What is the difference between an expert and a philosopher? An expert is someone who starts out knowing something about some things, goes on to know more and more about less and less, and ends up knowing everything about nothing. Whereas a philosopher is someone who starts out knowing something about some things, goes on to know less and less about more and more, and ends up knowing nothing about everything. Another Bohr definition: An expert is someone who in a given field has made all possible mistakes.

On several evenings, another house guest would join us: Bohr's Moster (aunt from mother's side) Hanna Adler, a spry little lady in her late eighties, and a well-known personality in Denmark. She had been one of the first two women to obtain a university master's degree in physics, had founded the first Danish coeducational school, and had barely escaped deportation as a Jew. One evening she told me of a long-ago experience when she sat in a Copenhagen streetcar together with Bohr's mother and the two young sons, Harald and Niels. The boys were hanging onto their mother's every word as she was telling a story. Apparently there was something peculiar about these two young faces (Bohr could look dumb when in deep concentration, even when I knew him), for Miss Adler overheard one lady in the streetcar remark to her neighbor: "*Stakkels mor*" (that poor mother).

On other occasions Bohr would read one or more of his favorite poems. I marked them in my own books: Goethe's "Zueignung," Schiller's "Sprüche des Konfuzius," "Breite und Tiefe," "Mädchens Klage," and so on. Bohr liked especially to quote the following lines by Schiller:

> Wer etwas Treffliches leisten will,
> Hätt' gern etwas Grosses geboren,
> Der sammle still und unerschlafft
> Im kleinsten Punkte die höchste Kraft.

These lines have been translated as

> Ah! he would achieve the fair,
> Or sow the embryo of the great,
> Must hoard—to wait the ripening hour—
> In the least point the loftiest power.[34]

Like everything Bohr did, large or small, he was able to put his whole being into it and he could convey beautifully how small the point was and how lofty the power.

Bohr was fond of good literature. He was well versed in the Danish classics and could quote extensively from the Icelandic *Eddas*. His knowledge and admiration for Goethe's poems and dramas were profound, but he did not care for his theory of colors.[35] His knowledge of German was good. Also of English, but he used some fixed and endearing mispronunciations.

The one I remember best was his way of referring to one of the great menaces of this century as the "atomic bum" (my attempt at phonetics). Also, he used to denote a well-known investigative agency by "FIB," which somehow seemed to take the sting out of J. Edgar Hoover's organization.

Bohr's knowledge of French was poor. I have it from an eyewitness that he once greeted the French ambassador to Denmark with a cordial *"Aujourd'hui."*

Bohr was an indefatigable worker. When he was in need of a break from discussions, he would go outside and apply himself to the pulling of weeds with what can only be called ferocity. At this point I can contribute a little item to the lore about Bohr the pipe smoker. It is well known that to him the operations of filling a pipe and lighting it were interchangeable, but the following situation was even more extreme. One day he was weeding again, his pipe between his teeth. At one point, unnoticed by Bohr, the bowl fell off the stem. Aage and I were lounging in the grass, expectantly awaiting further developments. It is hard to forget Bohr's look of stupefaction when he found himself holding a thoughtfully lit match against a pipe without a bowl.

I have already mentioned that Bohr and I worked together on his talk for the Cambridge conference. There was a further item of business: to help him prepare an address to the Royal Society of London, for the occasion of celebrations of the tercentenary of Newton's birth. Circumstances of war had necessitated postponement of that event from its proper year, 1942, to July 1946. A large part of the Tisvilde period was devoted to this second paper, entitled "Newton's Principles and Modern Atom Mechanics."

Bohr devoted tremendous effort and care to the composition of his articles. However, to perform the physical act of writing, pen or chalk in hand, was almost alien to him. He preferred to dictate. On one of the few occasions that I actually did see Bohr write, he performed the most remarkable act of calligraphy I shall ever witness. At one point during our discussion of the Newton paper, he went to the blackboard (wherever he dwelled, a blackboard was never far away) and wrote down some general themes to be discussed. One of them had to do with the harmony of something or other. So Bohr wrote down the word "harmony." It looked approximately like this:

However, as the discussion progressed, Bohr became dissatisfied with the use of "harmony." He walked around restlessly. Then he stopped and his face lit up. "Now I've got it. We must change harmony to uniformity." So he picked up the chalk again, stood there looking for a moment at what he had written before, and then made a single change

with one triumphant bang of the chalk on the blackboard.

When toward mid-July the two projects were in good shape, Bohr began to discuss with me my plans for the future. Soon after my arrival in Denmark, I had of course told him of my intention to be in Princeton in the autumn of 1946, a plan he had approved of. Now he told me that he too would be in Princeton around that time, and asked if I would like to travel together with him. I replied that even though the idea very much appealed to me I could not do so, since I had to go briefly to Holland before my departure for the States. Then he said that he would have to give a talk in Princeton—about which more later—and asked if I would be willing to help him once more with the preparations while over there. I said I would be happy to do so. He went on to express the hope that, after a year in Princeton, I would return to Copenhagen and continue to work with him for another year. He had the funds to support me for that period. I replied that that sounded immensely attractive to me. But the second year never materialized, for reasons I shall explain later.

Then the time came to return to Copenhagen. A few days earlier I had noted in my diary: "Got up early and went for a walk in the woods. I saw that it was beautiful but felt nothing." That inability to feel was an after-effect caused by still undigested memories of war. Yet it will be clear that I had just had wonderful experiences.

The trip back went by car, Bohr at the wheel, Margrethe next to him, I in the back. It was an act of faith to travel in an automobile driven by Bohr. On that particular occasion he complained that he felt too hot, and actually let go of the wheel to take off his jacket. Margrethe's rapid intervention saved the situation.

Shortly afterward, Bohr left for England. During the celebrations in London, held from July 15–19, he presented the Newton paper.[36] From there he went on to Cambridge where on July 22 he gave the opening address, "Problems in Elementary Particle Physics."[37]

Shortly after his return he came to the farewell party for me, organized by Frøken Have in her *pension*. I can still see Bohr running up the stairs. Good-byes and thank yous to him and others who had given me of their friend-ship came in due course. Then I packed my bags and in mid-August flew back to Amsterdam.

13.8 IN THE PRESENCE OF GREAT MEN

Late one evening, after Bohr and I had had a discussion that had led no-where, he turned to me with a smile and said: "Tomorrow will be a beauti-ful day." Completely puzzled, I asked why. "Because tonight I do not un-derstand anything."

Memories like these are precious remnants of the time Bohr and I grew close. I came to love him dearly. No other physicist, for that matter no one else, ever has stirred in me feelings of such high respect and deep affection. He has been my father figure.

Only later did I come to understand how fortunate I have been to spend a period with Bohr that was neither too short nor too long. Why not too long? Because it can be dangerous for a young man in his formative years to spend too much time in the presence of a personality as powerful as Bohr's. While always attentive to his coworkers' needs, Bohr was nevertheless rather over-whelming because, I think, he was simply unaware of the strength of his influence. I have known one physicist who, after having worked for some months with Bohr, came to him with a letter from his doctor, stating that he should be in his own home every evening not later than seven o'clock— which Bohr meticulously saw to. I have known another who unconsciously had adopted Bohr's mannerisms, the characteristic ways he would move his hands and his head. At the time I left Denmark in 1946, I had no inkling how lucky I was to escape such aftereffects, not because I was smart enough to see all of that then, but because of external circumstances.

As I write these lines, I hear Bohr reciting two lines of another of his favorite poems:

> Nur die Fülle führt zur Klarheit,
> Und im Abgrund wohnt die Wahrheit.

(Only fullness leads to clarity/And truth resides in the abyss.)

Book the second: America

14

It Is Time to Speak
of America

I HAVE MENTIONED several times before that in September 1946 I was planning to go to the United States. Already in Copenhagen I had heard of several interesting events that would take place that month. I had received a letter from John Wheeler and Eugene Wigner, both renowned physicists at Princeton University, asking me to give an invited paper at a meeting of the American Physical Society, to be held in New York City September 19–21, and I had replied that I was pleased to accept. The meeting was to be followed by academic festivities in Princeton, on September 23–25, to celebrate the university's bicentennial—to which I had also been invited. Also from Copenhagen I had written to Professor Adriaan Fokker in Holland to apply for financial support from the Dutch Lorentz fund to cover travel expenses, for which I had received a positive reply.[1] Finally, on August 2, I had obtained a temporary visitor's visa at the U.S. Legation in Copenhagen.

First, however, I went back briefly to Holland. Whenever I would return there, I would invariably be happy to be again in surroundings that were so profoundly familiar to me—the people, the city, the small talk. From the airport I went to my parents' apartment, where I would stay the next three weeks. I was warmly received, hugged them both, then we sat down with the inevitable cups of tea and cookies. We had regularly corresponded while I was in Denmark but I still had to tell them more and ask them how they had fared and what the local gossip was.

It was not more than perhaps twenty minutes later that I grew uncomfortable. I had told them all I could, heard all I wanted, and had nothing more to say or ask. Even my relatively short absence had greatly increased the distance between the flow of their lives and mine. I had genuinely looked forward to seeing them again, but already now—it is still hard for me to write this down half a century later—I only felt boredom. How would I be able to stand their company for several weeks? This sequence, happy anticipation quickly followed by a letdown, was to recur on all my later visits. Yet they had been good parents to me.

Those days in Holland were nevertheless full. Meetings with old friends. A visit to the Ministry of Education, Arts and Sciences in The Hague, where I was asked to pledge not to settle abroad until I had first been in touch with them. An interesting courtesy call on Fokker in Haarlem, which I remember in particular because of his stories about Bohr, whom he knew in 1914, right after the latter had formulated his theory of the hydrogen atom. A visit to the Nederlandsche Bank in Amsterdam, where, against payment of 53 guilders, I received 20 dollars—the first such bills I had ever seen—for "first expenses on arrival in the United States of America," all this duly recorded in my passport. Foreign currency was a sparse commodity at that time.

On the morning of September 4 I took a train from Amsterdam to Rotterdam. There I boarded the S.S. *Edam,* which that afternoon departed for the States.

In wartime the *Edam,* originally one of the smaller passenger liners of the Holland-Amerika fleet, had been converted to a troop ship. One could hardly call it a luxury liner when I came on board for its first postwar civilian voyage. The hold was divided in two by a large curtain, one half for women, the other for men. Forty-eight of us slept on bunks in the men's department. The smells were less than pleasant. Depending on the wind direction, we were exposed either to odors from the engine room or to those of the kitchens. I am happy to report, however, that nobody griped. To me, as presumably to most others, this was high adventure of a new kind. On that occasion as well as on later ocean crossings, I have always found life on board the most restful in my life's experience. I went for frequent half-hour walks on the sloop deck and slept extremely well.

My fellow passengers were pleasant. One young American presented me with a Reynolds pen, my first ballpoint, proudly telling me: "It writes under water." I wondered what the devil that was good for, but of course expressed my genuine thanks.

I had been on the high seas for a week when I met a very nice young American woman, Rachel, a war widow, who lived in New Brunswick, New Jersey. We talked a lot and planned to meet again after I had settled down in Princeton, which was only some fifteen miles from her house.

Only one passenger was an earlier acquaintance of mine: Mrs. Kramers, wife of my colleague and friend Hans (chapters 6 and 10, sec. 10.5), who was on her way to join her husband in New York. He was there for the following reason. In January 1946 the General Assembly of the United Nations had adopted a resolution calling for the establishment of the U.N. Atomic Energy Commission, which in turn had organized a scientific and technical subcommittee. Kramers had been elected its chairman.[2]

One more social item: one evening in the hold, I gave a well-attended lecture on atomic energy.

I can see from my diary that the voyage took at least ten days. I remember of course seeing the Statue of Liberty for the first time. Some hours later, disembarking toward evening, I was met on the pier, as had been planned, by a boyhood friend from Amsterdam who had emigrated to the U.S. before the war. That evening he and his wife gave me my very first glimpses of the New World.

14.2 A GREENHORN IN NEW YORK CITY

Imagine a young man who has lived through five hard war years, who next spent an idyllic year in Denmark, who has just been on the Atlantic for ten days, breathing the globe's finest air, and who then lands in New York Harbor on a miserably hot and humid Indian summer evening in September, a climate both new and unexpected to him—and you will understand that I was bewildered, to put it mildly.

Not just that. My friends had come by car to give me at once a brief tour of the city. Off we went to Times Square, which never fails to make a strong impression on a newcomer. I was overwhelmed. Imagine now that you have just come from ten days of peace and calm on an ocean vessel, and then are abruptly plunged amid those lights, that noise, the people, the traffic. It was, to use a pithy American expression, something else. My most vivid recollection of the sights was the Camel Man, the huge advertising billboard showing a man smoking a cigarette. There is a hole in the board where the man's mouth is, from which he blows smoke (actually steam) rings in the air. For years that sign used to dominate the Square.

Afterward we went to my friend's home, where I spent the night. The next morning he drove me to Riverside Drive, to the home of Bernhard Kurrelmeyer and his wife, who were to be my official hosts during the forthcoming Physical Society meeting. He was on the physics faculty of

Columbia University. Their apartment gave a beautiful view of the Hudson River, and they were kind and gracious to me.

On my first day I strolled around in the neighborhood and bought my first pack of American cigarettes. I remember well what happened. I stepped into a small tobacco shop on upper Broadway and said "Good morning" to the man behind the counter. He looked at me, a bit strangely I thought, and said nothing. I walked up to him and said: "May I please have a package of Camels." Again that strange look, once more not a word, the cigarettes were laid on the counter. I paid and said: "Thank you very much. Good-bye." Silence again. I had the distinct impression that I had not handled myself correctly, so I lingered on a few moments to see what the next customer would do. Then I knew. The next day I went back to the store, no salutation, walked up to the counter, merely said: "Pack o' Camels," paid, and walked out in silence. That's how you do it. It may seem unfriendly to the new arrival, but actually it is not. Those are the local codes of conduct.

My host smiled when I told him of that experience. He remarked that at least I spoke English well (although still rather stilted, I may add), then told me the first truly American joke, the kind I would hear often in later times. An immigrant who just arrived and speaks no English is hungry. He goes to a drugstore, sits down at the counter, and waits for the man next to him to order. That person asks for apple pie and a cuppa coffee. Our man also orders apple pie and a cuppa coffee. He likes it and orders the same every day for a week. Then he decides the time has come to try something else. He goes back to the same counter and again waits for the man next to him to order—he wants a ham sandwich and a Coca Cola. The new immigrant orders the same. The soda jerk asks: "On white or on rye?" Our man answers: "Apple pie and a cuppa coffee."

That is humor American style, lean, no words wasted. Want to hear another one? What is the origin of the Grand Canyon? A Scotsman lost a nickel. By now I have a vast repertoire of such jokes and, if I may say so, tell them well.

The next day I had been invited for lunch in midtown by Karl Darrow, the secretary of the Physical Society. Professor Kurrelmeyer explained to me how to get there by subway and reminded me to get off at 125th Street on the way back. The lunch was most pleasant. All who knew him will remember Darrow for his slow, deliberate way of speaking. Afterward I went back by subway and got off where I had been told—but became rather upset when I found myself in a strange part of town. My host had taken for granted that I knew I should take the Broadway line—which I had not done. So I found myself in the heart of Harlem. I asked for directions and began to walk westward. On my way I saw something absolutely marvelous. Walking by a fruit stand, I saw bananas. Bananas! I had not seen one in six years! I bought half a dozen, happily eating one after the other on my way back.

14.3 The Physical Society Meeting. First Encounter
with Oppenheimer

The next day, Thursday, September 19, 1946, the Physical Society meeting began. It was held in midtown, in the building of the Engineering Societies. From the minutes of the meeting:

> This was a meeting of unprecedented character in more than one respect. It was confined to papers on three topics: cosmic-ray phenomena, theories of elementary particles, and the design and operation of accelerators of nuclear particles and electrons. Disparate as these three subjects may appear to be, the trend of physics is rapidly uniting them. . . . Many guests from overseas were present, some of whom had timed their visits to the United States in order to attend our meeting, while we ourselves had timed the meeting so as to suit the convenience of others who came to attend the Princeton University conference on nuclear science.[3]

It was the biggest physics meeting I had ever attended—and the hottest. From the minutes again: "Over a thousand people attended the meeting, and the great auditorium of the Engineering Society was frequently jammed, in spite of tropical conditions indoors and outdoors; for the weather did not cooperate, inflicting upon us a heat-wave such as would have been excessive in midsummer." For several reasons this meeting has remained clearly etched in my memory.

First, I met Professor Uhlenbeck again, for the first time since the summer of 1939. I was touched by the warmth of his greeting. During the break, he invited me to lunch together with his dear friend Samuel ("Sem") Goudsmit, whom I had never met before but who knew who I was (chapter 12, sec. 12.2.). We talked. As a well-bred Dutchman, I answered Uhlenbeck's questions with yes professor, no professor. After a while he peered at me, then said: "Why don't you call me George?" I may well have blushed. In any event, that question marked another rite of passage for me.

Kramers was at the meeting, too, having broken away from his busy schedule at Lake Success, then the site of the United Nations. I was sitting next to him at one of the sessions when I saw him scribble something on a slip of paper which he handed to me. It read (verbatim): "Turn around and pay your respects to Robert Oppenheimer." I turned and there, right behind me, sat the great man, who up to that moment had been known to me only from newspaper pictures. He grinned pleasantly at me and stretched out his hand, which I shook. Most remarkably—or so I thought—he sat there in a short-sleeved open shirt. I felt I had entered a new civilization, where you call professors by their first names and where esteemed gentlemen appear in public wearing neither jacket nor tie.

But most important to me was the fact that I had to address this huge audience myself. I was the last scheduled speaker in a session of invited papers. Other speakers were Rudolf Peierls from Birmingham, Walter Heitler from Dublin, and Oppenheimer from the University of California at Berkeley. The title of my talk was "Some General Aspects of the Self-Energy Problem."[4]

I was naturally quite nervous before I had to go up to the podium but became quite collected from the moment I started to speak—a sequence of reactions that has repeated itself to this day whenever I have to speak in public. As my talk progressed, I noticed some commotion in the hall. The chairman motioned to me to stop speaking. What had happened was that Felix Ehrenhaft had come toward the podium, loudly demanding to be heard. He was a physicist near age seventy, who had done decent physics in earlier years but had developed the fixed idea that there exist "sub-electrons," particles lighter than the lightest massive particle known. Some people calmed him down and led him away. Otherwise I can relate only what I find in my diary: "My talk did not make a deep impression."

On Friday evening a conference dinner was held at the Men's Faculty Club of Columbia University. I was seated well, together with Blackett from Manchester (whom I had met before; chapter 12, sec. 12.3), Dean George Pegram of Columbia, Oliver Buckley, president of Bell Labs, and Isidor Rabi, Columbia's most renowned physicist.

It was my first meeting with Raab (as friends used to call him) who, after a few pleasantries, fired this question at me: "Do you think the polarization of the vacuum can be measured?" I recall my astonishment at being in a new land where experimentalists would know, let alone bother, about vacuum polarization. Nor did Rabi's question stem from idle curiosity. A month later there appeared in the Quarterly Progress Report of the Columbia University Radiation Laboratory a proposal entitled "Microwave Physics: Experiment to Determine the Fine Structure of the Hydrogen Atom (Lamb, Rutherford)."[5] (More later on this experiment; see chapter 17, sec. 17.4).

I liked Rabi from the start. He invited me to a party at his home the following evening. The next day, Sunday, September 22, I took a train to Princeton.

14.4 FIRST DAYS IN PRINCETON

I made the short trip in the company of a few other physicists whom I had met at the New York meeting. Local colleagues were present at the station in Princeton, all new faces to me: John Wheeler, Eugene Wigner, and Howard Robertson, whom I knew to be a distinguished contributor to the theory of relativity.

Well before I had begun my American journey, Wheeler had written to Rosenfeld that he would arrange to find me a place to stay in Princeton. After the group had exchanged pleasantries, Wheeler drove me to my first American residence: 148 Hodge Road. I did not yet know that this was an address in Princeton's wealthy western section. Mr. and Mrs. Hugh McNair Kahler, my hosts, were waiting for me; they extended a cordial welcome and took me upstairs to my quarters, a light, airy room with a private bath.

On the day of arrival I wrote in my diary: "Arrived at Hodge Road. A beautiful house, a beautiful room, in a wonderfully quiet town. Where one works a lot and goes out little." Pretty accurate for a first impression.

I had no kitchen privileges, so I had to go out for dinner that night. (Later I acquired a toaster and a hotplate to make my own breakfast.) After getting directions, I walked to Nassau Street, Princeton's main drag, where I found an eatery called The Balt (long gone). It was not exactly chic—white tiled and lit by neon. I soon had my own name for it: The Urinal. Then back home and early to bed. The next day was to be a busy one, the beginning of the bicentennial physics conference, which I was to attend.

Before turning to those events, I should like to relate what my material conditions were at that time. How, for example, could I afford to live in the fancy quarters I had just moved into?

I already mentioned (chapter 12, sec. 12.4) that I had been awarded an annual stipend of $1,800 and that "you will study under the auspices of the Institute of International Education [IIE]."[6] During the course of that academic year, I was required to submit two reports to the IIE. Fortunately I still have a copy of the first of these,[7] from which I can deduce that, in 1946, $1,800 was good money.

According to my report, my travel expenses to the U.S. were $175. I paid $40 rent per month, and about $2.50 per day for meals. Health insurance cost me $15 for a twelve-month period. I had of course no car yet.

Some prices of that time (1946): A nickel for a cup of coffee and for the New York subway. Three cents bought you a first-class mail stamp, also a copy of the daily *New York Times*. Thirty cents for a ticket to the Playhouse, Princeton's best movie theater at the time.

Clearly, then, I could not afford extravaganzas but could live comfortably and even save a little for sending parcels to Holland.

14.5 PRINCETON'S BICENTENNIAL CONFERENCE. BOHR AGAIN

Among the events arranged to celebrate Princeton University's bicentennial were a series of topical conferences, starting out with one on physics. Its subject was "The Future of Nuclear Science." The meeting was held at the Graduate College.

On a wall on the second floor of Jadwin Hall, the present physics building—in those days the physics building was good old Palmer Laboratory—you will find a picture of the physics conference participants. Notably absent: Einstein. It was otherwise an impressive collection, including Homi Bhabha, Blackett, Gregory Breit, Percy Bridgman (he received the Nobel Prize later that year), Subrahmanyan Chandrasekhar, Arthur Compton, James Conant, Dirac, Lee Dubridge, Luther Eisenhart, Enrico Fermi, Kramers, Oppenheimer, the great astronomer Henry Norris Russell, Glenn Seaborg, Harold Urey, Wheeler, and Wigner. On the fourth row from the front you may note yours truly, standing between Bhabha, director of the Tata Institute in Bombay, and Conant, president of Harvard. I had entered the big time. A few Soviet physicists were present too; I do not remember their names. Also in attendance were some of the younger Princeton physicists. On the photograph you will find one of Wheeler's students; his name was Richard Feynman.

And then there was Bohr. We greeted each other warmly, had dinner together that first Monday evening, after which he asked me again to help him prepare his talk for the conference. This I did, as I had already promised in Tisvilde (chapter 13, sec. 13.7). I so much enjoyed the familiar long hours of working hard together, that evening, and also part of the next day, on his paper entitled "Observation Problems in Atomic Physics,"[8] one of his many public presentations of his complementarity arguments.

I know how well prepared Bohr was with carefully structured arguments. However, I recall my amazement at the talk he actually gave, which was done without a worked-out manuscript before him. I should say that this amazement was due to the fact that till then I had never heard Bohr speak publicly.

In attempting to describe the experience of listening to Bohr in public, I am reminded of a story about the violinist Eugène Ysaye, who at one time had a member of a royal family as his pupil. Another musician of great renown (to whom I owe this tale) once asked Ysaye how this pupil was doing, whereupon Ysaye lifted his hands heavenward and sighed: "Ah, her royal highness, she plays divinely bad."

However different the background was in the two cases, these are the words which best characterize the situation. Bohr was divinely bad as a public speaker.[9] This was not due to his precept never to speak more clearly than one thinks. Had he done so, the outcome would have been quite different, as he was a man of the greatest lucidity of thought. Nor was it entirely due to the fact that Bohr's voice did not carry far, which made it impossible to hear him at the back of a large audience. The main reason was that he was in deep thought as he spoke. I remember how that day he had finished part of the argument, then said "And . . . and . . . ," then was silent for at most a second, then said, "But . . . ," and continued. Between the "and" and the "but" the next point had gone through his mind. However, he simply forgot to say it out loud and went on somewhere further down the road. To me, the story was continuous as I knew precisely how to fill in the gaps Bohr had left open. And so it came to pass more than once that I saw an audience leave a talk by Bohr in a mild state of bewilderment, even though he had toiled hard in preparing himself in great detail. Still, when he would come up to me afterwards with the characteristic question: *"Jeg håber det var nogenlunde"* (I hope it was tolerable), I could assure him that it was much more than that. In spite of all the linguistic shortcomings, this unrelenting struggle for truth was a powerful source of inspiration.

At the same time, it should be emphasized that Bohr's best way of communicating actually was the spoken word, but with just one or at most a few persons present. Bohr's need for verbal expression was great, as the following occurrence may illustrate. On a later occasion (1948) Bohr arrived in Princeton after a trip by sea from Denmark. For about a week he had had no opportunity to discuss scientific matters; he was quite pent up. Wolfgang Pauli and I were walking in a corridor at the Institute for Advanced Study when Bohr first came in. When he saw us, he practically pushed us into an office, made us sit down, said, "Pauli, *schweig!*" (Pauli, shut up!), and then talked for about two hours before either of us had a chance to interrupt him. Had Bohr's words been recorded, it would have constituted a fascinating document on the development of quantum theory.

Other memories are still alive from that conference. During a break I stood talking with Bohr when a man came up to him, who introduced himself as Paul Schilpp. (In later discussions Bohr would invariably call him Quilpp.) He asked if Bohr would be interested in contributing to a book he planned to present to Einstein on his seventieth birthday in 1949.[10] Bohr replied that in principle he was much interested. More later about what came of this.

During another break Rabi came up to me to ask if I might consider spending the second semester of that academic year as guest lecturer at Columbia. I ended up not doing so.

By Wednesday, when the conference was over, the time had come for me to present myself at the Institute.

15

The State of the Union, 1946: The U.S., Princeton, and the Institute for Advanced Study

15.1 USA 1946: A SHORT SOCIAL HISTORY

ON THE SUNDAY that I arrived in Princeton, the bicentennial had been officially opened with a sermon by the Archbishop of Canterbury in the University Chapel, followed by an academic procession.[1] Also on that day, Mayor William O'Dwyer of New York City had proclaimed the next day as "End Lynching Day, in the hope that it will focus attention of all true Americans on a cruel and murderous cancer."[2] Also on that Monday, a letter by Einstein to President Harry Truman was made public which contains the phrase: "Security against lynching is one of the most urgent tasks of our generation."[3] It was an America very different from today; to be sure, not all of our civil rights problems are solved yet, but a single lynching would certainly unleash civil war.

One cannot put a precise date on when that change began. It is quite significant, however, that, at the end of 1952, the Tuskegee Institute (now University) in Alabama could report that the past year had been the first without a lynching since 1882, when that famed college for blacks had begun to keep files on such crimes.[4]

What was 1946 life otherwise in the United States? America had emerged from World War II as the world's most powerful economic nation. The armament program had ended the Great Depression of the 1930s. American productivity, though reduced by strikes (notably the coal miners' strike in April–May 1946) was phenomenal compared to the rest of the world, both agriculturally and industrially. I had arrived in a country of 140 million inhabitants where vigor and optimism reigned.

In 1946 the United Nations held its first General Assembly, in London. Within a few days the Soviets cast their first veto. Also, the U.N. voted to establish its permanent headquarters in New York City. John D. Rockefeller donated $8.5 million to buy the site, then a cattle pen area on the East River. Truman created the U.S. Atomic Energy Commission. The first atomic bomb tests were held in Bikini. In Fulton, Missouri, Churchill gave his Iron-Curtain-is-coming-down speech. The average wholesale price for an automobile was just under $1,000.[5] In November the Republican party won majorities in both houses of Congress. Abroad, the verdicts at the Nuremberg trials were handed down.

In sports, the U.S. won the Davis Cup, and St. Louis beat Boston in seven innings in the World Series. In the arts, Edmund Wilson published *Memoirs of Hecate County,* and Eugene O'Neill's *The Iceman Cometh* had its premiere. *Annie Get Your Gun* was the year's new musical, *The Best Years of Our Lives* the most talked-about new film. The French weighed in with *Les enfants du paradis.* W. C. Fields died.

I interject a precious personal memory about film. In 1946 I saw *Casablanca* for the first time; it had premiered in 1942, and I became an instant fan even though, then as later, I did not care much for Ingrid Bergman's acting. Like many others, I can recall some of the film's great lines: "Here's looking at you kid," Humphrey Bogart toasting Bergman; "Round up the usual suspects," police chief Claude Rains to his underlings; the refugee couple practicing English—"Which watch?" asks he. "Ten watch," replies she. "Such much," he responds. And the immortal "Play it, Sam. Play 'As Time Goes By,'" Bergman to Dooley Wilson, the pianist at Bogart's café. (She did not ask, "Play it again, Sam," the line made famous by the 1972 Woody Allen comedy.)

What else? Hit songs of the time still had that inane quality. Most popular in 1946: "Zip-a-dee-doo-dah" and "Shoe-fly Pie and Apple Pan Dowdy." Still popular then, though already a few years old: "Marzy Doats."

In that year I also heard my first radio commercials, for which I at once acquired a lasting hatred. Among the singing commercials of that time: "Pepsi-Cola hits the spot, twelve full ounces, that's a lot . . . ," and one I did like:

> I am Chiquita Banana and I've come to say
> Bananas should be eaten in a special way.

When they are freckled brown and are a yellow-gold in hue,

Bananas taste the best and are the best for you.

You can put them in a salad,

You can put them in a pie, ay,

Any way you want to eat them

It's impossible to beat them.

But bananas like the climate of the very very tropical equator

So don't you never put bananas

In a refrigerator, no-no-no-no.

I would regale my friends with this song on my subsequent trips to Europe, to the accompaniment of my guitar.

15.2 PRINCETON IN 1946, TOWN AND GOWN

Princeton, in Mercer County, New Jersey, fifty miles southwest of New York City, played an important role in the American war of independence. In January 1776, General George Washington and his troops defeated three British regiments and three companies of light artillery in the Battle of Princeton. From June 30 to November 4, 1783, Nassau Hall (named after William III, prince of Orange-Nassau, king of England), then as now Princeton University's handsome main building, was the seat of the Continental Congress. It was there that the news of the peace treaty with Great Britain was first officially received. It was also from there that Washington issued his "Farewell Address to the Armies."

When I arrived in Princeton it was a small town with some 25,000 residents, with no public transportation. If I remember correctly, there was only one stoplight, on the corner of Nassau and Witherspoon Streets. The town housed four well-known institutes of learning: the university, the Institute for Advanced Study, the Theological (Presbyterian) Seminary, and Westminster Choir College (now part of Rider University).

The university, the oldest of these, received its charter as the College of New Jersey in October 1746. Until the Civil War it was attended mainly by Southerners. Even when I arrived it was still known as "the beginning of the South." Its present name dates from 1896. Its most renowned president (from 1902 to 1910) was Woodrow Wilson, class of 1879, the first layman (i.e., non-clergy) to hold that office and later (1912–1921) president of the

United States. Contiguous to the university is Lake Carnegie, an artificial widening of the Millstone River and the gift of Andrew Carnegie.

In 1946 the university was fairly small, with about 3,500 students and 250 faculty. Today total enrollment is about 6,500, with 675 faculty. It has never had schools of medicine or law. In 1946 the student body was still all male, and remained so until 1969. There were no blacks on campus when I arrived; the first black American graduated from Princeton in 1953.

It was not long after I had settled in Princeton that I was invited to a party at the home of Harry Smyth (he of the Smyth Report), who at that time was head of the university's physics department. That evening he told me how happy he was that a black American had been admitted to the University. "You mean just one?" I asked. "Yes," he said. Whereupon I expressed with righteous indignation my views on equal rights for all races. He smiled. "I agree, of course," he replied, "but you should understand the game plan. First we asked for three blacks and got one. Next time we shall ask for maybe six and, maybe, get two or three. And so we move on." I thanked him for this explanation and was silent for the rest of the evening, digesting this sensible piece of practical civil rights polity.

15.3 HOW THE INSTITUTE CAME INTO BEING

The Institute for Advanced Study owes its origins and immediate renown to a bizarre confluence of factors: generous philanthropy, the Wall Street crash of 1929, and the rise of Nazism in the early 1930s.[6]

In 1929 Louis Bamberger, a lifelong bachelor, and his sister, Julie Carrie Fuld, a childless widow, were living on the thirty-acre Fuld Estate in South Orange, near Newark, New Jersey. Years earlier the family had started a quite modest retail business, which in time became Newark's finest department store. In the summer of 1929 they decided to sell the store to R. H. Macy & Co. and to devote their time and fortune to philanthropy. The sale was consummated in early September. They received $11 million in cash plus 69,210 shares of Macy's stock, which on September 4 reached a high of $255.50 a share on the New York Stock Exchange.

Six weeks later, on October 29, the stock market crashed. On November 13 the Macy shares had fallen to $110; by June 1932 they had sunk to $17. Whatever the Bambergers did with their shares, they still had $11 million in the bank.

These events marked the beginning of a tragic period in world history, yet in those very same years they led to the founding of an institution that would leave its glorious mark on the world of thought and learning.

From the outset the Bambergers wanted to direct their philanthropy toward the support for higher learning. Accordingly, they sought counsel from a recognized expert on that subject, Abraham Flexner.

Years earlier Flexner had been commissioned by the Carnegie Foundation for the Advancement of Teaching to survey the quality of medical colleges in the United States and Canada. In 1910 the Foundation published their Bulletin No. 4, which became known as the Flexner Report.[7] It exposed American medicine to be a shallow enterprise and made its author internationally renowned. In 1930 he accepted the Bambergers' invitation to guide and direct their plans.

Flexner began by analyzing the patterns of European institutions such as All Souls College in Oxford and the Collège de France in Paris. These studies resulted in a confidential memorandum to the Bambergers in which he proposed the creation of an Institute for Advanced Study. From his report: "The Institute will be neither a current university nor a research institution. . . . It may be pictured as a wedge between the two—a small university in which a limited amount of teaching and a liberal amount of research are both to be found. It should be small, its staff and students should be few, the administration should be inconspicuous. . . . I should, one by one . . . create a series of schools—in mathematics, in economy, in history, etc. . . . [The faculty will] know their own minds. . . . No organizer can do more than furnish conditions favorable to the restless prowling of an enlightened and informed human spirit."

Those visions, which were to turn into reality, were acceptable to the Bambergers. Accordingly, on May 20, 1930, the certificate of incorporation of the Institute was signed.[8] An initial donation of $5 million was made. Bamberger became the first president of the Board of Trustees, Flexner the first director (until 1939). Five months later, a press account appeared with the headlines: "Dr. Flexner says Bamberger new Institute bans collegiate ideas/University will be without rules/Athletics also banned," and reported that it will be "somewhere in or near New Jersey."[9]

Next Flexner turned to the recruitment of faculty. For that purpose he went in January 1932 on a visit to the California Institute of Technology, invited by Robert Millikan. That institution was of particular interest to him for his present purposes. It had started out in 1891 as Throop College, and had only recently been modernized under its new name with a much-expanded prominent faculty—just what Flexner was after.

By Flexner's own account, it was serendipitous that there in Pasadena he met, for the first time, Albert Einstein, who was a guest professor that winter term. Flexner of course used the opportunity to consult with the great man on his projects. When they met again, in Oxford in the spring of 1932, he asked Einstein if he might be interested in joining the Institute himself. During a third encounter the next June, this time in Einstein's summer house in Caputh, near Berlin, Einstein expressed enthusiasm about coming and requested an annual salary of $3,000. "He asked . . . could I live on less?"[10] Formal negotiations began at once. In October 1932 the appointment was approved, with an annual salary of $15,000.[11] Also that autumn, the appointment was made of the mathematician Oswald Veblen—the nephew of the social scientist Thorstein Veblen—who had been on Princeton University's faculty since 1905.

Einstein made his definitive move to Princeton in October 1933. On the 17th, he, his wife Elsa, his secretary Helen Dukas, and an assistant arrived in New York harbor. There they were met by two Institute trustees, who handed Einstein a letter from Flexner, which read in part: "There is no doubt whatsoever that there are organized bands of irresponsible Nazis in this country. I have conferred with the authorities [who have] given me the advice that your safety in America depends on silence and refraining from attendance at public functions. . . . In the long run your safety will depend on your discretion."[12] The party was taken by special tugboat from quarantine to The Battery, from where they were driven by car directly to Princeton.

I cannot shake my conviction that Flexner's advice to Einstein to keep a low profile was less the result of consultation with authorities than of his own fear, shared by many other American Jews, that the arrival of Jews from Europe would raise the level of anti-Semitism in America, which was not all that dormant to begin with. I have mentioned earlier (chapter 5) similar reactions by Dutch Jews to the influx of German-Jewish immigrants. It had also been so earlier with German Jews responding to waves of their brethren coming from Poland and Russia. Now the time had come for American Jews to feel the pinch.

This, it seems to me, explains the dangerous step that Flexner took next. By prearrangement he had been answering mail addressed to Einstein at the Institute before his arrival, consistently declining invitations to speak, to dine, to attend meetings, to sponsor causes, and so on. He did not offer to reroute this mail while the Einsteins were, with some difficulty, settling into a rented house. Thus he continued to decline invitations, not consulting them even about an invitation tendered by the president of the United States. Instead, Flexner declined it in a letter to President Roosevelt.[13] When Einstein heard what had been happening, he talked to Flexner, insisting in no uncertain terms that he should be free to do in his own personal life as he saw fit, or he would leave Princeton. Shortly thereafter peace was reestablished on Einstein's terms.

Otherwise Einstein's reception in the U.S. was enthusiastic. Already in January 1933, before his arrival, the legislature of the State of New Jersey had passed a resolution to "welcome the eminent professor to the State of New Jersey." On March 28, 1934, the House of Representatives in Washington, D.C., had passed a similar resolution. Two months earlier the president had repeated his invitation to the White House; Einstein and his wife stayed with the Roosevelts and spent a night in the Franklin Room. Einstein's friend and colleague Paul Langevin is reported to have said about Einstein's move to America: "It is as important an event as would be the transfer of the Vatican from Rome to the New World. The pope of physics has moved and the United States will now become the center of the natural sciences."

Twelve more professional appointments were made in the 1930s. In mathematics (year of appointment and country of birth in parentheses): James Alexander (1933, U.S.), Marston Morse (1935, U.S.), John von Neumann (1933, Hungary), and Hermann Weyl (1933, Germany). In economics: David Mitrany (1933, Romania), Winfield Riefler (1935, U.S.), Walter Stewart (1938, U.S.), and Robert Warren (1939, U.S.). Also Edward Earle (1934, U.S.) in political history; Erwin Panofsky (1935, Germany) in history of art; Hetty Goldman in archeology; and Elias Lowe (1936, U.S.) in paleography. Hitler's contribution to this elite group will be obvious. Thus came into being the Institute's three initial schools: of mathematics, including physics; of economics and politics; and of humanistic studies. The Institute began operations in October 1933. From that time on through 1938 its official address was 20 Nassau Street, Princeton. The Institute was open year-round, but term times were short: from mid-September–mid-December, and from late January—late April. And so it has remained.

Additional temporary appointments of junior people were made from the start. Through 1935 Institute *Bulletins* listed them as "workers," initially all in the school of mathematics. The *Bulletin* for 1934 lists twenty-three: six from Europe, seventeen from the U.S. Beginning in 1936 they were called "members." Academic 1935–36 saw the arrival of the first non-mathematics members. By 1938, members from eighteen foreign countries had been in attendance. Furthermore, scientists of high distinction were invited to come; in physics: Dirac (in academic 1934–35), Pauli (1935–36; he also spent the war years in Princeton, from 1940 to 1946), Niels Bohr, and I. I. Rabi (both for part of 1938–39). Where did all these people find working space?

Arrangements were made with the university to rent space for the mathematicians and physicists in Fine Hall, the gracious old mathematics building (now Jones Hall). Humanists found their quarters in McCormick Hall. The Institute bought a large old residence at 69 Alexander Street and remodeled it for use as offices, where they installed the economists. (The house was sold during the war.)

Until late 1939 there were no meetings of the faculty as a whole—Flexner did not approve of them. Beginning on October 8, 1935, the School of Mathematics faculty did meet on its own, however, and Veblen became the powerful though unofficial leader of that group. It may be noted that he led opposition to Einstein, for example refusing funds for an assistant. The reason was presumably the mathematicians' insistence on keeping mathematics "pure" (more about that later). Einstein's lack of success in formulating a unified field theory and his critical position toward quantum theory may also have been contributing factors.

Aided by his appointment to the Board of Trustees, Veblen became the power broker of the faculty, often at odds with the director. He made himself responsible for many business affairs and played a role in the selection of new faculty members. His colleagues were complaisant with his control as long as they got what they needed—which was not always the case. And so, since its early years, the Institute has served as an apt example of the dictum that academic politics is such a big thing because its problems are so small.

Meanwhile a committee with the directive to choose a site for Institute buildings had been constituted. It had already begun its deliberations in December 1931. The founders had expressed the desire to house the Institute in Newark, preferably on the Fuld Estate. This idea was abandoned after outside advisers had opposed the idea. In 1935 a consensus developed to buy the Olden Farm in Princeton—265 acres of field, woodland, and meadows. Olden Manor, the old colonial house on the farm, would eventually become the director's home. In 1938 construction was put in the hands of the Hegemann-Harris firm of New York at an estimated cost of $312,000. By the time Fuld Hall, the main building, was completed, the total cost (including furnishings) had come to $520,000. The top floor of the Hall housed a cafeteria and a board room. The Bambergers provided additional funds, and by 1952 their total gifts had risen to $16 million, including the $9 million Bamberger had left as a residual estate upon his death in 1944.

In 1939, the year of completion of Fuld Hall, Flexner resigned as director, no doubt worn out by quarrels with his faculty. He was succeeded by Frank Aydelotte, president of Swarthmore College, who, on November 24, 1939, called the first full faculty meeting, held in Fuld Hall. It was fitting that the first order of business would deal with a resolution of thanks from faculty and trustees to Dr. Flexner.

The main contribution of Aydelotte was the introduction in 1944 of Institute Fellows, mainly recent postdocs appointed for one or two years. No further professional appointments were made during his tenure.

One last item concludes my brief account of the Institute's beginnings: the acquisition of the Gest Oriental Library.

Guion Moore Gest was the head of a New York engineering firm that had business abroad. On a journey to China he met Commander I. V. Gillis, the U.S. Naval Attaché in Peking, who interested him in Chinese books on eye medicine (Gest suffered from glaucoma). Gest left money with Gillis to procure the books for him. Thus began the Gest Oriental Library. Gillis inspired Gest to collect Chinese books far beyond the original scope. He later resigned his commission to become Gest's adviser and agent in the acquisition of books.

In 1937 the Institute purchased the Gest collection, assisted by a grant of $62,500 from the Rockefeller Foundation,[14] with the understanding that it was to be administered as part of the Princeton University Library. The collection was initially installed at 20 Nassau Street, but in 1948 it was moved into the Firestone Library. It is now on permanent loan in the library of the Gest Institute in the top floor of Palmer Hall.

The Gest collection is matchless among all Chinese collections outside of China and Japan. It contains books printed well before the appearance of the Gutenberg Bible (book shops have been recorded in China as early as the first century A.D.), and a large collection of manuscript volumes, the oldest of which dates from the sixth century and is a copy of chapters from a Buddhist *sutra*. The library contains some seven hundred books from the Sung (960–1279), 1,700 from the Yüan (1279–1368), and 24,000 from the Ming (1368–1644) dynasties. By 1965 the Gest collection comprised 190,000 books, of which over 100,000 are stitched volumes (ts'ê).[15]

This completes my outline of the Institute's history up to the time I set foot there.

16

Enter Einstein and Other
Interesting New Acquaintances

IN WESTERN EUROPE, the intense feelings of joy that had greeted the end of war had been short-lived. Fatigue, a sense of material impoverishment, and other grim realities of the early postwar period rapidly made themselves felt. The need for continued rationing did not help either.

These circumstances contributed mightily to anti-American sentiments of envy, widespread in those days. On my short trip to England in December 1945 (chapter 12), I had heard these feelings encapsulated like this: Americans are wonderful people. They have three shortcomings, however: they are overfed, oversexed, and over here. I am not sure when "Yankee go home" began to be a much-used slogan, which even today has not gone out of fashion. It could well date from that period.

Anti-American prejudice, common then in European intellectual circles—especially among the French, provincial as always, vide Jean-Paul Sartre—had also infected me. Did we not have better manners, were we not better educated—in a word, were we not more cultured than they? It would take some time before I could sufficiently distinguish between being better and being different. In fact, after having been in America for only a few months, I believed myself to be capable of writing an essay on American life and style. I did not do so then but now wish I had—so that today I could revisit those superficial and short-sighted early impressions. A line in a letter I wrote at that time from Princeton to Aage Bohr, Niels's son, gives some of the flavor of my preconceived notions: "It is certainly a great thing, this visit to the land of the Free. You remember the vaguely uncanny feelings I had about a land where everybody is crazy. It is not as bad as that. Some are far more crazy than I thought, some less."[1]

I already mentioned earlier (chapter 14) a couple of occasions at which I noticed cultural differences: for example, the style between Old World and New World professors, and the way you buy a pack of cigarettes. I now add a few more early experiences.

On baseball. During my first week in Princeton I took a break several times from the bicentennial conference to buy myself a cup of late afternoon tea, a pleasant European custom. I would walk from the Graduate College to Renwick's, an eatery on Nassau Street (it is now a jewelry store), sit down at one of the small tables in the back, and have my tea. One day, a man who was sitting at the next table turned to me and asked: "How is the game?" I asked: "What game?" He said: "The Series." I asked: "What is that?" The man looked at me as if he were seeing a creature from another planet—which, you might say, he indeed did—got up without saying another word, left his tip, and walked out. As I found out soon enough, that had been my first encounter with a baseball fan. If you are puzzled about the World Series being played in September, remember that until 1961 both major leagues consisted of eight clubs only and were not yet split into an Eastern and Western Division, so that the baseball season ended earlier than it does now. No Mister October in those days, my friends.

On my first acquaintance with *The New Yorker* weekly. Until then I had regarded the British weekly *Punch* as the epitome of wit. When I glanced through my first *New Yorker*s and studied their cartoons I could not understand the point of almost any of them. Why were they supposed to be funny? As I was to learn before long, I could not see their point because they referred to local situations, and, more generally, American and European humor is different. For example, I remember a cartoon by Curtis Arnoux Peters, who drew under the name Peter Arno. It showed a sexy young blonde sitting on a bar stool. Behind her stands a distinguished-looking older man. He says to the bartender: "Fill 'er up." I could understand the meaning of the words, but what was the joke? I did not yet know that, when you drive your car into a gas station and want the tank completely filled, that is what you say to the attendant. Gradually, I learned to appreciate highly the Arno cartoons, also those by Helen Hokinson. Now, when I see the low quality of today's *New Yorker* cartoons, for example those of Roz Chast, I can grow nostalgic for the good old days.

On student pranks. Princeton's best movie house (long gone) was the Playhouse, one of my favorite haunts. While I was there one evening, the show was interrupted by hysterical shrieks from women in the audience. It turned out that a student had smuggled in a greased little pig which he had let loose, to the delight of his friends and also of me. Lights went on, ushers went on a chase, order was restored. I regret to say that we European students were less exuberant back home.

On the harshness of the weather. On a day in December 1947, a young mathematician friend of mine from the Institute invited me to join him on a ski trip to New Hampshire, which I gladly accepted. On December 25 we drove in his car to New York, where we spent Christmas and the following night at his parents' home, and from where we would continue north the next day. When I got out of bed the next morning, December 26, and looked out of the window, all the parked cars were gone! There had been a blizzard during the night, 26.1 inches had fallen,[2] snow drifts had buried all cars on the street below. Having grown up in temperate climates, I had seen snow, of course, but never as much and coming down as abruptly as this. As I was to learn soon, temperature jumps within a few hours of twenty or thirty degrees Fahrenheit were not frequent, but not rare either. I had to adjust to a much more violent climate than I had been accustomed to.

We went down to dig out the car, as others were doing with theirs. I was struck by the way people would help each other. Dutch and Danes are friendly people too, yet the way Americans are always willing to lend a hand at moments of trouble has continued to impress me during later years. This blizzard was exceptional even by American standards. As I write this, shortly after the New York blizzard of March 13, 1993 (which I also had the pleasure of attending), the one of '47 remains the biggest one in the record books for the metropolitan area as far as snow accumulation is concerned.

In the beginning I regarded experiences such as these as minor curiosa. It would take some years before I began to realize them to be manifestations of more general cultural patterns.

Later I will say more about differences between the cultures of Europe and America. For now only one further comment. During the physics meetings in New York and Princeton, recounted earlier, I had been in touch with groups of highly distinguished scientists—hardly a typical cross-section of the American population. For better or worse, it has been my fate to spend the rest of my life, to this day, amidst the scholarly elite, most particularly in my Princeton years. That has no doubt marked me. Had that been my only contact with the outside world, I would never have acquired any grasp of American—or any other—realities. I regard it as most fortunate that I have never been content to confine myself to such a clannish lifestyle. Only a small fraction of my close friends are scientists.

As to America, I have crossed the country often, and have visited some forty of the fifty states for shorter or longer times. And still I would not presume to say that I know America. I do not even really know New York, where I have had residences for the last forty years. Among the great appeal the States have for me are their vastness, diversity—culturally, ethnically, geographically—and its unknowability, in full. I have surely learned a great deal about my new country—but am still in need of learning more.

I turn to my early times at the Institute.

16.2 Arrival at the Institute

My first day at the Institute began with a call on Frank Aydelotte, its director. He turned out to be an amiable man in his mid-sixties. I remember practically nothing about him, except that he had unusually large ears.

One of the first things Aydelotte told me was that Pauli had recently left for Zurich to reassume his professorship there. That was a real setback. Remember (chapter 12) that Pauli's presence in Princeton held the Institute's appeal for me.

Next I was told which office had been assigned to me. It was on the third floor of Fuld Hall and turned out to be a pleasant space. I emptied some papers from my briefcase on my new desk, and sat down. Work could begin.

It may well have been at that moment that the enormity of the transition from Europe to the United States sank in for the first time. The previous two weeks had been rich in new experiences, especially because I had just met so many new, highly interesting people. Such episodes do not lend themselves to quiet reflection. Now, at my desk, I was overwhelmed by intense feelings of loneliness—not a mood conducive to creative thought.

It would take some more time before I realized that there was an additional reason that kept me from getting to work right away: I was still suffering from postwar trauma. More about that in a while. In any event, my first year at the Institute was unproductive. That, for an ambitious young man, was of course painful. As will be evident shortly, however, it was otherwise a time rich in many new experiences.

By the time I arrived, the Institute was faced with a housing crisis. It had become impossible to find living quarters in town for the growing number of temporary members and visitors. Building was quite difficult since materials and labor were virtually unavailable. The problem was solved, at least for the time being, when the trustees were able to purchase from the Federal Public Housing Authority eleven prefab buildings containing apartments for thirty-eight families. During the summer of 1946 these were transported to Institute land from their location at Mineville, New York, and they were set up by late 1946. They were no bargain. Yet they had plumbing fixtures and other things which did not become available on the consumer's market for some time.

The following event will illustrate that their structure was less than solid. It happened one evening some years later that a colleague of mine and his wife were sitting in the living room of one of those apartments, reading quietly, when suddenly a wall of the room burst open and in rode a vigorous child of their neighbor's on his tricycle. These buildings have been torn down long since and were replaced by more modern brick and glass structures.

I made new acquaintances at the afternoon tea that was—and still is— served every weekday between three and four in the Common Room on the main floor in Fuld Hall. I would spend a good deal of that tea hour browsing through the foreign daily papers available there on racks—*Neue Zürcher Zeitung, Frankfurter Allgemeine,* and others. I became particularly fond of reading the Court Circular in the *London Times,* finding its elegance and irrelevance oddly entertaining. To know which of the Royals opened what exhibitions, which equerry or lady-in-waiting was in attendance, who used the Queen's Flight, might perhaps affect the course of Empire, but not much else.

During my first academic year at the Institute, hardly any junior physicists were there besides myself. I remember in fact only one: Shih-Tsun Ma, a gifted young Chinese man. I did have contact with some of the university's young people, however, notably with Arthur Wightman, one of John Wheeler's graduate students, who would develop into a prominent mathematical physicist at Princeton University and who would become a friend of mine. He and Anna-Greta, his wife, showed me the sights in the area. I recall in particular a visit to the Walker-Gordon dairy farm, where I saw its famous rotolactor in action, a contraption capable of milking fifty cows every ten minutes. One of the infamous smells that would hang over Princeton when the wind was "right" was that of the farm's cow dung.

My most interesting new experiences at that time, however, were meeting some of the senior people around.

16.3 A New Friend: Panofsky

It wasn't long before I met all the faculty members (listed in chapter 15, sec. 15.3). The ideal opportunity for doing so was to join them for lunch, which was then served in a space on the fourth floor of Fuld Hall. They were a group of uncommonly fascinating people.

It was a delight to have lunch with them. These occasions invariably turned into unplanned symposia. Someone would broach a topic, be it in history, art history, politics, economics, or what have you. In no time this led to animated discussions from which I learned a lot. Now, many years after having left the Institute, those lunches remain my fondest memory of my Princeton years.

One of the professors—we soon became friends—was the art historian Erwin Panofsky, Pan to his friends. His wife's first name was Dora, so it became inevitable that she was known as Pandora. They had two sons, very bright. The older, Hans, known as Paf, became a distinguished meteorologist; Wolfgang, the younger, known as Pief, became a renowned physicist. (Pief will reappear later in this book.) It must have been an unusual family circle, especially if you knew Pan's dictum: children should neither be seen nor heard until they can quote Virgil in Latin.

Pan's knowledge of Renaissance art was legendary already then. I will give an example. One day, on a visit to the Metropolitan Museum of Art in New York, I saw a painting entitled *The Miracles of San Zenobio* (I forget who was the artist). The canvas was divided into subpanels, each of which showed one or another miraculous act performed by the good saint. I had no idea what these were. So a few days later, back in Princeton, I called Pan to ask for enlightenment. He asked if I would be free that afternoon at four. Yes, I would be. Could I then come to his office. Yes, I could, and did. Whereupon Pan lectured to me for the next two hours, just about that one painting. It was private education at the highest level.

On March 21, 1968, I attended a commemorative gathering for Panofsky, who had died one week earlier, held at the Institute for Fine Arts of New York University. Short addresses were given by several friends and colleagues.[3] One of them quoted Pan's epitaph to himself, written in 1945, in a letter to a friend:

> He hated babies, gardening, and birds;
> But loved a few adults, all dogs, and words.

Another said: "All of us have passed our adult years in Panofsky's ambience. It has been like living next door to a lighthouse."

16.4 ANOTHER NEW FRIEND: VON NEUMANN

Before meeting John von Neumann, I got to know another faculty member, the German mathematician Carl Ludwig Siegel, appointed to the faculty in 1945 and at that time considered to be the most important mathematician in the world after Hermann Weyl, another faculty member.[4] He was also known for his bizarre sense of humor. One story about him goes like this. At one time he gave a course at some German university which was so advanced that only two students dared to follow it. These two lived in the same quarter of town and would come together to class by tram. One day the tram was delayed for twenty minutes by a traffic accident. When the students arrived belatedly in the classroom they found Siegel there, all alone, in the course of delivering his lectures before empty benches. Afterwards Siegel is supposed to have said triumphantly: "And they never caught up." My relations with him became friendly, though we did not become friends.

I did become good friends with another mathematics professor, John von Neumann, however. In my life I have met men even greater than Johnny, but none as brilliant. He shone not only in mathematics but was also fluently multilingual and particularly well versed in history. He also could recite a huge collection of limericks, and taught me the only one in French I have ever heard:

> Il y avait un jeune homme de Dijon,
> Qui ne croyait pas à la religion.
> Il disait: Bien ma foi,
> J'm'en fou d'tous les trois
> Le Père et le Fils et le Pigeon.

The day after he had told me that one I came back to him with an English translation:

> There was a young fellow from Digeon,
> Who did not believe in religion.
> He said: I admit
> I don't give a shit
> For the Father, the Son, and the Pigeon.

I also had a German translation ready, based on rhyming Glaube (faith) with Taube (dove).

Johnny was also deeply interested in current political events, but there our opinions differed sharply. I remember a party we both attended, it must have been sometime in 1947 or '48. The discussion turned on U.S.-Soviet relations. I was shocked to hear John proclaim, very calmly, that in his opinion the best thing to do was to annihilate Soviet power right away with atomic bombs. Like other Hungarian-born physicists I have come to know, Johnny was virulently anti-Communist.

Von Neumann was one of the rare mathematicians with whom I could talk physics. We physicists use mathematics as a tool and treat it with respect but not always with the same rigor that mathematicians do. As is well known in my profession, this often makes an exchange of views with mathematicians difficult if not impossible—but not with Johnny. Which explains, incidentally, why during the war he had been such a highly valued consultant at the Los Alamos atomic bomb laboratory. It was said that the Pentagon considered him as important as a whole army division.

I once came to him with a mathematics problem that had arisen in my own work and which I could not solve. He listened, then said he did not know the answer either but would think about it. Two weeks later (by that time I had figured it out by myself) I received an eight-page letter from him, posted in Los Alamos, in which he gave the solution.

At the time I first met von Neumann, his Electronic Computer Project had just begun. Computers have a long and venerable history, going back five thousand years to the abacus. I limit myself—if for no other reason than that my knowledge of this history is quite skimpy—to mentioning that automated devices appeared already in the seventeenth century, associated with such famous names as Blaise Pascal and Gottfried Leibnitz, who was the first to construct a machine that could automatically add, subtract, multiply, and divide. In the nineteenth century, Charles Babbage conceived of the first automated digital computer. The earliest prototype of a digital computer that used electronics was constructed shortly before World War II. The Princeton computer belongs to this class.

Records show that this enterprise had been broached for the first time to the Institute's faculty during its meeting of September 17, 1945; and that the Board of Trustees had first been briefed the following December. On May 3, 1946, von Neumann had proposed to house it in a separate building right next to the Institute. In the faculty meeting of May 14, 1946, Siegel commented famously that he did not see the need for such a computer.

When he needed a logarithm, he said, he did not even look it up in a table but rather computed it by hand.

The computer building was completed in early 1947. The construction was partly supported by the Office of Naval Research and by the Radio Corporation of America (now RCA), which recently had established its own laboratories near Princeton. The formal dedication of the computer, a gala affair, did not occur until June 10, 1952. By then the machine had already been in use for some time, however. The first large problem—dealing with thermonuclear processes—was run in 1951; it required hundreds of hours of computation. The expectation was that this computer would be a powerful research tool in the investigation of fundamental problems in dynamical meteorology, and would make possible for the first time a direct attack on the problems—which, Johnny once said, were too complex to solve on the back of an envelope—of weather prediction by numerical methods.

With the success of a series of numerical experiments leading to the development of a model in 1953 by which the generation of storms could be predicted, the civil and military forces of the government took over the project in meteorology and the men connected with it left the Institute in 1956. In 1957 the computer was given to Princeton University, where it was used for another three years, then decommissioned. Parts of the computer are now in the National Museum of American History (Smithsonian Institution), in Washington, D.C.

It is a fitting place for this totally obsolete machine to rest in peace. What was it like, what could it do? It weighed about one thousand pounds, occupied thirty-six cubic feet, and needed twenty-eight kilowatts power. Fifteen tons of air-conditioning kept down the heat generated by several thousand vacuum tubes (used also in radios in those days). It could perform a few thousand multiplications or divisions per second, about twenty times as many additions. Its principal novelty was that it was the first computer capable of storing programs in its innards.

What has happened since? Transistors, which made radio tubes obsolete, had already been discovered in 1948 but did not come on the market until 1959. Next, chips came into use in the late 1960s. The resulting, perhaps most revolutionary, advances in technology of our century have made computers faster, smaller, and cheaper. Example: a young colleague, working a few doors away from me, has a desk computer that costs less than $10,000 and digests 85 mips = millions of instructions per second.

A few more words on von Neumann. In 1954 he was invited to become a member of the Atomic Energy Commission (AEC). After approval by President Eisenhower, he took a leave from the Institute. In 1956 he was diagnosed to have cancer and entered Walter Reed Hospital in Bethesda, Maryland. He continued his duties by direct telephone line to the AEC offices, and was driven by ambulance to meetings he attended in a wheelchair. His health steadily declined, however, and on February 8, 1957, he died at Walter Reed, only fifty-three years old. He will briefly reappear in what follows.

16.5 GETTING TO KNOW DIRAC

I had first met Dirac on a visit to his home in England (chapter 12, sec. 12.3) but only began to know him really well during the fall term of 1946, which he spent at the Institute. We would frequently lunch together. In the course of these pleasant occasions I became exposed for the first time to Dirac's style of conversing: concise, crisp, no words minced, treating each topic exhaustively.

A first example. Still in the European mode, I would always have sandwiches for lunch. Having a huge appetite, I would get three of them. This led to the following dialogue between Dirac and me. You must imagine half a minute's pause between my response and his next query.

> DIRAC: Do you always have sandwiches for lunch?
> PAIS: Yes.
> D: Do you always have three sandwiches for lunch?
> P: Most of the time.
> D: Do you always choose the same three sandwiches for lunch?
> P: No. It depends on my taste that day.
> D: Do you eat your sandwiches in any fixed order?
> P: No.

When Dirac returned to the Institute to spend academic 1947–48, we would resume our joint lunches. By then my appetite had diminished somewhat and I now bought myself only two sandwiches. On the first day that we ate together again, Dirac looked at my plate and said, rather triumphantly, "You now eat only two sandwiches for lunch."

A few years later a young man came to the Institute from Cambridge, England. He called on me with a message: Professor Dirac sends best regards and wants to know if you still eat sandwiches for lunch. Typical Dirac.

One further example. During his 1946 stay, Dirac's office was next to mine. One day I was in my office when someone knocked on the door; it was Dirac. He said, "My wife wants to invite you for dinner tonight if you are free." I replied that I was grateful but could not make it because of another commitment. Whereupon he said, "Good-bye," and left. No social comment such as "I am sorry," or "Perhaps some other time." Nothing unfriendly implied. The question had been posed. The answer had been given. That sufficed. Typical Dirac.

We talked a lot together about physics. He was quite interested in my earlier work on quantum electrodynamics, a subject of which he was in fact the one and only founding father. I came to know his deep concern with the problem of the infinities (mentioned earlier, chapter 13, sec. 13.4), and his strong conviction—which he maintained throughout his life—that this indicated something so wrong with the theory that its basic tenets needed overhauling. I would say that I understood his point of view but did not share his hopes for the alternative approaches that had already consumed him for some time.

In the course of these encounters—and also later ones, to which I shall return—I came to know Dirac quite well. A friendship developed. He was a very private man, however, not much given to reminiscing about other personalities or past events. He would only rarely talk about himself. I, therefore, never felt close to having a well-rounded picture of his personality. In particular, much about the years of his youth has remained obscure to me. On a few occasions, he would reveal some of his emotions in his writings, however. Notable are his rare utterances about anxiety. When, at age sixty, he was asked about his feelings on discovering the Dirac equation (chapter 6), he replied: "Well, in the first place, it leads to great anxiety as to whether it's going to be correct or not . . . I expect that's the dominating feeling. It gets to be rather a fever."[5] At age sixty-seven: "Hopes are always accompanied by fears, and, in scientific research, the fears are liable to become dominant."[6] At age sixty-nine: "I think it is a general rule that the originator of a new idea is not the most suitable person to develop it, because his fears of something going wrong are really too strong."[7]

Finally, two more Dirac stories.

Once, Dirac and the famous British author Edward Morgan Forster met at a dinner in Cambridge. The tale of the exchange between them, in its entirety, has been told often:

> D: What happened in the cave?
> F: I don't know.

That version is apocryphal, however. The English physicist Rudolf Peierls told me that he had asked Dirac what was really said, and got this answer:

> D: Was there a third person in that cave?
> F: No.

The other story is not about Dirac, but one that I have heard Dirac tell more than once, with relish. In a small village, a newly appointed priest went to call on his parishioners. On a visit to a quite modest home, he was received by the lady of the house. He could not fail to notice that the place was teeming with children and asked her how many the couple had. Ten, she replied, five pairs of twins. Astonished, the priest asked: "You mean you always had twins?" To which the woman replied: "No, Father, sometimes we had nothing." Precision at that level had an immense appeal to Dirac.

16.6 OSWALD VEBLEN. BOHR AGAIN

One day in early 1947, Oswald Veblen asked my help in a delicate matter. He had received an indignant letter from the eminent Soviet theoretical physicist Vladimir Fok, in which it was alleged that a paper by a young member of the Institute that had come out in the November 1946 issue of the *Physical Review* had been plagiarized from an article by Fok.[8] Veblen asked me please to check that, which I did. My finding astonished me. The article was indeed a word-for-word translation of Fok's paper. I told Veblen, who took care of it. I do not recall the outcome of the case.

Veblen and I got along well. Once he invited me for lunch at the Nassau Club. During the meal he asked me about my scientific education. I told him that it had serious gaps, especially in mathematics, due to years of isolation during the war. Veblen was not moved. It is an advantage, he said, to be left alone for some time, because that frees the mind for its own pursuits. I have remembered that.

Our conversation turned to Einstein. Veblen clearly did not feel like discussing the great man's current research but made an interesting remark about Einstein's famous letter of August 1939 to Roosevelt, in which he drew the president's attention to the feasibility of atomic weapons.[9] Veblen told me that earlier in 1939 he had received a visit from Leo Szilard and Eugene Wigner, who wanted to ask his counsel on how to approach the president regarding the possibility of producing atomic bombs. Veblen suggested they involve Einstein, which they did, and which in turn led to the mentioned letter.

Another remark by Veblen that I recall: he told me that for many years he noted down titles of books he wanted to read, but not until his retirement; currently he was too busy with mathematics and administration. Unfortunately, he was going blind, and he had to have those books read to him.

A propos mathematics. One day Veblen asked me to give him my opinion about a physics manuscript by a young mathematician. I took it with me, sat down, and began to read. The first sentence began something like: Consider a Banach space. I got scared and said to myself, I must get out of here; I had never even heard of a Banach space. I returned the paper to Veblen, telling him I was ashamed to confess that it went over my head. Not to worry, he replied.

Veblen had also been present at a lecture on quantum field theory I had given at the Institute, in October 1946. So were Dirac, Weyl, von Neumann, Wheeler, and Alfred North Whitehead, the renowned mathematician from Harvard, who had deep interests in the foundations of physics, and who was on a short visit. Some audience.

Also present was Bohr, who expressed himself satisfied with the talk, and urged me to publish (which I did not).

After the Princeton bicentennial, Bohr had stayed on in the U.S. until late November, making his headquarters at the Institute but spending much of his time away on trips. Their main purpose was to contact politicians, Bernard Baruch and Trygve Lie, the secretary-general of the United Nations, for example, whom he tried to convince of his ideas on an open world.[10]

We did see each other numerous times, however. I find a note in my diary about an evening at the Smyths' during which Bohr told how, around 1936, Szilard came from England to see him about an idea he had about explosions caused by nuclear chain reactions initiated by slow neutrons. He proposed to organize a worldwide group of several hundred nuclear physicists who would circulate research papers on this subject among each other, but would otherwise keep this work secret, in order to leave the military out of it! His physical idea was dead wrong.[11] As Szilard's friend Wigner has written in an obituary: "The original basis of Szilard's conviction turned out to be erroneous, but he tenaciously held on to his idea, and indeed it came to fruition when nuclear fission, discovered in 1939, provided the missing key."[12]

It became clear to me that Bohr did not think much of Szilard, an opinion I came to share in later years, when I occasionally would meet him.

Also in that period I accompanied Bohr on a week's trip to MIT and Harvard, during which both he and I gave a lecture. On that occasion I met Victor ("Viki") Weisskopf for the first time. We got along famously from the beginning and to this day are good friends.

And, of course, Bohr and I talked at length about my plans for the future.

16.7 First Encounter with Einstein

One day, it was in October, Bohr came into my office. He was agitated, saying, "I am sick of myself, I am sick of myself." I was concerned, never having seen him upset before, and asked what had happened.

The reason for Bohr's despair was that he had just spent an hour with Einstein during which he had tried to convince him of his (Bohr's) complementarity concept. Once again he had failed, as he had many times before.

In briefest terms, the two men's intellectual conflict can be stated like this. In contravention to Bohr's view that a phenomenon is only defined if one specifies the experimental equipment with which observations are made,[13] Einstein maintained that a satisfactory physical description should be independent of that specification. He had coined the term "objective reality" for this notion of his.

Not long after that meeting, Bohr, wanting to talk some more with Einstein, proposed to take me along and introduce me. Until that day I had not even seen the great man. We went down to his office, one floor below mine. (That office is now a reading room for mathematical journals.) On that first encounter Einstein greeted a rather awed young man with a friendly smile and outstretched hand. The conversation turned to the quantum theory. I listened as the two of them argued. I recall no details but remember distinctly my first impressions. They liked and respected each other. With a fair amount of passion they were talking past each other. From our many previous discussions, I could follow Bohr's reasoning, but I did not understand what Einstein was talking about.

Not long thereafter I encountered Einstein in front of the Institute, told him that I had not followed his argument with Bohr, and asked if I could come to his office some time for further enlightenment. He invited me to walk home with him.

Thus began a series of discussions, always in German, that continued for nine years, until shortly before his death. I would visit him in his office or accompany him on his lunchtime walk home, often together with his good friend, the logician Kurt Goedel. Less often I would visit him at his home at

112 Mercer Street. He came to my apartment only once, to participate in a discussion on the Oppenheimer hearings (about which more later). In all I saw him about once every few weeks.

Whenever I met Einstein, our conversation might range far and wide but invariably the discussion would turn to physics. Such discussions would touch only occasionally on matters of past history. We talked mainly about the present and the future. When relativity was the issue, he would often talk of his efforts to unify gravitation and electromagnetism and of his hopes for the next steps. His faith rarely wavered in the path he had chosen. Only once did he express a reservation to me when he said, in essence, "I am not sure that differential geometry is the framework for further progress, but, if it is, then I believe I am on the right track." (This remark must have been made at some time during his last few years.)

The main topic of discussion, however, was quantum physics. Einstein never ceased to ponder the meaning of the quantum theory. Time and time again, the argument would turn to quantum mechanics and its interpretation. He was explicit in his opinion that the most commonly held views on this subject could not be the last word, but he also had more subtle ways of expressing his dissent. For example, he would never refer to a wave function as *die Wellenfunktion* but would always use the mathematical term *die Psifunktion*. I was never able to arouse much interest in him about the new particles that appeared on the scene in the late 1940s and especially in the early 1950s. It was apparent that he felt that the time was not ripe to worry about such things and that these particles would eventually appear as solutions to the equations of a future theory for which he kept ceaselessly and unsuccessfully searching.

It did not take long before I had a grasp of the points Einstein had debated with Bohr on that first occasion I had seen them together. I came to understand how wrong I had been in accepting a rather widespread belief that Einstein simply did not care anymore about the quantum theory. On the contrary, he wanted nothing more than to find a unified field theory that would not only join together gravitational and electromagnetic forces but would also provide the basis for a new interpretation of quantum phenomena. About relativity he spoke with detachment, about the quantum theory with passion. The quantum was his demon. I learned only much later that Einstein had once said to his friend Otto Stern, "I have thought a hundred times as much about the quantum problems as I have about general relativity theory."[14] From my own experiences I can only add that this statement does not surprise me.

We talked of things other than physics: politics, the bomb, the Jewish destiny, and also of less weighty matters. One day I told Einstein a Jewish joke. Since he relished it, I began to save good ones I heard for a next occasion. As I told these stories, his face would change. Suddenly he would look much younger, almost like a naughty schoolboy. When the punch line came, he would let go with contented laughter, a memory I particularly cherish.

Einstein's company was comfortable and comforting to those who knew him. Of course, he well knew that he was a legendary figure in the eyes of the world. He accepted this as a fact of life. There was nothing in his personality to promote his mythical stature; nor did he relish it. Privately he would express annoyance if he felt that his position was being misused. I recall the case of Professor X, who had been quoted by the newspapers as having found solutions to Einstein's generalized equations of gravitation. Einstein said to me, "Der Mann ist ein Narr" (the man is a fool), and added that, in his opinion, X could calculate but could not think. X had visited Einstein to discuss this work, and Einstein, always courteous, had said to him that his, X's, results would be important if true. Einstein was chagrined to have been quoted in the papers without this last provision. He said that he would keep silent on the matter but would not receive X again. According to Einstein, the whole thing started because X, in his enthusiasm, had repeated Einstein's opinion to some colleagues who saw the value of it as publicity for their university.

To those physicists who could follow his scientific thought and who knew him personally, the legendary aspect was never in the foreground— yet it was never wholly absent. I remember an occasion in 1947 when I was giving a talk at the Institute about the newly discovered π and μ mesons. Einstein walked in just after I had begun. I remember being speechless for the brief moment necessary to overcome a sense of the unreal. I recall a similar moment during a symposium held in Princeton on March 19, 1949, on the occasion of Einstein's seventieth birthday, at which Oppenheimer, Rabi, Robertson, Weyl, and Gerald Clemence spoke. Most of us were in our seats when Einstein entered the hall. Again there was a brief hush before we stood to greet him.

Nor do I believe that such reactions were typical only of those who were much younger than he. There were a few occasions when both Pauli and I were with him. Pauli, not known for an excess of awe, was just slightly different in Einstein's company. One could perceive his sense of reverence. Bohr, too, was affected in a similar way, differences in scientific outlook notwithstanding.

What was the nature of my personal relations with Einstein? A few reviewers of my Einstein biography have remarked that the book showed my love for Einstein. I cannot quite agree. Affection yes, respect certainly, but not love. Our relations were cordial and friendly, but I would not call myself a friend of Einstein.

In later chapters I shall have more to say about this remarkable figure.

16.8 SHOULD I STAY IN THE U.S.?

As mentioned before, my early days in Princeton were marked by loneliness, alleviated, however, by visits from Rachel (whom I had met on the crossing to the U.S., chapter 14) to Princeton, and by my visits to her in New Brunswick, pleasant events stopped after a few months. It may be noted that the all-male population of the university campus and the Institute made the absence of young women acutely felt, as I was not the only one to observe. Those days, if you went to the train station on a late Friday afternoon, you could see lots of students hungrily waiting for the arrival of their weekend dates. How much more refreshing and healthier are the scenes on campus today.

While an inner loneliness persisted, my life was far from dull, as the preceding already has made clear. In addition there was the stimulus, and also the confusion, of job offers. The first of these arrived already in September, when I received a letter from Maurice Goldhaber, inviting me to accept an assistant professorship at the University of Illinois in Urbana. In October I had visits from Vern Knudsen, chancellor of the University of California at Los Angeles, who proposed a similar position with an annual salary of $4,200; and of the president of the University of North Carolina in Chapel Hill, who also offered me an assistant professorship, to be combined with a position at Oak Ridge National Laboratory in Tennessee, the latter on condition that I become an American citizen.

In all these instances, I replied by expressing my appreciation but declining on the grounds that I had already made other arrangements, without specifying what these were. What in fact I had in mind was my intention to return to Copenhagen the next autumn, where another year's Rask Ørsted Fellowship was being held for me. I looked forward at that time to continuing to work with Bohr.

Not being familiar with the American negotiating style, I did not realize that my refusals, which appeared to become known via the grapevine, upped the ante. Thus in November, Rabi called me from New York with an offer of a visiting professorship at Columbia University; he gave me time to think it over. In December, I received a letter from Aydelotte offering me another year at the Institute with a raise in stipend to $2,500;[15] and one from John Van Vleck, chairman of the physics department at Harvard, offering me an assistant professorship.

It must have been one evening at about that time that I was lying in my bathtub when abruptly I sat up straight and said to myself, "I could stay in the United States!"

Before long even better offers were to come, to which I shall turn presently. First, however, I must relate an unpleasant development that December.

In the course of a joint discussion a while earlier among John Wheeler, Art Wightman, and myself, the question had been raised (not by me): How did my ideas on a modification of quantum electrodynamics affect the properties of mirror nuclei? These are pairs of atomic nuclei such that if one of them has a given number of protons and a given number of neutrons, then for the other these two numbers are interchanged; the number of protons (neutrons) in one equals the number of neutrons (protons) in the other. The simplest example of a pair of mirror nuclei is one single proton and one single neutron.

As noted earlier (chapter 12, sec. 12.2), my work had made it possible for the first time to calculate theoretically the neutron-proton mass difference. A new question, about which neither I nor those familiar with my work had thought before, came up in our discussion: What happens to the mass difference of mirror nuclei? For theoretical reasons I need not go into here, the latter can be and had been predicted from standard electromagnetic theory, with satisfactory results. What happens in my modified theory?

We decided that this was a nice problem for Wightman to work out. He did so. The results were a disaster.[16] My theory could not simultaneously account for the mass differences between neutron and proton and those between (heavier) mirror nuclei. Since the latter could satisfactorily be accounted for by the usual theory, the evidence was that my ideas were incorrect. Not that I had made mistakes of logic or in calculation. Rather, Nature simply did not like the idea.

I felt crushed. The work had received considerable attention in the physics community. I must confess to having had dreams of glory. Now these were replaced by shame and fear of contempt by others. For several weeks I was thoroughly downcast, until I realized that there was nothing to be ashamed of. I had not swindled anybody. In the event, no contempt followed either.

There is a saying among physicists that theories can be classed in decreasing order of importance like this: simple and right, simple and wrong, complicated and right, complicated and wrong. Mine belonged to the second class. It took some time, but in the end I have still come to feel good about these early efforts.

Like many, I look back and take stock toward year's end. Late December 1946 I wrote in my diary: "The year is almost gone. It was a great year." Indeed. I had had a wonderful time in Copenhagen. I had become close to Niels Bohr. I had made the move to the U.S., where job offers had reached me. I had met Panofsky, von Neumann, Einstein.

I had also had a bitter lesson that December but had not caved in. It seems perhaps most important to me now that in that year-end diary entry, I wrote of "vague new ideas" for further research.

17

In Which Oppenheimer Becomes Director and I a Long-Term Member of the Institute

17.1 Oppenheimer's Appointment
as Institute Director

In DECEMBER 1946, the *New York Times* reported that effective October 16, 1947, Aydelotte would retire as director of the Institute for Advanced Study.[1] Only recently did I learn details of the way his successor was selected and appointed.[2] I give next an outline of the procedures.

Already in October 1945, a Trustee Committee on Selection had been chosen, followed the next month by the establishment of a Faculty Committee on Succession. In February 1946, this committee sent a letter to all faculty members, including a list of nine suggested names. Two of those are of particular interest: Dr. J. Robert Oppenheimer, physicist, University of California; and Mr. (formerly Rear Admiral)[3] Lewis Strauss, a member of the Institute's Board of Trustees and chairman of its Selection Committee. (He pronounced his name "Straws," as they did back in Virginia, where he hailed from.) Oppenheimer had earlier been considered for a chair in the School of Mathematics, but no action had been taken.[4]

Matters were still in flux when Washington got into the act. In October 1946, President Truman announced the appointment of Strauss to the newly established United States Atomic Energy Commission (AEC).[5] In December the president appointed Oppenheimer to the General Advisory Committee (GAC) of the AEC. (He became the committee's chairman.) Obviously these were positions that would put great demands on these men's time. At any rate, by the end of 1946 no decision on the succession had yet been made.

The Board of Trustees' meeting was held on April 1, 1947. From its minutes:

> By unanimous vote, the . . . Committee authorized Admiral Strauss to approach first Dr. J. Robert Oppenheimer of the University of California. Admiral Strauss took the matter up informally with Dr. Oppenheimer,[6] and is now happy to report to the Trustees that Dr. Oppenheimer has expressed his willingness to accept the position of Director of the Institute for Advanced Study should the Trustees decide to offer it to him. In that event, Admiral Strauss reported that Dr. Oppenheimer has requested that in addition to administrative duties, he be permitted to devote some of his time to teaching in order that he may remain in direct contact with young scholars. . . .
>
> It was moved by Admiral Strauss and unanimously carried that Professor J. Robert Oppenheimer be appointed Director of the Institute for Advanced Study to succeed Dr. Aydelotte on his retirement, with the understanding that his duties and responsibilities will be the same as those of the present Director, and that he shall receive the same emoluments. It is expected that Dr. Oppenheimer will come into residence before the retirement of Dr. Aydelotte and during that period his status will be that of Director-Elect.

Oppenheimer must have accepted around April 1, for a few days later Aydelotte wrote to him that he "was delighted to get the good news by telephone from Admiral Strauss."[7] On April 17 the news appeared in leading New York and Philadelphia papers.

Oppenheimer has recorded his reactions to this offer:

> I did not accept at once. I like California very much. . . . Before I accepted the job, and a number of conversations took place, I told Mr. Strauss there was derogatory information about me. In the course of the confirmation hearings, on Mr. Lilienthal especially, and the rest of the Commissioners, I believe Mr. [J. Edgar] Hoover sent my file to the Commission, and Mr. Strauss told me that he had examined it rather carefully. I asked him whether this seemed in any way an argument against my accepting this job, and he said no, on the contrary—anyway, no.[8]

I shall come back later to this "derogatory information."

Driving across the bridge from San Francisco to Oakland one night in April, Oppenheimer first heard on his car radio that he had been appointed the Institute's new director. "Well," he said to his wife, "I guess that settles it." Some years later a faculty member was asked what his and his colleagues' impressions were on hearing the news. He replied: "Hell, this is a mecca for intellectuals and we were reading in the *New York Times* every day that Oppenheimer was the greatest intellectual in the world. Of course we wanted him—then."[9]

It so happened that Oppenheimer had fully informed me of his impending move before it became public.

17.2 OPPENHEIMER MAKES AN OFFER I CANNOT REFUSE

Early in 1947, Niels Bohr wrote to me from Copenhagen:

> We are all sending you our best wishes for the New Year. I need not say how much everybody here enjoyed your stay in Copenhagen last year and how great a support you were to me on my visit to U.S.A. . . . . I am also very anxious to learn about your personal plans and what the possibilities are for your coming back here, where you will always be so heartily welcomed. As soon as I know what your plans and wishes are, I shall take steps to secure the necessary funds.[10]

The offer was of course tempting, but so were the possibilities, still open, for joining a distinguished American faculty at the junior level. It was clear to me already then that the time might not be far for me to strike out on my own, with greater independence than was possible for me in Bohr's orbit. In any event, I decided to think things over carefully before replying to him.

A week or so after I had received the letter from Denmark, I had to include an important new option in my reflections.

On Friday, January 31, I took a train to New York in order to attend a session of an American Physical Society meeting at Columbia University. That afternoon Oppenheimer was to give an invited paper on mesons, in the McMillin Theatre.[11]

Oppenheimer spoke before a packed house. He was a rhetor rather than a speaker. Then, as on numerous occasions, I was struck by his priestly style. It was, one might say, as if he were aiming at initiating his audience into Nature's divine mysteries.

After the conclusion of his lecture I went to say hello to him. He greeted me and then said that he urgently needed to talk to me. Would I please give him a few moments until he could disengage himself from the crowd. As I stood waiting, I tried to play back what he had just said, and I recall my thought: What the hell do I remember about his talk? I had been intrigued, nay moved, by his words, but now found myself unable to reconstruct anything of substance. I would now say that this was not just a matter of stupidity on my part.

After a few minutes, Oppenheimer came up to me and said, "Let's walk down Broadway and find a bar"; and so we did. After having settled down, he explained why he wanted to see me: he had been offered the directorship of the Institute—which was unexpected news to me. He continued by saying that this news was confidential and urged me to keep open the possibility of remaining longer at the Institute and, in any case, not to make a move until he would call me with firm news on whether or not he would accept the Institute position, a decision which he expected not to be long in coming. Being anyway in an undecided frame of mind, I had nothing to lose by agreeing with his suggestion.

After a bit more chitchat we parted, and I took the subway to Pennsylvania Station. During the train ride back to Princeton I reflected on this new development. My thoughts went something like this. Here I am being pulled in two directions by two great men, Bohr and Oppenheimer. What is the matter with these guys? What do they expect from this young kid from Amsterdam? Recall that at that time I was still recovering from my disappointment about past work.

In February I wrote to Bohr, telling him about my nice job offers but not about my discussion with Oppenheimer, and added: "It might perhaps be healthy for me to do some regular teaching for some time. . . . After lots of thinking I have come to the conclusion, however, that I would feel much happier in Copenhagen. If you still feel like having me back, I would very much like to come in September."[12]

Meanwhile, back at the Institute, Dirac had left and Kramers had arrived. Having concluded his stint as chairman of the U.N. committee (chapter 14), Kramers had obtained a leave of absence enabling him to spend the 1947 spring term in Princeton. Evenings we spent many pleasant hours together, he telling me many of his fascinating reminiscences of physics and physicists. We went for long walks in wooded areas. To get there we had to go along streets. Frequently, cars would stop to offer a ride. It puzzled several drivers when we politely declined. We also did some work together, but that did not lead to much. I remember how deeply fatigued he was already then—he died in 1952 at the rather early age of fifty-eight.

Social life could be interesting. I recall in particular an evening at the home of Hermann Weyl during which he told of life in Zurich in the twenties. How in 1925 he had given a colloquium talk on matrix mechanics, the earliest version of quantum mechanics, just discovered by Werner Heisenberg. How Erwin Schrödinger, who was in the audience, had afterward said to Weyl: "I am against this but only because I do not know matrices." How a few months later Schroedinger had come forth with wave mechanics, his version of quantum mechanics, and how he had made that capital discovery during a late erotic outburst in his life.

Noted scientists would come on short visits. One of these, Théodor von Kármán, gave me the following definition of the Institute: "That magnificent place where science flourishes and never bears fruit."

It was becoming clear to me that von Kármán had a point. To be sure, my life among big shots in science was instructive and stimulating, but not all that conducive to doing work of my own. Doubts began to grow in my mind whether the Institute was the right place for me, if I were at all to stay in the U.S. longer.

At that time Rabi's offer of a visiting professorship at Columbia was still standing. Since it was a temporary position, leaving later options open, and also since I had heard nothing further from Oppenheimer, I decided to accept it. I called up Rabi, saying that I would like to come for a visit to discuss the matter further with him.

So one day in March I walked to the railway station to take a train to New York. On the platform in Princeton I met Veblen, who asked me where I was going. I told him of my intention to talk with Rabi about a stay in New York. He begged me to hold off from committing myself, since plans were in the making for offering me a long-term membership at the Institute, adding that for the moment this communication was unofficial and confidential. I noted this encounter in my diary, adding: "People must be crazy."

I had to keep my appointment with Rabi, however. I told him vaguely that in the last minute something had come up which was forcing me to postpone my decision a while longer. I do not know what Rabi thought of my dilly-dallying; I myself was uncomfortable during that visit.

When, a few weeks later, I still had not heard from Oppenheimer, I decided that, Veblen or no Veblen, I had to get out, since my discontent with the Institute kept growing. At that time the Harvard offer was also still open and began to appeal more and more to me. I therefore called Rabi, thanking him once more for his offer but declining it—his reply was gracious—and wrote a letter of acceptance to Van Vleck. As was my custom already then, I put the letter in my desk drawer to sleep over it a day or two longer. That was in early April.

One afternoon on one of the first days in April—the letter was still in my drawer—the telephone rang. I picked up. An operator asked if I was Dr.

Pais. "Yes, I am." She said: "Hold the line. Professor Oppenheimer is calling long distance from California."

In order to appreciate my reaction, you should know that, up till that moment, I had never in my young life received any long-distance call whatsoever. And here the great Oppenheimer was calling, all the way from California!

I remember verbatim not only what Oppenheimer said after he came on the line but also the way he said it, priestly, solemnly:

"This is Robert Oppenheimer. I have just accepted the directorship of the Institute for Advanced Study, and I desperately hope that you will be there next year, so that we can begin building up theoretical physics there."

Desperately, no less. What could I say? I said yes, of course. The man was such a consummate kingmaker.

Next I tore up the letter to Harvard, replacing it with another one in which I declined the tempting offer. I wrote to Bohr, telling him that I had decided to stay one more term in Princeton but would like to come to Copenhagen in January 1948, if that were acceptable.[13] A week later, Oppenheimer called me up again, this time from Los Alamos, confirming his earlier communication and adding further details. My fate for the next sixteen years was sealed.

From the Institute's records comes the following information. In the faculty meeting of April 21, Aydelotte announced that Oppenheimer would take up provisional residence in Princeton in July. Von Neumann proposed, and the faculty accepted, that Pais be given a five-year membership with annual salary of $6,000—tripling my earlier stipend.

On May 5, Aydelotte and Oppenheimer are both present at the faculty meeting, the latter as director-elect. It is announced that the trustees have approved Pais's five-year appointment.

From my diary, May 27: Lunch with the Oppenheimers and Trustee Herbert Maass and his wife, at the Aydelottes. It was my first meeting with Oppenheimer's wife, Kitty, née Puening, a vivacious, petite brunette. (Robert was her fourth husband.) Maass tells a story. When Einstein arrived in Princeton, Maass took care of his luggage. A bit later he receives an upset telephone call from Mrs. Einstein: something valuable got lost—five pounds of green peas for Einstein's favorite soup.

In mid-July of an unusually hot and humid summer, Oppenheimer, his wife, his son Peter (nicknamed Pronto, from the speed of his arrival after the marriage), and his daughter Toni arrived in Princeton to settle. On

December 8, Oppenheimer, now director, presided for the first time over a faculty meeting.

What was Oppenheimer like, in those days? He was forty-three years of age. In physical appearance he was slender if not thin, with slight features, but with piercing and imperturbable eyes. He was known for his forceful, quick repartee, immediately commanding attention and respect in any company. He was the owner of an extraordinary fine collection of paintings and prints, inherited from his father. He was widely read, and an uncommonly fine combination of science and the humanities.

Why would the Oppenheimers leave their beautiful house in the Berkeley hills overlooking the bay, with their two-and-a-half acres of gardens planted in profusion with many kinds of shrubs and flowers, tended mainly by Kitty, a passionate gardener, and situated in one of America's best climates? I think they came to Princeton not just because of the intellectual appeal of the Institute, but also because of the nearness to Washington, the center of world power, to which Oppenheimer felt so strongly drawn.

17.3 ASSORTED EVENTS IN 1947

Events in 1947 I well remember are the discovery of the Dead Sea Scrolls and two American firsts. On October 14, U.S. Air Force captain Charles ("Chuck") Yeager became the first person to break the sound barrier while flying over the Mojave Desert in the Bell X-1 plane (which is now in the Smithsonian Institution). On April 15, John Roosevelt ("Jackie") Robinson became the first Negro (as blacks were then politely called) to play in a major league baseball team, the Brooklyn Dodgers.

Robinson's debut affected me personally. Soon after I had had my first encounter with the culture of baseball (chapter 16, sec. 16.1), I came to understand that you had to root for a particular club. Since the Yankees were then the best team around, I decided to be a Yankee fan. But when I read in the papers about Robinson's first, and realized that I had been unaware of the color barrier in America's most popular sport, I immediately switched allegiance to the Dodgers.

In those days my views of baseball were rather too romantic. Some years later it came to pass that the Dodgers traded Sal ("The Barber") Maglie, one of their best pitchers, to their arch rivals, the New York Giants. That irritated me; how could they do that to my team? That event taught me that professional baseball is not just sport but also big business.

One more experience of mine of that year related to baseball. Some time in the early autumn, as I was sitting in the New York subway, a passenger opposite me opened his copy of the *Daily News*. I could read the front-page headline, printed in heavy capitals: BUMS TIE. What did that mean, I wondered. Then, suddenly, a wave of emotion came over me. Not only had I understood the meaning but also the capital importance of the message. That year the World Series was a battle between the Yankees and the Dodgers, the latter affectionately known as "Dem Bums." The headline meant that the Bums had evened the Series (which they eventually lost, 4 games to 3). My emotional response to grasping the contents of the headline was caused by the realization that my understanding of America had reached a deeper level.

I became good friends with Lars Gårding, a Swedish mathematician my age at the Institute, who would later become a distinguished professor in Lund. He had bought a second-hand car and proposed that we would use it for a joint long trip. I had never yet driven a car, so Lars gave me lessons. When I was ready to take the test for the driver's license, we drove together to the appropriate place. Lars got out and an inspector got in, and he told me where to go. I had not driven more than a few hundred yards when he ordered me to take a right turn. I gave the proper signal and made the turn—when something most unexpected happened. Just around the bend the car sank gently forward, like a camel going down on its front knees. I was perplexed but kept calm, turned off the engine and raised the emergency brake. After the inspector had stepped out to take a look, he told me I had a broken front axle. We walked back to his office where Lars was waiting and told him the bad news. The inspector then turned to me and said that I had reacted correctly to the emergency and that I was to receive my driver's license anyway. I hated to think what could have happened had the accident occurred a few miles earlier. The car was towed and fixed.

In late May we made our trip, driving south over the beautiful Skyline Drive to Roanoke, Virginia, then on to Atlanta. One evening we were driving in the dark through southern Georgia, I at the wheel, when I turned to Lars and said that I must have eye strain, since I had the impression of flickering light spots. So do I, he replied. Something had to be going on outside. We stopped the car and walked into the fields next to the road. No doubt, there were lights flickering on and off. Suddenly it came to me. "Fireflies!" I yelled. Neither of us had ever seen them before. We got wild, running through the fields, shouting. It was exhilarating.

We continued south until we hit the Mexican Gulf near Apalachicola, in western Florida. As we were driving along the coast I suggested we stop and take a swim. We had no trunks, but since nobody was in sight we stepped in the water in the nude. We had been swimming for several minutes when we heard a police siren. There was a cop, standing next to his car, waving at us to come out. We did and there we stood in the altogether, facing a fat officer wearing dark sunglasses who addressed us like this: "Don't you know that swimming in the nude is strictly forbidden? You each get a fine which you shall pay me right here." I said I was sorry, but I was a Dutchman and in my country everybody swam in the nude in the North Sea—which is a bloody lie. He replied that he could not care less what people did in Holland. In that case, I said, we request to be brought to court for sentencing. Whereupon he said, "Well, I guess you guys didn't mean any harm," and drove off.

We continued our trip, driving east, crossing Florida via Ocala, reaching the Atlantic at Daytona Beach, where we experienced another novelty: driving a car on the beach. Then home via St. Augustine, Savannah, and Washington, D.C. A grand and illuminating tour.

17.4 SCIENCE IN 1947, ESPECIALLY THE SHELTER ISLAND CONFERENCE

I now turn to my experiences with physics and physicists in that year.

As mentioned before, every few weeks I would go for a walk with Einstein. Only rarely did I make a note in my diary of our conversations, but here are two from that time.

Einstein on relativity theory: "If God would have been satisfied with inertial systems he would not have created gravitation." Explanation: Inertial systems are coordinate systems moving with constant velocity relative to each other—the motions treated in the special theory of relativity. Gravitation is included in the general relativity theory where one abandons the restriction to inertial systems and considers general relative motions. Note Einstein's imagery of God, whom he would often invoke.

On another occasion, Einstein expressed himself like this about his most recent efforts to generalize general relativity to a so-called unified field theory: "I believe that this is the God-given generalization of general relativity theory. Unfortunately the Devil comes into play, since one cannot solve the [new] equations." God again. If he could not obtain solutions, then why would Einstein nevertheless be so optimistic about his equations? Because in that late stage of his life, the elegance, the simplicity of equations had become the dominant criterion to him—actually a trap out of which he could not (or would not) escape.

Einstein on theories in general: "I do not like it when it can be done this way or that way. It should be: This way or not at all."

Also on that day, Einstein on Chaim Weizmann, the great statesman of Zionism, later the first president of Israel: "My feelings toward Weizmann are ambivalent, as Freud would say." I do not remember whether Einstein enlarged on that cryptic statement.

In late April I went to Washington, D.C., for the first time, to attend the spring meeting of the American Physical Society. I did a lot of walking. The sight that impressed me most was the Lincoln Memorial. I was quite moved to read Lincoln's words chiseled on the walls.

On that occasion I met Max Dresden my best friend from my youth (chapter 2), again. He had studied physics, obtained a Ph.D. with Uhlenbeck, and was to have a fine career as professor of physics, first in Lawrence, Kansas, then at the State University of New York, Stony Brook. We had a lot to catch up on. Since then, we have remained in contact.

The main physics event of the year was the conference held at Shelter Island.

The Manhansett Indians called their 7,700-acre island, tucked between Long Island's North and South Forks, "Manhansack-aha-quash-awamock," which means island sheltered by islands. They made their living by fishing. It had been British property, sold in 1651 to Barbados sugar merchants who saw Shelter Island's oak as ideal for making barrels. (The island was then heavily wooded, as was most of Long Island at that time.) They paid 1,600 pounds of sugar for the island, which later changed hands many times. It is now a favorite resort area.[14]

From June 1 to 3, 1947, twenty-one physicists, one chemist, and one mathematician[15] gathered at Shelter Island for a "Conference on the Foundations of Quantum Mechanics," sponsored and financed by the National Academy of Sciences. (Among the invited who did not attend was Einstein, who had declined for reasons of health.)

On the afternoon of Sunday, June 1, nearly all conferees met at the American Institute of Physics, then located at 55 East 55th Street, New York. There we boarded a bus which would take us to Greenport on Long Island's North Fork. We anticipated that it would be a rather lengthy trip along the old Montauk Road with its many stoplights. Neither the Long Island Expressway nor the Sunrise Highway existed as yet.

Unexpectedly, the ride went much faster than we had thought. As we entered Nassau County, the bus was stopped by a police trooper on a motorcycle who stuck his head in and asked: "Are you the scientists?" Yes, we were the scientists. "Follow me," he said to the driver, escorting us to the tune of sirens, passing unhindered through red lights, until we came to Suffolk County, where other troopers took over. We had no clue as to what this meant and speculated about scientific security, which in those days tended to take bizarre forms. All was cleared up after a fine dinner was served to us in Greenport and our host, the president of the local Chamber of Commerce, rose to give a short speech. He told us that, during the war, he had been a marine in the Pacific, and that he might well not have been alive had it not been for the atomic bomb. Not only the dinner but also the police escort had been tokens of his personal gratitude for what "the scientists" had meant in his life. After our meal, we were taken by ferry to Shelter Island, where another siren-shrieking police escort delivered us to the Ram's Head Inn, where we would stay the following days and hold our meeting. We had the place all to ourselves; the Inn had been opened ahead of its summer schedule to accommodate us.

In later years, one finds comments in letters by and interviews with participants to the effect that the Shelter Island Conference may well have been the most important event of its kind in their entire scientific career; this is also my opinion.[16] A newspaperman who covered the proceedings put it like this:

> Twenty-three of the country's best known theoretical physicists—the men who made the atomic bomb—gathered today in a rural inn to begin three days of discussion and study, during which they hope to straighten out a few of the difficulties that beset modern physics.
>
> It is doubtful if there has ever been a conference quite like this one. . . . The conference is taking place with almost complete informality, aided by the fact that the scientists have the inn all to themselves and feel that there is no one to mind if they take off their coats and get to work.[17]

The official chairman of the meeting was Darrow. As he noted in his diaries, however:

> As the conference went on, the ascendency of Oppenheimer became more evident—the analysis (often caustic) of nearly every argument, that magnifi-

cent English never marred by hesitation or groping for words (I never heard "catharsis" used in a discourse on [physics], or the clever word "mesoniferous" which is probably O's invention), the dry humor, the perpetually-recurring comment that one idea or another (incl. some of his own) was certainly wrong, and the respect with which he was heard.[18]

My own recollections confirm this. I had heard Oppenheimer speak before but had never yet seen him in action directing a group of physicists during their scientific deliberations. At that he was simply masterful, interrupting with leading questions (at physics gatherings interruptions are standard procedure), summarizing the main points just discussed, and suggesting how to proceed from there.

Oppenheimer's stature as a leader among men at that time was recognized not only by scientists, as the following story may illustrate.

> After Shelter Island Oppenheimer had to go to Harvard where he was to receive an honorary degree. Arrangements had been made to fly him and a few colleagues by seaplane from Shelter Island to Boston. However, bad weather forced the plane to come down at the New London Coast Guard Station, which is not open to civilian aircraft. The pilot was very worried since they were not supposed to land there. They were met by a naval officer who was clearly furious and ready to read them the riot act. As they opened up and jumped out, Oppenheimer told his very nervous pilot "Don't worry." Hand outstretched, he introduced himself to the ranting and raging officer with the statement: "My name is Oppenheimer." The bewildered officer queried: "The Oppenheimer?" To which came the reply: "An Oppenheimer!" After an "official" welcome in the officers' club, they were driven—with a military escort—to the New London railway station, where they boarded a train for Boston.[19]

Some time before the meeting, Darrow had asked Kramers, Oppenheimer, and Weisskopf to act as discussion leaders and to prepare abstracts for that purpose. These were distributed ahead of time to the participants. Those of the first two are too technical for present purposes, but Weisskopf's contains some remarks that give an accurate, broad picture of the mood of frustration as we arrived at the conference:

> The theory of elementary particles has reached an impasse. Certain well known attempts have been made in the last fifteen years to overcome a series of fundamental problems. All these attempts seem to have failed at an early stage. An agenda for a conference on these matters contains, necessarily, a list

of these attempts. After returning from war work, most of us went through just these attempts and tried to analyze the reason of failure. Therefore, the list which follows will be well known to everyone and will probably evoke a feeling of knocking a sore head against the same old wall. The success of the conference can be measured by the extent it deviates from this agenda.

It may perhaps be useful to divide the discussion into three parts:

A. The difficulties of quantum electrodynamics.
B. The difficulties of nuclear and meson phenomena.
C. The planning of experiments with high energy particles.[20]

Point A refers to the infinities—mentioned earlier—which the theory contains and on which I had been working hard during the war years. (I may note that this work received honorable mention at the meeting.) Point B addressed attempts to formulate the theory of nuclear forces in terms of a quantum field theory, the so-called meson theory. The purpose of Point C was to look forward toward future experiments that might help to throw light on the problematic status of current theory. Weisskopf anticipated that this part might become the most useful, because of "the small possibility that this conference may produce a new theoretical idea."

That guess proved to be much too pessimistic.

Already the very first presentation, by Lamb, brought, in fact, spectacular news. It dealt with his refined experiment on the spectrum of atomic hydrogen. His result: a small but definitive deviation, now known as the Lamb shift, from what Dirac's theory of the electron had predicted.[21] The next paper, by Rabi, was no less impressive. He reported another experimental deviation from Dirac which can be expressed by saying that the "magnetic moment"[22] of the electron was not exactly as predicted.[23] To give a sense of the precision of the results: the deviation from the theory quoted by Rabi is about $1/4$ percent—large compared to the limits on experimental accuracy, about $1/20$ percent. It was at once clear to all present that both experiments reported that morning were so fundamentally new that they would probably lead to Nobel prizes—as indeed they did, in 1955.

In the afternoon Rossi discussed recent cosmic ray experiments. The next day was devoted to fundamental theory, with talks by Kramers, Weisskopf, Bethe, and von Neumann. The third and last day was set apart for discussions, led by Oppenheimer. The main point of the debate was a serious-looking paradox in the behavior of mesons. If one knows the rate at which these particles are produced, then one can predict the rate at which they are subsequently absorbed in matter. The paradox was that experimentally the absorption rate was much smaller than theory indicated.

I was sitting next to Marshak during this discussion and can still remember how he suddenly got all red in the face. He got up and said: "Maybe there are two kinds of mesons. One kind is copiously produced, then disintegrates into a different kind which absorbs only weakly." This "two-meson hypothesis" was indeed the correct answer, to which I shall return presently.[24]

The final talk of the meeting was given by Richard Feynman, who presented an alternative formulation of quantum mechanics. As Darrow put it, the talk was given "with a clear voice, great rush of words, and gestures sometimes ebullient."[25] It was my first exposure to Feynman as a lecturer. My impression from that occasion remained through the years: a man who clowns while talking but who in fact is deeply serious.

I am sure I was not the only one who did not get the point of what Feynman was after. Since the subject very much interested me, I went up to him to ask for further explanation. We sat down. He began by drawing some pictures—my first look at what later became famously known as Feynman diagrams. I asked him to derive in his way some results known to me. He did so, with lightning speed. Whatever he was doing had to be important—but I still did not understand it.

A personal recollection: Julian Schwinger sitting quietly through all sessions, sort of hanging in his chair, his eyes half-closed, it seemed to me, a cigarette dangling from his mouth; we had several long late-night talks together, on quantum electrodynamics. Another memory: One late evening I was watching Kramers and Teller as they were sitting on the floor, engaged in a game of cribbage. One keeps score by moving a peg on a cribbage board. At one point Teller kicked over Kramers's peg. After apologizing, he returned it—several places back. I said, "Hey Teller, Kramers was much further along." Whereupon Teller burst out laughing and said: "Don't you know that in cribbage one cheats?" From that moment on I conceived a dislike for the man, reinforced by later events.

In July I went to Ann Arbor, Michigan, invited by Uhlenbeck to give a series of lectures on quantum field theory at one of their famous summer schools. There I taught, and I also learned. I attended lectures by Uhlenbeck on aerodynamics, by Weisskopf on nuclear physics, and by Mark Kac, a jovial Polish-born mathematician, on mathematical methods in physics. Afternoons were spent outdoors. I swam a lot, and once was invited to a golf game. My performance was disastrous; it was the only time I ever tried. I confess to have no interest in hitting a little ball, then walking a while. Why not just go for a nice walk?

Evenings were often spent with friends. We played a lot of poker. I fondly remember Mark's introduction of the term *les deux sauvages,* which is meant to be French for deuces wild.

In September I was to attend a small physics conference in Copenhagen, and would use my stay there to change my U.S. visitor's visa to permanent resident status. In mid-August I flew to Amsterdam. One had to make two intermediate stops in those days, first in Gander, Newfoundland, where you hang around for several hours, then to Prestwick in Scotland. The whole trip took about sixteen hours, which were particularly exhausting because of the vibrations of the prop plane. I stayed for about a month, visiting my parents, and seeing old friends, then took a train to Copenhagen.

I remember only one event of that visit to Denmark, but that one very vividly, since some years later it would mark a turning point in my scientific career. It was a talk by Cecil Powell given at the conference. He began with a quotation from Maxwell which is altogether fitting for the physics of the postwar era: "Experimental science is continually revealing to us new features of natural processes, and we are thus compelled to search for new forms of thought appropriate to these features." He went on to report results of his group in Bristol. They had made use of the fact that when a heavy charged particle passes through a photographic emulsion it leaves a succession of developed grains, a track. He reported two cases of a cosmic ray particle track which showed a big kink, indicating the decay of that particle into another one, also charged. The masses of the two particles, though not yet measurable with much precision, showed that one was dealing with two kinds of mesons. The two-meson hypothesis discussed at Shelter Island had been vindicated! No one at that earlier meeting knew that a preliminary report of this result had already been published in the May 24, 1947, issue of *Nature*,[26] just prior to our gathering at the Ram's Head Inn.

Powell noted further that the heavier type meson, which he called the π-meson or pion, had almost certainly been the particle proposed to account for nuclear forces (chapter 6). The secondary meson, which he called the μ-meson or muon,[27] was a particle no one had bargained for— apparently it had all the properties of an electron, only it was about two hundred times heavier. It was the first of a multitude of discoveries to follow before long which have revealed entirely unanticipated new forms of matter. Once again I had been present at the unveiling of a new discovery worthy of a Nobel Prize, indeed awarded in 1950.

For my trip back I had been able to secure a berth on a freighter that went directly from Copenhagen to New York. It was an inexpensive but long journey, ten days on the seas. The ship took along only a handful of passengers; we took our meals together with the captain and his officers.

Pacing up and down the deck, day after day, I had ample time for reflection. The question that preoccupied me above all was: What does Powell's discovery mean? Does the kinship between the electron and its heavy partner, the muon, mean that mass is quantized—as Møller and I had speculated a year earlier (chapter 13, sec. 13.3)? If that is true, I reasoned—again following Møller's and my earlier ideas—then the proton and neutron should also have heavier partners. Of these there is no sign, however. Hence mass quantization cannot be the answer.

A few years later I would change my mind about that conclusion.

Two final remarks. First, shortly after my return, Oppenheimer asked me to give a seminar on the Copenhagen meeting. I did so; it took place in the Institute's Common Room. A special seminar room was almost but not completely finished, in a new building still known as "Building D." I had been talking for maybe one minute, when in came Einstein and sat down. For a very brief moment I was tongue-tied. I experienced a sense of unreality at having to lecture to the century's greatest scientist. It passed, and I went on with an enthusiastic account of Powell's work. I may note that it was the only occasion in all my Institute years that I saw Einstein present at a physics seminar given by someone other than himself.

Second remark. As a result of the Shelter Island meeting, interest in quantum electrodynamics had increased in wide circles. Oppenheimer and Wheeler suggested that I edit a collection of reprints of earlier papers on the subject, and supply a detailed introductory essay. As a result, on December 5, 1947, I signed a contract with Princeton University Press for a book to be delivered on or before the first of March 1948.

For reasons I shall explain in the next chapter, that book never appeared. My introductory essay was printed by the Press as a separate pamphlet, however.[28] I am glad to report that it is still widely read.

18

Oppenheimer: Glimpses of a Complex Man

18.1 Oppenheimer as Director of the Institute for Advanced Study, the 1940s

OPPENHEIMER WAS nicknamed Oppie.[1] I was among those who always called him and spoke of him as Robert—the way I shall frequently refer to him here.

As already mentioned, Oppenheimer assumed the Institute's directorship in the fall of 1947, installing himself in what is still the director's office in Fuld Hall. Mrs. Eleanor Leary became his private secretary; before that she had worked for Robert's friend, Supreme Court Justice Felix Frankfurter.

New faculty appointments were made. In 1947 the archeologist Homer Thompson arrived. He was especially renowned for his dig in the Agora, ancient Athens' marketplace, which he had discovered by following the footsteps of Pausanias. This Greek traveler and geographer had recorded in Book One (of ten) of his *Description of Greece* the position of the marble stele which marks the entry to the Agora, rediscovered by Thompson by searching at the indicated place. The excavation of the Agora became Thompson's major lifework, assisted by his wife Dorothy and an able staff, headquartered at the Amerikaniki Skoli (American School of Archeology) in Athens, also for part of many years the home of the Thompsons themselves.

In 1948 Harold Cherniss was appointed to the faculty. He was America's foremost expert on Plato and Aristotle. We became very good friends. I think with gratitude of my many visits to his office, where I was always welcome, and where we discussed all kinds of topics, including his and my work.

At about that time a new rank was introduced: permanent member, with indefinite tenure but not a professorship. The first people appointed to this category were the mathematicians Deane Montgomery, in 1948, and Atle Selberg, in 1949. I shall come back later to my own promotion to this rank, which made me the first physicist on the permanent staff after Einstein and Oppenheimer.

Before Oppenheimer's arrival, mathematicians had formed the strongest group at the Institute; this remained so during his tenure. A few numbers: between 1948 and 1953, there were some three hundred mathematicians at the Institute, whose work produced more than five hundred papers in learned journals of mathematics.[2]

The first person to come to the Institute with support from the Director's Fund, newly established to support people who did not fit into existing programs, was the poet Thomas Stearns Eliot, who was at the Institute for most of the fall term of 1948. I had read and liked some of his poetry, none more than his *Old Possum's Book of Practical Cats,* the basis for *Cats,* one of the greatest and most popular musicals of the 1980s and 1990s. Naturally, I was eager to have conversations with Eliot but refrained from approaching him, less out of shyness than from an ingrained sense not to bother him with trivia. Yet we had one talk. One day, stepping into the Fuld Hall elevator on my way to the lunch room, I found one person already there: Eliot. I smiled politely, then pushed the button. Then he spoke: "This is a nice elevator." I replied: "Yes, this is a nice elevator." That was the extent of my conversation with Eliot, ever.

While in Princeton, Eliot completed work on his play *The Cocktail Party.* Oppenheimer once said to me he thought it was the worst thing Eliot ever wrote. He was awarded the Nobel Prize for literature in 1948.

In the autumn of 1950 George Frost Kennan arrived at the Institute for the academic year, also supported by the Director's Fund. He was the author of a famous anonymous article (signed "Mr. X") which stated the policy of containment regarding the Soviet Union.[3] Kennan and I developed friendly relations when we found out that both of us played the guitar. Every now and then after lunch we would repair to my office, where I kept one of my guitars. We would play in turn and sing, he Russian folk songs, I those from the West. He was a gentle man, a bit shy, I believe, but warmed up by music.

I conclude my account of the early uses of the Director's Fund by mentioning two psychologists. The first, who stayed through academic 1951–53, was David Levy, a noted psychiatrist who specialized in the relations between infant and mother. He told me how he made his preliminary diagnosis during his first visit with the two. He would say to the mother, "What a fine baby you have." The pleased mother would reply, "Thank you," looking at the same time lovingly at her child. If, however, she would say "thank you" and look at Levy, then there might be problems. At his invitation, I once went with him to his clinic in New York, where I could observe such interviews while sitting in an adjoining room and looking through a one-way transparent window.

The second psychologist to come (1951–52) was Jerome ("Jerry") Bruner, a professor of cognitive psychology. I had numerous discussions with him on his methods of testing. After one of these, he suggested that I visit his laboratory at Harvard with him to take tests myself—which I did. He put me in front of a lit, opaque glass screen, and pressed a button that caused a picture to appear on the screen for a fraction of a second. Whereafter he asked me to describe what I had seen. Then he showed the same picture again for double the time, asking me to report whether I had seen further details. We went through a sequence of such pictures. Afterward Jerry told me that I was the fastest person he had ever tested. We have kept in touch through the years. Clearly, the Director's Fund was a good idea well used, bringing in people whose work was stimulating to curious people like myself.

Among the early members of the School of Historical Studies I remember the historian Arnold Toynbee, who came in the spring of 1948 and a few more times thereafter on grants from the Rockefeller Foundation. I had a few discussions with him from which I came away with the impression that the man was an insufferable prick. I do not believe that anyone at the Institute derived much pleasure from his company, nor pride in his accomplishments.

18.2 OPPENHEIMER AS LEADER OF THE INSTITUTE'S PHYSICISTS

Robert's last position before coming to Princeton had been the directorship of the atomic bomb laboratory at Los Alamos, New Mexico, where some six thousand people had been doing his bidding. In his farewell address to the Association of Los Alamos Scientists, Robert had said: "When you come right down to it, the reason that we did this job is because it was an organic necessity. If you are a scientist you believe that it is good to find out how the world works; that it is good to find out what the realities are; that it is good to turn over to mankind at large the greatest possible power to control the world and to deal with it according to its lights and values"[4]—a first example of his literary style, which I have always greatly admired.

Now, in Princeton, Robert was lording it over just about one hundred people, as the third director of the Institute and the first to hold this position concurrently with a professorship there. The war had of course interrupted his research activities; after 1942 he did not publish in theoretical physics again until 1946. His total postwar physics output consists of four papers, the last of which appeared in 1949. His only later scientific publication (1959) is a digression into biophysics.[5]

Oppenheimer died at his home in Princeton on February 18, 1967. On the following April 24, a session of the Washington meeting of the American Physical Society was devoted to commemoration of him. I was one of the four speakers,[6] my assignment being to treat his Princeton period. In my eulogy I described Robert's role at the Institute in these words:

> Physics had been represented at the Institute since its inception—Einstein had been one of the first two professors appointed in 1933. Bohr and Dirac had been frequent visitors, and Pauli spent the war years there. In addition, a score of other physicists had worked at the institute at one time or another. But upon Oppenheimer's arrival a function and quality of the institute developed which had not been there before. It became a center for [theoretical] physics, in fact during the next decade the most important one of its kind in the world.
>
> Oppenheimer's outstanding talent for assembling the right people and stimulating them to great effort was the decisive factor, just as it had been at Los Alamos. Regular periods of residence for eminent physicists have continued to play an important role in the life of the institute. But from the very start Oppenheimer brought to physics at the institute a new emphasis on youth. In fact, on his arrival in Princeton, five research associates from Berkeley came with him as the first temporary physics members in the new style. This is characteristic for the continuity as well as for the transition in Oppenheimer's activities. For from then on, his principal activity was not so much his own research. Rather it was to be, in the original meaning, a director of physics.
>
> A director, rather than a teacher in the conventional sense, for there is no such teaching at the Institute. To be sure, we had our seminars. They were lively—sometimes very lively. And Oppenheimer's sharp insights played a major part in making them so. Yet Oppenheimer's main contribution to the work and the style of the institute was not merely the conducting of a seminar. His influence was far more important, more subtle perhaps, but no less

inspiriting. He could convey to young men a sense of extraordinary relevance of the physics of their day and give them a sense of their participation in a great adventure, as for example in the Richtmyer lecture:[7] "There are rich days ahead in physics; we may hope, I think, to be living in one of the heroic ages of physical science, whereas, in the past, a vast new field of experience has taught us its new lessons and its new order."[8] He could define and thereby enhance their dedication, by words such as these: "People who practice science, who try to learn, believe that knowledge is good. They have a sense of guilt when they do not try to acquire it. This keeps them busy. . . . It seems hard to live any other way than thinking that it was better to know something than not to know it; and that the more you know the better, provided you know it honestly."[9] To an unusual degree, Oppenheimer possessed the ability to instill such attitudes in the young physicists around him, to urge them not to let up. He could be critical, sharply critical at times, of their efforts. But there was no greater satisfaction for him than to see such efforts bear fruit and then to tell others of the good work that someone had done.

So much for my eulogy, written and spoken a quarter of a century ago. I distinctly recall my thoughts while preparing it: give honor where honor is due, do not perjure yourself, but leave a more rounded picture for later. That later time has now come.

18.3 OPPENHEIMER THE MAN

In all my life I have never known a personality more complex than Robert Oppenheimer. Which explains, I think, why different people reacted to him in such extremely varied ways. I have known those who worshipped him and those who detested him. Having been close to him for sixteen years, I can summarize my own response to him in one word: ambivalence. There have been times when I felt genuine affection for him, others when I felt compassion if not pity, still others when he deeply angered me by his conduct.

Oppenheimer's talents were manifest in the way he led the Institute's physics seminars. These were also his shortcomings. He would anger me by his arrogance if not cruelty when a young academic did not clarify a point or missed one, cutting him down with unnecessarily biting comments. There were one or two occasions when I had to console someone who would later come into my office, sobbing.

Nor, in the beginning, was I myself spared such treatment. It was probably about a year before this came to an end, when I was able to muster the courage of saying to him something like this: "Robert, I want you to know that I won't take any longer your unwarranted behavior." The outcome of this brief conversation was astonishing. Never again, in all the many years I was in close contact with him, did he expose me to his abrasiveness. I noticed a few other cases where Robert changed his tune after someone else let him have it.

In all, my most cherished recollections of Oppenheimer are the untold number of hours we spent together, mostly in his office, talking about physics, politics, literature, or what have you. Never in all this time would I raise a question about classified subjects, nor would he ever volunteer such information. I should note here that just outside his office stood safes containing top-secret documents, in front of which sat guards on twenty-four-hour duty, discreetly carrying a revolver. Also, as Robert told me, he knew that his phone was tapped and thought it was likely that his office was bugged.

From my discussions with Oppenheimer I have come away with great admiration for his talents of verbal expression, his mastery of the English language. I learned new turns of phrase from him, for example his use of the word "inspiriting." I knew the word "inspiring" but had never heard "inspiriting" before. I went to a dictionary, looked it up—and adopted it myself for occasional use.

I would come to Robert whenever I had finished a piece of physics research. Whenever I told him that I had found something new, he would at once briefly bite his nails. I would go to the blackboard in his office and sketch what I had done, then sit down and listen as he would eloquently play back what I had said, emphasizing the strong points and noting the weak ones. It was always a masterful summary. I realized quickly, however, that I should never discuss with him—as physicists often do with each other—the status of unfinished work that was causing me problems. That would only lead to confusion rather than clarification.

In private conversations Robert had uncommon powers of persuasion. I recall meeting a distinguished faculty member one day as he came out of Oppenheimer's office, shaking his head. I asked what was up. "Something odd just happened to me," he replied. "I had gone to see Oppenheimer regarding a certain issue on which I held firm opinions. As I left I found that I had agreed with the opposite point of view."

In those early years I knew him, Robert was strikingly handsome, as can best be seen from his photograph on the cover of *Life* magazine of October 10, 1949. That is the best picture I have seen of him—ever so much better than the ones taken later, where he looks like a martyr. He wore expensive suits (never sports jackets), which would look sloppy on his haggard frame.

No martyrdom was yet in evidence during the years I am now writing about. In fact, the man was then ablaze with power, as I would particularly notice when, in my presence, his secretary would knock on his door and say: "Dr. Oppenheimer, Senator Arthur Vandenberg [chairman of the Senate Foreign Relations Committee] is calling"; or "General Marshall is on the line." (I would of course step out during such phone conversations.) Such calls would electrify him. It was to prove unfortunate but true that Robert relished belonging to America's centers of temporal power. If he knew that politics is a saprogenic profession, he did not behave accordingly.

Oppenheimer was a very private person, not given to showing his feelings, though I have witnessed a few occasions when he did just that.

Some time in 1949, I gave my first big party, in my Dickinson Street apartment. Robert and Kitty were among my guests. At one point I said, "Everybody sit on the floor; we're going to sing folk songs." Robert sat down too, his air of hauteur clearly indicating that he thought this was an absurd situation for him to be in. I got out my guitar and started playing and singing. A while later I happened to look at Robert. I was touched to see that his attitude of superiority was gone; instead, he now looked like a man of feeling, hungry for simple comradeship.

Another occasion. I had gone to the Garden Theater, one of Princeton's two movie houses, to see *La Grande illusion,* that marvelous movie about comradeship among men during the First World War. As I walked toward the exit after the show, I saw Robert and Kitty sitting in a back row. I could see that he had wept.

One last instance. One day I had organized a crap game in my apartment. When I saw Robert that afternoon I said to him, "Please join us this evening for the game. It will be an all-male affair." Whereupon he made a characteristic gesture: he pressed his upper arms against his body, holding both elbows with his hands, then said, "But I am not all male." I cannot forget this response. Already then I was convinced that a strong, latent homosexuality was an important ingredient in Robert's emotional makeup. I have been in a position to ask several people who knew him in his early years if, to their knowledge, Oppenheimer had ever had a homosexual relation. From what I was told I concluded that there was no evidence whatsoever for this.

Robert properly considered it part of his obligations as director to invite new members to his house for afternoon cocktails. These poor people were not prepared for what was awaiting them: pitchers of viciously strong martinis. I have seen members stumbling dead drunk out of the house. (One faculty member had renamed the director's house "Bourbon Manor.") I never accepted such drinks, having always found the cocktail hour a barbaric custom.

Robert himself would join in the drinking. He invariably held his liquor well. Not so Kitty, who was an alcoholic as long as I knew her. Apparently that had already been the case in Los Alamos. Jackie, Kitty's sister-in-law, recalled those times: "On one occasion she asked me for cocktails. . . . When I arrived, there was Kitty and just four or five other women—drinking companions—and we just sat there with very little conversation—drinking. It was awful and I never went again."[10] From her experiences of dinners at the Princeton house: "You would sit in the kitchen, just gossiping and drinking, with nothing to eat. Then about ten o'clock Kitty would throw some eggs and chili into a pan and, with all that drink, that's all you had."[11]

I have my own recollections about those eating habits. Off and on Robert would invite me for dinner at home, just with the family. One summer evening, after drinks, Kitty appeared with a bowl of vichyssoise from which she served us. It was delicious. After having finished our soup, Robert and Kitty indulged in a rather extravagant exchange about its superb quality. Fine, I said to myself, now let's get on with the dinner. But nothing else came. That soup was the dinner. I waited for a civilized amount of time, then thanked my hosts and drove to town, starving. I treated myself to two hamburgers.

I have caught glimpses of Robert's reactions to Kitty's drinking. On several occasions when he and I were talking in his office, I saw her staggering drunkenly toward the door of the office, which gave out directly to the lawn. When Robert noticed her, all he would say to me was: "Don't go away." Those were moments when I hurt for him. It seems that he did all he could to overlook her problem. Robert's brother Frank has put it this way: "He knew of Kitty's traits but was unwilling to admit them—perhaps because he couldn't admit failure."[12]

Quite independently from her drinking I have found Kitty the most despicable female I have ever known, because of her cruelty. I shall give just one minor example. Every spring a dance evening was held at the Institute. At the end of one such occasion I went to Kitty, the hostess, to thank her. When I approached, she was talking to an Institute secretary. This is what I heard her say: "Mrs. T., for your next evening dress you should choose blue instead of the pink you are now wearing. Pink does not suit you at all." It caused me to tremble with rage but I said nothing, just thank you for the evening.

To an outsider like me, Oppenheimer's family life looked like hell on earth. The worst of it all was that inevitably the two children had to suffer. I have seen how Kitty and her son Peter did not get along well, and was not surprised when Peter left home for good in his late teens and broke all contact with his mother. Toni, the daughter, poor dear Toni, ended it all by taking her own life.

$$19$$

My Career Unfolds

T HE WORLD at large was in turmoil that year. In January, Mohandas Karamchandu Gandhi was murdered. On February 25, communists staged a successful coup in Czechoslovakia. In April, the U.S. Congress passed a bill authorizing the European Recovery Program, better known as the Marshall Plan, which in the next four years saw the United States disburse 13 billion dollars for aid to Western European nations. On May 15, the British mandate over Palestine came to an end, the State of Israel was proclaimed, and the new nation was attacked by Egypt, Transjordan, Syria, Lebanon, and Iraq. (The resulting War of Independence ended formally in July 1949, with defeat of the Arab alliance.)

In June, the Berlin airlift started in response to the USSR's blocking, without warning, of road and air traffic from that city to the West. (This air bridge was terminated in September 1949.) Also in June, New York's Idlewild (now J.F.K.) Airport opened for its first flights. At that time, the New York Port Authority estimated that it would have to handle seventy-eight international flights weekly.

In August, George Herman ("Babe") Ruth, baseball's greatest folk hero ever, died. In September, Queen Wilhelmina of the Netherlands abdicated for reasons of health, in favor of Juliana, her only child. Also in 1948 for the first time, pure natural gas in Dutch soil was discovered, and it soon became clear that Holland was situated on a huge gas bubble.

On November 2, Truman was reelected president, to everybody's astonishment (including mine). In December, Alger Hiss was indicted for perjury. Also in that year, the long-playing ("LP") record (33 rpm) was invented, and Alfred Charles Kinsey published *Sexual Behavior in the Human*

Male, which led to the ditty: "I looked you up in the Kinsey report/and you are the girl for me."

Of all those events, the one that concerned me most and which, in a way, I came nearest to, was the founding of Israel. One day in April, Chaim Pekeris, an acquaintance of mine at the Institute who was on the staff of the Weizmann Institute in Rehovoth, Palestine, came to ask me if I were interested in meeting Professor Weizmann, which of course I was. So one day we made our way to the Plaza Hotel in New York, where I was introduced to the leader of world Zionism. We had been talking for a while when an aide came in to tell the professor that there was a phone call from Lake Success, then the seat of the United Nations. Weizmann excused himself and went to an adjoining room. A while later he returned and told us what the call had been about. An observer at the U.N. session had informed him that the issue of the moment was how to partition the Negev. There are two ways in which that can be done, Weizmann commented. Either you draw a dividing line running east-west, which has the military advantage of a shorter border, or you make a split north-south. That would give Israel a Red Sea port, Elath. "We need that port," he continued, and he told our man at Lake Success to inform the U.N. Assembly accordingly.

All of this was said in the calmest way, as if he were discussing a scientific issue, one might say. The way he spoke, even more than what he said, gave me a slight shudder. Here was a man who for decades had devoted nearly all his energies to the Palestine question but who yet was able to discuss it in a most dispassionate way, to reason rather than let his emotions hold sway. It was clear to me that, after Bohr and Einstein, I had once again met a great man.

As we talked some more, Weizmann invited me to join the staff at Rehovoth. (I was told later that this had been the purpose of my invitation.) I replied politely in the negative, and in truth did not give that option a moment's thought.

Late on a cold Princeton night in the winter of 1948, I walked home from a party at the von Neumanns'. As usual I did not meet a soul on the streets. I remember the exact spot where I suddenly stopped and said out loud: "The war is over."

I was deeply astonished by my own words. At no moment on that day had I given any thought to that past period, nor had others brought up any related subject.

It was at once obvious to me that events from three or more years earlier were still astir in me that evening, though well below the surface. Nor was that a quite new insight. Ever since the end of the war I had had nightmares, roughly once a month. I would either dream that I was to be killed or that I would kill someone. Dreams like that have pursued me for decades; only in the recent past have they almost ceased. In general, my dreams have been of an unpleasant nature.

Through the years I have noted that these occurred most often if the evening before had been particularly pleasant and relaxing. It was as if that lessened the tight control in which I held unpleasant thoughts. I have learned how best to cope with bad dreams: turn on the lights, wash with cold water, and pace for a while.

My late-evening exclamation that the war is over kept haunting me. Already for some time I had suspected that undigested past emotions were impeding me, particularly my work. During the preceding two years I had learned a lot of physics, had had enriching encounters with many very interesting people, had not been lazy or idle, but had not produced anything scientific. I now became convinced that I had to do something about that.

In talking over these matters with a trusted acquaintance in Princeton, he suggested that a few sessions with a psychiatrist might be helpful, adding that he knew such a person in New York. My only question was whether this analyst was of the Freudian persuasion, the only one acceptable to me (chapter 4). That being the case, I asked for the person's phone number and made an appointment. I noted in my diary: "Already during the preceding days the prospect of this visit has had a stimulating influence."

I had a few sessions with this psychiatrist, a woman, whereafter we both agreed that she might not be the right person for me, particularly because she was American-born. She thought I might profit more from treatment by a man who had been her teacher, and who was European by birth. She offered to call him on my behalf, a suggestion which I gratefully accepted. So I came to meet Theodor Reik, a well-known and highly respected psychoanalyst (not to be confused with the man who would tell patients to sit in an ozone box and masturbate).

Reik, a native of Vienna, had studied with and been analyzed by Freud. He told me how his heart would beat with excitement every time he went up the stairs to the master's residence. During the next two years I visited him once a week, but I would go daily during the lengthy Institute vacation periods, when I remained in New York, staying in Hotel Harmony, a little hotel (long gone) on 110th Street east of Broadway, where I could have a small clean room with shower at the affordable price of $2.50 per night.

My sessions with Reik were very useful to me. While the war experiences were much discussed, it was inevitable that these brought me back to much earlier days in my life. I learned to relive early pains, a quite painful experience in itself, which I shall not attempt to describe here, not just because they are very private but also because they would not be all that interesting to third parties.

Pain or no pain, I think back on these sessions with Reik as enjoyable experiences. They frequently brought me into a state of great excitement, always followed by fatigue. As everyone knows, analysis of dreams is an integral part of the procedure. In those days I would pay great attention to them, noting down in the morning what I could remember from the past night's dreams. Even though practically everyone dreams almost every night, most people often lose the contents after waking up. These days I remember much less of what I dreamed than in those times of analysis. I am sure that is largely because by now I am no longer interested in what I produce that way, in what "it means."

The fact that Reik and I both hailed from Europe was indeed a strongly positive factor in the treatment. The distance between us, demanded by his profession, did not prevent us from having cordial relations. In one of his books, Reik has written of me (not using my name of course): "A very intelligent Dutch Jew had said: How pleasant it is to jump from one language to another and to be understood! Psychoanalysis was conducted in English, but the patient sometimes quoted French sentences he had read or the text of Viennese songs. He often inserted Hebrew words or used Yiddish expressions. In this particular session he had remembered some childhood scenes in Amsterdam and had repeated a dialogue then heard in his mother-tongue."[1] (I knew that he had spent several years in Holland.) Elsewhere in that book he wrote about me again: "My thoughts circled around the patient who had left me half an hour ago and the first words he had said in his psychoanalytic session mysteriously echoed within me. This highly intelligent man had been silent for a few minutes and had then said, 'We pause for station identification.' That phrase, well known from radio announcing, was meaningful in his case because he often experienced a feeling of self-alienation, of search for identity."[2] Of everything that Reik said to me, I only remember this. "Doctor Pais, you are trying to be Moses and Jesus Christ all in one. Don't you think that is overdoing it?"

There came a time when I felt it had been enough, and Reik concurred. Was I now "cured"? First of all, I had not really been sick. Second, I do not know what, in terms of psychoanalysis, it means to be cured. All I am clear about is that these hours have been of great help to me, not just in alleviating traumas of war, but also by giving me precious insights into the relations among people, including those of myself with others. I am grateful for all it has done for me.

Soon my analysis started to produce effects. From 1948 on I began to publish again; to this I shall come back shortly. Here I note quite another kind of event which, after the fact, I also attribute to my days with Reik: in the autumn of 1948 I fell in love for the first time in my life.

By then I had already enjoyed several relations with women, as mentioned earlier, which had meant more to me than their sexual aspect. As my new experience made clear to me, I had never had feelings as deep as those which had now welled up—feelings so new to me that I was unable to cope with them. Never before had I been at a loss for words, but this time I found myself unable to express myself to the young woman in question, who was kind but firmly kept me at a distance. In brief, I never got anywhere. It was a very painful experience which took quite a while to overcome.

More than forty years later I happened to learn that the woman in question was living in New York, as was I at that time. I called her up and invited her for dinner. She accepted, and we spent a few hours in a good restaurant, during which I finally told her in detail of the depth of my genuine earlier feelings for her. We also told each other in outline what had happened in the intervening decades. I could honestly tell her that I still could see why she had meant so much to me at one time. Both of us considered this a pleasant encounter. Then I hugged her and said farewell.

On May 19, 1948, my thirtieth birthday, I wrote in my diary: "I have never been young, yet am still a child."

19.2 MORE ON DIRAC AND BOHR

In academic 1947–48, old friends spent time at the Institute, Dirac the whole year, Bohr the spring term, during which his brother Harald, a famous mathematician, was also there. During those months I often saw the two brothers together and could observe their great mutual affection. Harald, however, would often poke fun at Niels, which the latter always took in good grace.

In February 1948 I noted in my diary: "This is an unreal place. Bohr comes into my office to talk. I look out of the window and see Einstein walking home with his assistant. Two offices away sits Dirac. Downstairs sits Oppenheimer . . ."

One day Bohr came in, shaking his head. I asked what was up. He told me that he had just come back from a walk with Dirac during which they had talked about the Cold War. Bohr had complained about the invective in the American press toward the Soviet Union. Dirac had replied that Bohr need not worry, since in a few weeks the press would have used up all terms of insult in the language, and then they would have to stop. Typical Dirac.

Another Dirac story. Once a week he and I would go wood chopping in the woods behind the Institute. (Tools were available in an Institute shed.) One day we went out again, in short sleeves since it was very hot. As we began our activities, I said to Dirac, "It is so hot that I will take off my shirt." I did so, hanging it on a twig. "Yes, indeed," said Dirac, "it is very hot," and proceeded to take off his tie and hang it next to my shirt.

In March 1948 I moved to the top floor of 14 Dickinson Street in Princeton, where I had a living room, bedroom, kitchen, and bath. (One time Feynman stayed there with me when he came for a brief visit.) The Institute had rented the whole house, initially reserving the two lower floors for distinguished short-term visitors. The first to use these were Bohr and his wife.

I spent many hours with Niels in his quarters, discussing what was on his mind. One evening, Bohr came upstairs to bring me a present, an old tomahawk he had bought at an Indian store near the Delaware Water Gap. The deadly weapon is still displayed in my New York office.

By that time Bohr's main concerns had become political, specifically the question—which I had known to be on his mind already in 1946 (see chapter 13, sec. 13.5)—how to ensure the peaceful application of atomic weapons. He told me that, recently, in Copenhagen, he had met John Jay McCloy, who had been U.S. Assistant Secretary of War from 1941 to 1945 and was now president of the World Bank. The two had discussed world affairs, Bohr explaining his views on the need for an open world. A second meeting followed in New York, in March 1948, during which McCloy suggested that Bohr talk to Secretary of State George Marshall and asked him to prepare a brief memorandum for the Secretary, describing his ideas. Bohr did so.[3] Oppenheimer personally delivered that document to McCloy. In May, McCloy asked Bohr to write more explicit comments, which Bohr also did. In that document Bohr noted the failure of U.N. efforts and the increasing distrust and suspicion among nations. Then he made his own proposal:

Under the circumstances it would appear that most careful consideration should be given to the consequences which might ensue from an offer, extended at a well-timed occasion, of immediate measures towards openness on a mutual basis. Such measures should in some suitable manner grant access to information, of any kind desired, about conditions and developments in the various countries and would thereby allow the partners to form proper judgement of the actual situation confronting them.

An initiative along such lines might seem beyond the scope of conventional diplomatic caution; yet it must be viewed against the background that, if the proposals should meet with consent, a radical improvement of world affairs would have been brought about, with entirely new opportunities for cooperation in confidence and for reaching agreement on effective measures to eliminate common dangers.[4]

I had helped Bohr prepare this document.

After having read Bohr's comments, Marshall met with him in private in McCloy's home in Washington. During their long and frank talk, Marshall entered on difficulties in preparing the American public and Congress for a policy of openness. In a letter to Marshall following this meeting, Bohr reiterated his position "to make a stand for free access on a mutual and world wide basis, and to make this a paramount issue."[5] He also raised questions regarding "observers admitted to the various territories" (verification!), and the dangers of bacteriological and biochemical warfare.

I find this letter of particular interest because of Bohr's expressed hope that his suggestions might lead the U.S. government to take an initiative which "would serve the true interests of this country as well as of humanity at large. . . . Your country possesses the strength required to take the lead in accepting the challenge with which civilization is confronted."[6]

Bohr did not meet Marshall again. It must have become clear to him that the U.S. government was not willing to speak in favor of his suggestions. He did not give up his efforts, however, as I shall explain later.

I reserve another Bohr story from 1948 for the end of the next section.

19.3 MY EARLY COLLABORATORS

In chapter 17, sec. 17.4, I told of spectacular experimental findings reported at the Shelter Island Conference, concerning deviations from predictions of Dirac's electron theory. A first step toward understanding these new effects was made immediately following the conference.[7] On the train back from the meeting, Bethe had made a calculation that strongly indicated, if not proved, that the Lamb shift is a consequence of ordinary quantum electrodynamics (QED). His paper was completed on June 9, 1947, and was circulated among the conference participants.[8] Even more decisive was Schwinger's refined calculation of the electron's magnetic moment (submitted to *Physical Review* on December 30), which quantitatively accounted for the effects reported by Rabi.[9]

I shall not give any details here of these important contributions and their sequels.[10] Suffice it to say here that the new methods for dealing with QED calculations initiated by Schwinger do not solve the problem of the infinities but rather shunt these difficulties aside, in such a way that it becomes possible to test QED to a hitherto inaccessible level of precision. In particular, the Lamb shift turned out to fit the theory as well. (This calculation is full of subtleties. The correct answer was not found until 1949.) This new so-called renormalization method was a distinct advance—but the problem of the infinities has remained unresolved to this day.

QED had therefore changed so much and was now in such flux that the earlier suggestion (chapter 17, sec. 17.4) that I edit a collection of earlier papers on this subject was clearly no longer timely. The idea of a book of this kind was therefore dropped. I had, however, already then prepared a lengthy introductory essay, which was indeed published, in 1948.[11] It pleases me that this paper is still in demand.

The 1948 annual winter meeting of the American Physical Society was held again at Columbia University, from January 29 to 31. Robert and I had gone up to attend a session on QED. One of the speakers[12] was a youngster from Cornell, where he had been working with Bethe and Feynman. As he proceeded to give his talk, Robert and I nodded at each other: this kid is smart. He looked a bit unusual: stiff white collar and light blue eyes that would intensely stare at you. His name was Freeman Dyson. I seem to remember that we talked with him afterward. In any event, Oppenheimer invited him for a year's stay at the Institute, which he accepted. In 1953 he became a professor, and he is still there.

Some time later I became Dyson's father confessor for a while. What he told me then I shall carry to my grave.

Among temporary members in 1948–49 I note first of all the physicist Hideki Yukawa, who later in 1949 would receive Japan's first Nobel Prize. He was a friendly but shy man, as was particularly noticeable when he gave seminars. Not only did he speak softly, but he would also turn his back to the audience and address the blackboard, pure torture for his listeners.

More important to me was Uhlenbeck's presence that year. We started a collaboration which produced some new results in renormalization theory.[13] Then we turned to another investigation, which would take us a year to complete. At issue was a critical examination of several recent attempts at eliminating the QED infinities, not by introducing an additional field (as I had tried), but by modifying the equations of the electromagnetic field itself by making the action nonlocal, that is, changing—in a variety of ways—the Maxwell equations by introducing higher derivatives. Our work led us to introduce some new mathematical techniques and to discover that these attempts led to unexpected other kinds of inadmissible results. This solid piece of work is still being used and quoted.[14]

That year Uhlenbeck did something marvelous for me: he introduced me to the game of squash. Twice a week we made our way to the university's Dillon Gym, which housed fifteen courts. (Institute members had free courtesy access to such facilities, also to the Olympic-size swimming pool, another favorite spot of mine.) Though he was almost twenty years older, George consistently kept beating me that year. He would position himself at the favored central position and from there hit the ball now in one corner, then in the other, so that I had to run my little ass off. In time I realized that the players must not only be physically fit but also mentally quick. I came to love the game, though I never became better than below average at it. I have played it every year until well into my seventies. I have also seen several championship games, always marveling at the players' rapid, ballet-like movements.

We all have fantasies about our favorite way of dying. Mine is to be on the court, place a soft drop shot just above the corner of the tin, then keel over.

My next collaborator and squash partner, Kenneth Case, is a member of my own generation. In 1950 we published work on nuclear forces.[15] At about that time I was also, for a year, a guest lecturer in nuclear physics at Princeton University.

Later Uhlenbeck came back to the Institute for one more academic year, in 1958–59. Once again we jointly tackled a tough problem, but now in a quite different field, a calculation of the third virial coefficient. Once again we had to introduce new methods and found new results that are still quoted.[16]

In the course of this work I had an experience unique in my life. We had come upon a mathematical problem which we could not solve despite trying for several weeks. Then I had to go to New York for a few days. I took the work along in my briefcase, sat down in the train, took out pen and pad, and tried again. Then something most unexpected happened. I wrote down the solution to our problem at once, just like that. In New York, I checked and rechecked. No question, the answer was correct.

Abrupt resolutions like this are not unknown.[17] They appear to come out of nowhere, but actually are the result of first trying hard, then abandoning the problem, after which subconscious activity leads to the apotheosis. Unfortunately, this does not happen every time one is stuck.

I conclude this recital of my early collaborators in Princeton with the most important one of all: Res Jost, whom I had met earlier in Copenhagen. Our deep friendship, mentioned earlier (chapter 13, sec. 13.3), began in 1949, after he had arrived at the Institute for a stay that would last until 1955. During that period we published two joint papers which I do not hesitate to call fundamental.

In the first of these,[18] dealing with the quantum theory of scattering processes, we elaborated a method first proposed by Max Born in 1946. Having concluded the work, we searched the literature for earlier contributions to our main result. We did not find anything until we came to Born's original paper,[19] where our problem was raised—but answered incorrectly.[20]

The other paper deals with a problem in particle physics.[21] It has played a crucial role in my later work, since it was the first occasion on which I learned to handle invariance principles, a mathematical technique that I shall not describe here.

My scientific activities in 1948 concluded with a kind of work I engaged in only once in my life: being the editor of a *Festschrift*. On December 9, 1948, I sent a letter to a number of prominent physicists which began like this:

> Professor Albert Einstein's seventieth birthday will be on March 14, 1949. The Council of the American Physical Society and the Board of Editors of the *Review of Modern Physics* have decided to dedicate to Einstein the June 1949 issue of that journal.
>
> On behalf of the Board of Editors it gives me great pleasure to ask you to contribute to this anniversary volume.
>
> It is planned that the first article of the volume shall be of a more personal nature and, written by a representative colleague, shall pay homage to Einstein on behalf of all contributors. You may wish to bear this in mind when writing your paper.

I then asked Robert Millikan to be the "representative colleague," and he accepted. It was decided later that Louis de Broglie, Max von Laue, and Philipp Frank would also contribute articles of a personal nature. In von Laue's piece it was written: "On March 14 [1949] physicists the world over direct their thoughts to Princeton." The anniversary issue of the *Review* appeared on July 1, 1949. The younger generation was represented by Feynman[22] and me.[23] I corresponded with Pauli about his and my contribution.[24]

Bohr did not contribute to this *Festschrift*. Recall (chapter 14, sec. 14.5) that he had accepted an invitation to contribute to a book, also meant for Einstein's seventieth birthday. When he arrived in Princeton he had with him an unfinished manuscript of this paper, which he wanted to finish with my help. In the course of doing so I witnessed a most unusual encounter between Bohr and Einstein.

One morning Bohr came into my office and started as follows: "Du er så klog . . ." (you are so wise). I started to laugh (no formality was called for with Bohr) and said: "All right, I understand." Bohr wanted me to come down to his office and talk, and we went there. I should explain that Bohr at that time used Einstein's own office in Fuld Hall, while Einstein himself used the smaller, adjoining assistant's office; he had a dislike of the big one and did not use it. (A photograph in the Einstein anniversary issue of the *Reviews of Modern Physics,* 1949, shows Einstein sitting in the assistant's office.) After we had entered, Bohr asked me to sit down ("I always need an origin for the coordinate system") and soon started to pace furiously around the oblong table in the center of the room. He then asked me if I could note down a few sentences as they emerged during his pacing, though it should be noted that, at such sessions, Bohr never had a full sentence ready. He would often dwell on one word, coax it, implore it, to find the continuation. This could go on for several minutes. At that moment the word was "Einstein." There was Bohr, almost running around the table and repeating: "Einstein . . . Einstein . . ." It would have been a curious sight for someone unfamiliar with his ways. After a little while he walked to the window, gazed out, repeating every now and then: "Einstein . . . Einstein . . ."

At that moment the door opened very softly and Einstein tiptoed in. He indicated to me with a finger on his lips to be very quiet, an urchin smile on his face. A few minutes later he explained the reason for his behavior. He was not allowed by his doctor to buy any tobacco. However, the doctor had not forbidden him to *steal* tobacco, and this was precisely what he set out to do now. Still on tiptoe, he made a beeline for Bohr's tobacco pot, which stood on the table at which I was sitting. Meanwhile Bohr, unaware of the new presence, was standing at the window, muttering "Einstein . . . Einstein . . ." I was at a loss about what to do, especially because I had at that moment not the faintest idea what Einstein was up to.

Then Bohr, with a firm "Einstein," turned around. There they were, face to face, as if Bohr had summoned him forth. It is an understatement to say that for a moment Bohr was speechless. I myself, who had seen it coming, had felt distinctly apprehensive for a moment, so I could well understand Bohr's own reaction. A moment later the spell was broken, Einstein explained his mission and soon the three of us were bursting with laughter.

Two postscripts to this story. One: Bohr's article, dealing with complementarity, is by far the best he ever wrote on that subject. Two: There exists a photograph of Einstein's desk the way it looked on the day he died; on the desk stands a tobacco pot—a gift from Bohr, the pot of my story.

19.4 POCONO. OLD STONE

By winter 1948, so much had recently happened in physics that another conference in Shelter Island style was called for. Oppenheimer had heard that there was a hotel in the Pocono Mountains in Pennsylvania that might be suitable for holding such a meeting. One morning he and I took off in his car (a blue Cadillac convertible) to check out the place, which indeed turned out to serve the purpose. On March 30 and April 1, 1948, the meeting came to be held in Pocono Manor. Many of the Shelter Island participants returned; newcomers included Bohr, Dirac, and Fermi.

There exists no printed version of the proceedings, but I have lying before me a dittoed copy of notes (dated April 2) taken at the meeting by John Wheeler. It is a 100-page document recording contributions by fifteen speakers (including one by yours truly).

Forty pages are devoted to a marathon talk by Schwinger, on QED of course, given on the first morning. It was a major tour de force in which he unveiled a detailed new calculus for dealing with renormalization. It strained the absorption capacity of his audience, which explains an inadvertent remark by Rabi that first afternoon: "Yesterday Enrico [Fermi] said. . . ." Schwinger's lecture led to this comment by Oppenheimer: "Now it does not matter anymore whether things are infinite"; and this one by Rabi: "What the hell should I measure now?"

The next longest (twelve pages) entry is by Feynman. It was his first public talk on an alternative formulation of QED, which he already had tried to explain to some of us at Shelter Island (chapter 17, sec. 17.4). It evoked the same reaction I had experienced on that earlier occasion: the speed with which Feynman could reproduce results also found by Schwinger convinced us that Feynman was on to something—but still no one could follow his arguments.

One reason for our bewilderment was that Feynman had not yet resolved all the technical problems that had arisen in this work. One of these had to do with the proper incorporation of the Pauli principle, a fundamental quantum mechanical theorem. So Feynman said in his flippant yet serious way: "Let us forget that principle." Whereupon Bohr rose and walked, nay strode, to the blackboard, causing a twenty-minute interruption in which he lectured Feynman and us about the importance of the Pauli principle—of which all of us were of course aware. It was an example of an older generation not capturing the spirit of what was going on.

Dirac spoke of magnetic poles (units of "magnetic charge"), illustrating his reasoning with a piece of string he pulled out of his pocket. When I met Dirac in Princeton the day after the conference, I asked him whether he had taken that string along to the meeting for the express purpose of demonstrating his point. I got a typical Dirac reply. No, he had already had that string in his pocket before he had started on this piece of work.

A few days after we were back, Oppenheimer sent off a letter to all conference members, from which I quote: "When I returned from the Pocono Conference I found a letter by [Sin-itiro] Tomonaga which seemed to me of such interest to us all that I am sending you a copy of it." The letter was of particular interest to me. I quote further: "During the wartime . . . Dr. [Shoichi] Sakata . . . made an attempt to [eliminate infinities] . . . which we afterwards found to be identical with Dr. Pais' theory."[25] It was astonishing. The Japanese work was an independent carbon copy of what I had done, including the calculation of the neutron-proton mass difference![26]

Not just that. Oppenheimer related further in his letter that Tomonaga[27] had also made calculations substantially identical with those we had just been told of by Schwinger! Oppenheimer at once called Tomonaga, suggesting that he promptly publish a summary of his findings in the *Physical Review,* which he did.[28] In the fall of 1949 he came to the Institute for a year's stay. I remember him as soft-spoken, serene, ascetic in appearance, and as the most profound of all the Japanese physicists I have known. In 1965 he shared the Nobel Prize with Schwinger and Feynman. In his Nobel lecture[29] he included reference to the Pais-Sakata efforts.

The Pocono meeting had again been sponsored by the National Academy of Sciences. So was one more conference, held from April 11 to 14, 1949, in an inn at Old Stone-on-the-Hudson, 60 km north of New York City.

By the time of Old Stone, interests of theorists had largely shifted to the physics of π-mesons, which had just been found to be copiously produced by the Berkeley accelerator known as a synchrocyclotron. QED remained a major item on the agenda, however, and this time it was Feynman's show. He had meanwhile worked out his methods systematically, and had sent in his first paper on that subject a few days before Old Stone.[30] Feynman's version, simpler and far easier to apply than Schwinger's, now began its rapid and never-waning rise in popularity.[31]

The third main theme at Old Stone was the application of renormalization methods to meson theories of nuclear forces. From the start this looked very bad. In fact, fundamental advances in the field theory of nuclear forces would not emerge until the 1970s.

My last recollection of Old Stone concerns my participation in an evening poker game. Others who participated were von Neumann, who played anxiously, Oppenheimer, very cautiously, and Teller, flamboyantly.

19.5 I Become an Institute Professor

According to the faculty minutes of April 19, 1949: "The Director proposed to change the present status of Dr. Pais by a) converting his $6,000 annual grant to $8,000 annual salary, b) giving Dr. P. permanent status rather than the present five-year tenure. On motion, seconded and carried, the appointment as recorded was approved." From the letter Oppenheimer sent me the next day: "Your appointment . . . will now be, if you care to accept it, a permanent appointment extending to the age of 65. . . . Whatever the future may have in store for physics, for you or for the Institute, one thing needs now to be recorded. That is my own deep sense of gratitude and that of all your other colleagues that you have elected at this time to continue your work with us here."[32]

Some time earlier, Robert had told me informally what plans for me were in the making. Since I felt content with my forthcoming permanent position—my own research had picked up well—the time seemed ripe to me for taking the first step toward becoming an American citizen. Accordingly, on April 18 I presented myself at the U.S. District Court, District of New Jersey, in Trenton, where I filed my "Declaration of Intention." This document states that I had to swear that "It is my intention in good faith to become a citizen of the United States and to reside permanently therein. I will, before being admitted to citizenship, renounce absolutely and forever all allegiance and fidelity to any foreign prince, potentate, state, or sovereignty of whom or which at the time of admission to citizenship I may be subject or citizen. I am not an anarchist; nor a believer in the unlawful damage, injury, or destruction of property, or sabotage; nor a disbeliever in or opposed to organized government; nor a member of or affiliated with any organization or body of persons teaching disbelief in or opposition to organized government. I do swear . . . ," etc.

Those requirements for naturalization, laid down in the Nationalities Act of 1906, were already then causing trouble as "guidelines," not only for the House Committee for Un-American Activities but also for nongovernmental loyalty programs. For example, in 1947 the association of motion picture producers had announced that it "will not knowingly employ a communist."[33] Driving to Trenton, I had reminded myself once again how deeply I disliked those outgrowths of the Cold War. It was only to get worse in 1950,[34] when, shortly after the outbreak of the Korean War, Congress imposed greater restrictions on naturalization by adopting—over a veto by Truman—the Internal Security Act of 1950, better known as the McCarran Act (after Pat McCarran, the controversial right-wing senator from Nevada). At any rate, I signed my declaration, paid three dollars to the County Clerk, and was now on record as a prospective citizen.

Some time in 1949 a British delegation of scientists involved in ongoing atomic bomb projects came to Princeton to call on Oppenheimer. Afterward I was introduced to these men. I remember in particular meeting Klaus Fuchs on that occasion. As is well known, a year later he was arrested, convicted of espionage in atomic matters, and jailed. Robert said to me, sometime thereafter, that he hoped Fuchs told the Russians of the status of the hydrogen bomb project as he (Fuchs) knew it, since that would set them back several years.

Shortly after his arrest I received a letter from Peierls, offering me Fuchs's position at Harwell, the British atomic energy center. My reply was thank you, but no thank you. I had no desire to become associated with weapons programs, nor could I accept the condition that I become a British citizen. Also in 1950 I received a letter from Mark Oliphant inviting me to head the theoretical physics group at the Australian National University in Canberra. I declined that, too, but told Robert of these offers. I believe that these invitations accelerated his decision to propose me for a full professorship at the Institute. He did so in the autumn of 1950, the first step being in the form of a written statement to the School of Mathematics professors. Forty years later I obtained a copy. It reads in part:

> The record of Dr. Pais' work in the last decade is almost a history of the efforts to clarify our understanding of basic atomic theory and the nature of elementary particles. Pais first proposed the compensation theories of elementary particles, and much of his work has been devoted to exploring the success and limitations of these theories, and indicating the radical character of the revisions which will be needed before they can successfully describe the subatomic world. Pais has made important contributions to nuclear theory and to electrodynamics. He is one of the few young theoretical physicists who within the last decade have enriched our understanding of physics.

In January 1951 I received the following letter from Oppenheimer: "It gives me great pleasure to inform you that on the unanimous vote of the Faculty and the Board of Trustees of the Institute for Advanced Study you have been appointed a Professor . . . of physics. . . . This step is taken in appreciation of your past work, in high hopes for the work of the future, and with the full recognition of the value which your counsel will be in guiding the Institute's policies." On July 1, I became the Institute's third professor of physics, after Einstein and Oppenheimer. On October 9, 1951, I was present for the first time as a regular member at a faculty meeting—too late to meet Einstein there. He had ceased attending in 1949.

Next to attending faculty meetings and pursuing science, I set myself a third, self-appointed task: the care and nursing of temporary junior physics members. These young people had come from their respective universities as the golden boys or girls, the best of the local crops. Now they found themselves in the company of similar golden kids from elsewhere. That, combined with the Institute's decompressed atmosphere—do what you like—was nothing less than a culture shock, as I knew so well from my own initial experiences. The result was what I came to call the November Depression, which almost invariably occurred after the excitement of arrival had worn off. It was during this time that I felt I had to keep a protective eye on the newcomers. I would drop in, ask them what they were doing and how it was going, tell them it takes some time to adjust to new surroundings, stress that this is a very peculiar place, that it takes time to get going here, and that they would be just fine in a while. That was the kind of support Oppenheimer was congenitally incapable of providing; nor did he try.

A fair number took this wisdom to heart and got their act together. Many of those have since risen to full professorships all over the world. Looking back on my Institute years, it is perhaps my greatest satisfaction to have helped the youngsters along in the beginning. There were also some who could not take it, who collapsed mentally. On rare occasions, one or two of these would simply pack up and vanish. As all of us know, starting a career is rarely easy.

It is perhaps possible that quite another event may have helped speed my promotions. Some time in 1949 I received a letter from The Hague signed by the Minister of Education which informed me that it had pleased her Majesty the Queen (Juliana) to appoint me to membership in the Royal Academy of Sciences of the Netherlands. On reading this, I blushed.

19.6 TALES OF A SUMMER JOURNEY

In the late 1940s the dollar was almighty. That enabled me, neither poor nor rich, to afford travel in Europe, not in luxury—which has never meant anything to me anyway—but in comfort. I made several interesting journeys in those years. Visas in my old Dutch passport have helped me reconstruct my comings and goings.

19.6.1 London

In June I crossed the Atlantic to England on the S.S. *Marine Jumper,* a student ship with inexpensive rates. On board I met Cliffie, a student from Radcliffe, the woman's college associated with Harvard. We spent pleasant hours and had long discussions. She was a student of Slavic languages, on her way to Prague for summer studies. She gave me her address in Czechoslovakia and we promised to write each other.

After arrival in Plymouth, I made my way to London, where I spent time with friends made during my 1945 visit there (chapter 12, sec. 12.3). One evening I went to the theater to see a puppet show performed by Russian artists who at the conclusion came out to take a bow. I remember saying to myself, astonished: "They look just like us, like ordinary people." I was ashamed to realize that this response was the result of having been influenced by the American press, which at that time used to paint Russians like ogres.

19.6.2 Paris

Some of my British friends had planned to go to France by car and ferry. I joined them. After arrival in Boulogne, we drove to Paris and checked in at the Hôtel Quai Voltaire, where I had a little room overlooking the Seine. I spent the next six days taking in the sights, especially the Louvre. I had coffee at the Café de Flore, a hangout of the existentialists, and attended a left-wing mass meeting in the Palais de la Mutualit on the topic "Will France Become an American Colony?" It was the time in which a wag had coined the term coca-colonization. I also discovered the French theater, which flourished in those years.

19.6.3 Prague

While in Paris the thought occurred to me: Why not fly to Prague and surprise my new friend, Cliffie? I went to the Czech Consulate, obtained a visa, and made plane reservations. After arriving in Prague, I proceeded to Hotel Axa, where Cliffie was staying, and checked in. The hotel was very inexpensive, 77 Kčs (Koruna) per night. At that time the dollar was worth 50 Kčs (now 28). Then I settled down in the lobby to await what was going to happen next.

After some time she came in and did a double take. I explained that I so much wished to see her again, promised not to interfere with her studies, but said I hoped we could spend her free time together, which we did.

My recollection of Prague is that it is the most beautiful city in Europe I have ever visited. The people were very pleasant and open. Thanks to my friend's knowledge of languages, I was able to learn what was on their minds. The mood was strongly pro-American and anti-Russian, the four-month-old new communist regime was not liked at all, even among many of the old-time communists. The U.S. was talked about as the land of milk and honey, probably under the influence of earlier help by the relief organization UNRRA. People knew remarkably little about America, however. The international position of the country was summarized for us by a woman who told us: "Balkan peoples are temperamental, but Czechs are cold. They are neither East nor West."

Our discussions with Czechs were dominated by the issue of individual freedom. As I walked down a street with a man and discussed the subject, he did talk freely but stopped the discussion every time someone passed by. Another man said: "It is not dangerous to be critical of the government but it is safer not to be that way." But a communist doctor told my friend: "We have less art and less science now, but we are in a period of transition, during which we must make sacrifices. We are in a state of war, we have to close ranks."

We found out that all newspapers were communist controlled, that the secret police were out to intimidate people. Workers received state pensions at age sixty but miners at age fifty. Food was rationed; people were divided into four categories: those who did very heavy, heavy, light, and very light work. University education was free, after the prospective student had signed a declaration of support for the regime. Just before I left, I heard that Czech students were forbidden to talk politics with American or Canadian students. On the other hand, Czechs could not go to the U.S. to study because the U.S. demanded that they swear they are noncommunists. I visited the university's physics laboratory, where I found the mood subdued and equipment to be very scarce.

I soon found out that the Czech language is a tongue twister. Every foreigner is regaled with the phrase: Push the finger through the neck; in Czech: *Strč prst skrz krk.* The food is heavy; the national dish is *hus a knedlyky,* goose with dumplings. Czechs consume inordinate amounts of *pivo,* beer. My souvenir of the trip is an ashtray with the exciting-sounding legend: *Mestanski Pivovar v Plzni,* which, however, only means: municipal beer factory of Pilsen.

As time to leave was drawing near, I proposed to my friend that we take a short trip to the Tatra Mountains. So we did, flying to Tatranska Lomnica in Slovakia, not far from the Russian border. We went there in a small plane, no seats, only two benches lengthwise. We flew low, it was extremely bumpy, and I got very airsick, making a mess. There were no airsickness bags; my friend took it kindly. We spent some wonderful days hiking. I also found time to visit the Statne Astronomical Observatory in nearby Skalnat, Plezo. Then I flew back to Prague and from there to Amsterdam, filled with enriching new experiences.

19.6.4 Amsterdam

Once again I stayed in my parents' apartment; I was glad to see them again. The looks of the city had begun to improve—there had been much reconstruction and painting of houses. The food situation was also much better now.

The main topic of conversation and in newspapers was the recent secession of the East Indian colonies. Recall that in 1945 the independent republic of Indonesia had been proclaimed, that initially there had been a military response by the Dutch, and that these matters were not settled until late 1949. During that summer of 1948, the situation was still messy. The Dutch had an army of 250,000 men in the region. The debate then raging in Holland centered on the choice: shall we first beat them, then talk, or shall we talk right away. The first option was preferred by a clear majority, "as long as my son will not have to go and fight." At that time the troops were still in possession of all ports and essential coastal areas, also in control of the rich tin mines on the small islands of Banka and Billiton, east of Sumatra. Unlike the British, the Dutch had not yet seen fit to yield on minor matters in order to be in the best long-term position. (The French were even worse.)

19.6.5 Copenhagen

Of my final destination that summer, a month in Denmark, I only remember spending a week with the Bohrs in Tisvilde. Niels and I spent much time discussing once again his political ideas. Evenings he read to us several times from his favorite poets, particularly from Friedrich von Schiller. I noted a few lines in my diary. From *Die Worte des Wahns* (The Words of Delusion):

> Es ist nicht draussen, da sucht es der Tor
> Es ist in dir, du bringst es ewig hervor.

(It is not outside, where the fool seeks it/It is within you, you produce it forever), and from *Breite und Tiefe* (Breadth and Depth):

> Der Stamm erhebt sich in die Luft
> Mit üppig prangenden Zweigen
> Die Blätter glänzen und hauchen Duft
> Doch können sie Frücht nicht zeugen
> Der Kern allein im schmalen Raum
> Verbirgt den Stolz des Waldes, den Baum.

(The trunk rises in the sky/Displaying lush branches/The leaves shine and
exhale a pleasant smell/But cannot produce any fruits/Only the seed in the
small space/Hides the pride of the forest, the tree.)

I went back to America by student ship again. During that voyage I encountered a young Indian who had been a disciple of and close to Gandhi. I
loved to listen to his stories. When someone came to Gandhi with a question, Gandhi would say, "Ha, ha, ha," then would reflect, then say: "Bolo,
bolo, speak, speak, repeat your question." Then he would answer. "He is
the most detached man I have ever met," the Indian said, "the most impersonal person. He listens with his whole personality. His ears almost flap,
like those of an elephant."

20

About Unexpected New Physics, Old Friends, and a Grand Tour

20.1 Physics Takes a Surprising Turn

THE SECOND WORLD WAR will be remembered above all for the human suffering it caused. On a more abstract level, it had been the physicists' war,[1] won by radar and ended by the atomic bomb.[2]

Among the physicists who returned from the wars were those who had contributed to victory, those who had been unable to stave off defeat, and those who, whether by design or circumstance, had been otherwise engaged. Some returned with many qualms about their participation in war work, others with none. International communication, severely disrupted for several years, was reestablished rather quickly.

All who had survived the calamities had to adjust to a different world, from politics to poetry. So it was in physics. As a colleague of mine wrote in 1947: "Gone was the reluctance to do big things, gone the sometimes valuable, sometimes hampering isolation of the research worker."[3]

Right after war's end, physics took a sharp turn rather than continuing on earlier trodden paths. There is an almost abrupt sense of novelty, in regard to instrumentation, new styles of cooperative experimental venture, discoveries of new forms of matter, and evolution of new theoretical methods.

In order to explain how this new style arose, it will help to recall some of the topics reported in 1947 at Shelter Island and in Copenhagen (chapter 17, sec. 17.4). I have already mentioned that great advances in QED had resulted from experiments by Lamb, Rabi, and their coworkers. These were performed with the help of tools originally devised in the course of war work on radar. We have also seen that new forms of matter, μ- and π-mesons, had been discovered in cosmic radiation experiments. It would obviously be desirable for further study to have these particles available in far greater quantities than cosmic rays can provide. That would demand accelerators capable of producing beams of protons or electrons (or other particles) with energies (per particle) much higher than those reached in the 1930s. The construction of these necessarily new machines began shortly after war's end. During the first postwar decade they drove the highest man-made energies up by a factor of over a hundred.

All that cost money, a lot of money. That demanded tapping new financial resources. The first of these was the United States military establishment, which had developed a benevolent attitude toward the scientific community because of its role in developing radar and the atomic bomb. Physicist Luis Alvarez told me: "Right after the war we had a blank check from the military because we had been so successful. Had it been otherwise, we would have been villains. As it was we never had to worry about money." The first military contributions to pure physics were authorized over the signature of General Leslie Groves, administrative head of the Manhattan Project. Meanwhile it had become evident that further progress in particle physics, and in other areas as well, demanded moneys that no single university could provide. As a result, consortia were founded for the purpose of jointly administering new facilities, funding to be provided by a government, or governments. The activities of the first of these groups led in 1946 to the establishment of Brookhaven National Laboratory on Long Island. In Western Europe, CERN, the European Center for Nuclear Research, began its official existence in 1954, governed by a multinational council. The Dubna Laboratory in the Soviet Union was another of the early international ventures. By the late 1950s these centers housed accelerators that could reach energies raised by yet another factor of about one hundred.

It is one of history's many quirks that experience gained during the war served to prepare scientists for dealing with high-cost projects demanding joint efforts at just about the time these factors became indispensable to the continuation of pure research in several areas. Also, before the war science could have profited from more funds, to be sure, yet the natural scientific scope of the enterprise at that time made it possible to keep research moving in single university context. That was out of the question after 1945. Once, years later, when I discussed these questions with I. I. Rabi, he said to me: "You people were fortunate to be the grandchildren of the atomic bomb and the children of Sputnik."

The new accelerators produced results that were very rich. They were also quite startling. New forms of matter were discovered that no one had previously conjectured nor even dreamed of. It is no exaggeration to say that in regard to the structure of matter, we were witnessing the unfolding of a revolution.

To lend perspective to this development, let me first relate what was known up to the beginning of the war. By then we believed the basic particles to be seven in number: electron, positron, proton, neutron, one meson (later called the μ-meson), photon, the quantum of light, one conjectured neutrino, a particle supposed to be (later shown to be) emitted in every so-called β-radioactive process. Quite a collection, but there was still hope that these particles might suffice for understanding the structure of all matter and the nature of all forces. One did not know then, nor does one know now, why these particles are there, why their masses stand in the ratios they do, or why the forces between them have the strengths they do. But one could still entertain the hope that those particles eventually would tell the whole story.

The discovery in 1947 of the π-meson and the realization that the μ-meson was not the particle responsible for the nuclear forces was a clear harbinger of greater complexity, however. What was the muon good for? Even today the muon continues to remind us how little we yet know of nature's particles. For that reason, physicists have long since ceased to speak of elementary or fundamental particles but rather use the term *particles tout court*.

In December 1947, George Rochester and Clifford Butler from Manchester published an article entitled "Evidence for the Existence of New Unstable Particles."[4] They had discovered two unusual events in a cloud chamber. One showed a forked track that they interpreted as the spontaneous decay of a neutral particle into two charged particles. The other showed a track with a marked kink, most probably the decay of a charged particle into a charged one and a neutral one. In both cases, the parent particle was heavier than the pion, lighter than the proton—which meant that they were "new" particles.

I may well have heard of these results soon after their publication, but do not recall their causing any stir or immediate awareness of a new era being upon us in regard to the structure of matter. They were certainly not even mentioned at the 1948 Pocono Conference (chapter 19, sec. 19.4). And so it remained until the spring of 1950, when I found a paper from Cal Tech reporting thirty forks and four kinks, both of the Manchester type.[5] In October of that year the first case was found[6] of another new particle (now called Λ) that is heavier than the proton. It was all startling and amazing—and it was just the beginning.

All these discoveries were made in the course of analyses of cosmic rays. Because they get rapidly absorbed in the atmosphere, it is advantageous to study cosmic rays at high altitudes, for example on mountain tops. This led to one physics publication with the most romantic title I have ever seen: "Four τ-Mesons[7] Observed on Kilimanjaro."[8]

None of these new particles were yet known when the new generation of accelerators was planned and their construction had begun. Since then, millions upon millions of these particles have been created in various laboratories on earth.

The arrival of the new particles changed my life. Recall (chapter 17, sec. 17.4) that in the summer of 1947, on board ship returning from Copenhagen to New York, I had been pacing the deck, reflecting on Powell's discovery of the muon and speculating about the possibility that, just as the muon appeared to be a heavy brother of the electron, there might well exist heavy partners of the proton and neutron—which had not yet been seen at that time. Now here was the Λ! That particle, I was immediately convinced, had to be related to the proton-neutron very much like the muon to the electron.

These visions were a consequence of my work done in 1946–47 in Copenhagen, in which each "prewar particle" appeared as the lowest mass particle of a "particle family" (see chapter 13, sec. 13.3.3). I had been the co-creator of the word "lepton" to denote a member of the electron-neutrino family. In 1953 I proposed to baptize the proton-neutron and its heavier brothers (the Λ was only the first of these to be discovered, as I shall discuss later) with the collective name "baryon" (from the Greek βαρύος = heavy). That word, like lepton, is now in the *Oxford English Dictionary*, where even the paper is quoted in which I first introduced the term.[9]

Visions such as the ones I had are precious—if they work out. In this case they did, even though the work from which they originated is rightfully forgotten. My convictions at that time were so strong that I decided: my future lies with these new particles. Drop everything else, I told myself, and devote yourself to what must be the beginning of a new chapter in the story of the structure of matter. I did and it was. Before long I became known as the father of particle physics. That was a bit of an exaggeration, but I certainly was the U.S. pioneer in this new field of theoretical research. In the next chapter I shall turn to my first paper on that subject, which appeared in June 1952.

From 1950 on, the new particles began to gain attention, though slowly at first. During a conference at Harwell, England, in September 1950, Blackett reported that his Manchester group had found ten more of the curious new events.[10] The next meeting where the subject might have been discussed, but was not, was the first Rochester Conference.

After the Old Stone meeting (chapter 19, sec. 19.4), Oppenheimer decided that the original purpose, to assess the current status and the prospects for further developments, had been accomplished. Thereupon Robert Marshak took a new initiative, to the lasting benefit of the high energy physics community. It was his belief that profitable meetings of the kind just ended should be continued but be more international in scope and have a better mix of experimentalists and theorists, especially in view of rapid developments in accelerator physics. The result was a series of seven annual conferences, beginning in 1950, with ever-growing attendance, all held in Rochester, New York, with financial support from local industry. During Rochester I, the 1950 meeting, the subject of quantum electrodynamics did not even come up (although Feynman was there). After these first seven conferences, the meetings continued in later years but were most often held in different places, in different countries. Nonetheless, they have continued to be called Rochester Conferences.

Since no published record exists for Rochester I, it may be of some use to state that it was a one-day meeting held on December 16, 1950, with an attendance of about fifty; that it consisted of morning, afternoon, and evening sessions chaired respectively by Pais, Oppenheimer, and Bethe, and that the topics discussed were accelerator results on the interaction of pions and nucleons with matter, muon physics, and cosmic ray physics. During the meeting, Oppenheimer suggested a discussion on the new mesons, but nothing came of that. I am grateful to the late Robert Marshak for making available to me an unedited transcript of that meeting.

During the two-day-long second Rochester Conference (January 11–12, 1952), one full day was devoted to the new particles. They have remained an important agenda item ever since.

20.2 PAULI IN PRINCETON

In November 1949, Pauli and his wife Franca (née Bertram) arrived at Idlewild (now JFK) Airport from Zurich for an academic year's stay at the Institute. Robert had asked me to pick them up at the airport, using an Institute station wagon with driver. After cordial greetings we went on our way to Princeton. In the car I asked Pauli what his plans were. He replied that he had come to the U.S. to find out what was happening in physics and to lose weight—he was not impressed with the American cuisine.

I had met Pauli earlier, in Copenhagen (chapter 13, sec. 13.3), but had not spent much time with him there. Now, in Princeton, we saw a good deal of each other. A friendship developed. We had numerous discussions on physics, often went for long walks, and frequently had lunch together. On such occasions he would often accompany his words with the characteristic oscillations described before. One day at lunch he made one of his rather outrageous statements, causing me to burst out laughing and to say: "You know, Pauli, there is no one like you." It was typical for him to reflect seriously about this banal statement, oscillating along. After a while he said: "Ja, es gibt mich nur einmal," then a pause, then "Und das ist vielleicht auch besser" (Yes, there is only one like me—and that is perhaps just as well). On another occasion, during a walk, he stopped, looked at the sky, then said: "Die weltfremden Physiker—die Menschen würden sich staunen" (The unworldly physicists—people would be surprised). During another walk he said to me: "I think we will get along well, because you think slowly, just as I do."

Yet another time he said that he could not understand why I would permanently settle in the United States, since he perceived me to be so very European in outlook and thought. I truthfully replied that, yes, I was aware of my continued strong ties to Europe but had also developed strong ties to America; and that I had begun to learn how to harmonize those sentiments which, superficially seen, looked contradictory. This led to interesting discussions about cultural diversity.

Thus our talks were not by any means confined to physics. Another frequent topic was psychoanalysis. I found out that Pauli was an adept of Jung. He had briefly and unhappily been married before, a relationship that had ended in divorce in November 1930. Shortly thereafter he had been analyzed by Jung himself. Since 1932 the two men had a correspondence (recently published)[11] that would last until 1958, the year of Pauli's death. As already mentioned, I was pro-Freud and strongly anti-Jung (chapter 3). The result was an intense debate between Pauli and me, always civilized but occasionally heated.

Pauli never talked to me about his relations with Jung, nor about his first marriage. He would, however, once in a while mention more personal matters. Thus he mentioned several times an extramarital affair he had had with one of his young students. It may have been on one such occasion that he said something to me which I vividly remember. "When I was young I thought that physics was easy and relations with women difficult. Now it is just the other way around."

As the end of Pauli's Princeton sojourn drew near, he invited me to come and stay with Franca and him in their home in Switzerland that coming summer. I was happy to accept.

In July I began my first consultantship at Brookhaven National Laboratory on Long Island. In the early years I would drive out twice a month for a day, together with Bob Serber. We went in his car, a sexy Jaguar XKE which he would allow me to drive part of the way. It was a tedious trip then, still along the old Montauk Highway. I remained a consultant there until 1977.

20.3 BOHR AND THE UNITED NATIONS

In February 1950, Bohr and his wife arrived once again in Princeton, after a crossing by sea from Denmark. For about a week he had had no opportunity to discuss scientific matters, and was therefore quite pent up. Pauli and I were walking in an Institute corridor when Bohr first came in. When he saw us he practically pushed us into an office and made us sit down. Before either Pauli or I could utter a word, Bohr said, "Pauli, *schweig*" (Pauli, shut up), which caused considerable mirth in all three of us. Then he talked for about two hours before either of us had a chance to interrupt him. Had Bohr's words been recorded, they would have constituted a fascinating document about the development of quantum theory.

The first subject Bohr wanted to discuss with me when just the two of us met shortly afterward was a draft he had brought along of an "Open Letter to the U.N." Would I help him to work further on that manuscript? I would.

The purpose of the letter was this. After Bohr's failed attempts in 1943 of convincing Churchill and Roosevelt (chapter 13, sec. 13.5) and, in 1948 (chapter 19, sec. 19.2), at spurring Secretary of State Marshall to act on his proposal for an open world, he had decided to desist from enlisting help from political leaders. Instead, he now planned to address the world at large directly.

I have vivid memories of many discussions during Bohr's visit that showed once again his deeply serious engagement in political matters. These would take place during evening hours at 14 Dickinson Street, where I still lived, and where the Bohrs once more occupied the lower floors. These sessions would invariably start in the following charming way. Bohr knew at what time I came home from having eaten out. When I came up to the house I could already see him pacing the downstairs corridor. When I opened the door he would always be walking away from me, so that it was I who would greet him first. Whereupon he would turn around in apparent surprise and ask if I would not like to come in for a glass of sherry, which I did. Then we would settle down for discussions that could last well into the night.

A story told to me by Oppenheimer dates from those days. At one point during this time Bohr called on Secretary of State Dean Acheson to discuss with him the content of his planned letter to the U.N. The meeting began at, say, two o'clock, with Bohr doing the talking. At about 2:30, Acheson spoke to Bohr something like this: "Professor Bohr, there are three things I must tell you at this time. First, whether I like it or not, I shall have to leave you at three for my next appointment. Secondly, I am deeply interested in your ideas. Thirdly, up till now I have not understood one word you have said." Whereupon, the story goes, Bohr got so enraged that he waxed eloquent for the remainder of the appointment.

In May, Bohr returned to Copenhagen. On June 9 at 10 A.M. New York time, Aage, who had been at Columbia University for some time, handed the Open Letter[12] to the Secretary-General, Trygve Lie. Simultaneously, Bohr held a press conference in Copenhagen. Right thereafter he sent copies of his letter to diplomats, politicians (one went to Churchill), newspapers, both national and foreign, physicists, friends. I was in Israel at that time and was supposed to brief President Weizmann but, as I wrote to Bohr,[13] my copy of the letter reached me too late to do so. Some press reactions were positive, others neutral if not negative.

The letter, written "without consultation with the government of any country," contains essential parts of Bohr's memorandum to Marshall (in particular the lines quoted previously, chapter 19, sec. 19.2), about which Bohr commented:

> The considerations in this memorandum may appear utopian, and the difficulties of surveying complications of non-conventional procedures may explain the hesitations of governments in demonstrating adherence to the course of full mutual openness. Nevertheless, such a course should be in the deepest interest of all nations, irrespective of differences in social and economic organization, and the hopes and aspirations for which it was attempted to give expression in the memorandum are no doubt shared by people all over the world.

The key phrases in the letter are as follows:

> The situation calls for the most unprejudiced attitude towards all questions of international relations. Indeed, proper appreciation of the duties and respon-

sibilities implied in world citizenship is in our time more necessary than ever before. On the one hand, the progress of science and technology has tied the fate of all nations inseparably together, on the other hand, it is on a most different cultural background that vigorous endeavors for national self-assertion and social development are being made in the various parts of our globe.

An open world where each nation can assert itself solely by the extent to which it can contribute to the common culture and is able to help others with experience and resources must be the goal to be put above everything else. . . . The arguments presented suggest that every initiative from any side towards the removal of obstacles for free mutual information and intercourse would be of the greatest importance in breaking the present deadlock and encouraging others to take steps in the same direction.

Within weeks Bohr's initiative was overshadowed by dramatic developments.

On June 24 the Korean War broke out.

On November 1 the U.S. exploded its first thermonuclear device in the Pacific.

Bohr was defeated by overwhelming historical forces.

Even then he did not give up. In 1956, during the crisis caused by events in Hungary and Suez, he made a second approach to the U.N., in another open letter to Secretary-General Dag Hammarskjöld. This letter, again privately printed and distributed, caused even less response than his earlier one. Indeed, in Bohr's lifetime his noble cause never received the public attention it deserved.

In October 1985, the centenary of Bohr's birth was celebrated with several conferences in Copenhagen. The proceedings of one of these, devoted to the challenge of nuclear armaments, are recorded in a book of essays "dedicated to Niels Bohr and his appeal for an open world."[14] A follow-up meeting took place in 1989.[15]

Of all the centennial tributes paid to Bohr, those he himself would have appreciated most are, I think, the public discussions during international symposia of his pleas for openness.

Shortly before the Paulis returned to Europe, I invited them and Niels and his wife for an evening in my apartment with coffee and dessert. I have before me a letter from Franca to me (I always called her Mrs. Pauli) dated November 9, 1976. After Pauli's death she and I would occasionally correspond (in German). In that letter she reminisced about the evening just mentioned: "I recall the unforgettable, unique evening which we, Niels Bohr, Margrethe, you, Wolfgang and I passed in Princeton, when Niels talked about complementarity until dawn. You too were deeply moved and said: 'It is like Jesus with his disciples.'" The last letter before her death which Mrs. Pauli wrote to me ends as follows: "It was during his last three days in the hospital [before his death in 1958] that a visitor, an old acquaintance, asked Pauli whether there was someone he would like to talk with. Pauli answered: 'Niels Bohr.'"[16]

20.4 MY GRAND TOUR OF 1950

My perceptions of our times have been enhanced by extensive travels, through America from coast to coast, through Europe from Madrid to Moscow, twice around the world. I have learned of other customs and seen much beauty, especially art treasures which are ever more important to me; also squalor. I must refrain—not always easy—from recording the things you can find in guidebooks and will confine myself to experiences of a more personal nature.

Please join me now in the first of several trips.

20.4.1 Israel

Via Holland, where I spent a few days with my parents, I flew to Israel, where I arrived on May 9. I was fetched from Lud Airport by Pekeris, who had invited me to lecture at the Weizmann Institute. He informed me that we were going to Tel Aviv, to attend the wedding of Ezer Weizmann, commander of the fledgling Israeli air force during the 1948 War of Independence. As we came to his parents' home, carloads of Israeli Air Force men and women were also arriving. I was introduced to the bride and groom, then Israel's chief (Ashkenazi) rabbi officiated at the *chuppah,* the marriage ceremony. Afterwards there was food and dancing. I joined in one of the *horrahs* proceeding simultaneously on several floors of the house, which was shaking with jumping Israelis. It certainly was the liveliest wedding I ever attended.

At this writing, Ezer Weizmann is president (the seventh) of Israel (since 1993), so he was its fifth president whom I have known personally. I had already met Shazar, the third president, in Holland, as well as Ezer's uncle,

Chaim (chapter 19, sec. 19.1), the first president. Meanwhile, in Princeton, I had met the Katchalsky (Katzir) brothers, Aharon and Ephraim, very bright, burly, and amiable fellows. Before Aharon, who had accepted to become Israel's president, could be formally elected, he was brutally assassinated on May 30, 1972, in a terrorist attack at Lud Airport by members of the Japanese Red Star organization, acting on instructions from the Popular Front for the Liberation of Palestine. His brother Ephraim was chosen in his place to be the fourth president (from 1973 to 78). The last president I met was Itzhak Navon, Israel's fifth (1978–83), whom I met in 1979 during the Einstein centennial celebration in Jerusalem. No country except Israel has had so many presidents who were (and are) outstanding intellectuals.

I spent my first night in Israel in Tel Aviv. The first thing I noticed on waking up the next morning was that people outside were making much noise. Perhaps it was some holiday, I thought, but on opening the curtains I saw nothing but a regular street crowd. I had to get used to everyday Israeli exuberance.

Then we drove on to Rehovoth, where, I found out, a private room in a guest house on the Weizmann Institute's pretty campus was waiting for me. A day or so later I started my lectures, always held in the early morning. I soon learned that after lunch I needed to take a siesta. The intense heat and light fatigued me.

One day I was invited to call on President Weizmann, who had his own office at the Institute. I was surprised to note that he remembered me from our meeting in New York. After some small talk he invited me once again to join the Institute faculty. I remember so well one of the reasons he gave me for doing so. When you come to live in Israel, he said, you will notice that you, like all Jews here, will walk straighter, a poetic way, I thought, of expressing how Israelis responded to their new freedom. He also pointed out the green fields and plants one could see from his window, adding with evident pride that, when he first came to Rehovoth, all you saw was barren sand.

Weizmann's arguments are the best I have ever heard for settling in Israel, yet I could not imagine, then or later, that I would feel at home in his country, the main reason being that in the U.S. I was living at the center of science. That meant far more to me than my ancestral roots.

From Rehovoth I made several trips to Jerusalem, always using public transportation. It was very enjoyable and moving to talk with other passengers. Noting that I was a foreign visitor, they would point out sites of interest to me, with great pride in the progress their young nation was making. There reigned a spirit of community in those early years, of confidence that together they would successfully master the enormous problems Israel was facing.

Jerusalem itself was still a city divided. My hosts, physicists, walked me to the barricades marking the limits of Israel. Cautioned to be careful, I clambered on debris to have a look at the other side. Their warning was not idle; when I stuck my head over the rim of rubble, an Arab who saw me aimed a rifle at me.

Another recollection of that time: seeing the ultra-orthodox Jews from the quarter known as *me'ah she'arim* (a hundred portals). To my eyes they were a weird-looking crowd, the men dressed in black garb that harks back to the days of the Polish ghettos. I consider them a pathetic lot, still clinging to messianic visions, and therefore not recognizing (to this day) the secular state of Israel. An Israeli joke from that time goes as follows. During the War of Independence, the black Jews (as they are called) organized a parade, marching behind a banner that said: "Don't believe in miracles. Pray."

In Jerusalem I met Giulio Racah, the head of the theoretical physics department at the Hebrew University. I was told that from his fluent Hebrew one could hear that he was a native of Florence. I knew of Racah's major contributions to group theoretical methods in atomic physics, published during the 1940s. He died in Florence, on August 28, 1965, as the result of a freak accident. I was privileged to contribute to a memorial volume in his honor.[17]

Some time into my stay, the Weizmann Institute graciously put at my disposal a car with driver, who also served as guide, for a trip of several days through the country.

We went north to Galilee for a visit to Tsefat (Safed), one of Judaism's four holy cities in Israel (the others being Hebron, Tiberias, and of course Jerusalem) and visited nearby Meron, the site of what one might perhaps call a Kabbalist monastery. Inside I saw bearded old men dressed fully in white, engaged in the study of the *Sefer ha Zohar* (the book of splendor), their most sacred text, a farrago of mystical speculation and philosophy. While there, my companion spoke to a man who was a local guide. He took us for a walk to a nearby ravine. Pointing to a large gaping hole in one of the rocky hills, he said: "There was the House of Hillel," then to another hole on the opposite side: "And there was the House of Shammai."

I was moved and surprised. I knew that these two were great rabbinical teachers from the second half of the first century, Shammai the adherent of an austere, strictly literal interpretation, Hillel more liberal and humane, a teacher of Jewish laws. I had heard of their schools, but was startled to see that these were nothing but large caves.

Then our guide said something which was to be my strongest memory of my whole first stay in Israel. Pointing to a nearby large rock he said: "This is Elijah's rock, on which the prophet will descend from the heavens to proclaim the coming of the Messiah and the restoration of Israel." I shivered. The man had spoken almost casually, without noticeable great reverence. It was obvious that he lived in daily contact with biblical events, the return of the ninth-century-B.C. Elijah being prophesied both in the Old (Malachi 4:5–6) and the New (Luke 9:8) Testaments.

Shortly afterward I departed for Greece, carrying with me in my mind strong images of what is so rightfully called the Holy Land.

20.4.2 Greece

Flying to Athens on July 5, I had pleasant fantasies of relief from the Israeli heat, of cooling Mediterranean breezes. Not so; I arrived during a heat wave. The temperature at Athens Airport was 108°F; the airfield was covered with metal grids to prevent the wheels of planes from getting stuck in the melting tar of the tarmac. Homer Thompson, my archeologist friend from Princeton, was at the airport to pick me up and drive me to the Amerikaniki Skoli, where I stayed.

The next morning, armed with a guidebook, I made my way to the Acropolis, its view dominated by the Parthenon. On arrival I sat down on the steps of the *propylaea*, read for a while, then took a stroll, read again, and so on. In the evening I told Homer what I had seen and asked for more information, which he gave me in his quiet, expert way, then invited me for a tour under his own guidance, which I happily accepted.

The next morning we took off, first passing the Theseum, then on to the Agora, located in a hollow near the Acropolis. Homer pointed out the stele mentioned by Pausanias, the starting point of his own excavations (chapter 18, sec. 18.1). As we strolled around the Agora that morning, Homer showed me its sites and explained their origins and meanings. We had lunch with the workmen there—one of whom was named Pythagoras. After lunch Homer took me to the nearby hill of the Pnyx, the ancient meeting place for popular assembly. It was there that Demosthenes, the famed Attic orator and statesman, roused the Athenians with his forensic speeches on public and private causes. On the Pnyx one walks along a wall hewn out of the rock. Just a wall, I thought, until Homer would stop, now here, now there, pointing out details, holes, protrusions, each of which had a story to tell. He made that wall come to life.

On the way back I noticed a decorated shard lying on the ground. I picked it up and said excitedly to Homer: "Look what I found." "Oh, that's only a seventeenth-century Byzantine pottery fragment," he said. I dropped it. There are not many places in the world where such a find would be treated that casually.

Then my time in Greece was up. In little more than two months I had been at the two cradles of Western culture. Those were intense and unforgettable experiences. Before leaving I expressed my profound gratitude to Homer.

20.4.3 Zurich

On July 12, I flew from Athens to Zurich. The first thing I noticed on arrival was the name of its airport, Klooten, which must strike any Dutchman as funny, since it is one of the vulgar Dutch terms for testicles. Pauli had come to fetch me. We took a taxi to his home, where I was to stay.

Most days Pauli and I would go to the physics institute, which then was located at Gloriastrasse 35 in old Zurich. Evenings were spent with the Paulis at home. I had met Franca a number of times before, but now I got to know her much better and could observe how she dealt with her husband—not the easiest of customers—with affection, but firmly. Margrethe Bohr has told the following story of the two. When Pauli came home in the afternoon he would always ask Franca what was new. (He never read newspapers.) She prepared herself for this questioning, but one day had nothing to tell. When she so informed Pauli, he said: "Nah ja, man kann sich auch langweilen" (Oh well, one can also be bored).

When the time came to leave, Pauli handed me a present. It was volume 7 of Jung's *Psychologische Abhandlungen,* which had just appeared.[18] Pauli had inscribed it: "Seinem jüngeren Freund Pais als Gegenwicht gegen Freud, zur Erinnerung an dem Sommer 1950 in Zürich" (To his younger friend Pais as counterweight to Freud, in memory of the summer of 1950 in Zurich). I was moved by this gesture of friendship. The book still stands on my shelves in New York.

20.4.4 France and Belgium

On July 18 I flew from Zurich to Paris, where Stephen White was waiting for me at the airport. I should explain that I had known him since Shelter Island, where he was the one newspaper man present. Steve and I drove to his home near Paris, a cottage on the estate of ex-prime minister Léon Blum, who had died just a few months earlier and whose widow I met. I greeted Steve's wife and settled down for what I expected to be a few days of peace and quiet. It turned out quite otherwise.

Early on the 20th we were sitting outside with our morning coffee when the phone rang. Steve went in and came back a few minutes later. That was the New York main office, he said. He had been told to proceed on the double to Brussels in order to cover the serious unrest expected on the return of the king. He asked if I wanted to come along. "Very much so," I replied, "provided that I shall not be in your way." "That will be no problem," he said. "I shall get you reporter's credentials. You can in fact be of help in interviewing since you understand Flemish."

An hour or so later he and I took off by car. On the way he filled me in on the political situation. Leopold III, king of Belgium since 1934, had remained after the capitulation of his country in May 1940 as prisoner in his own palace in Laeken, a Brussels suburb, rather than join his government-in-exile in London. In 1944 he had been taken to Germany, from where he went to Geneva after war's end, to await the calming down of loud voices demanding his abdication. Actually he stayed in Switzerland until 1950, when Parliament voted to recall him; he returned on July 24.

Whereupon serious unrest began. Steve on the front page of the *New York Herald Tribune* of the 26th: "Anti-Leopoldist bombs disrupt Belgian trains." On the 28th: "Crowds invade the grounds of Laeken," the Royal Palace. I was eyewitness to those events. Crowds marching through Brussels, chanting: "Léopold, au poteau" (Leopold to the gallows), and, rhythmically: "Ab-di-ca-tion." We decided to drive out to Liège, where we found a city looking as if it were under siege. Because I knew French I could assist Steve in interviewing one of the rebellion's leaders. On that trip, a press photographer, Mark (I forgot his last name), went along. One of his pictures taken that day won a Pulitzer Prize. On it you see a chair flying in the air, thrown by an irate citizen at a mounted policeman.

One day I accompanied Steve to a press conference at the office of Prime

Minister Jean-Pierre Devieusart. After he entered, while rowdy crowds shouted outside, he pompously started proceedings with "Messieurs, vos porteplumes" (gentlemen, your fountain pens). By observing Steve, I learned something valuable about the distinction between gathering objective information and writing an article. Whenever there was an interview with a group of reporters, Steve would walk up and down and listen, but would not take notes, unlike most others. When I asked him about this, he said that he could get all that was said from the wire services, and that meanwhile he was more interested in reflecting on the general flavor of events—like the better historian who gathers his objective information from existing documents and only then sits down to give his own subjective account. Information is necessary but not sufficient for insight. I also made my contribution by personally interviewing the Home Secretary, who was Flemish.

Most of the reporters who were there to cover the story stayed in the same hotel as we did. They were a lively group, but every day around three or four in the afternoon they would become very quiet. When I asked Steve why that was so, he told me that everybody was thinking about his lead, the crucial opening sentence that had to draw the reader into his or her article.

The next day I warmly thanked Steve for the unforgettable times we had spent together (to this day we greet each other with "Léopold, au poteau" when we meet), and took a train to Amsterdam. After months of strong experiences, ranging from Elijah's rock to Liège's riots, I was in need of decompression and digestion.

20.4.5 England

My R and R in Holland lasted until September 6, when I took a plane to London to start the last phase of the summer's tour. After arrival I took a train to Oxford, where as per instructions I presented myself to the porter of Brasenose College, who handed me the key to a pleasant room. All conference participants were housed there.

The next day an international physics conference started. I presented a review of the theoretical problems of interpreting theoretically the data on neutron-proton and proton-proton scattering, especially at high energies. Niels Bohr also attended and we had several discussions on the fate of his Open Letter.

My only other recollection of that pleasant week was participating in an evening poker game in one of the Brasenose rooms. Others who joined were Luis ("Luie") Alvarez, whom I met there for the first time, and Philip Dee, a physics professor from Glasgow. Alvarez turned out to be a seasoned, tough player, Dee had never played the game until that evening. Nevertheless, the good professor from Scotland managed to bluff Luie out of a very strong hand.

What happened was hilarious. After having invited Dee to join us, and having been informed that he did not know the rules of the game, we said we would help him by preparing a list of betting hands: one pair, two pairs, etc. There came a moment when all of us had folded except Alvarez and Dee. Luie raised Dee, who studied the list lying before him, then raised Luie by more. Alvarez raised Dee again, Dee took another long serious look at his list and raised Alvarez by more. After another repeat, Alvarez folded. After it was all over, we asked Dee what his hand was. It turned out to be a pair of jacks and a pair of eights with which he had managed to outplay Luie's straight! Ah, the virtues of innocence.

Then I took the boat train via Dieppe to Paris, where I arrived on the 14th.

20.4.6 Paris

I stayed at the same hotel as Viki Weisskopf; I don't recall why. I remember an evening spent at the Caveau des Oubliettes on Rue St. Julien le Pauvre. It was a small place where one drank wine and listened to the wonderful ballads sung by one or another of the waiters. I still know by heart the "Ballade des quatre vingt chasseurs" (Ballad of the Eighty Hunters).

As I walked by a fine print shop on the Left Bank one day, I noticed a small pen drawing by Picasso in the window. I stepped inside and asked the proprietor whether it was an original; it was. What was the price? Fifty dollars. We talked some more, I telling him how much I admired the painter. Would I like to see some more of his work? Yes, please. I saw bigger prints and then he said, "Now I will show you some museum pieces." Reverently he opened a huge portfolio. It contained two large Picasso prints, one a Pan figure, one a copy of *Le Repas frugal*, number one of the Saltimbanque series of 1904. That second one transfixed me. I knew I had to have it. Was it for sale? Yes, the price was 250 dollars. Now I had a problem. As it was toward the end of a long trip I did not have that much cash left (credit cards came later). I asked the owner to please hold this one for just one hour—I would get the money.

I ran back to the hotel, which was not far away, and knocked on Weisskopf's door. Fortunately he was in. "Viki," I said, "can you lend me 250 dollars? I shall be back in the States in just a few days and will immediately deposit that amount in your bank." I told him why I needed the cash, and he was able to help me. I gave him a grateful hug and ran back. The shopkeeper accepted the money, then asked me to please make myself comfortable in the store while he would dash over to the U.S. Embassy to have a certificate of authenticity notarized. That paper would enable me to get through customs without paying duty. He went, I sat, he came back with the stamped certificate. I took off with my treasure in a big cardboard role under my arm.

Little did I know then that I had just made the best financial investment of my life. I bought that print just prior to the precipitous rise in prices of objets d'art, when investors took over from art lovers. When in 1993 I had my print appraised at Sotheby's, its price had risen almost four hundred times what I had paid.

Nor did I then or ever after buy art for investment. Just as had happened with the Picasso, I never went shopping for art but rather would stumble on something, take one look, and know that was it.

I left Paris on the 21st.

20.4.7 Iceland

The reason I had returned to Paris was that it was a natural stopover on my way to Luxembourg, from where I was to fly back to New York on a non-scheduled airliner.

We had to make a refueling stop at Keflavik Airport, where we landed at night in the dark. Winds made it bitter cold. We were shepherded into a help-yourself cafeteria. In a lousy mood, like my fellow-travelers, I took a tray, put something on it, and shuffled to the cashier—who turned out to be an absolutely gorgeous blonde. My spirits were raised at once. When it came my turn to pay, I said to her: "Good morning. How do you say 'good morning' in Icelandic?" To which she replied, verbatim: "How the hell should I know?" She turned out to be an American-born employee from Minnesota. So much for my Icelandic experiences.

20.4.8 Coming Home

After we landed at Idlewild Airport I proceeded to customs. When my turn came, the inspector wanted to know what was in the roll under my arm. A Picasso, I said, producing my certificate. He asked to see it, whereafter he stared at me and asked: "What the hell is an owner of a Picasso doing on a nonscheduled flight?" I explained that I'd rather spend money on art than on travel tickets. He laughed and said: "Welcome home."

Shortly after my return to Princeton I moved from Dickinson Street to the upper floor of a white clapboard house on South Olden Lane. It had a private entrance via outdoor wooden stairs. I had one wall thrown out, making a large living room which I had painted a soft warm brown. Earth colors are my favorite.

Since I now lived very close to the Institute, I thought it better to go for a walk before getting to work. So I walked to Mercer Street, had a cup of coffee at The Balt, then went to the Institute, in all about a 45-minute walk. That way of starting the day agreed so well with me that up to the present I have kept up the daily routine of a morning walk first. I have estimated that in this way I have covered a distance twice around the equator.

Soon after my return I noticed a phenomenon I have since called the "Princeton fog." Upon returning from wonderful experiences overseas, it was as if a fog rose over the Atlantic, crept on till it surrounded Princeton, which itself kept clear. Memories from the outside world faded—I was back in what Einstein once called "that quaint ceremonious village of puny demigods on stilts."

21

Of the Beginnings of Theoretical
Particle Physics, Some Baseball History,
and Two Long Summer Journeys

21.1 ABOUT PHYSICS' NEW TOYS, BRIEFLY

IN SECTION 20.1 of the preceding chapter, I recalled the great changes in style and content of post-World War II physics as compared to the state of affairs in the 1930s. I noted in particular how experimental particle physics had to be pursued by consortia of universities because accelerators had become too costly to be funded by individual institutions.

An accelerator by itself only "comes to life" when detectors—tools for observing and measuring what the machines produce—are emplaced nearby. This is not the place for even a brief sketch of most important developments of new kinds of detectors designed to analyze events at ever higher energies and ever increasing numbers. One example must suffice.

In 1960 my friend Don Glaser received the physics Nobel Prize "for the invention of the bubble chamber," a new kind of detector he had proposed in 1952. His idea was to enclose a liquid in a vessel under pressure, then heat it above the liquid's normal boiling point. Upon expanding the volume, vapor bubbles can be formed along the path of an electrically charged particle traversing the chamber and occasionally scattering off a molecule of the liquid. This track is then photographed.

Glaser's first bubble chamber had a two-cubic-centimeter volume. Along came Luis Alvarez, who in 1955 proposed to build a 500-liter chamber filled with liquid hydrogen, an ideal target for studying fundamental processes. Four years and two and a half million dollars later, the chamber was operational, complete with elaborate cryogenics for keeping hydrogen at

$-250°C$, a 15,000-gauss magnetic field for bending tracks, its own separate building, and its elaborate safety precautions.

That still was not all. As Alvarez had further emphasized, data analysis would be the bottleneck in future cloud chamber work. Thus, he concluded, track scanning and analysis needed to become semiautomatic; computers should be used for analysis and storage of data. And that is exactly what happened.

I well recall the initial reservations of quite a few members of the profession in regard to Alvarez's managerial approach which, they felt, would remove physicists yet another step from experimentation done in the old ways. They were right, and so was Alvarez. It came to be recognized that either one accepts the new style as indispensable, or particle physics will languish. How else could the Berkeley group alone have measured 1.5 million events in 1968?

If you think that was as far as it went, hear this. In 1975, BEBC, the Big European Bubble Chamber, hydrogen filled, was completed at CERN; its volume was 35,000 liters. As to detectors, many new types are now in use: spark chambers, multiwire proportional chambers, drift chambers, streamer chambers, others.

So much for experimental developments which, I hope, will give the reader a glimpse of the complexity and costliness of these endeavors.[1]

In the preceding chapter I mentioned that the coming of particle physics changed my life, and I alluded to my first publication in this field in 1951. I shall now expand on this after first recounting my adventures during the summer of 1952.

21.2 THE SUMMER OF 1951: TO THE WEST AND BACK

Early in 1951 I received an invitation to be guest lecturer at the forthcoming summer school at Stanford University in California. I accepted and thought it might be a new experience to go there by car. Before taking off I joined the American Automobile Association (AAA), which provided me with route sheets. I had my car, a solid Pontiac, thoroughly checked and ran trials at changing tires. Sometime in June I went on my way. I can easily retrace my itinerary since I still have my old battered copy of the Rand-McNally atlas on which I marked my route and stops. I spent the first night at a motel near Pittsburgh, having covered about 250 miles and feeling quite ex-

hausted. My next stops, always at motels, were Columbus, Ohio, Spring-
field, Illinois, and Kansas City, Kansas.

I had no memorable experiences so far except for one: I had begun to
feel, viscerally, how large these United States were. I knew of course that
my native Holland fits more than three times into New York State; also that
driving south from Amsterdam over the distance just covered I would have
found myself somewhere in Spain, having crossed three borders on the way.
Yet these were just numbers that do not match the direct experience of
driving through this great land, without ever having to stop for border
inspection.

Beyond Kansas City, I entered the real Midwest, the plains, with wheat
fields as far as the eye could see. Some may find that too monotonous, dull.
One wag has in fact called the United States a desert of boredom stretching
between the oases of New York and San Francisco. I do not share that
judgment. On my trip I found it exhilarating to drive at high speed through
this expanse, windows open, my radio at high volume, listening to ballads
sung in a rather nasal voice with guitar accompaniment.

Coming to western Kansas I began to see mountains rising up at the far
horizon. I was nearing the Rockies. I stopped at Limon, Colorado, then
drove on to Denver and crossed the Continental Divide at Loveland Pass. I
had to be careful since driving at this considerable altitude I became quite
sleepy. Next stop: Steamboat Springs, a short distance beyond the Rockies.
It had been a hard day's drive.

My next stop was in Wells, just over the border of Nevada, the land of the
ubiquitous slot machines, where I also saw my first silver dollars. Wherever
I stopped, for a meal, for gas, I would waste a few quarters on the one-
armed bandits.

Leaving Wells I arrived in Elko, where I had the great good luck to find
out that there would be a rodeo that afternoon, which of course I would not
want to miss for the world. It was a spectacle ever so much better in vivo
than the clips familiar from television. Sitting there on wooden benches
amid a raucous crowd, munching hot dogs, having sodas, in that hot but
dry air—I still smile when I think about it.

After the rodeo I drove on till late that evening, so on that day I attended
one rodeo and covered five hundred miles, all the way to Reno, yet I was no
longer exhausted. I had caught on to a new rhythm.

My next stop was near Lake Tahoe, where I took off one day to swim and
sun myself on a rock. Having the Rockies well behind me, I looked forward
to an easy last phase of the trip, through the plains to the Pacific Coast. Fool

that I was, I had entirely forgotten that the minor matter of crossing the Sierras lay still ahead of me. That traversal was easier, however, than doing the Rockies. Also, the vistas were much more beautiful. Via Sacramento and San Francisco I reached my destination city of Stanford. I went straight to the physics department, where an envelope marked with my local address was waiting for me, keys inside. I found the place to be a delightful studio apartment.

I had never yet seen a campus as enchanting as that of Stanford, where shortly afterward I started my lectures on QED. One of my students was a young man by the name of Sidney Drell. I am proud to report that he learned his first quantum field theory from me, a subject on which in the 1960s he co-authored one of the best-known textbooks.[2] I should also mention that Uhlenbeck was the other guest lecturer that summer.

Well before I left, I had heard that Ma Koehorst, my hostess from my hiding days in Amsterdam (chapter 10, sec. 10.2), was now divorced and living in San Mateo, not far from Palo Alto, together with her daughter Alwien. I gave her a call soon after having settled down in my summer residence. She was pleased to hear from me and invited me for dinner. I went, had a nice evening—and I had a long talk with Alwien. The result was that she and I spent all my California weekends together in my studio apartment. We would make occasional trips by car, mainly to San Francisco, where I parked in the underground garage on beautiful Union Square, and where we delighted in trips on the fabled cable cars and delicious dinners at Fisherman's Wharf. It was an idyllic summer.

In addition I had a fairly active social life in Palo Alto. With particular pleasure I remember meeting Felix Bloch and Leonard Schiff, distinguished members of the physics faculty. I also recall a cocktail party in the home of the university's president. At one point Uhlenbeck and I wandered out on the roof garden, where we encountered George Polya, a well-known mathematician. We talked so animatedly that we lost track of time—until we realized that we had considerably overstayed our welcome. We went down, passed through the living room, where we startled the president and his wife in quiet conversation with personal guests, mumbled apologies, and left.

During that summer Alwien told me of her plans to find work in New York. I suggested that we drive back together, leisurely, making detours to see some sights. She thought that was a fine idea.

We took off in early September, going north on Highway 101, I seeing my first giant redwood trees. First stop: Eureka. Then into Oregon, driving through magnificent evergreen forests to Crater Lake, our next stop. The next day to Portland, then into the Yakima Valley of Washington State, with high flat-topped volcanic formations on both sides; stop in Yakima. On we went to a crossing of the Columbia River, where we saw a stirring spectacle: Indians catching salmon (for which they had a monopoly) as the fish were swimming upstream to their spawning areas. It was an astonishing sight, men standing on rocks in the riverbed, simply scooping up in nets large numbers of quite sizable fish. On to the Grand Coulee Dam, next stop Spokane. Into northern Montana, a stop in Kalispell, then to Glacier National Park, where we spent three days hiking, to Iceberg Lake, and to the Grinnell Glacier. Then south via Missoula to Yellowstone Park, where we spent another three days, watching the geysers and loafing.

Then we turned eastward through northern Wyoming, stopping near Devil's Tower, that imposing, solitary high rock. Into South Dakota next, with the obligatory visit to Mount Rushmore, with its huge carvings of four presidents' heads. East thereof begin the Badlands, an eerie barren landscape that does not fail to leave a lasting impression.

That was the last memorable experience of our trip. We drove next through Minnesota and Wisconsin to Milwaukee, where we crossed Lake Michigan by car ferry. Then via Detroit and Pittsburgh to New York City, where one early evening I delivered Alwien to a friend's apartment in the fifties, just west of Fifth Avenue.

I parked the car on the street, took out Alwien's luggage, locked the car, accompanied her upstairs, had a cup of coffee with her and her friend, then kissed her au revoir, planning to drive on to Princeton that night. That, however, would not come to pass.

Returning to my car, I was shocked to find that my big suitcase with all my clothes had been stolen from the back seat. It was very upsetting, yet I felt fortunate that all my papers were locked in the trunk. I lost one highly valued possession, however: an expensive fine French flute, which I had bought on my last trip to Holland. I had taken lessons in Princeton, not getting all that far, but I was able to entertain myself by playing simple melodies.

I never bought another flute, but now, more acutely, I had no clothes left to speak of, except for the dirty jeans I was wearing. I went back up to the apartment and asked if I could sleep on a couch so that the next day I could shop for some apparel; permission was granted. The next morning I borrowed some cash, bought one suit and one shirt, then returned to the Princeton fog.

As everyone knows who has had a similar experience, theft of property may be painful but more lasting is the sense of invasion of privacy. Yet this unpleasant journey's end has in no way detracted from the rich memories I brought home from my first good long look at these United States.

I still had some clothes in Princeton. Soon after my return I donned an old pair of slacks and a sweater, then went to Langrock on Nassau Street, the finest men's clothing store in town, to get myself a new pair of slacks and a sports jacket. As I entered, two men looked me up and down, then the shorter one said, clearly audible, to his colleague: "Well, look at that." That was Mr. Decker, the head salesman, a well-known fixture of that Princeton period. I took to him at once, very sympathetic to his exclamation. Then and for years thereafter, Mr. Decker was my sartorial guide. On a wall in the back of the store he had autographed pictures of his best-known clients: Oppenheimer, von Neumann, William Faulkner, and others.

21.3 BASEBALL'S FINEST HOUR

Baseball fans will remember the third of October 1951 for the most dramatic game ever played. It was televised, but I heard it over the radio since I did not yet own a set.

On the preceding August 11, the Brooklyn Dodgers had been leading the National League, followed by the New York Giants, thirteen and a half games behind. Then the Dodgers started losing, the Giants winning, greatly helped by their new center fielder, the nineteen-year-old Willie Howard ("The Say Hey Kid") Mays, a black, who became rookie of the year for 1951 and turned into one of the game's greatest players.

On September 30, at the end of the regular season, the two teams ended in a dead heat. A best-of-three play-off series had to decide who would be National League champion. On the next day the Dodgers won, on October 2 it was the Giants. On the third day, the deciding game took place.

The bottom of the ninth inning came, the Dodgers leading, 4–2, the Giants at bat. They managed to get runners on 2nd and 3rd with one out. Then Robert Brown ("Bobbie") Thomson came to the plate.

Strike one. Bobbie swung at the next pitch. The ball sailed high up, landing in the lower left seats, 320 feet from home plate. Home run. On its front page, the *New York Times* called it "the blow of blows."[3] The Giants had won, 5–4, and were the League champion.

"Thomson's home run instantly became a moment in the consciousness of a nation, without equal in American sport."[4] On October 4, the baseball columnist of the *New York Herald Tribune* wrote: "Now it is done. Now the story ends. And there is no way to tell it. The art of fiction is dead. Reality has strangled invention. Only the utterly impossible, the inexpressibly fantastic, can ever be plausible again." There have been other exciting end-it-all home runs, most recently Carter's in 1993, which finished the World Series with a victory of Toronto over the Phillies, but never, repeat *never*, as dramatic as Thomson's.

In the 1951 World Series, the New York Yankees beat the Giants in six. That series marked the end of the baseball career of Joe ("The Yankee Clipper") DiMaggio. On the next December 12, the *New York Times* reported on its front page that Joltin' Joe had announced his retirement from the game. On that day, the paper also devoted an editorial to him: "The proficiency and exquisite grace he brought to the art of playing center field must have been seen to be believed."

*21.4 INTO THE PARTICLE JUNGLE

Scientists are like pickpockets. God has all the secrets in his pockets, and we try to pick them. You make an assumption in science—and it is an assumption—that there are fundamental laws you can find out. You have an idea you think can be proved and you try to prove it. Depending on how it goes, you make a step forward or you make a fool of yourself. Nature doesn't care whether you're right or wrong. Nature is the way it is, and you had better be smart enough to get a little glimpse.

—A. PAIS, The Rockefeller
University Research Profiles,
1982–83

Early in October 1951 I attended my first faculty meeting as full professor. The next day, Robert and I discussed plans for physics over lunch. I recorded in my diary one of his pungent comments: "It is the question whether we should emphasize the work of people done here or whether we should continue our thin but pleasant life with visitors, discussions, and the like," which reminded me of my own experiences during my first two years at the Institute. By the time of that luncheon I had become an active professional, however.

By spring 1951 my joint paper with Jost on scattering theory (chapter 19, sec. 19.3) had been sent in for publication. It had been hard labor. At that time both of us were late workers. It happened frequently that we ended our joint efforts at three or four in the morning. As a result, I did not get up until about noon. By that time, children attending a kindergarten near my South Olden Lane apartment were just leaving their morning session. They loved running up and down my outdoor steps on their way home, so that I would be awakened by their yelling outside my bedroom. One morning I had enough of that, stepped outside in my pajamas, completely unkempt, and yelled back: "Go away." I must have scared them since they never used my stairs again. One parent told me in fact that I had become known to them as the Bad Man.

I mentioned earlier (chapter 20, sec. 20.1), the strong impression a Cal Tech paper of 1950 on the new particles had made on me and how I felt that my future lay in them. At that time there was not much for a theorist to get his teeth into, however. Also, I was fruitfully engaged in my work with Jost. So my labors in this new area did not begin until early 1951.

It was known by then that "V-particles"—the early collective name for the new particles, meant to symbolize the kinks in their tracks when decaying—are produced at a copious rate, roughly comparable to that of pion production in nucleon-nucleon collisions, that is, they were produced by a "strong" interaction. Their half-life, the time it takes on average for a particle to decay, had also roughly been measured by then, for example for the decay of a Λ-particle into a proton plus a pion. Since from production processes it was known that Λ's, protons, and pions all participate in strong interactions, one might think that also Λ-decay is a process ruled by these same interactions. If so, one can easily estimate that the Λ half-life would be in the neighborhood of 10^{-21} seconds (one divided by ten to the power of twenty-one). It was actually found to be very much larger, about 10^{-10} seconds! In the physicist's language—which must sound bizarre to the non-initiate—Λ-particles, indeed V-particles of all kinds, are very long-lived, showing that the forces causing their decays have to be very weak.

Such weak forces, or processes, had been known to exist in other contexts. They are responsible for the long-known β-radioactive decay processes, in which, for example, a neutron decays into proton + electron + neutrino. It might therefore seem as if one were on familiar ground: V-particle production is ruled by strong interactions, their decay by weak ones. That is true, but it does not yet address the cardinal new issue: What forbids the strong interactions from causing far more rapid V-particle decay? One must further ask: What forbids electromagnetic interactions—weaker than the strong but much stronger than the weak interactions—from causing far more rapid V-particle decay?

It would take several years before the fundamental nature of these questions was appreciated by the physics community at large. In fact, in 1951 the new particles "were not considered respectable, especially among theorists."[5] When some time later one theorist had completed an excellent paper on the subject, he "was warned that [its publication] might adversely affect his career, because he would be known as the sort of person who worked on that kind of thing."[6]

Nevertheless, in 1951, a few excellent physicists (Feynman and Fermi among them) had begun to speculate that the strong suppression of strong interactions in decay processes was due to a complicated V-particle structure, which allows the strong interactions to act in full force at the high energies at which their production takes place but strongly inhibits them at the low energies at which decays occur.[7]

I did not much care for such ideas. As indicated earlier (chapter 20, sec. 20.1), I had the idea that the Λ is related to the nucleon as the muon is to the electron. If so, one should seek a resolution in which "the heavy fermion [Λ] is as elementary as the nucleon."[8]

My familiarity with atomic and nuclear physics provided me with a lead to another approach. In these domains of physics it happens rather often that reactions that are conceivable are in fact strictly prohibited by systematic principles known as "selection rules." None of the earlier known rules could be of use for what I needed here, however. To cope with the situation—strong production, weak decay—I needed a rule that would forbid strong and electromagnetic but not weak decays. In other words, the rule could not be strict, could not be universal, and it should hold for some but not all processes—a novel situation. That line of thought, which has proved to be correct, marks the birth of theoretical particle physics.

So far, so good—but how to formulate the new rule? The existing corpus of theory was of no use to me, and the only guide I had was experimental facts. These facts led me to introduce a postulate[9] that can be phrased (a bit loosely) in simple language: the new particles interact strongly only when pairs of them are involved, but weakly when interacting alone. This hypothesis has become known as the "principle of associated production." The evidence for it was still dubious at the time I first stated it; I recall being told by some experimentalists that it was wrong. The first convincing experiments were not published until 1953.[10] Associated production has in fact proved to be of the ages.

On the other hand, it is not surprising that my attempts of 1951 at casting my rule in a more concrete mathematical form did not survive. As the next years were to show, the data were too incomplete at that time. I had anticipated that. As I wrote in my first paper on the subject: "The search for ordering principles at the moment may . . . ultimately have to be likened to a chemist's attempt at building up the periodic system if he were given only a dozen odd elements."[11]

Still, I had found the right direction. As has been written of those efforts: "Although encumbered by . . . a wholly incorrect model, a program for the next generation lies swaddled within the nervous evidence of Pais's creativity."[12] My friend Sam Treiman has commented: "This observation [associated production] broke a logjam of understanding and led to the discovery of new quantum numbers and to a first round of organization."[13] I shall come back in a while to those new numbers, noting here only that "logjam" was no exaggeration. Starting in about 1952, new particles kept being discovered at an awesome rate. We had entered a veritable jungle.

In the autumn of 1951, I lectured on these ideas at the Institute, and again at the Second Rochester Conference (January 11–12, 1952).[14] At that meeting discussions of the new particles were "the hottest item on the agenda."[15] I am not responsible for the title of my paper as it appears in the proceedings: "An ordering principle for megalomorphian zoology." That fickle title was the creation of Oppenheimer, who, by the way, was also the inventor of the term "megalopolis."

In concluding my report I noted that perhaps we are witnessing "the unfolding of an ordering in which one talks of families of elementary particles rather than of elementary particles themselves. [I] would hope ultimately for a master equation for each family which, essentially by means of a quantization process would give not only a set of mass values but also contain selection rules that go with new quantum numbers." This remark led in the 1980s to the comment by Marshak, "Pais certainly paved the way

for the new era of the 'additive strangeness quantum number' that com-
menced in 1953."[16] I shall turn to that era in the next chapter.

Early in 1952 my friend and colleague Harold Cherniss and I conceived of
the idea to organize a supper club that would meet once in a while in a
reserved room in the Nassau Tavern (now Inn). As permanent core we co-
opted Ernst Kantorowicz, the distinguished historian appointed to our faculty in 1951, Erwin Panofsky, and John von Neumann, and further decided
to invite one or two guests each time. There would never be an agenda, we
would just see what happened.

   Our supper club proved to be a tremendous success. Among the guests I
recall George Kennan; Perry Miller, the American intellectual historian; and
Edward Tolman, the psychologist. We kept the enterprise going for several
years, after which it petered out.

21.5 THE SUMMER OF 1952: ANOTHER GRAND TOUR

21.5.1 Denmark

As usual I first went to Holland, leaving New York on May 16, 1951, for a
crossing on board the *Nieuw Amsterdam,* which still took eight days. I spent
two weeks in Amsterdam, staying with my parents, seeing old friends, visiting favorite places. On June 7 I flew on to Copenhagen, to attend a conference. On the 9th I gave a talk on nuclear forces,[17] on the 10th on "Heavy
Unstable Particles,"[18] and on the 12th on the scattering of pions.[19] I met
old friends: Bohr, Møller, the Josts, Pauli. I also met Heisenberg for the first
time, with whom I talked physics; never, either then nor on later occasions,
did I raise political issues with him.

   I stayed in Copenhagen until the end of July. I had been able to rent a house
known as Struensee's Gaard (farm), after its original owner, an eighteenth-
century count who became prime minister of Denmark. I spent most of my
time reading: *Unpopular Essays* by Bertrand Russell; *Civilization of the Renaissance in Italy* (in German), the masterpiece by Jacob Burckhardt; poetry by
Rilke; and several volumes by my favorite author, Charles Morgan. From his
essay "On Singleness of Mind," an appendix to his *The Flashing Stream:*
"Singleness of mind is not an end but a beginning. It is a receptive state, the
converse of hardness of heart. It is the womb of reason."

I tuned the radio regularly to the American Armed Forces Network's news programs. One evening I heard a political address that literally made me jump. Here, for the first time since settling in the United States, I was hearing eloquent words of reason. It was the address by Adlai Stevenson, governor of Illinois, welcoming the Democratic National Convention, also held in Chicago, to his state. I had no right to vote yet, but all the same I told myself: Stevenson is my man.

21.5.2 Germany

On July 31 I took a train to Hamburg, where I was met at the station by a friend from Princeton. To my surprise she took me to a waiting limousine with chauffeur, who drove us to an elegant house where, it turned out, she lived together with a wealthy industrialist. I was their house guest for the next three days.

This was my first visit to Germany. Understandably, I felt rather queasy which, however, did not prevent me from spending some interesting, in fact pleasant, days. I remember most particularly a visit to an art museum that houses the finest collection of paintings by Max Lieberman, a Jew and leader of the German Impressionist movement. Not until that day did I realize what an excellent painter he was.

On August 2 my friend accompanied me to Bergen-Belsen. It was bizarre to be driven there in a chauffeured Mercedes-Benz. We walked around for a while in this now barren, desolate place. I was somber as I walked past large mass graves where untold many Jews lay buried, wondering all along: Could I be near the remains of my dear sister Annie? I did not yet know about Sobibor (chapter 10, sec. 10.3).

My friend accompanied me to Braunschweig, where I said a grateful good-bye and took a train to Salzburg.

21.5.3 Austria

Jerry Bruner and his wife, other friends made in Princeton, welcomed me at the station, and informed me that they had rented a room for me on the Kaigasse. My original plan had been to spend a few days there. As it happened I stayed for three glorious weeks of immersion in music.

The next morning I walked over the Mönchsberg to Schloss Leopolds-
kron, a small château by a lake where, under American auspices, the
summer school was in progress at which Jerry lectured to students of various nationalities. I got to know other members of the teaching staff, all
American, including Milton Babbitt, a Princeton professor of music and
mathematics, a leading figure in electronic music composition which, I
regret to say, I never took to. Also the well-known poet Robert Lowell
and his wife, the author Elizabeth Hardwick. He suffered from serious depression and had to be hospitalized in Munich that summer. I attended
various classes and also gave an evening lecture on physics in the Vene-
tian Room of the Schloss, ate with the students, and participated in evening dances.

My main Salzburg experiences were musical, however, particularly hearing Mozart played in his native town. Never in all my life, before or after,
have I heard so much and such good music as in those few weeks. My
strongest memory is hearing "The Marriage of Figaro" with Elisabeth
Schwarzkopf and Irmgard Seefried in the female lead roles, beautiful
women with wonderful voices. After the final curtain I said to myself: Never
in your life will you hear a more beautiful performance. I was right. Finally,
I attended an open-air performance of *Jedermann* (Everyman).

In the middle of it all, the Bruners and I went for a three-day visit to
Vienna, then still divided into zones, each one governed by one of the four
Allied powers (as in *The Third Man*). A special visa for entering Vienna was
required. On the way back we again had to show our passport and special
visa to the Russian border police. A soldier took one look at my visa, then
yelled at me: "Zuruck, kaputt!" (Back, ruined.) I trembled until the soldier
burst out laughing and explained, in broken German, that my visa was valid
for three more days, and I should go back and use them up. Not a funny
moment.

My three grand weeks came to an end. I told the Bruners how immensely
grateful I was to them for my rich experiences. Next stop: Berne in Switzerland.

21.5.4 Switzerland

In Berne I met my friends the Josts. We had planned to take some days of
vacation together in the mountains. Accordingly we went by car to Pon-

tresina in Canton Graubünden, where we settled down in Pension Remi. Res and I had made a plan to climb the nearby Piz Albris. We estimated that the ascent would take some five hours, so, leaving early, we could be back by dinnertime. That, however, did not come to pass.

All went as planned on the way up. The climb was not very technical, yet did require that now and then Res, an expert in the mountains, had to belay me. After we reached the top we had a piece of bread and sausage and some water. Looking over the beautiful landscape, we noticed another possible way back to the valley, steeper but considerably shorter. We decided to try that one and began our slow descent. There came a point where I, in front, belayed by Res, saw trouble ahead. "If we continue this way," I told him, "we will hit a good-sized waterfall." We retraced our steps part of the way until we found a narrow lateral ledge along which we proceeded sideways, stepping very carefully. The going was slow, the sun went down, we were still on the slope. Whereupon Res decided that safety demanded that we spend the night there to wait for sunrise before going farther. We sat for quite a while until I felt like moving a little bit. That was lucky, since I discovered a safe way to get down. Slowly, slowly, we descended, reaching the road by eleven in the evening. We still had to walk another hour to reach our *Pension*. On we went, when a car stopped next to us. "Are you the two men from Pension Remi who were on the Albris?" Indeed we were. Shouts of joy from the car.

What had happened meanwhile was that Res's wife Hilde, seriously alarmed, had called a local three-man mountain rescue squad who were on their way to save us when we met them. Together we drove to the *Pension*, where we were embraced by a tearful Hilde. All of us were given food and hot tea, then sat for hours as the locals told stories of other rescues that did not end as happily as ours.

We spent the next days loafing. One morning I walked into the village to buy the latest *International Herald Tribune*. I read through it, sitting on a terrace with coffee, when my eyes fell on a small ad in the "Miscellaneous" column. It read: "Buick '63 going to Casablanca by Barcelona, Madrid, will take passengers. Share expenses. John Pinto, Hôtel Quai Voltaire." I sat transfixed, staring at the ad. Now wouldn't that be something, to go to Casablanca, an almost mystical name that drew me irresistibly? I returned to the *Pension* and announced to my friends that the next day I was leaving for North Africa. They thought I was mildly mad. Early next morning I said au revoir and took off.

21.5.5 France

Late that night I arrived at the Hôtel Quai Voltaire, dropped off my luggage, and called John Pinto over the house phone. He was in, and turned out to be a good-looking Sephardic Jew in his late twenties, born in Tunis, now a toy salesman in Washington, D.C. We quickly agreed to terms.

We took off on September 8, taking turns at the wheel. Jacques, as he preferred to be called, was a maniacal speed driver, scaring me a bit but causing no mishaps. In Paris I had told him of an article I had recently read in the *New Yorker* which described in lyrical terms the delights of a dinner at Les Pyramides in Vienne, twenty miles south of Lyon. We planned to reach that restaurant the first evening. That demanded covering over 250 miles along roads that were not exactly superhighways. But we made it.

We were led to a table for two on a delightful outdoor terrace. The waiter came, without menus—there were no written menus, one was counseled on the options. Toward the end of our unspeakably marvelous dinner, a portly gentleman approached us who turned out to be the great Fernand Point, the restaurateur, known all over France as "Le Roi," the king, considered by experts to be the greatest of the living French chefs. We rose and I thanked him for the honor of coming to our table and for the privilege of dining in his establishment. I then asked him if the waiter could please dictate to me the courses we had been served. We shall do better, Point replied, called the waiter and asked him to write out our menu, which I received a few minutes later. To this day this document, record of my life's finest meal, hangs, framed, in my New York kitchen.

21.5.6 Spain

The following day we crossed the border at le Perthus. The first thing I saw on Spanish soil was a large vertical granite slab on which words of wisdom by Generalissimo Franco were chiseled. "There you have the son-of-a-bitch," I loudly exclaimed. Jacques turned to me and said: "If you don't like it you can go back. Otherwise you better keep your foul mouth shut." Sensible advice, which I followed.

Sightseeing on the way, we reached Madrid. There Jacques went his own way into the city during the morning hours while I visited the Prado museum, which houses one of the world's principal collections of paintings—

poorly hung, but what art! Large collections of painters I knew but, I now realized, only superficially: El Greco, Francisco Goya, Diego Velazquez, and others familiar to me only by name: José de Ribera, Francesco Zurbaran, Bartolomé Murillo. Clearly that museum by itself is worth a visit to Spain.

After my morning visits to the museum I would step outside and sit on a stone bench while waiting for Jacques to pick me up. After one of my first visits I sat there leafing through my guidebook, when I noticed a very attractive young lady also sitting on that bench. I gazed at her with interest, then continued browsing. When Jacques arrived, he suggested he take a picture of me on the Prado steps. I left my book lying on the bench and went up to pose. Then we had lunch followed, as always, by a siesta.

When I woke up I picked up my guidebook again. A sheet of paper fell out. On it was written: "Please call me"; a phone number was given, signed Nelly Ruiz de Arcaute y Ruigómez.

I was astonished. It had to be from the woman on the bench. I grabbed the phone and called. A pleasant voice said: "I should like to invite you for tea this afternoon to meet my mother." She gave me her address. I said, "Thank you, I shall be delighted to come." By now I was flabbergasted.

I dressed, took a cab, rang the bell. A servant came and I explained that Miss Nelly was expecting me. She led me to a handsome room where I waited. I was clearly in an aristocratic milieu. The door opened, Nelly came in with an older elegant lady on her arm. Introductions followed, tea was served, then the mamma rose, excused herself, and left.

I turned to Nelly and said, "I am so pleased with your invitation but hope you will understand that I am completely bewildered by what is happening." She smiled and explained. She had been educated at a convent school, where she had received instruction in English. She had, however, never had an opportunity to speak the language. When she heard my exchanges with Jacques, she decided to invite me and to ask if I would speak with her. I said, "I'll make you a deal. I speak English with you, you show me Madrid." That, she thought, was a fine plan. We made a date the next afternoon. All of which shows again, incidentally, how rare foreign tourists still were.

Back at the hotel I told Jacques what had happened, adding that I hoped he would not mind if I would not join him on the trip to Casablanca. Madrid was too rich for me to leave. He replied that he understood fully and departed by himself the next day.

The next few days were instructive and delightful. Nelly told me of her education. "We are taught to act stupid"—this in relation to men. She taught me Spanish proverbs, like: *Nunca te acostaras sin saber una cosa mas*

(Never go to bed without having learned one more thing). She took me shopping. I bought two sixteenth-century wooden statuettes, one from a convent in Salamanca, the other from a private home in Toledo—both still in my living room.

Then Nelly invited me to Las Ventas, the Madrid bullring, to attend a *novillada,* a bullfight where the fighters are apprentice killers (it was not the season for *corridas,* where graduated matadors appear). I gave her a rather impassioned speech about cruelty to animals. She smiled and said I might like to see for myself. Which I did and did not regret. On the contrary.

My words fail to describe the elegance, the controlled passion, the technical skill of the events. I shall never argue against anyone who condemns such fights as senseless killings, but I personally changed my position after attending that one fight in my life. My position is best described by quoting from my favorite book on the subject, written by someone who likewise started out by being against the fights: "Now the bullfight seems to me a logical extension of all the impulses my temperament holds—love of grace and valor, of poise and pride; and, beyond these, the capacity to be exhilarated by mastery of technique."[20]

21.5.7 The Return Home

On September 19 Nelly accompanied me in a taxi to the Madrid airport. It will be clear that she was a woman one played neither hanky nor panky with. The extent of our intimacy was an exchange of chaste kisses in that taxi. I told her of my genuine gratitude; we wrote each other for some years but that gently faded out.

On the plane to Paris I was filling out the entry forms for France when the man seated next to me asked if he could borrow my pen. We got into conversation. I asked him was this his first visit to Spain. He replied: "I am Sidney Franklin." I had no clue who that was but had the presence of mind to say: "Are you really?" That broke the ice. He was the first American bullfighter, born (he told me) in Brooklyn, the son of a Talmud scholar. At age seventeen he had graduated in physics from Columbia University. For three years he had worked with Ernest Hemingway on *Death in the Afternoon.*

I spent a few days in Paris and, on the 23rd, arrived in New York.

A few items from that autumn.

October 24. I was invited to attend the U.N. anniversary ball at the Plaza. Elsa Maxwell was the hostess, Edith Piaf sang, and Marlene Dietrich gave the birthday speech. From my diary: "A pretty grandmother she was."

November 5. Eisenhower wins the presidential election with 55.1 percent of the vote against Stevenson's 44.4 percent. I sobbed when I heard the news over the radio. The Institute looked like a graveyard the next morning. I met Kennan in a corridor; we just looked at each other, not saying a word. The following weeks I thought a lot about my emotional response, coming to the conclusion that there was nothing wrong with it but that it served no purpose either. My interests in politics have remained intense but have also become more detached as the years have gone by.

22

Of Symmetry and My Longest Journey

22.1 STAGE STRUCK. NEL MEZZO DEL CAMMIN

SOME TIME in the early 1950s I made the acquaintance of Kim Hunter, an actress best known for her role of Stella in the original Broadway version of *A Streetcar Named Desire.* She was also in the movie version, for which she won an Oscar as best supporting actress. I became good friends with her and her family. In 1953 I saw her on Broadway in a revival of *The Children's Hour,* a play by Lillian Hellman. Often I would visit her backstage, where I met Patricia Neal, who played the other lead role. I also became friendly with her as well. I remember in particular a party in her apartment where I met Lillian Hellman, whom I found to be a smart but bitchy little lady.

Some years later Kim called me up. She had been invited to attend the Oscar award ceremonies which that year were held partly in Los Angeles, partly in New York, with a TV linkup. Would I be willing to be her escort, since her husband had to be out of town that day? Of course I would. When the evening came, I presented myself at her apartment, where we were fetched by a Cadillac limousine—the first time I rode in such a vehicle— and driven to a Broadway theater. It was a pretty fancy occasion.

These were but a couple of the events that marked the period—the early 1950s—during which I was stagestruck for some years. There were also other reasons for that.

One evening in January 1953 I was walking along midtown Broadway on my way to Penn Station. I was in a bad mood, since the day's snow had turned into slush. As I made my way I noticed a sign on a theater marquee which said *Guys and Dolls.* I knew it was a musical, a type of show I had never yet seen. I decided to buy a ticket, for the one and only reason to escape from the cold and wetness.

As, some hours later, I came out, the weather was still miserable, but now

I could not care less. Frank Loesser's music and lyrics had raised my spirits very high. I still think it is the best musical I have seen, and can still sing "Sit down, you're rockin' the boat." And so, in the fifties, I used every opportunity to see other musicals.

Also from the early fifties date some of my all-time favorite movies: *The African Queen, The Quiet Man, High Noon,* and *Le Salaire de la peur* (The Wages of Fear).

On May 19, 1953, I wrote in my diary: *Nel mezzo del cammin,* to the middle of the road. I had reached the ripe age of thirty-five. As I write these lines I am more than twice that age—and counting.

*22.2 ABOUT SYMMETRIES AND THE LEIDEN CONFERENCE

Returning to Princeton after the January 1952 Rochester Conference (chapter 21, sec. 21.4), I began my second collaboration with Jost. As already mentioned (chapter 19, sec. 19.3), at that time we discovered a new quantum number in particle physics (G-parity), along with its selection rules. For what follows next, the results of that work are less important than the methods by which they were derived: arguments of symmetry.

Symmetry concepts made their initial appearance in physics as the result of observations of everyday natural phenomena, both animate and inanimate. Group theory, the rich branch of mathematics that encodes symmetries in abstract form, has played, and still does, an important role in theoretical physics. I have been fortunate to know well the pioneers: Weyl, Wigner, and later, Racah, who applied that discipline to quantum mechanics, the part of physics for which group theory has yielded particularly powerful results.

I already knew some group theory before setting out to work with Jost. While I am fond and respectful of mathematics, I have never been inclined to learn more of it for its own sake, however; I like to think that I was a decent theoretical but not a mathematical physicist. On the other hand, when my research in physics made clear that I should dig deeper into one or another part of mathematics, I would be motivated to do so enthusiastically. That was the case after having completed my paper with Jost. The link between group theory, symmetry, and selection rules was right up my alley at that time. Had I not, just a few months ago, been searching for a new selection rule? (Chapter 21, sec. 21.4.) As noted before, initially my only guide had been experimental facts. Now the possibility dawned on me to try and give that new rule a group theoretical foundation.

In the early 1930s a group had already made its appearance in nuclear physics, the so-called isospin group, code named SU(2).[1] The initial reason for introducing SU(2) had been the very near equality of the proton and neutron masses, which indicated the existence of a symmetry not heretofore known. If SU(2) were strictly valid, then these two masses should be strictly equal—which they are not. Since the proton but not the neutron carries an electric charge, it stood to reason that SU(2) would be the group governing strong interactions only, while electromagnetic interactions would violate SU(2) symmetry, thereby causing a small neutron-proton mass difference. In modern parlance, SU(2) had to be a broken symmetry.

Simple mathematical considerations easily showed that there was "no room" in this SU(2) to incorporate my new selection rule. So, slowly, the following program became clear to me. One should enlarge SU(2) to a "bigger group" which should yield (at least) one additional quantum number that should not be violated by the strong and electromagnetic interactions (see chapter 19, sec. 19.4), but should only be broken by weak interactions. The notion of a bigger group or, which is the same, a higher symmetry, which thus made its entrance in physics, was first mentioned in my paper published in the autumn of 1953.[2] That concept has been central to particle physics ever since. So has the idea of "a hierarchy of interactions corresponding to the symmetry classes of the [intrinsic] variables":[3] Strong interactions have the highest symmetry, electromagnetic ones a lower one, weak ones a still lower one.

While group theory is a subject of study for mathematicians and physicists, there are nevertheless groups that are familiar to all of us, though we may not be used to calling them that. A simple example: consider a sphere in the world in which we live. Make it rotate around any axis of your choice and with any size of angle of rotation of your choice. This assembly of rotations forms a group, technically known as the three-dimensional real orthogonal group. The mathematician says that this group "acts on" the sphere.

What is the higher symmetry group I was looking for and what does it act on? Already since the days of the isospin group SU(2), it had been clear that symmetries of this kind demand some sort of extension of the standard description of nature in terms of the variables that define the behavior of particles in terms of its location of points in space and time. I therefore proposed that "the element of space-time is not a point but it is a mani-fold,"[4] that is, one had to extend the age-old description of phenomena by imagining that at each familiar space-time one should "hang" another space—not part of our visualizable daily world.

What could one guess about the character of that other space? I sug-gested that one "consider a minimum extension needed for our purposes, an extension which, I am sure, will itself have to be enlarged and refined eventually," a wise proviso, as it has turned out. That extension turned out to look like the surface of a sphere such as a billiard ball. The higher sym-metry group was the assembly of rotations and reflections of that sphere. "Thus the full manifold employed that way is a 6-dimensional one: it involves the four space-time dimensions and the two dimensions of [the sphere]."[5] I was unaware at that time that the full manifold I had in mind was an elementary example of structures already then studied by mathe-maticians, and known as "fibre bundles."

In June 1953, a conference was to take place to commemorate the cen-tennial of the births of two of Holland's great physicists, H. A. Lorentz and Heike Kamerlingh Onnes, discoverer, in 1911, of superconductivity. I had been invited to give a talk at that meeting and decided to give a paper on the ideas just described.

On June 18 I flew to Amsterdam via Gander and Prestwick. It was my tenth ocean crossing. (Since that time I have lost count of the number of my transcontinental journeys.) After visiting with my parents I went to the seaside resort of Noordwÿk, where all conferees were housed in Hotel Noordzee. I was happy to meet Bohr, Dirac, and Pauli there again.

The conference began on the 22nd. On the 24th, a commemoration meeting was held in the Aula of Leiden University, followed by a fine din-ner. On the 26th I gave my talk.[6] I was of course very pleased with Pauli's comment afterward: "I am very much in favor of the general principle to bring empirical conservation laws and invariance properties in connection with mathematical groups of transformations of the laws of nature."[7] Heisenberg, who gave a paper on QED (as did Felix Bloch and Willis Lamb), remarked: "We can work from two sides, either from the experiments or from the mathematical methods. If one starts from the experiments, I think the most useful attempt will be of the kind which has been presented by Pais."[8]

The Leiden meeting ended on the 26th. The next day I drove to Amster-dam, together with Bohr and Bloch, where I spent two weeks vacationing.

During that time I gave a lecture at the physics institute, visited my high school, where I met a few of my old teachers, heard some music, and took my parents to dinner in a kosher restaurant.

On July 14, I sailed from Rotterdam on the *Nieuw Amsterdam*. This time I traveled first class, on my favorite principle that one should try everything at least once. In this instance it turned out that once was more than enough. Neither the passengers nor the overabundant food and free champagne appealed to me.

On the 22nd I was back in New York, which lay silently in the summer heat. From there I took a train to funny little Princeton. A few days later the Korean armistice was signed. In August we learned that the Russians had exploded an H-bomb device.

22.3 FIRST TRIP AROUND THE WORLD

In September 1953 I was to attend a physics conference in Japan. I had planned to take the shortest route there and back, via the West Coast. When I called my travel agent to make arrangements, she asked whether I had a few hundred dollars to spare. When I replied affirmatively, she said, "Then why don't you make a trip around the world?" At once my instincts told me: Go. I did.

My readers will not be surprised to learn that my adventures on this trip do not match those described by Jules Verne. Yet they are more interesting than experiences on a similar modern journey could be. The more recent marked trends toward homogenization of the world's cultures have diminished the old sense of novelty on visiting foreign lands. Also, these days package tours are crowding out the vanishing breed of real travelers. At any rate, on this trip I did not yet see some of those sweet, blue-haired, elderly American ladies, nor any males in shorts and loud shirts looking at the world through the viewfinders of their cameras, more interested in "having been there" than in living through exciting experiences in foreign places. The 1950s were probably the last decade before the onslaught of tourism as a mass phenomenon. Thus I remember overhearing in 1965 two of the blue-haired ladies in Faaa Airport on Tahiti comparing only their notes on the local shopping. While I shall defend to the death the rights of such people to move about in our global village, they make it ever harder for the aficionados to escape the spirit of suburbia.

22.3.1 Turkey

On August 22 I left by plane for London. After brief stopovers there and in Rome and Athens, I arrived on the evening of the 23rd at the Park Otel in Istanbul, the site of fourth-century Byzantium. I had decided to use this trip to explore new territory, and therefore to bypass Western Europe. It had taken me a day and a half to get there; now you can do it in nine and a half hours.

I slept long that night. At breakfast the waiter offered me a good black-market rate for the dollar, which I accepted. He also told me of a French-speaking guide he knew, suggesting that he arrange for the man to come to the hotel. I said that was fine, could the guide meet me at dinnertime to plan for the next day. As always, I first liked to stroll around on my own.

I took a tram to the Galata Bridge near the chief business center, looked around over the spice market, then entered the "blue" (Ahmat) mosque, the finest of its kind I was to see. I was struck by the serenity of its uncluttered interior, took off my shoes, and sat for awhile. Then to the Aya Sofia (which means Holy Wisdom), which dates from the sixth century. Its height, 225 feet to the top of the dome, is impressive, especially when looking upward from inside. I did not find it as beautiful, however, as the blue mosque. Then to the old serail and the Topkapi Museum.

On return to the hotel I found the guide waiting for me. We negotiated a price and a plan for the next day. Since I found him *sympathique,* I invited him for dinner. Whereafter he suggested that we visit a nightclub. That is not my usual pastime, but I said all right. So we went to the Rita bar. After we had settled down with a drink, the guide pointed to some young ladies and asked if I would be interested in some female company. That is even less my speed, but I said okay, going by my oft-mentioned principle to try everything at least once.

Two came over, I bought them a glass of champagne, and all of us engaged in some amiable chat, also in French. After an hour or so, I said that I wanted to return to the hotel and called the waiter for the check. I was prepared to have to pay more than the usual price for drinks but was outraged when I saw the charges, which were truly exorbitant. I called the waiter back, said these rates were scandalous and I was not going to pay that much. He said that this is the normal price. I said I won't pay that, and to call the owner, which he did. I thereupon engaged with him in an argument, eyeball to eyeball. Both parties became increasingly aggressive, when suddenly the owner stopped, stared at me, then said: *Bista a Yid?* (Yiddish: Are you a Jew?)

It is a moment I have never forgotten. Abruptly the atmosphere changed from hostility among strangers to brotherly feelings. We sat down together, started to talk, and he called over the band leader, who turned out to be a Brooklyn Jew. There we were, a Jew from Amsterdam, one from Galicia, and one from New York, having a fine time. Then he came down on the amount of the check, I still paid more than usual, and we parted with warm feelings. It was the instance which underscored, more than any other in my whole life, that Jews are bound together primarily by tribal rather than religious feelings.

The next morning my guide and I took off. First we climbed up the Galata tower, from where one has a fine view of the city. Next to the Fatih and Suleiman mosques and the university. Then out of town, up a hill to a cottage that had belonged to Pierre Loti, where he had done much of his writing. After lunch, we crossed the Bosporus to Scutari in Asia.

The next morning I went, by myself again, to the Grand Bazaar, which had nothing to offer to my taste; then I attended noon service in a mosque; in the afternoon, by boat to the island of Büyükada, once known as Prinkipo, in the Sea of Marmara, where Istanbul's *beau monde* has its villas.

22.3.2 India

From Turkey I went for a week to Israel. The flight from Istanbul to Tel Aviv now takes an easy two hours but at that time the political situation made the direct connection impossible. The next best route was via Ankara and Nicosia, on Cyprus. In Israel I visited old friends and lectured at the Hebrew University. Then on to Karachi, by Philippine Airlines. Boarding the plane I felt for the first time that I had left the West behind, for there I saw my first heavily veiled women, and men with beards painted red, signifying that they had completed the *hadj* (pilgrimage) to Mecca. I stayed over at the Airport Hotel and continued the next morning to Bombay to spend my first full day in the tropics. I proceeded to the famed Hotel Taj Mahal (all my hotel reservations had been arranged in New York), right on the bay, near to the so-called Gate to India.

I had hardly arrived in my room when there was a knock on my door. When I opened, I was puzzled to see some half dozen Indians standing there. Each one offered me his service as servant, which I politely declined. Next I took a bath in the largest and most luxurious bathroom I have ever used, all marble.

After a rest and dinner I stepped out for a stroll around the block, when a well-dressed Sikh, umbrella over his arm, approached me and courteously asked: "Sir, would you be interested in a woman? Chinese? French? English? Or would you perhaps like a boy?" I declined, giving as my way out that I had just arrived and was too tired. The next morning, a local paper happened to carry this item: "A bill was introduced . . . any person carrying on prostitution within 150 yards of a place of worship, playground, or cinema is to be punishable with three months imprisonment."

The next morning I visited the Tata Institute of Physics, where I had long talks with the lively cosmic ray group, and with Bhabha, its director, whom I had met at the Princeton bicentennial (chapter 14, sec. 14.5). I found out that he was a member of the very wealthy and influential Tata family.

I was glad to accept an offer from one of the junior physicists to show me some sights. After lunch we walked up Malabar Hill, on top of which stands the Tower of Silence, in which the remains of deceased Parsees are placed. I was told of the funeral procedures of this sect, which follows the precepts of Zoroaster (Zarathustra). A dead person's body is draped in cloth, then placed on a bier that is carried to the tower. There it is left for vultures to denude it of all flesh. The remaining bones drop through a grill and are thereafter collected.

The next morning my new young friend picked me up for an excursion by boat to Elephanta, a small island six miles into the bay. It is famous for its caves, in which one finds colossal figures cut out of the rock, a triform representation of Shiva, a four-faced Buddha, a huge *lingam* (penis), many others. A deep silence enhances the serenity of the place.

On the way back to the hotel we passed a garden in which I saw a crowd of people sitting on a lawn and listening attentively to a man who was talking. When I asked my guide what was happening, he told me that the man was reciting verses from the Bhagavad Gita. I felt the nearness of another civilization.

I took my companion to dinner, after which we walked to an unusual place: Falkland Street, a long row of narrow cages opening toward the street but locked off with a metal grill. Inside each cage stood a prostitute. The procedure, I was told, was for a man to first hand over money through the grill, after which the client was allowed to enter and a curtain was drawn.

The next day, September 7, I flew to New Delhi, where I settled in the

Imperial Hotel and spent the first day walking around. Government buildings have a Western allure, the Memorial Arch looks like the Étoile with the Concorde fountains moved up there. The following day I left for an excursion to Agra, first to Akbar's tomb at Sikandra, then on to the ghost city Fatipur Sikri. After lunch to the Taj Mahal, the monument built by the Mogul emperor Shah Jahan (who reigned from 1627 until 1658) to house the tomb of his much beloved wife, Mumtaz Mahal; he himself was later buried by her side. Coming through the gate and seeing it there before you is an unforgettably beautiful sight. I believe it is the serene whiteness of its Rajpur marble that produces the lasting impact of purity and chasteness. Its architecture does not differ that much from other Indian tombs or temples, most of which, however, are decorated in colors which to my eyes are quite gaudy. At nine in the evening I was back in my hotel.

I spent all of the next day visiting old Delhi, the Jama Mashid or Great Mosque, also built by Shah Jahan; the thirteenth-century tower called Kutb Minar, one of the world's most perfect pillars; the Old Fort, at one time an imperial palace; a Sikh temple. Then I went on to pay my respects at Raj Ghat, the place where Gandhi's remains had been cremated. While there, I witnessed two cremations in actual progress—a strange, strong experience.

I saw a great deal, those few days in India, yet knew that I had been exposed to only a few glimpses of the subcontinent's riches—and poverty. I do regret never having visited India again.

22.3.3 Hong Kong

On September 10 I flew to Hong Kong, landing at Kai Tak airport, the hairiest descent in my experience. Until the last moment you feel sure that the plane will hit surrounding rock slopes. I stayed three days in the Hotel Peninsula in Kowloon. I could afford to stay in all such renowned hotels because tourism was still a pastime of the happy few, so that the prices of hotel rooms had not yet risen to their later astronomical heights.

After dinner I followed my standard routine of taking a walk to reconnoitre the neighborhood. I was not gone for long before I was accosted by a young woman who offered me her services for the night. I replied politely that I had traveled the whole day and was too tired. Whereupon she told me that she was distressed. I was the first man she had propositioned that evening, and a refusal in that case would bring her bad luck. We walked along for a while, and I asked her about her life. She was in fact a sweet, poor thing.

Otherwise, there is little to tell about my stay in Hong Kong. I went up the Peak, and had a meal in one of the floating restaurants in nearby Aberdeen. Shopping, especially for clothes, is Hong Kong's real folly. In practically no time one can acquire a bespoke suit or coat. I was offered a camel hair coat for very little money, but what does a man like me do with such a luxury item? I did get myself some custom-fitted shirts, however.

22.3.4 Japan

On September 13, I flew from Hong Kong to Tokyo, my ultimate destination. By then I had spent sixty-two hours in the air since leaving New York.

Two physicists fetched me at the airport, delivered me to my hotel, and informed me that they would collect me from there in an hour to bring me to a banquet for foreign participants of the conference, courtesy of the Japan Chamber of Commerce and Industry.

I went to my room to wash up. While doing so I listened to the radio, catching what apparently was a news program. I was astonished to hear several times the words Oppenheimer *san,* and even more so to hear Pais *san.* When the two men returned to collect me as well as Dick Feynman, I asked if they could please explain what that was about. They informed me that at the last minute Oppenheimer had canceled his plan to attend and chair the scientific opening session, and that I had been chosen to replace him.

That was my first intimation that our meeting was treated as an event of national importance, being the first postwar conference at which foreign scientists, some sixty of them, were to participate. I was also told that, some days earlier, lectures for the general public had been arranged to explain what the meetings would be about; and that people had started queuing up at seven in the morning to get in at 1 P.M.

The next two days were devoted to various activities in Tokyo, beginning with a visit to the imperial gardens and palace. After lunch we were taken to see a *Noh* play (*Noh* means "performance"), a classic form of Japanese theater dating back to the thirteenth century. It is really pantomime, performed by actors in magnificent costumes, wearing one or another of four prescribed chiseled masks. We lacked the knowledge for interpreting the meaning of the intricate gestures used. It is a form of theater which, as far as I know, is not seen in the West. Feynman and I, seated next to each other, got the giggles.

Then we went to the prime minister's official residence for cocktails and a buffet dinner given by the ministers of foreign affairs and of education. In the evening we went to the Kabuki in the Kabukiza Theater, another kind of Japanese theater that originated in the sixteenth century, also distinctly different from Western styles, though recently shown in New York. All women's roles are played by men, all costumes are sumptuous. Movements tend to be slow and stately, and every once in a while they are completely frozen in a stately tableau. Men seated on the floor at the side of the stage produce occasional noises unfamiliar to Western ears, either vocally or by rhythmically hitting wooden clappers (called *ki*) on the stage floor with varying speeds that indicate the levels of tension of the particular moment. Feynman and I got the giggles again. Afterward, in our hotel rooms, we gave our own rendition of all those uncommon sounds.

The next morning the official opening session of the conference was held in the main auditorium of Tokyo University, in the presence of over one thousand scientists and guests, including representatives of the diplomatic corps and of the Japanese government. Speakers included Yukawa, the conference president. In the evening a formal dinner was given by the president of the Japan Academy.

On September 16 and 17 we traveled by train from Tokyo to Kyoto. First stop: Nagoya, for a public lecture. Then on to Gifu, a city on a tributary of the Kiso River, where we were housed in an old and (we were told) famous inn; I roomed with Feynman. In the evening, after a sumptuous fish dinner, we were treated to an unusual spectacle: cormorant fishing on the river, using an ancient method first mentioned in the eighth century. We boarded boats lit by a torch on the bow, where a fisherman was seated who held a cormorant with a long string loosely tied around its neck. When we had reached the middle of the stream he let go of the bird, which took a dive to catch fish. Next the bird was pulled in by the string, now held taut around the neck, whereafter the fisherman grabbed the animal around the neck and pulled upward so that fish dropped out on the boat's floor. The procedure was repeated several times.

The next day a train took us to Kyoto, where we boarded a bus at the station. I shall let Feynman tell what happened next.

> In the bus on the way to Kyoto I told my friend Abraham Pais about the Japanese-style hotel, and he wanted to try it. We stayed at the Hotel Miyako, which had both American-style and Japanese-style rooms, and Pais shared a

Japanese-style room with me. (The room was named Yuki no ma, which, if I remember correctly, means snow room.)

The next morning the young woman taking care of our room fixes the bath, which was right in our room. Sometime later she returns with a tray to deliver breakfast. I'm partly dressed. She turns to me and says, politely, "*Ohayo, gozai masu*," which means, "Good morning."

Pais is just coming out of the bath, sopping wet and completely nude. She turns to him and with equal composure says, "*Ohayo, gozai masu*," and puts the tray down for us.

Pais looks at me and says, "God, are we uncivilized!"

We realized that in America if the maid was delivering breakfast and the guy's standing there, stark naked, there would be little screams and a big fuss. But in Japan they were completely used to it, and we felt that they were much more advanced and civilized about those things than we were.[9]

That day, September 18, the scientific part of the meetings finally began, held in three parallel sessions. The one I was to chair was held in the main room of Yukawa Hall, which was built in 1951 to commemorate the Nobel Prize for Yukawa, and in which the Research Institute for Fundamental Physics was established in April 1953. Before the start of business I had the pleasure of meeting for the first time Professor Sakata, whose work had so much paralleled my own (chapter 19, sec. 19.4). We exchanged cordial greetings. We were also exposed to a battery of cameramen with flashbulbs popping (electronic flash came later). Then Tomonaga spoke brief words of welcome, after which I took the chair of a session devoted to "Non-Local Field Theory," quoting for openers a line from Maxwell: "Let us be neither drawn aside from the subject in pursuit of analytical subtleties, nor carried beyond the truth by a favorite hypothesis."

The afternoon session on field theory was chaired by Feynman. When that was over, we were subjected to a press conference. I was told that a leading Japanese physicist had conducted two months of prior briefings with reporters of the Asahi press.

On the next morning I gave my own paper,[10] a variant of what I had reported in Leiden, with Bhabha in the chair. Feynman has recounted what happened that afternoon.

I was in my room and the telephone rang. It was *Time* magazine. The guy on the line said, "We're very interested in your work. Do you have a copy of it you could send us?"

I had never been in *Time* and was very excited. I was proud of my work, which had been received well at the meeting, so I said, "Sure!"

"Fine. Please send it to our Tokyo bureau." The guy gave me the address. I was feeling great.

I repeated the address, and the guy said, "That's right. Thank you very much, Mr. Pais."

"Oh, no!" I said, startled. "I'm not Pais; it's Pais you want? Excuse me. I'll tell him that you want to speak to him when he comes back."

A few hours later Pais came in: "Hey, Pais! Pais!" I said, in an excited voice. "*Time* magazine called! They want you to send 'em a copy of the paper you're giving."

"Aw!" he says. "Publicity is a whore!"

I was doubly taken aback.

I've since found out that Pais was right, but in those days I thought it would be wonderful to have my name in *Time* magazine.[11]

(On September 30, I noted in my diary that *Time* had carried "a crazy note" about my work.)

That evening, Feynman and I were taken to a geisha house in the Gion district, followed by press photographers, whose ever-presence by now had begun to pain me. We had a charming time, being entertained by *maikos*, apprentice geishas. Today a picture of that evening, showing Feynman, myself, and company hangs in my New York office, and is reproduced in this book.

The next day, a Sunday, we went for an excursion to Nara, the first (eighth century) permanent capital of Japan. It is a place of great physical beauty and extraordinary monuments. Its main temple, called Todai-ji, is thirteen hundred years old. It contains a colossal statue of Buddha, 53 feet high and weighing 450 tons. Elsewhere, one sees effigies of Brahma and Indra. In the temple park tame deer wander around. A museum displays antique objects of great interest as well as work by more recent artists. Qua beauty, it was my finest day in Japan.

I had asked Yukawa about places where I might perhaps be able to acquire some objets d'art. He urged me to pay a call to the shop of a Mr. Imai on Kyoto's Shinmonzen Street and had given me a letter of introduction to him. The next day I went there, playing hookey from the conference. I entered and was greeted by the owner, an elderly, dignified man to whom I handed the letter which evidently greatly impressed him. Note that, after the emperor, Yukawa was considered to be the country's most prominent personality. We sat down and were served tea. Then I spoke of the reasons for my call. He began by showing me some small sculptures, of which I bought two. One, dating from the Kamakura period (fourteenth century), is a granite head of Jizo, protector of children, which moved me by its great simplicity and purity of line. The other, a thirteenth-century Korean piece, a seated altar boy, holding a baby tiger between his knees, and inscribed: "A gift to the temple from a pious merchant."

Then Mr. Imai came with folders of woodblock prints. I bought a small Hiroshige of a kingfisher diving down, and also a triptych by Utamaro, in his characteristic pale colors, showing a young man at a gate, coming to court a young lady, also shown, playing a *koto*, surrounded by her attendants. These acquisitions, which are now in my New York apartment, cost me less than one hundred dollars apiece. When, many years later, I showed them to a Japanese visitor, the son of a diplomat, he gazed at the triptych, then said that it was now worth its weight in gold. (Shortly after my visit to Kyoto the export of Japanese classical art was forbidden by the government.)

Then Mr. Imai showed me a complete first printing of the *Tokkaido* by Hiroshige, the well-known set of scenes along the road from Kyoto to Edo (the old name for Tokyo). It cost five hundred dollars. I told him that unfortunately I could not afford that sum. Later I have often regretted not to have scrounged the money together; the set is now worth a small fortune.

After the conclusion of the meetings, on the 23rd, we took off on a trip arranged by the conference organizers. First to Osaka, where we visited the sixteenth-century castle, and then were given a special treat: a performance by the Bunraku-za, the famed Osaka puppet theater. Its unusual feature is that one does not only see the richly dressed puppets but also the upper bodies of the puppeteers, dressed and hooded in black. The ensemble exerts a hypnotic effect.

All during these excursions we were followed by reporters and press photographers, who on occasion made a nuisance of themselves. How is one supposed to answer the question put to me when we got off the train at Osaka station: "What is your impression of Osaka?" Before we went sightseeing, we were served lunch, which was pleasant enough until one photographer managed to pop a flashbulb in my soup. This caused me to address him in rather fierce terms.

By then I had spent ten days in Japan, long enough to correct my first distinct impression that all Japanese look alike. I found it interesting to note that this process of differentiation took a little time.

From Osaka we continued to Hiroshima. On September 25 I noted in my diary: "It is strange to be here. Hiroshima has always been an abstract concept to me, and now it is a city. Try in vain to read people's faces for hate reactions—none. Maybe we can't read."

I had found the Japanese people to be friendly but considered this not surprising since I had nearly always been in the presence of colleagues and their families. But now we walked through a city recently devastated by the first atomic bomb, large areas still in ruins, and well aware that press publicity had made it quite clear to the populace that foreigners, American scientists among them, were in their midst. We had been uncomfortable with the prospect of this visit, yet wherever we went we had friendly receptions, saw smiling faces. It was not until shortly after my return to America that I began to grasp the underlying Japanese psychology. That came about as the result of my reading a splendid book on Japan by Ruth Benedict,[12] commissioned by the U.S. Office of War Information for the benefit of occupying forces.

The key to understanding Japanese mentality is the appreciation of the role that obligations play in their lives, expressed by the word *on*, which means "an indebtedness, a burden, which one carries as best one may. . . . People do not like to shoulder casually the debt of gratitude which an *on* implies."[13]

To get a sense of Japanese behavior one needs to be familiar with their complex scheme of the rank of obligations. Most important are *gimu*, obligations that can never be fully repaid. These include *chu*, the duty to obey the emperor, and *ko*, duties to parents and ancestors. Then there are *giri*, obligations including those to people other than family and emperor, which can be paid in kind.

My colleagues and I had been the subject of *giri*, since our mere presence laid an *on* on our Japanese hosts. These they repaid by showering us with presents wherever we came, acts which at the time I found overdone, but which I now understand to be *giri*. Quite another example is what happened when we left the old inn at Gifu. Yukawa expressed our appreciation to the innkeeper, a distinguished old woman. He bowed respectfully to her, and she did likewise to her famous compatriot. In such situations the superior person raises his body back up first. Now here there was a manifest problem: Should fame defer to age or vice versa? There these two people stood bowing, slightly raising the head to see whether the other had raised. It was a touching scene.

Giri also explains the common term *arigato* for "thank you"—but which literally means "oh, this difficult thing." It also makes clear the politeness our hosts showed us foreigners and which, to my taste, sometimes went too far. For example, when entering an elevator the Japanese, men as well as women, stood bowing until we visitors had gone in first. One day I had too much of all this and addressed a quite distinguished Japanese woman approximately as follows: "Madam, I do appreciate your courtesy, but please realize that in my country it is most impolite to enter an elevator before a lady. So I beg you to enter first." She smiled and did so. My polite request had reversed her mode of expressing *giri*.

Chu found its most extraordinary expression in the reaction of the Japanese to the war's end: "During the War the Japanese had stopped at nothing and they are a warlike people. . . . [Then] the Emperor spoke and the War ceased. . . . Our troops landed at the airfields and were greeted with courtesy. Foreign correspondents, as one of them wrote, might land in the morning fingering their small arms but by noon they had put these aside and by evening they were shopping for trinkets. The Japanese were now 'easing the Emperor's heart' by following the ways of peace."[14]

That abrupt change in attitude is also the explanation for our friendly reception in Hiroshima.

Now to our experiences in Hiroshima. After a reception by the president of the university, we were taken for a tour of the city, which today is entirely rebuilt and enlarged. We visited the remains of the Exhibition Gallery, a building 100 meters from the bomb's epicenter, which has been maintained in its almost destroyed state to this day, as an eloquent memento. Nearby stands a large stone with the inscription: "Sleep safely and soundly. We will not commit a mistake any more in the future."

The next morning we went for a boat trip on the Inland Sea, going in particular around Miyajima Island, where one is treated to the uncommon sight of a Shinto temple that stands in the middle of water ("Miya" means shrine devoted to the cult of departed ancestors). After this beautiful morning we were treated to lunch by the mayor of Hiroshima, then went to visit the ABCC, the American Bomb Casualty Center, an institution devoted to the care and study of survivors of the blast. An American M.D. showed us around and explained what they were doing. Seeing bomb casualties is a powerfully grim sight.

Then to a sumptuous dinner offered by the governor of Hiroshima prefecture.

The next day we continued southward to Fukuoka on Kyusha Island, and did some sightseeing. I bought a little Hakata doll, a Japanese favorite.

When you put it on the table you see a pretty geisha figure, but when you turn it upside down you see something quite obscene.

22.3.5 Going Home

From Fukuoka we went back nonstop to Tokyo where, after some last-minute shopping, I boarded a Pan American plane for the return trip. It was a sleeper plane, with berths above regular seats. I was happy to have one of those, since in those days it was a very long journey, seven and a half hours in the air from Tokyo to Wake Island, a one-hour fuel stop, then nine hours from there to Honolulu. I spent a portion of that time in my berth, did not get any real sleep, but was quite content to be able to stretch out. In Honolulu we spent a night in a hotel, then went on to San Francisco—another eight and a half hours. Finally, San Francisco–New York, with inning-by-inning results of the ongoing Yankee-Dodgers World Series game over the public address system. I arrived on October 2, having gone around the world in fifty-six days. The net flying time Tokyo–New York added up to thirty-four hours. Forty years later I would make the same trip nonstop in thirteen.

It took me one full month to overcome time lag and travel fatigue.

I was eager to obtain good prints of the many pictures I had taken on this trip with my beloved Leica. Following someone's advice to visit Bernard Hoffman's photo lab on West 50th Street, I went there and found him to be a pleasant person. The prints turned out very well. He found them so good that he advised me to submit the best ones to *Modern Photography,* a monthly magazine well known to camera fans. I am proud to report that they bought several of my pictures.

Stimulated by this success, I joined the Greenwich Village Camera Club, which gave me access to darkroom facilities. I was instructed on how to make prints and enthusiastically went to it, but not for long. I found out that one can easily spend a whole afternoon with one negative, varying exposure, developer, et cetera. I found this absorbing but also very tiring, and soon concluded that this was a worthy but too demanding undertaking, which I had better give up.

Meeting Mr. Hoffman again some time later, he told me of a large photo exhibit planned for 1955 at the Museum of Modern Art, to be called "The Family of Man," and that the organizers were on the lookout for suitable pictures. He suggested that I submit my best picture, a street scene in Hong

Kong showing children at play, which I did. A month later I received a phone call informing me that my picture had survived the selection process until the last round, when it had been rejected, but that I was invited to meet with the assistant of Edward Steichen, the main organizer. On my visit to him he told me that my picture was good and showed promise, but that it was too conventional. I took his point. He advised me to capture scenes such as a man shaving, or a married couple having an argument. I thanked him for his advice, though I found no opportunity to pursue it.

22.4 A FEW OTHER EVENTS IN 1953

On March 5, the *New York Times* reported the death of Stalin and, the next day, that the Tennessee legislature had adopted this resolution: "Whereas Josef Stalin is dead, long live America"—a typical sample of Cold War silliness.

The news that on May 29 Edmund Hillary, together with his *sirdar* Tenzing Norgay had successfully completed the first ascent of Mount Everest moved me profoundly.

On June 19 the Rosenbergs, Julius and Ethel, convicted of atomic espionage, went to Sing Sing's electric chair. Whatever they were guilty of, their execution was a blemish on the United States.

On November 12, the *New York Times* reproduced a brilliant cartoon from the British *Daily Telegraph*. Two U.S. senators are standing under a bust of Washington. One says to the other: "Personally, senator, I'd like to reopen the whole cherry tree inquiry. I figure he was shielding someone." Joe McCarthy was in full swing—more about that in the next chapter.

Finally, a personal note. In the autumn I attended a colloquium on transistors. Until then I had not paid much attention to those gadgets. As I sat and listened, it became obvious to me that their discovery, dating back to 1948, would cause a revolution in the manufacturing of such everyday goods as radios. By that time I had already begun to invest in the stock market, very modestly of course. I immediately called my broker in New York. Had he heard of transistors? He had. Did he know of a good company that was producing them? Yes, Texas Instruments. How much were the shares? About five dollars. I took a deep breath, then asked him to buy me two hundred shares. I still have the buy slip, at $5\frac{3}{8}$, dated November 13. I kept following the stock in the daily papers. It kept going up and up. By the time it had reached twenty dollars, I decided that a fourfold return on investment was enough and proudly ordered them sold. Had I hung onto them, they would have climbed to $250, accounting for splits. Also in later years I have had smart ideas on what to buy, but have been stupid about when to sell.

Once a year around Christmas my broker would invite me for lunch, always at Fraunces' Tavern. I would ask him about the market, he would query me about new prospects. On one such occasion he suggested that we reverse roles, I telling him about the market. I gave him a ten-minute summary of my thoughts. Afterward he remained silent for a few moments, then turned to me and said: "Why don't you make $100,000 a year?" I replied: "Because I have no time for that."

ILLUSTRATIONS

1. My fourth-grade class picture, 1928. I am in the bottom row, third from left, age 10.

3. With my paranymphs, Sieg Gitler (*left*) and Lion Nordheim (*right*), awaiting the start of my doctoral thesis defense, July 1941. Lion was executed later during the war.

2. On the beach in Holland, 1940.

4. In Amsterdam with my lifelong friend Tineke Buchter, the day after I received my doctoral degree, July 1941.

5. Dinner celebrating my doctoral degree, July 1941. On the far left is my mother; seated fourth from the left, next to me, is Tineke, and behind her is my father. Lion stands to my right, and standing next to him are my sister Annie and her fiancé, Herman de Leeuw.

6. Wedding picture of Annie and Herman, 1942.

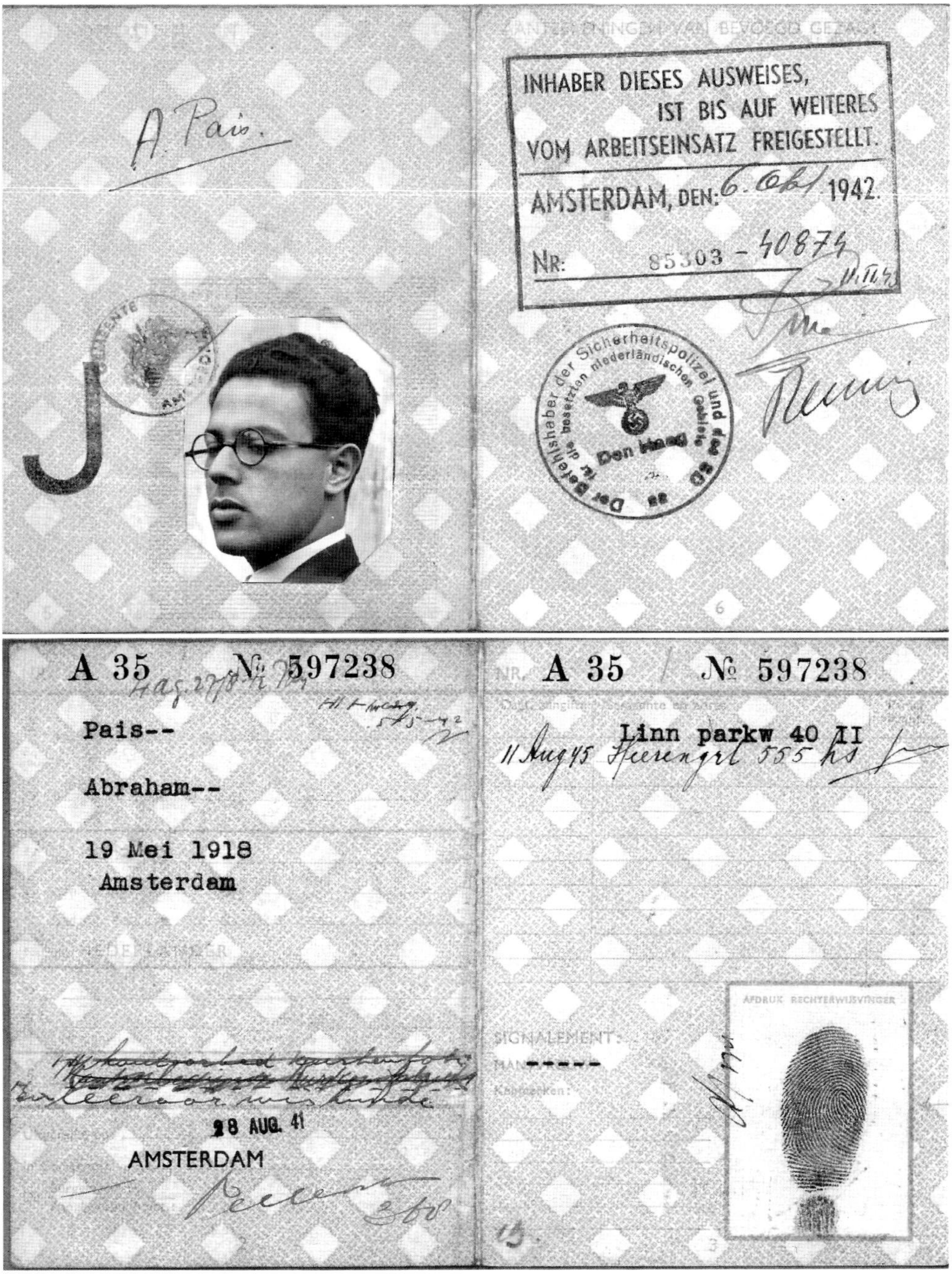

A. Pais.

INHABER DIESES AUSWEISES,
IST BIS AUF WEITERES
VOM ARBEITSEINSATZ FREIGESTELLT.

AMSTERDAM, DEN: 6. Okt 1942.

NR: 85303 - 40874

J

A 35   № 597238

Pais--

Abraham--

19 Mei 1918
Amsterdam

28 AUG. 41
AMSTERDAM

NR. **A 35   № 597238**

Linn parkw 40 II

11 Aug 45 Heerengrt 555 hs

SIGNALEMENT:

7. My identification card exempting me, "until further notice," from "mobilization for wartime labor," a euphemism for transport to concentration camps, dated October 6, 1942.

8. Fiddling around, Norway, 1946.

9. In Einstein's living room, Princeton, late 1940s. *From left to right:* Mrs. Weisgal, Bram Pais, Einstein, Helen Dukas (Einstein's secretary/housekeeper), and Meyer Weisgal, fund-raiser for the Weizmann Institute in Israel. (Empire News Photos)

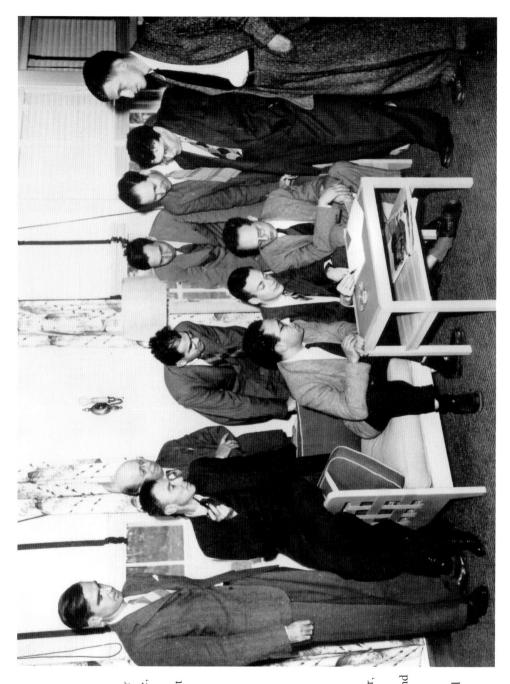

10. At the Shelter Island Conference, June 1947, at the Ram's Head Inn at the tip of Long Island. Left to right, *standing:* W. Lamb, Jr., K. K. Darrow, V. Weisskopf, G. E. Uhlenbeck, R. E. Marshak, J. Schwinger, and D. Bohm; *seated:* J. R. Oppenheimer, A. Pais, R. P. Feynman, and H. Feshbach. (Courtesy of Archives, National Academy of Sciences)

11. With Oppenheimer and Dirac in the Common Room, Institute for Advanced Study, Princeton, spring 1948. (Courtesy of Florida State University)

12. With Oppenheimer in the lecture room of the Institute for Advanced Study, Princeton, circa 1950.

13. My mother at home and father in his office in Amsterdam, early 1950s.

14. With Richard Feynman and geishas in Kyoto, 1953.

15. With my parents in Amsterdam, circa 1954. In the background: the Mint Tower.

16. Standing at the dais of the Supreme Soviet Hall in the Kremlin, 1956.

17. On top of Mont Blanc with my guide, 1960.

18. On top of the Matterhorn, 1962.

19. Lecturing at the Du Pont Company, Wilmington, Delaware, 1968.

20. With Helen Dukas in Princeton, September 12, 1981, a few months before her death.

21. Ida and I on our farm near the Baltic Sea, 1986. (Photo by Ellen Land-Weber © 1986, reprinted with permission)

22. Ida and I on our way to the Nobel ceremonies in Stockholm, December 10, 1989.

23. At the symposium honoring my seventieth birthday, 1988, Rockefeller University.

24. With Mitchell Feigenbaum at the reception following my seventieth birthday celebration, 1988.

25. My son Joshua, his wife Lisa, and my grandson, Zane Abraham, 1995. (Photo by Shonna Valeska © 1995, reprinted with permission)

26. Joshua and Zane, 1995. (Photo by Shonna Valeska © 1995, reprinted with permission)

23

Greenwich Village, American Citizenship, and the Oppenheimer Affair

23.1 The Yang-Mills Theory Unveiled

IN THE SPRING TERM of 1954 two important seminars were given at the Institute for Advanced Study. One, on February 23, was by Chen Ning ("Frank") Yang, a brilliant young Chinese physicist who in 1949 had been appointed to a five-year Institute membership. (In 1955 he was promoted to professor.) It was the first talk in which Frank reported on his work with Robert Mills dealing with so-called non-abelian gauge fields, which came to be known more popularly as "Yang-Mills fields." It is too technical a subject for this book.

The Yang-Mills theory was initially received with skepticism, to put it mildly. The reason was that the quanta of the new field appeared to have zero mass (like the light quantum), which for many reasons is wholly unacceptable. In their paper on the subject, a piece of chutzpah for that time, the authors simply stated that they had "no satisfactory answer" to that difficulty.[1]

Two weeks earlier, on February 10, Pauli (back for that term) had given a talk on the same subject! This work is very little known because he never published it.[2]

Pauli's interest in this problem was the result of my talk at the Leiden conference. As noted in chapter 22, section 22.2, he had found my work interesting and in the subsequent discussion had raised the technical question: "I would like to ask . . . whether the transformation group with constant phases can be amplified in a way analogous to the gauge group for the electromagnetic field in such a way that the meson-nucleon interaction is connected with the amplified group"[3]—precisely the problem Yang and Mills had addressed!

Pauli kept pondering his question. A few weeks after the Leiden conference he sent me a manuscript entitled "Meson-Nucleon Interaction and Differential Geometry," which begins: "Written down July 21 till 25 [1953] in order to see how it is looking." In December 1953 he sent me an important mathematical appendix to his earlier letter.[4] These documents contain the correct equations for the Yang-Mills field strengths. But later in 1953 Pauli's enthusiasm began to wane. "If one tries to formulate field equations . . . one will always obtain *vector mesons with rest mass zero*" [his italics].[5]

The mass problem caused the theory to be almost completely forgotten until about twenty years later, when it was resolved. Since then, Yang-Mills fields have become crucially important for the description of the weak as well as the strong interactions. This development is as profound as were Maxwell's nineteenth-century equations for electromagnetism. I shall come back later to this subject.

23.2 I Acquire a New York Apartment and Become an American Citizen: The McCarthy Era

I have always been quite comfortable in Princeton, where to this day I have very good friends. Yet, then as now, I have found it to be a town with character but without soul. As a colleague of mine once said to a student who came to ask him if it was a good place to do graduate studies: "It is one of the very best. But if you are single, you'll go crazy; or, if you are married, your wife will go crazy." In 1960, while I was married, my mother came to visit us in Princeton. One evening, on an after-dinner walk, I asked her what she thought of the place. Her reply is unforgettable: "It is the most beautiful limbo I have ever seen."

My life therefore took a drastic change for the better when, in January 1954, I acquired a sublet on 47 Perry Street, Apt. 5C, in Greenwich Village, while also holding on to my Princeton place. It has always struck me how feeble the Jewish element in Princeton is compared to New York. As Henry Louis Mencken has so neatly noted,[6] in 1955 the most common surnames in the U.S. overall were Smith, Johnson, Brown, Williams, Jones; in New York City, Smith, Cohen, Miller, Brown, Schwartz. I paid fifty-six dollars a month for my very sweet and quiet apartment, a fifth-floor walkup near the corner of 4th Street. It consisted of a living room with kitchenette, a bedroom, and a bath. Most weeks on Thursday afternoons I would fill a big briefcase with papers and books and drive from Princeton to the City, where I stayed until early Monday. No need to move my car all that time: alternate-side-of-the-street parking rules came only later. The following June, the people from whom I had sublet vacated the premises and I got my own lease.

I now had two residences, a luxury that, one way or another, I have been able to indulge for the last forty years, even though I stayed on Perry Street for only ten of those. I do not find it difficult at all to move between one place and another: all you need are double sets of a few basic items, such as a toothbrush and a raincoat. I find this arrangement most stimulating. In particular, when you are at A you get a better perspective on B, and vice versa.

Some time after I had settled down on Perry Street, I opened the issue of *The New Yorker* that had just arrived in the mail. I started reading and remember jumping up and down and dancing excitedly through my little apartment: the issue was entirely filled with Edmund Wilson's account of the discovery of the Dead Sea scrolls.

In 1954 the United States was, on the whole, a nation of conspicuous wealth. It was sixth among the world's nations in population size but had sixty percent of all cars, fifty-eight percent of all telephones, forty-five percent of all radio sets, thirty-four percent of all railroad tracks.

At the same time, it was a dystopia.

In January 1950, Joseph McCarthy, junior U.S. senator from Wisconsin, a ruthless, phenomenal demagogue and liar, fraudulently claimed in a radio broadcast aired in Wheeling, West Virginia, that he had in his hand a list of 205 people known to the secretary of state to be members of the Communist Party and still working at the State Department. It was the opening salvo of the McCarthy era, which would last for over four years.

Being a resident alien, a guest in America, I was in no position to express publicly my outrage at the situation during those years. I concluded that under these circumstances I had only two options: either return to Europe or become a U.S. citizen. After some reflection I decided against going back, for two reasons. First, I knew that many European friends, intelligent though they may be, would make cheap judgments like fascism against America, and I would be unable to convey to them that the political situation was miserable but, I was deeply convinced, not hopeless, that sanity would prevail. Second and even more important, I realized how strong my American identity had become as a reaction to this adversity. It reminded me of the first time I saw German soldiers in Amsterdam, when for the first time ever I had said to myself: I am a Dutchman. I had to become a citizen.

Already in 1949 I had taken the first steps in that direction, and I had in the meantime satisfied the residency requirements. Accordingly, sometime in 1953, I presented myself to an office of the Immigration and Naturalization Service to apply for a hearing on citizenship. I was duly fingerprinted and given an instruction sheet, which included the following: "You must be able to speak English in ordinary conversation and to write your name. . . . You must have a fair knowledge of the fundamental principles of the United States Constitution and the government which is based thereon." I therefore bought a two-volume history of the United States which I studied diligently.

On September 22, 1954, I appeared on the third floor of the new post office building in Trenton, bringing along various documents as well as two Institute friends as witnesses. I was ready to be queried on my knowledge of English and of the Constitution. My examination went as follows. An officer asked me: "Do you speak English?" "Yes, I do." Whereupon he let me go. I was deeply disappointed not to have had an opportunity to vent more knowledge. No doubt the interrogation was so cursory because the officer had noted my profession and affiliation. On the way back to Princeton, one of my witnesses told a story of a colleague who, after having been naturalized, was asked for his first reaction on having become an American. His reply: "There are too many damn foreigners in this country."

On November 11 I had to appear in the U.S. District Court in that same building for the "final hearing," that is, the naturalization ceremony. It is a day I shall never forget. I was in Princeton, and when I woke up I was sick to my stomach. I was also confused, could not find a decent shirt, and had to drive to town to buy one. Then I pulled myself together, took the car and drove to Trenton. I entered a hall where another seventy or so people were likewise waiting to be inducted. Then the judge, Phillip Forman, entered. He greeted us, then said that he wished to address us briefly before swearing us in. He began by saying that he realized how important this day was for each of us, then explained the meaning of the oath we were about to swear, and ended with words I shall not forget as long as I live: "Before you take the oath there is something I want you to understand. The grass will never be greener than in the country where you were born."

Deep emotions welled up in me after he said that. I now understood why I had been so unwell earlier that morning. I must have felt that I was about to betray Holland, which I continued to love so strongly. The judge's words meant, of course, that such feelings demanded no apology. I now felt ready to take the oath.

As we were filing out after the ceremony, a clerk of the court came up to me and said that Judge Forman would like to see me in his chambers. Here I told the judge how immensely grateful I was for his words and recounted my morning's experiences. He smiled and said that, having performed the ceremony many times, he had increasingly become aware of such emotions and that that was in fact why he had said those words. I told him I would always remember them.

Then the judge explained that he had wanted to see me in order to tell me of a colleague of mine he had also sworn in. He pointed to a photograph on the wall. It was Einstein, who in October 1940 had become a citizen in that same hall.

A week later I received in the mail my Certificate of Naturalization, No. 7117792, issued at the Trenton Court, November 11, 1954. By that day, McCarthyism already belonged to the past. For thirty-six days, beginning the preceding April 22, the nation had followed on television the congressional hearings of *McCarthy vs. the U.S. Army*. On December 2, the U.S. Senate passed a motion of censure against him. In 1957 he died of drink.

In 1954 other political events of great importance occurred in the United States, some good, some bad.

First the good news. In May, the Supreme Court unanimously found in *Brown vs. Board of Education* that segregation in American public schools is unconstitutional. That decision marked the beginning of desegregation, a process that has made great strides forward since, although even now it is not completed.

Now the bad news.

23.3 THE OPPENHEIMER CASE

23.3.1 April 11–22, 1954

On April 11, 1954, a column entitled "Next McCarthy target: the leading physicists" by the Alsop brothers appeared in the *New York Herald Tribune*. It began by stating that the junior senator from Wisconsin was getting ready to play his ace in the hole "when he charged [quoted in the same column] that there had been an 'eighteen-month deliberate delay' in the development of the hydrogen bomb." Further down the article it stated: "One extremely distinguished American physicist, who made great contributions to the American atomic program, is known in his younger years to have committed acts of political folly unworthy of the intelligence of a five-year-old child." I knew that the Oppenheimer case was about to break.

That Sunday evening I was working in my office at the Institute when the phone rang and a Washington operator asked to speak to Dr. Oppenheimer. I replied that Oppenheimer was out of town. (In fact, he was in Washington.) The operator asked for Dr. Einstein. I told her that Einstein was not at the office and that his home number was unlisted. The operator told me next that her party wished to speak to me. Mr. Henry Raymont of the United Press came on the line and told me that the Oppenheimer case would be all over the papers on Tuesday morning. He was eager for a statement by Einstein as soon as possible. I realized that pandemonium on Mercer Street the next morning might be avoided by a brief statement that evening, and so said that I would talk it over with Einstein and would call back in any event. I drove to Mercer Street and rang the bell. Helen Dukas, Einstein's secretary, let me in. I apologized for appearing at such a late hour and said it would be good if I could talk briefly with the professor, who meanwhile had appeared at the top of the stairs dressed in his bathrobe, asking, "Was ist los?" (What is going on?) He came down and so did his stepdaughter, Margot. After I told him the reason for my call, he burst out laughing. I was taken aback a bit and asked him what was so funny. He said that the problem was simple: all Oppenheimer needed to do was go to Washington, tell the officials that they were fools, and then go home. On further discussion, we decided that a brief statement was called for. We drew it up, then I went to one phone, to call Mr. Raymont, and Einstein to another to read his statement: "I have the greatest respect and the warmest feelings for Oppenheimer. I admire him not only as a scientist but also as a great human being."

That done, Raymont asked Einstein what he believed the impact on the scientific community would be. Having stayed on the phone, I heard Einstein take a deep breath, whereupon I broke in before he could say a further word. I said in the phone that the statement ought to suffice for this evening, doing so because I felt the situation was too delicate to let Einstein loose with a statement of the kind he had earlier made to me.

Not to be misunderstood: I think Einstein's initial response to me was correct, even though his suggestion would not and could not be followed. I remember once attending a seminar by Bertrand de Jouvenel in which he singled out the main characteristic of a political problem; it has no answer, only a compromise. Nothing was more alien to Einstein than to settle any issue by compromise, in his life or in his science.

On April 12, a specially appointed board started the hearings, "In the Matter of J. Robert Oppenheimer," to examine whether or not Robert was a security risk.

23.3.2 The Hearings

Ever since 1947, when Oppenheimer had been appointed to the General Advisory Committee (GAC) (chapter 17, sec. 17.1), he had found himself in the middle of more important military-political problems than had ever been faced before by any scientist. To mention but one major issue, considered by the Board: Should the U.S. proceed to make hydrogen bombs? In 1949 Oppenheimer had advised against it, on both moral and technical grounds. The Board also dragged up past sympathies with leftist causes by Robert, his wife, and his brother. In my judgment he could have weathered controversy and personal attack had it not been for his damned arrogance, which had contributed to his making powerful enemies. One of these was Lewis Strauss, chairman of the Atomic Energy Commission (AEC) since July 1953, whom he had gratuitously insulted before a congressional committee. Moreover, Strauss was a trustee of the Institute—in which capacity he had nominated Oppenheimer for the directorship (chapter 17, sec. 17.1)—and he had in the meantime become president of the Institute's Corporation.

I met Strauss a few times because of his Institute connections. I recall in particular the day when he flew in from Washington and his helicopter landed right smack on the Institute's front lawn. As I witnessed that event, it appeared to me as what in ice hockey is called a power play. Along with a few faculty colleagues, I was on hand when he disembarked. I was struck by his appearance, suave if not slick, and had the instinctive reaction: Watch out for what is behind this fellow's deportment.

The hearings, which lasted through May 6, were held in the AEC's dilapidated building T-3, near the Washington Monument. Forty witnesses testified under oath, including Robert, who was on the stand for twenty-seven hours in all, and his wife. Writings about the hearings are voluminous.[7] These include the transcript of the hearings, a 992-page government publication that appeared in 1954, after it was all over.[8] It may well be out of print by now, but not to worry, an inexpensive reprint was published in

1971,[9] which has the added advantages of an index and an intelligent fore-word, in which it is written: "In those 750,000 words are history, drama, conflict, personalities, villains and heroes, injustice, brutality, courage, and eloquence,"[10] words with which I heartily concur.

It neither can nor should be my task to give a detailed account of these proceedings. I can only add a few personal recollections. On April 22, the Thursday of the second week of the Oppenheimer hearings, the McCarthy hearings also started and Robert reached the age of fifty. On that day, the members of our supper club had a case of good wine delivered to his Princeton home, and brought a telegram to his Institute office with the request to send it on to him. It read: "*De natali tuo tibi tuisque nobisque nec non imprimis patriae gratulamur. Macte virtute*" (On your birthday, you and yours and all of us, and not least your own country, send you congratulations. More power to you). *Macte virtute* is what Cato is reputed to have said to a young man he saw coming out of a whorehouse.

The Oppenheimer hearings wound down in the fourth week. Oppenheimer took the stand to answer follow-up questions and deliver his final comments. Kitty spoke briefly.[11] On Thursday, May 6, the nineteenth day, the hearings were concluded.

23.4 THE VERDICT. THE AFTERMATH

23.4.1 May 12–June 29

From my diary. May 12: "Went to greet O. at his Institute office. He tells me that a transcript of the hearing will be made public. Is weary and preoccupied, so I didn't stay long." May 25: "Visited Robert and Kitty at their home this afternoon. Extraordinary experience. There they sit glued to their TV, watching the McCarthy hearings. Have the feeling I was watching a play within a play. A line from *Hamlet* flashed through my mind: 'What's Hecuba to him or he to Hecuba . . .' Robert remarks: 'Many people expect war. But it seems hard to rent a battlefield.'"

On May 28, the general manager of the AEC sent a letter to Oppenheimer enclosing the findings of the Security Board, advising him that he had until June 7 to appeal their conclusions, which were two against, one (the chemist) for reinstatement of clearance, and reminding him that the final recommendation would come from the AEC.[12] The main conclusion of the Board's majority was: "We have . . . been unable to arrive at the conclusion that it would be clearly consistent with the security interests of the United States to reinstate Dr. Oppenheimer's clearance, and, therefore, do not so recommend." From the minority report: Oppenheimer is "naive but extremely honest . . . our failure to clear him will be a black mark on the escutcheon of our country."[13]

On June 2, while I was in New York, the *New York Times* had an extensive front page story, from which I learned what had happened. I sent a telegram to Princeton at once: "This is disillusion but Robert and Kitty it may not hurt you stop this madness cannot last all my good wishes accompany you."

On June 14 I had a long discussion with my faculty colleague Cherniss. It seemed to me that the Institute faculty should prepare a statement of support for its director. Cherniss agreed but wisely added that we should hold off such a statement until the AEC's verdict was in. In the meantime, we convened the faculty for several meetings. Von Neumann refused to sign at first, but in the end agreed to go along. The final meeting was held in my apartment. It was the only time that Einstein visited my home.

The AEC's verdict, dated for release on June 29, upheld the Board's findings with a four-to-one vote. The majority report ends with: "Dr. J. R. Oppenheimer is hereby denied access to restricted data." It clears him of the accusation regarding the H-bomb program but contains such gems as "proof of fundamental defects in his character," "placed himself outside the rules which govern others," "wilful disregard of the normal and proper obligations of security." The dissenting vote came from my late friend, the physicist Henry De Wolf Smyth, bless his memory: "I have voted to reinstate clearance. . . . His further employ will continue to strengthen the United States."[14] Years later, Lloyd Garrison, Robert's defense attorney—whom I met several times—said to me: "They slayed him, inch by inch."

23.4.2 At the Institute

After the verdict, a formal statement was issued to the press, signed by all twenty-six permanent members and professors emeriti at the Institute, of which I quote the following part:

> Dr. Oppenheimer has performed for this country services of another kind, more indirect and less conspicuous but nevertheless, we believe, of great sig-

nificance. For seven years now he has with inspired devotion directed the work at the Institute for Advanced Study, for which he has proved himself singularly well suited by the unique combination of his personality, his broad scientific interests and his acute scholarship. We are proud to give public expression at this time to our loyal appreciation of the many benefits that we all derive from our association with him in this capacity.

From my diary, July 2: "Talked in the afternoon and evening with O. He is tired and edgy, more so than I have ever seen him." In the evening, while I was with him, he said: "Worse than the denial of my clearance is that now the president gets the wrong advice on the atom." Then the phone rang. He picked it up, listened, said, "Thank you so much for your words," hung up, then turned to me: "That was Groves. He wanted to tell me that he had of course heard the verdict and was deeply sorry for this outcome." General Leslie Groves had been the administrative head of the Manhattan Project at Los Alamos.

23.4.3 *"See It Now"*

In November, Edward R. Murrow spent some days at the Institute in preparation for an interview with Oppenheimer, to be aired on television in his marvelous series of programs, *See It Now*. He and I had lunch one day, during which Murrow remarked: "This is the goddamndest place I have ever seen." When I asked why, he replied: "Because here I am supposed to be at the Olympus of learning, yet I have never been at a place where people say so often: 'I don't know.'"

The actual filming took place on December 15 in Robert's office. While that was in progress I heard a knock on my office door. It was Rabi, who had come to see Robert but had to wait until Murrow was finished. We sat in my office and talked a while until Rabi got impatient and said, "Let's go down," which we did. We tiptoed into Robert's office and sat silently in a corner, watching the proceedings. When it was over and Murrow had left, Rabi turned to Oppenheimer and said: "Robert, you're a ham." I don't think Oppenheimer quite liked that but he didn't let on.

On January 4, 1955, the program was shown on CBS; public response was ecstatic. If you ever see a replay, you will notice a blackboard filled with formulas—written by me.

23.4.4 Oppenheimer as Martyr

Robert may well have missed the role of guru he had played on the American political scene not only because it had given him a sense of power, which he craved, but also because he had a genuine and deep love of country. The latter had made the hearings into such a spectacle of cruelty and stupidity.

There was now another love to which he could return, however: physics. Remember that his Berkeley days of research and teaching had been the happiest in his life. New power was also beckoning, derived from his martyrdom, which would give him even greater charisma than he had ever had before, enhanced by his now ascetically frail looks.

It must have been a great relief to Oppenheimer to have the hearings behind him. I had known only little of what was revealed by that circus, but I had been aware even earlier that trouble was brewing. For example, when I returned from Japan and told Robert that he had been much missed at the conference, he replied that he had been unable to attend because difficulties might be waiting for him in Washington. Not for nothing had he given his dog the name "Worry." It must also have been an emotional relief to him to see so many good people rally to his defense, both during and after the hearings. To me he seemed calmer, more balanced now.

Though he never told me so, I know it gratified him greatly to be seen as a martyr. For example, when in 1958 he went to France to lecture at the University of Paris he was treated like a film star. Cars with reporters and cameramen followed him along in the streets; his lectures were packed. High public recognition in the United States began some years later. In April 1962 he received an invitation from the White House to a formal dinner honoring American Nobel laureates. In the fall of 1963 it was announced that he was that year's recipient of the Fermi Award, given by the AEC;[15] on November 22, the New York Times reported that President Kennedy had signed the citation and would personally present the award. On that same day Kennedy was assassinated in Dallas. On December 2, President Lyndon Johnson presented Robert with his citation, a gold medal, and a check for $50,000 "on behalf of . . . the people of the United States." In his reply, Robert said: "I think it is just possible, Mr. President, that it has taken some charity and some courage for you to make this award today."[16]

On January 23, 1964, German television premiered a play on the hearings. When, some time later, Oppenheimer had read the book version,[17] he said to me: "The author is trying to make a tragedy of something that was nothing but a farce." The play was staged with great acclaim in Berlin and Munich and, in translation, in Paris, London, and New York, where I saw it in the Lincoln Center Repertory Theater. It was a schizophrenic experience. The man who played Robert had an uncanny knack for imitating his body language, presumably from screening film and TV clips. When he spoke, I heard an alien voice, however. The result was that I came out of the theater with a splitting headache. Oppenheimer's eidolon later appeared in films such as *The Day after Trinity* and in TV programs.

Oppenheimer consistently refused all honorary degrees except the one from Princeton University, which he received in June 1966. Half a year later he died.

24

Of My Best Work and a Year's Leave of Absence. Death of Einstein

24.1 PROGRESS IN PARTICLE PHYSICS, 1954–55

24.1.1 Experimental Advances until 1954

BAGNÈRES DE BIGORRE, a resort at the foot of the French Pyrenees, has for centuries been one of the principal watering places in France, already frequented by the Romans. When physicists gathered there in July 1953, it was not for such frivolous pursuits, however, but to hold a conference on particle physics. The meeting place had been chosen because of its nearness to the Pic du Midi de Bigorre, on top of which (alt. 2,850 m) an observatory had served as the site of many important early cosmic ray experiments on the new particles.

The dittoed notes of the conference proceedings[1]—which I believe to be a collector's item—list me among the participants. In fact, I did not go, since I had my hands full with the summer 1953 conferences in Leiden and Kyoto. The conference notes show a rapid expansion of experimental activities. About twenty groups, with sites ranging from Berne to Bombay, could now actively study the new particles, possible because particle beams, in the form of cosmic rays, were available worldwide, and no special new instrumentation was needed to study them.

The conference offered a rich menu of new results. The number of new heavy mesons appeared to be increasing rapidly. They had code names like θ, τ, κ, χ, etc. At that time, von Neumann said to me, "If you run out of Greek letters, you can always use names of Pullman cars." Their masses all clustered around 500 Mev. It did not take deep insight to posit that these objects, identified by their specific decay mode, were in fact alternative decays of one and the same particle—though it would take a revolution in fundamental physical concepts (to which I shall turn in the next chapter) to implement that idea fully. At that conference the term "K-particle," embracing all decay modes, was agreed on, as was the name "hyperon."

In his closing remarks at Bagnères, C. F. Powell said: "Gentlemen, we have been invaded . . . the accelerators are here."[2] In the preceding April the first man-made new particles produced by the big machines had been reported. From then on accelerators took over. One should never forget, however, the debt owed to the cosmic ray pioneers.

24.1.2 Theoretical Advances

Early in 1951 a young physicist by the name of Murray Gell-Mann came to the Institute to spend the calendar year. A professor's quarter consisted of two spaces: an office for the professor, and an adjoining one for a visiting member, the idea being that the latter would serve as assistant. Gell-Mann occupied my assistant's office, though he never played that role. Our physical proximity caused us to have more joint discussions than usual, mainly about the new particles. It did not take me long to recognize that he was unusually bright. By fall of 1951 I was busy preparing my paper on associated production,[3] which Gell-Mann and I discussed at length. Shortly afterward he went to Chicago as an instructor.

As already told (chapter 22, sec. 22.2), early in 1953 I became interested in the possible connection between new selection rules and group theory and produced a paper[4] on that subject, on which I reported in Leiden and Kyoto. When I came back from Japan I found two preprints by Gell-Mann with new ideas on the game of the new particles.[5] The first of these, entitled "Isotopic Spin and Curious Particles," appeared in print in November 1953.[6] The second, "On the Classification of Particles," was never published. In simplest terms, the main idea of this work was this: nucleons have isotopic spin $\frac{1}{2}$, pions 1. Suppose now that hyperons have integer, K-particles have half-integer isotopic spin ($\frac{1}{2}$, in fact). This new, simple, and ingenious remark resolves the dichotomy of strong production/weak decay. It has turned out that this solution is correct. The same idea was put forward independently by a Japanese team.[7]

Meanwhile, experimental discoveries of new hyperons heavier than the Λ had shown my first guess about extending the isotopic spin group (chapter

22, sec. 22.2) to be incorrect. It was natural to try next to represent Gell-Mann's proposal in terms of another group. In the spring of 1954 I found a way of doing this,[8] in which his idea is once again expressed in terms of a new quantum number. I of course sent an early copy of my new manuscript to Gell-Mann. This resulted in correspondence back and forth. In April he wrote to me that he was "quite enthusiastic about your new scheme."[9]

In the spring I had received an invitation to give a talk at an international conference on particles, to be held in Glasgow July 12–17. It seemed to me a good opportunity to summarize all that had been concocted so far to explain the behavior of the new particles. I therefore called Gell-Mann in Chicago, asking if he might be interested in coming East to join me in preparing a two-author report on our various efforts. He thought that was a good idea. Accordingly we spent May 14–18 together in Princeton, discussing and drafting, about our own work as well as schemes proposed by others. During those days I recognized again how smart a fellow he was. We ended up with a decent first draft, to be polished in Britain. In the course of our deliberations, in a seminar room at the Institute, we found one new result which astonished us so much that we did not yet dare to insert it in our report.[10] On the 18th I drove him back to LaGuardia.

The next day, my thirty-sixth birthday, I copied in my diary a quotation from Schopenhauer's *Vom Unterschiede der Lebensalter* (On the Difference between Periods of Life): "In regard to vitality we are, up till the 36th year, comparable to those who live on their interest. What is spent today is back tomorrow. But from that time on . . ."

24.1.3 The Glasgow Meeting. London

On July 10 I left by plane for Scotland. The usual refueling stop at Gander dragged on for five hours. Fortunately I had my copy of the transcript of the Oppenheimer hearings with me, so I did a good deal of reading.

On the 12th the conference opened in Kelvin Hall, Glasgow University. The next day I had a long talk with Heisenberg on his new ideas. On the 17th, the final day, I gave the paper on behalf of Gell-Mann and me. On the 18th we worked on our manuscript all day. Since we still had more to do, we agreed to reconvene in London.

On the 19th, I took a train for a short excursion to Edinburgh together with some friends from the conference. Then back to Glasgow and from there by plane to London, where I settled in the Great Western Royal Hotel at Paddington Station for a two weeks' stay. Gell-Mann joined me there for two days, putting the final touches to the Glasgow report. This paper contains several new points about the Gell-Mann scheme. The first dealt with "the apparent existence of both a positive and a negative hyperon, which we shall call $\Sigma^{\pm}$,"[11] the names they have gone by ever since. The scheme predicted that these particles should have a neutral partner, discovered later.

At that time, a further, still heavier hyperon had been discovered. How to name it? At that moment an idiotic association came to my mind, "The Darling of Sigma Xi," the title of a song then popular. And that is why that hyperon has been known ever since as Ξ (Xi). Finally, the report states that in decay processes, isotopic spin changes by half a unit, a prediction since confirmed, although the deeper reasons for this rule elude us to this day.

When all that had been put to paper, we had a long discussion about the meaning of the Gell-Mann scheme. In the spirit of my own ideas I said (approximately) that the relative displacements of isotopic spin values from nucleon to the various hyperons, and from the pions to the K-particles, should be expressed in terms of a new quantum number. Gell-Mann said, "Why so, why not just state what the isotopic spin values are?" As a result there is no explicit mention of a new quantum number in the Glasgow report. Only in 1956, when Gell-Mann presented the definite version of his scheme, did this quantum number appear in print. He called it "strangeness."[12]

After those days of work in London, Gell-Mann left for a hiking tour and I continued my vacation. Then I left London by boat train, boarded the *Liberté,* and was back in Manhattan on August 9.

24.1.4 Encounters with Delbrück and Francis Crick.

Seeing Bohr Again

In September, I spent a week at Brookhaven National Laboratory on Long Island, where for the first time I saw the Cosmotron in operation. At that time and for a brief period it was the world's highest energy accelerator. While there, I had my first experience with a hurricane, that one named Edna. That day I came to the lab so completely drenched that I had to take off my pants, and so did Uhlenbeck, who was also there. It became the only occasion in my life that a colleague and I would discuss physics in our underwear.

Later that month Bohr came to the Institute for the fall term. As always, it was great to see him again, but I noted that this man who not so long ago had been the exalted father figure of my life was now merely a lovable old man to me. That autumn he gave a series of lectures on complementarity at the Institute. They were not good. Only those who were or had been close to him could have known what he was hinting at.

In November I made the acquaintance of Max Delbrück, physicist-turned-distinguished-biologist, who had come for a brief visit to Bohr. It was he who told me the news of the DNA discovery by James Watson and Francis Crick, which of course greatly excited me.

Sometime later I met Crick at a party at the Oppenheimers'. I began raving to him about his discovery, how we would soon understand every-thing about life. Whereupon he looked at me with a mildly contemptuous smile, put his elbow on a table, stuck up his hand, and said: "See my hand? Five fingers? If you think I have the faintest clue why I have five and only five fingers you are badly mistaken."

The major event in my life that autumn, already recounted, was my be-coming a U.S. citizen. It was also the time of my last collaboration with Gell-Mann.

*24.1.5 The Theory of Neutral K-Particles

In section 24.1.2 I alluded to an astonishing result Gell-Mann and I had come upon while preparing the Glasgow report. In October we spent some days together in New York, where, in my Greenwich Village apartment, we worked out more details and then wrote a short paper on the subject. It appeared in March 1955.[13]

An experimentalist has described the first reaction to that paper: At "a remarkable seminar in the early part of [1955] . . . Abraham Pais walked in on a meeting at the Cosmotron and [the chairman] asked him to give us a talk. 'I have nothing to say,' said Pais. You know that cannot have been true; Pais had always something to say. This time it was about a 'funny' paper that he and Murray Gell-Mann had written."[14]

The problem we had addressed was this. According to the strangeness scheme, there should exist *two* neutral K-particles, called K^0 and $\bar{K}^0$, with almost the same mass but with opposite values for the strangeness quantum number S. Since S is conserved in strong production reactions, in such reactions one will produce either a K^0 or a $\bar{K}^0$. How do you know which one?[15] The production process in and by itself cannot tell. So the only possibility is: distinct ways of decay, which was already known to be via neutral $K \rightarrow \pi^+ + \pi^-$. But which neutral K?

It was the answer to that question which had surprised us. To understand what we did demands the brief discussion of some quantum mechanical concepts, which I shall do next, departing briefly from my plan to refrain from all reference to such technical issues in this book. If you do not care to follow along, dear reader, just skip the next few paragraphs.

A general quantum mechanical symmetry principle, called charge conjugation, or C-invariance, with an associated quantum number C, was already known at that time. The value of C is equal in magnitude but of opposite sign for particle and "antiparticle," such as electron and positron, or proton and antiproton—or K^o and $\bar{K}^o$. The principle of C-invariance says that the laws of physics are the same in our world as in a world in which all particles are interchanged with their antiparticles.

What is the charge conjugate reaction to $K^o \rightarrow \pi^+ + \pi^-$? It is $\bar{K}^o \rightarrow \pi^+ + \pi^-$, since the system $\pi^+ \pi^-$ is its own antisystem. So it seemed that decays could not distinguish between K^o and $\bar{K}^o$ either!

Then came the liberating idea. K^o and $\bar{K}^o$ are "states" in the sense of quantum mechanics. States can be superposed, added, or subtracted. Consider now the states (normalized by a factor of $1/\sqrt{2}$) $K_1 = K^o + \bar{K}^o$, $K_2 = K_0 - \bar{K}_0$. Then it is easily seen from C-invariance that K_1 can decay into $\pi^+ + \pi^-$ while K_2 *cannot decay at all* that way. That does not mean that K_2 is stable but rather that it will decay into other final products. We were "led to suspect" that K_2 would live much longer than K_1.[16]

The physicist calls "a particle" a thing that has a definite mass and, if unstable, one or more definite decay modes. Hence K_1 and K_2 are particles, but not so K^o and ($\bar{K}^o$), which are proportional to the sum (difference) of K_1 and K_2. In other words, the K^o and $\bar{K}^o$, produced in strong production processes, are particle *mixtures*, a type of prediction never before encountered in physics!

As often happens with scientific novelties, our conclusion drew considerable initial skepticism. For example, shortly after our paper had appeared, I received a letter from Racah in Jerusalem, telling me that our logic was in error. I did not reply since I did not know what else to say than what had been written in the paper. A week later I received another letter from him, stating that meanwhile he had thought more about it and now agreed.

In 1956, a year and a half after we had submitted our paper, a Columbia University group of experimentalists published a letter reporting that the "rather startling properties [of neutral K's] . . . predicted by Gell-Mann–

Pais . . . have been confirmed."[17] In particular, they corroborated our conjecture that K_2 lives much longer than K_1. "[Further] confirmation of those results . . . came thick and fast. They started to appear everywhere."[18] At that time, Freeman Dyson came to congratulate me, adding that until then he had not believed what we had done.

The writing of this paper marked the end of my collaboration with Gell-Mann. It was about then that I noticed first signs of his hostility toward me, which has become more explicit in later years, when colleagues told me of his claims that I had stolen ideas from him.[19] Initially such statements caused me anger, not diminished when distinguished friends informed me of similar accusations against them. He has remained brilliant as a scientist, better than I, but has remained a controversial figure. As to me, I would not advertise myself as having been likable at all times, but I have never behaved that way, nor have others ever reacted similarly to me.

Some years later, on a visit to Baltimore, I entered the old Saint Paul's Church, which dates from 1692. There I came upon an inscription that reminded me of the events just recorded. I copied it:

> As far as possible without surrender be on good terms with all persons. Speak your truth quietly and clearly; and listen to others, even the dull & ignorant; they too have their story. Avoid loud & aggressive persons, they are vexations to the spirit. If you compare yourself with others, you may become vain & bitter; for always there will be greater & lesser persons than yourself. Enjoy your achievements as well as your plans. Keep interested in your own career, however humble; it is a real possession in the changing fortunes of time.

I liked that.

24.2 Farewell to Einstein

By late 1954 I had spent eight and a half academic years at the Institute and felt ready for a leave, not so much because Institute duties had been such a burden but rather because by now a temporary change of scenery seemed healthy to me. New York was of course my choice, because of my Perry Street apartment. The physicists at Columbia were happy to have me, and the Institute did not object to my proposal. And so, as of December 17, the end of term, my leave began. I once and for all vacated my South Olden Lane apartment and a week later was ready to go.

On December 21, before taking off, I paid a visit to Einstein. As he had not been well, he had for some weeks been absent from the Institute, where he normally spent a few hours each morning. Since I was about to take off, I called Helen Dukas and asked her to be kind enough to give my best wishes to Professor Einstein. She suggested I come to the house for a brief visit and a cup of tea. I was, of course, glad to accept. After I arrived, I went upstairs and knocked at the door of his study, then heard his gentle "Come." As I entered, he was seated in his armchair, a blanket over his knees, a pad on the blanket. He was working. He put his pad aside at once and greeted me. We spent a pleasant half hour or so together; I do not recall what was discussed. Then I told him I should not stay any longer. We shook hands, and I said good-bye. I walked to the door of the study, not more than four or five steps away. I turned around as I opened the door. I saw him in his chair, his pad back on his lap, a pencil in his hand, oblivious to his surroundings.

He was back at work. It was the last time I saw him.

24.3 A BREAK IN JAMAICA

Also before leaving Princeton I had called on my doctor for his medical opinion, since I had felt unusually weary. He checked me over, then asked when I had had my last true, lazy vacation. I could not count my long travels of past years as such, so I replied: "Perhaps never." "Well, my friend," he said, "that's what you need right now. You're in good health but run down. Go to the Caribbean for a week." That idea somewhat upset me. "But Marvin," I replied, "the Caribbean is for rich old people, not for my kind." "I don't care what you think," he shot back at me in his usual friendly but brusque way. "You asked my advice, you got it." What the hell, I said to myself, why not.

So it came about that on January 11 I flew from New York, temperature twenty degrees, to Montego Bay in Jamaica, temperature eighty-one degrees. The next day I had my first exposure to calypso as sung by natives. I took a great liking to these songs, which would follow me that whole vacation—the music, the lovely pronunciation of English, the singers' body language. Here is one I liked:

> There was a little fly
> He flew into a store

He dood it on the ceiling
He dood it on the floor
He dood it on the bacon
He dood it on the ham
He dood it on the head of the little grocery man
The little grocery man
Took out his gatling gun
He said I kill the fly
Before the day is done
But before he could count
From one to ten
The little fly dood it on the grocery man again.

One evening I came upon an outdoor meeting of the Salvation Army in Montego Bay and had the delight of hearing "Jesus Is Our Savior" sung in a calypso rhythm.

The next morning I took a swim before breakfast, a new experience which, I decided, was the ultimate luxury. (I still think so.) In the evening I began reading the journals of André Gide, which greatly impressed me. Somewhere early he writes the line: "Le dégoût de relire le journal" (the disgust at rereading the journal). Which caused me to write in my own diary: "Why the hell do I chronicle like this? Do I really believe that I have a destiny, and that people, other people, would ever read this?" The next morning I woke up violently depressed, feeling completely out of touch with the "real" world. Another expression from Gide fitted my mood: "Enfermé, avec la Nature" (locked in with Nature).

On the morning of the following day, I saw a man die, apparently from a heart attack while swimming. Looking in his wallet, we bystanders found his name: Baron Louis de Rothschild. There was also a little German poem written on a slip of paper. I remember only one word: Meeresstille, the silence of the sea. There was a silence on the beach. And then life went on and we took our next swim.

The obituary in the Times international edition, January 16, read: "Baron de R. for whose freedom the Nazis obtained what is believed to be history's highest ransom . . . When the Nazis annexed Austria in March 1938 he was taken into custody and held until May 1939 as a prisoner of the secret police in the former Metropole Hotel. He was released only after his family had paid a ransom of 21 million dollars."

That afternoon, after another swim, I sat sunning myself on a raft when a young man came out of the water, seated himself next to me, and without preliminaries addressed me like this: "How about going crocodile hunting on the river tomorrow morning?" I was at once taken with him. He was a New Yorker named Neil Cooper. We went up to the hotel to inquire; it turned out that the hunt could not be done. So instead we went spearfishing—another first for me. I loved snorkeling between coral reefs and seeing beautiful fish, and tried to spear one, without success.

After lunch we took Neil's car and drove to Round Hill, a chic resort hotel some twenty miles away, where I met some models I had encountered on the plane. I had developed a shine for one of them and took her out for a drink, but never got anywhere. Then Neil and I attended a polo game—it was that kind of a place—where I saw two actresses in the stands, Shirley Booth and Hedy Lamarr, the latter known as the "Ecstasy girl," after the movie in which she swam in the nude—never done before on screen.

The next day we took a ride along the North Shore. We passed Discovery Bay, where, so the locals have it, Columbus made his first landfall in the New World.[20] We also saw Runaway Bay, where the retreating Spaniards had their last sight of Jamaica; Ocho Rios; and finally, Tower Isle, a hotel of the kind one should avoid. Then back to Montego Bay.

The next morning Neil and I took a swim at Round Hill. We liked the place and decided to move there for my last three days. My stay at Round Hill was pleasant and uneventful except for the afternoon on which I nearly drowned. I had swum out a good distance, then lay floating for a while. On the swim back I came to a point where I could not move closer to the shore, however hard I tried. Then I saw the problem: I was caught in a vortex. I had the strong sensation to either get help or it would be all over. I started to wave frantically and was lucky enough to be noticed. Several men jumped into a canoe and came paddling in my direction—but their boat capsized. A second canoe was launched, reached me, and dragged me in. When I was safely on the beach I was given a big shot of much-needed brandy. I sat on the beach for a while with my saviors (I left them a large tip), who told me what to do when caught in a vortex: dive down as deep as you can, then start swimming, underneath the vortex. As a souvenir, I took with me a piece of coral from Round Hill Bay, which I still have in my New York living room.

On January 22 I took a cab to the airport and boarded the plane back, half drunk from a farewell rum drink, and from the sun.

24.4 MY YEAR AT COLUMBIA

24.4.1 Spring Term

Two days later I started at Columbia, took occupancy of a pleasant office on the eighth floor of Pupin Laboratory, and joined the Faculty Club. On February 4 I started my course, designated "Advanced Quantum Mechanics," devoted more specifically to QED. By May 11, the end of term, I had gone through complete calculations of Schwinger's anomalous magnetic moment and of the Lamb shift (chapter 19, sec. 19.4), teaching all the tricks I knew of this complicated trade. I had some excellent students. Gary Feinberg would later become full professor at Columbia and for some years head of the department. Mel Schwartz would share the 1988 Nobel Prize for his experimental contributions to neutrino physics. Several others became full professors too.

I had good contacts with the faculty, particularly with Rabi. We spent many hours talking together, either in his office or mine, or in his apartment on Riverside Drive. A recurring topic was the foundations of quantum mechanics. He knew and accepted full well the powers of that theory yet often confessed to a sense of discomfort about its basis. Also in later years, indeed until shortly before his death in 1988, he would want to discuss these issues with me, time and again.

Soon after my arrival at Columbia I began a collaboration with Robert Serber, another Columbia professor. Our first project was an analysis of "K-fragments," possible bound states of K-particles to ordinary nuclear matter. A paper on that subject appeared that September.[21]

In the autumn, Serber and I tackled another problem. It was a time of deep malaise in quantum field theory. It was clear by then that the methods that had been so highly successful for QED failed entirely when applied to strong interactions. Was it because field theory simply did not apply in these cases—as some unfortunate souls believed—or that other computational methods were called for? It seemed worthwhile to us to explore that second alternative further, in particular the so-called "strong coupling method," devised as early as 1940. We embarked on a careful methodological study of that method.[22] It was a pretty tough problem, which we brought to interesting conclusions only after I had returned to Princeton.[23]

In mid-March I received a phone call from Oppenheimer concerning

George Kennan, who had first come to the Institute in 1950 on a temporary appointment (chapter 18, sec. 18.1), interrupted in 1952 when he served as U.S. ambassador in Moscow. After that year he had resigned from the Foreign Service and returned to Princeton. Robert had recently put him up for a permanent Institute professorship in diplomatic history but had hit upon strong resistance from the mathematics faculty. He asked me for help in a forthcoming faculty meeting at which the matter would come up for formal discussion. Strictly, he had no right to do so, since I was on leave, but he sounded so desperate that I said I would come. It was an unpleasant meeting, the opposition tearing hard into the proposal on the grounds that Kennan's publications to date could not be called scholarly contributions. Things got rather nasty; I did not say much but afterward told Robert that I would talk privately with the mathematicians, who considered me reasonably unbiased. I tried to calm them down.

The matter ended the following November, when the appointment was approved with a vote of 13 for and 5 mathematicians against. This contretemps marked the beginning of a lasting hostility of the mathematics group toward Oppenheimer. As to Kennan, his appointment has proved to be fully justified. The books he wrote while at the Institute have received wide acclaim and numerous high honors.

24.4.2 Death of Einstein

Early in the morning of April 18 I was woken up by a phone call from a friend, a physics professor at Johns Hopkins. "Do you think you could help us get Einstein's brain for our medical department?" he asked.

"What the devil are you talking about?"

"Haven't you heard? Einstein died in the night."

No, I had not heard. I do not recall the rest of the conversation, only that I had to sit down to digest the news. Because of my absence from Princeton, I had not been aware of the past week's events there.

I knew that during the preceding years Einstein had not been well. An exploratory operation in 1948 had revealed a large intact aneurysm in his abdominal aorta which, two years later, was found to be growing. From then on, "We around him knew . . . of the sword of Damocles hanging over us. He knew it, too, and waited for it, calmly and smilingly."[24]

This is what I later learned about Einstein's last days.

On the morning of Wednesday, April 13, the Israeli consul called on

Einstein at his home in order to discuss the draft of a statement Einstein intended to make on television and radio on the occasion of the forthcoming anniversary of Israel's independence. The incomplete draft ends as follows: "No statesman in a position of responsibility has dared to take the only promising course [toward a stable peace] of supranational security, since this would surely mean his political death. For the political passions, aroused everywhere, demand their victims." These may well be the last phrases Einstein committed to paper.

That afternoon Einstein collapsed at home. The aneurysm had ruptured. His personal physician was called immediately. On Thursday, a cardiac and aortic surgeon from New York Hospital was also called in for consultation. After the doctors had deliberated, Einstein asked his doctor if it would be a horrible death. "Perhaps; one does not know," he was told. Perhaps it will be minutes, perhaps hours, perhaps days.[25] "He was very stoical under pain," his doctor said a few days later.[26] During this period, Einstein often resisted being given morphine injections and firmly refused all suggestions for an operation. "I want to go when I want. It is tasteless to prolong life artificially; I have done my share, it is time to go. I will do it elegantly."[27] On Friday he was moved to Princeton Hospital. That evening a call was made to his son Hans Albert in Berkeley, who immediately left for Princeton and arrived on Saturday afternoon. "On Saturday and Sunday, I was together quite a lot with my father, who much enjoyed my company."[28] On Saturday, Einstein called the house to ask for his glasses. On Sunday, he called for writing material. That evening he appeared to be resting comfortably.

A night nurse at the hospital was the last person to see Einstein alive. At 1:10 A.M. on April 18, "She noted that he was breathing differently."[29] She summoned another nurse, who helped her roll up the head of the bed. Right after the other nurse left, Einstein mumbled in German. Then, as the nurse put it, "He gave two deep breaths and expired."[30] It was 1:15 in the morning.

The news was made public at 8 A.M. The autopsy performed that morning showed that death had been caused by "a big blister on the aorta, which broke finally like a worn-out inner tube."[31]

At 2 P.M. the body was removed to the Mather Funeral Home in Princeton and from there, ninety minutes later, to the Ewing Crematorium in Trenton, where twelve Einstein intimates gathered. One of them spoke briefly, reciting lines from Goethe's *Epilog zu Schiller's Glocke*. The body was cremated after removal (without consent of next of kin, as best I know) of vital organs, including the brain, for scientific study. The ashes were scattered at an undisclosed place.

Back to April 18. After I had collected myself, I went to Columbia and looked up Rabi, who had also heard. From my diary: "Together we sat *shiva* today." In my class that afternoon I said that this time I would not continue my regular course but would rather talk about Einstein. Rabi also came to this impromptu talk.

Some days later I went to Princeton to call on Helen Dukas. Toward the end of our long talk I asked her for a personal favor, a memento from Einstein, nothing fancy. She said she'd think about it. Sometime thereafter she gave me Einstein's last pipe. It had a clay head and a strawlike stem, and had cost a dime. It still stands in my office.[32]

24.4.3 Summer

In July I went to Brookhaven National Laboratory on a six-week summer appointment. I got an apartment on the site and took meals in a dilapidated but pleasant cafeteria (since replaced by a modern version). It was the first of many summers I was to spend there. Those stays have invariably been profitable for my work. Late afternoons I would always go for a swim at a nearby Fire Island beach, easily reached by car, crossing a bridge.

In the middle of that stay I was able to rent a beach house on Dune Road in Westhampton, for two weeks only, all I could afford, rents were really steep. Those were days of luxury, starting with a swim, followed by breakfast, which I took on my sundeck near the ocean. I also spent a weekend with Willis Lamb and his wife at their cottage elsewhere on Fire Island, sailing and crabbing.

I spent the rest of that summer in New York. When the first breeze of autumn came, it was as if a curtain was raised from over my brain. I never could think clearly during the hot, humid summers on the Eastern seaboard.

24.4.4 Fall Term

In the autumn I gave a course on particle physics. A couple of memorable events occurred those months. On October 4, the Dodgers beat the Yankees 2–0 in the seventh game of the World Series, to earn their first world championship. I can still see little Sandy Amoros, Dodger outfielder, leaning into the stands to catch a Yankee hit, a feat that has been called the most outstanding play in World Series history. Note from my diary: "It was all very much human drama in miniature and I am glad it is the Dodgers." In November, there was joy at Columbia with the announcement that two of their physics faculty had won Nobel prizes: Polykarp Kusch "for his precise determination of the magnetic moment of the electron," and Willis Lamb "for his discoveries concerning the structure of the hydrogen spectrum."

24.5 THE PAIS-PICCIONI EFFECT

In the preceding March I had given a colloquium at Columbia on the neutral K-particles that was recalled by Leon Lederman, one of the discoverers of the long-lived K_2, in his 1988 Nobel lecture.[33] I remember that occasion in particular because of the discussion at the blackboard afterward with Oreste Piccioni, then a staff member at Brookhaven. It marked the beginning of a collaboration of ours that began in New York, ended in Brookhaven, and resulted in a joint paper that came out in December,[34] dealing with "bizarre manifestations of the mixing of K^o and $\bar{K}^o$,"[35] specifically the fate of a freshly created K^o-beam.

As noted in section 24.1.4, in strong production reactions either a beam of K^o's or a beam of $\bar{K}^o$'s is created. For definiteness consider the K^o-case, a mixture of K_1 and K_2. Evidently one can choose a later time such that almost all K_1's have decayed, so that the beam has turned into almost purely the much longer-lived K_2's. At that later time, let this beam of K_2's, a mixture of K^o and $\bar{K}^o$, fall on an absorbing plate of matter. The rules of strangeness dictate that only $\bar{K}^o$, not K^o, can be absorbed. As a result, what comes out of the absorber is a beam enriched in K^o-content—which, to repeat, is a mixture of K_1 and K_2. Result: a *regeneration* of K_1 has occurred, manifested by the reappearance of the decay $K_1 \rightarrow 2\pi$. This prediction, which has become known as the Pais-Piccioni effect, was verified a few years later.[36]

A more detailed analysis—which I will skip here—shows moreover that from the time evolution of the beam it is possible to measure the extremely small mass difference between K_1 and K_2, about a hundred thousandth of a millionth of the electron mass. This, the smallest mass difference between particles ever detected, was first measured in 1961.[37]

Feynman has called these predictions "one of the greatest achievements of theoretical physics. It is not based on an elegant hocus-pocus . . . yet the predictions are just as important as, say, the prediction of the positron."[38] It is certainly the best physics I have done in my whole life.

25

My First Trip to Russia
and My First Marriage

25.1 How I Met Lila and How
We Went to Haiti

ONE EVENING in the spring of 1955, Sammy Eilenberg took me along to a dinner party given by friends of his, a young couple living near Columbia University. At the table I was seated opposite a young woman of rare beauty, a redhead, blue-eyed, with a lovely voice and an enchanting smile, who seemed to have stepped out of a Botticelli painting. Her name was Lila Atwill. She was a friend of Viki, our hostess; both were high-fashion models. I could not keep my eyes off her, and decided to give her a call some time later. So it came about that one evening that autumn I took her out for dinner and a movie. That marked the beginning of a courtship. I took her for a drive upstate to see the gorgeous fall colors. She invited me to her apartment on 49th Street near the East River, and also to a glamorous fashion show in town, at which I sat feeling extremely self-conscious.

I was happy when Lila accepted my invitation to spend two weeks together in Haiti. On December 23 we arrived at Port-au-Prince, settling in the Villa Créole, a hotel in nearby Pétionville, a small town favored by the Haitian elite, who turned out to be of no help whatever in helping us understand the local culture; they frowned on Africanism.

The next day we went to cockfights, held in a cockpit (I suddenly understood the origin of that word), locally called *gaguère*. It is immensely cruel, without the ennobling element of danger I had seen at bullfights, and with high financial stakes. Some time thereafter, we took a little plane which in twelve minutes brought us to Jacmel, on the south shore, for a three-day stay. Of that visit I only remember an afternoon excursion by *camionette,* a local public transport vehicle. You sit packed together with many people, some carrying live chickens, some with pigs. It was great colorful fun.

Another three-day side trip by plane brought us to Cap Haitien, ninety miles to the north, Haiti's second most important town. In the early nineteenth century it had been the capital of the then newly independent nation, ruled by the black king, Henry Christophe. First we went to Sans-Souci, one of Christophe's monuments, completed in 1813. At that time it had marble and mosaic floors, walls of mahogany, and (unusual for that time) numerous bathrooms. Then, for one and a half hours, up the steep trail to the Citadelle, the other monument, an almost menacing-looking fortress. Its walls are 140 feet high and more than 20 feet thick. It can house a garrison of 15,000 men. Giant cannon, smaller guns, and piles of cannonballs litter the battlements. Eight huge cisterns solve the water problem. Christophe's tomb is found on the ramparts.

On January 7, 1956, we flew back. Temperature at departure was 90°, at arrival 20°.

During those weeks I had gotten to know Lila much better. I learned of her troubled youth and her previous brief marriage. Also, there were moments when I could sense in her a deep helplessness in confronting the world. These and other insights caused me to develop a strong, protective tenderness for her, feelings I had not before experienced toward a woman.

On returning from Haiti I still had to finish my course at Columbia and give the final exam. Meanwhile I had gone to Princeton to arrange for a new place to live and found a pleasant room in a house on Hibben Road. I noticed that my leave had caused me to develop a greater detachment toward my Princeton environment. The Institute now looked like a doll's house to me.

I continued to spend weekends in New York, driving back and forth. One day in March, Lila called. Friends had two tickets to *My Fair Lady* which they were unable to use. "Buy them," I said. This musical, which had opened on the 15th of that month in the Mark Hellinger Theater, was the hottest show in town, sold out long in advance. One critic has written that it was the best musical of the century. So we went, to one of the most memorable theater evenings of my life. Rex Harrison and Julie Andrews were superb, the music was melodious, the score witty, the costumes by Cecil Beaton for the Ascot scene the most elegant I have ever seen on stage.

25.2 ROCHESTER VI: A QUESTION OF PARITY

On April 2, 1956, I went by train to Rochester for its sixth annual physics conference. It was a historic meeting, for several reasons. It was the first one in which Soviet physicists participated, who spoke on their work in Russian, with translation. This welcome development was of course post-Stalin, in the Nikita Khrushchev era. It was also the first meeting where the recent experimental discovery in Berkeley of the anti-proton was reported. Most memorable was the first mention of possible parity violation. I should explain what parity is.

Ancient philosophers had already debated whether Nature exhibits a symmetry between left and right, that is, in modern terms, whether the basic laws of physics are the same in our world as they would be in a mirrored world. Nothing seemed to contradict this symmetry, which in fact was already a useful tool in classical physics, for example in the classification of crystal types. No one doubted the universal validity of parity conservation—until the Sixth Rochester Conference, where the Θ-τ puzzle was formulated.

Charged K-particles can decay into two pions, the Θ-mode, also into three pions, the τ-mode. Increasingly, accurate measurements had shown that Θ and τ have the same mass and the same lifetime. Therefore, it seemed obvious that Θ and τ are alternative decays of the *same* K-particle. It had meanwhile been shown, however, that Θ and τ have opposite parity.[1] Since parity was supposed to be a unique attribute, Θ and τ could *not* be the same particle. That was the Θ-τ puzzle, first seriously debated in Rochester. Feynman raised the question whether in K-decays parity might not be conserved—which at the time seemed a high price to pay for saving the simplicity of having one and only one K-particle.[2] Oppenheimer said: "The τ-meson will have either domestic or foreign complications. It will not be simple on both fronts."[3]

In 1958 I wrote: "Be it recorded here that, on the train back from Rochester, Professor Yang and the writer each bet Professor Wheeler one dollar that the Θ- and the τ-meson were distinct particles; and that Professor Wheeler has since collected the two dollars."[4] I shall explain in the next chapter how that insight had come about.

25.3 First Visit to the Soviet Union

25.3.1 The Road to Moscow

One last remark about the Rochester meeting. It was announced that in May the "First All-Union Conference on the Physics of Particles at High Energies" would take place in Moscow. It was the first postwar conference with American participation, and fourteen of us, including yours truly, had been invited. At Rochester, the physicist Edwin McMillan from Berkeley gave us our first briefing on that forthcoming event.

On May 11 I arrived in Helsinki, en route to Moscow. On May 13 I went to the airport again, where I met a number of physicists from the West who were also there, on their way to the meeting. We flew on to Moscow by Aeroflot—no seat belts.

25.3.2 Moscow

At Sheremetyovo Airport, some of Russia's leading physicists were on hand to greet us, including Lev Davidovich Landau, Igor Tamm, and Vladimir Veksler, all of them future Nobel laureates. They led us into what I supposed to be a VIP reception room. I was amazed at its furniture: very heavy, very plush, very much what my grandparents would have liked. I had somehow expected stark, modern furniture, but that was nowhere seen at any official function I attended there. We sat down and started talking (in English, no interpreters). I vividly remember my feeling that within minutes we knew each other well. That was due to the fact that I knew their work and they mine.

A little later we were driven to Hotel Moskva, just off Red Square. In its cavernous lobby, which reminded me of the old Penn Station, stood an oversize statue of Stalin. It was actually removed during my ten-day stay there, no doubt a consequence of Khrushchev's "secret" address to the Twentieth Congress of the Communist Party the preceding February, in which he had denounced Stalin's policies.

The conference started the next day. Headphones for translations were provided. The main speaker was Landau, Russia's most brilliant theorist, who discussed issues in QED. In the discussion he and Nikolai Nikolaievitch Bogoliubov got into an argument. It was my first experience of hearing

Russians debate, impassioned and uninhibited. Later I would see Russians from the audience get up and walk toward the speaker, with fists raised as if for a physical fight—which never did occur. Afterward, all involved would smile as if nothing had happened—behavior not familiar to us Westerners. The next day I gave a talk on my work with Serber. In the evening we were taken to the Bolshoi for a performance of *Prince Igor*, with Petrov, a "People's Artist" (the highest honor) singing the lead role. The stage is broader and deeper than any I have ever seen elsewhere, well suited for the apparent Russian fondness of spectaculars. That evening I saw horses galloping up on stage, and a castle burn down. Caviar and champagne during the intermission. Dinner at midnight.

During the next day's break, the Americans were taken to the U.S. Embassy, Spasso House on Chaikowsky Street, for lunch with Ambassador Charles ("Chip") Bohlen. We had many questions, which he answered frankly but within diplomatic constraints. He also told us of an exchange with Khrushchev at a reception where a young woman from *Life* magazine was taking pictures. K: "She looks nice even though she is American." B: "She looks nice *because* she is American." K asks the girl if she agrees; she says yes. K: "She has to agree with you because she is afraid of you." B: "The only person in this room she is afraid to disagree with is *you*." Bohlen also told us that Moscow is a diplomatic hardship post—much of their food was flown in from Berlin.

The following day began with an interview by Daniel Schorr of CBS. Lunch was at Landau's, who loves jokes, practical and otherwise. He gave me an example of Armenian humor: "Why can my old blind horse jump higher than St. Basil's Cathedral?" "Because the cathedral cannot jump." Also from Landau: American scholars, about to attend a conference, settle down in their hotel. At breakfast the next morning they compare notes about their rooms. The first tells that his window was painted shut so that he could not let any air in. The second tells that his faucet kept dripping all night, disturbing his sleep. The third tells that he checked his room for hidden microphones, found one under the center of the carpet, cut the wires with pliers. The fourth says: "I had just gone to bed and was about to fall asleep when the damned chandelier came crashing down."

After lunch I excused myself to go to the bathroom. Looking for paper I found no roll but instead a book out of which you had to tear pages. Looking more closely, I saw that the book, in Russian, was a history of the 1917 Communist revolution. I tore out a few extra pages to take home as souvenirs. Landau was badly injured in a car accident in 1962. He never fully recovered and died six years later.

In the evening our interpreters asked what we wanted to do after dinner. "Ride the subway," we replied. Tania Bulgakova, my interpreter, looked at me, clearly thinking that we were slightly mad, then said: "I must ask a certain person," evidently some sort of superior, who had to give permission. The Moscow subways are one of Russia's great prides. Imagine, stations with marble walls, decorated with murals, lit by chandeliers.

The next day, Sunday, we were taken to a visit inside the Kremlin, accompanied by our interpreters, who were quite excited since they had never been inside the principal buildings. Our VIP tour included visits to Lenin's apartment, maintained the way it was in his lifetime; to the cabinet room, where we left a message for Khrushchev; to the assembly hall of the Supreme Soviet, where I had my picture taken on the dais; to the Kremlin palace, with reception rooms reminiscent of the subways. As a conclusion to that visit came the high point: the visit to the truly magnificent churches, also inside the Kremlin walls, with their superb icons and tombs.

Finally, to the mausoleum, right outside the walls. I was wearing a raincoat under which I had hidden my camera, hoping to take a picture of the tombs of Lenin and Stalin by slightly opening my coat. Nothing came of that after one of several soldiers lining the steps down to the main room pointed his bayonet to my coat and shook his head: no dice. In the evening, to the Bolshoi, to see *Giselle*. As before, we had excellent box seats. Looking sideways, I saw Andrei Gromyko sitting a few yards away from me.

25.3.3 Zagorsk, Leningrad, Kiev

Our hosts had been good enough to prepare several tours for us, beginning with a one-day excursion to Zagorsk, forty miles from Moscow, the most beautiful experience of my Russian trip. It was one of four active theological seminaries in Russia. Of lasting memory was hearing religious melodies rendered by a male choir, the voices and melodies simply magnificent. That same day we drove back to Moscow and boarded the Red Arrow, the night train to Leningrad, for a ten-hour journey. There were two sleeping berths in each compartment. Tea and caviar sandwiches could be bought on the train.

The next day, a Sunday, there was time enough for a few hours at the

Hermitage. I walked over by myself, opened the front doors, when an attendant explained in sign language that the museum was closed. I was much
taken aback, then inspiration hit me. I said: "Akademia Nauk" (Academy of
Sciences). As if I had pronounced a magical formula, the doors were opened
for me and I could enter unattended, having the collections all to myself.
Marvelous.

In the afternoon we boarded a plane for a miserable six-hour flight to
Kiev. We spent the next day sightseeing, notably the Sofia Cathedral, still in
ruins. After lunch, a speedboat ride on the Dniepr River, then a swim in it.

The next day it was back to the West. I was still in a daze due to the strong
Russian experiences, but also felt intense relief upon departing from Soviet
soil. True, we had been given the red carpet treatment and everywhere had
been well received. True, we had been able to talk freely with our Soviet
colleagues, including touching on sensitive political subjects. Yet I had felt
hemmed in, oppressed, wherever I went, as did my American colleagues.
Why? Perhaps that is best expressed by a witty but very profound remark
made to me by a Soviet colleague: "Our future looks bright but our past is
unpredictable." Think about that. On July 6 I was back in New York.

25.4 MARRIAGE

After my return I called Lila in Missouri, where she was on a family visit—
she hailed from the Ozark region. Both of us sounded rather tentative—no
surprise after my two months' absence. After she returned to New York, I
told her that I would have to spend some of the coming time at Brookhaven
National Laboratory and proposed we drive to Long Island to find a house
to rent for us for that time. That brought us to Montauk, where we found an
ideal little place on a hill overlooking the Sound, to be ours until Labor Day.

By then the question of marriage had begun to loom. While I still felt
tenderly toward Lila, that question started to cause me considerable discomfort, mainly because it meant a level of commitment that I had always
evaded so far. Also, I had begun to realize that her helplessness, as noted
earlier, would occasionally lead to instability, which, though of short duration, nevertheless disturbed me. All of which led to a period of ups and
downs, not uncommon at this stage, which included a temporary separation.

That troubled time had subsided when September came. I now suggested
that I find quarters in Princeton which we could share. My room on Hibben

Road was not suitable, so I went hunting once more and found space in a house on Battle Road.

In late September a solemn moment came for me: I registered to vote. Neither in Holland nor in America had I ever done that before. On November 6, I turned the lever of a voting machine for the first time, casting my vote for Stevenson, knowing very well, however, that he did not stand a chance against Eisenhower, who indeed won by a landslide.

In mid-November I proposed to Lila to become my lawfully wedded wife, which she accepted. The first time we told others was the next evening, at a dinner party in the home of Hume Cronyn and his wife, Jessica Tandy, who, after the demise of the Lunts, were to become America's premier theater couple. In the beginning of December we moved Lila's belongings to my Perry Street apartment.

From then on I took charge of all wedding arrangements—not Lila's forte—including buying the gorgeous wedding dress she had chosen. (Her mother and stepfather, who lived near New York, were friendly but tightfisted.) On December 15, our wedding day, I got up quite early and went for a long walk in Central Park, trying to master my uncertainties about the coming events, and to control my nerves. I came back calmed and went to the house of friends, where the civil ceremony was to be performed by a judge.

After our guests had assembled (there were more than sixty of them) and I stood waiting, Lila entered on the arm of her stepfather. I was deeply moved and profoundly happy when I saw her. She looked more beautiful and radiant than I had ever seen her before. The judge officiated. That done, a friend broke a glass, after which those who knew the custom cried "Mazzeltov," good luck. Afterwards I said: "My wife and I want to raise our glass to drink to you and to thank you for being with us and for your friendship. And now I propose a toast, to Helen, Lila's mother, and to my parents in Amsterdam." Our guests included the Oppenheimers, the Cronyns, the Frank Yangs, and the Tsung Dao Lees.

The next morning we took off for our two-week honeymoon in Jamaica, where we stayed in the Shaw Park Hotel in Ocho Rios, which turned out to be fancy but dull. Days of swimming quickly unwound us. I took two lessons in water-skiing, which I was proud to master and enjoyed doing, on two skis only. I tried but never made it on a single ski. One evening, pleasant people whom we met at the hotel took us along to a very fancy party where I met Noel Coward, dressed in a pink dinner jacket and pink bow tie. We had a pleasant chat during which he explained his living arrangements: a house on a hill above the nearby town of Port Maria, where he receives guests; a cottage on the beach below, where he spends his days all alone, after having had breakfast with his guests, whom he meets again at dinner.

On December 30 we flew back, departing in eighty-five degree temperature, arriving in fifteen. By midnight I carried Lila over the threshold of our apartment. I noted in my diary: "End of honeymoon. I am a married man, a regular guy."

26

Enter Joshua.
The 1950s, Concluded

26.1 THE PARITY QUESTION RESOLVED

SHORTLY after Lila and I returned from Jamaica, we moved into a new apartment in Princeton. We had kept the Perry Street apartment for use over the weekends. As the humdrum of the wedding and this new move receded, I began to worry whether married life would give me the peace of mind to think and work.

For me, the most important event in January 1957 occurred at a party given by Viki and her husband (where Lila and I had first met, chapter 25, sec. 25.1). There I encountered my friend and collaborator Robert Serber, who asked me: "What do you think of the parity situation?" I countered: "What are you talking about?" "Haven't you heard that Lee and Yang's proposals have shown that parity is violated?" I could only reply: "I need a drink," a most unusual request since already then I barely touched alcohol.

During my time in Jamaica, a fundamental leap in physics had taken place. The news reached the papers a few days after Serber told me. On January 16, the *New York Times* carried on its front page an article head-lined: "Basic concept in physics is reported upset in tests/Conservation of parity in nuclear theory challenged by scientists at Columbia and Princeton Institute."

As my need for a drink showed, the news of that change in basic concepts had shaken me profoundly, even though, as I had gone on my honeymoon in mid-December, I had already been fully aware of the option of parity violation, and had in fact already written a paper in which that possibility was taken into account.

We already briefly met Frank Yang (chapter 23, sec. 23.1), but not yet

Tsung Dao Lee, "T. D." to his friends. Lee's arrival at the Institute in 1951 marked the beginning of an intimate and intense collaboration between him and Yang, ranging from fundamental particle physics to the theory of phase transitions. Here I will discuss only their seminal work on the parity question, published in June 1956.[1]

I already noted that the issue of parity conservation or violation had first been raised at the Sixth Rochester Conference (chapter 25, sec. 25.2). What Lee and Yang had done, right after that meeting, was to begin a systematic investigation of the status of experimental knowledge concerning the verification of space reflection (parity or P-) invariance and also of charge conjugation (C-) invariance (see chapter 24, sec. 24.1.5). This study led to a most surprising result: there existed as yet no experimental evidence for or against either P- or C-invariance for all weak processes (a term defined in chapter 21, sec. 21.4), that is, neither for the long-known β-radioactive decays, nor for the decays of pions or muons, nor for any of the more recently discovered weak decays of the strange particles. Thus what had begun as the Θ-τ puzzle (chapter 25, sec. 25.2), a question of parity seemingly confined to one single phenomenon, now had become a quite broad issue.

That is where matters stood in the summer of 1956. The first time I had occasion to get involved with questions of P- and C-invariance or noninvariance was in the autumn of that year, when Sam Treiman and I produced a paper[2] that was sent off in December, a week before I got married. (To the best of my knowledge it was the first submitted paper in which the ideas of Lee and Yang played a role.) Treiman, who had begun his academic career in 1952 as an instructor at Princeton University, was now an assistant professor there and has since climbed through the ranks. More important to me is that he has become my best American friend.

The question Sam and I addressed concerned a decay mode named K^0_{e3}, the decay of a long-lived neutral K into a charged pion plus an electron plus a neutrino. Details need not be of concern here, except for our remark that our results are "independent of whether or not parity is conserved or not . . . [and of] whether charge conjugation invariance is valid or not in weak interactions."[3] Obviously we were prepared for either eventuality.

Then, in late December, came the great news: experiment had shown that P and C are violated, first in a β-decay process, a few days later likewise in the decays of pion and muon, shortly thereafter also in the decay of the Λ-hyperon. The Θ-τ puzzle had been solved. The January 1957 issue of *Fortune* magazine carried a very good article entitled "The Magnificent

Riddle" on recent developments in particle theory, which included photographs of Gell-Mann, Lee, Yang, and me.

Even before the experimental observation of P-violation, the following question had been raised: Suppose P is violated; is there a weaker but nevertheless elegant symmetry (physicists cannot do without elegance) that could take its place? It had occurred to several physicists that combined CP-invariance might serve that purpose: look in a mirror and flip the charge and all will be symmetric.[4]

Now that C is violated, what remained of the theory of the K_1-K_2 particle mixture which had made use of C-invariance (chapter 24, sec. 24.1)? All is saved, verbatim, by replacing the requirement that K_1, K_2 are eigenstates of C by the condition that they be eigenstates of CP. It is easily seen that this suffices to allow K_1 but forbids K_2 to decay into two pions.

Treiman and I were the first to note[5] that the switch from C to CP importantly affects the 3π-decay modes of neutral K's, however. Before long, experiment confirmed our findings. Other tests of CP were also successful, within the experimental errors. As a result, in the late 1950s, "even though parity had been overthrown a few years earlier, one was quite confident about CP-symmetry."[6] I reported on our work at the Seventh Rochester Conference (April 15–19, 1957).[7]

In 1957, Lee and Yang shared the Nobel Prize in physics "for their penetrating studies of the parity laws which have led to important discoveries concerning elementary particles." I am pretty sure that never before or since has the time interval between work done and this high recognition been as short.

I responded with pleasure to the request by the editor of *Nuclear Physics* to write for the journal an appreciation of the scientific work of the two men.[8]

One sunny but freezing morning that January 1957 I went to the cemetery on Witherspoon Street in Princeton to attend the burial of Johnny von Neumann. A brief prayer was said by the Roman Catholic priest who had converted him shortly before. Thus came to an end the life of a Jewish wunderkind from Hungary.

26.2 Physics' Years of Glamour

By the 1950s we reached the years when the particle physics literature began its tremendous growth. On the subject of weak interactions alone, approximately 1,000 experimental and 3,500 theoretical articles, as well as one hundred reviews, appeared between 1950 and 1972, written by authors from fifty countries.[9] The distribution in time shows a large peak immediately following the discovery of parity violation.

This outpouring of papers was due to a complex of reasons. First, physics across the board had become a glamorous subject because of physicists' spectacular role in developing atomic weapons and radar. I already noted (chapter 20, sec. 20.1) that as a result, funding agencies were ready, nay eager, to support physics research. Thus, more than before, physics attracted young people, eager to see their name in print. Particle physics in particular exerted great appeal since meanwhile it had been recognized as one of the new frontiers in science, which was the second reason for the increase in the literature.

Physics' new glamour caused changes not only in the field itself but also in its perception by the public at large. Physics as front-page news was basically a new phenomenon, dating from about the 1950s, with major exceptions such as references to Einstein and Roentgen. In the preceding section we met a first example: the announcement of parity violations. Also from that time the headline announcements of Nobel prizes, as was, for example, the case with Lee and Yang's award.

It had not always been like that. As a striking example of different earlier coverage, turn to the November 10, 1922, edition of the *New York Times,* where, on page 4, middle of column 2, one finds, in its entirety, the following item:

NOBEL PRIZE FOR EINSTEIN

The Nobel Committee has awarded the physics prize for 1921 to Albert Einstein, identified with the theory of relativity, and that for 1922 to Professor Neils [*sic*] Bohr of Copenhagen.

Thus, without the flourishes so familiar in modern coverage, did the good citizens of New York and elsewhere hear of the honors bestowed on the century's two greatest physicists.

Then, in 1957, public awareness of and support for science received another great boost. On October 5, the *New York Times* carried a headline spanning the entire front page: "Soviet fires earth satellite into space; it is circling the globe at 18000 mph; sphere tracked in 4 crossings over US." Sputnik I had gone into orbit. Once again the glamour of science rose steeply. As Rabi once said to me during those years: "You younger physicists are the children of Sputnik and the grandchildren of the atomic bomb." This glamorous period lasted well into the 1960s.

CHAPTER TWENTY-SIX

26.3 ANOTHER EUROPEAN TOUR

During the first week of May 1957, Sam Treiman and I finished yet another paper, this one on "hyperfragments," hyperons bound to nuclear matter.[10] Some days later, Lila and I boarded a steamer bound for Rotterdam. During the next peaceful week on the ocean I found the quiet I needed to take stock of my relationship with her. She was still as lovely as ever to me, but as a daily companion I found her dull. It began to dawn on me what deeper feelings had caused me to marry her: it was an attempt at redemption for the loss of my sister, Annie. Lila's frequent helplessness, which in some imprecise way resonated with Annie's behavior as a young girl, aroused strong protective feelings in me—still, after all these years, my dominant recollection of her. Taking care of Lila was an attempt at expiating the guilt I continued to feel for not having done enough for my late sister.

One aspect of Lila's behavior troubled me much. At moments of instability she would take to the bottle and drink a great deal. She was by no means an alcoholic. Those bouts would last a day, after which she would remain sober for weeks on end.

All through that crossing a line from André Gide's journals kept coming back to me: "Ce bonheur médiocre qui est le plus grand ennemi du vrai bonheur" (That mediocre happiness which is the greatest enemy of true happiness).

Our first stop was Amsterdam, where my parents met Lila for the first time. Both my father and my mother took to her at once, and she to them. The fact that she was not Jewish caused no friction. A week later we took off by car, first for a month's stay in Denmark, where I introduced Lila to the Bohrs, and where Niels, now almost seventy-two, still struck me with his strength. Then through Germany to Saas Fee in Switzerland, where we caught up with the Josts. Then down to the French Riviera, where we had planned to stay several weeks. I did not like St. Tropez and Ste. Maxime one bit, as people seemed to be almost crawling over one another. So we turned west, moving from one rental agency to the next until we had luck in Le Rayol, where we rented the Villa Sarabelle.

I came to like the little village, my quiet room, the inhabitants I came to know, the sweet girl at the Bureau de Tabacs, where I bought my stamps, the incredibly slow post office with a stern young woman behind the counter. Above all, the fish market, where you go to order very fresh fish for the next day. The fishermen take off at five in the morning, and get what you ordered. I grew to love the specialty of the region, *soupe de poissons,* fish soup of one kind or another.

We made an excursion by boat to some small islands in a nearby bay, to Port-Cros, subtropical with flowering yuccas, and to the village of Hélio-polis on the Ile du Levant, a favorite of the *naturistes,* according to my guidebook. I did not know what these were, and said to Lila that probably they were bird watchers. As the boat entered the little port, I saw people coming down to the dock from the hills, evidently to collect mail. All of them were nude! We had arrived at a nudist colony. We had a drink in a bar on the village square, where the bartender as well as his customers, except for us, were in the altogether. We of course were normally dressed. I learned something from that experience: the majority sets the norm, the others look and feel rather odd.

In early September we drove back through France. Most memorable: din-ner in the famed three-star Ousteau Baumanière. The high point of the superb meal was a *truite au bleu* in a sauce *au beurre blanc.* I was so moved by the quality of that sauce that I asked to see the saucier. When he came to our table, I rose and thanked him, saying that I had never before tasted a sauce of such perfection. When I asked how it was made, he replied: "Sur-tout pas d'oeufs, monsieur, pas de crème" (Above all, no eggs, Sir, and no cream). One could afford a meal like that in those days: twenty dollars for food, wine, a brandy, and tip.

Then on to Geneva. There I put Lila on a plane to Amsterdam, where she would spend two weeks with my parents while I would work at CERN, and then drive the car back to join her.

As already mentioned (chapter 20, sec. 20.1), CERN is the multinational European high energy physics laboratory. At the time of my arrival, its director general was Cornelius ("Cor") Bakker, an Amsterdamer whom I knew from my Dutch years. We spent much time together, discussing the future of physics in general and of CERN in particular. He asked me if I would be interested in heading its Theory Division. I replied that I would be glad to consider that offer, which I eventually declined, however.

Then I drove to Amsterdam for the reunion with Lila and my parents. There I saw Dutch television for the first time, notably the excellent cover-age of the opening of Parliament by the queen on the traditional third Tues-day in September. A few days later we were back in New York.

26.4 1958: THE ARRIVAL OF JOSHUA

Not long after our return from Europe we learned that Lila was pregnant.

It was a grand turn in my life, as it was in Lila's. A serenity I had not seen before descended upon her. Gone were her instabilities and bouts with the bottle. She had always been beautiful but now there was a quiet radiance about her which made me love her more than ever.

The time was now ripe to stop moving around from one rented apartment to another and find a more permanent home. I went to the Institute's business office, where I was informed of the procedure to obtain faculty housing. Someone on its staff would look for a house, and if something turned up we would be asked to have a look. If we liked it, it would be bought as Institute property; I would get a mortgage of $6\frac{1}{2}$ percent. It would be ours for as long as we wanted, but the Institute would have first refusal if we wished to vacate. The staff did find a beautiful house for us at 94 Battle Road, close to the Institute, right behind the director's home. In January 1958 we moved in.

There was a lot to do now—arrange what little furniture we had, buy new things. I loved working in the fine garden but could not manage it all when springtime came. We had to get a gardener. I was jealous of his expertise the first time he went into action.

I read a lot those months, particularly the *Alexandria Quartet* by Lawrence Durrell. I often used to stop in the middle of a page to let its exquisite prose sink in. Also poetry by W. H. Auden. I copied these lines from his "Under which Lyre": "Professors back from secret missions/Resume their proper eruditions/Though some regret it/They liked their dictaphones a lot/They met some big wheels and do not/Let you forget it." Right on, Mr. Auden.

As to my work, it became more prolific. In 1958 I published four articles on an old love of mine: symmetry properties of strong interactions.[11] In mid-April, I went to Copenhagen once more for a month's stay, leaving Lila with her mother. One purpose of that trip was to buy furniture, which I did at Den Permanente, a joint exhibition space on Vesterbrogade of several furniture firms, now, alas, defunct. I bought quite a lot, including a desk which to this day I use in New York.

Came the evening of May 18. I sat by myself in my hotel room in Vestersøhus, frightened and depressed: that midnight I would turn forty. I was irrationally scared that something bad might happen to me at that moment.

Then the townhall clock on Rådhuspladsen struck twelve. I was deeply relieved when the moment passed without incident.

On my return later in May I found Lila bulging; she was in her eighth month now, and more radiant than ever. Her pregnancy had proceeded without complications. We sat down to decide on a name for the baby, whose sex we did not know. If it was a boy, he should be named after my father. (Only American, not European, Jews do so only if the grandfather is deceased.) But my father's name, Isaiah, did not appeal to us; we thought it was too solemn. He was called Jacques by one and all, but that was too French, and we did not like Jack one bit (with apologies to other Jacks). So we began to think about other names starting with J, whereupon Lila suggested Joshua. I thought that was a marvelous choice. I did have a girl's name ready, Tamar, which is Hebrew for the fruit of the date palm, a name that occurs in the *Song of Songs*. Lila concurred.

On June 20 Lila's contractions were coming at five-minute intervals. By late evening the frequency had risen considerably. I called Ray Stone, her gynecologist, and asked for advice. He said: "Relax, give her a bourbon, call me in two hours," which I did. On June 21 at 1:30 A.M. I drove her to Princeton Hospital. She was still in good shape; I stayed with her in her room. At 4 A.M. the nurse checked the contractions. At 8 A.M. Stone took me aside to tell me that a Caesarian was called for and to ask me for permission to do so, which of course I gave. Later he told me that he had known for a long time that a Caesarian birth was inevitable, but that he nevertheless deeply believed that a woman should have the satisfaction of full labor, since that would mean a great deal to her in later life. My instincts told me how wise that was. "She fought bravely," Stone said later. (I never told Lila what Stone and I had discussed.)

At 1 P.M. Lila was put on a rolling bed to go to the operating room. I walked with her to the door, kissed her, and left for a waiting room—I was not allowed to be present during the delivery. So there I sat, until at 2:30 some doctor came in to turn on a baseball game on TV—it will probably be rained out, he said. Then he turned to me and asked if I was waiting for the Caesarian baby. Yes, I was. "It was already born and is in the nursery now. I believe it is a boy." A little later the obstetrician came in to congratulate me. Indeed, I had a son, as I so fiercely had hoped for all along. "He weighs 7 pounds ten, is 19½ inches long, and he is perfect."

Half an hour later I had my first look at Joshua. I was shocked. His skin was dark, with hair all over his face. "I helped create a mongrel," I thought. Then I went to Lila's room and found her in deep sleep, looking infinitely relieved. I went home for a few hours of sleep too, having been up for more than twenty-four hours.

At six I was back at the nursery for another look. All the facial hair was gone; Josh now had a beautiful, rosy skin. He was perfect, it was incredible. I went to see Lila, who was only barely awake, kissed her, sat with her for a while, and said I would be back early in the morning. That evening I spent at my friends the Chernisses. All I remember is being totally manic.

Josh was an easy baby from the beginning, nearly always sleeping through the night. Around six I would hear a whimper, jump out of bed, have a look at him, then wake Lila. From that time dates my permanent change in working hours, from late at night to early morning.

All through 1958 Josh kept thriving. From the beginning I would go upstairs after coming home in the afternoon from my office, sit down next to his crib and talk to him about what I had done that day, science and all. He would just lie there, looking at me with his beautiful dark eyes. He developed a coloring just like mine. To this day people say that he looks very much like me. Oddly, I have never been able to see that resemblance myself.

In June 1959 the three of us flew to San Francisco. It was Joshua's baptism by air, and mine by jet plane, a most comfortable experience, feeling like sailing, no more exposure to long hours of engine vibrations. We were on our way to a two months' stay in Berkeley, where I was to work in the Radiation Laboratory (now the Lawrence Radiation Laboratory) as visiting professor. The house rented for us had been built by Bernard Maybeck, a distinguished California architect. It was spacious, with a large sleeping porch. Josh was now crawling everywhere at full speed. We soon celebrated his first birthday with an excursion to Stinson Beach in Marin County. Another night Lila and I joined friends for a dinner at the Blue Fox in San Francisco, where I ordered something new: *faggianino a la creta,* pheasant baked in clay. Afterwards we saw Lenny Bruce perform at the Hungry I nightclub.

In August some physicist friends and I drove to the Sierra Nevadas for a mountaineering expedition, complete with ropes and crampons. We climbed the Polemonium Pass, I as the novice being the last on the rope on the way up, the first on the way down. During the descent we had a hair-raising experience. The man on the top, belaying us all, fell. I saw him slide down past me, then the next man, and the next likewise. I stood there knowing that in no time my turn to be pulled down would come. Fortunately there was a deep snow pile at the bottom of the rather long slope, where we all piled up on top of one another. The danger came from the crampons, which cut into our legs. When it was all over, we washed the blood off with snow, then laughed hysterically. When, during later years, members of that little expedition met, we would ceremoniously roll up our pant legs to show our scars.

Earlier that year, Hawaii had been admitted to the Union, and the American Physical Society therefore decided to hold its annual West Coast meeting in Honolulu. In late August a contingent of us flew out. The whole meeting was pleasantly absurd; all we wanted to do was to go to the beach. Deals were struck: if you'll be my audience, I'll be yours. I gave an invited paper on weak interactions. Other memories: the afternoon at Waikiki Beach when my friend Don Glaser and I desperately tried to stay up on our rented surfboards. Glaser and I decided to explore the nearby island of Kawaii, flew out for a couple of days, rented a car. Drove up along the Waihua River to a very fine rain forest, then to the Waimea canyon, known as the Grand Canyon of the Pacific.

Back in Berkeley I had a quite unexpected experience: I quit cigarette smoking. For years I had been a one-pack-a-day smoker. Then, one morning, as I was shaving, I suddenly stopped and said out loud to myself in the mirror: "You have just stopped cigarette smoking." I do not know where that came from, then and there. As usual I put an open pack of cigarettes in my shirt pocket and kept doing so for several more weeks without ever taking one out. Then I said to myself, "Now the test is over," and threw the pack away. I still cannot explain what came over me then. I have never smoked cigarettes since, that is, I will have an occasional one when offered by a friend, but this has never led to a relapse. The explanation may be that I had begun to smoke a pipe—which I still do, along with an occasional cigar.

At about that time, the main interest at the Berkeley laboratory was the large number of pions, most often five or six, produced when anti-protons from the incoming beam were annihilated upon colliding with the chamber's protons. Such complicated states had not been seen before, so a new question arose: What can one learn from them? I noted that those states with many particles yield simple new ways for checking whether or not parity and charge conjugation are conserved in strong interactions at these high energies.[12]

One of the first experimental results found in Berkeley regarding multi-pion systems was that the angular distribution of pions with like charge (all plus or all minus) was noticeably different from the one for angles between pions of opposite charge. Some experimentalist colleagues came to ask me for an explanation. I sent them back, saying that I would think about it. The next day I called them with an idea: the effect could be a consequence of the quantum statistics for pions (the so-called Bose-Einstein statistics), which implies that pions would tend to go in the same direction if and only if they have the same charge. This led to a collaboration that involved a fair amount of computer calculation. A paper resulted,[13] its contents now being commonly referred to as the GGLP effect (after the authors' initials). Our conclusions, checked often through the years, have turned out to be qualitatively correct.

Other experimentalists came knocking at my door with another question: What are the theoretical predictions for branching ratios? I can explain with an example. Consider the annihilation into six pions. These can appear in four versions: (006), (114), (222), (330), where the three numbers denote, in that order, the number of positive, negative, and neutral pions. Branching ratios are the relative probabilities for annihilation into each of these four states. What are they? For two or three pions, isospin is a great help, but otherwise that quantum number is not enough. For example, for a 6π-system, there are fifty-one states with the relevant isospin values 0 or 1. What to do?

Then I remembered what Eugene Wigner once had told me when, in the 1920s, he had begun to think about many-electron systems, where similar questions arise. He asked his mathematician friend von Neumann, who— Wigner told me—walked to a corner of the room, faced the wall, and started mumbling to himself. After a while he turned around and said: "You need the theory of group characters." Never mind what these are, but that answer would also serve me, I thought.

I knew those characters only by name, so I had to do some studying. I took home Wigner's book on group theory and quantum mechanics and began reading it.[14] I had tried to do so before but didn't get far—I had no motivation then, as I did now. I read through the whole book as if it were a detective story, picking up clues for what I needed on the way. When I finished, I was ready to attack my own problem. It turned out that isospin plays only a secondary role here, and that the branching ratios can be fully specified by a triple of new quantum numbers.

After my return from Berkeley to Princeton I worked out the theory in detail and produced tables that deal with up to eight pions. In December I submitted a long paper on this subject entitled "The Many π-Meson Problem."[15] It still gives me pleasure to reread it.

27

Times of Great Change:
The Early 1960s

ON JANUARY 15, 1960, as I had begun mapping out a sequel to my paper[1] on many-meson systems,[2] I received a letter from Holland telling me that my father had a slight heart ailment. On the 22nd, at 11:30 in the morning, a telegram arrived: "Father worse." One-half hour later another: "Father peacefully deceased."

My first reaction was as if time stood still. My next one: I must go to Amsterdam immediately. I made calls to reserve a ticket for a nine o'clock flight that evening. Then I went to talk to Lila. I cannot forget what happened next. She told me that she wasn't feeling well, and went to bed. I am perfectly capable of packing my own bag, but this time I felt lame and would have appreciated some support.

When I arrived the next morning, my mother told me what had happened. The doctors had diagnosed a heart irregularity and had advised that my father have a month of absolute rest in a hospital. "No," said my mother, "He will go home with me; I shall take care of him." On the morning of the 22nd he sat propped up in bed, reading a newspaper. The bell rang; it was the milkman. "I shall be back in a minute," my mother said. When she returned, he was gone. "He died in peace and comfort."

When I arrived, my father had, according to Jewish tradition, already been laid on the floor of the bedroom, arms and hands extended down alongside his body, feet toward the door, covered with a sheet. Jews do not view a dead body. I sat down on the floor next to him and talked to him.

Next morning was the *Tehera,* the ritual washing of the body, which no one is permitted to witness and which is performed by the religious members of the community. The washing takes place by lifting only a part of the sheet, so the washers do not see the body either. Our family and close friends sat silently in the living room. A washer came in, whispering to me to come along: I should put a sock on one of my father's feet—the last part of him that I would see. I do so, sobbing. The washer whispers to me to fetch my mother to put on the other sock. I walk up to her and whisper the message. My mother speaks up, firmly: "No, I won't do that. I have done enough for him." I am stunned, and put on the other sock myself. A while later I am called in again to help fasten the pins that close the coffin. It is put on a rack, and two lit candles are placed on top. That evening I sit with the coffin—a dead body may not be left alone.

The next day we bury him. First we sing psalms at home. I am told that a quite unusual ceremony will be performed in his honor. We drive close to our Sephardic synagogue. The coffin is taken out of the hearse and carried to the synagogue, where it is placed in front of the main door—according to Jewish tradition, a dead body cannot be brought into a place of worship. The doors are opened wide; inside many candles have been lit. We sing for him. Then the chief rabbi pronounces him to be posthumously a rabbi, with the added title "*Tsofer umaskir shel kehilatenu, shehistadel leharbits betoch amenu*" (Scribe and secretary of our community who endeavored to spread the Torah amongst the sons of our people).

Returning to the cars, we drive to the three hundred-year-old Sephardic cemetery (like the synagogue, untouched by the war) in the nearby village of Ouderkerk. The coffin is first put in a small hall, where I speak briefly, then it is carried to the open grave, where it is lowered in these infinitely serene surroundings. Afterwards we are served tea and the traditional hard-boiled eggs in the hall.

Then back home, to start the *shiva* (= seven), the days of mourning. I wear a good jacket, which I first rent, as tradition demands, and pronounce the formula: *Baruch dayyan ha-emet* (Blessed be the true judge). We sit on the floor, on cushions, my mother, my father's sister, a cousin, and I.

Around seven in the evening, visitors come. They are to sit in silence until one of the mourners starts a conversation. Refreshments are not served. A while later I rise to say the *Kaddish*, the prayer for the deceased. The first evening I break down completely, then collect myself and finish. The next evening my voice only trembles, thereafter I speak firmly. There is great wisdom in these mourning rituals; they help so very much to readjust to life that has to go on.

There came an evening toward the end of the week when all the visitors had left. After which my mother said, "Let's all get up and sit around the table. I'll make tea." We sat and talked and, for some reason, I started telling Jewish jokes. We burst with laughter—when the bell rang: an unexpected late visitor. "Quick," my mother said, "cups and all to the kitchen. Sit down on the floor again." I vividly remember the effort it took to force myself back into a serious mien. That, in itself, was a lesson in the virtues of mourning together.

I stayed on for a few more days. As I came into the living room one evening, I found my mother crying quietly. As I tried to console her, she said: "I am more unhappy because of my loneliness than because he is gone." That, and her reaction to being asked to put on a sock, taught me lessons about the woman's hard-boiled sense of reality. While my first response was again shock and amazement, I realized later how admirably honest her reactions had been.

Those nights in Holland I had strange dreams, in which my father often appeared as if he were still alive. Death penetrates only gradually into the deeper consciousness. In later days I often wondered why I cried so much those days. Was it because of the pain of loss? Or because I had lost the "buffer" of an older generation so that next time it would be my own death? I do not know.

I suggested to my mother that she settle in the United States. She declined, saying that she still felt most comfortable in Amsterdam, surrounded by her friends. My parents had planned a trip to Princeton that spring. I urged her to come by herself, an idea she liked very much.

In early April my mother arrived in Princeton for a month's stay. As always, I was happy to see her. As always, after a day or two I felt we had nothing more to say to each other.

Passover came. I decided to give a Seder, the traditional evening of celebration in the home with prayers, songs, and a meal. We had invited several guests, including Helen Dukas, the late Einstein's secretary, and the Treimans. Lila had to make preparations, in the middle of which she fell to pieces. Women guests came to her assistance. Her lack of composure hurt me very much. I conducted the Seder, in Aramaic and in Hebrew, interrupting with English translations and commentary.

In April I received word that I had been awarded the Guggenheim fellowship for which I had applied earlier. That fixed my plans for the rest of the year. In early May I brought my mother, Lila, and Joshua to Hoboken in northeastern New Jersey, where they boarded ship for Holland. I stayed behind, preparing to go to CERN in Switzerland, where I would spend the first part of my Guggenheim. Lila and Josh would join me there; my mother would also come later for a visit.

In early June I flew to Geneva. With the help of the CERN housing office I found a wonderful apartment in the Vieille Ville (old city), at 39 Grand'Rue, next to City Hall and the Cathédrale Saint Pierre. Our apartment had the only balcony on that street.

In August my mother came for a week's visit. Of those days I remember the evening I took the family out to dinner, during which my mother reminisced about my father. As she had done so often before in my presence, she spoke critically of him: he ate too much and too fast, his hearing was poor, etc. Whereupon I put down my knife and fork and said to her: "Mother, now it is enough." She never spoke to me again in that vein.

I spent part of my days in my nice little office at CERN, working on symmetries shared by strong and weak interactions. By August I had completed and sent off a paper on that subject.[3] I had a nice view from my office, in particular, on clear days, of Mont Blanc. I would stand in front of my window, staring, almost hypnotized, at that majestic peak. Which seemed to draw me so much to it that I made up my mind: I had to climb it.

27.2 UP MONT BLANC, OR THE TALE OF TWO KINDS OF FOOLS

In the middle of August, I put Lila and Josh on a plane to the States, where they would visit with her mother, while I would stay two more weeks, mainly to make my climb. After the family's departure, I began preparations for my big expedition. I should confess that I anticipated the whole enterprise with some trepidation. I live, however, by this general principle: if something scares me, do it anyway, it is good for the soul. So I went to the Bureau des Guides in Chamonix to hire a guide. Henri Dufour was willing to take me, and we settled such matters as agreeing on his fee and on a date. When I mentioned my plans to Mr. Guillot, a *hotelier* from Chamonix with whom I had become friendly, he told me that he had lived in this valley virtually all his life but had never climbed the mountain. Would I permit him to join me? "Talk it over with Dufour," I replied, "It's okay with me if he agrees." Dufour agreed.

The day before we were to go, Dufour called me in Geneva to cancel: the weather was terrible, too cold, too much wind. I must confess to feeling great relief. But we fixed another date, and this time executed our plan.

This is how it went. Guillot and I meet Dufour at the Bureau des Guides. We go by car to Les Houches, where we take a *téléférique*, then a little cable train which at 8:45 A.M. brings us to the Nid d'Aigle (Eagle's Nest). We start our climb at a clip which is fast for me. At ten we are at the Tête Rousse, where we take a meal.

We leave at 11:30, rope up, cross a snow field, then come to the *couloir* (corridor) of the Aiguille du Gouter, the crossing of which is the most perilous part of the trip, because of crumbling rock. I knew about this spot because recently a CERN colleague of mine had fallen 300 meters at this point, hurting himself rather badly. Dufour gives instructions: we unrope here, because if one of us falls, he would pull down the others as well. Then we cross the *couloir* at a run. Dufour goes first, then Guillot, then I. We make it safely, but afterward I feel momentarily weak in the knees. On we go until, at 2:15 P.M., we reach the *refuge* (hut) du Gouter, at 3,800 meters where we eat and rest for the remainder of the day.

The views from up there are grandiose. Behind the *refuge* lies the snow-cap of the Gouter. Inside, against one wall, are three tiers of bunk beds where we will sleep, packed in like sardines; several other groups are on their way up as well. After we lie down, I get up again to view the sunset. I do not sleep well at all, tension, but also—as those who have been high up know—when you are asleep, the heart slows down and you wake up mildly asphyxiated because of the thin air. A while later, a Frenchman lying next to me piped up: "There are two kinds of fools: those who climb mountains and those who don't." These words of deep wisdom can be applied, as I often have done later, to practically any human activity.

We get up at 2 A.M. and have breakfast: a piece of bread and jam, ovaltine, a lump of chèvre. I feel great self-pity. "Quick, quick," urges the impatient Dufour—which makes me mad—"put on your crampons." At 3 A.M. we take off, roped together, the guide with a miner's lamp on his cap, spreading an impish light that I'll never forget.

It is full daylight when we reach the unmanned *refuge* Vallot, an aluminum shack at 4,300 meters, built as a meteorology station on Les Bosses du Dromadaire. Dufour puts down his backpack and tells us to do likewise—we will pick them up again on the way down. Guillot refuses to part with his. Now comes a steep part, La grande Bosse. We make it. "Now," Dufour says, "we are all right. This slope is the hardest when the winds are strong." I feel a bit faint but plod on.

At seven we reach the top of Mont Blanc, at 4,800 meters a flat, narrow strip. The view is spectacular, from the Monte Rosa in Italy to the Matterhorn in Switzerland. Dufour takes off his gloves, puts an arm around my shoulders, and congratulates me. "Vous avez fait une belle course" (You have made a good climb). We take pictures. I turn aside and cry tears of freedom and liberation.

Then the inimitable Guillot opens his backpack, which turns out to contain only a fine bottle of Heidsieck; he pops the cork and passes the bottle around. I feel fine but, let me tell you now, drinking champagne is the dumbest thing one can do at high altitude. The climb causes dehydration; that and the thin air cause immediate drunkenness. Inexperienced as I was, I had focused on getting up, forgetting that getting down is hard labor as well.

My legs feel completely leaden as we begin our descent along crevasses and seracs toward the *refuge* Le grand Mulet (3,000 m). I get exhausted and tumble now and then. Dufour keeps pushing: "Dépêchons nous, dépêchons nous" (hurry, hurry). I'm ready to kill him. We reach the *refuge* at nine. I sit down with my head between my hands. We get hot soup, also a steak which I'm too tired to eat.

An hour later, as we descend further to the Plan de l'Aiguille (2,300 m), I am, remarkably, fully restored. We take a *téléferique* down from there to Chamonix (which, incidentally, lies at the 1,000 m level). Guillot takes off, Dufour and I sit down for a cold drink; I pay him. Then he explains his behavior to me. He knew quite well, he said, that pushing me along the way would get me angry. But he did this on purpose, since the anger would urge me on, to show him I can do it. Also, it was important to go down fast because melting snow in the midday sun could cause serious problems.

Then we walked to the Bureau des Guides, where Dufour and the *chef guide* signed, then handed to me, a certificate stating that on August 23, Monsieur A. Pais successfully completed the ascent of Mont Blanc. (That document now hangs in my Copenhagen office.) We parted after I had thanked Dufour warmly for the unforgettable experiences.

I walked around in Chamonix a while longer, looking up at the mountain I no longer had to climb, feeling very virile, bronzed, and bearded, and having the curious sensation that I had left some of my troubles behind up there. Then I drove back to Geneva, had a bath, a meal, and took in a movie. I was in bed at midnight, after a twenty-two-hour day.

The next day I felt fit and rested, no after-fatigue at all. I called my mother: "Guess what I did!" After I told her, she was briefly silent, then said: "Don't you think that's enough now?" It took me quite a while to overcome the letdown of her response.

On August 29 I was back in New York.

In early September we went back to Berkeley for the second half of my Guggenheim fellowship. Here I finished a sequel to my CERN paper.[4] I met several interesting people. The physicist Otto Stern, a Nobel laureate, lived in retirement in the area. He had known Einstein well when both were in Prague, where—he told me—they would visit bordellos together, "quiet places for discussing physics." Also there were Bertrand de Jouvenel, the political scientist (already mentioned in chapter 23, sec. 23.3) and Charles P. Snow, the author, both of whom were visiting professors like myself. Snow gave a lecture in the physics department on "The Moral Unneutrality of Science." It was a pompous and trivial talk; moreover, I had the distinct impression that the speaker was mildly inebriated. Afterward I walked back with Emilio Segrè, who said that Snow had wasted an hour on what could have been said in half a minute: If you kill your father and your mother, that is your problem. But if you knowingly publish a faked result, you're done for.

One November morning I stood in the shower when the doorbell rang. Lila went to open the door. Someone stormed into our bedroom. It was Don Glaser, beside himself with excitement. "I just received word that I've been awarded the Nobel Prize! Now I'm a free man, I can leave physics." He did not care at all for the recent style of doing experiments in large teams. Indeed, soon after he returned from Stockholm he became a molecular biologist.

In late December I spoke at an international physics conference in Berkeley.[5] By year's end we were back East.

27.3 DIVORCE

27.3.1 Stunning Advice

On a cold winter day in January 1987, Josh and I viewed Lila for the last time, as she lay on a slab in the morgue of a hospital in New York. She still looked beautiful.

That moment haunts me as I am about to write next how, thirty years earlier, our marriage came to an end. By now the memories of those days are more painful to me than those of the grim war events told earlier. I shall spare the reader and myself most of the details.

Earlier in this chapter I had alluded to Lila's odd behavior when my father had died, and also when I gave a Seder in Princeton. Let that suffice as indications of disturbed behavior that became increasingly frequent. I felt that she needed help and therefore consulted with a psychiatrist friend in New York, who gave me the name of a colleague who practiced in Pennington, near Princeton. There came a day when I suggested to Lila that it might be good for her to get help and see this man. She burst out crying, then agreed.

I called to make an appointment for her, then we drove together to Pennington. I waited till her hour was over. Afterward the doctor came out and said that he would like to see her a few times, after which he would call me.

I managed to finish a paper on nuclear reactions before that call came.[6] I drove to the doctor's office, we sat down together, and I asked for his opinion. He replied that he first wanted to hear my own impressions. After I gave them, he was silent for a while, then said to me, verbatim: "You have done time and a half . . . Better follow your own road. Have you ever considered that it might be better for *both* of you if you were not married?" He added that deep analysis was counterindicated.

I was stunned. Thoughts of divorce had occurred to me before, but never from the point of view of Lila's possible advantage. Moreover, I had always rejected such an idea. How could I do that to Joshua, my marvelous little son? Worst of all, how could he live with Lila without my protection against her emotional troubles, even though, then and later, she was a good mother? Finally, divorce was unknown in my family. So I had always said to myself, better stick it out, tough as it is.

After seeing the doctor, I went for a ride in the countryside to reflect on what I had been told. I fully realized that I might not be the easiest man to be married to, but Lila had held her own quite well in the rather uppity Princeton milieu. True, she had not had enough to occupy herself in an environment that was new to her, and I could not share with her my intense preoccupation with science. I had hoped she would follow her avocation in painting, for which she showed talent, and even helped her arrange one room in our house as a private studio. Still, in spite of my support and strong protective feelings, I was perhaps not the ideal mate for her.

27.3.2 *Puerto Rico. Meeting Casals*

Soon afterward, I made up my mind: we had to separate, in as friendly a way as possible. When I returned after a trip to Berkeley, I suggested that the three of us take a ten-day vacation in Puerto Rico. Out there, on the beach, I broke the silence. When I suggested separation, Lila took it fairly calmly, as if she had anticipated that eventuality.

At that time the issue absorbed me more than anything else, yet, looking back now, the greatest experience of that vacation was the afternoon I spent with Pablo Casals.

When a New York friend had heard where I was going, she asked whether I would deliver a small package to Casals. I demurred, saying I would be happy to help but felt it would be presumptuous of me to call on the great cellist. But she assured me it would be all right, adding that she would send off a note to him announcing my visit. So, on a day in early June, I presented myself at Canto des Ocells (Catalan for "Song of the Birds"), the Casals home at 79 Atlantic View in Santurce. My first impression of Casals, then already eighty-five years old, was his amazingly strong handshake. He wore a white shirt and blue seersucker slacks. I handed him the package, expecting to take my leave after a few pleasantries. He invited me to sit down in the living room, however, which opened to the sea. So began a visit of several hours, during which tea was served while Casals incessantly puffed on his pipe.

During our discussions, which ranged far and wide, I noted his serenity, lucidity, broad interests, and the intensity with which he would listen. He would sit up straight when a point interested him particularly. He was the last of the truly great men I have met in my life. (The others were Einstein, Bohr, and Weizmann.) These four different personalities had one trait in common: simplicity. Now he was deeply serious, then he would burst out in hearty laughter, with a touch of boyishness in his mien.

Casals wanted to know about Einstein, whom he had known in the Berlin days. When I told him of my visit to Russia, he said he had not been there since 1914. He had known Anna Pavlova and had vivid memories of seeing her dance. About Russians: a people of great feeling; they still write him, send presents. "Some people think I am pro-Communist because I am anti-Franco—I am not, I am not, I am not." He did not want to make a return visit to Russia, "which is ruled by a small minority." He lost several friends in the Revolution. There is an absence of anger, he has passed beyond that.

About Eisenhower: "He was certainly a great general." About Ike's visit to Puerto Rico: "He seemed to have been mainly interested in playing golf at Dorado Beach." About Kennedy: "I have two letters from him, not just thank you notes [he had been invited to play at the White House] but with thoughts in them." About Franco: does he think his regime will change? "Not for the time being."

The deepest impression that has remained of that afternoon was a story Casals told me. One day he had gone for a hike in the French Alps. At one point he slipped on the icy path and fell down several meters, ending unharmed on a snow bank. While falling, the thought flashed through his mind: "If I fall on my hands and hurt them, then I do not have to play that damned cello again." That is what he said, "damned." Astonishing and revealing.

Sometime during those hours, his third wife, the much younger Martita, née Montañes, joined us. It was touching to see how they responded to each other, with great mutual affection and respect. She told me that his only diversion was watching TV. She talked about him in his presence in a devoted, yet ever so slightly impersonal way. She was manifestly dedicated to his work. "We have rehearsals."

As the encounter drew to an end, Casals asked me if I would come to the music festival in San Juan. Indeed I would. I asked if they would take some vacation afterward. No, they were going on to the Prades Festival. Then I rose to leave. I warmly thanked them for the wonderful hours, then gathered my courage and asked if I could perhaps have a photo of him. "With pleasure," he replied. Shortly afterward I received one, sent to Princeton, with the dedication: "To Prof. A. Pais, cordial souvenirs, Pablo Casals." It now hangs in a place of honor in my New York apartment.

27.3.3 Reims

I had several obligations in Europe that summer. I therefore proposed to Lila that we separate: I would go by myself, she and Josh would stay in the Princeton house. She agreed.

In late June I flew to London, where I picked up the car I had ordered earlier in New York: a convertible Austin Healy Mark II, the sexiest sports car I have ever owned. I had made transport arrangements in advance. I drove to Lydd, where the car and I were put on a Silver City Airlines plane, then we flew to Le Touquet on the French coast. My final destination was CERN. I had decided to bypass Paris and stop at Reims for my first view of its famed cathedral Notre Dame. I went there right after I had found a hotel. I walked down a street, then turned a corner. There it was.

As I stood in awe looking at its facade, one of the most perfect masterpieces from the Middle Ages, I noticed commotion. People were stopping at a table outside, then entering. When I went to inquire I learned that the boychoir of Rome's Sistine Chapel would sing there that evening—for the first time in Reims' history! What incredible luck. I bought a ticket, ran to a nearby store to buy a sandwich, ate it on the run, and entered the nearly full church. It was a most beautiful concert, music by Giovanni Palestrina, Orlando Lasso, Francesco Balducci. The next morning I drove on, and two days later I was in Geneva.

A week later I wrote to Lila, formally asking for a divorce. Another week thereafter she gave her consent by letter. In my reply I wrote that I would soon come to Princeton for a week, that I would find a room to rent someplace, and that she and Josh could keep the house for as long as she wanted.

This stay in Geneva was not memorable. I managed to complete my first, not very successful paper on physics with neutrino beams.[7] I also did some climbing, the finest being the ascent of the Wildhorn with Res Jost and a guide.

27.3.4 A Room without a View

Back in Princeton, I rented a room at 172 Nassau Street. All I took from the house was a mattress, a desk lamp, a wastepaper basket, and my clothes.

Then came a very difficult moment: I had to tell Joshua. He was only three years old, bright and vigorous to be sure, but how does one explain the situation to a child who still lives in prelapsarian innocence? I do not remember how I did it, only that I told him that I loved him, and that we would continue to be together a good deal. Afterward I went to another room and cried bitterly. Fifteen years later, when I told him the background of my actions, he said, "Why didn't you tell me that before?" "Because," I replied, "you could not have grasped it much earlier."

Late in August I flew back to CERN, and from there to Holland, to be with my mother on her seventieth birthday, and to tell her of the separation. When I told her, she said: "Why don't you stay together but take a lover?" Once again she greatly astonished me; it was the last thing I had expected to hear from a woman of her generation.

27.3.5 The Twelfth Solvay Conference

I had been invited to give a talk at the Twelfth Solvay Congress, so in early October I went to Brussels. It was the fiftieth anniversary of the first of these meetings, where the cream of physicists would gather. We were housed in Hotel Amigo, one of the best hotels I ever stayed in. Its name has an amusing origin. During the years of Spanish rule it had been the site of a prison.

Soldiers patrolling the streets would pick up drunks, grab them by their neck, and say, "Amigo, come along."

At the meeting I gave a review of the status of weak interactions.[8] It was a chic affair, with two good wines at lunch. One evening we were invited to a gala dinner given by the king and queen of Belgium. I remember Feynman trying to explain quantum mechanics to Queen Fabiola.

The conference opened with an account by Bohr, both charming and fascinating, of the developments in physics during the past half century.[9] Afterward we walked up and down in the corridor and talked about the future of particle physics. It was the last time I saw him.

At the conference it was announced that, as part of the fiftieth anniversary celebrations, a Solvay professorship had been established. I was asked to be the first Solvay professor. Also, Heisenberg invited me to spend time in Munich. I declined both invitations, if only because I did not want to be that far away from Josh at that time.

When I returned to Princeton, Lila told me that she and Josh were about to move to New York. She had rented a pleasant apartment at 270 West 11th Street, around the corner from the Perry Street apartment. That made it convenient for me to spend time with Josh. Lila never objected to my doing so. I spent most of my Christmas vacation with him and also took him to register at a nursery school.

From then on he would spend weekends with me. For a while he would ask: "Will you play with me?" I would answer, "Of course, dear Josh." After a number of such exchanges there came a time, I had put him to bed, when he looked at me with his big dark eyes and said, "You will play with me." I gave him a hug and walked out, so that he would not see my tears.

Meanwhile I spent the weekdays in Princeton. At night I would lie down on my mattress, light the desk lamp which was standing on the floor, and read. A number of times I would heave a sigh of deep relief while lying there. Yet my general state of mind at that time is best described by the finest pun I know: He felt his Kraft ebbing.[10] I managed, however, to finish a paper on meson physics before the tumultuous year of 1961 came to an end.[11]

27.3.6 Reno

In February 1962, I sold the house on Battle Road, which caused me to have a resounding depression followed by deep relief. In March, Yang and I sent a letter to the powers that be, proposing Oppenheimer for the Fermi Award in recognition of his contributions to the war effort and of his scientific career. We sent copies to distinguished colleagues, suggesting they might write in support of our proposal. Also that month I finished the first of two papers on meson decays, a collaboration with Gerald Feinberg.[12]

In April, I packed up clothes and papers and went to Reno, Nevada, for a six-week stay in preparation for my legal divorce. I had reserved a cottage at the Casson Hotel on Forest Street, a motel-type of place. One of my first experiences there was to be awakened by police sirens. Looking out my window I saw great commotion, then a handcuffed man being led to a police car. It turned out that he was on the FBI's list of the ten most wanted criminals. Never a dull moment.

All the others at the motel waiting for their divorces happened to be women. (I had been advised to go there instead of Lila because of her mental instabilities.) I became intimate with one of them, her name was Mary, a lovely, intelligent woman.

In the middle of my stay in Reno, I received a telegram of congratulations from Oppenheimer. I had been elected to the National Academy of Sciences, happy news that could not have come at a better moment. Also in Reno I received an invitation to participate in a celebration in Copenhagen, in July 1963, to commemorate the fiftieth anniversary of Bohr's first paper on the quantum theory of atoms.

Many evenings I went to one of the casinos to gamble at roulette or craps. After having won eighty dollars at roulette one evening, I decided to splurge and spent the money on a fancy wallet. The next evening I lost eighty dollars at the wheel. Live and learn. When it was all over I had broken about even—and never afterward felt the urge to indulge in gambling again.

I got some decent work done while out there, finishing one of my rare papers on a mathematical problem,[13] and one on statistical mechanics, which I published in the *Proceedings of the National Academy of Sciences* in honor of my election.[14]

On May 21 I went to the Washoe County Court House to get my divorce. As I entered, I noticed a sign making reference to the marriage bureau, also housed in that building: "Members of the Washoe County Ministerial Association do not perform marriages in hotels, motels, or guest houses; do not make 'deals' with cab drivers or others to solicit marriages; do not 'compete' for marriages." I presented myself to the Honorable

Judge John W. Barrett of the Second Judicial District Court in and for the County of Washoe who "ordered, adjudged, and decreed" that I was granted a decree of divorce.

Next to me lies a letter from Lila from that time, in which she wrote: "I remain your faithful friend . . . bless you, dear Bram." Hers was a troubled life, yet what a gentle person she was. I shall always remember her with love and with gratitude. She gave me one of life's greatest gifts: a son.

27.4 THE REST OF MY YEAR

27.4.1 Summer at Brookhaven

I used to call Joshua every day he was not with me. Moreover, Lila and I had agreed that he would spend weekends and a stretch of time during summers with me.

In early June the two of us took off for a six-week stay at Brookhaven National Laboratory, where spacious apartments for summer visitors are available on site. It was an ideal setup in my situation. The lab area, several thousand acres, was safe since it was fenced in and patrolled by lab police, and provided playgrounds, a swimming pool, tennis courts, and a cafeteria. Because of the children, the speed limit in the apartment area was five miles per hour. There were plenty of children from other summer visitors to play with. Moreover, there was a fine ocean beach nearby, Smith Point on Fire Island, reached across a bridge by car. Every afternoon, weather permitting, we would go out there for a swim and play on the beach. For the next twelve years Josh and I spent part of every summer there, in all more than a year of our life together.

That first time out there was rough on me, however. I was quite tense because of my new responsibilities even though I had acquired the house-keeping and child care services of a young woman. Moreover, my mother had come, so I had a full house. It worked out well, also because Brookhaven has always been profitable for me in getting work done. It was stimulating to be together with other physicists, those on the local staff as well as the visitors. While there, I finished a short paper on weak interactions at very high energies.[15] Then time was up. I brought Josh back to Lila, and took my mother to the boat for her return to Holland.

27.4.2 Up the Matterhorn

In early August, I took a plane to Milan, my destination being Trieste, where I was to give a series of lectures. Then on for a brief stay at CERN, where I had stored my climbing gear, which I picked up on my way to Zermatt. I had arranged by phone for a guide to lead me on my summer's last adventure: the ascent of the Matterhorn.

In Zermatt I spend the first day loafing. I fall when I walk down the stairs of my small hotel, a clear sign of nervousness about the coming event. I am too old to believe that this climb would prove anything but young enough to feel failure if I didn't try. The Matterhorn is in sight as I stroll through the village, particularly majestic because it is a solitary mountain, not part of a range.

The next morning I pack my gear and take off, completely composed now. First by cable car to Schwarzsee (2,600 m), then a walk to the Hotel Belvedére (3,400 m), where I meet my guide. The next morning at five we take off. We rope up, then follow the Whymper route along the Hörnligrad, at some point into the Ostwand. It is largely a rock climb. My guide is a pleasant, patient man who knows every crack in the wall. The sights from the Grad are creepy at times. We reach the Solvay hut in 2½ hours and the summit (14,800 ft) in another two hours. The last part is made easy by fixed ropes—no doubt garnering patronizing smiles from true mountaineers. We sit a while, eat a little, I gaze at the marvelous view. I am better prepared for the descent this time—no champagne—which is a slow, long affair. By 2 o'clock we are back at the Belvedére.

I spent one more day of leisure in Zermatt, also paying my respects at the cemetery, where townsfolk as well as those who fell are buried. A quotation from Psalm 121 is on one of the tombstones: "I will lift my eyes unto the hills." A few days later, in early September, I was back in the States.

27.4.3 The Death of Niels Bohr

In November I gave a lecture on "The Structure of Matter" in the Delaware Seminar on Philosophy.[16] I was pleased with my epigraph: "Dig we must," the ubiquitous sign put up by New York's Con Edison utility service whenever they dig a hole in the streets. Then, on the 19th of that month, I received a telegram from Copenhagen, informing me that Bohr had died the day before.

I sent a telegram to Margrethe at once: "All my feelings are with you and your family. I knew no greater man."

In December I received a letter from Margrethe, dated the 18th: "Dear Bram Pais, my heartfelt thanks for your warm words of sympathy in my deep sorrow by my beloved husband's death." And a letter from Aage with the same date: "Thanks for your warm words. Many memories return, of fine hours all of us spent together, in Tisvilde, Copenhagen, and Princeton. I need not add that my father enjoyed your company."

As I write these lines, warm feelings of gratitude well up again for having known Bohr so well. To this day it remains true what I wrote then: I knew no greater man.

28

Changing My Workplace from
Princeton to New York

ONE DAY, early in 1963, I left my office around eleven to have my morning coffee in the cafeteria. As I sat there, smoking a cigar and looking out over the peaceful landscape, a very unexpected thought came to me: I am in great danger.

What I felt at that moment was that I had arrived. I was a professor at the Institute, a highly competitive milieu, respected by my faculty colleagues, by the ever-renewed group of young postdocs, as well as by the physics community at large. I had been productive, though not by any means at the level I had aspired to.

What then was the danger? It was the realization that, after years of struggle, I was about to become too content with myself, and to stop striving toward new goals. It certainly was pleasant enough to sit down with midmorning coffee and a cigar, but that was not my aim in life. It may well have been that morning that for the first time I became fully aware that I had received much from the Institute, had also given much, but that now I could neither receive nor give much more. It started to dawn on me that I had better move on.

There were other contributing factors to these considerations. Starting the single man's life all over again in Princeton was hardly appealing, most especially because Joshua was living in New York. Also, just about then, Oppenheimer was in trouble again with the faculty because of his vacillations in regard to two new faculty appointments in mathematics, which had taken days of mediation on my part, whereafter I said to myself: No more.

But where to go?

In 1961 my old teacher, the physicist George Uhlenbeck, had joined the faculty of the Rockefeller Institute in New York City. As I visited him several times I could not fail to notice that this small campus was an island of tranquillity within bustling New York City. When in later years friends and colleagues came to visit me there, they were amazed at this oasis, unknown even to most New Yorkers, with its handsome plantings and landscaping.

When I began to think about leaving Princeton, New York, already my second home in America, was of course my first choice, and the Rockefeller became my leading option. It was ideal for several reasons. It could provide me with a place to think and work in an atmosphere about as peaceful as Princeton's Institute for Advanced Study, yet in the midst of activities, especially cultural, that suited my tastes. It would bring me close to Joshua. Furthermore, it would appear to offer possibilities for the realization of an idea that now kept growing in my mind: to try and build up a group in theoretical high energy physics, using my experiences of successes and failures learned from Bohr and Oppenheimer. Until then Uhlenbeck was the only physicist there and I already knew that he was not inclined to spend any effort in attracting young people. (Incidentally, in June 1962 Bohr had paid his last visit to the U.S. in order to collect the last of his many honorary degrees—this one from the Rockefeller Institute.)

In April 1963 I made up my mind. First I broached the idea to Uhlenbeck, who was wildly enthusiastic and said he would immediately discuss the matter with President Detlev Bronk. A week later the three of us had lunch together, my first encounter with Det (as I was soon to call him). I immediately realized that he was, what I have since liked to call, the last of the great romantics in science. He, too, was enthusiastic about the possibility of my joining the faculty and liked the idea of building up my own physics group. That luncheon marked the beginning of my close friendship with Det, which would last until his death.

Then came the hardest part. I had to inform Oppenheimer that I wanted to resign and leave right away. That talk went well; we parted in friendship. Then I called Bronk, telling him that I accepted his offer. He said that he had warm feelings for me. Finally I called Uhlenbeck, who expressed relief that my talk with Robert had gone well. All that done, my reaction was, perhaps not surprisingly, that I was scared. What have I done?

My letter of resignation from the Institute is dated May 15. That month I had several meetings with Bronk and his staff about my New York office, which was to be on the ninth floor of a barely finished building, then called

South Lab, now Bronk Lab. It was to be the largest office of my career, in fact rather absurdly big.

I started the chore of packing twenty-nine cartons of books and papers from my Institute office, plus the little I had in my Nassau Street room. On May 28, movers came to transport all that to Rockefeller. The next day I left. From my notes: "Now I am home. The mood fluctuates, sometimes I am tense, sometimes very happy."

I have maintained good contacts with Princeton in later years, where to this day I have good friends, though many of those are now gone.

28.2 THE BOHR MEMORIAL CONFERENCE

When in June 1963 the Russians shot a woman into earth's orbit, the following story became popular. The first human to land on the moon is a Russian woman. She returns pregnant. The Russians now face a dilemma: they must either accept immaculate conception or else admit that Americans had been there first.

In July I went to Copenhagen. As mentioned earlier, a celebration of the fiftieth anniversary of Bohr's first paper on the quantum theory of atomic structure had been planned there. After Bohr's death in 1962 it was decided to hold the meeting anyway, but now as a memorial conference, to be held from July 8 to 12. Before leaving I had finished and sent off an invited contribution to a book of essays on Bohr by his close coworkers of earlier times.[1]

Many earlier and later Copenhagen coworkers from all over the world came to the meeting. In Bohr's spirit, only a few of the presented papers dealt with the past, all others were devoted to current developments. For example, Heisenberg and I discussed the status of particle physics.[2] A number of the old guard got together to prepare a present for Mrs. Bohr, a silver tray engraved with our autographs. I have before me my copy of the letter which Margrethe sent the following September to all contributors. It reads in part:

> I am deeply moved to receive the beautiful silver tray with the autographs so well known to me through many many years. . . . Nothing could make me happier than this opportunity often to look at the names so beautifully arranged on the tray, they will bring for my eyes treasured remembrances from the years you spent here and worked at the Institute and from the unforgetful days during the memorial meeting.

During the conference week, I called on Mrs. Bohr, who at that time was still living in Carlsberg. I felt uneasy as I went over there. Margrethe and Niels had been so close. Would she now feel lost, downcast? It turned out to be quite otherwise. She was in very good spirits and exuded even more energy than I had noted in earlier years. (I was of course not surprised when others told me that on other occasions she would miss Niels very much.)

Not long after these events, I visited an old friend, the psychoanalyst Theodor Reik, in New York. I told him of my visit and expressed puzzlement about Mrs. Bohr's demeanor. Reik smiled. If one partner in a good marriage dies, he said, the other will feel a sense of fulfillment because she or he has brought a vital task to good conclusion. If, on the other hand, the marriage was bad, then the survivor is ridden with guilt and a sense of failure.

Every Christmastime in later years I would write to Mrs. Bohr to send good wishes and tell her what had happened to me the past year; she always wrote back. I also visited her a few times in later years. Just before Christmas 1984 she died peacefully. Her remains rest close to those of her beloved Niels.

28.3 THE KILLING OF OUR PRESIDENT

From October 21 to 23, 1963, I attended the centennial festivities of the National Academy of Sciences, a symposium in Washington, D.C., celebrating a century's advances in science. Topics ranged from "The Origin of the Elements" to "The Origins of Life" to "Science and Public Policy."[3] On the 22nd we marched in academic procession to the Centennial Convocation in Constitution Hall, where President John F. Kennedy gave a talk. His eloquent, forceful speech, chiastic prose, delivered in his clipped Boston accent, ended like this.

> Even though some of your experiments may not bring fruition right away, I hope that they will be carried out immediately.
>
> It reminds us of what the great French Marshal Lyautey once said to his gardener: "Plant a tree tomorrow." And the gardener said, "It won't bear fruit for a hundred years." "In that case," Lyautey said to the gardener, "plant it this afternoon." That is how I feel about your work.

I shall never forget that address by our young president, one of those festive moments so rare in the academic world. On my way back I kept thinking: this president is one of us, caring more about how the game is played than about who wins or loses.

One month to the day after that event, I read in the *New York Times* that on December 2 Kennedy would personally hand the Fermi Award to Oppenheimer. That same afternoon, a secretary burst into my office with the news that Kennedy had been shot in Dallas, Texas.

It was totally unbelievable.

I stopped working, took my briefcase, and drove downtown. After parking the car, I walked to the newsstand on Sheridan Square, where I stood, waiting silently for the afternoon papers to arrive. I could not accept the news until I had seen it in print. When I read my paper, I believed.

I went home and turned on the TV, saw the arrival of the coffin at Andrews Air Force Base, Mrs. Kennedy and brother Robert Kennedy walking alongside. I heard that Lyndon Johnson had been sworn in on *Air Force One,* the presidential aircraft, and saw and heard his brief speech to the nation from the Base.

I wrote in my diary: "Now it is all over. And, I guess, the jerks will be back again." One reporter wrote: "There never was a time like that in American history."

The whole world shared in America's grief. It was written in a South African magazine: "In this way was murdered the first real chance in this century for an intelligent and new leadership to the world. . . . More than any other person, he achieved the intellectual's ideal of a man in action. His death leaves us unprepared and in darkness."

From my notes, the day after: "A deep depression has engulfed everyone I know."

On December 2, 1963, President Johnson presented Oppenheimer with the citation, the medal, and a check for $50,000, the Fermi Award, "on behalf of the people of the United States." He also said: "One of President Kennedy's most important acts was to give this award."

28.4 SYMMETRIES COME, SYMMETRIES GO

In previous chapters I attempted to sketch the twentieth-century searches for new symmetries in the strong interactions and for the violation of old ones (parity) in the weak interactions of basic particles (see chapters 21, sec. 21.4; 22, sec. 22.2; 24, sec. 24.1; 26, sec. 26.1). In the 1960s important new discoveries were made in this area.

28.4.1 New Accelerators

The new developments were in large part due to the advent of new accelerators in that decade. Variants of old-style machines but with much higher energies (up to 70 billion electron volts) went into operation. New types of accelerators appeared on the scene, notably high energy linear accelerators and colliders. These are circular machines in which not one but two beams of particles, one consisting of electrons and one of positrons or protons, or both of protons, are accelerated in opposite directions. Beams of neutrinos became a new experimental tool.[4]

28.4.2 Strong Interactions: SU(3)

In the early 1960s the search for a needed extension (see chapter 22, sec. 22.2) of isospin symmetry in strong interactions came to a preliminary conclusion with the introduction of a group named SU(3). This advance led, in turn, to the proposal that protons and neutrons as well as hyperons have a further substructure, each one being built up out of three "quarks"; and that mesons are built up out of a "quark" and an "antiquark."[5] Several decades of experimental searches have never produced evidence for the existence of free quarks, that is, quarks not bound inside baryons or mesons. As we shall see later, that negative result is actually in accordance with more recent theoretical views.

28.4.3 Weak Interactions: CP-Violation

One morning in the spring of 1964 I was having breakfast in the Brookhaven National Laboratory when James ("Jim") Cronin and Val Fitch came to the table to talk to me about their recent, as yet unpublished, experiment. That was the first time I heard of their discovery that about two in a thousand of all decays of the long-lived neutral K-particles into charged secondary particles take place into $\pi^+ + \pi^-$.[6]

How can that be, I asked. It violates CP-invariance, the elegant new symmetry introduced in 1956, after parity had turned out to be violated (chapter 26, sec. 26.1), and which had appeared to work well for almost eight years. They knew that, Fitch and Cronin said, but there it was. Why was the effect not due to regeneration of short-lived K's (chapter 24, sec. 24.5), I wanted to know. Because, they said, that effect was far too small in the helium bag where the 2π events had been found. I asked many more questions: Why were they not seeing $2\pi\gamma$ decays with a soft photon, or $\pi\mu\nu$ decays with a soft neutrino and perhaps some confusion about mass? They had thought long and hard about these and other alternatives (the actual experiment had been concluded the previous July) and had ruled them out one by one. After they left, I had another cup of coffee. I was shaken by the news. I knew quite well that a small amount of CP-violation would not drastically alter the earlier discussions, based on CP-invariance, of the neutral K-complex. Also, the experience of seeing a symmetry fall by the wayside was not new to anyone who had lived through the 1956–57 period. At that time, however, there had at once been the consolation that P- and C-violation could be embraced by a new and pretty concept, CP-invariance. What unsettled everyone now was that with CP gone, there was nothing elegant to replace it with. The very smallness of the 2π rate, CP-invariance as a near miss, made the news even harder to digest.

It has been an obvious great challenge in later years to look for CP-violations at places other than the long-lived neutral K-particle. As I write these lines, thirty years after that discovery, serious, hard-working experimentalists have not (not yet?!) found any such effect elsewhere. It is thought by many (including me) that the weakness of CP-violating effects, even on the scale of weak interactions, constitutes the headiest challenge, both for experimentalists and for theorists, at the physics frontier. As Cronin put it: "We must continue to seek the origin of CP-violation by all means at our disposal. We know that improvements in detector technology and quality of accelerators will permit even more sensitive experiments in the coming decades. We are hopeful, then, that at some epoch, perhaps distant, this cryptic message from nature will be deciphered."[7]

28.4.4 Strong Interactions: SU(6)

In August 1964 the next international conference, in the Rochester style, on high energy physics, was to be held in Dubna, in the Soviet Union. I had been invited to give the rapporteur's talk on weak interactions. The preceding June, when Joshua and I had gone to Brookhaven again, I had taken along material for preparing that talk, an assignment that demanded particular care because of the great novelty: the recent discovery of CP-violation.

Among the papers I wished to summarize I found one which mentioned a group SU(6), which, if "of any use as an approximate symmetry . . . would arrange particles of different spins and parities in super-super-super multiplets."[8] I mentioned this remark to Feza Gürsey, also at Brookhaven, suggesting that he look further into this while I finished my Dubna report.

On July 1 Luigi Radicati arrived. He had only recently been working on the supermultiplet theory for atomic nuclei (originally proposed by Wigner in the 1930s) in which one marries, so to say, ordinary spin with isospin, resulting in a symmetry group, SU(4). From this curious confluence of circumstances was born the generalization of Wigner's SU(4)-theory for nuclei to the SU(6)-theory in particle physics (which has nothing to do with the SU(6) suggested in the paper just mentioned),[9] the result of another marriage, this time of spin with the recently proposed group SU(3).

A week after Radicati's arrival, he and Gürsey came to see me, to tell me about this SU(6) idea.[10] Whereupon they and I joined forces to work out the consequences of that proposal.

The month that followed was the most intense period of my later-life scientific activity. The first exciting results came rolling out within weeks.[11] I was simply glued to my desk—so what to do about Dubna? In late July I called Sam Treiman, who was also going to Russia, told him what I was up to, and asked whether he would be willing to take over my rapporteur's talk if I sent him the incomplete notes I had made so far. Sam agreed, good friend that he is.[12]

I kept going on with SU(6), spurred on further by the fact that others had independently gotten hold of similar ideas. By mid-September I, together with two colleagues, found a most spectacular result. Using SU(6), we could compute the ratio of the magnetic moments of the good old neutron and proton, finding it to be equal to minus 3/2, within three percent of the experimental value.[13]

SU(6) became the hottest theoretical topic of 1964, including brief but considerable confusion caused by conjectures about extensions of these ideas to include relativity theory.[14] Finally I note that SU(6) led to the proposal, as a by-product one might say, that each species of quark should carry an additional label, capable of taking on three distinct values. That label soon acquired the picturesque name "color" so, one said, each quark species actually can be "either red, or white, or blue." As will be noted later, in the 1980s this notion of color was to take on a most fundamental role. At that later time I polled the experts, asking whether they had had any inkling of the importance of color when the idea first appeared twenty years earlier. It was with them as it was with me: the idea had barely registered and so lay almost forgotten for two decades. So do incomplete but profound thoughts seep barely noticed into the body of physics.

28.5 EARLY YEARS AT THE ROCKEFELLER

Most of the events reported in the previous section had taken place after June 1963, the month during which I had moved to the Rockefeller Institute. Going back to that time, I had first of all been busy settling in, unpacking books and papers, then starting to think about people I'd like to join me in my undertakings. That, of course, took time, but after two years a group had begun to take shape. Two of the physicists I initially hired for junior positions eventually became full professors at the Rockefeller: Nicola ("Nick") Khuri and Baqi Bēg. As time went by, a group stabilized consisting of three full professors (including me), an associate professor, one or two assistant professors, and three or four postdocs. All in all, it became a respectable and respected enterprise. Later a number of our young people became full professors, some in America, some elsewhere. Looking back on this aspect of my life's activities, I feel that I could have done better but did well.

We also had a few graduate students—in all, there were only about one hundred of them at the university (in 1965 it changed its name from Institute to University). In the early years I gave courses but students were mainly educated by tutorials. The only degree awarded at the Rockefeller is the Ph.D. I delivered two of these: one recipient is now a full professor in physics, the other switched fields afterwards and became a respected medical person. Two is not a large number, but then I had enough to do with research and with keeping the group going. Also, in the beginning I took charge of organizing weekly seminars with speakers from elsewhere, as well as making arrangements for temporary visitors whose stay might vary from a week to an academic year. I have always encouraged our students and postdocs to come and talk with me.

My own productivity visibly benefited as well from my fresh start at a new institution. In the previous section I already mentioned my role in the SU(6) adventure in 1964. I also had occasion to contribute scientific papers to Festschrifts for two men who had played an important role in my life and who both had turned sixty that year: Léon Rosenfeld,[15] with whom I had studied for my Ph.D.; and Robert Oppenheimer.[16] In April 1964 I went to Princeton for a festive evening celebrating Robert's birthday.

Also in April my mother came to New York for a three weeks' stay. I had reserved a pleasant room with bath and kitchenette for her in the Fifth Avenue Hotel, a nice old-fashioned establishment on downtown Fifth Avenue. Before her arrival I had brought some little gifts to her room, a bowl of fruit, magazines, flowers, items for breakfast. I picked her up at the airport and drove her to the hotel right away. As she entered her room, she went straight to the bathroom, lifted the toilet lid, then said: "It is all right, it is clean." Not a word about my gifts or how nice the room was.

Every morning after breakfast I would pick her up at her hotel, drive her to some place in the city, explain what was nice to see there, and where she could have some coffee. Late afternoon, back from work, I would call for her at her hotel and take her for dinner. One day I drove her near the Plaza Hotel at Fifth Avenue and 59th Street, pointed out a nice walk in Central Park, and showed her where she could board a bus to take her back. When I met her that evening, I asked if she had had a nice day. Oh yes, very nice. Had she found her bus? No, she had decided to walk back—fifty blocks. Not bad for a lady of seventy.

In 1965 I moved out of my Perry Street apartment, which had served me so well. I felt the need for more space, which I found at 36 Gramercy Park East, Apartment 8W, a two-tower building designed by Stanford White. On July 15 I moved in, celebrating that transition by reading *Here Is New York* by E. B. White, where I found the line: "No one should come to New York unless he is willing to be lucky."

28.6 TRAVELS IN THE MID-SIXTIES

I conclude this chapter with an account of major work-related travels in the years 1964–67.

28.6.1 The German Experience

In the spring of 1964 I received an invitation to give an invited address to the main annual meeting of the Deutsche Physikalische Gesellschaft (German Physical Society), to be held in October in Düsseldorf. That letter brought back memories of the war once again. Should I accept? I decided I would, but—perhaps it was a bit juvenile—would also request that they pay me for first class airfare, not the way we physicists generally travel. The request was honored. I also decided that I would immediately leave if I noticed the slightest signs of anti-Semitism. In the event, I did not, and actually had an enjoyable few days, especially in talking to younger Germans who did not at all shun discussing the war: they said the war was the sin of a previous generation. I gave a lecture on CP-violation, starting out in English, then continuing in German, a gesture that was much appreciated.[17]

28.6.2 Sicilian Sojourn

In 1965 I continued work on elaborations of SU(6).[18] That was also the subject of my article in a book honoring Weisskopf;[19] and of a series of lectures I gave in the autumn, first in Sicily, then in Dubna in the Soviet Union.[20]

As a diversion from my lectures in Sicily, some colleagues and I would drive down for a swim at a beach near Trapani. There I was treated to some unfamiliar delicacies: *gelsomino* (jasmin) ice cream on bread, sea eggs on the half-shell.

When time was up, a car with driver took me to the Palermo airport, but first we made one stop, at Segesta. The view seen from a distance of its solitary Doric temple ruins (5th century B.C.) was like entering the valley of a fairy tale.

28.6.3 To Dubna and Serpukhov

I then flew to Vienna, where I boarded a Topulev 124—Russia's answer to the Caravelle—for the flight to Moscow, where I was fetched by a colleague who drove me to a hotel in Dubna, north of Moscow, where I had been asked to give a series of lectures. I arrived on an early Sunday afternoon. A little later, at 5 P.M., I watched on the TV in my room three ladies (two over fifty) do simple physical exercises—in prime time.

The next day I met an old acquaintance, Bogoliubov, the director of Dubna's Joint Institute for Nuclear Research, an international Eastern Bloc institution modeled after CERN. He told me: "We have many foreigners here. . . . Chinese students arrive without knowing a word of Russian nor any physics. In one year they speak Russian and know field theory. They sit at their desks calculating madly. Sometimes they faint and a doctor has to be called in. . . . We understand when foreigners are happy, when sad; but we don't know with the Chinese."

After the conclusion of my lectures (in English), I was taken by car to the Institute of High Energy Physics, 160 miles to the south. It had been created out of nothing in a beautiful forested area (mainly birches) much beloved by Russian painters. At that time the institution was still under construction but four thousand people already lived there. It was to be the site of a 76 billion volt accelerator. Finished in 1967, for the next five years it became the world's largest accelerator. The construction was assisted by soldiers. In a high school, I saw a bulletin board with a sign: WE LEARN ENGLISH. Both in Dubna and in Serpukhov I was struck by the desire for contact with the West. "We are now inviting people from the U.S., and not just for conferences." The reception was cordial everywhere, the students quite bright.

After my one-week visit to the two laboratories, I returned to Moscow for a few days of sightseeing and shopping. On a walk, I passed by a movie house where *Westsideskaya Istoria* was shown. I did go to another movie, a Russian one, just to see what it was like. As in television, the camera work was quite static and the play was largely dialogue.

In early October I was back in New York.

28.6.4 Australian Journey

I had accepted an invitation to lecture at a summer school in Canberra. On January 20, 1967, at 7 A.M., I left my apartment and the next morning at 5 A.M. New York time (having gained many hours) arrived at Faaa, the airport of Papeete, the capital of Tahiti. I spent the first day resting and strolling around town. To my disappointment, there was nothing romantic about it. It was a dusty and noisy place, traffic was heavy, lots of Vespas.

At my hotel I met a man from the U.S. Embassy in Canberra. We decided on a side trip to the island of Bora Bora, a one-hour flight from Tahiti. That turned out to be a simply divine experience, wonderfully clean air, gorgeous beaches, great swimming.

Then I flew on to Canberra with a stop in Sydney. I found a room waiting for me in University House. Waking up the next morning and drawing the curtains I was amazed and delighted to see several beautifully feathered cockatoos sitting in a tree right in front of me.

I gave four lectures, part on SU(6), part on new topics on which I had recently started to publish.[21] I note in passing that in 1967 I published my first book review, on a book written by Eugene Wigner.[22]

Finally, it was out to the outback, the main excursion of that trip, with Steward Butler, one of the leading local physicists. First we went by car to the Sydney airport, then by small plane via Coonabarabran and Coonamble to Wallgett, where we were to be guests of friends of Butler. The heat hit hard on arrival, but it was dry, and soon I found the climate invigorating. A T-bone steak (for ninety cents) for lunch at the RSL (Returned Servicemen's League) Club, then on to their 7,000-acre property. It is hard to describe the outback landscape; it is tough and dry and dusty, the sky is hard blue, the greens are grayish, coolabah trees are all around, it is flat and goes on and on. You know there are animals there, somewhere, but you see nothing. It suggests a mysterious emptiness.

That afternoon we went to the property of other friends and had the chance to witness some sheep shearing. "We get a good screw out of it," our host said, which is Australian for making good money. The shearers made twenty dollars per one hundred animals shorn. They looked like a tough bunch, yet have that nonsubservient friendliness one finds here all over.

Then by Land Rover into the bush to get a peek at the roos, as kangaroos are called here. Big ones are known as "old men," baby ones as "joeys." The car stirred them out of their hiding places and the landscape became alive with them, left and right and ahead of us. An emu was surprised by us as well and ran along frantically. Then back to the ranch and beer (I never drank more beer than in Australia), grace, dinner, joke telling, and bed.

Next morning we took off for the opal mines at Lightning Ridge. I knew it was an open mine and had pictured it as a gaping mouth in the earth. Nothing like it. Instead, many small holes wide enough to let one man down and move his pick ax. I got a glimpse of my first opals there, and was entranced. Turning them in my hand, I noticed red flashes of light. I bought two of them. Words cannot do justice in describing this tiny settlement, somewhere, nowhere, where people get the fever for this fiery gem. All along, the same casual air permeates the area, as everywhere else in Australia.

On the 11,000-mile trip back to New York, I allowed myself a two-day stop on the Fiji Islands. Walking around in Suva, the capital, I became aware of the great racial varieties of the Pacific. The Fijian men are handsome and have a martial bearing, but they are a friendly people. After stops in Hawaii and San Francisco, I was finally approaching New York. Coming over the city, the "fasten your seat belt" sign went on, and we descended. But then the plane veered abruptly upward. The captain announced that a snow blizzard had just started, we could not land, and we must fly all the way to Montreal to deplane. It was an abrupt change in temperature: from ninety degrees in Fiji to nine degrees in Montreal. We were given blankets to keep warm, then transported to a Holiday Inn, where I stayed in bed for a day to keep warm. I only got up for meals. So ended my three-week Australian journey.

$$29$$

What Befell Me in the Late 1960s

TEN DAYS after my return from Australia, I received a phone call early in the morning from a colleague telling me that the night before, on February 18, 1967, Oppenheimer had died in his Princeton home. After fetching the *New York Times,* I found a brief news item about his death on the front page. The next day, February 20, the same paper carried a long essay on Robert's life and numerous short eulogies—by Glenn Seaborg, chairman of the Atomic Energy Commission, David Lilienthal, and many others. The *Times* of February 29 carried a statement by President Johnson: "The world will miss his genius." The March 3 issue of *Life* magazine contained a long article about him.

His ashes were flown to the Virgin Islands, where they were scattered on the sea, off St. John's.

In April 1965, two days after his sixty-first birthday, it had been announced that, effective June 1966, Oppenheimer would retire as director of the Institute but "will continue as a senior professor of theoretical physics. . . . Despite the controversy about Dr. Oppenheimer there has been no disagreement about his brilliance."[1] On his retirement the faculty gave him a beautifully bound four-volume edition of the poems of Gerard Manley Hopkins.

Already in 1965 Robert's health had turned poor. In 1966 throat cancer was diagnosed, causing him to give up his heavy cigarette smoking and to receive radiation therapy at the Sloan-Kettering Institute in New York, situated across the street from the Rockefeller University. One day I met him there to drive to Princeton. His haggard looks of many years were now accentuated by emaciation. I hurt for him that last time I saw him alive.

In June 1966 Oppenheimer could only walk with a stick and a leg brace. A sad yet superb photo of him, shows him leaning on a stick and showing the ravages of his final illness.[2] It was taken on the day he received an honorary degree from Princeton University, the only such degree he ever accepted among the many offered him. In October he wrote to a friend that the cancer was spreading rapidly. A few days before his death he wrote that his hearing and speech had become very poor.[3]

On February 25, 1967, an intensely cold day, some six hundred friends and associates gathered in Alexander Hall on the Princeton University campus for a memorial meeting.[4] Those present included some of Oppenheimer's ex-students from Berkeley and colleagues from Los Alamos and the Institute. Retired General Leslie Groves had chartered a plane from Washington in order to attend. Harry Smyth had flown in from an International Atomic Energy Agency meeting in Vienna. I was there too.

Three speakers had been chosen to address the gathering, which started at three o'clock.[5] First came Bethe, who spoke of Robert the scientist and teacher: "He did more than any other man to make American theoretical physics great. . . . He brought out the best in us like a good host with his guests. . . . I have seldom heard a speaker, scientist or otherwise, who had such command of the English language."

Then followed Smyth, who recalled Oppenheimer's many contributions in the service of his government, and also the Oppenheimer hearings (chapter 23, sec. 23.3), of which he said: "Such a wrong can never be righted; such a blot on our history never erased. . . . We regret that his great work for his country was repaid so shabbily and that he felt impelled to quote these lines from Shakespeare:

'The sad account . . .
Which I now pay as if not paid before.'

He paid heavily."

Finally, George Kennan:

In preserving and developing the Institute as a seat of the purest and highest sort of intellectual effort . . . he was rendering a service of great importance. In the dark days of the early fifties, when troubles crowded in upon him from many sides and when he found himself harassed by his position at the center of controversy, I drew his attention to the fact that he would be welcome in a hundred academic centers abroad and asked him whether he had not thought of taking residence outside this country. His answer, given to me with tears in his eyes: Damn it, I happen to love this country. The truth is that the U.S. Government never had a servant more devoted at heart than this one. . . .

The arrogance which to many appeared to be a part of his personality masked in reality an overpowering desire to bestow and receive affection. Neither circumstances nor at times the asperities of his own temperament permitted the gratification of this need in a measure remotely approaching its intensity. . . . Such was the nature of his predicament.

After these eulogies, the Julliard Quartet played Beethoven's quartet No. 14 in C-sharp Minor. We sat in silence throughout it all. After the music ended, we rose and filed out into the biting cold.

On April 24, 1967, the American Physical Society held an Oppenheimer Memorial Session at its Washington, D.C., meeting. The speakers were, in order, Serber on the early years, Weisskopf on the Los Alamos years, Pais on the Princeton period, and Seaborg on "Public Service and Human Contributions." I ended my talk (from which I quoted earlier)[6] as follows:

We honor Oppenheimer as a great leader of science in our time. When all is interwoven with the dramatic events that centered around him, we remember Oppenheimer as one of the most remarkable personalities of this century. In the years to come the physicist will speak of him. So will the historian and the psychologist, the playwright and the poet. But it would take the singular combination of talents of this extraordinary man himself to characterize his life in brief. Perhaps Robert has done just that. I shall conclude by reading a few lines which he wrote fourteen years ago: "The wealth and variety of physics itself, the greater wealth of the natural sciences taken as a whole, the more familiar, yet still strange and far wider wealth of the life of the human spirit, enriched by complementary, not at once compatible ways, irreducible one to the other, have a greater harmony. They are the elements of man's sorrow and his splendour, his frailty and his power, his death and his passing, and his undying deeds."[7]

29.2 MY LIFE IN THE LATE 1960S

29.2.1 Of Art and of Physics

The next summer, during my usual stay in Brookhaven with Josh, a colleague and his wife, an artist, took me on a visit to Tatiana Grossman, who lived in nearby Islip. She was an unusual sort of art agent. Attached to her home was a studio where some of the best American artists would come to make lithographs on stones she made available. She sold their prints, a number of which she showed us. One, entitled "Vision Number 4," attracted me at once. I asked who had made it. Robert Rauschenberg, she said. Having never yet heard of him, I asked if he was well known. She replied that he was perhaps the best of the American moderns. I bought it, number 29 of a drawing of 44. Years later I saw the same print in the Metropolitan Museum. I also bought an abstract expressionist print by Helen Frankenthaler, number 2 of 21. Later I saw number 1 in the Museum of Modern Art collection. Those were my only acquisitions of postwar art, as I have never cared for most of it one bit.

During the summer I wrote to Rauschenberg (I had obtained his address in Islip) to tell him how happy I was to own one of his lithos. I also invited him to an orientation lecture on physics I would be giving in October for all students at our university. He accepted my invitation and enjoyed the talk. We had lunch afterward, during which we talked of neutrinos and of art, particularly of "happenings," a new form of theater in which he was actively interested. That autumn I also met another artist, the poet Anne Sexton, to whom I was introduced after having listened to one of her readings. I had a physics book under my arm and asked her to autograph it, which she did with the dedication: "The hell with everything else." She was a tragic figure.

For me the main event and pleasure of that autumn was the presence of Sam Treiman as a one-term visitor at my university. Right away we went to work together on a technically complex problem dealing with a rare decay mode of charged K-particles (the decays $K^+ \rightarrow e^+ + \nu + \pi^+ + \pi-$) which, we found, yields new information on the scattering of pions by pions. For days on end we first completely filled my huge blackboard, then went across the hall to Sam's office, where we continued on his huge blackboard, then finally copying on paper the main results. By December we were ready to submit a paper on the subject.[8] Thus began another period of our fruitful collaboration, this one lasting about ten years, yielding fifteen publications.

Before 1967 was over, I completed another paper of a different sort. In 1968 the journal *Physics Today* was to celebrate its twentieth anniversary with an issue of general articles by specialists on progress made during the last twenty years in a variety of areas in physics. I wrote the one on "Twenty Years of Particle Physics."[9]

Sam and I worked together again during the summer of 1968 when, along with about eighty other physicists, we were at the Center of Physics in Aspen, Colorado, to attend the first of a series of summer study programs organized by the National Accelerator Laboratory, a new institution to be situated in Batavia, Illinois (ground for its first building was broken the following December), and since 1974 known as Fermilab.[10] While there we finished a paper on certain other rare decay modes of K-particles.[11]

Joshua had come along to Colorado. We made a fine car trip together, visiting Mesa Verde, to my taste America's most impressive national monument, riding the narrow-gauge train at Durango, and touring through Utah. For the rest, he had a good time at a day camp in Aspen.

Sam's and my next joint enterprise, a rather elegant brief note on a general property of neutrino reactions, was mainly negotiated by phone calls between New York and Princeton. It was published in Moscow in a Festschrift in honor of Bogoliubov.[12] Meanwhile I had published two other papers as well.[13]

In 1969 we wrote two papers on the issue of charge conjugation tests in colliding beam experiments.[14] The second of these, my last one published in the 1960s, was written when we were once again in Aspen. At that year's summer study we organized a series of seminars on lepton physics.[15]

Josh had come with me to Aspen again. I had rented a house on a hill behind the Copper Kettle restaurant. To my son's delight, it was reached by private chairlift. Again we made an excursion, this time driving to Taos, visiting the pueblo, then on to the gorge of the Rio Grande. From there to Santa Fe and nearby Los Alamos, where we saw the A-bomb models in the science museum, then to Bandelier National Park, finally on a visit to friends in Albuquerque, then back.

One last item on physics in the sixties. In January 1968, while attending a conference in Coral Gables, I was approached by a man from the Air Force's Office of Scientific Research who suggested that I apply for a grant— something new for me. After returning to New York I sent off a proposal, feeling quite uncomfortable about asking for money. Some time later I got a call—my proposal sounded reasonable, but would I not be interested in more money? Now I smelled blood and sent off a modified version in which I asked for a lot more. Half a year later I got it all. So began my career as contract applicant, a task later taken over by Khuri. My group has continued to be treated well by one funding agency or another.

29.2.2 I Turn Fifty

In the preceding pages I have refrained from boring my readers with accounts of the many times I felt lonely or low. I must now make one exception, my reactions preceding my fiftieth birthday, on May 19, 1968, when fear of old age must have caused a genuine depression.

Only those who have had such an experience will appreciate what that was like: trouble getting out of bed in the morning, shuffling rather than walking, unable to work, no desires of any kind, with past and future life looking bleak and lonely. I once read somewhere a good description of that state of mind: it is as if one looks at a seabed, all water has receded, one only sees wreckage on the bottom. One looks at one's life with merciless lucidity. Since I had heard that depression is a physical illness, I went to see my doctor, who prescribed Tofranil, a medication. The episode lasted for about two months. Then, as I woke up one morning before my birthday, it was completely gone, just like that. That time now feels to me like a bad dream; I recall that it happened but cannot relive the feelings I had. Nor have I ever had a relapse.

On that May 19, a Nobel symposium on elementary particle physics was to start in Aspenäsgården, near Göteborg in Sweden, which I had been invited to attend. On the 15th, Josh and I flew to Amsterdam, to celebrate my birthday with my mother. Joshua made interesting observations on that trip. "The houses are friendlier here; they don't jump at you like in New York." After two days: "It seems as if only now I can believe that I'm here." On the 19th we spent the early day together. After lunch I took off for Sweden, Josh staying with my mother until my return on the 25th. The symposium was a pleasant event held in peaceful surroundings. Even the matchboxes bore Nobel's name. I presented a paper on some of my recent work.[16]

29.2.3 Apollo 9 and Apollo 11

By late 1968 the Apollo program, designed to land man on the moon, had gone into high gear. On December 24, Apollo 8 had gone into lunar orbit, carrying three astronauts farther from the earth than any man before.

One evening around that time I had dinner with Robert Jastrow, a physicist I had known since the 1950s when he had been an Institute fellow, and who now held a high position in the space program. He told me that next February he was going to Cape Kennedy to watch the liftoff of Apollo 9, which was to undertake a prolonged mission in earth orbit to check out the LM, the lunar module, and invited me to join him. I accepted enthusiastically.

When we arrived at the Quality Courts Motel in Titusville, Florida, we were much disappointed to learn that the liftoff, scheduled for February 20, had to be postponed for three days because the astronauts had headcolds. We could not stay that long but felt privileged all the same to be given a guided tour of the launching area. At the Kennedy Space Center, I noted parking spaces marked "For Astronauts Only." We were led to the VAB, the Vehicle Assembly Building, three city blocks in size, on Merritt Island. Inside, looking down from the thirty-fourth floor, the people below looked like ants. We visited Pad 39A, where we saw Apollo 9 from various angles, standing there essentially lonely, totally quiet and static. Then to the MSOB, the Manned Spacecraft Operations Building, where I came as close to Apollo 11 and to the landing module, both in altitude chambers, as any noninvolved layman will ever be. Next to the VAB is the LCC, the Launch Control Center, with its four firing rooms, as many as there are bays in the VAB. Standing nearby was the incredible six-million-pound transporter, the size of a baseball field with its own road, the width of an eight-lane highway, from the VAB to the launching pad. There is a new, special poetry to it all, including the herons in the wildlife preserve which comprises Merritt Island.

We were invited to sit in on a staff meeting, convened to discuss the delay in the Apollo 10 launch caused by the delay of 9. I was awed by the low pressure and utter calmness of all present. These men exuded a certainty free of cockiness. They did not play it cool, they *were* cool. I spoke with the deputy director of the program, who showed neither tension nor irritation. Representatives of industry, also present (20,000 contractors contributed to the program), interacted comfortably with the NASA people. "What does IBM say? Does TWA have comments?"

Clearly, the disappointment of missing the liftoff was royally compensated by those other experiences, which I never would have had if everything had gone according to the original plan.

Apollo 10, the next flight, journeyed to within ten miles of the moon's surface, to test the LM. Then, in July 1969, came the great event. Apollo 11 would land men on the moon. Jastrow invited me again for that takeoff; and of course I went.

This happened during my second stay in Aspen. I arranged for Josh to stay with friends during my four-day absence, then flew from Denver to Dallas to Orlando, meeting Jastrow in the Caravelle Inn at Cocoa Beach. On July 16 I went to bed just before midnight and was up again at 4 A.M. to set out for the liftoff.

It was pitch dark but, looking out from the Inn, I saw one starkly illuminated shining white object: the bird, as each satellite is called. It inspired me to write a poem, with a jab at TV commercials, beginning: "On its pad, uninterrupted by a word from Gulf Oil, stands the bird."

Off we went in chartered buses, traffic moving well, thanks to help from NASA staff. We arrived at the stands: one for diplomats, governors, and members of Congress—I saw LBJ and his wife—others for little people like us. The atmosphere was like that of a county fair. People sat on the grass with coffee and Danish bought on the site; there were latrines, also a post office where I bought and sent Apollo 11 postcards with a special cancelation. Among the milling crowds I saw some French staff officers, with *kepi* and a baton under the arm, looking ludicrously out of place. I also met a few astronauts, being again struck by their almost palpable calm and their no-nonsense way of talking. The astronauts for this flight were already in their capsule. I was told that their eeriest moment is when they go up in an elevator and the crowds are no longer around.

We sat waiting on the stand. Next to me was the author Herman Wouk, with whom I talked books. The crowd grew very quiet as the moment neared. Then it came: liftoff. Memories of the next few minutes will forever be grafted on my memory. The flames—then the rise, slow at first. Then the sound waves, which made my shirt rattle against my chest. I looked up to see the bird go. What amazed me above all was this: I had seen liftoffs before on TV, when cameras zoom in and give an impression of the enormous size of the satellite plus booster. As I now saw it live, it was just the opposite: you see a tiny object moving outward into the huge blue sky, a deeply moving sensation. A few little men are out to conquer big space.

Then came the wait for the flight's progress, which I followed on television along with half a billion others all over the world. On July 20 the *New York Times* carried a banner headline informing its readers that the astronauts had swung into moon's orbit.

Then, at 2:17 P.M., Eastern daylight time, came the laconic message from the LM: "The Eagle has landed." At 10:56 P.M., Neil Armstrong stood on the moon. After another sixty hours: splashdown in the Pacific. All over the world church bells rang and whistles blew. It was a proud moment for mankind, particularly for Americans, for whom this was a great unifying moment—the last one to date on this scale.

29.2.4 New Homes

In 1969 I began preparations for procuring a new office and two new homes. My group was going to move into a new building on campus that was nearly completed. In June the chief engineer invited me for a visit to the

"Tower building," to inspect the space assigned to us on the thirteenth floor, after which he took me up to the roof for a view of the city. I shall forever remember the graffiti written by a workman on an unfinished wall of the top floor: "Time is money, so take your time."

Since meanwhile my financial situation had improved, I decided to look for another apartment, and finally settled on one on York Avenue, across the street from the university, in a building jointly owned by nearby academic institutions, including Rockefeller. That made my rent quite reasonable. I have lived there happily ever since.

By then I had lived in New York for six years, and had traveled far and wide, but missed a place outside but near the city, where I could go on weekends, like my earlier Princeton–Perry Street arrangement, but in reverse. After some weekends of searching I found an ideal solution in Zena, a township near Woodstock, just over one hundred miles north of New York, satisfying my desideratum of being in easy reach but too far for a daily commute. The property consisted of several acres of forest in the center of which lay a clearing, on which stood a small house, log cabin style, pretty, and isolated from all traffic. Joshua and I fell in love with it.

30

The 1970s

30.1 MY MOTHER'S DEATH

IN MID-JANUARY 1970 I received a phone call from my mother's doctor in Amsterdam, who told me that she was not well. There were no immediate fears for her life but I would be well advised to come over right away for a visit. Which I did. There she was, lucid as ever but moving poorly. I felt overwhelming tenderness for her.

I was convinced that the time had come for her to leave her apartment, where she lived by herself and which had steep steps to the outside. But she would have none of it—she had lived there for twenty-five years and was perfectly comfortable. I argued to no avail. After a week's stay, I went back home.

On February 20 I had another call from Holland. Mother had fallen, broken a collarbone, and was hospitalized. The next day at six in the morning the phone rang again. At eleven the previous evening she had suddenly lost consciousness and passed away fifteen minutes later.

I turned on all the lights in my apartment, made coffee, sat down, and reflected. I could not escape the thought that Mother had known that she could not go back to her old home, and had told herself: Now it is enough.

I flew to Holland and went to her apartment, where neighbors let me in. I sat alone at her coffin in that silent home and cried. On the 24th we buried her in Ouderkerk, next to Father.

I did not sit *shiva* for her. The next of kin who had joined Mother and me after my father's death had also died meanwhile, and I felt it made no sense to sit there all by myself. There were also many practical arrangements to be made, including the dismantling of the apartment. I selected a handful of mementos for shipment to the U.S.: photographs, the clock that had stood in the room where I was born, a small Persian rug, a light crown—all these items are still in my New York apartment—and a few of Mother's personal belongings.

Then, as I closed the door behind me, the existence of the Dutch branch of the Pais family came to an end.

A year later I received a check from Amsterdam—my modest inheritance. I used it to improve the looks of my apartment. I bought beautiful curtains, had part of the interior wallpapered and the rest painted, after which my quarters looked much ·warmer and homier.

Other events in 1970. Joshua was admitted to Manhattan's Dalton School, one of the best in New York. I was appointed to the Scientific Policy Committee (SPC) of the Stanford Linear Accelerator Center (SLAC) and attended my first meeting in May. This brought me to California two or three times a year. In 1974 I was appointed chairman of the SPC, serving for three years.

In July 1970, a small number of Rockefeller professors were invited to meet with David Rockefeller, chairman of the Board of Trustees, at his residence in Pocantico, to discuss future plans for the university. I was among them and got along quite well with him then and also later. Some of our many discussions have illuminated the lifestyle of the powerful for me. For example, once Rockefeller told me of a trip he took to Beijing, where he was to meet with China's leaders. He took off from New York in his private plane, which brought him as far as Hong Kong, where he became upset when told that his plane was not allowed into China's air space; he was to take one of theirs to Beijing. Once he was there, he was treated like royalty; in fact, one Chinese leader told him he was considered to be the emperor of America. Rockefeller told me quite seriously: "But that is not true, you know." Curious.

30.2 Travels in the Early Seventies

30.2.1 Honolulu

In March 1971 I went to Stanford again for an SPC meeting. Physicists from the University of Hawaii had invited me to come from there to Honolulu for a few lectures. They would pay expenses from San Francisco and back. I accepted, gave my lecture, and had a few days of sun and swimming for free. That same arrangement was repeated a number of times in later years.

Shortly thereafter I met Jorge Luis Borges in New York after a poetry reading, a man whose writings I admire enormously. At age seventy-two his face was still smooth and full of vitality. We talked about the resemblance between science and literature—beginning in a myth and ending in it as well (see his essay on Cervantes in *Labyrinths*). I remember one other curious comment of his: "Sometimes I have the haunting fear of being immortal."

30.2.2 Copenhagen

In late April 1971 I went to Copenhagen to attend a symposium celebrating the fiftieth anniversary of Niels Bohr's Institute. The talks were on philosophical themes and included a dialogue between physicists and psychologists. The affair turned out to be a friendly sort of disaster, but it was pleasant to meet old friends. Mrs. Bohr was marvelously handsome at age eighty-one. Of new acquaintances I remember only some discussions with Jean Piaget, who had spoken on "Causality and Probability." I found him to be a rather arrogant old man. Afterward I flew to Amsterdam to present a paper on colliding beam physics at a conference.[1]

30.2.3 Sausalito

In February 1972, while back in California for an SPC meeting, I took the opportunity for a side trip to Sausalito, to visit my friend Olga Burns, the mother of a friend of mine in New York. The memorable event of that trip was the dinner we had at the Valhalla Restaurant owned by Sally Stanford, the renowned ex-madam of what was, in the 1930s and 1940s, San Francisco's most celebrated bordello. Miss Stanford, a friend of Olga's, joined us at dinner, during which she reminisced about her experiences. She spoke of the order she maintained in her earlier establishment: rigid cleanliness, weekly medical examinations of her "staff," gentlemen thrown out if they became drunk. She was clearly an intelligent, articulate, and no-nonsense woman. As a souvenir she gave me an autographed copy of her wonderfully witty memoirs,[2] which begin like this: "I didn't set out to be a madam any more than Arthur Michael Ramsey, when he was a kid, set out to be Archbishop of Canterbury. Things just happened to both of us, I guess." Later she became the mayor of Sausalito.

30.2.4 Uzbekistan

In the autumn of 1971 I received an invitation to participate in a conference to be held in Tashkent the following May. I was tempted to decline since that would interrupt my usual working season. Then, however, I read the small print, which said that an excursion was planned to Bukhara and Samarkand.

Samarkand! One of those magic place names of which one dreams. It brought back to me lines from a poem by James Elroy Flecker:

> We travel not for trafficking alone,
> By hotter winds our fiery hearts are fanned.
> For lust of knowing what should not be known,
> We take the golden road to Samarkand.

I had to go.

Just before leaving I received a nice piece of news. I had been elected a member of the American Academy of Arts and Sciences. A year later I went to Cambridge, Massachusetts, to take my bow before the Academy's membership.

In May 1972 I arrived at Tashkent, a city of one and a half million inhabitants which, I was told, has seven trees for each resident. The next morning I chaired a session. In the afternoon we were taken to the Madrassah Barak Chana, where the oldest Koran, dating from Mohammed's times, is kept. (A *madrassah* is a Muslim university.)

A few days later we got up at five in the morning, went to the airport, from where a one and a half hour flight brought us to the Holy City of Bukhara. Here we were taken on a guided tour to the Emir's summer palace, and then to his winter palace, where we were shown the "room of cruelty." There we saw the executioner's knife, so worn out through use that not much of the blade was left, and a photograph of a beheading. Then to the madrassahs and the bazaar, filled with Uzbeks, squatting, colorful square skullcaps on their heads, drinking green tea, exuding a wise calm. Then we walked to the Bolo-i-Khauz mosque, made of wood, a rarity in Muslim architecture, with beautifully ornamental exterior walls. Thereafter we were served a plate of *kroschka*, then back to the airport again.

I had had fantasies about seeing fine Bukhara rugs, perhaps buying one. None of the above. The only rug I saw was on a donkey carrying a man who was seated on a folded, worthless little carpet.

From Bukhara we flew to Samarkand, where we arrived at four that same afternoon. We were housed at the quite modern Hotel Samarkand. That evening we were invited to join a party in the hotel's dining room, where I met the writer Alberto Moravia. The next day I had a long discussion with him about politics and about Japanese literature. After dinner we went for a moonlight stroll to the Gur Emir, the tomb of the warriors, where Timur, also known as Tamerlane, is buried. The next day, Irena, a pretty young Russian woman who spoke good English, a student from the University of Samarkand (student body 30,000), took us on a guided tour. First to the Gur Emir. Before the entrance to the mausoleum there is an inscription with Timur's words: "Happy is he who renounced the world before the world renounced him." Inside we saw his tomb covered by a large stone of green nephrite, the mineral from which the finest jade is cut. According to Irena, this stone was brought from China as proof of the wealth of that land. Legend has it that the Chinese will not rest until the stone is returned to their country. The tomb was first opened on June 19, 1941. It had been foretold that a great war would start if the tomb was entered. Two days later Hitler's armies invaded Russia.

Next we walked down a narrow street with exquisite mausoleums on both sides, executed in turquoise-blue stone. One, called Shadi-mulkh-akbah, is the burial place of Timur's sixteen-year-old niece. Over its doors is written: "She was as beautiful as the moon and as slender as a cypress." Another tomb was that of Kussam ibn Abbas, considered a holy shrine by orthodox Muslims; to visit his tomb twice is equivalent to going to Mecca. Irena tells: One day, as Kussam was preaching the Koran, he was attacked by an angry mob that beheaded him. But his head kept preaching. After he was finished, he took his head under his arm and descended into a well.

From there we went to the Righistan, a square at the center of old Samarkand. It is fenced in by the three madrassahs of Ulugh Beg, Shir-dar, and Tilla-Kari. It is an area of great architectural symmetry and beauty, matching Europe's finest squares.

Our final visit was to the remains of the mosque of Bibi-Hanoum, Timur's favorite wife. Irena tells its romantic legend. As Timur went on one of his war expeditions, his wife ordered that a huge mosque be built in his honor, as a surprise when he returned. All went along well until suddenly the work slowed down considerably. She soon found out why. The young architect in charge had passionately fallen in love with her, and soon expressed his ardor. Bibi-Hanoum warned him not to think such thoughts and reminded him of Timur's terrible cruelty. But the young man kept insisting, so she sent him a basket of eggs of different colors and said: "Outside they look different, inside they are all the same." Whereupon the young man sent her two bowls, one filled with water, the other with white wine, and said: "These look the same, but one arouses passion, the other does not." Then he insisted that even an exchange of one kiss would satisfy his passion. Bibi refused, but after much ado she consented to putting a hand on her cheek so the man could kiss her hand there. This he did, but so great was his passion that the kiss left a mark on her cheek. When Timur returned and saw the mark, he had the mosque laid in ruins and ordered all women veiled. (Some time after the 1917 revolution, when Uzbekistan became a Soviet republic, the wearing of the veil was prohibited, prompting a number of men to kill their wives.)

30.2.5 Mexico

In mid-June, Joshua and I arrived in Mexico City, where I was to lecture on particle physics at the National University, for a three-week visit. We stayed in a hotel in the Zona Rosa. We did a lot of sightseeing, becoming acquainted with cultures that were new to us. In preparation I had read the book by William Prescott on the conquest of Mexico which had moved me very much. Our first outing was to the city's anthropological museum. It was indeed as beautiful from the outside and as fascinating inside as I had been told.

One weekend friends drove us to Puebla, where we visited the hidden convent of Santa Monica, operated secretly for over seventy years by 120 nuns until it was accidentally discovered in 1934. For lunch we had a local specialty, chicken *mole Poblano,* chicken in a strongly spiced thick chocolate sauce (*mole* means sauce in Nalunatl)—delicious. There I learned that the word "chocolate" is of Aztec origin, derived from *chocolatl.* From Puebla we drove to the ancient sacred Toltec city of Cholula, where 294 of its 365 churches were still in business. Then to Hvejotzingo, with its nearly purely Aztec population. And back home.

This concluded my unusually heavy year of travel, during which, I calculated, I had covered over 23,000 miles. It was also the year in which Josh reached a height equal to mine. He was blossoming.

30.2.6 London

The only trip of interest in 1973 was my trip to London with Joshua that summer, to show him the sights and to go to Hempstead to call on Anna Freud, Sigmund's youngest daughter and a well-known psychiatrist in her own right, the founder of child psychoanalysis. Once again (as earlier with Casals), a New York friend had asked me to deliver a package to her, and had written her of my impending visit.

I found Miss Freud to be a vivacious woman with intensely alive eyes that exuded sunniness. She showed me her father's study, which, she told me, was arranged exactly as it had been in Vienna, and which had been left untouched after his death. Most notable in that room was her father's sculpture collection, nearly all small pieces, some superb Chinese items, a few Greek ones, but largely of Egyptian provenance. He had bought "a bag of fragments" of Pompeian mosaics; she could "dimly remember" the hours her father had spent putting them together. Each piece had an "emigration number" (said Miss Freud), dating the time when the German authorities had permitted their exportation from Vienna to London. The sculpture collection was a dense clutter in an otherwise serene and spacious room. It was a memorable afternoon.

30.3 JOSHUA BECOMES AN ACTOR

Thinking back on what I saw in the theater and the movies in the 1970s, I am struck by the intelligence and inventiveness of much that was produced in those years, especially when compared with large parts of today's offerings. In my opinion there has never before nor since been a musical like *A Chorus Line,* nor a film like *Nashville,* which I remember as the best of that decade. Among foreign films of that time my favorite has been *Amarcord* by Federico Fellini.

During one of his weekend stays with me, in the beginning of his senior year in high school, Josh told me that he had made up his mind about his future. He wanted to become an actor. My instant reply was: "That is the dumbest idea I have ever heard," whereupon I fired my objections at him, one after the other. He had already thought of all of them, and came back with thoughtful replies. I suggested we continue the argument the next weekend. When that time came, I sang the same song: "Josh, your idea of becoming an actor is one of the stupidest things I have ever heard," giving him yet more reasons to forget the idea, to which he again responded sensibly. By then it was clear to me that he was deeply serious, so I said: "OK, I'll underwrite you in your studies at a performing arts department of a good university. After that you are on your own." We shook hands on that.

One June 11, 1976, after five years at the Dalton School, Joshua graduated. Meanwhile, we had gone through the routine of college applications. He had been accepted at several places and chose to go to Syracuse University, which has a very good theater school.

Josh did well in college. While a sophomore, he was selected for a year's study at the Royal Academy of Dramatic Arts in London in his junior year. I found him to be thriving when I visited him there. We spent a festive evening visiting a London theater to see Julie Harris in a marvelous one-woman show, *The Belle of Amherst*.

That summer Josh would turn twenty. During my visit I presented him with my gift for this special anniversary: a Eurail pass for three weeks' travel on all European trains and ferries plus a reasonable per diem for his trip. I expected that he might make a tour through France. No sir. The first postcard I received was from Venice, the second from Crete, where, he wrote, he was sleeping out on the beach. I liked that.

Back in Syracuse he was given his senior-year assignment: the lead role in a college production of *One Flew over the Cuckoo's Nest*. From Jack Nicholson's performance in the movie you may recall that this was a major enterprise. I went to see him. As the show went on I realized for the first time how talented an actor my son is. I went to Syracuse again for his graduation. Later I will tell of his further career.

30.4 I REMARRY

Most parents are left with intense feelings of emptiness when a child takes off for college. And so it was with me. After more than a decade, my weekends were mine, alone. No more Brookhaven summers, either.

I had had lady friends those past years, some of whom knew Josh and got along well with him. Yet my social life was constrained in that period; Josh always came first. I was simply not prepared for personal attachments.

Those feelings, of which I became increasingly conscious as the time of Josh's departure for college grew near, no doubt played a role when, in the spring of 1975, I made the acquaintance of a woman who held a junior faculty position in Princeton, teaching French. Her name was Sara. She was attractive and vivacious. Her fluent French and academic credentials appealed to me, as did the contrast in personality with Lila. To cut a long story short, after a year of courtship, we married. To cut an even longer story short, the relation had its better moments but did not work out. We shared two residences, mine in New York, hers in Princeton, where I spent a year (during a leave of absence) at my old Institute. Shortly after marriage I sold my house near Woodstock. Travels in those years were sometimes together, other times by myself. Early in 1985 we parted and were divorced soon afterward. It would take a while—not long—before I realized that her running off was the best thing she had ever done for me.

One good thing has survived from that period. Sara had a young son, Daniel, from a previous marriage. My relations with him were not easy in the beginning but have improved ever since. We still see each other and are the best of friends. I love him.

30.5 MISCELLANEA

A handful of assorted personal items from the later 1970s.

In 1976 I was approached for possible interest in being nominated as director of the Institute for Advanced Study in Princeton. I declined, having never been drawn to administrative positions.

In May 1977 I went to Israel for a series of lectures as the James Arthur Balfour guest professor at the Weizmann Institute of Rehovoth. In September of that year I lectured in Karlsruhe.

In January 1979 I received the Robert Oppenheimer Memorial Prize "in recognition of [my] contributions to elementary particle physics." The signatories of the accompanying diploma included three Nobel laureates. The ceremony took place during a physics conference at the Institute of Theoretical Physics in Coral Gables, Florida, where I gave a technical talk[3] and spoke on Oppenheimer after the medal was handed to me. Dirac was in the audience and commented afterward: "Even those who knew Robert Oppenheimer learned much from it."

*30.6 My Last Decade as a Research Physicist

30.6.1 The Early 1970s

That time will be remembered for its spectacular developments in the physics of particles and fields, both experimentally and theoretically. It was the last decade in which I was active in physics research. I was quite productive during those years, completing some forty papers. The last research paper I co-authored was submitted in July 1980. After that I did not, by any means, sit still, as will be seen in the next chapter.

I wrote some of these papers by myself, quite a few others with collaborators. First and foremost of these was Sam Treiman; the others were some of my junior research associates at the Rockefeller University. All of them have later obtained senior positions elsewhere, some of high distinction. Thus Chris Llewellyn Smith is at this writing director general of CERN. Howard Georgi has at this time just completed his term as chairman at Harvard's physics department. Otto Nachtmann and Vladimir Rittenberg are now senior professors in Heidelberg and Bonn, respectively.

The content of all this work is technical and will hardly be of interest to the general reader who is hereby cordially invited to skip the remainder of this section—no hard feelings—which is a quite cursory account of how one physicist kept busy in those times.

My work in the 1970s began with applications to lepton-nucleon collisions of methods developed in the 1960s (the so-called Regge models) for the analysis of strong interactions.[4] Next, Treiman and I continued our theoretical studies of electron-positron collisions,[5] which we had also worked on earlier.[6] Some time later I published a review article on this subject.[7] My writings in 1971 concluded with a lengthy review of weak interactions at high energies,[8] and two papers on another aspect of lepton-nucleon scattering.[9]

In 1972 I produced several papers, two of those in collaboration with Llewellyn Smith, on applications of isospin to proton-antiproton as well as lepton-proton collisions.[10] At Fermilab I completed a collaboration on the application of a method, then modern (the so-called light cone approach) to inelastic lepton-nucleon scattering,[11] and wrote a contribution to a book published by Brookhaven National Laboratory on the prospects of physics with Isabelle, a planned accelerator which unfortunately was never completed.[12]

All the work sketched above was based on concepts and methods current before the onset of the spectacular developments referred to above. After those began, I threw myself enthusiastically into the new theoretical prospects now lying before us. Let me first indicate the general nature of these new directions.

30.6.2 A Great Leap Forward in Particle Physics

In the preceding we encountered three kinds of forces: electromagnetic, strong, and weak (for the last two, see chapters 21, sec. 21.4, and 28, sec. 28.4). Their analysis is based on techniques collectively called quantum field theory (QFT). I had first become acquainted with that discipline when working on my doctoral thesis (chapter 6), which contains applications of meson theory, the QFT for strong interactions of that time, now largely obsolete.

I had again become active in QFT while in hiding during the war years, that time in quantum electrodynamics, that is, QFT applied to electromagnetic forces. That work had been an attempt to get rid of a difficulty in that theory, to wit, that it predicts the masses and electric charges of basic particles like the electron and proton to be infinitely large, a thorny problem encountered in any QFT for any particle, which neither I nor anyone else has satisfactorily resolved to this day.

Right after the Second World War, major progress was scored, however, when it was shown that the infinities in quantum electrodynamics can be bypassed, though not eliminated, when applying the theory to all other problems besides the particles' mass and charge. This method is called "renormalization," and one calls quantum electrodynamics "renormalizable" (chapter 19, sec. 19.3). Once that idea was digested, it became possible to reach ever higher precision in theoretical predictions. For example, by the 1970s the calculated value of the magnetic moment of the electron agreed with ever-improving experiment to ten decimal places—the highest level of agreement reached anywhere in physics.

Up to that decade, the theory of weak and strong forces had been lagging woefully behind.

From the very beginning of the introduction of weak forces by Fermi in the 1930s, one encounters the idea that also here QFT should provide the tools for their description. Good methods for codifying experimental data on these forces soon became available, yet all attempts at their more basic treatment, on the level of quantum electrodynamics, seemed doomed to failure, essentially because renormalization appeared to be inapplicable to weak forces.

And so it remained for decades, although theoretical work done in the meantime[13] does contain important elements that could be incorporated in a theory which emerged in the late 1960s, where two seemingly independent pursuits transformed the theory of weak forces from a descriptive stage to a successful field theory. One was the search for a renormalizable field theory, the other the desire for a theory that would unify the various fundamental forces, in some ways similar to the nineteenth-century unification of electricity and magnetism into classical electromagnetic field theory.

The key to this advance, one of the most important in physics in the second half of the twentieth century, was to make use of the discovery, in 1954, of the non-abelian gauge fields (Yang-Mills fields), which I had earlier referred to as "a development as profound as were Maxwell's nineteenth-century equations of electromagnetism," but which had passed almost unnoticed for the next twenty years (chapter 23, sec. 23.1). As noted before, that was because it appeared that the quanta of these fields had to be massless, whereas they ought to be quite massive for the application of such fields as intermediary of weak forces, somewhat analogous to the (massless) electromagnetic field quanta, the photons, that mediate forces between electrically charged particles.

In order to use these gauge fields for weak interactions, it was necessary, therefore, to find a way to give their quanta a mass. That mechanism turned out to have been available since 1964 and goes by the name of "spontaneous symmetry breaking."[14]

It came to pass in 1967 that a theory was proposed that, with the help of these ingredients, unified weak and electromagnetic forces.[15] This "electroweak" theory contains four quantum fields. One is the electromagnetic field. Two more, with quite massive quanta, are called W^+ and W^-, or, collectively, "charged heavy bosons," because they themselves carry electric charge. The W's translate into field-theoretic language the ideas proposed long ago by Fermi. Finally, there is one more field with massive quanta, called Z, or "neutral heavy boson," because it carries no electric charge and mediates "neutral current" processes, corresponding to a weak force that had not been observed up to that time. In 1967 it was conjectured,[16] but not yet shown, that this theory is renormalizable. When in 1971 that proof was produced, one had a full-fledged workable theory.[17]

That time interval, 1967–1971, explains in part why the number of citations of the new theory was only one from 1967 to 1970.[18] Another reason was that in these years there was as yet no firm experimental evidence for the new neutral current, the first sighting of which, using beams of neutrinos, an experimental tool producing important physics since 1962, dates from 1973. In that single year the citation record of the theory rose to 162.[19]

That same year, 1973, marks the beginnings of a new, most promising (many would say "correct") field theory for strong forces, called quantum chromodynamics (QCD). It is once again a Yang-Mills-type of field theory, in which the quantum number "color" (mentioned in chapter 28, sec. 28.4.4) plays a central role. Potent results have been obtained regarding the solutions of that theory, but some central issues still demand proof.

Earlier I had mentioned that in the early 1960s it was proposed that baryons are built up out of quarks, and mesons out of quarks and antiquarks (chapter 28, sec. 28.4.2). These subunits of matter have become the indispensable basis both for electroweak theory and for QCD. It is one of the major achievements of QCD that it explains why free quarks cannot be seen. They are forever confined, the theory says, inside baryons and mesons. I shall not describe QCD in further detail here since (with one exception) all my own further work deals with the electroweak theory.

One final remark about unification. As soon as one had gotten hold of QCD, the search was on for "grand unification," the union of electroweak theory with QCD. Promising efforts in this direction have been made, but we do not as yet know how to implement this strongly appealing idea.[20]

30.6.3 How Particles Proliferated in the Late 1970s

Sam Treiman and I went to work on neutral currents after they had been proposed but already before they had been detected. We were interested in the ratio of probabilities for the process neutrino + nucleon → neutrino + whatever else, mediated by Z, and the process neutrino + nucleon → negative muon + whatever else, mediated by W^-, and were able to find a useful lower limit for this ratio.[21] Two further papers deal with the structure of neutral currents.[22]

Then I turned to a question that interested me more than any other (and it still does): Can the new gauge field theories shed light on the origins of

CP-violation (chapter 28, sec. 28.4.3)? I made an attempt (not successful)[23] by enlarging the number of electroweak gauge fields, and studied possible new manifestations of CP-violation.[24] In the course of that work I also noticed a way of understanding the fact that the number of baryons is conserved in all physical processes.[25]

My best work on gauge theories was done in collaboration with H. Georgi, during 1974–79. We addressed a series of issues of principle, one paper dealing once again with CP violation,[26] another with what is calculable with the help of gauge fields,[27] and three more on quite delicate issues of symmetry which arise in these new theories.[28]

Meanwhile, I kept active in other areas, publishing on pion production in electron-positron collisions,[29] and, together with V. Rittenberg, a pioneering article of a mathematical nature (on semi-simple graded Lie algebras), a piece of work that still pleases me.[30]

On November 11, 1974, a period in particle physics of a kind rarely witnessed in the postwar era began. It was not only the rapid sequence of spectacular experimental discoveries that, by itself, made the difference; above all, the novelty lay in the intensity and immediacy of the interplay between experimental progress and theoretical predictions based on fundamental dynamical principles rather than, as in earlier years, on phenomenological regularities ingeniously guessed at. The general pandemonium following these discoveries compares only, in my experience, to what happened during the parity days of late 1956.

On that November day, I received phone calls from the West Coast and the East Coast informing me of a joint announcement of a discovery made at practically the same time at the Stanford Linear Accelerator (SLAC) and at Brookhaven. A new meson had been found with a mass of about three times that of the proton, eventually named J/Ψ, a symbol that I had seen much earlier on the label of Valdespino, the distinguished Spanish sherry. Even more exciting than its large mass was the fact that this new particle had a lifetime about one thousand times longer than one would anticipate. What was going on? Theorists delved in their grab bag of exotica. I recall early discussions of several options.

The answer was charmonium.

In 1963–64 a flurry of papers had appeared in which, for various reasons, the existence of a new kind of quark had been postulated, supposed to carry a new quantum number dubbed "charm." Shortly before the discovery of J/Ψ it had been predicted that this quark could bind to its antiquark, forming a long-lived compound, baptized "charmonium." J/Ψ just fitted that bill.

Shortly afterward, in 1975, another experimental discovery was announced, that one entirely unanticipated: at SLAC another new particle had been found, named τ, which was a heavy brother of the electron and muon—a heavy lepton. In 1977 still another new meson was discovered, the upsilon, three times as heavy as charmonium, which turned out to be yet another quark-antiquark bound system, demanding the introduction of a still further new quantum number, that one called "bottom."

All this novelty opened up rich new fields for theoretical research. The final phase of my own work in physics deals with explorations in this area.

In the summer of 1975, Sam Treiman and I (and Joshua, of course) were in Brookhaven, where we busied ourselves with the physics of the newfound particles. We began by writing the first paper on what they might teach us about CP-violation,[31] an issue that now, twenty years later, remains of great experimental interest. Then we turned our attention to neutrino physics. Experiments had shown that neutrino-induced reactions can produce events in which both a positive and a negative muon appear. An important question at that time was whether some of these events could be due to the decay of a neutral heavy lepton. We found what became known as the Pais-Treiman criterion for deciding that issue.[32] Continuing our collaboration when back at our universities, Sam and I worked on the question of how many new quantum numbers of the charm variety there are.[33] That autumn I reported at a conference on the status of gauge theories.[34]

In later years Sam and I discussed the production and decay of charged heavy leptons,[35] and the ratios of charmed lifetimes.[36] Otto Nachtmann and I devoted two papers to the production of charmed mesons and heavy leptons in electron-positron annihilation.[37]

My final research paper, together with Georgi and one of his postdocs, deals with the role of CP-violation in QCD.[38]

30.6.4 The First Unveiling of the W and the Z

On January 26, 1983, I left my office at the Rockefeller University for an early lunch, then walked to the New York Hilton on Sixth Avenue, where the winter meeting of the American Physical Society was in progress. Carlo Rubbia was to give an invited paper in Section HB. No title for his talk had been announced but word had come from CERN, the European Center for Nuclear Research in Geneva, that the subject was to be the discovery, long anticipated, of the W-boson by the UA1 team (UA = underground area) led by Rubbia.

The search for the W and the Z, the supreme test for the electroweak theory, had not been a surprise party. It is in fact dubious whether this enormous enterprise would have been funded and executed had there not been excellent theoretical reasons for knowing where to look: near 80 GeV for M_W, near 90 GeV for M_Z (recall that one GeV is a billion electron volts). These values had meanwhile been predicted from the wealth of data on a variety of electroweak processes. They are high indeed, ten times larger than any encountered so far in particle physics. Remember, a proton weighs a bit less than 1 GeV, thus the W-mass was expected to be about equal to that of a rubidium atom, the Z-mass that of a molybdenum atom! It was necessary to build completely new equipment to reach these high values.

Back to that cold January day. I entered the Hilton's Sutton Ballroom, joined an audience of several hundred, and listened. First came a report from UA2, another group at CERN. They too were hunting for the W, had promising results, but were not yet ready to commit themselves. Rubbia spoke next. He began by explaining the experimental arrangement. Antiprotons with a moderate energy of 3.5 GeV were collected in the AA, the antiproton accumulator. (Modern physics, like other enterprises, has its own abundance of acronyms.) This is a roughly square doughnut-like ring held at a vacuum of about one ten-billionth of a torr. The pressure had to be low since otherwise the antiprotons would be lost in collisions with gas molecules in the ring. Although this was by no means the lowest pressure then attained at CERN, it sufficed for the purpose because of a brilliant invention by Simon van der Meer, "our best accelerator man," for keeping antiprotons moving in a disciplined manner. Once every twenty-four hours the AA releases its antiprotons, which are then accelerated in two stages, the second of which takes place inside a high-vacuum ring, six kilometers in circumference, in which these particles reach an energy of 270 GeV. Inside that ring they collide with protons moving in the opposite direction with that same energy. The collisions were analyzed by means of a complex detector, ten meters high by five meters wide, weighing two thousand tons. Rubbia explained next how six events out of one billion recorded had been singled out as bearing the indubitable "signature" of the W-particle. This production rate, six in a billion, agreed well with theoretical expectations, as did the first crude determination of the W-mass.

Next to me sat an expert in high-energy neutrino physics. As the talk drew to a close, we looked at each other and nodded: they had it. Afterward

I talked with Rubbia. He asked me whether I believed it; I said I did. He gave me a preprint of the first UA1 publication on the W, signed by 135 authors from twelve European and two American institutions.[39]

The next time I met Rubbia was the following May 9. We were in Princeton where that day he was to give a lecture on UA1's further progress. During a long conversation before his talk he told me that the first example had been found of an event that looked just like the signature of a Z-boson. I asked him whether the report he was about to give would be the first in the United States to mention the Z. "It is indeed," he replied. "We found this event only a few days ago."

Much has happened since then. To date one has observed about 100,000 W's and over ten million Z's.

At the time I ended the writing of *Inward Bound* with the discoveries of the W and the Z, I could not know that this was a natural place to stop. Experimentalists have not sat still after those discoveries, but to date (I am writing this in 1995), nothing as momentous has been found in the high energy laboratories except for the discovery of a further type of quark, called the "top." As of 1995, forty-three examples of top quark productions have been seen in six trillion proton-antiproton collisions, a most impressive illustration of what it takes to find such rare events. Much worse than that, in 1994 the U.S. high energy experimental program suffered a tremendous setback when Congress in its wisdom decided to kill the funding for the so-called SSC project, which had aimed at creating the nation's next higher energy laboratory, the supercollider. For the remainder of this century, there are no prospects for an independent American effort in this frontier domain.

Nor does high energy theory look any rosier at this time. After 1983, theorists have not sat still either, having moved into new territory known as superstring theory. Their mathematics has been impressive, but there is as yet not the slightest indication that these explorations have anything to do with phenomena as they occur in the real world.

So, with very deep regret, I must end on a note of gloom my account of what was during my career the most flourishing part of physics.

31

A Career Change

31.1 I Switch from Physics Research to Physics History

Since the late 1930s I had put my energies and devotion into theoretical physics research and had produced an oeuvre which was, I may say, highly creative in some parts, routine in others. So it continued until into the 1970s, when I changed fields—not abruptly but gradually, until toward the end of that decade the transition was complete. I shall first relate what led to this change.

During most of my life, history has been among my favorite topics for leisure reading, not only because of an interest in the past but, perhaps even more so, because of the grand literary style of the great historians. My taste, indeed my need, for reading history is best explained in the eloquent words of George Steiner, whom I consider to be the greatest living literary critic: "The writing of history achieves classic status less by its documentary exactitude or its sobriety of judgment than its literary power. Thucydides, Tacitus, Gibbon, Michelet are the masters of history because they are very great writers, because they have made the language live and made remembrance eloquent."[1] These lines also express my own opinion that writing history is a great art which, however, like all arts, demands its own technical knowledge. That linkage is so well expressed by the terminology of the ancient Greeks, who coined the words *histor* for a learned man, *historeon* for a seeker after knowledge, but also *historikos* for a reciter of stories. Note further that our word "story" is nothing but an apheptic derivative of the word "history."

I should like to tell next how that interest made me, more or less acciden-

tally, stumble into writing about the history of science. This brings me back
to 1972.

In that year, while actively engaged in research dealing with the gauge
theory of weak interactions, I was invited by the editor of a prestigious journal
to write a review article on that subject. The idea appealed to me, and I decided
to work on it that coming summer at Brookhaven. When that time came, I
started to make an outline when the thought struck me that it might be fun to
begin with a brief sketch, just a few pages, on the history of weak interactions.

But how had that branch of physics begun? I knew of course that this
would bring me back to the turn of the century, to the discoveries of radioactivity by Henri Becquerel and the Curies, but I did not have the vaguest
idea what they had done and why. I did not even know the year in which
they had begun their work. So I went to the laboratory's librarian to ask
how I could find out. She suggested that I look into the *Encyclopaedia Britannica*. There I found the year: 1896. When I went back to thank her, she
suggested that I might next look at the microfilm of the *Comptes Rendus de
l'Académie des Sciences de Paris*. It turned out that, for reasons I don't understand, the library had a complete set dating back to 1850. So, for the first
time in my life, I sat down in front of a reader with the film for 1896, and
soon found the first papers by Becquerel. As I read them, I was simply
stunned to learn of the truly bizarre motivation for his work and of the
equally bizarre way in which it was discovered, a few years later, that radio-
active radiation can harm living organisms.

More surprises followed as I kept on reading about that early research.
All that old stuff was new to me and, I would bet, to many if not all of my
physics colleagues. Therefore it seemed worthwhile to tell them of this
work by our ancestors that lies at the root of their own current efforts. That,
however, would demand much more space than a few pages in a review
article. I therefore called the editor of the journal, told him of my inten-
tions, and begged off from my assignment in order to devote a few months
to this historical project. He was sympathetic to my plan. And that is how
my writing on history of science began.

As you may know, the decade 1895–1905 was exceedingly rich in fundamental advances in physics. X rays, radioactivity, the electron, the substructure of the atom, quantum theory, relativity theory—all these were discovered in that period. I conceived the ambitious idea to enlarge my project
and write a short book about the history of that decade regarding all particles and all forces then known. I did this during evening hours, keeping
busy on my current research in the daytime.

I still have the manuscript of what I wrote in those days. It was a disaster—facts piled one upon another in breathless style. I came as far as Einstein's first paper of 1905 on relativity. Then I got stuck.

It was clearly impossible to fit this vast subject, which has its own fascinating prehistory, into my planned book without throwing the whole enterprise out of balance. Not knowing how to cope with this, I stopped, put the manuscript in a drawer, and forgot the whole project. These early forays did, however, result in publications on the early puzzles posed by the discovery of radioactivity.[2]

So it remained until 1978.

31.2 'SUBTLE IS THE LORD'

In that year, I was elected a member of the committee to prepare the scientific program for the Einstein centennial conference to be held in 1979 at the Institute for Advanced Study in Princeton. I was unanimously chosen to report on Einstein's contributions to and thoughts about quantum physics, of which I knew a great deal from personal discussions both with Einstein and with Niels Bohr. I had in fact more than once been locked in a room together with those two men, as they argued, and talked past each other, about issues of fundamental principle in quantum mechanics.

My lengthy report to the conference,[3] followed by wise invited comments from my good friend Res Jost,[4] was quite well received. This stimulated the thought: Why not go for the whole enchilada and write a full-fledged biography of Einstein's science and his life? That would demand full-time devotion—which in fact suited me. I was past sixty now, and felt that I could no longer contribute sufficiently original ideas to modern research. So for the next three years I worked on my first book, day in, day out. In July 1982 I held in my hands the first printed copy of *Subtle is the Lord*.

Before turning to details of that work, I will first tell something about my experiences in putting together books on history, in particular about the differences between that kind of work and physics research.

31.3 KEEPING TRACK OF THE WRITTEN RECORD

In the course of preparing four fairly lengthy works on the history of science—which I now have under my belt—I have of course frequently been faced with questions familiar to all who write: how to keep track of information from outside sources which I may need right now, or which I know to be relevant for what will come later, or which oblige me to rewrite what I had already committed to paper.

Each of us so engaged has his or her own way of coping with these problems, which are as mundane as they are important. I have at times been curious as to how others proceed. Since they may well wonder likewise, I thought it would be all right to tell something about how I have resolved these questions to my satisfaction, without advertising my way as better. It is all very much a matter of personal style and custom.

First of all, in the case of each of my books, I spent about a year thinking, reading, and browsing. I do not actually start until I have in my head a beginning, a middle, and an end. Having come that far, I get myself a loose-leaf notebook in which I write down a title for chapter 1 on the first page, for chapter 2 on the second, and so on. Next I jot down, under each chapter heading (which itself may change in the course of time), thoughts about what should go there, references to books, papers, and letters I should use, sometimes a phrase or two that I think may be appropriate—all this in random order.

As time goes by, I inevitably come to realize that chapters 5 and 6 should really be put together into one, and I adjust my loose-leaf pages. More often I decide that chapter 3 should actually be split into two chapters. Accordingly I insert a new page and split my notes for what was to be chapter 3 under two new headings. That takes time, but I find it well worth the trouble. So things grow until there comes a day when I feel I could begin the actual writing. Since I like to have an opening chapter in which I outline the contents of the whole book, I always reserve that one for the end, when everything else is on paper. Only then do I in fact know what I had been trying to write.

When I start on a new chapter, I believe—not always correctly—that I have all the necessary material in hand. Yet very often nothing spills out as I sit down—an experience which must be familiar to many. Practice has taught me that patience is now called for. Most often I stop trying, go for a walk or do something else. After some time, it may be days, a beginning announces itself, as it were. Thereafter I may still falter but never again as long as it took me to write the opening lines.

Doing original physics research and writing books both demand patience, but each of a different kind. When doing physics, one can get stuck, too, sometimes badly, but more on technical issues, less on matters of language. When doing history, one can also get stuck on what may be called technical points, but these are of a quite different nature. First, in my kind of physics research I rarely needed to consult literature that dates back to more than a few years and thus is readily at hand, while in history one often needs to go back to sources that are much older. This often demands patience while obtaining access to sources that are much less readily available. Second, one may have to consult letters and other documents that first have to be located, and then have to be retrieved or copied. All these circumstances demand kinds of patience I had not been familiar with from my physics research work.

Another quantitative difference between writing a research paper and historical work lies in what is sometimes called the iceberg principle: never write all you know, just show the tip of the iceberg, yet convey—and that is a subtle task—that you are aware of much more that lies beneath the surface. The judicious use of this principle distinguishes hacks from good writers.

31.4 THE ACTUAL WRITING

I have never learned to type; I can do no better than use my two index fingers. Nor have I ever mastered the use of a word processor. I need not be convinced of the tremendous advantages of the new technologies, but for me they do not work. Speed is of no advantage to me since I think and write slowly. I am of course aware of the possibilities for correcting and moving around sentences or paragraphs or whole pages. For that I have been blessed with a good secretary who does use a word processor and patiently throws things around at my request.

As to the actual writing, I soon found out that having published some 150 research papers had not in the least prepared me for writing history. All one needs by way of language for writing any physics research article, even a good one, is in essence a quite limited set of stock English phrases.

To illustrate for a typical theoretical paper. Start a section 1, called Introduction, in the following way: It has recently been observed [or pointed out] that . . . . Earlier analyses of these phenomena [slew of references] had led to the conclusion that . . . . In the light of the more recent data it appears, however, that these previous results need to be extended [or modified or revised]. It is the purpose of the present paper to do so.

In section 2 we summarize previous answers. In section 3 we introduce the following new feature [. . .] and leave a number of more technical points for an appendix. In section 4 we summarize our conclusions and present a further outlook.

Sections 2 and 3 are basically mathematical, with the merest connective linguistic tissue. Section 4 consists of a few assertions plus a conjecture or two.

Writing of this kind does little, if anything, to prepare oneself for writing history, where language rather than mathematical formalism is of the essence. I have found it stimulating and refreshing to tackle this new type of task in my later years. I have grown more attentive than I was earlier to the writing style of others, and have come to compare a good sentence with a piece of sculpture. Writing and chiseling in marble or stone seem to me to have similarities. I have also become much more aware of minute details of language. Thus I recall my pleasure when I learned to appreciate the difference between "my son John" and "my son, John."

Like every writer, I adopted my own technique for committing fact and thought to paper. In practice I proceed as follows. First I make a scribble, writing down things as they come to mind, correcting and changing things around, until I am the only one who can make sense of my sheets. When I have done so for a chapter, the pages go into a drawer for a month, say, and I move on to some other part. Then I go back to my scribbles and write them in neat longhand, thinking over once more every sentence, every word, as I go along. Again the pages go into a drawer, now maybe only for a week. Having done that, I have a draft which in my experience is final at the ninety percent level. Next, I give it to a typist. So my only physical tools are paper and my beloved Mont Blanc fountain pen. I actually find the physical act of writing quite pleasurable, especially because it makes less noise than using any form of machine.

Writing is for me an experience so intense that I am incapable of profitably writing for longer than about two hours each day. I never continue thereafter, since for me writing demands the most optimal freshness of mind I can muster. So the rest of the day is devoted to more routine tasks. It can of course happen that, while being otherwise engaged, a thought comes to mind that I would like to retain. For that purpose I always carry a small piece of paper and a pencil stub in my front shirt pocket on which I jot down whatever comes along. In general I can only remember what I write down. I have trained myself to have at any given time as little floating around in my head as possible. Even so, I do carry around more thoughts, most of them garbage, than I care to.

I derive pleasure from getting acquainted with the etymology of words, not necessarily fancy ones. (I am in fact averse to the use of polysyllabics or unnecessary use of sophisticated terms.) For example, I remember my joy at suddenly realizing that "breakfast" and "déjeuné" mean the same thing.

I also find it great fun to learn new words. When I do not know a word, I go at once to my small-print *Oxford English Dictionary* to look it up, magnifying glass in hand. For example, not so long ago I came across the word "ventripotent" (which means corpulent) in Lawrence Durrell's *Quincunx*, which contains a wealth of uncommon but good English words. I looked it up, liked it, and decided to save it for future use, once and only once. I like to use quaint words in my writing, but only very sparsely. As to "ventripotent," a splendid occasion for using it arose when I had to characterize the qualifications of the physicist Wolfgang Pauli. Accordingly you can find in print my reference to his "brilliance, erudition, and ventripotence."[5] The use of incommensurable qualifiers is a trick I learned from Gibbon.

I express myself best in English, though it is not my native tongue. During preparatory stages I often need to read material in other languages. As I do so, I often think back with immense gratitude to my Dutch high school education, where I was taught five years of German and French and four years of English. At age seventeen I could read these three languages with reasonable ease and also speak them fairly well. Later I learned Danish, in which I am now also comfortable. I also read Spanish, Italian, Norwegian, and Swedish, though none of these without a dictionary at hand. I can read Hebrew, but with little understanding of the text. Likewise with Russian, in which I once took a one-year course at Princeton University. My knowledge of languages has been a decided help to me in my writing.

Reading and understanding a foreign text well is one thing, translating it into English is quite something else. All those familiar with that predicament will know how it can come to pass that one reads a phrase in another language, perfectly grasps its content, yet finds oneself at a total loss on how to translate it. Each language has its own delicate nuance that is often difficult if not impossible to translate. One of my favorite phrases that I offer for translation to those fluent in another language is: "What the hell?"

It has also happened to me that, having read an author first in translation, then in his or her native tongue, I find that only after that second reading do I acquire a real feeling for the intent. This is true of the stories by the Danish writer Hans Christian Andersen. I first read and enjoyed them as a boy, in Dutch translation. Years later I read them in the original, and only then did I understand that these tales are meant for adults rather than children.

Thus acquaintance with a foreign language adds a new dimension to experiencing the power of the word.

31.5 On Indexes, Titles, and Illustrations

My books have two indexes: one on subjects, one on names. The latter, which carries the marvelously quaint title onomasticon, includes years of birth and, where applicable, of death. I never include those years in the body of the text since that to me seems a mild form of scholarly pedantry, distracting rather than helping the reader.

I prepare a preliminary version of the name index, using again a loose-leaf notebook with pages marked A to Z on which I write down names as I encounter them for the first time in my main text. I send the result, a semi-ordered array, to the publisher, who hires an indexer who puts the names in order, adds the page numbers, and also prepares a subject index. I do not touch that stuff, having been blessed with grants from the A. P. Sloan Foundation for each of my books. From these funds the indexer gets paid.

I recall an evening in the summer of 1981, when I was sitting with some of my historian friends at a table in the City Hall of Vienna while a reception was in progress for members of a conference on Ludwig Boltzmann. Someone asked me how far along I was with my Einstein biography. "It is finished," I said. "Including the indexes?" I was asked. "I do not intend to make indexes," I replied, rather snottily. As a man, my friends jumped on me, telling me how stupid an idea that was, if only because it would give reviewers a good reason for being critical. I was taken aback and said, "I guess you are right." I mended my ways and, as a matter of fact, now find my own name indexes very helpful.

I give careful thought to chapter titles, which should carry both information and a touch of intrigue. The ones I like best are: "Portrait of the Physicist as a Young Man," copying Joyce, and "The Suddenly Famous Doctor Einstein," a quote from the New York Times, both used in my Einstein biography; "It Was the Epoch of Belief, It Was the Epoch of Incredulity," a line from Dickens, and "Pitfalls of Simplicity," in Inward Bound; and "In Denmark I Was Born," a line from a poem by H. C. Andersen, and "A Modern Viking Who Comes on a Great Errand," another quote from the New York Times, in my book on Niels Bohr.

I attach great importance to my choice of book titles, which I like to imbue with an element of ambiguity, followed by a subtitle that is precise and matter of fact. When in the course of writing one idea or another for a title comes to mind, I jot those down on a piece of paper I keep in a drawer. My ultimate titles were sprung on me, as it were, in unexpected moments.

I spent the final year of working on my Einstein biography on leave at the Institute for Advanced Study in Princeton. As is my daily custom, I walk for an hour in the morning before settling down at my desk. One of these walks led me to Mercer Street. I was not far from the late Einstein's house when suddenly I stopped in my tracks and said out loud: "Subtle is the Lord," a quotation from Einstein himself.[6] I had found my title but still cannot explain how that came about at that time and at that place, which I can still pinpoint.

When I told the editor at Oxford University Press of my choice, he said: "It is a great title, a wonderful title. We can't use it." "What do you mean?" I asked, my temperature rising. "Well," he replied, "a book with a title like that will end up on the stores' religion shelves." I shot back: "So what? That will mean selling even more books." The long and short of it was that he gave in and now agrees wholeheartedly with my choice. (By the way, sales have been good: so far a quarter of a million copies in ten languages.)

When I have a manuscript in hand at the ninety percent level, I allow myself to turn to a fun part of the work: choosing the illustrations. I have been singularly fortunate to have access to many sources for all of my books.

When I had come to that point with my Einstein biography, I went to see Helen Dukas, the late Einstein's secretary and housekeeper, in her little office at the top floor of the Institute for Advanced Study's Fuld Hall. "Helen," I said to her, "I need your help once again, but now for something else. I need photographs." Whereupon she opened her desk drawer, took out a small key, handed it to me, and said: "Do you see that big suitcase standing over there in the corner?" Yes, I did. "Put it down flat and open it," she said. I did so and was stunned. There before me lay hundreds of photographs. That morning and the next I sat on the floor of Helen's office, going through them one by one, accompanied by her illuminating commentary, and selecting a number of those that in my opinion were not only among the best but had also either rarely or never been published. I put aside some twenty items, then asked Helen for permission to borrow them for some days, to show them to my editor. She let me do so. The final decision fell on twelve for the book, including such items as Einstein with Charlie Chaplin; Einstein near the Grand Canyon wearing an Indian feather headdress and holding a calumet; Einstein and his sister Maja; Einstein sitting at the induction ceremony for U.S. citizenship wearing a neat suit and tie but no socks; and more.

One in particular caught my fancy. It was taken in 1931, in California, by a photographer from one of the Hollywood studios. It shows Einstein wearing a Panama hat presented to him when his ship had made a stop in Balboa, in the Panama Canal Zone. He is looking heavenward, clearly comfortable. I always call this photograph the butterfly picture, associating his intent stare with that of someone following those little creatures. I decided on the spot that this one was ideally suited for the dust jacket. I asked and received Helen's permission to take this sepia picture to Bloomingdale's in New York for reproduction. One exemplar now hangs in my New York office, another is in the entrance hall of the home of my good friend Sam Treiman.

As far as I know, the suitcase with photographs is now at the Hebrew University in Jerusalem.

31.6 'SUBTLE IS THE LORD,' CONTINUED

31.6.1 The Jerusalem Symposium

I return to the year 1979 of the Einstein centennial. Right after the Princeton celebrations I took off for Jerusalem, where another memorial symposium was to be held on March 14–23. On March 12 I landed in Athens, to go from there to Israel. We took off for Ben Gurion Airport but had to turn back after forty-five minutes of flight. It turned out that Carter was in Jerusalem to negotiate with Begin on what was soon to be known as the Camp David Accord, and that the airport near Tel Aviv would be closed until after his departure. After some waiting we tried again, successfully this time although, as it turned out, Carter was still in Jerusalem when we arrived. After settling in, I strolled over to the King David Hotel, where he was staying, but found the surroundings barricaded. I caught a glimpse of the two leaders, however, as they drove by in a large cortège. I heard on the evening news that Carter would leave the next day.

The meetings opened on the evening of March 14, Einstein's actual birthday, with a ceremonial session in the Jerusalem Theatre. The program included an address by Isaiah Berlin and music performed by Isaac Stern with the Israel Chamber Orchestra. The next morning the regular program began with a session, which I chaired, devoted to historical perspectives on Einstein's scientific contributions.[7]

There were official receptions by Teddy Kollek, the beloved mayor of Jerusalem, and by Yitzhak Navon, Israel's president from 1970 to 1983. In my New York office hangs a picture of that last event, showing yours truly explaining to Navon how to run the country. On the morning of March 20, an Einstein plaque was unveiled on Albert Einstein Square, in front of the Israel Academy of Sciences and Humanities. On that occasion I met Elizabeth Einstein (née Roboz), the widow of Einstein's older son Hans Albert, not one of the most pleasant ladies I have ever met.

The meetings were devoted not only to scientific issues, but also included reports on other areas of culture where Einstein's impact had been felt. Correspondingly, among those attending were renowned non-physicists. I remember in particular a long talk I had with Gershom Scholem, the famous scholar of the Kabbalah and of Jewish mysticism. I had read some of his books and was deeply impressed by his personality.

On my return I found an Einstein centenary volume waiting for me, a book to which I had contributed a short essay on "Einstein, Newton and Success,"[8] which, in turn, was included in a long paper[9] that came out in October, a considerably extended version of my Princeton talk.[10] In April I went to Washington twice to lecture on Einstein, first at the Smithsonian Institution, then at a ceremonial meeting of the American Physical Society.

31.6.2 Browsing in Zurich, Berne, and Jena

In June I went to CERN, and from there made a side trip to Zurich to visit the library of the Elektrotechnische Hochschule, which houses several unique Einstein documents. Another excursion brought me to Berne, to visit Kramgasse 49, Einstein's house in 1905, where he had written his explosive series of papers that had marked the beginning of his rise to fame. Then my life quieted down, and I could work full time on my planned book.

When I was far along, the question came to my mind whether it would not be a good idea to sketch progress in general relativity, Einstein's greatest contribution, from the time he developed it in 1915 to the present. I knew that this part of physics had become a very lively area of research only after Einstein's death in 1955, mainly because of great experimental advances in radioastronomy and X-ray astronomy. In 1963 quasars had been discovered, and in 1965 a radiation (the so-called three-degree radiation) that gave experimental evidence for the big bang theory of the origin of the universe. Pulsars were first seen in 1967. The existence of black holes had first been suggested in the 1930s but "these exotic objects remained a textbook curiosity until the 1960s, when the combined efforts of radio and optical astronomers began to reveal a great many strange new things in the sky."[11] There had been major theoretical advances as well, mainly in the application of general relativity to cosmology.

I had followed all these developments, but not as a specialist. I knew of several good books that could be helpful to me but felt that that was not enough. I wanted in addition to attend a major conference on these subjects to give me up-to-date impressions of what my esteemed colleagues were up to.

That brought me to Jena in East Germany, where in June an international conference code-named GR 9 (GR = general relativity) took place. The growth of this field is demonstrated by the fact that this meeting was attended by about eight hundred participants from fifty-three countries. All through the meeting I sat silently, made notes, and learned about all the topics listed above, and also about the status of the search for gravitational waves. While I did not participate at all during the sessions, I talked a good deal with the experts afterward. These stimulating experiences enabled me to write the chapter "The New Dynamics" for my book.[12]

The only recollections from the city of Jena I have are of large, gaudy, red banners inscribed with inane communist slogans, which I saw hanging from buildings everywhere. I do remember well, however, our excursion to Weimar, twelve miles northwest of Jena, the intellectual center of Germany in the late eighteenth and early nineteenth centuries, for many years the residence of Johann von Goethe and Friedrich von Schiller, the city that gave its name to the republic of Germany founded in 1919, because it was there that its constitution was signed. We walked through Weimar's narrow, winding, pretty streets, bordered by picturesque houses with high-pitched gables and roofs, and visited the Goethe National Museum, which had once been his home.

In the afternoon we visited nearby Buchenwald, at one time an infamous concentration camp, the remains of which are now a National Memorial, a place that brings back grim memories to many.

The way back brought me by train to East Berlin for a short visit. In the late afternoon I arrived at my hotel, a modern highrise built in impersonal Western style whose interior was luxurious, even by Western standards.

Everything had to be paid in dollars, including the *International Tribune* which was for sale in the lobby.

That evening I took a long walk along streets and historic places that up till then were familiar to me only by name: Unter den Linden, the Friedrichstrasse, the Brandenburger Tor. It was cool and drizzling when I arrived at Checkpoint Charlie—just the kind of weather to create the right atmosphere. It was a stirring moment to stand there, the neighborhood shrouded in half-darkness, the crossing area harshly lit. From East Berlin I flew to Amsterdam and from there back to New York.

31.6.3 Responses to the Einstein Biography

Physicists tend to be sparing, to put it mildly, in complimenting colleagues on their achievements. I was therefore amazed, even taken aback, when letters from them began to arrive soon after the book was out, expressing not only enthusiasm, but even gratitude for my work. My initial silent reaction was, maybe they are just kidding me. Letters from non-physicists also kept coming (they still do), from clergymen, lawyers, businessmen, the man in the street. It took me about a year before I could say to myself: you know, they mean it.

In the early 1980s I received several recognitions, most if not all stimulated by the publication of the Einstein biography.

In the fall of 1981 I was named the Detlev W. Bronk Professor at the Rockefeller University. The announcement said some friendly words about my physics career and ended by noting that the book on Einstein would be published in mid-1982.[13] Then in April 1983 I was elected to the American Philosophical Society, America's oldest learned academy, founded in 1743 by Benjamin Franklin. George Washington and John Quincy Adams were early members, as was the Marquis de Condorcet, the mathematician who was then perpetual secretary of the French Académie. When Thomas Jefferson, then the president of the United States, was informed of his election also as president of the Society, he wrote, on January 28, 1797: "The suffrage of a body, which comprehends whatever the American world has of distinction in philosophy and science in general, is the most flattering incident of my life, and that to which I am the most sensible." The Society is housed in a part of Independence Hall in Philadelphia, where I attended numerous meetings. On one such occasion I remarked to an older member that I found those gatherings to be friendly and relaxed, never noticing any one-upmanship so common in academic circles. He smiled and replied: "Well, you see, to be elected you have to be so smart that there is no need to show that afterward."

That April was a busy month. I was also Loeb Lecturer at Harvard,[14] and received the American Book Award for biography. The award was presented on April 28 at the New York Public Library. I made the following brief acceptance speech:

> When somebody once told Einstein how modest one of his colleagues was, he replied: "Why should that man be modest? He has not achieved that much." Mindful of this story, which perhaps is true and certainly could be true, I cannot be modest on this festive evening. Having exquisite taste, I cannot be arrogant either. Therefore I would only like to say that, for a man whose professional language is mathematics and whose native tongue is Dutch, it is a moving experience to be deemed worthy of the American Book Award. I am honored and grateful.

In October 1983 I received the American Institute of Physics–United States Steel writing award in physics and astronomy.

Finally I note that, as of now, translations have appeared in Brazil,[15] and in the Chinese,[16] French,[17] German,[18] Italian,[19] Japanese,[20] Portuguese,[21] Russian,[22] and Spanish[23] languages.

31.6.4 Einstein Lived Here

Twelve years after the publication of 'Subtle is the Lord,' I published another book on Einstein, this one entitled *Einstein Lived Here*.[24] This title is copied from a marvelous cartoon by Herblock which also serves as the frontispiece of the book.

A number of reasons led me to write once again about the man. First, material had surfaced that had not yet been available in 1982, when my earlier book on Einstein was concluded, notably that he had an illegitimate daughter by the woman who later became his first wife, a fact that entered the public domain only in 1986. In that year, a number of high school classmates of Edward Einstein published a collection of reminiscences about this younger son of Einstein's who had become manifestly schizophrenic just after their years of close contact with him. This book has so far been published only in German. Also of recent vintage are publications in which it is alleged that Einstein's first wife played an important role in his formulation of relativity theory.

Second, as I browsed further in the Einstein archives in Boston as well as in Jerusalem, I found items which I had not dealt with before. For example, there was what Einstein has called "die komische Mappe," the funny folder, a collection of a variety of letters from others, from congratulatory notes to requests for help or additional information to thoughtful comments to lunatic utterances to expressions of hate, and threats. I also found documents dealing with his contacts with the Indian poet Rabindranath Tagore and with Mohandas Gandhi.

Finally, it had become evident to me already in the course of writing my previous book that the worldwide nature of Einstein's renown was the result of the attention he had received from the media. The thought had occurred to me already then that it might be quite illuminating to explore this press coverage even more fully. Accordingly I had, every now and then during the following ten years, delved into newspaper and magazine archives, beginning with microfilm of the *New York Times* from 1919, the year in which Einstein made his first appearance in that newspaper of record, until the present. By the late 1980s, many hours of searching had produced some fifty sheets of tightly handwritten notes.

Meanwhile, I had become convinced that I should try to extend this material as far back in Einstein's life as possible and also try to make efforts at obtaining clippings from the foreign press. With wonderful help from local spies I found out that as early as 1902 Einstein had made his first appearance in a newspaper. Fascinating tidbits emerged from Swiss, Czech, and German dailies—the countries where Einstein had held academic positions prior to his coming to the United States; also from newspapers in Austria, Britain, France, Holland, Palestine, and Spain, countries he had visited. This motley collection of topics, and more, was assembled into a series of essays that form the content of *Einstein Lived Here.*

31.6 INWARD BOUND

I return to the year 1982, when *'Subtle is the Lord'* was published.

Having written at length about relativity, I was prepared to return to my earlier project, the history of physics at the turn of the century, since now readers could turn to my Einstein book for the specific subject of relativity. This I did, extending the period covered from 1895 to 1983. Another four years of hard labor resulted in my next book, the one I personally like best.

Once again, its title appeared to me out of nowhere. I never read newspapers in the morning—I find it too distracting. When I come home around 5 P.M. I make tea and settle down with the *New York Times.* One day, I had the paper in my hands, reading an article on I do not recall what, when suddenly I looked up and said out loud: "Inward bound." Again I still do not have a clue why that happened then and there.

Having decided that that was it, the following thoughts began to trouble me. If someone else used that title before, can I then legally use it again? Should I use it again? I found out that one can request a title search by the Library of Congress in Washington, D.C., by just writing there, enclosing a check for ten dollars. I did so, and after a while received an answer. Yes, the title had been used before, in 1938, as the title of a short play reproduced in a book. I called the woman in Washington who had signed the letter, thanked her for her help, and asked if I was legally permitted to use that title again. Her reply was illuminating: book titles cannot be copyrighted. That I had not known. I asked her next: "Does that mean I can use anything I like for a title?" She replied, "Yes, indeed you can, though you might run into some problems if you were to choose a title like 'Gone with the Wind.'"

Selecting pictures for *Inward Bound* caused me some problems. The book deals with so many personalities, so whom should I choose for a picture gallery? It also deals with so many photogenic pieces of apparatus and laboratory sites. Again, which to choose? I simply could not make up my mind and ultimately chose a way out which perhaps was too easy: none of the above. As a result the book has no pictures at all.

Except for one on the dust jacket. One day I received my copy of the CERN *Courier,* opened it and there saw, without a moment's doubt, the picture I had vaguely been looking for. It shows a piece of fairly abstract metal sculpture, depicting a man playing a cello. In the background one sees an enlarged photograph of a set of particle tracks as seen in a bubble chamber. (This ensemble had for some time been on exhibit in CERN.) This combination expressed to me what an ancient poet has called the music of the spheres. That was it. A copy now hangs in my study on our farm in Denmark.

31.7 *Niels Bohr's Times. First Appearance of Ida*

The writing of *Inward Bound* had tired me out, especially the last chapter, which alone had taken me four months of arduous study. Moreover, divorce procedures regarding my second marriage had begun at the time the book was finished. Medical examinations revealed that I was pretty run down physically. Rest was urgently prescribed.

Joshua was greatly concerned when I told him of the state of my health, and suggested that we two take off for some vacation in the sun and near beaches. I was moved by his response and proposed that we find a country neither of us had ever visited as a place of rest and recreation. We settled on the Algarve (from the Arabic "Al Gharb," land of the West), at the southern shore of Portugal.

First, however, I had to spend a week in Oxford to talk business with my publishers. I arrived there on July 21, 1985. The next days were largely devoted to matters concerning my forthcoming book. I found time for some diversions, however, notably to attend a concert in the Sheldonian, and to read a good bit—*Brideshead Revisited* and the memoirs of Robert Browning, from which I copied a line from his comment on his poem "Sordello": "When I wrote it God and I knew what it is about. Now God only knows." A week later Joshua arrived in Oxford. I showed him the sights, the college courts, tea at the Randolph, the Bodleian Library, evensong at Christ Church. One evening we were invited to dinner at the high table in St. John's College. I took delight in the brevity of grace: *benedictus benedicatus,* let what is to be blessed be blessed; after the meal, *benedicti benedicatur,* what had to be blessed having been blessed. At dinner a sociologist told me that Pais means petticoat in Welsh, derived from the Latin *pexa.* A week later we enjoyed our vacation at the Algarve and I returned home reinvigorated.

Having sufficiently recovered, I began to think about what to do next, after *Inward Bound.* Since I had been in close contact with Bohr during the last sixteen years of his life and had become good friends with his wife and sons, it was natural to consider doing a biography of him; in fact, many friends and colleagues had urged me to do so. I was reticent, however. The subject had great appeal to me but would demand that I spend considerable time in Copenhagen, in and by itself a pleasant prospect were it not that I was single again. Given that situation I had many reservations about spending a long period abroad by myself.

One month later, all such gloomy thoughts had vanished, when my life had taken a most unexpected, marvelous turn.

Danish colleagues had organized an international meeting to commemorate the centenary of Niels Bohr's birth on October 7, 1985. Invitations had been sent to all surviving members of the old guard, to which I now belonged. Of those, some of the major figures had since passed away: Heisenberg, Kramers, Pauli, Dirac, others.

I spent a week in Copenhagen. Festivities began on the evening of October 3 with two commemorative lectures at Det Kongelige Dansk Videnskabernes Selskab, the Royal Danish Academy of Sciences and Letters.[25] The next morning, the three-day centenary symposium began, held in the lecture hall of the Panum Institute, close to the Bohr Institute. On the afternoon of that first day we were invited to a reception at Copenhagen's Town Hall, where I had been assigned the task of giving a brief speech on behalf of the symposium's participants. The meetings were largely devoted to current developments in physics, which was in Bohr's own spirit. It has been written of him: "However great a scientist he was, he was even a rarer phenomenon as a noble character."[26] I could have wished that that second aspect of the man had been better illuminated in those proceedings.

Evenings were filled with official receptions here and there, except for the evening of October 6. The senior local physicists had decided to divide the guests from abroad into groups of about ten, each of which was to be invited that free evening to one or another of their homes for supper and some hours together afterward. I had been chosen by Stefan Rozental and his wife, Hanna, friends of mine ever since my Copenhagen days as a young postdoc. I was bushed when I returned to my little hotel room that afternoon and felt much more inclined to take off my shoes, stretch out on my bed, and read a novel than to go out again. I went all the same, of course, since it would have been most discourteous to be absent. Never has my virtue been so richly rewarded.

As I was told later, on the morning of that day Hanna had called a younger friend of hers, Ida Nicolaisen, who was in her country home on Lolland, the southernmost of the Danish islands. She told her about the party that evening and asked if she could possibly come and help. As I found out afterward, Ida was also tired and had hoped to spend a few restful days in the country, but felt that she could not refuse to assist her much older friend. So it came about that both she and I came to the Rozental party somewhat against our wishes.

I shall leave for the last chapter the story of Ida's and my blessed union, but needed to introduce her here to indicate how it came about that, from shortly after that party on, I came to live roughly half my life in Denmark. It was not the most important consequence of that turn of events that I was now in an ideal situation for starting a Bohr biography, which I began in August 1986 on my return to Copenhagen, yet I am not sure if I would have undertaken that enterprise if I had not met Ida.

The first task I set myself was to delve into Bohr's background. I found out that he was fifth-generation Danish from his father's side and descended from a German soldier who in 1770 had settled in Helsingør (Elsinore), where he became a gardener. Following the line of descent I learned that his father had been the first to pursue an academic career, in medicine, was rector of Copenhagen University for two years, and was nominated for (but did not receive) a Nobel Prize, in 1907 and 1908. From his mother's side he was a descendant of a wealthy banker's family of Anglo-Jewish origin. His maternal grandfather had been cofounder of major Danish banks that exist to this day, and had been a member of Parliament, first of the Folketing (Lower House), then of the Landsting (Upper House). Nothing of this had been known to me earlier, nor had I been aware that Niels had had not only a younger brother, Harald, but also an older sister, Jenny.

I went to the homes and houses where Bohr had lived: to the palatial residence of his maternal grandparents at Ved Stranden, where he was born; to the professorial apartment on Bredgade, where he grew up; to Nærumgaard, an estate ten miles north of Copenhagen, acquired by his maternal grandfather, where he spent summers (it is now a home for under-privileged children); to the school on Toldbodgade (now an office build-ing), where he had stayed until the end of high school; to Garnisonskirken, the church where he was baptized when he was six (he left the Lutheran church at age twenty-seven). I became familiar with sources of information that were new to me, such as *Kirkebøger* (church records), and the *Borgerlig Vielsesbog* of Copenhagen, a record of civil marriages. Studies like these contributed in important ways to familiarize me with Danish history and culture. Moreover, I came to know (and write) of the growth of physics in Denmark, from a fifteenth-century college for the clergy to modern times; and of the history of the Danish nation from the 1864 war with Prussia until after the Second World War.

As the work went on, I also realized how limited my knowledge of Bohr's activities had been earlier. A composite picture began to emerge of a life so full and dedicated that one wonders how a single individual could have accomplished so much. First of all, of course, I developed a grasp of all his contributions to physics, but now I also came to understand Bohr as a philosopher, administrator of his Institute, fund-raiser, catalyst in promoting physical applications to biology, helper of political refugees, cofounder of international physics institutes and of the nuclear power projects in Denmark.

Finally, I should mention Bohr's main concern during the last twenty years of his life, his service in a noble cause which, in his lifetime, never received the public attention it deserved: his ceaseless striving for political understanding and openness between East and West.

On October 24, 1957, I was in Washington, D.C., to attend a ceremony in which Bohr was honored with the first Atoms for Peace Award. The closing line of the award citation is the most succinct and eloquent characterization of Bohr I have seen:

> In your profession, in your teaching, in your public life, you have shown that the domain of science and the domain of the humanities are in reality of single realm. In all your career you have exemplified the humility, the wisdom, the humaneness, the intellectual splendor which the Atoms for Peace Award would recognize.

It took me five years to write Bohr's biography. When I was almost finished I began to think of a title. This caused me trouble. For a while I had in mind to use "Niels Bohr, Father of the Atom." As the manuscript began to take shape, I realized that this title would illuminate only one of the book's several central themes. I did retain the above title for a chapter, however. Next I came up with "Niels Bohr, Father of the Atom, Pioneer of Glasnost," in order to include Bohr's concern with an open world. Several of my friends pointed out to me that "glasnost" might become a forgotten word—no one could prophesy whether Gorbachev's wonderfully bold initiative would long survive. How right they were. Out with glasnost, but once again used in a chapter title. As I came to the late stages of my book I finally understood Bohr's importance as a philosopher. Then it all became clear: Use *Niels Bohr's Times* as the title, end it with a comma, and continue with a subtitle: *In Physics, Philosophy, and Polity.* That last word once again came to me out of nowhere. I immediately liked it, and not only because it would send many of my future readers to a dictionary. When I submitted this title to my editor for his opinion, he stared at it, then looked up and said: "Polity . . . h'm, not bad for a Dutchman."

The way to the pictures for my Bohr biography was much like that for the case of Einstein. This time I put my request for photographs to another good friend, Hilde Levi, who works in the Bohr archive in Copenhagen and is in charge of the photo collection, among other things. Hilde took me to some bookshelves on which stand more than thirty photo albums. Choosing was a pleasure. Again I sought out pictures that had never been published—some family shots, some of Bohr with other prominent people, Heisenberg, Dirac, the Danish and British royal families, Ben-Gurion, Martin Buber, Louis Armstrong, others. I also included a famous Bohr cartoon by the renowned Danish artist Bo Bøjesen.

One picture of the thirty-three that appear in the book came from elsewhere. I knew that Bohr and his great mentor, the New Zealander Ernest Rutherford (later Lord Rutherford of Nelson), had first met at a festive dinner in the Cavendish Laboratory in Cambridge, England. So I wrote to my friend Sir Sam Edwards, the current director of the laboratory, asking him if there existed any mementos he knew of from that occasion. He responded by sending me a copy of the printed menu for that dinner, along with the texts of some jolly songs rendered as the evening progressed. Then I saw the gem: on the back of the menu someone had collected the signatures of all those present. The list, which includes the names of Bohr, Rutherford, and J. J. Thomson, is proudly reproduced for the first time in my book.

Finally there came the choice of a picture for the dust jacket. Brooding over that one, I suddenly remembered the photograph, taken by a professional, that to this day hangs in "Auditorium A" of the Niels Bohr Institute, the lecture hall famous for the splendid physics conferences held there in Bohr's lifetime. With permission, I took the picture from the wall and had an expert reproduce the photo which now graces the cover of the book.

31.8 THE LONELINESS OF WRITING

Writing books is a delicious but painful undertaking. As has often been said, it is the loneliest of professions. My own way of minimizing the years-long sense of isolation is to send a copy of each chapter separately to a few readers, right after it is all finished. Thus Sam Treiman of Princeton saw all chapters of all my books right away. As did Res Jost in Zurich. These were my closest friends (Res has since passed away, in 1990), quite interested in what I was doing and unsparing in their criticisms, just the ideal combination for critical reviewers.

Last but not least, I have had the enormous benefit of a patient and critical listener in my dear wife, Ida.

32

My Final Years—So Far

IN PRECEDING chapters I have written of my beginnings—a carefree youth followed by grim days of war—in Holland. Whereafter I have given an account of how I established a new base in the United States, that dynamic, sometimes crass, but always wonderful nation, of which I am now a citizen—where I made my career, and to which, to this day, I have a strong sense of belonging.

Never, in all my American years, did I lose touch with my roots, however. Countless are the trips I have made to Europe in the past fifty years, always comfortable to be there, always comfortable to return. That was my rhythm until, in 1985, I found, along with my home in New York, a second home in Copenhagen.

It was in 1991, now four years ago, that I started writing of my experiences during the Second World War. As, at that time, I began sorting out my recollections of those past years, I was forcefully struck by the disparity between those days and my present life. By way of counterpoint it appeared sensible to me to start my memories of the war days with a brief comment on my present life. This I did in what became the opening pages of chapter 9, where I noted that witnesses are less concerned with the past than with a sense of that past in the present. As I put it there: "I cannot think of a greater contrast than that between my present life, so full of happiness and contentment, and those years of the past, so full of suffering and sorrow." I wrote those lines in Copenhagen, sitting "at my desk . . . feeling at peace with myself and the world, turbulent though it is today."

That state of grace is due above all else to the presence in my life of Ida, whose full name is Agnes Ida Benedicte Nicolaisen. But after 1991 my life was even more enriched. I have acquired a lovely daughter-in-law, Lisa Emery. I am now the grandfather of a wonderful little boy, Zane Abraham. That is still not all, however. Ida has brought along her large family into my life: her mother, two sisters and their husbands and children, and a brother. I am the oldest male of that entire clan and therefore have become its patriarch.

I turn now to the main topic of this chapter, my personal story of the years 1985 to the present.

32.2 IDA

They who another keep
Alive, ne'er parted be.
—JOHN DONNE

In the preceding chapter (sec. 31.2) I mentioned, but only in passing, how on October 6, 1985, I came to meet Ida, and how that encounter led to our marriage. Briefly postponing what happened to us in the next five years, I turn to the month of March 1990, when Ida and I sent the following announcement to our family and friends:

> To all Friends to whom these Presents shall come,
> Greeting.
> Having for years happily lived together in sin,
> we are even happier to announce that on
> March 15, 1990, we were married at the
> South Rim of the Grand Canyon.

To which we added our names and our Copenhagen and New York addresses.

On the following June 9, Ida and I had one hundred guests for dinner at Kongekilden (the King's Well), an old Copenhagen restaurant. On that occasion I gave the following after-dinner speech:

> It has been said that the life of a man passes through three stages. In the first, a woman can make a man very happy or very unhappy. That is youth. In the second, a woman can make a man very happy. That is middle age. In the third, a woman can no longer make a man very happy. That is old age.
>
> My own life has been rather different. Middle age came late and, though one day my life must end, I shall never pass through old age.

That, dearest Ida, will, I think, be your fate as well, as is expressed in Shakespeare's 104th sonnet, from which I quote.

[Pull piece of paper out of my pocket.]

"Let me not to the marriage of true minds
Admit impediments."

Oops! Wrong, that is sonnet 116.

[Pull out other piece of paper.]

"Let not my love be called idolatry.
Nor my beloved as an idol show."

Wrong again! That is 105. Ah, here it is.

"To me, fair friend, you never can be old,
For such as you were when first your eye I eyed,
Such seems your beauty still."

If I had to characterize Ida's and my own life together in one word, I would choose "harmony." It is and remains astonishing to us that we have so much in common in spite of different backgrounds and upbringing. We know of each other's past joys but also of past sorrows. In particular, Ida has told me much about Johannes Nicolaisen, her first husband.[1] I never knew him personally but from Ida's accounts I have vivid impressions of a man whom I would have liked and respected very much.

I first proposed marriage to Ida after having known her for only two weeks. She was pleased but noncommittal. Thereafter I proposed to her about once a month, but without a firm response. I soon realized, however, that she very much liked being proposed to.

So it continued until the summer of 1989, when she accepted.

Then we were faced with new problems.

Should we be married in a synagogue or in a Lutheran church? While we highly respect each other's religious background, we felt that neither would do for us. And where should we be married? In Copenhagen? Then we would miss our family and good friends from New York and environs. In New York? Then we would miss our family and good friends from Denmark.

Then Ida hit upon a brilliant idea: we elope. So it came to pass that on March 15, 1990, shortly after two o'clock in the afternoon, we were married at the South Rim of the Grand Canyon by Judge James J. Sedillo. It was a brief, beautiful ceremony, ending with the judge reciting marriage prayers of American Indians.

Of course we wished also to share our happiness with friends, so it came about that on April 9 we gave a dinner party at the Knickerbocker Club in New York for our family and closest American friends. So it has also come about that on this evening, we celebrate not only Ida's fiftieth birthday— which will be tomorrow—but also, with all of you here, our recent marriage.

I cannot recite here, dear Ida, all the ways in which you have enriched my life, but will single out just one. You have brought along to me your family and a large circle of friends. Nearly all of them are here. So this is an excellent opportunity for me to thank you, all of you, for the warmth with which you have received me in your midst.

Whatever else I could say of you, Ida, is once again written in a Shakespearean sonnet, the 84th:

"Who is it that says most which can say more
Than this rich praise—that you alone are you?
But he that writes of you if he can tell
That you are you, so dignifies his story.
Let him but copy what in you is writ.
Not making worse what nature made so clear.
And such a counterpart shall fame his wit,
Making his style admired everywhere."

At a moment like this one wonders what the future will have in store. That reminds me of a story. A visitor to Washington, D.C., was riding in a cab along Pennsylvania Avenue when he noticed at the back of the National Archives building a statue of a seated woman holding an open book on her lap. He was puzzled by the inscription on the statue's base: WHAT IS PAST IS PRO-LOGUE. What does that mean, he asked his cab driver. To which the cabbie replied: "You ain't seen nothing yet."

Among Ida's ancestors—which she can trace back to the seventeenth century—one finds farmers, priests, marine officers, and civil servants. Her father, who died before we met, was the governor of Ribe.[2] A brother of his, an ethnographer, participated in expeditions to Afghanistan and Nuristan. At the beginning of this century, Ida's mother's father was governor of South Greenland. He had named a fjord he had discovered after one of Ida's uncles. We count several Greenlanders among our friends, also the Danish Greenland explorer who owns the world's northernmost house. In 1863 one of Ida's great-grandfathers, an industrialist, saw to it that Copenhagen became one of the first European cities to acquire horse-drawn streetcars. A brother of her great-great-grandfather was governor of St. Croix, one of the Virgin Islands, which were Danish at that time.

Ida is now an associate professor of anthropology at the University of Copenhagen. She has done substantial fieldwork. She accompanied her first husband, who was Denmark's first professor of anthropology, to Chad and to the Sahara to study the Tuareg tribe. In the course of these expeditions she became an accomplished camel rider. Her main interest is in a small tribe in Borneo, however, with whom she has spent three years in all, counting together the rather shorter stretches of time. (More about that later.)

Ida is currently the chief editor of a twelve-volume series of books on nomadic studies conducted by Danes since the middle of the nineteenth century. She herself has published on a variety of anthropological topics, for which she has received several awards. On November 16, 1989, she gave the traditional scientific lecture, on *Kulturens Gave* (the gift of culture), at the annual celebration of the founding of the University of Copenhagen, the first woman in that institution's 510-year-long history to be chosen for that honor.

Ida has traveled extensively in Africa as adviser to Danida, a Danish government organization aiming to support developing nations. She is a member of numerous boards, including the World Wide Fund for Nature, and of the Foundation of Crown Prince Frederick, for which she selects candidates for travel grants for academic studies. That last membership led to her being named, in 1995, Knight of the Order of Dannebrog, whereafter she was received in audience by Queen Margrethe II to express the traditional thanks for that honor. On that occasion the two women, who know each other well (they were born in the same year), spent some time chatting amiably.

Having now properly introduced my dear wife, I turn to the period from the day we met to the time we married.

I return again to October 6, 1985, the evening when Ida and I first met at a party for foreign guests at the Niels Bohr centennial.

It was an informal buffet dinner, where you filled your plate and found a place to sit. Ida and I came to be seated next to each other. We started talking. After some ten minutes I had the unusual experience of knowing nothing about the woman at my side yet sensing that I understood who she was. Even stranger, she knew nothing about me but I felt that she understood me perfectly as well.

Returning to my little hotel that evening, I went for a walk around

Copenhagen's town square, pondering about the beautiful and highly intelligent lady I had met. I wanted to see her again but had only one day left in Denmark. Moreover, the afternoon was already filled with a festive meeting at the Great Hall of Copenhagen University—it was Bohr's actual birthday. So I had to be quick.

Early the next morning I called Ida at her home to invite her for lunch at the Angleterre, Copenhagen's finest hotel. I noticed her hesitation before she accepted.

We had lunch together and talked and talked. When we parted I told her: "You will hear from me." Then I went to the Great Hall and sat down, too filled with new feelings to hear a word of the speeches delivered. It was clear to me by now that a most important event had occurred in my life.

On my way back to New York I composed a long letter to her in which I made my feelings clear, but in a very guarded way. She was, I felt, a woman who should be treated with the utmost respect and should in no way be pushed. I mainly told her more about myself, making clear that I was in the process of getting divorced, that I had not at all been looking for a new companion, and that our encounter had been a complete and happy surprise to me. I ended by expressing my sentiments with the words "that I may hope."

I mailed the letter from New York and right away called Joshua to tell him that I had met a very wonderful woman. He was happily excited and kept calling me the following days to ask if I had heard further from her. Some weeks later Ida's reply arrived, telling me that my letter had confused her, also that she would be in New York the first week of December, where she would stay with friends and would attend meetings on foreign aid at the United Nations, in her function as consultant to Danida. She suggested that perhaps we could have dinner some evening that week. I called her up, saying that I would be quite delighted to see her in New York and that I would fetch her from the airport.

We saw much more of each other that week than just one dinner. We visited museums, ate together, and above all talked and felt comfortable together. At the end of her stay I proposed. As said, she was pleased but noncommittal.

Shortly after Ida's return I called her again in Denmark, suggesting that we spend the Christmas vacation together in New York. She thought that was a lovely idea but unfortunately she could not accept because she had to be in Borneo that time. Borneo? What did she have to do there? "I have to buy a tree." I was confounded and begged her to explain.

That may have been the first time I learned how, ever since 1973, she had spent considerable time with the Punan Bah, a small tribe of about fifteen hundred people who live in the rain forests of central Sarawak, and who had been headhunters until well into the twentieth century; how a colleague had suggested that they might be an interesting subject for anthropological study; how she had arrived in Long Bah, a settlement consisting of two longhouses built on stilts, homes to about four hundred people; how she came there for the first time without knowing a word of their language—of which meanwhile she has composed the only extant dictionary—which belongs to the Malayo-Polynesian language group; how initially she was helped by a Punan Bah girl who knew English; how they took to her and how she came to be adopted as a sister in one of the families.

What about the tree?

The principal mode of transportation of the tribe is over a river by means of long canoes of a type now no longer used in Borneo. Ida had decided to invite an expert canoe builder from the tribe to come to Denmark with his wife and a nephew, to build a canoe in the Viking ship museum in Roskilde, where the process was to be filmed. Ritual demanded that a Bornean tree be used, cut down following complex ceremonies, whereafter it had to be shipped to Denmark. So there.

Through the later years, Ida has continued to tell me about the little tribe from the rain forest. During my own many travels I have learned much about other cultures but never of one so utterly distinct from our own. My genuine interest in Ida's work and hers in mine are a continuing source of mutual respect and stimulation in our lives.

The next time Ida and I met was in February 1986, when I paid my first (two months') visit to her in Copenhagen. I shall never forget the first time I entered her home, a two-story villa in the part of Copenhagen called Frederiksberg. I was overwhelmed by its beauty, spaciousness, tasteful interior, and its lovely garden. Never in my life had I been offered so much, including a beautiful study all my own. In the beginning I would call that house "your" home. Right away Ida would correct me: it is "our" home. It took me quite a while to get used to that.

And there was more. Ida also owned a farmhouse dating from the seventeenth century which she wanted to show me. It lies in a hamlet called Tågense, a hundred miles south of Copenhagen, on Lolland, the southernmost island of the Danish archipelago. Shortly after my arrival in Copenhagen we drove there.

Once again I was overwhelmed, to see this lovely one-story house with its thatched roof and its comfortable rooms with low ceilings, in old-fashioned Danish style. Two hundred yards behind it lies the Baltic Sea. Depending on the season, one sees seals sunning themselves on rocks in the water, masses of swans, birds of many other kinds, especially during the migration seasons, partridges nesting on the land. In springtime we hear nightingales sing in the evenings. Fruit trees surround the house— apples, pears, mirabelles. Eight acres of arable land go with the house. Animals abound there; deer, hares, ducks, partridges, sheldrakes. The land is rented to a farmer who lives nearby, at a low rate but with the understanding that he and his family keep an eye on the house in our absence, and that in wintertime they turn on the heat the day before we arrive. A few years later we sent out Christmas cards showing me on a combine, helping with the harvest.

The Lolland landscape is undramatic but of a beautiful serenity which I have grown to love very much. Most of our neighbors are farmers, with whom I have become friends. They have their own kind of wisdom, stemming from living a life so different from mine. I love to talk with them and be edified by their stories.

To complete the tale of my private spaces, I note that I go to the Niels Bohr Institute every working day I am in Denmark. I now have my own office in the Niels Bohr Archive with my name on the door. So now I have, in all, five offices: at home and at the Rockefeller University in New York, and at our two homes and the Bohr Institute in Denmark.

I shall next introduce another important creature: our dog. For many years, Ida has had one dachshund after another. The present one is Sidse, a female name of Danish origin. To have a dog was a new experience for me. I have become very attached to Sidse, a beautiful pedigreed animal, quite intelligent and with a will of her own, as, I am told, is typical for that breed. I take her for walks and have been assigned the task of feeding her. She travels with us from Europe to America and back. I cannot count the number of times she has crossed the Atlantic, always with great ease. Our home feels empty to us when she is not there.

In 1986 we also began to become acquainted with each other's circle of friends, Ida during two visits to New York. (I was unfortunately not present when her Punan Bah friends came to Denmark to build their canoe.) It was gratifying to us both to see how well my friends took to her, and hers to me. We began to give dinner parties for them in both countries. I take great pride in Ida's graciousness as hostess. In November we went to Philadelphia, where I introduced her to the members of the American Philosophical Society.

Most important to me is the way Ida has taken to Joshua. I interrupt my story about Ida to update my account of what has happened in my son's life.

32.3 JOSHUA'S CAREER, HIS MARRIAGE, AND HIS SON

At last mention, Joshua had just graduated from college in the spring of 1980 (chapter 30, sec. 30.3) and was now ready to face the realities of life as an actor. He was well aware that the going would be tough: interminable auditions, rarely a callback, even more rarely an acceptance. I have always admired my son for his persistence, not to be discouraged but to keep on trying in the face of many rejections.

Josh started his career in the customary way by taking roles in so-called showcases, in which actors perform without pay. In those early years he made his living by renovating brownstones, together with a small group of friends. That brought in enough to live on. As a concerned father, I would ask him off and on how he was doing financially, telling him that I would be glad to lend a hand when needed. He never took me up on that offer except once when, after a year of frugal living, he was offered two floors in a New York East Village brownstone. He permitted me to buy that space for him under the condition that this would be the last time I would help him that way. It was then that I saw him in action as a renovator in his new home, tearing out floors, walls, and ceilings, putting in new ones, installing new kitchens and bathrooms, rewiring the whole place. I was greatly impressed with the beautiful outcome.

Sometime thereafter, Joshua got a paying role in *Brecht on Brecht,* a play produced under the auspices of Actors' Equity, the actors' trade union. That allowed him to become a member of Equity, an important step forward. At this time the union has 37,000 members, of whom about fifteen percent are employed. Later he was also able to join the Screen Actors Guild, which now has 80,000 members, of whom only about ten percent are employed.

Now, slowly but steadily, his acting career took off. I remember seeing him in Maxim Gorky's *The Lower Depths,* in *Heart of a Dog,* an adaptation of a story by Mikhail Bulgakov, *in Short Change,* and in *Waco Woman,* a Circle Rep production, all off-Broadway productions. I also saw him play parts in major network TV series such as *Law and Order, Murphy Brown,*

The Cosby Show, and once in an interview on the Letterman show. His movies have been *Jackknife* and *Five Corners.*

Then came his big break, a role on Broadway in *I Am Not Rappaport,* the play that won the Emmy Award for best Broadway play of 1986.

In 1990 Josh and I went together to the New York world premiere of the movie *Teenage Mutant Ninja Turtles,* in which he played the role of Raphael, the chief turtle. I was a proud father as, after that show, I watched Joshua being interviewed by several TV networks. In the early nineties, the Ninja turtles were a tremendous hit with young people. People would often ask me if I was the father of the famous actor who played Raphael. Nothing made me happier than my son's success.

Meanwhile, Joshua has become interested in creating and developing his own style of play direction, landing him a teaching position at New York University. All told, he has done very well in a difficult profession.

In November 1986 Joshua invited Ida and me for Thanksgiving dinner. Lila (my first wife), who lived nearby, also came. At that time she was already terminally ill. She had asked to meet Ida, so Ida and I went to her home before dinner. After spending a while with the two women, I left them alone. Later Ida told me how much she had enjoyed that meeting and how they had had a long heart-to-heart discussion. When I asked her what they had talked about, she replied that that was none of my business, but I felt sure that Joshua was their main topic of conversation. At the end of the following December, Lila died.

Enter Lisa, whom Josh had met in 1982. She is an actress, a very good one. I have seen her often on stage, notably in the lead role in *Burn This* on Broadway, and in *Marvin's Room* and *Talley and Son,* off-Broadway, all of them good plays. From the start she and I got along famously. She is bright, beautiful, and has a wonderful sense of humor. I love her dearly and am proud of her. In 1989 Josh and Lisa bought some property in upstate New York, a bungalow with forty acres of land, all of which they have meanwhile beautified. I much enjoy my occasional visits there. Josh and Lisa had lived together for many years when, in August 1990, they followed Ida's and my example, eloped and got married, in California.

On the morning of September 22, 1990, Lisa entered Lenox Hill Hospital to give birth. At one o'clock that afternoon I installed myself in a waiting room there, in anticipation of the blessed moment. Joshua was with her in her room and would come out every once in a while to report progress to me. At one time he brought me a written message that said: "Dear Poppy, ooh shit fuck fuck, ouch shit, love, your lovely daughter-in-law." That note now hangs, framed, on a wall in my New York apartment.

Then, at eleven that evening, Josh came out, radiant, and said to me: "You have a grandson." We embraced, I wept with joy.

Long before Zane appeared, I had told Josh that if ever he had children he would be a very good father, in fact a better one than I because he would be more patient. And so he is, and Lisa is a fine mother. Zane is a healthy, bright, and sweet boy. He was talking already at age two, calling me Papa Bram. I glow every time he says that.

32.4 MY HAPPIEST YEARS

32.4.1 Our Lifestyle

Since Ida and I started our life together, not a day has passed on which I have not been astonished about my good luck to have met her and been accepted by her. Earlier I called our life harmonious. We are in fact delighted when an occasional minor dispute arises, since that gives us an opportunity to "fight." To this I should add further that our togetherness stimulates both of us, and this not only because we are intrigued by each other's work. She has given me a home in Europe, I gave one to her in America. Neither continent had been new to us (she had paid brief visits to the States before meeting me), but now we had roots in both places. It is our good fortune that we are fond of each country and find much to explore in both.

Our life in Denmark and in the States provides ideal opportunities for reflecting on their distinct strengths, especially when we are "in the other place." Thus Denmark's advantage of not being a world power adds greatly to the economic strength within its borders. Its small size leads to closer bonds between its people compared to America. We have learned to appreciate that the States derive their strength from cultural inhomogeneity, Denmark from its cultural homogeneity. Another contrast which has struck us concerns the degree of taxation: low in America, the highest in the world in Denmark, but compensated for by levels of free social services that are astoundingly generous by American standards.

Ida finds New York a better place than Copenhagen to get work done— "it is calmer" because she is less interrupted there, especially by the telephone. For the same reason, I prefer Copenhagen. She likes to cook—American style in New York, Danish in Copenhagen, though we also eat out once in a while. Some of our favorite spots are Karen Kik's Slotskælderen in Copenhagen, which to me is the world's best place for a lunch of smørrebrød (open sandwiches). As portraits on the walls show, it has been a preferred haunt of prime ministers and of the prince consort. In New York we enjoy the ethnic mix of the restaurants, and particularly like Sushi-Hatsu on First Avenue, around the corner from us, where you get the finest sushi I have ever tasted.

In Copenhagen we enjoy strolling through the pretty narrow streets of the old city, around Trinitatis, the old church we attend on Christmas Eve. On such walks I often notice how well known Ida is. This is largely due to her frequent appearances on a highly popular Danish quiz show. My favorite story is of the man who came up to her, doffed his hat, and said, "Madam, you are even more beautiful in real life than on TV," then walked on.

It demands some careful planning for us to be together, now here, now there. This problem simplified greatly when, in 1988, I became much more mobile because of my status of emeritus professor.

32.4.2 An Operation

In March 1988 I went to visit my doctor for my annual checkup. On such occasions I am usually told that all is in good order. But not this time. After the stethoscope examination the doctor looked worried and told me that he would call New York Hospital, across the street, where I should immediately go for an abdominal sonogram, wait for the pictures, then come right back with them. After my return he inspected the photographs, then told me it was just as he thought: I had a sizable aortic aneurysm with a large amount of thrombus inside. He told me next that I should undergo surgery immediately and proposed that he make the necessary arrangements. I told him that was impossible, since in a few days I would be leaving for Denmark, and I suggested that I be operated on there. He reluctantly concurred.

My principal reason for not wishing to change my travel plans was that it seemed inhuman to me just to pick up the phone to tell Ida what was going on. I felt that I had to do so face to face. So I continued my standard travel preparations, which always include a game of squash prior to departure—something that makes subsequent air travel more comfortable for me.

When, some months later, I told my New York doctor of that squash game, he declared that I had been quite mad to have done that in my physical state.

Upon arrival in Copenhagen, I waited one day before telling Ida, since I wished for her to see first that I was not on the point of falling apart. Nevertheless, she was shaken when I told her the next day. At once she called a medical friend who arranged that I would be operated on as soon as possible in the Rigshospital by Denmark's best specialist. As it turned out, all went well. The operation, standard procedure by now, was of rather recent origin. In the 1950s, an aneurysm had cost Einstein his life . . . .

I spent one week in the hospital. During one of these nights a nurse was startled to see me walking in a corridor, tubes hanging all around me. "Herr Pais, what are you doing?" she asked. "I have to go to the post office," I replied. She brought me back to my bed and reconnected the tubes. The next morning Ida told me of my excursion, about which she had heard from the nurse. To this day I have no personal recollection of that escapade. After leaving the hospital I spent another week resting at home, then went back to work. There have been no postoperative complications.

32.4.3 Retirement

On May 19, 1988, I turned seventy, the mandatory age of retirement, to go in effect as of the next July 1. Friends arranged a symposium in my honor, held at the Rockefeller University on May 13 and devoted to a retrospective review of current trends in particle physics. The speakers, all personal friends, represented a roster of the finest American particle physicists. In addition, Robert Merton, the distinguished social scientist, gave a fascinating talk about the genesis of the term "scientist."

At the conclusion of the program I thanked everyone for honoring me with their presence and expressed particular gratitude to the speakers: Treiman and Georgi, close friends and past coworkers; Lee and Yang, colleagues from the Princeton days; Fitch and Cronin, discoverers of CP-violation; Nick Samios, an ex-student of mine from my year's leave at Columbia University and now director of Brookhaven National Laboratory; David Gross, a colleague from Princeton University; and Martin Klein, the historian of science.

That evening, more than a hundred people attended a festive dinner at the Rockefeller University. Many speeches were made; I got up after each one to express thanks. I have only incomplete recollections of who spoke and what was said—with one exception. Tineke, my dear friend from the war days, attended as well (see chapter 10, sec. 10.5). Many guests wept as, in her quiet, unprepossessing way, she spoke of our war experiences, and so did I. At the end I spoke of my happiness to have my family with me that evening—Ida, Joshua and Lisa. I was quite tired when it was all over. It had been an emotional day for me and I was still feeling fatigue from my recent operation.

My years as professor had been good, but to be emeritus is paradise. Without interruption from administrative matters, I have been able to devote myself to writing, and to traveling with Ida.

32.4.4 Honors

When I was young, I craved recognition. Now that I have passed beyond the age of ambition, it still pleases me of course to receive tokens of esteem. It is perhaps just as well, however, that I no longer attach as much importance to honors as I did in earlier years. Yet a few still came my way.

In 1988 I was elected Foreign Member of the Royal Danish Academy of Sciences and Letters. In 1992 I was in Holland to receive the Physica Prize of the Dutch Physical Society, in recognition of my contributions "as historian-physicist and physicist-historian." Also in that spring I received a letter (in Dutch) stating that "Her Majesty the Queen has by her decree of May 11, 1992, appointed Professor Abraham Pais to Officer in the Order of Oranje Nassau." In 1993 I was presented with the Medal of Science of the Royal Dutch Academy of Sciences "for meritorious contributions to the arts and sciences in the Netherlands." In April 1994 I went to Washington, D.C., to be given the Gemant Award of the American Physical Society.

Most recently, in May 1995, I received the Lewis Thomas Prize, established by the trustees of the Rockefeller University, which recognizes "the scientist whose voice and vision can tell us of science's aesthetic and philosophical dimensions"—big words that would not be my choice to characterize my writings. On the day I received the award I gave a lecture, "On History, That Little Conjectural Science, That Great Art."

Two years earlier, on May 19, 1993, I was honored in a different and personally more meaningful way. On that day Ida had organized in our Copenhagen home the mother of all birthday parties to celebrate my seventy-fifth birthday. We were particularly happy that Josh and Lisa, heavily pregnant, had come over for the occasion. There was an afternoon reception for some hundred friends followed by a dinner for forty. It was a glorious spring day, much of which we spent in our garden. Among Ida's presents to me was a flying lesson, which I received some days later. I did not do well—I'll spare you the details.

32.5 Travels Together

Ida is a cheery and efficient travel companion, even more curious about new places than I am. Only rarely did we take off separately since we have been together, such as when Ida went to Borneo, Singapore, and Yemen, and I went to lecture in Karachi. Here is an account of our main joint trips.

32.5.1 Moscow. Meeting Sakharov

When I discussed with Ida my invitation from the Academy Sinica to lecture in China, she proposed that we go there by Transsiberian Railroad. I said that's a great idea. She did not yet know at that time that I have the habit of masking anxiety by enthusiasm. In this case, I was scared by the idea of being shut in a train for a week, away from my desk and papers.

First we flew from New York to Copenhagen, from where I called Sakharov's residence in Moscow. I got Yelena Bonner, his wife, on the phone, told her that I was a physicist colleague of her husband, and asked whether my wife and I might call on them in Moscow. "Wait," she said, then came back to the phone and, in her no-nonsense style, familiar to all who have met her, gave me a day and hour on which we could visit.

We spent two days in Moscow doing some sightseeing—to Red Square, where smoking is now forbidden, to the Kremlin, and to the Pushkin Museum with its fine Picasso collection. We spent hours acquiring our visas for Outer Mongolia. On the afternoon of the second day we went by taxi to Ulitza Chkalova, where the Sakharovs lived, showing the driver the address written on a piece of paper. When we arrived it turned out that their home was in a large complex with many entrances. I asked someone for Entrance B—no response. So it went a few times until a man asked, "Sakharov?" "*Da*," I replied. With a smile he led us to the correct entry. We went in, noting the dilapidated state of the hallways, then rang the doorbell. Yelena opened the door.

It was a most pleasant visit. Sakharov's English was poor, so we spoke in German. We talked animatedly of physics and of colleagues—no politics. I did not want to cause problems because his home might well be wired; moreover, I was certain we saw eye to eye about major issues anyway. I found Sakharov to be a serene person, with a soft, gentle voice. He showed no noticeable trace of bitterness for what he had been through.

Ida and Yelena conversed in English, at which our hostess was quite good, and the two women got along famously. After some time, the four of us came together for tea and a cake which Yelena had baked for the occasion. As we left, the women embraced warmly.

That evening around midnight we boarded the train for the six-day, 4,915-mile ride to Beijing.

32.5.2 A Physicist on the Transsiberian

There are two Transsiberian trains, one Russian, one Chinese. We had followed the advice to take the latter because, we were told, they are much cleaner. The dining room served Russian meals, however—nourishing, simple food.

Our compartment for two was small but cozy, one lower, one upper bunk bed, an easy chair, and a small table with a lamp. In the corridor a bulletin was posted marking place, time, and duration of stops, the latter to enable passengers to stretch their legs, which we did at fifteen stops, including Sverdlovsk in the Urals; Omsk, Novosibirsk, Krasnoyarsk, and Irkutsk in Siberia; and Ulan Bator in Mongolia.

My fears of claustrophobia turned out to be unfounded. The ride was a lesson in the enormous extent and emptiness of the former Soviet Union. The monotony of the landscape was curiously fascinating, varying from tundra to taiga, interrupted only by sporadic industrial centers. In Siberia we drove along Lake Baikal, the deepest (one mile) freshwater lake on earth; in Mongolia we saw occasional yurts, rode through the Gobi Desert. On our stop in Ulan Bator we saw vigorous, handsome Mongolians, women holding babies swaddled in bundles.

I learned physics on the Transsiberian from reading Richard Rhodes' excellent, nine hundred-page book on the making of the atomic bomb. Most interesting of all were the bonds created with fellow passengers. I was particularly struck by the facts that in this international and racial mix of people I turned out to be the only American on board, and that the fraction of young Europeans was so large. We would visit them in their compartments, they would come calling on us. We would ask them where they were going and staying, and were astonished by their replies. All were going to Beijing first, none had any ideas about lodging. That was no problem, they said, because they would simply go to the nearest big square, where they were sure to find other young people who would either take them in or else would help find others who would do so. Their plans for further travels in China ranged from stays of a few weeks to several months. In my own young days, I had belonged to the adventurous first generation of hitch-hikers in Europe. Today's youth impressed me by operating similarly, but on a global scale.

On entering Mongolia, the Russian dining car was replaced by a Mongolian one, with its own staff and cuisine, replaced in turn by a Chinese crew on entering China.

32.5.3 Chinese Sojourn

Throughout our stay in China we received VIP treatment; a car with driver was always at our disposal. We were of course grateful for such courtesies, even though that mode of transportation kept us at some distance from the people. More important in that respect was the language barrier, and the fact that we were not able to explore on our own. Therefore I cannot pontificate on the Chinese character and psyche. All I can say is that we invariably found those we met to be friendly and open.

The next day we went sightseeing, to Tiananmen Square, the Forbidden City, Beihai Park, and the Heavenly Temple—overwhelming experiences. The day thereafter I started lecturing, having, then and later, Chinese interpreters at my side who were not always very good. Their translations caused my talks to last long hours. The next morning we drove the thirty miles to Zhou Kou Dian, the cave called Dragon Bone Hill by the locals, where in the 1920s the remains of *Homo erectus Pekinensis*, or Peking man, had been found. A professor in paleoanthropology, who served as our guide, explained that the collective term "Peking Man" represents the remains of forty individuals of various ages and both sexes, one of the greatest archeological finds of the century. More lecturing occurred that afternoon, and sightseeing the next day at the Summer Palace, the Lamasery. The mix of lectures and tourism continued throughout our stay.

After one of my talks, a physicist in his early fifties came up to me and said, "My name is Fang Li Zhi. I'd like to talk with you." I knew who he was, a leader of the Chinese dissidents, sometimes called the Chinese Sakharov.[3] I invited him for lunch, also with Ida, where he arrived carrying a magazine, exclaiming: "I have made the cover of *Time*." He is a cheery, lively fellow, his English is good. We spent hours discussing the political situation in his country.

On our last day in Beijing we were taken by car to the Great Wall and the Ming tombs. Two Chinese students joined us. During the ride one of them asked what I thought of Chinese communism. I paused a moment—it was a delicate issue—then said, tactfully I thought: "I think that communism has its virtues as a transitional stage." The student exploded, replying in a fury: "You really think there is something good about communism?" That was two years before the tragedy at Tiananmen Square.

The next day we flew to Xian for a four-day stay of more lectures and tourism, including a visit to the six thousand entombed warriors, surely one of the world's most astounding sights. From Xian by sleeper to Nanjing. The landscape changed; we now passed rice fields and saw many water buffalo and geese. We visited the mausoleum of Sun Yat Sen, the tomb of the first Ming emperor, the bridge over the Yangtze River.

Two days later we continued via Shanghai to Hangzhou, described by Marco Polo as the most beautiful city in the world. We loved walking along the promenade bordering the West Lake and were rowed over its waters to the fairytale Island of the Three Pools Mirroring the Moon. One evening we were entertained at a banquet given by the mayor of the city.

Our last main stop was Shanghai, from which I remember the extraordinary density of people and bicycles on the streets; the finest tea served at the four hundred-year-old Wu Santing Tea House; the walks along the Bund, the boulevard bordering the sea. Once again I lectured. We made a side trip to Szuchow, famed for its gardens, and the Tiger Hill Pagoda, a tenth-century temple reputed to be one of the finest in the country.

Then it was time to go home. We were driven to Shanghai's Hongqiao Airport, flew to Tokyo, and from there nonstop to New York, where we returned a month after having left. I had completed my second trip around the world, a journey richer in new experiences than any other I have made.

32.5.4 Shorter Trips and Other Varia

In 1988 we went to Berlin—in time for Ida to see the wall before it went down the next year. Also that year we went to Cambridge, where I gave the Scott Lectures. We stayed in Gonville and Caius College.

In 1989 we vacationed at St. Croix, then went to Blois in France, where I gave the opening address at a conference, held at the famed Renaissance château, commemorating the twenty-fifth anniversary of the discovery of CP-violation.[4]

In December of that year we went to Stockholm, invited to attend the Nobel ceremonies. I had done that before, in 1982. On both occasions I lectured at the Swedish Academy of Sciences, the first time on Nobel prizes. At that earlier event I had congratulated Gabriel García Márquez on his literature prize and urged him to nominate Jorge Luis Borges for that same honor, an idea with which he heartily agreed.

After our marriage at the Grand Canyon, in March 1990, we honeymooned in Arizona, visiting Navajo country and attending Indian dances in a *kiva* in a Hopi village. The month thereafter we went to Israel for a conference in Jerusalem, staying at the Mishkenot Sha'ananim, the mayor's guesthouse. From our balcony we could see the wall of the Old City, built by Suleiman the Magnificent. It was Ida's first visit there, and she could not get enough of walking in the Old City. We went to Massada, swam in the Dead Sea near Ein Geddi, visited the caves at Qumran, where the Dead Sea scrolls had been found, went to Yad Vashem. That summer we made a short trip to Bornholm, a beautiful Danish island in the Baltic.

Of our May 1991 visit to Venice I remember in particular the small church of Santa Maria dei Miracoli, and our boat trip to the island of Torcello with its seventh-century cathedral, Santa Maria dell' Assunta. A year later we went to Ireland, flying to Shannon, where we rented a car and drove eastward, first to the cliffs of Moher, then through the Barrens to Galway. From there to Cong in County Mayo, where I was happy to visit Cohan's Bar, which I had first seen in the movie *The Quiet Man*. Then on to Kells and New Grange, the burial chamber from 3000 B.C., and from there to Dublin, where I lectured at Trinity College and saw the Book of Kells in its library. During that short trip I grew to love Ireland's beauty, its historic monuments, and the charm of its people.

In May 1994 we went to Israel again, where I lectured once more. Our excursion by car was to the north this time. We passed through the roadblocks at Jericho, had lunch at Lake Tiberias, went up the Golan Heights (the most moving event of that trip), swam in the Sea of Galilee, visited the crusaders' fort at Acra.

In August 1994 we joined a group of friends for a vacation on Bozcaada, a small Turkish island in the Aegean Sea. We flew to Istanbul, rented two cars and drove west, first along the Sea of Marmara. On the way we stopped for visits of historic sites: the ruins of Troy, the battlefields and cemeteries of Gallipoli, very strong experiences. I was deeply moved by an inscription on one gravestone: "I have fought a good fight, I have finished my course." Then by ferry across the Dardanelles into Asia and by another ferry to our island, not yet overrun by tourists, where we spent an idyllic week, swimming and loafing.

On November 13, 1995, a plaque commemorating my friend the physicist Dirac was to be unveiled in Westminster Abbey. I had been invited to give a lecture that day at the Royal Society on Dirac's life and work. Afterward, Ida and I and those attending the lecture walked over to the Abbey for the unveiling ceremony, held after Evensong. It was a solemn, tasteful occasion. We added excursions to our trip, to Cambridge, to Oxford, where we admired the anthropological collections in the Pitt-Rivers Museum, and to Stratford-upon-Avon, where we attended a superb performance of *Richard III.*

Two final items of a different character.

One day I received a call from my Oxford editor. "You have reached the masses," he said. "What's up?" I asked. He told me he had lying before him a card from the game Trivial Pursuit, on which appears the question: "Which scientist is portrayed in the biography '*Subtle is the Lord?*'" A copy of that card now hangs, framed, in my Copenhagen office.

In August 1993 two members of the Punan Bah tribe came to us as one-month houseguests. To explain the reason for their visit, I quote from a circular letter sent the previous July by the National Museum in Copenhagen:

A TOTEM POLE IS MADE—MEETING WITH BORNEO

From August 3 to 31 the National Museum has as guests the Punan Bah carvers Kojan Kavang and his nephew, Thomas Bugi Seng, from Borneo. In that period you can see the two men carve and paint a 6.5-meter-high statue [actually they carved two], a so-called *Kelamen,* in the Museum's great hall. Such totem poles were traditionally raised during the Punan Bah's headhunting rituals but were thrown in the river after use. This project assures a *Kela-men* for the future.

Project, idea, exhibition and catalogue: Lektor, mag. art., Ida Nicolaisen.

I had been a bit nervous about that visit. How would I communicate with our guests? But things went well. Kojan did not speak English, but Bugi did—quite well. I became very fond of them; they were friendly men with great dignity. It was fascinating to see them work, beginning with Kojan's blessing in the museum hall of two as-yet-uncut huge trees (Danish ones, this time), with a sword, an egg, and beer. The hall was filled with visitors on August 27, the day of the raising ceremony, a complex ritual that included the beheading of a live chicken. Kojan addressed the animal approximately as follows, Ida translating: "Have no fear, chicken, you will soon join my ancestors in heaven."

During one of those August nights I was awakened by singing coming from our guests' room. "What's happening?" I asked Ida. "He is singing to his ancestors," she explained.

Throughout this book I have told of travels to foreign lands, from which I have learned much about other people's mores. The singing of the Punan Bah tribesman brought home to me, however, how much I still have to learn about other cultures, a fitting thought to conclude the tales of my life—so far.

33

Approaching
the Millennium

T HE CENTURY now approaching its end has been one of indiscrimi-
nate violence, it has been perhaps the most murderous one in Western
history of which we have record. Yet I would think that what will strike
people most when, hundreds of years from now, they will look back on our
days is that this was the age when the exploration of space began, the molecular basis of genetics was laid, the microchip was invented, revolutions
in transport and communication virtually annihilated time and distance,
transforming the world into a "global village," and relativity theory, quantum mechanics, and the structure of the atom and its nucleus were
discovered—in brief, that this has been the century of science and
technology.

Enough of such speculations about judgments by our far descendants. I
shall now conclude this book with some of my own reflections—written at
the rim of the millennium—on the recent past.[1]

Our century has not ended well. Today we live in the midst of upheaval and
crisis. We do not know where we are going, nor even where we ought to be
going. Awareness is spreading that our future cannot be a straight extension
of the past or the present, that in the late 1980s an era in world history has
ended and a new one has begun.

New technologies continue to squeeze human labor out from the production of goods and services without providing either enough work for those
it has jettisoned or guaranteeing a rate of economic growth sufficient to
absorb them. The political situation exhibits instability worldwide, its major problem being not how to multiply the wealth of nations but how to
distribute it equitably. Politics has increasingly become an exercise in eva-

sion, as politicians are afraid to tell voters what they do not want to hear. It does not take great wisdom to appreciate that many of the policy decisions that will have to be taken early in the next century will be unpopular. In this decision process there are only very few among the voters and the elected who are qualified to express opinions on major issues, such as, for example, the future of nuclear industry.

The conflicts between capitalism and socialism that have dominated most of the twentieth century's political scene can already now be seen as an ideological relic of a bygone era, not only because the communist bloc has largely disintegrated (but watch China), but also because the titanic economic and techno-scientific process of the development of capitalism, which has dominated the past several centuries, has reached a point of historic crisis. The forces generated by the capitalist economy are now strong enough to destroy the material foundation of human life. Capitalism as we have known it simply cannot go on *ad infinitum*. Painful as it may be, the time is at hand to reconsider the validity of the right of self-determination, which has always been at the core of the theory of capitalist economy.

I add a few brief comments on more specific events.

ARMED CONFLICTS

From 1816 to 1965, 144 countries have fought wars during 4,500 "nation months," leaving 29 million men killed on battlefields and the high seas. As to the United States, by early 1968, toward the end of the Johnson administration, the Vietnam conflict had become the longest war in American history. The fighting came to a conclusion on April 29, 1975, with the unconditional surrender of Saigon.

Thus ended the U.S.'s catastrophic two decades of military involvement in Vietnam, which had cost the lives of over 58,000 Americans and an estimated 1.5 million Vietnamese. Thus also ended the many years of phony military communiqués from Southeast Asia. Americans now had to face hard facts: for the first time in history they had lost a war. If there is one good thing that has come out of this enormous disaster, it is, I think, the nation's maturing realization that it is not invincible.

I feel no need to comment on the United States' involvements in other military operations during the recent past, all minor compared to the Vietnam tragedy. Regarding battles fought by other nations, I shall confine my-self to remarks on conflicts involving Israel.

On May 6, 1967, Cairo radio broadcast this message: "The battle has come in which we shall destroy Israel." Two weeks later, the king of Jordan placed his forces under Egyptian control. Saudi and Iraqi forces moved into Jordan, Algerian and Kuwaiti troops into Egypt.

Israel could not delay. On June 5 its air force attacked, destroying 450 enemy planes in less than three hours and achieving complete air superi-ority. The war ended in six days with the rout of Arab forces, the capture of the Old City of Jerusalem, the control of the Sinai Peninsula, the capture of the Golan Heights, and deep penetration into Syria.

These events profoundly affected many Jews, including me. For once there was pride in Israel because Jews had shed their passive role. To a Jewish friend I wrote: "It has been a rough 2000 years."

In 1968 I celebrated the Passover Seder with the Bennahum family and other guests, which included Uzzi Narkiss, the general who had com-manded the capture of Jerusalem. At one point in the ritual, the phrase "Next year in Jerusalem" is recited. All of us wept when we sang that age-old line; we stood up and kissed Uzzi.

On September 13, 1993, I watched on TV as Itzhak Rabin, prime minister of Israel, and Muhammad Abdel Raouf Arafat al-Qudwa al-Husseini— Arafat's full name—chairman of the Palestine Liberation Organization, shook hands on the White House lawn (with some coaxing from President Clinton) on the occasion of the signing of the peace accord between Israel and the PLO. I was moved to hear Rabin say, after nearly half a century of Arab-Israeli conflicts: "Enough of blood and tears. Enough." Furthermore, in 1994 Israel and Jordan signed a peace treaty, the first event of its kind in the Near East since the treaty with Egypt in 1979.

These recent events give hope—even though blood is still let and tears are still shed.

UPHEAVALS IN EASTERN EUROPE

In retrospect one may perhaps see the founding, in 1980, of Solidarity, a new Polish independent trade union, led by Lech Walesa, as a prelude to the immense changes that were about to start in Eastern Europe. In 1980 one was not quite there yet, however, as witness the fact that in that same year Andrei Sakharov was sent into internal exile in Gorki; and that in 1982 Solidarity was outlawed. (It was legalized in 1988.)

The beginning of the end of Eurocommunism came in 1985 when Mikhail Sergyevitch Gorbachev took over the leadership of the Soviet Union. He must be credited more than anyone else for bringing the Cold War to an end.

Western capitalism saw these changes as opportunities for opening new markets. Sample: in 1988 the McDonald's chain opened twenty restaurants in Moscow.

From then on, the decay of communism spread all over the Eastern bloc, reaching a high point of drama on November 10, 1989, the day on which hundreds of thousands of East Germans swarmed through gaps made in the Berlin Wall, an event avidly watched on television in the West.

At that time I was a member of the board of overseers of Berlin's Wissenschaftskolleg, an institution modeled after the Institute for Advanced Study in Princeton. That brought me to Berlin twice a year. I vividly recall a very moving experience: to walk through the Brandenburg Gate, where the Berlin Wall had blocked passage until a few months earlier.

That year, 1989, marked the time of high optimism that now a new era of peace and progress was at hand—expectations which did not last long, however.

A change of mood became apparent already in 1990, when West and East Germany were reunified. Almost at once the ignorance regarding Western life-styles of peoples in nations until then under communist rule began to show. They believed democracy to be a magic wand that brings affluence and did not seem to realize that improving living standards required them to work, work *hard*. Nor had West Germans anticipated the high financial burdens that reunification would visit on them. All of this resulted in great unrest all over Germany, fueled further by the presence of asylum seekers from the East, more than a million by 1989. Nazi thugs began roaming the streets of Germany, causing chaos and fear.

Attempts at democratic rule in the Soviet Union caused tremendous upheavals in a population that for seventy years had been ordered from above what to do, how to think. Individual freedom was hard to take for many, and communism was still alive in their souls. The result was the coup of August 1991 by members of the old régime, which eventually led to the end of the Gorbachev era; the country dissolved from under him. On December 25 he resigned and Boris Yeltsin took over. The next day the Soviet Union disbanded into a loose commonwealth of independent states.

None of these developments had we, the optimists of 1989, foreseen. Nor had we reckoned with the steep rise in the crime rate (Russians speak of the *mafiyah*) and the resurgence of ancient ethnic rivalries, remnants of ghoulish myths and tribal memory, long suppressed during the reign of communism when different nationalities had been pressed into overarching political structures. Revolts broke out in many parts of the now extinct Soviet Union, in Moldova, in the Caucasus and Transcaucasus, in ex-Soviet central Asia.

It is inevitable that this turmoil has led to movements that desperately try to cling to the past, such as the rise of the ultra-Right, of fundamentalism both in the Western and Eastern world, the unexpected revival of support for the heirs of the old régime in the ex-communist countries—reactionary responses which are as understandable as they are futile.

In 1991, Yugoslavia, a state created in 1918 by the League of Nations, fell apart when Slovenia and Croatia declared independence. In April 1992, Bosnian Serbs began the siege of Sarajevo, a city that had never been Serbian, not even in medieval times. A new grim term entered the language: *ethnic cleansing,* short for evictions, killings, and rapes. The United Nations responded by sending in troops charged with humanitarian aid only, and with creating "safe zones," gestures that served to ease Western conscience rather than create order. Untold many armistice proposals were proposed, all broken. And so Bosnia became for the United Nations what Abessynia had been for the League of Nations: the foreign field where honor was lost beyond recall. At this time the area remains a powder keg.

Upheavals Elsewhere

The year 1989 also brought havoc to Communist China, where since 1980 Chairman Deng Xiaoping had pursued far-reaching changes in political and economic institutions. In April 1989 some 100,000 students and workers demanded more changes and marched on Tiananmen Square in Beijing, where students camped out. On June 3–4, army troops crushed these protests, killing or injuring more than 10,000 people.

The years after 1989 have seen more brutal armed conflicts than anyone can remember, savage civil wars in Angola and Liberia, the hacking to death of Tutsis by Hutus in Rwanda, the failed attempt by the United Nations to sanitize the situation in Somalia, to mention but some. Moreover, quite small groups of political or other dissidents were causing disruption and wreckage all over the globe. At this time the term "the international community of nations" sounds like exalted fiction.

Currently, all these tragic events have led to a widespread sense of malaise. And yet, and yet—one should bear in mind the progress in the Middle East after a deeply troubled half-century, and, above all, the fact that in 1994 Nelson Mandela was elected the first black president of South Africa by democratic process in which all races participated. The long times it has taken for these events to mature may serve as a reminder that there is hope—and need for patience.

UPHEAVALS AT HOME

In the early 1960s there was optimism and hope in the land. Kennedy and his beautiful young wife Jacqueline were raising spirits and setting a new style.

It did not last. Later in the sixties, Kennedy, his brother Robert, Martin Luther King, Malcolm X, Mary Jo Kopechne, and many young Americans in Vietnam would all die violently. Soon bitterness began to divide Americans.

In August 1968 the Democrats held their national convention in Chicago. Trouble was expected, the National Guard was alerted, U.S. Army troops were standing by. Trouble came, less the fault of the anti-Vietnam demonstrators than of the police, who tore into crowds with nightsticks and tear gas. There was bloodshed.

The ultimate importance of these events lies in the fact that an estimated 90 million Americans watched this mayhem on television. Viewing this spectacle must have contributed to another disaster: the election of Nixon the next November. Evidently the assassinations of 1968 have changed the course of history.

The mid-1960s saw very serious race riots in America. These often began with a minor incident that erupted into devastation, as in August 1965, when hell broke loose in the Watts section of Los Angeles, blacks fighting police and National Guardsmen, looting and burning their own homes. Large black communities rebelled against society, in Washington, D.C., Chicago, Detroit, Brooklyn, and elsewhere. Militant black groups emerged, such as the Black Panthers in 1966. "Black power" became their cry of battle, "radical chic" was the appellation for some supportive white liberals. It should be remembered, however, that the Black Panthers also introduced a very positive element, summarized in the slogan "Black is beautiful."

These activities overshadowed the calls for peaceful action led, above all, by Martin Luther King.

After the assassination of King, President Johnson ordered flags at half-mast, the first time that had been done for a black man. I was one of the 120 million Americans who watched on television the funeral march of over 50,000 people, including many of the nation's leaders.

On King's marble tomb in Atlanta are hewn the words with which, five years earlier, he had closed his historic oration at a Washington demonstration:

> Free at last, free at last,
> Thank God Almighty, free at last.

Since midcentury, our world has also changed in less violent but no less profound ways.

The 1950s saw the dawn of the Age of Television. Coast-to-coast telecasts began in 1951, TV dinners appeared in 1954. Suburban living was on the rise; so was the American custom of people addressing each other by first names. Throughout the decade, over a million American farmers were leaving their land each year.

The sexual revolution may be said to have started in May 1960, when the U.S. Food and Drug Administration approved the Pill. The publication in 1963 of *The Feminine Mystique* by my friend Betty Friedan signaled the beginning of the modern women's movement.

1963 is perhaps the best choice of year for marking the beginnings of the drug culture. In that year Timothy Leary was dismissed from the Harvard faculty for using LSD on himself and others. At about that time new expressions entered the vernacular: tripping, freaking out, blowing one's mind. The Beatles' songs "Yellow Submarine" and "Strawberry Fields" set this new vogue to music. I never felt any inclination to take hard drugs. On the contrary. However, I did try a few sticks of marijuana, and once a little hashish. I only remember that I reacted by becoming a bit giggly.

Student disorders started in the U.S. in 1964 with turmoil in Berkeley, but only in 1968 did it spread, and not just to universities all over America. Helped by the speed of modern communication, campus eruptions that had begun in the U.S. rapidly spread to Europe, even behind the Iron Curtain, and to Asia. It may never be fully understood why this revolution started *when* it did. One reason is obvious, however: the intensely anti-Vietnam mood among students.

There must have been other reasons as well, however, for that uprising of the young. It seems plausible that the explosive increase of the size of the university's student body in those years was another contributing factor—especially as it brought elements to campus whose interests in higher learning were, shall we say, limited. Now, a quarter of a century later, I venture a further thought, having to do with two scales of time. One is the period after which the leadership of one generation is taken over by the next one, typically about twenty years and fairly constant. The second is the ever-shortening period after which existing information and technology become obsolete. A critical point is reached when the second period becomes shorter than the first. At that juncture the experience of the older generation is no longer all that helpful. Perhaps that crucial changeover fell in the sixties?

It is quite striking how, in recent decades, our consciousness of world events has been shaped by television. Its impact cannot be matched by the printed word. For example, we were there, so to speak, when in 1972 terrorists held Israeli athletes hostage at the Munich Olympics, killing two directly, with nine dying later; or when Sadat's plane landed on Israeli soil—which made me cry. The footage from Vietnam, the first television war in history, did more than the press could possibly manage to bring home—literally, the brutality of war. No statistics can rival the shocking pictures, shown in 1972, of the little girl running naked along a road near Trang Bang. She had torn off her flaming clothes after being napalmed in error by a South Vietnamese plane. Images like these, which have contributed so much to shaping public opinion, are among the indelible icons of history. The media are now a more important component of the political process than parties and electoral systems—think of the presidential debates or of the Watergate hearings—and are likely to remain so.

THE ENVIRONMENT

The last of my fairly random and scattered reflections concerns the environment. In 1969 a Gallup poll found that 70 percent of Americans put the environment issue first among the country's domestic problems. Pollution had become unconscionable. Combustion in the U.S. was disgorging 140 million tons of grime per year into the air. Pollutants cost 10 billion dollars annually in property damage. Marine life was being destroyed. Protests began, the first actions were taken, and so it has continued until this day. It is true that the problems of ecology have often been discussed in exaggerated terms of an imminent collapse. Nevertheless, it is evident that if humanity is to have a future, then the untrammeled capitalism we have known, and which is at the root of the environment's decline, can have none.

Until twenty, maybe thirty, years ago, I would open the morning papers and read about the world's problems. There was plenty to ruminate about. Remember, for example, that in the second half of the twentieth century, imperialism had come to an end, and colonialism had become a thing of the past. I would say to myself this problem I would solve like this, that one like that. Never mind that I was wrong more often than not. I had opinions. Now, when I read the papers, I have a reaction which is much more painful: I have no ideas at all what I would do were it in my power.

All I can offer, to conclude, is to repeat the words written in the fifth century B.C. by Pindar in his Sixth Nemean Ode:

> Though we know not what the day will bring,
> what course after nightfall
> destiny has written that we must run to the
> end.

Notes and References

PROLOGUE

1. A. Pais, *Subtle is the Lord* (Oxford University Press, New York, 1982).

2. A. Pais, *Niels Bohr's Times: In Physics, Philosophy, and Polity* (Oxford University Press, New York, 1991).

3. A. Pais, *Inward Bound* (Oxford University Press, New York, 1986).

1. DESCENT

1. Dutch spelling of Isaiah.

2. These data were compiled by the Centraal Bureau voor genealogie, The Hague, Netherlands.

3. Quoted in M. H. Gans, *Memorbook* (Bosch and Keuning, Baarn, Holland, 1977); distributed by Wayne State University Press, Detroit), p. 10. This book is a superbly illustrated history, written in English, of the history of Dutch Jewry from the Renaissance to 1940.

4. J. L. Motley, *The Rise of the Dutch Republic,* vol. 1 (Routledge and Sons, London, 1889), part 2, chapter 3.

5. See ibid. for a history of the Inquisition in the Netherlands, and W. H. Prescott, *History of the Reign of Philip the Second* (Lippincott and Co., Philadelphia, 1864), for the reign of Philip II.

6. Gans, *Memorbook*, p. 19.

7. Ibid., p. 29.

8. A canal that was later dammed to become a square, the Waterlooplein.

9. Gans, *Memorbook*, p. 47.

10. Ibid., p. 87.

11. Ibid., p. 569.

12. Ibid., p. 570.

3. Bachelor's Degrees in Amsterdam

1. R. Weitzenböck, *Invariantentheorie* (Noordhoff, Groningen, 1923).

5. First Contacts with Zionism

1. For the early history of the Zionist movement, see A. Böhm, *Die zionistische Bewegung,* 2 vols. (Hozaah Ivrith Co., Jerusalem, 1937).

2. See L. Giebels, *De Zionistische beweging in Nederland 1899–1941* (Van Gorcum, Assen, 1975), p. 23.

3. Term coined from some of the letters of the Hebrew words *merkaz ruhani,* which mean "spiritual center." At the same time, *mizrach* means "east."

4. Meaning "one of the people," the pen name of Asher Ginzburg, born in Skriva near Kiev of well-to-do chassidic parents, died in Tel Aviv. For a biography of Ahad Ha'am, see note 5 below.

5. L. Simon, *Ahad Ha'am* (Horovitz Publishing Co., London, 1960).

6. See the instructive essay on Ahad Ha'am by A. Hertzberg, *The New York Times Book Review,* March 31, 1991.

7. Ibid.

8. Ibid.

9. Giebels, *Zionistische beweging,* pp. 178, 179.

10. Ibid., p. 171.

6. Utrecht: M.Sc. and Ph.D.

1. L. Landau and G. Rumer, Proc. Roy. Soc. *A166,* 213, 1938.

2. For more on Casimir, see his book *Haphazard Reality* (Harper and Row, New York, 1983); also A. Pais in *Physics in the Making,* ed. A. Sarlemyn and M. J. Sparnaay (North-Holland, New York, 1989), p. 45.

3. For more on this Washington meeting, see A. Pais, *Niels Bohr's Times* (Oxford University Press, New York, 1991), chapter 20.

4. A. Nordsieck, W. E. Lamb, and G. E. Uhlenbeck, Physica 7, 344, 1940.

5. K. van Lier and G. E. Uhlenbeck, Physica *4,* 531, 1937.

6. C. Møller and L. Rosenfeld, Nature *143,* 241, 1939; Det Danske Vid. Selsk. math.-fys. Medd. *17,* No. 8, 1940.

7. C. Møller and L. Rosenfeld, Nature *144,* 476, 1939.

8. W. Pauli, letter to W. Heisenberg, May 13, 1954, W. Pauli, *Scientific Correspondence* (Springer, New York, in press), vol. 4.

9. Copy in the Rosenfeld Papers, Niels Bohr Archive, Copenhagen.

10. A. Pais, letters to L. Rosenfeld, May 8, 9, 1940, copies in ibid.

11. A. Pais, letter to L. Rosenfeld, August 11, 1940, in ibid.

12. Ibid.

13. C. Møller, Phys. Rev. *58*, 1118, 1940; Det Danske Vid. Selsk. math.-fys. Medd. *18*, no. 6, 1941.

14. The motivation was that in the Møller-Rosenfeld theory two kinds of mesons appear: vector mesons described by four fields, and pseudoscalar mesons by one field. The totality of these five fields can be very compactly handled in a five-dimension theory.

15. The subject has an international flavor. The general idea of a five-dimensional description is due to Theodor Kaluza a German, and Oskar Klein a Swede (see Th. Kaluza, S. B. Akad. Wiss. Berlin 1921, p. 966, and O. Klein, Z. Phys. *37*, 895, 1926; *46*, 188, 1927). Projective relativity is an invention of two Americans, Oswald Veblen and Banesh Hoffmann (see O. Veblen and B. Hoffmann, Phys. Rev. *36*, 810, 1931). Willem de Sitter was a Dutchman.

16. W. Pauli, Ann. der Phys. *18*, 305, 337, 1933.

17. A. Pais, *Subtle is the Lord* (Oxford University Press, Oxford, 1982), chapter 17.

18. A. Pais, *Projective theory of meson fields and electromagnetic properties of atomic nuclei* (Noord Hollandsche Uitgeversmaatsch., Amsterdam, 1941).

19. A. Pais, Physica *8*, 1137, 1941.

20. A. Pais, Physica *9*, 267, 407, 1942.

21. A. Pais, Det Danske Vid. Selsk. math.-fys. Medd. *20*, no. 17, 1943.

7. War

1. W. L. Shirer, *The Rise and Fall of the Third Reich* (Simon and Schuster, New York, 1960), pp. 471ff, where one also finds excerpts from that speech.

2. Ibid., pp. 456, 468.

3. Ibid., pp. 540–42.

4. Ibid., p. 1143.

5. Ibid., p. 715.

6. R. Petrow, *The Bitter Years* (Morrow, New York, 1974), p. 49.

7. W. Warmbrunn, *The Dutch under German Occupation 1940–1945* (Stanford University Press, Stanford, Calif., 1963), p. 7.

8. *New York Times,* May 11, 1940.

9. Shirer, *Rise and Fall,* p. 721.

10. In order to refresh my memory, I consulted Warmbrunn, *The Dutch under German Occupation,* and *Onderdrukking en Verzet,* 4 vols. (Meulenhoff, Amsterdam, 1949–54).

11. Shirer, *Rise and Fall,* p. 721.

12. *Onderdrukking en Verzet,* vol. 1, p. 206.

13. Ibid., p. 208.

14. Ibid., p. 264.

15. Warmbrunn, *Dutch under German Occupation,* chapter 9.

8. Occupation of Holland

1. W. L. Shirer, *The Rise and Fall of the Third Reich* (Simon and Schuster, New York, 1960), p. 943.

2. The best and most accessible account of the fate of the Dutch Jews is the English translation of a 500-page book by the Dutch-Jewish professor of history and author, Jacob Presser, who himself lived through the entire period of Holland's occupation. See J. Presser, *Ashes in the Wind* (Souvenir Press, London, 1968, and Wayne State University Press, Detroit, 1988).

3. R. Rashke, *Escape from Sobibor* (Houghton Mifflin, Boston, 1982), chapter 15.

4. Presser, *Ashes in the Wind,* p. 495.

5. *Onderdrukking en Verzet,* 4 vols. (Meulenhoff, Amsterdam, 1949–54), vol. 2, pp. 621–28.

6. See ibid., vol. 3, pp. 301–37, for the role of universities during the occupation.

7. Presser, *Ashes in the Wind,* p. 27.

8. Ibid., p. 89.

9. Ibid., p. 46.

10. *Onderdrukking en Verzet,* vol. 3, p. 84.

11. Presser, *Ashes in the Wind,* p. 388.

12. *Onderdrukking en Verzet,* vol. 3, pp. 567ff.

13. W. Warmbrunn, *The Dutch under German Occupation 1940–1945* (Stanford University Press, Stanford, Calif., 1963), p. 7.

14. Ibid.

15. Ibid.

16. W. S. Churchill, *Triumph and Tragedy* (Houghton Mifflin, Boston, 1953), pp. 5–6.

17. Ibid., p. 39.

18. In addition to my own recollections, I have used the following for details: *Onderdrukking en Verzet,* vol. 3, pp. 632ff; vol. 4, pp. 662ff.

19. Warmbrunn, *Dutch under German Occupation,* p. 7.

20. *Onderdrukking en Verzet,* vol. 2, p. 648; vol. 4, p. 670.

21. Ibid., vol. 2, p. 623.

22. Ibid., p. 648.

23. Churchill, *Triumph and Tragedy,* p. 468.

24. Ibid., p. 478.

9. SHO'AH

1. R. Langer, *Holocaust Testimonies* (Yale University Press, New Haven, 1991), p. 40.

2. Ibid., p. xiii.

3. Ibid., p. 40.

4. M. Blanchot, *The Writing of the Disaster* (University of Nebraska Press, Lincoln, 1986).

5. R. Rashke, *Escape from Sobibor* (Houghton Mifflin, Boston, 1982), chapter 15.

6. Ibid.

7. Langer, *Holocaust.*

8. *Shiva,* meaning "seven," refers to the number of days Orthodox Jews sit in mourning for the death of a next-of-kin.

9. G. Reitlinger, *The Final Solution* (Vallentine and Mitchell, London, 1953), appendix 1. This prodigious work contains, country by country, the most detailed statistical summary I have come across of the number of Jews who disappeared.

10. M. Gilbert, *The Macmillan Atlas of the Holocaust* (Macmillan, New York, 1982), pp. 11, 141.

11. Cf. R. Hilberg, *The Destruction of the European Jews* (Allen, London, 1961), chapter 11.

12. Ibid.

13. J. Presser, *Ashes in the Wind* (Souvenir Press, London, 1968, and Wayne State University Press, Detroit, 1988), p. 126.

14. W. L. Shirer, *The Rise and Fall of the Third Reich* (Simon and Schuster, New York, 1960), pp. 965ff.

15. For more on the Wannsee meeting, see R. Kempner, *Eichmann und Komplizen* (Zurich, 1961).

16. See D. Lipstadt, *Beyond Belief* (Macmillan, New York, 1986), chapter 8, for more details on press reaction to the atrocities.

17. Hilberg, *The Destruction,* pp. 717, 718.

18. E. Bliss, *The Broadcasts of Edward R. Murrow* (Knopf, New York, 1967), pp. 56–57.

19. Hilberg, *The Destruction*, pp. 717, 718.

20. *PM*, April 30, 1943.

21. M. N. Penkower, *The Jews Were Expendable* (University of Illinois Press, Chicago, 1983).

22. Presser, *Ashes in the Wind*, p. 331.

23. W. Churchill, *The Second World War* (Houghton Mifflin, Boston, 1953), vol. 6, p. 693.

24. Hilberg, *The Destruction*, p. 728.

25. *New York Times*, November 29, 1943.

26. *Washington Post*, April 24, 1945.

27. Churchill, *The Second World War*, vol. 6, p. 766.

28. *Baltimore Sun*, April 7, 1945.

29. Anne Frank, *The Diary of a Young Girl* (Washington Square Press, New York, 1972).

30. In writing the remainder of this section, Presser's *Ashes in the Wind* has been a great help in refreshing my memory.

31. Ibid., pp. 34, 35.

32. Ibid., pp. 93, 94.

33. Ibid., p. 103.

34. Ibid., p. 121.

35. Ibid., p. 136.

36. *Onterdrukking en Verzet*, 4 vols. (Mewenhoff, Amsterdam, 1949–54), vol. 3, p. 105.

37. Presser, *Ashes in the Wind*, p. 167.

38. Ibid., p. 228.

39. Ibid., p. 308.

40. Ibid., p. 535.

41. Ibid., p. 328.

42. Ibid., p. 333.

43. Frank, *Diary*.

44. Presser, *Ashes in the Wind*, p. 334.

45. A. J. Herzberg in *Onterdrukking en Verzet*, vol. 3, pp. 162–63.

46. See H. Arendt, *Eichmann in Jerusalem* (the edition I used is Penguin books, 1977), a controversial book in which she discusses the actions of various JRs—in my opinion short on vision and sloppy in historical detail. See *Uit het werk van J. Presser* (Polak and Van Gennep, Amsterdam, 1969), p. 179, for a detailed critique.

10. Wartime Experiences

1. J. Presser, *Ashes in the Wind* (Souvenir Press, London, 1968, and Wayne State University Press, Detroit, 1988), p. 235.

2. Literally *baldachin,* under which the betrothed sit during the ceremony. The word has come to mean the marriage ritual as a whole.

3. See further *Onderdrukking en Verzet,* 4 vols. (Meulenhoff, Amsterdam, 1949–54), vol. 3, pp. 131ff; and Presser, *Ashes in the Wind,* pp. 234ff.

4. R. Hilberg, *The Destruction of the European Jews* (Allen, London, 1961), p. 564.

5. See ibid., p. 573, for a map.

6. W. L. Shirer, *The Rise and Fall of the Third Reich* (Simon and Schuster, New York, 1960), p. 664.

7. G. Reitlinger, *The Final Solution* (Vallentine and Mitchell, London, 1953), pp. 460, 461.

8. Hilberg, *The Destruction,* p. 632.

9. Ibid., p. 633; Reitlinger, *Final Solution,* pp. 463ff.

10. E. A. Cohen, *De negentien treinen naar Sobibor* (Elsevier, Amsterdam, 1979), p. 22.

11. Hilberg, *The Destruction,* p. 572.

12. Ibid., p. 630.

13. R. Rashke, *Escape from Sobibor* (Houghton Mifflin, Boston, 1982), p. vii.

14. Ibid., p. 363.

15. Ibid., p. vii.

16. Ibid., p. 372.

17. For a list of references, see ibid., p. 369.

18. L. de Jong in *Encounter,* December 1978, p. 20.

19. For a map of Camp Sobibor, drawn from memory, see Rashke, *Escape from Sobibor,* pp. 54, 55.

20. De Jong, *Encounter,* p. 20.

21. Ibid.

22. Ibid.

23. Report reproduced in English in M. Novitch, "Sobibor, Martyrdom and Revolt" (Holocaust Library, New York, 1980), p. 168.

24. Reitlinger, *Final Solution,* p. 337.

25. Cohen, *De negentien,* p. 23.

26. Rashke, *Escape from Sobibor,* pp. 108, 109.

27. De Jong, *Encounter,* p. 20.

28. For a history of the Institute, see *De onderzoekers van de oorlog* (SDU Publishers, The Hague, 1989).

29. Cohen, *De negentien,* p. 21.

30. See A. Pais, *Inward Bound* (Oxford University Press, New York, 1988), pp. 448–49, for more details.

31. These were the mathematical method of fluxions; the law of composition of light; and the law of universal gravitation—not bad for a graduate student in his early twenties. It was during those Woolsthorpe years that, as alleged, he hit upon his fundamental idea of gravity after having seen an apple fall from a tree.

32. L. T. More, *Isaac Newton* (Dover, New York, 1962), p. 41.

33. See E. Verheÿ, *Om het joodse kind* (Nÿgh and van Ditmar, Amsterdam, 1991), chapter 4, for a history of this bill.

34. B. Braber, *Zelfs als wÿ zullen verliezen* (Balans, Amsterdam, 1990), pp. 128, 129.

35. *New York Times,* April 29, 1945.

36. Ibid., July 23, 1945.

37. Ibid., May 6, 1945.

38. Ibid., May 10, 1945.

11. WAR'S AFTERMATH: A LAST LESSON IN DUTCH HISTORY

1. *New York Times,* May 8, 1945.

2. See Z. Stein, M. Susser, G. Saenger, and F. Marolla, *Famine and Human Development: The Dutch Hunger Winter of 1944–45* (Oxford University Press, Oxford, 1975), p. 47, a book entirely devoted to medical studies of that catastrophe.

3. Ibid., pp. 45, 46, 52, 53.

4. Ibid., pp. 73, 76.

5. Ibid., p. 75.

6. Ibid., p. 83.

7. L. de Jong, *Het Koninkrÿk der Nederlanden in de twede wereldoorlog* (SDU Publishers, The Hague, 1988), vol. 12, pp. 280ff.

8. Ibid., p. 285.

9. Ibid., p. 154.

10. J. Presser, *Ashes in the Wind* (Souvenir Press, London, 1968, and Wayne State University Press, Detroit, 1988), pp. 539, 540.

11. Ibid., pp. 536, 537.

12. J. Kater in *Algemeen Handelsblad,* May 30, 1946.

13. Ibid.

14. Presser, *Ashes in the Wind*, p. 544.

15. Ibid., p. 543.

16. D. Hondius, *Terugkeer* (SDU Publishers, The Hague, 1990). This book is entirely devoted to the experiences of returning Dutch Jews.

17. Ibid., pp. 79–85.

18. De Jong, *Het Koninkrÿk*, p. 660.

19. *Het Parool*, March 10, 1945, edition published in Eindhoven, which had been liberated in the autumn of 1944.

20. Presser, *Ashes in the Wind*, p. 544.

21. Ibid., p. 545; Hondius, *Terugkeer*, pp. 118ff.

22. Hondius, *Terugkeer*, p. 110.

23. J. G. van Donselaar, "Fout na de oorlog," Ph.D. diss., University of Utrecht, 1991. This thesis is entirely devoted to discussing postwar fascist organizations in the Netherlands.

24. Ibid., pp. 55, 56.

25. Ibid., pp. 74, 75.

26. Hondius, *Terugkeer*, p. 110.

12. MY FINAL MONTHS IN HOLLAND

1. E.g., *Het Parool*, May 19, 1945.

2. *New York Times*, September 5, 1945.

3. A. Pais, Proc. Cambr. Phil. Soc. 42, 45, 1945. This was a refinement of the Born approximation derived by variational methods.

4. L. J. F. Broer and A. Pais, Proc. Kon. Ak. Wetensch. Amsterdam 48, 190, 1945. The question was how to go to the zero mass limit of a neutral vector meson, in particular how to understand that the vector meson has three states of polarization, however small, though non-zero, its mass, while the photon only has two.

5. See A. Pais, *Inward Bound* (Oxford University Press, New York, 1988), pp. 448–49.

6. A. Pais, Trans. Kon. Ak. Wetensch. Amsterdam 19, 1, 1946.

7. A. Pais, Physical Review 68, 227, 1945. These results included a calculation of the proton-neutron mass difference. Among the technical points summarized was my finding that the introduction of a "subtractive vector field" leads to physical inconsistencies. Such fields were rediscovered a few years later, when they became known as "regulators" and were used as handy mathematical (but not physical) tools. See W. Pauli and F. Villars, Rev. Mod. Phys. 21, 434, 1949.

8. A. Pais, Nature 156, 715, 1945.

9. A. Pais, Physica *12*, 2, 81, 1946.

10. L. Onsager, Phys. Rev. *62*, 559, 1942; *65*, 117, 1944.

11. A. Pais, Phys. Today *43*, August 1990, p. 13.

12. A. Pais, *De Vrÿe Katheder 5*, 154, 1945.

13. A. Pais, ibid., *5*, 234, 1945.

14. A. Pais, ibid., *5*, 360, 1945.

15. Published by Princeton University Press, 1945.

16. W. Pauli, letter to A. Pais, October 23, 1945; reprinted in *W. Pauli, Wissenschaftliche Korrespondenz* (Springer, New York, 1992), vol. 3, letter no. 782.

13. GETTING TO KNOW NIELS BOHR

1. *Politiken*, February 3, 1946.

2. T. Fink, *Deutschland als Problem Dänemarks* (Christian Wolff Verlag, Flensburg, 1968), p. 116.

3. R. Petrow, *The Bitter Years* (Morrow, New York, 1974), p. 49.

4. For a detailed account of the fate of the Danish Jews, see Petrow, *The Bitter Years,* chapters 14 and 15.

5. See *Besættelsen's hvem hvad hvor* (Politikens Forlag, Copenhagen, 1965).

6. *Dansk Social Historie* (Gyldendal, Copenhagen, 1980), vol. 7.

7. M. and A. Bohr, interviewed by L. Rosenfeld and T. S. Kuhn, January 30, 1963, Niels Bohr Archives (NBA), Copenhagen.

8. A. Pais, Proc. Cambr. Phil. Soc. *42*, 45, 1945.

9. L. Hulthén and A. Pais, *Proceedings of the Cambridge Conference on Fundamental Particles and Low Temperatures* (Taylor and Francis, London, 1947), p. 177.

10. C. Møller, Phys. Rev. *58*, 1118, 1940; Det Danske Vid. Selsk. math.-fys. Medd. *18*, no. 6, 1941.

11. C. Møller and A. Pais, *Proceedings,* p. 181.

12. Oskar Klein, interview by L. Rosenfeld and J. Kalckar, November 7, 1968, NBA.

13. N. Bohr, letter to A. Einstein, April 13, 1927, NBA.

14. N. Bohr, letter to M. Born, January 22, 1927, NBA.

15. R. Feynman, *Lectures in Physics* (Addison-Wesley, Reading, Mass., 1965).

16. W. Pauli, letter to W. Heisenberg, May 13, 1954, in W. Pauli, *Scientific Correspondence* (Springer, New York, in press), vol. 4.

17. Two or more substances occupying the same place in the periodic table of elements but having different atomic weights—commonly expressed in terms of the weight of the hydrogen nucleus as a unit—are called isotopes. The most abundant isotope of uranium has weight 238.

18. A. Pais, *Niels Bohr's Times: In Physics, Philosophy, and Polity* (Oxford University Press, New York, 1991).

19. J. Chadwick, letter to N. Bohr, January 25, 1943, reprinted in full in Pais, *Bohr*, p. 486.

20. Pais, *Bohr*, p. 487.

21. Ibid., chapter 21, sec. (e).

22. *Berlingske Tidende*, October 8, 1955.

23. *New York Times*, October 25, 1957.

24. Reprinted in *Berlingske Tidende*, November 21, 1962.

25. *Politiken*, November 21, 1962.

26. Sir Nevill Mott, *A Life in Science* (Taylor and Francis, London and Philadelphia, 1986), p. 28.

27. Recall that this was said in 1946. The Russians exploded their first test bomb in August 1949.

28. Bernard Baruch had been the U.S. member of the U.N. Atomic Energy Commission, established in January 1946. In June 1946 he presented a U.S. proposal for international control of atomic energy—which never got anywhere. The U.N. Commission disbanded its activities in 1948.

29. A more detailed but nontechnical account of Bohr's ideas can be found in Pais, *Bohr*, chapters 14 and 19, including a survey of Bohr's speculations on the applicability of complementarity in fields other than physics.

30. N. Bohr, Nature *121* (Suppl.), 580, 1928.

31. Ibid.

32. N. Bohr, Dialectica 2, 312, 1948.

33. Hans Bohr, in *Niels Bohr, His Life and Work*, ed. S. Rozental (North-Holland, Amsterdam, 1968), p. 325.

34. Translation by P. E. Pinkerton of Heinrich Düntzer's *Poetical Works: Life of Schiller* (Dana Estes, Boston, 1902).

35. Cf. J. Kalckar, *Det inkommensurable* (Rhodos, Copenhagen, 1985).

36. *Proceedings* printed for the Royal Society, p. 56, 1946; see also Nature *158*, 90, 1946.

37. In Hulthén and Pais, *Proceedings*, p. 1.

14. IT IS TIME TO SPEAK OF AMERICA

1. A. D. Fokker, letter to A. Pais, June 6, 1946.

2. As a consequence of the developing Cold War, the UNAEC recommended on May 17, 1948, the suspension of its own activities.

3. Phys. Rev. 70, 784, 1946.

4. A. Pais, Phys. Rev. 70, 796, 1946.

5. W. E. Lamb, reprinted in *A Festschrift for I. I. Rabi*, ed. L. Motz, p. 82, Trans. N.Y. Ac. Sc. Series II, vol. 38, 1977.

6. Institute of International Education (IIE), letter to A. Pais, December 14, 1945.

7. A. Pais, letter to IIE, January 7, 1947.

8. The proceedings of the conference, which came out in book form (see *Physical Science and Human Values,* ed. E. P. Wigner [Princeton University Press, 1947]), do not contain Bohr's contributions. A transcript of a dictograph record of his talk has been preserved in the Niels Bohr Archive, Copenhagen, however.

9. Bohr might not have agreed. Léon Rosenfeld was sitting next to him at the Maxwell celebrations in Cambridge in 1931 when one of the speakers commented on Maxwell's reputation as a poor lecturer and added: "So perhaps with our friend Bohr: he might want to instruct us about the correlation of too many things at once." Whereupon Bohr whispered to Rosenfeld: "Imagine! He thinks I'm a poor lecturer." See L. Rosenfeld, *Quantum Theory in 1929* (Rhodos, Copenhagen, 1971).

10. See also P. Schilpp, letter to N. Bohr, October 7, 1946, Niels Bohr Archive, Copenhagen.

15. The State of the Union, 1946

1. *New York Times* (NYT), September 23, 1946.

2. *NYT,* September 22, 1946.

3. *NYT,* September 23, 1946.

4. *NYT,* December 31, 1952.

5. *Ward's Automotive Yearbook* for 1947.

6. In preparing this section I used two documents. In the early 1950s Oppenheimer commissioned Mrs. Beatrice Stern to write the Institute's early history. During 1955–57 she interviewed a number of people, including me. In 1964 she completed a manuscript, "A History of the Institute for Advanced Study, 1930–1950," which has been suppressed on grounds which I understand but do not consider reasonable. In 1980, *A Community of Scholars* was published by the Institute, printed by Princeton University Press.

7. A. Flexner, "Medical Education in the United States and Canada."

8. Its complete text is found in Bulletin No. 1, published in December 1930 by the Institute, the address for which was given as 100 East 42nd Street, New York.

9. *NYT,* October 12, 1930.

10. *NYT,* April 19, 1955.

11. Institute for Advanced Study, minutes of October 10, 1932.

12. A. Flexner, letter to A. Einstein, October 13, 1933, in Mrs. Stein's manuscript.

13. A. Flexner, letter to Roosevelt, November 3, 1933, ibid.

14. The Rockefeller Foundation Annual Report for 1936, pp. 46, 290, 351, and 379 (49 West 49th Street, New York).

15. Most of my information on the Gest Library comes from Hu Shih, Princeton University Library Chronicle *15,* Spring 1954, reprinted in 1967, with a preface by W. S. Dix.

16. Interesting New Acquaintances

1. A. Pais, letter to A. Bohr, November 9, 1946, Niels Bohr Archive, Copenhagen.

2. *New York Times,* December 27, 1947.

3. *Erwin Panofsky* (The Spiral Press, New York, 1968).

4. See A. Borel, in *A Century of Mathematics in America,* ed. P. Duren et al. (American Mathematical Society, Providence, R.I., 1989), part 3, p. 119, for a history of mathematics at the Institute.

5. T. Kuhn, interview with Dirac, May 7, 1963, transcript in Niels Bohr Library, American Institute of Physics, College Park, Md.

6. P.A.M. Dirac, *Eureka,* no. 32, 2–4, October 1969.

7. P. A. M. Dirac, *The Development of Quantum Theory* (Gordon and Breach, New York, 1971).

8. E. Corson, Phys. Rev. *70,* 728, 1946.

9. See, e.g., Pais, *'Subtle is the Lord'* (Oxford University Press, New York, 1982), p. 454.

10. See chapter 13, sec. 13.5, for Bohr's political creed and his contacts with Baruch.

11. For experts: At that time the so-called (n,2n) reactions had been discovered, in which one neutron hits an atomic nucleus, causing the release of two neutrons. The energetics of those processes do not lend themselves to initiating a chain reaction, however.

12. E. Wigner, Biogr. Mem. Nat. Acad. Sci. *40,* 337, 1969.

13. See chapter 13, sec. 13.6, for the definition of complementarity and the accompanying definition of phenomenon.

14. R. Jost, letter to A. Pais, August 17, 1977.

15. F. Aydelotte, letter to A. Pais, December 6, 1946.

16. A. Wightman, Phys. Rev. *71,* 447, 1947.

17. In Which Oppenheimer Becomes Director

and I a Long-Term Member of the Institute

1. *New York Times,* December 23, 1946.

2. Much of the information given here on this subject is from chapter 11 of Mrs. Stern's history of the Institute, referred to in chapter 15.

3. A rank he was given following his appointment as chief of the Naval Ordnance Division at the beginning of World War II.

4. Minutes, School of Mathematics, Institute for Advanced Study, September 25, 1945.

5. *New York Times,* October 29, 1946.

6. Strauss recalled that he did so during a meeting with Oppenheimer at San Francisco Airport. See L. Strauss, *Men and Decisions* (Doubleday, New York, 1962), pp. 270, 271.

7. F. Aydelotte, letter to R. Oppenheimer, April 5, 1947.

8. AEC Personnel Security Board, *In the Matter of J. Robert Oppenheimer,* transcript of the hearing (Washington, D.C., 1954), pp. 26, 27.

9. P. Michelmore, *The Swift Years* (Dodd, Mead and Co., New York, 1969), p. 142.

10. N. Bohr, letter to A. Pais, January 15, 1947, Niels Bohr Archive (NBA).

11. R. Oppenheimer, Phys. Rev. 71, 460, 1947.

12. A. Pais, letter to N. Bohr, February 16, 1947, NBA.

13. A. Pais, letter to N. Bohr, April 3, 1947, NBA.

14. This information is part of a write-up distributed by the local press to participants of "Shelter Island II," a conference held June 1–4, 1988, to commemorate the conference I am about to describe.

15. They were Hans Bethe, David Bohm, Gregory Breit, Darrow, Herman Feshbach, Feynman, Kramers, Willis Lamb, Robert Marshak, von Neumann, Arnold Nordsieck, Oppenheimer, Pais, Linus Pauling, Rabi, Bruno Rossi, Julian Schwinger, Robert Serber, Edward Teller, Uhlenbeck, Van Vleck, Weisskopf, and Wheeler.

16. The best historical accounts of the conference are by S. Schweber, in *Relativistic Groups and Topology,* ed. B. de Witt and S. Stora (Elsevier, New York, 1984), p. 40; and in *Shelter Island II,* ed. N. Khuri et al. (MIT Press, Cambridge, Mass., 1985), p. 301.

17. *New York Herald Tribune,* June 3, 1947. See also the September 29, 1947, issues of both *Newsweek* and *Time.*

18. K. K. Darrow, diary entry for June 3, 1947. Diaries deposited in Niels Bohr Library, New York.

19. V. Weisskopf, interview by S. Schweber, February 14, 1981.

20. From Weisskopf's abstract of his report.

21. See W. E. Lamb and R. Retherford, Phys. Rev. 72, 241, 1947. Some deviation has been expected, the result of vacuum polarization (Rabi's question, see chapter 14, sec. 14.3), but the effect actually found was much larger.

22. This quantity is a measure for the fact that the electron acts as a tiny magnet.

23. J. Nafe, E. Nelson, and I. Rabi, Phys. Rev. 72, 914, 1947; P. Kusch and H. Foley, ibid. 72, 1256, 1947.

24. A. Pais, *Inward Bound* (Oxford University Press, New York, 1988), chapter 18, sec. (b), contains a history of these events, including the independent contribution of Japanese physicists.

25. K. K. Darrow diary, entry for June 4, 1947.

26. C. Lattes et al., Nature 154, 694, 1947.

27. The symbols π and μ appeared for the first time in C. Lattes et al., Nature 160, 453, 486, 1947.

28. A. Pais, *Developments in the Theory of the Electron* (Princeton University Press, Princeton, 1948).

18. OPPENHEIMER: GLIMPSES OF A COMPLEX MAN

1. Sometimes written Opje, the Dutch diminutive of his name, given him in 1928, when Oppenheimer spent several months as a National Research Fellow working with Ehrenfest in Leiden. "Oppie" is the slightly more vulgar version of Opje, also Dutch.

2. "Director's Report for 1948–1953," published by the Institute for Advanced Study, 1954.

3. G. Kennan, in "Foreign Affairs," July 1947.

4. Full text in A. K. Smith and C. Weiner, *Robert Oppenheimer* (Harvard University Press, Cambridge, Mass.), 1980, p. 315.

5. W. Arnold and R. Oppenheimer, J. of Gen. Physiology, 33, 423, 1959.

6. The others were Serber on the early years, Weisskopf on Los Alamos, and Glenn Seaborg on "Public Science and Human Contributions." The texts of all of these talks were published in *Physics Today,* vol. 20, October 1967. They have also appeared as a book which I particularly recommend because of the sensitive introduction written by Rabi: *Oppenheimer* (Scribner's, New York, 1969).

7. R. Oppenheimer, Phys. Rev. 71, 462, 1947.

8. From the unpublished manuscript of the Richtmyer lecture.

9. R. Oppenheimer, "Knowledge and the Structure of Culture," The Helen Kenyon Lecture, Vassar College, October 1958.

10. P. Goodchild, *Oppenheimer, Shatterer of Worlds* (Houghton Mifflin, Boston, 1981), p. 128.

11. Ibid., p. 72.

12. Ibid., p. 272.

19. MY CAREER UNFOLDS

1. Theodor Reik, *Jewish Wit* (Gamut Press, New York, 1962), p. 36.

2. Ibid., p. 13.

3. N. Bohr, letter to J. J. McCloy, March 22, 1948.

4. N. Bohr, manuscript entitled "Comments," copy in Niels Bohr Archive, Copenhagen.

5. N. Bohr, letter to G. Marshall, June 10, 1948, NBA.

6. Ibid.

7. See S. Schweber, in *Shelter Island II,* ed. N. Khuri et al. (MIT Press, Cambridge, Mass., 1985), p. 301, for a history of the period following Shelter Island.

8. H. Bethe, Phys. Rev. 72, 339, 1947.

9. J. Schwinger, Phys. Rev. 73, 416, 1948.

10. For details, see Pais, *Inward Bound* (Oxford University Press, New York, 1988), chapter 18, sec. (c).

11. A. Pais, *Developments in the Theory of the Electron* (Princeton University Press, Princeton, 1948).

12. F. J. Dyson, Phys. Rev. 73, 1272, 1948.

13. A. Pais and G. E. Uhlenbeck, Phys. Rev. 75, 1321, 1949.

14. A. Pais and G. E. Uhlenbeck, Phys. Rev. 79, 145, 1950.

15. K. M. Case and A. Pais, Phys. Rev. 79, 185, 1950; 80, 203, 1950.

16. A. Pais and G. E. Uhlenbeck, Phys. Rev. 116, 250, 1959.

17. The mathematician H. Poincaré, has written a wonderful account of another such instance.

18. R. Jost and A. Pais, Phys. Rev. 82, 840, 1951.

19. M. Born, Zeitschr. f. Phys. 38, 803, 1926, esp. p. 816.

20. At issue was the convergence of the Born expansion. Born had given a correct proof for the one-dimensional problem, and had concluded without proof that the extension to three dimensions would be straightforward, which is not the case, however.

21. See A. Pais and R. Jost, Phys. Rev. 87, 871, 1952. It was the first paper to introduce selection rules as a consequence of what has become known as G-parity. For more on G-parity, see Pais, *Inward Bound,* p. 489.

22. J. A. Wheeler and R. P. Feynman, Rev. Mod. Phys. *21*, 425, 1949.

23. A. Pais and S. T. Epstein, Rev. Mod. Phys. *21*, 445, 1949.

24. See *W. Pauli, wissenschaftlicher Briefwechsel*, document nos. 993, 1012, 1024, 1026, 1028 (Springer, New York, 1993).

25. R. Oppenheimer, letter dated April 5, 1948.

26. S. Sakata, Progr. Theor. Phys. *2*, 30, 145, 1947.

27. S. Tomonaga, Progr. Theor. Phys. *1*, 27, 1946; *3*, 1, 1948.

28. S. Tomonaga, Phys. Rev. *74*, 224, 1948.

29. S. Tomonaga, in *Les Prix Nobel en 1965* (Norstedt, Stockholm, 1966), p. 151.

30. R. P. Feynman, Phys. Rev. *76*, 749, 1949; see further Feynman, ibid., *76*, 769, 1949; *80*, 440, 1950.

31. The equivalence between Feynman's and Schwinger's formulation had meanwhile been demonstrated by Dyson. See F. J. Dyson, Phys. Rev. *75*, 486, 1949.

32. R. Oppenheimer, letter to A. Pais, April 20, 1949.

33. *New York Times*, November 26, 1947.

34. See T. Emerson and D. Haber, *Political and Civil Rights in the United States* (Dennis and Co., Buffalo, N.Y., 1952), for a legal history of this subject until 1952.

20. About Unexpected New Physics

1. D. J. Kevles, *The Physicists* (Vintage Books, New York, 1979), chapter 20.

2. As L. DuBridge put it; see J. S. Rigden, *Rabi* (Basic Books, New York, 1987), p. 164.

3. P. Morrison, J. App. Phys. *18*, 133, 1947.

4. G. Rochester and C. Butler, Nature *160*, 855, 1947.

5. A. J. Seriff et al., Phys. Rev. *78*, 290, 1950.

6. V. Hopper and S. Biswas, Phys. Rev. *80*, 1099, 1950.

7. The term for one of the particles with mass between that of pion and proton.

8. R. Dixit, Zeitschr. f. Naturf. *9a*, 355, 1954.

9. A. Pais, Progr. Theor. Phys. *10*, 457, 1953.

10. P. M. S. Blackett, Proc. Harwell Nuclear Phys. Conf. 1950, p. 20, Ministry of Supply Report AERE, G/M68.

11. *Wolfgang Pauli und C. G. Jung, ein Briefwechsel 1932–1958*, ed. G. A. Meier (Springer, New York, 1992).

12. N. Bohr, open letter to the United Nations, dated June 9, 1950, printed as a pamphlet by Schultz, Copenhagen.

13. A. Pais, letter to N. Bohr, July 4, 1950, Niels Bohr Archive, Copenhagen.

14. *The Challenge of Nuclear Armaments,* ed. A. Boserup et al. (Rhodos, Copenhagen, 1986).

15. *The Challenge of an Open World,* ed. N. Barfoed et al. (Munksgaard, Copenhagen, 1989).

16. Franca Pauli, letter to A. Pais, April 12, 1986.

17. A. Pais, in *Spectroscopic and Group Theoretical Methods in Physics,* ed. F. Bloch et al. (North-Holland, Amsterdam, 1968), p. 317.

18. C. G. Jung, *Gestaltungen des Unbewussten* (Rascher Verlag, Zurich, 1950).

21. OF THE BEGINNINGS OF THEORETICAL PARTICLE PHYSICS

1. For more details on postwar high energy experimental physics, see Pais, *Inward Bound* (Oxford University Press, New York, 1988), chapter 19, secs. (a), (e); chapter 21, sec. (c).

2. J. Bjorken and S. Drell, *Relativistic Quantum Fields* (McGraw-Hill, New York, 1965).

3. *New York Times,* October 4, 1951.

4. R. Kahn, *The Era* (Ticknor and Fields, New York, 1993), p. 280.

5. M. Gell-Mann, in "International Colloquium on the History of Particle Physics," J. de Physique *43,* p. C 8-395, 1982.

6. Ibid.

7. See M. Gell-Mann and A. Pais, *Proceedings of the Glasgow Conference on Nuclear and Meson Physics,* July 1954 (Pergamon, Oxford, 1955), p. 342.

8. A. Pais, Phys. Rev. *86,* 663, 1952; it also contains references to related efforts by Japanese colleagues.

9. Ibid.

10. W. B. Fowler et al., Phys. Rev. *93,* 861, 1953.

11. A. Pais, Phys. Rev. *86,* 663, 1952.

12. R. Crease and C. Mann, *Makers of the Revolution in Twentieth-Century Physics* (Macmillan, New York, 1986), pp. 174–75.

13. S. B. Treiman, quoted in *Rockefeller University Research Profiles, 1982–83.*

14. A. Pais, *Proc. 2nd Rochester Conf.,* University of Rochester Report NYO-3046, p. 87.

15. R. Marshak, in *The Birth of Particle Physics,* ed. L. Brown and L. Hoddeson (Cambridge University Press, New York, 1983), p. 376.

16. Ibid.

17. A. Pais, in "Report on the International Physics Conference, Copenhagen, June 3–17, 1952," p. 27, mimeographed report.

18. Ibid., p. 33.

19. Ibid., p. 45.

20. K. Tynan, *Bull Fever* (Harper, New York, 1955).

22. OF SYMMETRY AND MY LONGEST JOURNEY

1. For more details on SU(2), see Pais, *Inward Bound* (Oxford University Press, New York, 1988), chapter 17, sec. (f).

2. A. Pais, Physica *19*, 869, 1953.

3. Ibid., p. 885.

4. Ibid., p. 869.

5. Ibid.

6. Ibid.

7. W. Pauli, Physica *19*, 887, 1953.

8. W. Heisenberg, Physica *19*, 905, 1953.

9. R. P. Feynman, *Surely You're Joking, Mr. Feynman!* (Norton, New York, 1985), p. 242.

10. A. Pais, in *Proceedings of the International Conference on Theoretical Physics* (Nippon Bunka Insatsusha, Tokyo, 1954), p. 156.

11. Feynman, *Surely You're Joking,* p. 243.

12. R. Benedict, *The Chrysanthemum and the Sword* (Houghton Mifflin, Boston, 1946).

13. Ibid., pp. 99, 104.

14. Ibid., p. 131.

23. GREENWICH VILLAGE, AMERICAN CITIZENSHIP,
AND THE OPPENHEIMER AFFAIR

1. C. N. Yang and R. Mills, Phys. Rev. *96*, 191, 1954; see also Phys. Rev. *95*, 631, 1954.

2. Notes of his lectures on this subject, given in autumn 1953, later appeared in print, however; see P. Gulmanelli, *Su una teoria dello spin isotopico,* publication of the National Institute of Physics, Milan (Case Editrice, Milan, n.d., probably 1954). The Cambridge Ph.D. thesis of Ronald Shaw, submitted in August 1955, contains very similar results. A footnote in that dissertation reads: "The work described in this chapter was completed, except for its extension [to a four-dimensional case] in Section 3, in January 1954, but was not published. In October 1954, Yang and Mills

adopted independently the same postulate and derived similar consequences"; see R. Shaw, "The Problem of Particle Types and Other Contributions to the Theory of Elementary Particles," Cambridge University, 1955.

3. W. Pauli, Physica 19, 869, 1953.

4. These documents are reproduced in W. Pauli, *Scientific Correspondence* (Springer, New York, in press), vol. 4.

5. W. Pauli, letter to A. Pais, December 6, 1953, reprinted in ibid.

6. H. L. Mencken, *The American Language,* 4th ed. (Knopf, New York, 1955), p. 477.

7. Philip Stern, *The Oppenheimer Case* (Harper and Row, New York, 1969).

8. Full text of the letter by W. L. Borden is in *In the Matter of J. Robert Oppenheimer, Transcript of Hearing* (U.S. Government Printing Office, Washington, D.C., 1954), pp. 837–38.

9. By MIT Press, interchangeable with n. 8.

10. Ibid.

11. *In the Matter of JRO,* pp. 915–21.

12. Ibid., p. 1025.

13. Reports in full in ibid., p. 999.

14. Ibid., p. 1049.

15. I had something to do with that event. Some time in 1962 I met with Freeman Dyson, Tsung Dao Lee, and Frank Yang to suggest that we nominate Robert for this award. We sent a letter to that effect to the nominating committee, with copies to a number of prominent colleagues, requesting that they write in support of the nomination if they felt so inclined. The response was enthusiastic.

16. *New York Times,* December 3, 1963.

17. H. Kipphardt, *In der Sache J. Robert Oppenheimer* (Suhrkamp Verlag, Frankfurt, 1964).

24. OF MY BEST WORK AND A YEAR'S LEAVE OF ABSENCE.

DEATH OF EINSTEIN

1. "Congrès sur le rayonnement cosmique, Bagnère de Bigorre, July 1953," unpublished.

2. Ibid.

3. A. Pais, Phys. Rev. 86, 663, 1952.

4. A. Pais, Physica 19, 869, 1953.

5. For what follows, the reader is advised to consult also Gell-Mann's account in Journal de Physique *43*, p. C 8-395, 1982.

6. M. Gell-Mann, Phys. Rev. *92*, 833, 1953. The stodgy editors of the *Physical Review* had replaced "curious" with a more neutral term, however. For some time, Gell-Mann was clearly searching for an appropriate adjective. In correspondence with me (1954) he would sometimes use "queerness."

7. T. Nakano and K. Nishijima, Progr. Theor. Phys. *10*, 581, 1953.

8. A. Pais, Proc. Nat. Acad. Sci., *40*, 484, 1954, and *40*, 835, 1954.

9. M. Gell-Mann, letter to A. Pais, April 30, 1954.

10. Except for a cryptic remark and a footnote (see M. Gell-Mann and A. Pais, *Proceedings of the Glasgow Conference on Nuclear and Meson Physics* [Pergamon, Oxford, 1955]), referring to a forthcoming paper.

11. Gell-Mann and Pais, *Proceedings*.

12. M. Gell-Mann, Nuovo Cim. Suppl. *4*, 2848, 1956. Independently by K. Nishijima, Progr. Theor. Phys. *13*, 285, 1955, who used the term "η-charge" for "strangeness."

13. M. Gell-Mann and A. Pais, Phys. Rev. *97*, 1387, 1955.

14. See the fine historical account of the early strange particle experiments by W. Chinowsky, in *Pions and Quarks* (Cambridge University Press, New York, 1989), p. 331.

15. A question apparently raised by Fermi.

16. Gell-Mann and Pais, Phys. Rev. *97*, 1387, 1955.

17. K. Landé, E. T. Booth, J. Impeduglia, L. Lederman, and W. Chinowsky, Phys. Rev. *103*, 1901, 1956.

18. Chinowsky, *Pions and Quarks*, p. 331.

19. Later he wrote: "Jealousy was [one] reason why I decided I would put forward the strangeness scheme"; see Gell-Mann, Journal de Physique *43*, p. C 8-395.

20. Not so. Columbus did discover Jamaica, however, and called the island Santiago. The current name is derived from the Indian "Jaymaca," which means "island of springs."

21. A. Pais and R. Serber, Phys. Rev. *99*, 1551, 1955.

22. For that purpose we analyzed so-called scalar meson theories, useful for trying out new techniques, though too simple to account for real phenomena. Some years later we completed a similar study for the more realistic so-called symmetrical pseudo-scalar theory. See A. Pais and R. Serber, Phys. Rev. *113*, 955, 1959.

23. A. Pais and R. Serber, Phys. Rev. *105*, 1636, 1957.

24. H. Dukas, letter to A. Pais, April 30, 1955.

25. H. Dukas, letter to C. Seelig, May 8, 1955.

26. G. K. Dean, *New York Times,* April 19, 1955.

27. H. Dukas, letter to A. Pais, April 30, 1955.

28. H. A. Einstein, letter to C. Seelig, April 18, 1955.

29. G. K. Dean, *New York Times,* April 19, 1955.

30. *New York Times,* April 19, 1955.

31. Ibid.

32. See A. Pais, *Subtle is the Lord* (Oxford University Press, 1982), for more on Einstein's last decade.

33. *Les Prix Nobel, 1988* (Almquist and Wiksell, Stockholm, 1989), p. 61.

34. A. Pais and O. Piccioni, Phys. Rev. *100,* 1487, 1955.

35. J. D. Jackson, *The Theory of Elementary Particles* (Princeton University Press, 1958), p. 75.

36. W. Fowler, P. Lander, and W. Powell, Phys. Rev. *113,* 928, 1959.

37. R. H. Good et al., Phys. Rev. *124,* 1223, 1961.

38. R. P. Feynman, *The Theory of Fundamental Processes* (Benjamin, New York, 1961), p. 50.

25. My First Trip to Russia and My First Marriage

1. R. Dalitz, *Proceedings of the Sixth Rochester Conference, April 3–7, 1956* (Interscience, New York, 1956), p. 56.

2. R. Feynman, in ibid., p. 27.

3. R. Oppenheimer, in ibid., p. 22.

4. A. Pais, Nucl. Phys. *5,* 297, 1958.

26. Enter Joshua. The 1950s, Concluded

1. T. D. Lee and C. N. Yang, Phys. Rev. *104,* 254, 1956.

2. A. Pais and S. B. Treiman, Phys. Rev. *105,* 1616, 1957.

3. Ibid.

4. Cf. C. N. Yang, Rev. Mod. Phys. *29,* 231, 1957; L. D. Landau, Sov. Phys. JETP *32,* 405, 1957.

5. A. Pais and S. B. Treiman, Phys. Rev. *106,* 1106, 1957.

6. J. Cronin, Phys. Today *35,* July 1982, p. 38.

7. A. Pais, in *Proceedings of the Seventh Rochester Conference* (Interscience, New York, 1957), sec. 8, p. 1.

8. See A. Pais, Nucl. Phys. *5,* 297, 1958, and also the editor's prefatory note.

9. D. White and D. Sullivan, Phys. Today *32*, April 1979, p. 40.

10. A. Pais and S. B. Treiman, Phys. Rev. *107*, 1396, 1957.

11. A. Pais, Phys. Rev. *110*, 574, 1480; *112*, 624; Phys. Rev. Lett. *1*, 418, all in 1958.

12. A. Pais, Phys. Rev. Lett. *3*, 242, 1959.

13. G. and S. Goldhaber, W. Y. Lee, and A. Pais, Phys. Rev. *120*, 300, 1960.

14. E. P. Wigner, *Group Theory and Its Application to the Quantum Mechanics of Atomic Spectra* (Academic Press, New York, 1959).

15. A. Pais, Annals of Phys. *9*, 548, 1960.

27. Times of Great Change: The Early 1960s

1. A. Pais, Annals of Phys. *9*, 548, 1960.

2. A. Pais, Annals of Phys. *22*, 274, 1963.

3. A. Pais, Nuovo Cim. *18*, 1003, 1960.

4. A. Pais, Phys. Rev. *122*, 317, 1960.

5. A. Pais, Rev. Mod. Phys. *33*, 493, 1961.

6. A. Pais, Phys. Rev. *123*, 1058, 1961.

7. G. Feinberg, F. Gürsey, and A. Pais, Phys. Rev. Lett. *7*, 1208, 1961.

8. A. Pais, in *La Théorie quantique des champs,* ed. R. Stoops (Interscience, New York, 1962), p. 101.

9. N. Bohr, in ibid., p. 18.

10. Richard Krafft-Ebbing was a psychiatrist best remembered for his book on sexual pathology.

11. M. Nauenberg and A. Pais, Phys. Rev. Lett. *8*, 82, 1962.

12. G. Feinberg and A. Pais, Phys. Rev. Lett. *8*, 341; *9*, 45, 1962.

13. On spinors in n-dimensions; see A. Pais, J. Math. Phys. *3*, 1135, 1962.

14. A. Pais, Proc. Nat. Acad. Sci. *49*, 34, 1963.

15. A. Pais, Phys. Rev. Lett. *9*, 117, 1962.

16. A. Pais, in *Philosophy of Science* (Interscience, New York, 1963), vol. 2, p. 291.

28. Changing My Workplace from Princeton to New York

1. A. Pais, in *Niels Bohr,* ed. S. Rozenthal (North-Holland, Amsterdam, 1967), p. 215.

2. All talks were collected in a dittoed, unpublished report. My talk was pub-

lished later in slightly modified form; see A. Pais, in *Spectroscopic and Group Theoretical Methods in Physics*, ed. F. Bloch et al. (North-Holland, Amsterdam, 1968), p. 317.

3. All contributions, including Kennedy's speech, are in *The Scientific Endeavor* (Rockefeller University Press, 1964).

4. See Pais, *Inward Bound* (Oxford University Press, New York, 1988), chapter 21, sec. (c), for more on these experimental advances.

5. See ibid., sec. (b), for the rather complicated history of the discovery of SU(3) and of quarks.

6. J. H. Christenson et al., Phys. Rev. Lett. *13*, 138, 1964.

7. J. W. Cronin, Rev. Mod. Phys. *53*, 373, 1981. For more details on CP-violation, see Pais, *Inward Bound*, chapter 20, sec. (e).

8. M. Gell-Mann, Physics *1*, 63, 1964.

9. Ibid.

10. F. Gürsey and L. Radicati, Phys. Rev. Lett. *13*, 173, 1964.

11. A. Pais, Phys. Rev. Lett. *13*, 175, 1964; F. Gürsey, A. Pais, and L. Radicati, ibid., *13*, 299, 1964.

12. A. Pais and S. Treiman, "Weak Interactions," in *Proceedings of the 1964 High Energy Conference at Dubna* (Atomirdat, Moscow, 1966), vol. 2, p. 213.

13. B. Bég, B. Lee, and A. Pais, Phys. Rev. Lett. *13*, 514, 1964.

14. See A. Pais, Rev. Mod. Phys. *38*, 215, 1966, for my review of SU(6) theory.

15. A. Pais, Nucl. Phys. *57*, 96, 1964.

16. N. Khuri and A. Pais, Rev. Mod. Phys. *36*, 590, 1964. Both papers dealt with so-called singular potentials, i.e., those which increase at small distances with a power of distance smaller than minus two. Also in 1964 I published two more papers on that subject: A. Pais and T. T. Wu, J. Math. Phys. *5*, 799, 1964; and Phys. Rev. *B134*, 1303, 1964.

17. A. Pais, "Fachbericht über schwache Wechselwirkungen," in *Plenarvorträge der Physiker Tagung* (Düsseldorf, 1964).

18. Together with B. Bég, Phys. Rev. *B137*, 1514, 1965; *B138*, 692, 1965; Phys. Rev. Lett. *14*, 51, 267, 509, 577(E), 1965.

19. A. Pais, in *Preludes in Theoretical Physics*, ed. A. de Shalit et al. (North-Holland, Amsterdam, 1966), p. 302.

20. A. Pais, in *Recent Developments in Particle Symmetries* (Academic Press, New York, 1966), p. 13.

21. Dealing with so-called low energy theorems (A. Pais, Phys. Rev. Lett. *18*, 17, 1967; *19*, 544, 1967), and sum rules (with B. Bég, Phys. Rev. *160*, 1479, 1967).

22. A. Pais, Science *157*, 911, 1967.

29. What Befell Me in the Late 1960s

1. *New York Times,* April 25, 1965.

2. P. Goodchild, *Oppenheimer: Shatterer of Worlds* (Houghton Mifflin, Boston, 1981), p. 280.

3. Ibid., pp. 279, 281.

4. *New York Times,* February 26, 1967.

5. Reprinted in a pamphlet, "Three Tributes to J. Robert Oppenheimer," Institute for Advanced Study, Princeton, 1967.

6. See chapter 28, sec. 28.2. All talks were published in Phys. Today *20,* October 1967, and reprinted in *Oppenheimer* (Scribner's, New York, 1969).

7. R. Oppenheimer, in *Science and the Common Understanding,* the BBC Reith Lectures (Oxford University Press, Oxford, 1954).

8. A. Pais and S. Treiman, Phys. Rev. *168,* 1858, 1968; also A. Pais, Proc. Fifth Coral Gables Conf. 1968, p. 7.

9. A. Pais, Phys. Today *21,* May 1968, p. 24.

10. See Pais, *Inward Bound* (Oxford University Press, New York, 1988), pp. 476–77, for the early history of Fermilab.

11. A. Pais and S. Treiman, Phys. Rev. *176,* 1974, 1968.

12. A. Pais and S. Treiman, "Full Content of Lepton Pair Locality," in *Problems of Theoretical Physics* (Nauka, Moscow, 1969), p. 257.

13. A. Pais, Phys. Rev. *173,* 1587, 1968; *178,* 2365, 1969.

14. A. Pais and S. Treiman, Phys. Lett. *29B,* 308, 1969; Phys. Rev. *187,* 2076, 1969.

15. *1969 Summer Study* (National Accelerator Lab., Batavia, Ill., 1969), vol. 1, p. iii.

16. A. Pais, "Dynamical Asymmetry in Octet Space," in *Elementary Particle Physics* (Wiley and Sons, New York, 1968), p. 215.

30. The 1970s

1. A. Pais, in *Proceedings of the Amsterdam Conference on High Energy Physics, 1971* (North-Holland, Amsterdam, 1972), p. 391.

2. S. Stanford, *The Lady of the House* (Ballantine Books, New York, 1966).

3. A. Pais, "Physics after Tau and Upsilon," in *High Energy Physics in the Einstein Centennial Year* (Plenum Press, New York, 1979), p. 79.

4. A. Pais and S. Treiman, Phys. Rev. *D1,* 907, 1970, and *D1,* 1349, 1970.

5. A. Pais and S. Treiman, Phys. Rev. Lett. *25*, 975, 1970.

6. A. Pais and S. Treiman, Phys. Lett. *29B*, 308, 1969; Phys. Rev. *187*, 2076, 1969.

7. A. Pais, Comments Nucl. and Particle Phys. *5*, 26, 1972.

8. A. Pais, Ann. of Phys. *63*, 361, 1971.

9. A. Pais, Phys. Rev. Lett. *26*, 51, 1971; with M. Elitzur, Phys. Rev. *D3*, 2897, 1971.

10. A. Pais, Phys. Rev. *D5*, 1170, 1972; with C. Llewellyn Smith, Phys. Rev. Lett. *28*, 865, 1972, and Phys. Rev. *D6*, 2625, 1972.

11. With C. Callan, M. Gronau, E. Paschos, and S. Treiman, Phys. Rev. *D6*, 387, 1972.

12. A. Pais, "Reflections on BNL's Spirit of 1976," Isabelle Physics Prospects, BNL report 17-522, p. 3, 1972.

13. See A. Pais, *Inward Bound* (Oxford University Press, New York, 1988), and A. Pickering, *Constructing Quarks* (Edinburgh University Press, Edinburgh, 1984), chapter 6, for a history of that period.

14. Ibid.

15. S. Weinberg, Phys. Rev. Lett. *19*, 1264, 1967; see also A. Salam, in *Elementary Particle Physics* (Wiley and Sons, New York, 1968), p. 367.

16. Ibid.

17. G. t'Hooft, Nucl. Phys. *35*, 167, 1971.

18. Cf. S. Coleman, Science *206*, 1290, 1979.

19. See S. Weinberg, Sci. Am. *231*, July 1974, p. 50, for a popular account of that period.

20. See H. Georgi, Sci. Am. *244*, April 1981, p. 44, for a popular account.

21. A. Pais and S. Treiman, Phys. Rev. *D6*, 2700, 1972.

22. A. Pais, Phys. Lett. *48B*, 326, 1974; A. Pais and S. Treiman, Phys. Rev. *D9*, 1459, 1974.

23. A. Pais, Phys. Rev. Lett. *29*, 1712, 1972; Phys. Rev. *D8*, 625, 1973.

24. At issue were electric dipole moments of spin-$\frac{1}{2}$ particles; see A. Pais and J. Primack, Phys. Rev. *D8*, 3063, 1973.

25. A. Pais, Phys. Rev. *D8*, 1844, 1973.

26. H. Georgi and A. Pais, Phys. Rev. *D10*, 1246, 1974.

27. H. Georgi and A. Pais, Phys. Rev. *D10*, 539, 1974.

28. H. Georgi and A. Pais, Phys. Rev. *D12*, 508, 1975; *D16*, 3520, 1977; *D19*, 2746, 1979.

29. A. Pais, Phys. Rev. Lett. *32*, 108, 1974; Phys. Rev. *D10*, 2147, 1974.

30. A. Pais and V. Rittenberg, J. Math. Phys. *16*, 2062, 1975.

31. A. Pais and S. Treiman, Phys. Rev. *D12*, 2744, 1975.

32. A. Pais and S. Treiman, Phys. Rev. Lett. *35*, 1206, 1975.

33. A. Pais and S. Treiman, Phys. Rev. Lett. *35*, 1556, 1975.

34. A. Pais, in *Proceedings of a Conference on Gauge Theories* (Northeastern University, Boston, and MIT Press, Cambridge, Mass., 1975), p. 211.

35. A. Pais and S. Treiman, Phys. Rev. *D14*, 293, 1976.

36. A. Pais and S. Treiman, Phys. Rev. *D15*, 2529, 1977.

37. O. Nachtmann and A. Pais, Phys. Lett. *65B*, 59, 1976; Phys. Rev. *D16*, 630, 1977.

38. H. Georgi, A. Pais, and T. Tomaras, Phys. Rev. *D23*, 469, 1981.

39. G. Arnison et al., Phys. Lett. *122B*, 103, 1983.

31. A Career Change

1. G. Steiner, *The New Yorker*, March 11, 1991.

2. A. Pais, Rev. Mod. Phys. *49*, 925, 1977; also in "A Festschrift for I. I. Rabi," *Trans. N.Y. Acad. Sci.*, series II, vol. 48, p. 116; German translation in Physik u. Didaktic *4*, 300, 1980.

3. A. Pais, in *Some Strangeness in the Proportion*, ed. H. Woolf (Addison-Wesley, Reading, Mass., 1980), p. 197.

4. R. Jost, in ibid., p. 252.

5. A. Pais, *Niels Bohr's Times* (Oxford University Press, New York, 1991), p. 200.

6. In 1921 Einstein paid his first visit to the United States, during which he lectured on relativity theory at Princeton University. While there, word reached him that an American experiment was in conflict with relativity. This led him to comment: "Raffiniert ist der Herr Gott, aber boshaft ist er nicht" (subtle is the Lord, but malicious He is not). Oswald Veblen, a professor of mathematics at Princeton who had overheard Einstein's comment about the subtlety of the Lord, wrote to him in 1930, asking his permission to have this statement chiseled, in German, in the stone frame of the fireplace in the common room of Fine Hall, the newly constructed mathematics building at the university. Einstein consented. The mathematics department has since moved to new quarters, but the inscription in stone has remained in its original place, Room 202 in what is now called Jones Hall, home of the East Asian Studies Program.

7. The proceedings of the conference are in *Albert Einstein: Historical and Cultural Perspectives*, ed. G. Holton and Y. Elkana (Princeton University Press, Princeton, 1982).

8. A. Pais, in *Einstein: A Centenary Volume*, ed. A. French (Heinemann, London, and Harvard University Press, Cambridge, Mass., 1979).

9. A. Pais, Rev. Mod. Phys. *51*, 863, 1979.

10. Pais, in *Some Strangeness*, p. 197.

11. S. Weinberg, *Gravitation and Cosmology* (Wiley and Sons, New York, 1972), p. 297.

12. A. Pais, *Subtle is the Lord* (Oxford University Press, New York, 1982), chapter 15.

13. The Rockefeller University *News and Notes*, vol. 13, no. 2, December 1981.

14. The lecture was entitled "The Origins of the Einstein Legend," delivered on April 27, 1983.

15. *Sutil é o Senhor* (Editora Nova Frontera, Rio de Janeiro, 1995).

16. *Shangdi ShiWeimiao de Aiyinstan de Kexue yu Shengping* (Publishing Company of Literature on Science and Technology, Beijing, 1988).

17. *Albert Einstein, la vie et l'oeuvre* (Interéditions, Paris, 1993).

18. *Raffiniert ist der Herrgott* (Vieweg, Braunschweig, 1986).

19. *Sottile è il Signore* (Boringhieri, Turin, 1986).

20. *Kami wa rokai nishite, Einstein no hito to gakumon* (Sangyo Tosho, Tokyo, 1987).

21. *Sutil é o Senhor* (Gradiva, Lisbon, 1993).

22. *Nauchnayah deyatelvnost i shyzn Alberta Einsteina* (Nauka, Moscow, 1989).

23. *El Señor es sutil* (Ariel, Barcelona, 1984).

24. A. Pais, *Einstein Lived Here* (Oxford University Press, New York, 1994).

25. The lectures, as well as others given over the next few days, have been collected in *The Lesson of Quantum Theory*, ed. J. de Boer et al. (Elsevier Science, New York, 1986).

26. F. Frankfurter, *Of Law and Life and Other Things That Matter* (Kurland, New York, 1969), p. 251.

32. My Final Years—So Far

1. Ida has kept Nicolaisen as her surname. Her maiden name is Edelberg.

2. Denmark is divided into *amter*, somewhat similar to provinces. Ida's father was governor of Ribe Amt.

3. Fang Li Zhi, *Bringing Down the Great Wall* (Knopf, New York, 1991).

4. A. Pais, "CP-Violation: The First 25 Years," in *CP-Violation*, ed. T. T. Van (Éditions Frontières, Paris, 1990), p. 4.

33. Approaching the Millennium

1. The writing of this chapter has been helped by information and quotations contained in E. Hobsbawn, *The Age of Extremes* (Pantheon Books, New York, 1994).

Onomasticon